SELECTED LETTERS OF
JAMES JOYCE

Selected Letters
of
JAMES JOYCE

edited by

RICHARD ELLMANN

THE VIKING PRESS · NEW YORK

First published in a hardbound and
a paperbound edition in 1975
by The Viking Press, Inc.,
625 Madison Avenue,
New York, N.Y. 10022

Distributed in Canada
by The Macmillan Company of Canada Limited

LIBRARY OF CONGRESS CATALOGING IN PUBLICATION DATA
Joyce, James, 1882-1941.
Selected letters of James Joyce.
Includes bibliographical references and index.
1. Joyce, James, 1882- 1941—Correspondence.
PR6019.09Z52 1975   823'.9'12   71-83240
ISBN 0-670-63190-6
ISBN 0-670-00276-3 pbk.

Printed in U.S.A.

CONTENTS

PREFACE

This selection of James Joyce's letters has been drawn from three volumes: the first, edited by Stuart Gilbert, appeared in 1957; the second and third, edited by me, in 1966. An eventual edition of all Joyce's letters, including many not previously known, is contemplated. But in the meantime ten letters not published before, and unpublished passages heretofore omitted from many others, are gathered together in this book.

Of the new letters, two are addressed to Lady Gregory at an interval of twenty years, the second denying her permission to publish the first (21 December 1902 and 8 August 1922); one, about Joyce's first attack of glaucoma, is to Ezra Pound (20 August 1917); and one, a postcard to Stanislaus Joyce (16 June 1915), announces a chapter arrangement for *Ulysses* from which the book itself sharply diverges.

Two of the new letters were written by Joyce to his wife on 8 and 9 December 1909. At the time when my Volume II appeared, there were several obstacles to publication in its entirety of Joyce's correspondence with his wife, and of the total of 64 letters, I was permitted to give the complete text of 54, a partial text of 8, and no text at all of the remaining 2. Publication of the missing correspondence has now been authorized. The eight letters containing restored passages are those of 7 September, 2, 3, 6, ?13, 15, 16, and 20 December 1909. To make the context of the letters to Nora Joyce continuous and clear, I have included with the new material all the letters Joyce wrote to his wife in 1909. This correspondence commands respect for its intensity and candour, and for its fulfilment of Joyce's avowed determination to express his whole mind. I hope that readers will not only countenance it but recognize its value as an extreme of Joyce's, and perhaps of human, utterance. The part these letters played in his life is set forth in the Introduction to this volume (pp. xi–xxix). They had their effect upon the sexual imagery of his books, where, however, their blunt ardour was made more subtle.

Out of five new letters to Harriet Shaw Weaver, four (12 October 1923, 13 May and 26 July 1927, and 26 March 1928) contain explanations of passages in *Finnegans Wake*; readers of that book will wish immediate acquaintance with them. The fifth (6 March 1917) is Joyce's thanks to her as his still anonymous patron. These letters form part of the much larger collection which Miss Weaver willed to the British Museum under a ten-year seal. In a covering note dated 5 July 1960, which she sent with the letters, she stated, 'I destroyed 3 or 4 [letters] including a long one written on February 6, 1932.' This last must have had to do with Lucia Joyce's unhappy condition. Miss Weaver was Joyce's archivist, but she had her feelings too, and one must allow her conviction that three or four among Joyce's hundreds of letters to her, many of personally painful context, were unbearable.

In the same note she also remarked that 'deletions where needed' had been made in her earlier transcriptions of the letters. It is now clear that they were needed principally because of her sympathy for Joyce, her modesty about her own role in his life, and her reluctance to consider money matters important. The ten years being up, her transcriptions have been corrected, with the deleted passages restored, in this book. Of the 44 letters to her included here, most contain minor changes, and substantive additions have been made in the following 15: 20 July 1919, 6 January 1920, 24 June and 10 December 1921, 19 November 1923, 27 January and 13 June 1925, 20 September 1928, 28 May 1929, 18 March and 22 November 1930, 15 December 1931, 17 January 1932, 1 May 1935, 9 June 1936.

In making this selection I have chosen letters which seemed to me the most interesting, rather than those most conspicuous for information. Readers familiar with the other volumes may miss one letter or another as, confronted by exigencies of space, I do myself, but they will recognize here Joyce's principal assertions of his character and of his literary aims.

The procedures outlined in the preface to Volume II have been followed again in this book. Letters drawn from Volume I have been retranscribed whenever possible, and some footnotes and manuscript locations added; letters included there in translation only are given here in the original as well. Letters are reproduced with their original spelling and punctuation; only where confusion might result has the bracketed word *sic* been inserted. A word underlined once by Joyce appears here in italic type; a word underlined more than once appears in roman with a black line underneath it. References to Joyce's books are made first to the standard London edition, then, in parenthesis, to the standard New York edition.

In the preparation of this book I have been particularly aided by Ottocaro Weiss, whose recent death I greatly regret. For many suggestions I wish to thank Robert E. Scholes. John V. Kelleher aided me with some Irish problems. Charles P. Noyes provided valuable editorial help at an early stage. Later Catharine Carver, with her customary skill, ironed out difficulties of every kind. I am grateful to Mary T. Reynolds for making, with such dexterity and patience, the elaborate index.

R.E.

New College,
Oxford
15 *March* 1974

MANUSCRIPT LOCATIONS

When the present owner is not known, the previous owner is listed

Institutions

Bibliothèque Municipale, Vichy
British Museum
Buffalo—Lockwood Memorial
Library, State University of
New York at Buffalo
Colby College (Healy Collection)
Cornell University Library
Faber & Faber, Ltd
Harvard—Houghton Library,
Harvard University
Library of Congress
National Library of Ireland,
Dublin
New York Public Library
(Henry W. and Albert A. Berg
Collection)

New York Public Library
(Manuscript Division)
Royal Literary Fund
Southern Illinois University
Library (H. K. Croessmann
Collection)
Southern Illinois University
Library (Charles A. Feinberg
Collection)
University College Library,
Galway
University of Texas Library
Yale University Library
Zurich City Archives

Private Owners

Dámaso Alonso
Mrs Olga Brauchbar
Signora Emma Cuzzi Brocchi
Daniel Brody
Estate of Frank Budgen
Jørgen Budtz-Jørgensen
C. P. Curran
Richard Ellmann
David Fleischman
Signora Letizia Fonda Savio
Mme Moune Gilbert
Mrs Maria Jolas

Mrs Nelly Joyce
Stephen Joyce
Robert Kastor
Mrs John McCormack
Jacques Mercanton
Professor Norman Holmes
Pearson
Rachewiltz Trust
Professor George Rogers
Professor Heinrich Straumann
Dario de Tuoni
Senator Michael B. Yeats

x

INTRODUCTION

Letter-writing imposes its small ceremonies even upon those who disdain the medium. An audience of one requires confrontation too, and even a perfunctory message discloses a little with what candour, modesty, or self-esteem its writer ranks himself in the world. Some accompanying hint of his appraisal of that world is bound to appear in the way he asserts or beseeches a tie with his correspondent, the degree of familiarity he takes for granted, the extent to which he solicits action or approbation, the alacrity and tenacity with which he joins issue. He may present himself in various guises, as machine, badger, deer, spider, bird. Whatever his mode, if he is a practising writer his assembling of words can never be totally negligent; once enslaved by language forever enslaved.

Joyce did not regard the letter or its brazen sister, the postcard, as a literary form of any consequence, but almost every day he burdened mailmen in different parts of his hemisphere with his sedulous correspondence. At letter's length he felt comfortable, and wrote sparely and to the point. His letters adopt a stance which at first may appear the reverse of that in his books. His creative works are humorous, lyrical, daring. These qualities appear from time to time in his correspondence, but its prevailing tenor is wry, terse, pressed down. 'I am in double trouble, mental and material,' he writes,[1] and says in another letter, 'my spiritual barque is on the rocks.'[2] In both of these the statement has a sweep and finality which paradoxically imply that all may not be lost. His summaries of his condition are sometimes more epigrammatic: 'My mouth is full of decayed teeth and my soul of decayed ambitions.'[3] And sometimes he relents a little to joke: 'Well! (as Mr Pater beautifully says) I have reached the low-water mark in Xmases this 'ere time.'[4] He is fond of deflating his life into a vista of ludicrous confusion. As Joyce writes later of Shem, 'O! the lowness of him was beneath all up to that sunk to!'[5] In an early letter he wrote that he could not enter

---

[1] II, 50. References to *Letters of James Joyce*, ed. Stuart Gilbert and Richard Ellmann, 3 vols. (London and New York, 1957, 1966) are indicated by volume and page number; references to this book by page number only.
[2] P. 150.   [3] II, 216.
[4] II, 204.   [5] *Finnegans Wake* (London and New York, 1939), p. 171.

society except as a vagabond, and there is perhaps always a submerged pleasure in his not being an upstanding British subject.

The sense of contradiction between his works and his letters is illusory. The attitude of resignation is not so far removed from that of confidence as it first appears. It contains, in fact, a peremptory note. Underneath themes which are favourites of Joyce from beginning to end—the meticulous exposition of his penury, his physical weakness, or his discouragement—there is the conviction that he expresses rarely because he holds it so unshakably, that his needs are trivial when weighed with his deserts. The letters simultaneously plead and berate. He tells his brother, 'Do not delay so long executing my requests as I waste a lot of ink.'[1] He demands patronage rather than charity. Joyce's conviction of merit was justified in the event, yet he was imbued with it long before there were publications or even manuscripts to confirm it; confidence in his powers may be said to have antedated their manifestation.

Because of this confidence, he has little patience with those who fail to pay tribute to his talent, and is likely to shift suddenly from supplicant to renunciant. He is regularly on the verge of scorning the help he requires. This readiness to 'doff the world aside' is characteristic of him. He is like Stephen in *A Portrait of the Artist as a Young Man*, who counters his girl's practical questions about his future by making 'a sudden gesture of a revolutionary nature',[2] evidently a dismissal of everything in his present life. Joyce was given to such gestures, as when he went to Paris in 1902 and again in 1903, when he eloped with Nora Barnacle in 1904, when he left Trieste for Rome in 1906 and Rome for Trieste in 1907. A mood of this sort impelled him to write his brother from Trieste, at the age of twenty-three, 'If I once convince myself that this kind of life is suicidal to my soul, I will make everything and everybody stand out of my way as I did before now.'[3] In a letter to his aunt Josephine Murray he threatened to leave his new family as he had left his old one: 'I suppose you will shake your head now over my coldness of heart which is probably only an unjust name for a certain perspicacity of temper or mind.'[4] In later life, angered and pained by his friends' dislike for *Finnegans Wake*, he said he would abandon the writing of the book to James Stephens. Many of these intentions were not carried out; Joyce did not leave his wife, and while Stephens was more or less willing to complete the book, in the end he was mysteriously not called

[1] II, 78.
[2] *A Portrait of the Artist as a Young Man* (London, 1960; New York, 1964), p. 256 (252).
[3] P. 74.   [4] P. 81.

upon. In retrospect, it is clear that Joyce's secret motive in making most of his threats, though not all, was to compel the contrapuntal encouragement which would warrant his not fulfilling them. But the urge to renounce was always present in his mind as a strong possibility, and no doubt reinforced him in repudiating easy solutions to artistic as well as personal problems, thus making possible his elaborate and great solutions. As he said himself of his literary work, he wanted to feel that he had overcome difficulties.

Though his gestures of renunciation, and threats of gestures, might argue that Joyce was as he called Ibsen, an 'egoarch',[1] they must somehow be reconciled with his other qualities. Joyce was gregarious, filial, fraternal, uxorious, paternal, in varying degrees, and surrounded himself with relatives and friends. His letters to his son Giorgio and his daughter Lucia demonstrate his talent, when they were in the dumps, for finding miseries of his own equivalent to theirs, with which he proposed to cheer them up. He needed to return from hours of isolation, it would seem, and to feel that a few people were in rapport with him. This handshaking (and Joyce ends most of his letters in Italian with '*una stretta di mano*') affects his work as well, mitigating its more savage extremes. Accordingly, Stephen mocks his own gesture of renunciation by comparing it to 'a fellow throwing a handful of peas up into the air',[2] just as Lynch mocks Stephen's Flaubertian view of the artist, as a god paring his fingernails, by suggesting that these too may be 'refined out of existence'.[3] This comic questioning does not disprove the rhetoric, but lightens it, and effects a rapprochement which ostensibly was disdained. The rebel's jokes, many of them on himself, allow him back into the human family.

Joyce's lifelong reluctance to comment publicly on his work gives unusual value to these letters as evocations of his mental scenery. They do not, however, offer more than fragments of self-analysis, and we must relate them ourselves. Certain expressions appear often enough to claim special notice. Among them the word 'artist' thrusts itself forward as a starting-point. Joyce's conception of himself as artist had origins in his early life; if *A Portrait of the Artist* may be said to plead for anything, it is for the continuity of the artistic temperament almost from infancy. He apparently first articulated this vocation soon after he passed from childhood to adolescence. The words 'artist' and 'puberty' had, in fact, a relation that is several times hinted at in these letters. As early as the age of fourteen, Joyce said,[4] he began to go to brothels, initially with a

---

[1] P. 142.   [2] *A Portrait of the Artist*, p. 256 (252).   [3] Ibid., p. 219 (215).
[4] To his brother Stanislaus, who noted it down in a diary.

strong sense of guilt. The Church urged him to master these impulses, but he found himself unable, and at heart unwilling, to do so. At confession he could find comfort and pardon, but not sanction. He was unwilling to give up either the spiritual idealism which had sustained him as a child, or the erotic drive which was agitating his adolescence. If debauchery was a part of his character, and he sometimes said it was,[1] then it must be justified. The word 'artist', which in the late nineteenth century had been invested with a secular awe, offered a profession which would protect all his soul instead of only its idealistic side, and might yet give it a profane sanctity. He thought of it as denoting something solid, unitary, and radiant, compounding into a new purity the errant flesh and the moral nature.

In early youth Joyce began to formulate the relation of art and the spiritual self into an aesthetic, as these letters testify; this aesthetic would vindicate him by establishing the primacy of the poet over the priest through a system rival to theology's. The artist was to be shown as devoted to integrating human experience on a level higher than the priest's, and without external or supernatural authority to make his work easier. This conscious definition of the principles of his art finds an accompaniment in these letters in Joyce's reiterated insistence that his own behaviour has been defensible and even praiseworthy. He tells his brother that his struggle with conventions 'was not entered into by me so much as a protest against these conventions as with the intention of living in conformity with my moral nature'.[2] He granted contemptuously, 'There are some people in Ireland who would call my moral nature oblique, people who think that the whole duty of man consists in paying one's debts.'[3] He is not less but more moral than other people. A year before he had written Nora Barnacle, 'Six years ago I left the Catholic Church, hating it most fervently. I found it impossible for me to remain in it on account of the impulses of my nature. . . . I made myself a beggar but I retained my pride.'[4] The words 'nature', 'moral nature', and 'pride' stand for him as aspects of the one substance, the artist's soul.

Although Joyce does not bother to mention his moral nature often, his awareness of it lies behind most of his letters. It enables him to assert to Grant Richards, *Dubliners* is 'a chapter of the moral history of my country'.[5] It underlies his criticism of other writers, such as Thomas Hardy. He writes his brother in December 1906 to complain of a book of Hardy's stories called *Life's Little Ironies*, and says:

[1] P. 48.   [2] P. 70.   [3] Ibid.
[4] Pp. 25–6; cf. p. 125.   [5] P. 83.

One story is about a lawyer on the circuit who seduces a servant, then receives letters from her so beautifully written that he decides to marry her. The letters are written by the servant's mistress who is in love with the lawyer. After the marriage (servant is accompanied to London by mistress) husband says fondly 'Now, dear J. K.-S-&c, will you write a little note to my dear sister, A. B X. etc and send her a piece of the wedding-cake. One of those nice little letters you know so well how to write, love.' Exit of servant wife. She goes out and sits at a table somewhere and, I suppose, writes something like this 'Dear Mrs X—I enclose a piece of wedding-cake.' Enter husband— lawyer, genial. Genially he says 'Well, love, how have you written' and then the whole discovery is found out. Servant-wife blows her nose in the letter and lawyer confronts the mistress. She confesses. Then they talk a page or so of copybook talk (as distinguished from servant's ditto). She weeps but he is stern. Is this as near as T.H. can get to life, I wonder? O my poor fledglings, poor Corley, poor Ignatius Gallaher! . . . What is wrong with these English writers is that they always keep beating about the bush.[1]

In discountenancing Hardy, Joyce was attacking not only a kind of fiction but a way of seeing or failing to see. Hardy appeared to him to lack the directness which he had taught himself by accepting nothing because it had been accepted before. As a result, the characterization in Hardy's stories was a false one based upon conventional ideas of class. Joyce, living himself with someone who had once been in service, was particularly entitled to detect the improbability here. He rejected as well the whole idiom as 'copybook talk'. For Joyce Hardy had lacked the courage to break through, and so was already dated, the moral fault breeding a literary one.

In his first years away Joyce associated artistic intrepidity with political self-consciousness, and he declared himself emphatically to be a 'socialistic artist'.[2] The character of his socialism was never made clear; he mentions Wilde and Lassalle rather than Marx, and planned to translate Wilde's essay on the subject into Italian. He was closest to Wilde in conceiving of socialism as a means of protecting the self and enabling it to be free. The particular abuses in society which made socialism necessary were the property system, which offered no provision for writers; religion, with its burdensome load of belief; and marriage, perpetuating property arrangements and disregarding individual freedom. Joyce does not condescend to argue the case for socialism on

[1] P. 137.   [2] P. 61.

an abstract level, but he names rich and church-married Oliver Gogarty as his epitome of the 'stupid, dishonest, tyrannical and cowardly burgher class'.[1] Gogarty appears in these letters as a kind of mythical adversary, a Hayley to Joyce's Blake, and the later use of him as Buck Mulligan was not accidental in the moral scheme of *Ulysses*.

Joyce did not hesitate to disclose that his socialism had a personal motivation, the hope of securing for himself a subsidy from the state. He wrote his brother, 'Some people would answer that while professing to be a socialist I am trying to make money: but this is not quite true at least as they mean it. If I made a fortune it is by no means certain that I would keep it. What I wish to do is to secure a competence on which I can rely, and why I expect to have this is because I cannot believe that any State requires my energy for the work I am at present engaged in.'[2] Stanislaus objected that this socialism was thin, and his brother unexpectedly agreed, 'Of course you find my socialism thin. It is so and unsteady and ill-informed.'[3] But any other system was tyranny, he maintained. Then on 1 March (?) 1907, he reported, 'The interest I took in socialism and the rest has left me. . . . I have no wish to codify myself as anarchist or socialist or reactionary.'[4] He never calls himself a socialist again.

He gave temporary allegiance to one other political programme, that of Sinn Féin; this Irish movement proposed to attack England by an economic boycott, a method which pleased Joyce more than armed revolution. Not joining an army, and annoying England, were equally desirable in his mind. Apart from the Irish language programme, he said, he was a nationalist. This interest in Sinn Féin also languished after a short time, however. At heart he was incapable of belonging to any political party, but he continued to make war in his own indirect way upon tyrannical authority.

Sometimes the moral note of Joyce's letters is more equivocal. There is, for example, the extraordinary letter he sent his mother from Paris soon after his twenty-first birthday:

Dear Mother Your order for 3s/4d of Tuesday last was very welcome as I had been without food for 42 hours (forty-two). Today I am twenty hours without food. But these spells of fasting are common with me now and when I get money I am so damnably hungry that I eat a fortune (1s/-) before you could say knife. I hope this new system of living won't injure my digestion. I have no news from 'Speaker' or 'Express'. If I had money I could buy a little oil stove

---

[1] P. 103.   [2] P. 61.   [3] P. 125.   [4] Pp. 151–2.

(I have a lamp) and cook macaroni for myself with bread when I am hard beat. I hope you are doing what I said about Stannie—but I daresay you are not. I hope the carpet that was sold is not one of the new purchases that you are selling to feed me. If this is so sell no more or I'll send the money back to you by return of post. I think I am doing the best I can for myself but it's pulling the devil by the tail the greater part of the time. I expect to be served with my bill (£1–6–0 with oil) any day and then my happiness is complete. My condition is so exciting that I cannot go asleep at night often till four in the morning and when I wake I look at once under the door to see if there is a letter from my editors and I assure you when I see the wooden floor only morning and morning I sigh and turn back to sleep off part of my hunger. I have not gone to Miss Gonne nor do I intend to go. With the utmost stretching your last order will keep me Monday midday (postage half a franc probably)—then, I suppose, I must do another fast. I regret this as Monday and Tuesday are carnival days and I shall probably be the only one starving in Paris.   Jim[1]

On the back of the letter Joyce transcribed a few bars of a song called 'Upa-Upa', which he said was played 'before the queen of some Indian island on occasions of state'.

This letter does not inspire an instant sympathy or a desire to join in singing 'Upa-Upa'. Its young writer is not self-sacrificing, not virtuous, not sensible, although he waves his hand distantly at these attributes. At first we see only self-pity and heartlessness in this assertion of his own needs as paramount. He takes unfair advantage of the fact that his mother's love is large enough to accept even the abuse of it. Yet there are twinges of conscience, sudden moments of concern for her, and there is evidence that he depends upon her for more than money, as if he could not live outside the environment of family affection, badly as he acts within it. The postscript about 'Upa-Upa' is a kind of humorous palinode; it seems to say, 'Never mind. We can still sing.'

Throughout the letter the emphasis is on his lenten fasts for his art. In other correspondence with her too, Joyce asks his mother to approve his artistic plans while he is fully aware that they are beyond her grasp, just as later he makes the same demands of his less educated wife. He writes that he will publish a book of songs in 1907, a comedy in 1912, and an aesthetic system five years after that. 'This *must* interest you!' he insists,[2] fearful that she may regard him as a starveling rather than as a starved hero. Her reply to many such pleas is a naked statement of

---

[1] II, 29–30.   [2] P. 19.

maternal love: 'My dear Jim if you are disappointed in my letter and if as usual I fail to understand what you would wish to explain, believe me it is not from any want of a longing desire to do so and speak the words you want but as you so often said I am stupid and cannot grasp the great thoughts which are yours much as I desire to do so. Do not wear your soul out with tears but be as usually brave and look hopefully to the future.'[1] To his harshness, and the defence of harshness by reference to his art, and the muted note of apology in her son's letters to her, May Joyce responded with a faultless simplicity.

The subdued ferocity of Joyce's letter was consistent enough with his consciousness of the difficulties of the life he had chosen. In his private phantasmagoria, which he never laid aside but had less use for later, he saw the world as giant and himself as Jack. He must evade, hide away in Pola and Trieste, and scheme (in 'silence, exile and cunning'),[2] and one day the world would topple at his feet. To get out of Ireland was a step of this strategy. It was justified in two ways: the loftier was Rousseau's, 'If one wishes to devote one's books to the true benefit of one's country, one must write them abroad.'[3] Joyce rephrased this as, 'The shortest way to Tara is *via* Holyhead.'[4] A Parnell of art, he would create 'at last a conscience in the soul of this wretched race'.[5] He predicted in a 1912 letter to his wife, 'I hope that the day may come when I shall be able to give you the fame of being beside me when I have entered into my Kingdom.'[6] His images of departure evoked balancing images of return, which displayed themselves not only in his trips back to Dublin but in the ironical homecoming of *Exiles*, the 'eternal return' of *Finnegans Wake*, and the saturation of almost all his work in Irish times and places.

The second means of justifying departure was more reactive than independent. Joyce felt he had been 'betrayed' by his countrymen, not of course by all but by those on whom he might have expected to rely, his friends. The letter he wrote to Ibsen when he was eighteen indicates he already expected trouble from this quarter and was set to follow his master's example by 'absolute indifference' to them.[7] But absolute indifference was not his mode. In certain moments he conceded that his decision did not depend upon his friends' behaviour; he wrote his brother that it was 'a youthfully exaggerated feeling of this mal-disposition of affairs which urged me to pounce upon the falsehood in their attitude towards me as an excuse for escape'.[8] We may even add

---

[1] II, 22.
[2] *A Portrait of the Artist*, p. 251 (247).
[3] Jean-Jacques Rousseau, *Confessions*.
[4] *A Portrait of the Artist*, p. 254 (250).
[5] P. 204. [6] P. 203. [7] P. 7. [8] P. 62.

that, without meaning to, he courted betrayal. As if to prepare the ground, he made great demands upon his friends, and in asserting his own freedom of action, he hampered theirs, to draw them into what he himself described as 'the Daedalean spell'.[1] He tested their loyalty by making them his creditors, by leaning upon them, by asking their responses to his works and acts. The demands grew greater. His friends were like his readers, who had only to accept one difficult work when he devised another much harder for them to accept, in an ascending series. They, for their part, had never met anyone so enveloping, at once so contemptuous of their abilities and so avid for their allegiances. Their own individuality seemed jeopardized by Joyce's quiet importunacy. As signs of their resistance multiplied, Joyce saw these as inevitable; he did not recognize that the friendship he required of them was inordinate, yet his own doubts that they would persist in it contributed to that failure of which he then complained.

Sometimes he granted that he might himself be a little at fault, and this admission, rare as it was, lends support to his claim that he could free himself from his preconceptions when necessary. He allowed to Nora Barnacle that he had 'a contemptuous suspicious nature'.[2] His habit of representing himself as worse than he was also offered encouragement to those who wanted to leave him. Before he went away from Dublin with her in 1904, he admitted that he had a propensity 'a little devilish . . . that makes me delight in breaking down people's ideas of me and proving to them that I am really selfish, proud, cunning and regardless of others'.[3] But even as he denigrated his own character, he mustered support for it. So he wrote his brother in a burst of anger, 'My irregularities can easily be made the excuse of your conduct.'[4] Others, with more faults than he, dared not risk his candour. He has only to ask, in self-depreciation, could I deserve more from the world than exile? when the question changes to: could I deserve less? as if to ask, who would want to be anything but an outcast?

His ironies may therefore be said to compete with each other. At one end of the scale he filters self-abasement through mockery; at the other, he approaches grandeur, feels it verging on grandiosity, and turns abruptly away. He wrote to inform his friend in Trieste, Alessandro Francini Bruni, of the magnificent praise which Valery Larbaud had lavished upon *Ulysses*, then wryly concluded: '*Son diventato un monumento—anzi vespasiano!*'[5] ('I have become a monument—no, a vespasian!') When he announced to his brother that his situation in

---

[1] P. 46.   [2] P. 25.   [3] P. 28.
[4] P. 196.   [5] P. 280.

Trieste was a 'voluntary exile',[1] he meant it, though the word 'voluntary' before 'exile' begged the question a little. But when he spoke of his departure with Nora Barnacle from Dublin to Pola as a 'hegira',[2] the mood of self-mockery was in the ascendant.

The title of his autobiographical novel imposed the problem of reconciling two persistent attitudes towards himself. He had named it *Stephen Hero* in ironic allusion, perhaps, to Byron's *Childe Harold* as well as to the ballad of 'Turpin Hero', but the brag, archaically inverted, began to trouble him as too sceptical of its own vaingloriousness. His letters show that he thought about the matter a good deal. He wrote Stanislaus to say flatly, 'the whole structure of heroism is, and always was, a damned lie and . . . there cannot be any substitute for the individual passion as the motive power of everything—art and philosophy included.'[3] All talk of selflessness and social purpose was poppycock. In response to a compliment about steadfastness in adversity, he replied, 'I dislike to hear of any stray heroics on the prowl for me.'[4] Yet the issue was not dismissed so flippantly. He had written to Ibsen in 1900 that the quality most admirable in that artist was an 'inward heroism' which had for one aspect the 'wilful resolution to wrest the secret from life', and for another the 'absolute indifference to public canons of art, friends and shibboleths'.[5] Now, writing to Stanislaus again, he mused, 'Do you not think the search for heroics damn vulgar— and yet how are we to describe Ibsen ?'[6] The upshot of these ruminations was that he changed the title of his novel to *A Portrait of the Artist as a Young Man*, a title less likely to be misinterpreted, although the term 'young man' was meant humorously (he wrote Dámaso Alonso) insofar as it was applied to the infant on the first page.[7]

Joyce did regard himself as a hero, but thought it advisable not to say so explicitly; he thought of himself also as in some ways a martyr, but as usual his way of saying so is by seeming to repudiate the idea. Referring to this Christlike resemblance, he wrote his brother, 'I must get rid of some of these Jewish bowels I have in me yet.'[8] And in another letter he said, 'I am not likely to die of bashfulness but neither am I prepared to be crucified to attest the perfection of my art.'[9] The figure pleased him, and a year later he remarked once more, 'I have written quite enough and before I do any more in that line I must see some reason why—I am not a literary Jesus Christ.'[10] But three disavowals of the crown are less convincing than one. Whatever he might say in the cold mutton of letters, Joyce was fascinated by the Christlike analogies

---

[1] P. 56; cf. p. 125.   [2] P. 132; III, 217.   [3] P. 54.   [4] P. 56.   [5] P. 7.
[6] P. 53.   [7] P. 311.   [8] P. 76.   [9] P. 56.   [10] P. 106.

of the artist, and developed them fully in *A Portrait of the Artist*. A powerful sacrificial feeling sustained him as he fought for a literary foothold around southern Europe, staving off mosquitoes in Pola, instilling an alien tongue into Triestines, cashing cheques for other people in Rome. But he undercut it with modesty by jokingly or grimly calling attention to his defects and failures.

His behaviour with his books was a similar combination of aloofness and self-advertisement. The enormous pride of the artist was compatible with enormous exertions. He had his own press notices printed up and sent them, with chilling formality, to possible reviewers. He did not condescend to explain his own work, but through letters and conversations he laid down, as he told Harriet Shaw Weaver, the terms in which *Ulysses* was subsequently discussed. He was equally skilful with *Finnegans Wake*. There were earlier schemes which mixed self-exculpation with promotion, such as his letter to the press in 1911, complaining that publishers had broken contracts with him for *Dubliners* because of the book's forthrightness.[1] Another was his public letter in 1919 protesting against mistreatment by the British Consulate General in Zurich.[2] The protest in 1928 against the piracy of *Ulysses*, in which a hundred and fifty eminent men joined,[3] was one of his shrewdest mixtures of publicity with high principle. He could never think of his works as popular, or as popular enough, and he felt justified in overcoming middle-class torpor and hostility by any means he could devise.

Sometimes his epistolary campaigns moved outside literature. One of these was on behalf of the tenor John Sullivan, whom Joyce regarded as a kind of alter ego. Others involved such schemes of enrichment as importing Irish tweeds to Trieste, establishing a cinema in Dublin, managing a troupe of actors in Zurich. These projects had much the same place in Joyce's mind as the Sardinian silver mines in Balzac's, and like those came to nothing, though they were also good ideas. His attitude in them exhibited a combination of effrontery and involvement, supplication and reserve.

This mixture permeates his letters and is somewhat explained by them. Joyce often appeared to be cold and aloof, but in his own view these qualities were less fundamental than others. He thought of himself most fondly as fragile and vulnerable. Once this part of his self-portrait becomes visible, other elements take shape around it. The 'enigma of a manner', which he speaks in the first draft of *A Portrait*[4]

---

[1] Pp. 197–9.   [2] II, 438–40.   [3] III, 151–3.

[4] 'A Portrait of the Artist,' in Robert Scholes and Richard M. Kain, *The Workshop of Dedalus* (Evanston, Illinois, 1965), pp. 60–8.

of consciously fabricating, is seen as an attempt at self-protection. 'Can you not see the simplicity which is at the back of all my disguises? We all wear masks,' he writes to Nora Barnacle,[1] and he is pleased, at least temporarily, when she pierces his 'magnificent poses' and recognizes him to be an 'impostor'.[2] His asperities show as attempts to overcome an indulgence to which he feels so apt to become prey, and the method of his prose books is a kind of absorption of the universe rather than a facing up to it; he seems to draw it bit by bit inside him, and conceives of the imagination as a womb.

Joyce liked to think of himself as weak and of others as stronger than he. Like Shem, he 'disliked anything anyway approaching a plain straightforward standup or knockdown row'.[3] Men were stronger physically and women stronger spiritually. 'I am so helpless tonight, helpless, helpless!' he writes his wife,[4] and in his poem, 'A Prayer', he begs, 'Take me, save me, soothe me, O spare me.' This attitude is the one he regularly assumes in his letters to his wife, and is the more surprising in that she might have been expected to take it towards him. The letters to Nora Barnacle Joyce, which make this position plain, are psychologically the most important in this volume; they move gradually towards self-surrender as if it were a kind of Ultima Thule.

At first their tone is jaunty, with some of that 'assumed dongiovannism' which he attributed to the young Shakespeare.[5] But within a month of the beginning of their courtship, the tone is solemnized. She must become his mistress, to be sure, but he seems more occupied with something else, that she become his fellow-conspirator against the established order. 'My mind rejects the whole present social order and Christianity—home, the recognised virtues, classes of life, and religious doctrines,' he writes her in August 1904.[6] His intransigence to the world is related to his submission to her. Their elopement must not be sportive but agonized, a sign and portent of his future work. He was aware that to his father, and to many of his friends, the relationship with Nora Barnacle was a misalliance. Though he pretended to be impervious to their criticism, 'their least word,' he told her, 'tumbles my heart about like a bird in a storm.'[7] Yet like Heine, as he says,[8] and like others he does not trouble to name, he had the courage to see that the world was wrong about this as about other things. By virtue of being poor and in love with him, Nora became the banned sweetheart of a banned artist. 'It seemed to me that I was fighting a battle with every

---

[1] P. 27.   [2] P. 194.   [3] *Finnegans Wake*, p. 174.   [4] P. 195.
[5] *Ulysses* (London, 1960; New York, 1961), p. 251 (196).
[6] P. 25.   [7] P. 27.   [8] P. 51.

religious and social force in Ireland for you and that I had nothing to rely on but myself.'[1] Chambermaid and prodigal son might make a match of it; obloquy was a state they might share like pleasures of the bed.

Joyce's affection for Nora Barnacle developed rapidly, though she complained it lagged behind her own. He was already unconsciously altering his role in the affair from active to passive. 'Allow me, dearest Nora,' he wrote her, 'to tell you how much I desire that you should share any happiness that may be mine and to assure you of my great respect for that love of yours which it is my wish to deserve and to answer.'[2] The word 'love' was one that mustered up all his doubts, doubts of his own sincerity, doubts of the emotion itself. To talk of 'spiritual love', he informed Stanislaus, was 'lying drivel',[3] though in a few years he used the phrase without irony.[4] But as he said, he was deeply impressed by the unqualified feeling Nora Barnacle had for him, and the fact that she expressed it without the coyness he had come to expect in girls of his age. 'I never could speak to the girls I used to meet at houses,' he wrote her later. 'Their false manners checked me at once.'[5] Stephen Dedalus represents Shakespeare as equally shy. If Nora was untutored she was also unspoiled, a 'simple honorable soul',[6] and one 'incapable of any of the deceits which pass for current morality'.[7] It was very important for him, knowing with what intricate devices he met most people, to have in her someone he could trust. His reserve, his sense of watching his own dignity, are involved in almost all his other relationships. With Miss Weaver, for example, he seems to want not only to act politely towards her, but to see himself as meeting the English Protestant middle class with adequate decorum. A certain gentleness comes through regardless, but almost against his will. With Nora there was the possibility available to him nowhere else, of complete self-revelation, a great relief to a suspicious man. He came to feel that she was more than wife or mistress; she must triple as a symbol of Ireland and a more genuine one than Yeats's Maud Gonne. In her he saw, as he said, 'the beauty and the doom of the race of whom I am a child',[8] and he asked her, 'O take me into your soul of souls and then I will become indeed the poet of my race.'[9]

This yielding of himself was not achieved without difficulty. Joyce had to pass through stages of amusement, perplexity, boredom, and even distrust. The last was of course the most serious. In 1909, on his first trip back to Dublin, he was led mistakenly to believe that Nora had been faithless to him during a period which he held sacred, the early

[1] P. 30. [2] Ibid. [3] P. 129. [4] Pp. 169, 181. [5] P. 161.
[6] P. 167. [7] P. 66. [8] P. 179. [9] P. 169.

months of their love. In a few days he was undeceived, and felt guilty
for having so misjudged her. His first letters were filled with remorse:
'What a worthless fellow I am!'[1] But gradually he tried to turn the
incident to advantage by ushering her into a greater intimacy. His
letters became a turbulent mixture of erotic imagery and apologies for
it, the apologies being accompanied by equally extreme flights of
adoration. His relationship with her had to counterbalance all his rifts
with other people. Having become partners in spiritual love, they must
now share an onanistic complicity, agitating each other to sexual climax
by means of their letters. In this way Joyce renewed the conspiratorial
and passionate understanding that they had had when they first left
Ireland together.

These letters of 1909 and 1912 present Joyce with more intensity
than any others. Often they transfer habitual attitudes to a different
plane; he does not ask her for more money, as he does others, but for
more proof of affection. He reminds her constantly of his art, often
combining it with love tokens: the first present he brings her from
Dublin is a necklace inscribed with a line from one of his poems, and
the next is a manuscript of *Chamber Music* laboriously copied out on
parchment. His art is the lofty counterpart of that deeper nature which
he will divulge otherwise only to her. And he mixes his pleas with tender
rebuke, scolding her for scolding him. She is too rude to him, ruder than
he deserves. To vary the note, he sometimes delights in acknowledging
his faults, including his infidelities with prostitutes, in imagining her as
even more merciless to him, as whipping him like the ladies of Sacher-
Masoch,[2] and with furs on to complete the picture.[3] 'You have me
completely in your power,'[4] he enjoys telling her, pleased to have, as
whipping-boy, her undivided attention. Then, to renew his innocence
and hers, he leans upon her as if she were a mother, and longs to be her
child or even her unborn infant: 'take me into the dark sanctuary of
your womb. Shelter me, dear, from harm!'[5]

Yet one route of distrust remains: he can never quite understand her
implacable unlikeness to him. He finds himself suspicious again: 'Are
you with me, Nora, or are you secretly against me?'[6] When most
allayed, this feeling can tease itself almost pleasurably with a curiosity
like John Donne's about her body's life before she knew him, but she
cannot reassure him enough: 'I am sure there are finer fellows in Galway
than your poor lover but O, darling, one day you will see that I will be
something in my country.'[7] And he writes again, in a letter three years

---

[1] P. 160.　　　[2] Pp. 166, 188.　　　[3] Pp. 172, 175, 176.　　　[4] P. 173.
[5] P. 195.　　　[6] P. 174.　　　[7] P. 195.

later, 'Can your friend in the sodawater factory or the priesteen write my verses?'[1] He adores her as 'my beautiful wild flower of the hedges, my dark-blue rain-drenched flower',[2] and compares her to the Virgin,[3] then desecrates this romantic lyricism by naming her his 'fuckbird'[4] instead. One moment he is an angel, the next a frog, and then back again. He likes to boast of his prudishness with men, at whose dirty stories he never even smiles, to give a greater secretive value to his outspokenness with her, and to indicate that this erotic singleness must prove the essential innocence of his nature.

The atmosphere is not one of Catholic guilt, but it is certainly not one of pagan insouciance either. He feels compelled to set images of purity against images of impurity. He dwells upon the association of the sexual and excretory organs, then fears she will consider him corrupt, although he has found learned sanction in Spinoza, yet he also wants corruption to be a part of their love as well as incorruption. 'Are you too, then, like me,' he asks hopefully, 'one moment high as the stars, the next lower than the lowest wretches?'[5] They must share in shame, shamelessness, and unashamedness.

Frank as these letters are, their psychology can easily be misunderstood. They were intended to accomplish sexual gratification in him and inspire the same in her, and at moments they fasten intently on peculiarities of sexual behaviour, some of which might be technically called perverse. They display traces of fetishism, anality, paranoia, and masochism, but before quartering Joyce into these categories and consigning him to their tyranny we must remember that he was capable, in his work, of ridiculing them all as Circean beguilements, of turning them into vaudeville routines. Then too, the letters rebuke such obvious labels by an ulterior purpose; besides the immediate physical goal, Joyce wishes to anatomize and reconstitute and crystallize the emotion of love. He goes further still; like Richard Rowan in *Exiles*, he wishes to possess his wife's soul, and have her possess his, in utter nakedness.[6] To know someone else beyond love and hate, beyond vanity and remorse, beyond human possibility almost, is his extravagant desire.

In later life Joyce evidently wrote Nora in a similar vein, but with more sense of human limitations. Their relationship never achieved the complete understanding for which he had striven. The only letter of importance that has survived was one sent her in April 1922, when against his will she took their two children to Galway. She seems to have

---

[1] II, 304.   [2] Pp. 179, 180, 181, 183, 188,193.   [3] P. 165.
[4] P. 185.   [5] P. 167   [6] *Exiles* (London, 1936; New York, 1961), p. 157 (112).

said she would not return, and wrote to ask him for money to remain. He replied:

8.30 a.m. Thursday

My darling, my love, my queen: I jump out of bed to send you this. Your wire is postmarked 18 hours later than your letter which I have just received. A cheque for your fur will follow in a few hours, and also money for yourself. If you wish to live there (as you ask me to send you two pounds a week) I will send that amount (£8 and £4) rent on the first of every month. But you also ask me if I would go to London with you. I would go anywhere in the world if I could be sure that I could be alone with your dear self without family and without friends. Either this must occur or we must part forever, though it will break my heart. Evidently it is impossible to describe to you the despair I have been in since you left. Yesterday I got a fainting fit in Miss Beach's shop and she had to run and get me some kind of a drug. Your image is always in my heart. How glad I am to hear you are looking younger! O my dearest, if you would only turn to me now and read that terrible book which has now broken the heart in my breast and take me to yourself alone to do with me what you will! I have only 10 minutes to write this so forgive me. Will write again before noon and also wire. These few words for the moment and my undying unhappy love.   JIM[1]

This letter, written while *Ulysses* was meeting with great success, is humourless and sad like almost all Joyce's love letters. It assumes the old humility of subject to queen, but as usual it is the subject who controls the royal treasury. He is as eager now as fifteen years before to buy furs for her. Each sign of weakness has its implicit limit: he begs for more affection, but is still able to threaten that without it they must part forever. His heart is broken, so she must read his book. His 'undying unhappy love' and his physical collapse are proofs of his dependence upon her, but they are also curiously self-regarding. With all his testimony of surrender, Joyce utterly dominated that scene.

A more complete picture of his mind though not of his emotions can be elicited from his imperfect and rather eerie liaison with Martha Fleischmann in Zurich in 1918 and 1919. Joyce wrote this young Swiss woman quite a few letters, of which four have survived. Their idiom is a less intense copy of that which he employed with his wife; he writes pitiably, with many references to physical weakness, and he prostrates

[1] III, 63.

himself before Martha. Though well aware that women are not neces-
sarily susceptible to advances of this sort, Joyce seems to have been
able to use no others. The letters make Martha his Virgin and Madonna
like Nora before her; he suggests she might be Jewish but asks her not
to take offence, since Jesus was born from the womb of a Jewess.[1] And
throughout he calls attention to his art, as in his slightly inaccurate
remark that, at the age of thirty-five, he was at the same point as Dante
when he began the *Divine Comedy* and Shakespeare when he had his
affair with the Dark Lady of the Sonnets.[2] He was actually thirty-six.

Joyce knew he was behaving absurdly, but he had never halted any
line of action merely to avoid possible folly, and it is not necessary to
doubt his statement in one letter that he was passing sleepless nights
over her. That he intended only a clandestine affair, however, and so
was not offering himself completely, is indicated by his caution in
disguising his handwriting by using Greek e's, as Bloom does in writing
another Martha in *Ulysses*. The affair never came to much: these
letters, and other information, suggest that Joyce engaged in a good
deal of peering through windows at Martha Fleischmann, and that the
chief pleasure he arrived at was probably voyeuristic like Earwicker's
in the Phoenix Park. He recognized the implicit comedy afterwards by
depicting a similar episode in Bloom's day, in which Gerty McDowell,
like Martha Fleischmann, has a limp. There also a men's retreat is
going on at the Star of the Sea Church, and the prayers to the Virgin
are amusingly juxtaposed with Bloom's profane adoration of Gerty.
Joyce, in turn, seems to have written Martha letters that contained
obscene words,[3] and his behaviour also admixed detachment and passion.

The later parody of the emotions does not prove that earlier they
were false, and it is unlikely that Joyce laughed at the time. But even
though he kept his sense of comedy in abeyance as he clutched tenta-
tively for support at another female figure, it must have existed in
reserve as a defence against possible humiliation, ready if called upon
to turn amorous defeat into artistic triumph when his original feelings
had run their course.

The dip and sway of Joyce's love letters make an amusing counter-
point to his letters to men. With Nora the effort is to rip away pretences,
with men Joyce is very bespectacled and walking-sticked. There are
exceptions, such as his bantering notes to Frank Budgen and Ezra
Pound, but usually he pushes the correspondent away a little by
continuing to employ 'Mr' after long association, by pretending some
indifference to the things that most oppress him, by half-anticipating

[1] P. 233.   [2] Ibid.   [3] II, 430.

defeat in arguments, as with publishers, though he wishes to appear bold and steadfast.

Because of his disinclination to collide with men, or to be informal with more than two or three, Joyce's correspondence with his brother Stanislaus, especially from 1902 to 1912, stands almost by itself as a fairly frank expression of his intellectual position. It is comparable to the letters setting forth his emotional position to Nora. James, as older brother, asserted himself freely, and Stanislaus, as younger, disputed his conclusions but admired most of them; he considered James superior only in literary matters, not in politics or domestic behaviour. The relationship of the two was set from the first as one in which Stanislaus was to pay heavily. These letters make clear that by and large he accepted this arrangement to which he sometimes objected, and that James assumed it as a matter of course. From their correspondence Stanislaus emerges as a solid figure, helpful and cantankerous, roused by his brother to intellectual emulation as well as to envy and impatience.

The hints and declarations in these letters enable us to see Joyce a little as he saw himself. While he considered that rebellion had been for him the beginning of wisdom, a kind of birth of consciousness, he did not regard himself primarily as a rebel. His dominant image of himself was one of delicacy and fragility, of perpetual ill health and ill-luck, of a tenor among basses. It led him to imagine himself as like a deer or a bird or a woman, or like a Gandhian Christ. He reacted against varieties of power by juxtaposing the strong with the weak, Boylan with Bloom or the Ondt with the Gracehoper. Then his wit challenged the powerful masculine energies until they had lost their strength. He wished to protect the lyrical centre of his work by acknowledging with laughter all the absurdities of human conduct through which it must draw its breath. He counters a possible contempt for his almost effeminate delicacy by examining in the fullest and liveliest way its inescapably comic embodiment. Where other writers, like Wells, appear always to be thrusting, Joyce characterized himself more nearly by the parry. Each of his works concludes in a lyrical assertion, which is made possible by the undermining of maleness by comedy, as if brute force had to be overcome by subtler devices. In *Finnegans Wake* the Crimean War is reduced to a scatological joke, the Battle of Waterloo to an extravaganza in a waxworks museum, and the World War to a prizefight; in *Ulysses* the Cyclops is defeated; in *A Portrait* Ireland is left. Joyce's distaste for war, crime, and brutality relate to this preference for all that is not the bully. His work is not conceived as a blow in the face, but, these letters help us to perceive, as a matrical envelopment.

But this appraisal of Joyce which his letters sponsor is not entirely satisfactory. His disclaimers of masculinity, his assumption of 'feminine' weakness, were secondary manifestations. After all, strong men have hidden themselves among women before. His succession of mewing exhortations always sprang from initial decisions inflexibly pursued. He cared for his daughter with a solicitude that could be called feminine, but his delicate coaxing and joking were directed to twist her mind back to sanity, like a resistant piece of iron. Though he lived in discouragement like a bad climate, and sporadically thought of not finishing his books, he needle-and-threaded each one to its conclusion. As if adjusting himself to his pliant, jointless body, which was basically tough and wiry, he imagined himself in the state of being malleable and passive, and commenced to live there, like a second residence. The mixture of such qualities as pride and plaintiveness, the flashes of candour amid stretches of tortuous reticence or confessions that are off the point, lend his spare self-portraiture in these letters an interest quite different from that to be found in the shaped nuances of Henry James or the open-collared eloquence of D. H. Lawrence. An urge to the immoderate is always there, but at various distances from the surface. Read in this light, these letters—the best of them—are among the most interesting, and insinuating, ever written.

SELECTED LETTERS OF
JAMES JOYCE

Part I

DUBLIN AND PARIS

1882–1904

Dublin and Paris (1882–1904)

James Joyce was born on 2 February 1882 at 41 Brighton Square West in Rathgar, a township of Dublin. He was the oldest of ten children (five others failed to survive infancy) born to John Stanislaus Joyce (1849–1931) and Mary Jane Murray Joyce (1859–1903). Joyce's father was a profligate, witty, sentimental man who, after several false starts, obtained by political influence a well-paid job in the office of the Collector of Rates. He held this position from 1880 until 1892, when it was abolished and he was put on a small and predictably insufficient pension. During the rest of his long life he had occasional jobs but no regular occupation.

John Joyce was ambitious for his oldest son, and sent him from 1888 to 1891, while the family was still comfortably off, to the best Catholic preparatory school, Clongowes Wood College, in Sallins, County Kildare. When this financial burden became too great, he sent James to Belvedere College, a Catholic day school in Dublin, where he studied from 1893 to 1898. James was soon known as the most gifted pupil there, though his Jesuit teachers detected signs in him of irreligion. He then went on to University College, Dublin, from which he received his Bachelor of Arts degree in 1902.

James Joyce's career as a writer began when he was nine years old. The death of Charles Stewart Parnell on 6 October 1891 roused him to write a poem, 'Et Tu, Healy', in which he contrasted the heroic chief with his treacherous followers. While a pupil at Belvedere Joyce made his mark by his prize-winning compositions in the Intermediate Examinations. He tried writing stories, and began a series of prose sketches called *Silhouettes* and a series of poems entitled *Moods*. The titles, innocuous in themselves, perhaps suggest in retrospect the tangential method he was to adopt in *Dubliners* and the wavelike insubstantiality of the poems of *Chamber Music*. Meanwhile he read widely and found in the works of Ibsen a model for his own ideals of blunt subject-matter, artistic self-possession, and symbolically ordered work.

At University College, Dublin, Joyce made evident his ambition as a writer, and was quick to speak up for art when his classmates celebrated morality or the national movement. He read a paper, 'Drama and Life', before the Literary and Historical Society of the College on 20 January

1900; he now insubordinately took the part of Ibsen, who in Ireland was still thought to be of questionable moral tendency, against Shakespeare and the Greek dramatists. At the age of eighteen he published an article on 'Ibsen's New Drama' (*When We Dead Awaken*) in the *Fortnightly Review* for 1 April 1900. The same year he tried his hand at a play in prose, *A Brilliant Career*, and at one in verse, *Dream Stuff*; he composed a number of lyrics under the title *Shine and Dark*, and began a series of prose poems which he named *Epiphanies*. By this term he meant the sudden disclosure of a hidden aspect of personality or of the inner meaning of a scene, in a style sometimes lyrical and sometimes expressionless. In 1901 Joyce wrote an article, 'The Day of the Rabblement', protesting against the Irish Literary Theatre, which W. B. Yeats, George Moore, and Edward Martyn had got under way, because of its intolerable provinciality. He felt that they were making Ireland quaint when it should be European.

After Joyce completed his studies in 1902 he resolved to make himself known to Irish writers. He first approached George Russell (AE), through Russell met Yeats, and through Yeats met Lady Gregory, impressing them all with his arrogance as well as his talent. During the fall of 1902 he decided to go to France and take up medical studies at the École de Médecine of the University of Paris. He intended to support himself by his writing and by contributions from home. On 1 December 1902 he left Dublin, stopped in London to see Yeats and some editors of reviews, and went on to Paris. He was quickly homesick enough to be persuaded by his family to return for the Christmas holidays; but when these were over he ventured to Paris again, arriving there on 23 January 1903. This time he discarded the notion of studying medicine; he wrote poems and epiphanies, assembled the elements of his 'esthetic philosophy', and set himself for an artistic career. He stayed in Paris until his father telegraphed him on 10 April to come home because his mother was dying.

Mrs Joyce's fatal illness, which proved to be cancer, did not end until 13 August 1903. During those months, and for more than a year afterwards, Joyce gave the impression of idleness; he consorted a good deal with Oliver St John Gogarty and other young men who later served as models for his generally unoccupied fictional characters. But on 7 January 1904 he abruptly wrote an essay, 'A Portrait of the Artist', which gave an account of the spiritual development of a nameless but largely autobiographical hero. Although the new magazine *Dana*, to which he submitted it, rejected the essay, he determined to extend it into an autobiographical novel, *Stephen Hero*. At this he wrote steadily during 1904. Early in the summer of that year George Russell suggested that Joyce write some simple stories for the *Irish Homestead*, and this invitation spurred him to begin the composition, in a style enigmatically simple, of *Dubliners*.

Shortly before, on 10 June 1904, Joyce met for the first time Nora Barnacle, a young woman of twenty from Galway who was employed in Finn's Hotel. They first went walking together almost certainly on 16 June, and liked each other well. Joyce remembered the date with sacramental precision and used it as the day of *Ulysses*; he encouraged his admirers to call it 'Bloomsday'. While he had doubts and misgivings about Nora Barnacle, he overcame them and proposed that she run away with him to the Continent. When she bravely agreed, they left Dublin on Saturday night, 8 October 1904. Joyce had been assured by a teachers' employment agency that a position in the Berlitz School in Zurich awaited him. He and Nora Barnacle set out for Switzerland, stopping in Paris to borrow money so they could continue their journey.

From WILLIAM ARCHER[1]   MS. Cornell

23 April 1900   *2 Vernon Chambers, Southampton Row, W.C.*

Dear Sir I think it will interest you to know that in a letter I had from
Henrik Ibsen a day or two ago[2] he says 'I have read, or rather spelt out,
a review by Mr James Joyce in the *Fortnightly Review*[3] which is very
benevolent ("velvillig") and for which I should greatly like to thank the
author if only I had sufficient knowledge of the language.' Yours truly

WILLIAM ARCHER

To WILLIAM ARCHER   MS. British Museum

28 April 1900   *13 Richmond Avenue, Fairview, Dublin*

Dear Sir I wish to thank you for your kindness in writing to me. I am a
young Irishman, eighteen years old, and the words of Ibsen I shall keep
in my heart all my life. Faithfully yours   JAS A. JOYCE

To HENRIK IBSEN   MS. Cornell

March 1901   *8 Royal Terrace, Fairfield, Dublin*

Honoured Sir: I write to you to give you greeting on your seventy-third
birthday and to join my voice to those of your well-wishers in all lands.
You may remember that shortly after the publication of your latest
play, *When We Dead Awaken,* an appreciation of it appeared in one of
the English reviews—*The Fortnightly Review*—over my name. I know
that you have seen it because some short time afterwards Mr William
Archer wrote to me and told me that in a letter he had had from you
some days before, you had written, 'I have read or rather spelled out a
review in *The Fortnightly Review* by Mr James Joyce which is very
benevolent and for which I should greatly like to thank the author if
only I had sufficient knowledge of the language.' (My own knowledge of

---

[1] William Archer (1856–1924), Ibsen's translator and principal champion in England.

[2] Ibsen's letter to Archer, dated 16 April 1900 at Christiania, is now in the British
Museum.

[3] Joyce's first published article 'Ibsen's New Drama', appeared in the *Fortnightly
Review*, n.s. v. 67 (1 April 1900), 575–90. It is included in *The Critical Writings of
James Joyce*, ed. Ellsworth Mason and Richard Ellmann (London and New York, 1959),
pp. 47–67.

your language is not, as you see, great but I trust you will be able to decipher my meaning.)[1] I can hardly tell you how moved I was by your message. I am a young, a very young man, and perhaps the telling of such tricks of the nerves will make you smile. But I am sure if you go back along your own life to the time when you were an undergraduate at the University as I am, and if you think what it would have meant to you to have earned a word from one who held as high a place in your esteem as you hold in mine, you will understand my feeling. One thing only I regret, namely, that an immature and hasty article should have met your eye rather than something better and worthier of your praise. There may not have been any wilful stupidity in it, but truly I can say no more. It may annoy you to have your works at the mercy of striplings but I am sure you would prefer hotheadedness to nerveless and 'cultured' paradoxes.

What shall I say more? I have sounded your name defiantly through the college where it was either unknown or known faintly and darkly. I have claimed for you your rightful place in the history of the drama. I have shown what, as it seemed to me, was your highest excellence— your lofty impersonal power. Your minor claims—your satire, your technique and orchestral harmony—these, too, I advanced. Do not think me a hero-worshipper—I am not so. And when I spoke of you in debating societies and so forth, I enforced attention by no futile ranting.

But we always keep the dearest things to ourselves. I did not tell them what bound me closest to you. I did not say how what I could discern dimly of your life was my pride to see, how your battles inspired me—not the obvious material battles but those that were fought and won behind your forehead, how your wilful resolution to wrest the secret from life gave me heart and how in your absolute indifference to public canons of art, friends and shibboleths you walked in the light of your inward heroism. And this is what I write to you of now. Your work on earth draws to a close and you are near the silence. It is growing dark for you. Many write of such things, but they do not know. You have only opened the way—though you have gone as far as you could upon it—to the end of 'John Gabriel Borkman' and its spiritual truth— for your last play stands, I take it, apart. But I am sure that higher and holier enlightenment lies—onward.

As one of the young generation for whom you have spoken I give you greeting—not humbly, because I am obscure and you in the glare, not sadly, because you are an old man and I a young man, not

---

[1] Only the English draft of this letter, which Joyce translated into Dano-Norwegian, has survived.

presumptuously, nor sentimentally—but joyfully, with hope and with love, I give you greeting. Faithfully yours,   JAMES A. JOYCE

To LADY GREGORY   TS. Yeats[1]

[*November 1902*]   *7 S. Peter's Terrace, Cabra, Dublin*

Dear Lady Gregory: I have broken off my medical studies here and am going to trouble you with a history. I have a degree of B.A. from the Royal University, and I had made plans to study medicine here. But the college authorities are determined I shall not do so, wishing I dare say to prevent me from securing any position of ease from which I might speak out my heart. To be quite frank I am without means to pay my medical fees and they refuse to get me any grinding or tuitions or examining—alleging inability—although they have done and are doing so for men who were stuck in the exams I passed. I want to get a degree in medicine, for then I can build up my work securely. I want to achieve myself—little or great as I may be—for I know that there is no heresy or no philosophy which is so abhorrent to my church as a human being, and accordingly I am going to Paris. I intend to study medicine at the University of Paris supporting myself there by teaching English. I am going alone and friendless—I know of a man who used to live somewhere near Montmartre but I have never met him—into another country, and I am writing to you to know can you help me in any way. I do not know what will happen to me in Paris but my case can hardly be worse than it is here. I am leaving Dublin by the night boat on Monday 1st December and my train leaves Victoria Station for Newhaven the same night. I am not despondent however for I know that even if I fail to make my way such failure proves very little. I shall try myself against the powers of the world. All things are inconstant except the faith in the soul, which changes all things and fills their inconstancy with light. And though I seem to have been driven out of my country here as a misbeliever I have found no man yet with a faith like mine. Faithfully yours,   JAMES JOYCE

To his FAMILY in Dublin   MS. Cornell

6 December 1902   *Grand Hotel Corneille, Paris*

Dear Everybody, Mr Yeats[2] went to see the editor[3] of 'The Speaker' in

[1] From a typewritten copy found among the papers of W. B. Yeats.
[2] W. B. Yeats (1865–1939), the Irish poet.
[3] Richard Barry O'Brien (1847–1918), Irish barrister and author, best known for *The Life of Charles Stewart Parnell*, 2 vols. (London, 1899).

London but he was ill and I expect a letter every day: he is also to go to the editor of the 'Academy'.[1] He wrote to Miss Gonne,[2] a letter of whose I enclose. He also introduced me to Arthur Symons[3] and wants me to review for the Speaker a book of Symons's—a translation of *Francesca da Rimini*.[4] I breakfasted, lunched and dined with him and he paid all the hansoms and busses. I sent in my reviews to the 'Express' a day or two ago, so look out in the Express at the beginning of the week. I have certain definite information about the medical course. The first thing is to have a French baccalauréat but those who have foreign degrees may be dispensed therefrom by the Minister of Public Instruction. I have written to the Minister and this morning called at the Ministry and was told there that the dispensation would probably be accorded me in a few days. Thereupon I went to the Secretary of the Faculty of Science at the Sorbonne and he gave me a provisional card of admission to the course for the certificate in physics, chemistry and biology (the whole year's work). There are no fees to pay for lectures but the lectures begin at 9 in the morning continuing for an hour or two hours and practical work begins in the afternoon at 1.30 and goes on for two or three hours. There are no written exams: all exams are oral and last about a quarter of a[n] hour. My exam for the certificate will come off July next. I am somewhat late as the last day for demands to the Minister was 1 Dec, but I daresay, as I am a foreigner, I will be excused. I can therefore have a fortnight or so to work between this and Christmas. I have bought an alarm-clock (4 francs) to waken me in time in the mornings as the school is some distance away. I had a bath just now ($7\frac{1}{2}$): warm. I can get breakfast for 3d, dejeuner (soup, meat, dessert, coffee) for 8d or 9d and dinner (soup, fish, meat and vegetables, dessert, coffee) for 1s/-. But I am obliged to take coffee constantly through the day. Coffee is taken here during the day without milk but with sugar. This I find to my taste as the weather here is very severe, sometimes going down to 7 or 9 degrees below zero. The wind too is very keen but there is neither fog nor rain. Tell Stannie to go to Eason's in Abbey St where I ordered and paid for a certain quantity of paper, and tell them to forward it to me. They will do this if the carriage is paid. I forgot it in the hurry of going away. I have not had time yet to work up

[1] Charles Lewis Hind (1862–1927).

[2] Maud Gonne (1866–1953), Irish patriot, to whom most of Yeats's early love poems are addressed.

[3] Arthur Symons (1865–1945), English poet and critic. He and Yeats had shared rooms for a year in 1894–5. Symons, at this first meeting with Joyce, promised help in finding a publisher for him.

[4] Symons's translation of Gabriele D'Annunzio's *Francesca da Rimini* (1901) was published in London in 1902.

my letters of introduction—except some—but I shall do so during the week. I have to get an apron and sleeves and a dissecting case at once if I begin work on Monday, and my money will not be due in Paris from Lloyd's till Thursday. However I daresay I shall manage. I intend next week to look around for a room at about 7£ or 8£ the year—35s/- the three months and engage it from January 1st, and my month will be up in the hotel here on January 3rd and I think the courses will begin again on January 4th. There is magnificent Norman furniture in a shop here—heavy wooden presses with panelled doors—5£ for one about twice as big as your wardrobe and though I cannot buy these yet for my room I shall certainly get them as soon as I can when I have definitely settled myself in Paris for my medical course. No information is to be given about me to anybody except—'O, Very Nicely, thank you.' Tell Stannie to send me the December no of S. Stephen's[1] and to write to the Unicorn Press and to be careful of the books in my room.   JIM

To MRS JOHN STANISLAUS JOYCE   MS. Cornell

15 December 1902   *Grand Hotel Corneille, Paris*

Dear Mother I enclose a letter I had a day or two ago from Mr Yeats. I answered saying I had left my manuscripts in Ireland but sent him a poem. I have at my disposal a position in the Ecole Berlitz, beginning at 150 francs a month (£7–10–0), but I should be at the school all day. However I am giving two or three lessons a week to a M Douce[2] who gives me or will give me 20 or 25 francs a month (£1 or £1–5–0).

The weather is milder. I hardly know if I have anything to say. I received both your letters and see that I have alarmed you very much. My curious state has been followed by an equally curious weariness which is however painless. For instance I would prefer you wrote and I read. Write again if you like and say if I should go home for Christmas. Please ask Stannie to go to Hodges, Figgis, say I am here and have written to him to order 'A Book of British Song' by I don't know whom, published recently by John Murray, London.[3] I would like to go asleep now yet I did not get up till eleven, and it is now only two. I also feel as

---

[1] The student magazine at University College, Dublin.

[2] Joseph Douce, a champagne manufacturer who took lessons in English from Joyce and brought him a second pupil, A. Auvergniot. It was Douce who lent Joyce the money to return home in April 1903; the Cornell collection has letters from Douce which indicate that John Joyce ceremoniously repaid the debt.

[3] Cecil James Sharp, *A Book of British Song for Home and School* (London: John Murray, 1902).

if I should not seek to express but simply listen to people. I am afraid I shall not easily settle down. I should not like to live in Paris but I should like to divide my existence. I shall set you some music in a few days which I want you to learn. M Douce will give me 10^s/, the 'Express' £1–1–0, and the Academy, I daresay, £1–0–0: that is £2–11–0. Could you get a set of teeth for that? Do not be offended please because I cannot write.   JIM

To LADY GREGORY   MS. N.Y. Public Library (Berg)

21 December 1902   *Hotel Corneille, Paris*

Dear Lady Gregory Your letter has been forwarded to me but I have yet no definite news to give you except that I am going back to Dublin for the Christmas and leave Paris tomorrow night. Your friend Mr Longworth[1] asked me to review two books. I did so, the reviews appeared a fortnight ago but I have received no money. My prospects for studying medicine here are not inviting. Mr Yeats is to see the editor of 'The Speaker' some time after Christmas and he suggested to the editor of the 'Academy' to take verses of mine but the editor of the 'Academy' wants columns of 'really good verse'. When I have any definite news be sure I shall tell you. O yes—I am teaching a man here and he gives me 10 fr every fortnight. Paris amuses me very much but I quite understand why there is no poetry in French literature; for to create poetry out of French life is impossible. I have no sympathy with the 'gallant' French. I am glad the Germans beat them and hope they will beat them again. But heaven forbid the French should perish and the world lose such cooks and dancing masters. But—

> Es war ein Konig in Thule
> Gar treu bis an das Grab[2]

the whole menagerie, beginning with round little M Loubet,[3] couldn't produce that because the Kingdom of God cometh not with observation
Faithfully yours   JAMES A JOYCE

[1] Ernest Victor Longworth (1874–1935) was editor of the *Daily Express* (Dublin) from 1901 to 1904.
[2] 'There was a king in Thule, Faithful even to the grave.' Gretchen's song in Goethe, *Faust*, First Part, 'Evening' scene.
[3] Emile François Loubet (1838–1929) was president of the French Republic from 1899 to 1906.

To JOHN STANISLAUS JOYCE (Postcard)   MS. Cornell

21 January 1903[1]   *London*

I have been appointed writer of literary and dramatic notes in Paris
(with a suggestion that I should become Paris correspondent if my work
pleases) for a new sixpenny weekly but the first no. will not appear till
March. I have however to submit my contribution as soon as possible
and the payment is very high (£2–2–0 per 1000 words or twice the pay of
the 'Academy') I have seen the editor of the 'Academy'[2] too and have
left my article with him and he is to tell me whether he thinks I will suit
his paper. I cannot see Mr Tuohy[3] till late tonight. Be sure to push on
the 'Irish Times' and to let me know how the matter is going and also
what exactly O'Hara[4] said. I have written also to Courtney[5] and expect
letters from him and from Archer (if he is in London) in the morning.

                                                              JIM

To MRS JOHN STANISLAUS JOYCE   MS. Cornell

25 January 1903   *Grand Hotel Corneille, Paris*

Dear Mother I didn't write before this as I was expecting the parcel
which has not yet (Monday morning) arrived. I have sent in the review
of that book[6] to the Express so let Stannie look out for it. The name of
the new paper is 'Men and Women' and the editor described it to me as
something between the 'Spectator' and the 'Tatler' so if you buy these
papers you can see for yourself. It will be a weekly, price sixpence. Tell
Stannie to send me *at once* (so that I may have it by Thursday night) my
copy of Wagner's operas and if he can to enclose with it a copy of Grant
Allen's 'Paris'.[7] By the way at page 100 of 'La Femme en Gris'[8] he will

---

[1] After spending the Christmas holidays with his family in Dublin, Joyce stopped in
London for two days (21 and 22 January) before returning to Paris.

[2] C. Lewis Hind. When Hind did not accept the article, Joyce treated him with scorn.
Yeats afterwards rebuked the young man for relinquishing, by this behaviour, any
chance of writing for the *Academy*.

[3] James Tuohy, a London friend of Joyce's father.

[4] Matthew O'Hara, a reporter for the *Irish Times*, and a friend of Joyce's father.
It was probably through his good offices that Joyce's article, 'The Motor Derby', was
published in that newspaper on 7 April 1903.

[5] William Leonard Courtney (1850–1928), English journalist and author, was editor of
the *Fortnightly Review* from 1894.

[6] Stephen Gwynn, *To-day and To-morrow in Ireland: Essays on Irish Subjects* (Dublin
and London, 1903). Joyce's review of it appeared in the *Daily Express* (Dublin) on
29 January 1903.

[7] Grant Allen (1848–99), Canadian-born writer, best known for his novel, *The Woman
Who Did* (1895). His book *Paris* was published in London in 1900.

[8] *La Femme en Gris* (Paris, 1895), a translation of the novel *Frau Sorge* (1887) by
Hermann Sudermann (1857–1928).

find a pawn-ticket for two books which must be seen to without delay. I am afraid I have let it lie too long. I hope Stannie is recovered by now and I hope you are doing what I told you. I met Archer at the Liberal Club but our talk though it lasted a long time was not very business-like. I also met Lady Gregory and had just time to see Mr O'Connell[1] before I caught my train. The 'Speaker', I understand, though a good paper is a poor paper and so is the 'Academy' but perhaps I shall send them something. However I intend to explore among papers myself without any introduction. Don't forget to urge on matters at home—I mean about Charlie's preparing for that exam (sometime in the spring) and about Stannie. I hope you will write to me and if you do write also about the things that interest us. Tell Pappie I expect to hear how he is getting on with the 'Irish Times'.   JIM

I delayed this letter till today (Tuesday) thinking there might be a letter in the parcel which would require an answer.

To STANISLAUS JOYCE   MS. Cornell

8 February 1903   *Grand Hotel Corneille, Paris*

Dear Stannie, I send you two poems. The first one is for the second part[2] and I fancy it will pique Eglinton's curiosity. By the way I wrote nothing in my review of Everyman's book (damn Everyman anyhow!) about the printing and binding.[3] My little editor must have added that but I wrote about the people 'who are beginning to talk a little vaguely about their friends the French'[4] which is pretty well—Was that in it?— I am feeling very intellectual these times and up to my eyes in Aristotle's Psychology. If the editor of the 'Speaker' puts in my review of 'Catilina' you will see some of the fruits thereof.[5] Words cannot measure my

[1] Presumably a London relation of Joyce on his father's side; possibly Sir Ross O'Connell, Bart., M.P. for County Kerry in 1902.

[2] This letter, and a postcard to Byrne of 15 December 1902, indicate that Joyce planned to divide his poems into two parts, the first being relatively simple and innocent, the second more complicated and experienced. The second group would commemorate his departure from Dublin, though the poem, 'When the shy star goes forth in heaven', evidently belonged to the first group even if written in Paris.

[3] Joyce's review of Gwynn's *To-day and Tomorrow in Ireland* appeared with the final sentence, 'The volume, admirably bound and printed, is a credit to the Dublin firm to whose enterprise its publication is due.' *Critical Writings*, p. 92. The Dublin firm was Hodges, Figgis & Co.

[4] Joyce said that Gwynn was 'too consistently Gaelic for the Parliamentarians, and too mild for the true patriots, who are beginning to speak a little vaguely about their friends the French'. Ibid., p. 90. He was probably referring to Maud Gonne and her faction, who had been hoping to secure the support of French arms for an Irish revolution.

[5] Aristotle's *De Anima* is not mentioned in the review of Ibsen's *Catalina* (see p. 15n.), but some phrases are perhaps indebted to it. Joyce later used this work as the basis of much of the *Proteus* episode of *Ulysses*.

contempt for AE[1] at present (I believe he didn't write to Lady Gregory)[2] and his spiritual friends. I did well however to leave my MSS with him for I had a motive. However I shall take them back as my latest additions to 'Epiphany' might not be to his liking. And so help me devil I will write only the things that approve themselves to me and I will write them the best way I can. It is the same way with boots. O, I have revelled in ties, coats, boots, hats since I came here—all imaginary! So damn Russell, damn Yeats, damn Skeffington,[3] damn Darlington,[4] damn editors, damn free-thinkers, damn vegetable verse and double damn vegetable philosophy![5]   JIM

> I hear an army charging upon the land
> And the thunder of horses plunging, foam about their knees,
> Arrogant, in black armour, behind them stand,
> Disdaining the reins, with fluttering whips, the charioteers.
>
> They cry amid the night their battle-name;
> I moan in sleep, hearing afar their whirling laughter.
> They ride through the gloom of dreams, a blinding flame,
> With hoofs clanging upon the heart, as upon an anvil.
>
> They come triumphantly shaking their long green hair,
> They come out of the sea and run shouting by the shore—
> My heart, have you no wisdom thus to despair?
> Little white breast, O why have you left me alone?[6]

> When the shy star goes forth in heaven,
> All maidenly, disconsolate,
> Hear you amid the drowsy even,
> One who is singing by your gate.
> His song is softer than the dew
> And he is come to visit you.

[1] George William Russell (1867–1935), Irish poet and mystic, who wrote under the pseudonym of 'AE'.

[2] Possibly to ask for money for Joyce.

[3] Francis Skeffington, later Sheehy-Skeffington (1878–1916), a friend of Joyce at University College, Dublin, and collaborator in the private publication (1901) of which Joyce's 'The Day of the Rabblement' was one part, and an essay of Skeffington, 'A Forgotten Aspect of the University Question', was the other. He had evidently annoyed Joyce in some way during the latter's short stay in Dublin from December 1902 to January 1903.

[4] Rev. Joseph Darlington, S.J. (1850–1939), dean of studies at University College, Dublin. He had perhaps urged Joyce to stay sensibly in Dublin.

[5] Both Russell and Skeffington were vegetarians: Skeffington was probably the free-thinker.

[6] This and the following poem appear, with slight changes, as *Chamber Music*, xxxvi and iv.

O bend no more in revery
When he at eventide is calling,
Nor muse who may this singer be
Whose song about my heart is falling?
Know you by this, the lover's chant,
'Tis I that am your visitant.

JAJ
Paris, 1903

To JOHN STANISLAUS JOYCE   MS. Cornell

26 February 1903   *Grand Hotel Corneille, Paris*

Dear Pappie I received your telegraph order on Tuesday afternoon and
dined. As it was the evening of the carnival, I allowed myself some
luxuries—a cigar, confetti to throw, and a supper. I bought a stove, a
saucepan, a plate, a cup, a saucer, a knife, a fork, a small spoon, a big
spoon, a bowl, salt, sugar, figs, macaroni, cocoa &c and got my linen
from the laundry. I now try to do my own cooking. For instance last
night for dinner I had two hard-boiled eggs (these are sold here hard-
boiled during Lent in red shells) bread and butter, macaroni; a few figs
and a cup of cocoa. Today for dejeuner I had some cold ham, bread and
butter, Swiss cream with sugar; for dinner I had two poached eggs
and Vienna bread, macaroni and milk, a cup of cocoa and a few figs. On
Sunday for dinner I shall make a mutton stew—mutton, a few potatoes,
mushrooms and lentils, with cocoa and biscuits after. Tomorrow (for
dejeuner) I shall finish my ham with bread and butter, Swiss cream and
sugar, and finish my figs. I think I shall reduce my expenses in this way.
Anyhow I hope I shall not fall asleep now as I used dreaming of rice-
pudding, which for one who is fasting is not a nice dream. I am sorry to
say that after my dinner on Tuesday I became very ill and at night I had
a fit of vomiting. I felt very bad the whole of the following day but I am
better today except for attacks of neuralgia—induced, I imagine, by
my constant periods of fasting.

On Tuesday morning I received from the 'Speaker' the proof-sheets
of my article which will therefore appear Sat. Feb. 28th if I am right.[1]
I suppose I shall be paid some time next week. I have no news from the

---

[1] Joyce's review of *Catalina*, by Henrik Ibsen, did not appear in the *Speaker* until
21 March 1903.

'Express'. Stannie tells me my four reviews[1] appeared. I sent them a fortnight ago a criticism of a performance of Sarah Bernhardt's, as I told you, and a letter with it. I sent today an account of the carnival.[2] As for my other paper it has not come out yet and until the Syndicate approves of the dummy copy no appointments can be made and there is no money. I understand that this dummy is now ready and I have consequently to wait. I shall try to let my tuition money (20 francs and 10 frs) remain intact till the end of March so as to pay my hotel-bill. I was favoured with my hotel-bill on Tuesday (£1–10–0 as I used seven candles (3s/-) before I got a lamp) I hope you will send this to me on the 1ST as the lady here is rather black in the face and has a whimsical way of looking at me when she sees me going up the stairs with milk sticking out of one pocket and bread and provisions out of another. I hope I won't have to bother you for any more money if I get on all right. I am 18s/- in debt but that be hanged for the present. Your (and my) good friend Mr Tuohy took no notice of my letter as I told you. I see that nothing has been done at the 'Irish Times' and if I am [a] good judge of heavy heads nothing will be done with its manager who is, I think, very heavy in the head. I am seriously thinking of entering the church if I find editors and managers and 'practical' people so very stubborn as they appear to be.
                                                                                    JIM

To [MRS JOHN STANISLAUS JOYCE]   MS. Cornell

[? 8 March 1903] Sunday 2.30 p.m.   *[Paris]*

I cannot cash your order today. I do not understand in the least what you write about Gaze's.[3] When you spend only three minutes at a letter it cannot be very intelligible. In any case Gaze's was shut. My next meal therefore will be at 11 a.m. tomorrow (Monday): my last meal was 7 pm last (Saturday) night. So I have another fast of 40 hours—No, not a fast, for I have eaten a pennyworth of dry bread. My second last meal was 20 hours before my last. 20 and 40 = 60—Two meals in 60 hours is not bad, I think. As my lenten regulations have made me somewhat weak I shall go up to my room and sit there till it is time to go to bed.

---

[1] Joyce had three reviews in the *Daily Express* (Dublin), 6 February 1903: 'A Suave Philosophy', on H. Fielding Hall, *The Soul of a People*; 'An Effort at Precision in Thinking', on James Anstie, *Colloquies of Common People*; and 'Colonial Verses', on Clive Phillips-Wolley, *Songs of an English Esau*. The fourth review was the earlier one, published on 29 January, of Gwynn's *To-day and To-morrow in Ireland*.

[2] This account was not published, nor was Joyce's criticism of Sarah Bernhardt, presumably as Hermione in Racine's *Andromache*.

[3] A Dublin travel agency.

Your order will last me till Tuesday morning, as I shall be very hungry tomorrow. Douce has already paid me—how else did you think I was living so the only money coming to me here is 5 francs from my new pupil, Auvergniot. JIM

To STANISLAUS JOYCE MS. Cornell

9 March 1903 *Grand Hotel Corneille, Paris*

Dear Stannie I enclose you self-explaining documents though it costs something to send them. Write at once to the 'Unicorn Press'. Get also the following books if you possibly can. 'Everyman'[1] 1s/- and 12 Elizabethan Songs (edited with original music by Janet Dodge)[2] 3s/6— both published A H Bullen, 47 Great Russell St, London. I have written fifteen epiphanies—of which twelve are insertions and three additions. I was paid 25 frs on Sat—of which 8 went to pay off a part of my debts.—I shall have to use my tuition money when I am paid, I fear. Synge[3] is here for a few days selling out—he can't get on either and is going back to Ireland. He says the 'Speaker' is always slow but once you get a proof the article is sure to appear. He has written four plays—one of which 'Riders to the Sea' Arthur Symons and W B Yeats admire very much—Yeats told me it was quite Greek: and I suppose Synge will be boomed now by the Irish Theatre—the plays are all in one act. Synge gave me the MS of 'Riders to the Sea' and I have read it: it is a play of Aran in peasant dialect. I am glad to say that ever since I read it I have been riddling it mentally till it has [not] a sound spot. It is tragic about all the men that are drowned in the islands: but thanks be to God Synge isn't an Aristotelian.[4] I told him part of my esthetic:[5] he says I have a mind like Spinosa. I cannot write a long letter as I am running for the post. I shall write to Charlie at the end of the week: tell him so. If you can knock out a few shillings on your own hook, do so and send them in God his name. I am half planning an entertainment. Tell me what you think of all this. Tell mother to go out now that spring is come and take walks. Damnably cold here.[6] JIM

[1] The fifteenth-century morality play.

[2] *Twelve Elizabethan Songs*, ed. Janet Dodge (London, 1902).

[3] John Millington Synge (1871–1909), Irish dramatist.

[4] As Joyce was.

[5] Joyce was developing his aesthetic theories in a notebook which he kept in Paris in February and March 1903. See *Critical Writings*, pp. 143–6. He used them later in *A Portrait of the Artist*.

[6] The last two sentences were inserted after the letter was signed.

To MRS JOHN STANISLAUS JOYCE   MS. Cornell

20 March 1903   *Grand Hotel Corneille, Paris*

Dear Mother I have not heard anything yet from the paper you call
'Men and Women' but I shall write early next month—perhaps next
week. I still continue with M Douce and M Auvergniot but I do not see
any likelihood of my getting any more tuitions. I have drawn on my
tuition money and am paid by M Douce up to 27 March and by M
Auvergniot up to 16 March. Therefore when my hotel bill falls due I
cannot meet it as I thought I could. However last night I made up my
second month's account and I have reduced my expenses from 161
francs to 106 francs (Hotel bills included)—a reduction that is of 56
francs—about £2–3–0. As against this however my debts in France
remain now 19 francs: they were 18 francs at the end of last month. I
paid off 7 francs as I told you and borrowed as much again. My reduction of expenses, however, is accompanied by a lack of clean linen—
I have had one handkerchief for three weeks—but I have a grey tie
which is something under a mile in length—it floats all over me so that
it is difficult for the world to discover the state of my shirt. One boot is
beginning to go—I knew that that bootmaker wouldn't put leather in
them. I have taken to wearing the 'good' black suit as the 'other' is
impossible. The trouser-buttons of the 'good' black suit are falling out
one after the other—however I have two safety pins and I shall stitch in
buttons now that I have money to buy them. As for the food I get—I do
not always get food only when I can. Sometimes I take one meal in the
day and buy potatoes cooked and dry bread in the street. I do not know
if I am getting lean or not. But, I can assure you, I have a most villainous
hunger. Today I came laughing and singing to myself down the
Boulevard Saint-Michel without a care in the world because I felt I was
going to have a dinner—my first dinner (properly speaking) for three
days. This shows what simpletons we all are. I sent in my review of Lady
Gregory's book a week ago. I do not know if Longworth put it in as I
sent it:[1] the review was very severe. I shall write to Lady Gregory one of
these days. I am sending the two other reviews with this letter. I have
not shaved nor do I intend to. When the 'Speaker' pays me I shall have

---

[1] E. V. Longworth, the editor of the *Daily Express*, published the review under
the title, 'The Soul of Ireland', on 26 March 1903, but added to it the initials 'J.J.'
to make Joyce's responsibility for it clear. In *Ulysses*, pp. 277–8 (216) Mulligan
expostulates with Stephen, 'Longworth is awfully sick . . . after what you wrote about
that old hake Gregory. O you inquisitional drunken jew jesuit! She gets you a job on the
paper and then you go and slate her drivel to Jaysus.'

a bath. I answered Fr Ghezzi's letter.[1] I shall answer Aunt Josephine on
Monday. Every Sunday I try and get out into the country. Last Sunday
I went out to the woods of Clamart and walked through them to Sèvres
—coming back by steamer. I read every day in the Bibliothèque
Nationale and every night in the Bibliothèque Sainte-Geneviève. I often
go to vespers at Notre Dame or at Saint-Germain l'Auxerrois. I never go
to the theatre—as I have no money. I have no money either to buy
books. Synge was over here selling out and gave me his play to read—a
play which is to be produced by the Irish Literary Theatre. I criticised
it. Synge says I have a mind like Spinoza! (Spinoza was a great Hebrew
philosopher): I am at present up to the neck in Aristotle's Metaphysics,
and read only him and Ben Jonson (a writer of songs and plays).
Gogarty[2] wrote to me a day or two [ago] and tells me that 'John
Eglinton' said the other day (Stannie will tell you who he is) 'There is
something sublime in Joyce's standing alone.' My book of songs will be
published in the spring of 1907. My first comedy about five years later.
My 'Esthetic' about five years later again. (This *must* interest you!)
Yeats (who is impressionable) said he knew me only a little time and in
that time I had roared laughing at the mention of Balzac, Swinburne &c.
I have more than once upset a whole French café by laughing. An old
woman shook her umbrella in my face one day in Dublin—I was
laughing so loudly. Come what may I will lunch tomorrow. You will
oblige me very much if you will write to me and tell what you think of
me. I shall read your letter with great anxiety.   Jim

Ask Benson about your own glasses, I am sure they are ruining your
sight. Get him to prescribe *proper* glasses for you. Don't fail to do this.
Do you go out as I told you? I think you are in good health. I never saw
you look better than the night I went home and you came into the hall.
I never saw Pappie look better than on S. Stephen's Day. Tell him so.
He looked brown and healthy and neat. I hope he is still in good health.
I was sorry to hear about poor old Thornton.[3] However no-one that has
raised up a family has failed utterly in my opinion. You understand

[1] Rev. Charles Ghezzi, S.J., was Joyce's professor of Italian at University College,
Dublin.
[2] Oliver St John Gogarty (1878–1957), the Irish writer and surgeon, a member of the
Irish Senate from 1922 to 1934. He and Joyce had met during the Christmas holidays in
1902–3. Gogarty was about to go up to Oxford, in January, for two terms.
[3] Ned Thornton, a tea-taster, was a neighbour of the Joyce family when they lived in
North Richmond Street from 1894 to about 1898. He served as a model for Mr Kernan
in the story 'Grace' and in *Ulysses*.

this, I think. Why did you ask Stannie about the Irish Literary Theatre
plays?   JIM

Georgie[1] understood me, I am beginning to think.

To MRS JOHN STANISLAUS JOYCE (Postcard)   MS. Cornell

10 April 1903   *[Paris]*

Dear Mother Please write to me at once if you can and tell me what is
wrong.[2]   JIM

To [JOHN STANISLAUS] JOYCE (Telegram)   MS. Cornell

11 April 1903   *[Paris]*

Arrive morning   Jim

To OLIVER ST JOHN GOGARTY   MS. Colby College

3 June 1904   *60 Shelbourne Road, Dublin*

Dear Gogarty I sent you back the budget. I am still alive. Here is a
more reasonable request. I am singing at a garden fête on Friday and if
you have a decent suit to spare or a cricket shirt send it or them. I am
trying to get an engagement in the Kingstown Pavilion. Do you know
anyone there? My idea for July and August is this—to get Dolmetsch[3]
to make me a lute and to coast the south of England from Falmouth to
Margate singing old English songs. When are you leaving Oxford? I
wish I could see it. I don't understand your allusion. 'Chamber Music' is
the title for the suite. I suppose Jenny[4] is leaving in a day or so. I shall
call to say farewell and adieu. Her letter did not annoy me. The others

---

[1] George Alfred Joyce (1887–1902) was the fifth child in the family. He died from
typhoid fever and peritonitis. The description of the death of Stephen's sister Isabel in
Stephen Hero is based somewhat on George's death.

[2] Joyce's mother had fallen gravely ill from cancer of the liver. His father sent him a
telegram, 'Mother dying come home Father', and on funds borrowed from his pupil,
Joseph Douce, Joyce returned home on Easter Sunday, 12 April 1903. His mother died
on 13 August of that year.

[3] Arnold Dolmetsch (1858–1940), expert on old musical instruments and their music.

[4] Possibly, as Stuart Gilbert suggests, the same Jenny—an acrobat with a taste for
exotic lingerie—of whom Gogarty writes in *Mourning Becomes Mrs Spendlove* (New
York, 1948).

did. I enclose one lest you should plume yourself. Ellwood[1] is nearly
cured. I have a rendezvous with Annie Langton. But you forget her?
I have no news to report. Their Intensities[2] and Their Bullockships[3]
continue to flourish. His Particular Intensity[4] walks now unencumbered.[5] MacAuliffe is going for Greenwood Pim's job in C P I[6]—desires
to be remembered to you. You will not have me faithfully. Adieu then,
Inconsequent.   STEPHEN DAEDALUS

To NORA BARNACLE[7]   MS. Cornell

15 June 1904   *60 Shelbourne Road*

I may be blind. I looked for a long time at a head of reddish-brown hair
and decided it was not yours. I went home quite dejected. I would like
to make an appointment but it might not suit you. I hope you will be
kind enough to make one with me—if you have not forgotten me!
                                                          JAMES A JOYCE

To C. P. CURRAN[8]   MS. Curran

23 June 1904   *[Dublin]*

Dear Curran: The Accountant-General would not like me at present—
black eye, sprained wrist, sprained ankle, cut chin, cut hand. I enclose
eloquent note from *Saturday Review*.[9] For one rôle at least I seem unfit

[1] John Rudolf Elwood (d. 1931?), a medical student of Joyce's acquaintance in Dublin.
He could not finish medical school but became a Licentiate of the Apothecaries' Hall in
1915 and was thereby qualified to practise medicine. He is a model for Temple in
A Portrait of the Artist.
[2] Earnest Sinn Féiners.
[3] Countrified louts, or perhaps, as Stanislaus Joyce suggests, priests.
[4] John Francis Byrne (1879–1960), later a journalist in the United States, and at one
time Joyce's closest friend. He is a model for Cranly in *A Portrait*.
[5] Without his usual companion, Vincent Cosgrave (1878?–d. probably late 1920s),
a model for Lynch in *A Portrait* and *Ulysses*.
[6] Pim was secretary to the committee of management of Conjoint (Medical)
Examinations Office, Royal College of Physicians, Ireland (C.P.I.).
[7] Nora Barnacle (21 March 1884–10 April 1951), who was to become Joyce's wife.
She was the daughter of Thomas Barnacle, a baker, and Annie Barnacle, both of Galway
City. As a result of family dissension, she had left Galway a few months before, and came
to Dublin to work as a chambermaid at Finn's Hotel, 1 and 2 Leinster Street. Joyce met
her shortly before the date of this letter, and arranged to see her on 14 June. She failed to
turn up at the promised time, and their first walk together took place almost certainly
on 16 June, to be commemorated later as the date of the action of *Ulysses*.
[8] Constantine Peter Curran (1883–1972), a classmate of Joyce, had just joined the
Four Courts (Dublin) service and been posted to the Accountant-General's office. He
later became Registrar of the Supreme Court.
[9] A note expressing 'cordial thanks' for his contribution ('Silently she's combing',
reprinted in *Chamber Music*).

—that of man of honour. However I will not groan through the post. Here is the marvellous novel[1] delivered upon you by my twenty-third sister. An amiable creditor waited on me at breakfast yesterday for the return of fourpence which he had 'lent' me. If you are too busy to read the novel now, no harm. But as soon as you have read it send me word to meet you on some altitude where we can utter our souls unmolested. The 'Titania' people paid me in nods & becks & wreathed smiles. The Celbridge concert fell through. Nok sagt![2] Yours heroically,

STEPHEN DAEDALUS

To C. P. CURRAN (Postcard)   MS. Curran

Postmark 3 July 1904   [*Dublin*]

Je serai à votre bureau demain. Suis dans un trou sanguinaire. J.A.J.[3]

To C. P. CURRAN   MS. Curran

[*Early July 1904*]   *The Rain, Friday*

Dear Curran: Invaluable! A thousand feudal thanks! I have finished the awful chapter—102 pages—and Russell (A.E.) has the book now. I shall send you the chapter in a week. I am writing a series of epicleti[4]— ten—for a paper. I have written one. I call the series *Dubliners* to betray the soul of that hemiplegia or paralysis which many consider a city. Look out for an edition de luxe of all my limericks instantly. More anon   S. D.

SD [sic]

To NORA BARNACLE   MS. Cornell

[? *12 July 1904*][5]   *60 Shelbourne Rd, Dublin*

My dear little Goodie-Brown-Shoes   I forgot—I can't meet you to-morrow (Wednesday) but will on Thursday at same hour. I hope you put my letter to bed properly. Your glove lay beside me all night— unbuttoned—but otherwise conducted itself very properly—like Nora. *Please* leave off that breastplate as I do not like embracing a letter-box.

---

[1] *Stephen Hero.*   [2] Meaning 'Enough said' (Danish).
[3] (Translation)
     'I will be at your office tomorrow. Am in a bloody hole. J.A.J.'
[4] Derived from *epiclesis* (invocation).
[5] The date is conjectural. Tuesdays fell on 5, 12, 19, and 26 July in 1904.

Do you hear now? (She is beginning to laugh). My heart—as you say—
yes—quite so

   A twenty-five-minutes kiss upon thy neck   AUJEY[1]

To GEORGE ROBERTS[2] (Postcard)   MS. S. Illinois (Feinberg)

Postmark 13 July 1904   *G.P.O. [Dublin]*

Dear Roberts: Be in the 'Ship' tomorrow at 3.30 with £1. My piano is
threatened. It is absurd that my superb voice should suffer. You
recognise a plain duty—Well then—   JAMES OVERMAN[3]

To NORA BARNACLE   MS. Cornell

[? Late July 1904]   *60 Shelbourne Road, Dublin*

My particular pouting Nora, I told you I would write to you. Now you
write to me and tell me what the deuce was the matter with you last
night. I am sure something was wrong. You looked to me as if you were
sorry for something which had *not* happened—that would would [sic] be
very like you. I have been trying to console my hand ever since but can't.
Where will you be on Saturday night, Sunday night, Monday night,
that I can't see you? Now, adieu, dearest. I kiss the miraculous dimple
at thy neck, Thy Christian Brother-in-Luxuriousness   J.A.J.

When you come next leave sulks at home—also stays

To NORA BARNACLE   MS. Cornell

[Late July? 1904]   *[Dublin]*

My dear Nora I found myself sighing deeply tonight as I walked along
and I thought of an old song written three hundred years ago by the
English King Henry VIII—a brutal and lustful king. The song is so
sweet and fresh and seems to have come from such a simple grieving
heart that I send it to you, hoping it may please you. It is strange from
what muddy pools the angels call forth a spirit of beauty. The words

---

[1] This signature is almost impossible to read. It may be a pig-Latin anagram of
James Augustine. Written across the bottom of the letter is the word 'tooth-ache' in
Joyce's hand.

[2] George Roberts (d. 1953), born in County Down, came to Dublin in 1904 and
became one of the young writers who clustered around George Russell. He soon
founded the Dublin firm Maunsel & Company, and as its managing director published
Synge, Lady Gregory, and James Stephens, and all but published *Dubliners*.

[3] In reference to Nietzsche's '*Übermensch*'.

express very delicately and musically the vague and tired loneliness which I feel. It is a song written for the lute.   JIM

Song
(for music)

Ah, the sighs that come from my heart
They grieve me passing sore!
Sith I must from my love depart
Farewell, my joy, for evermore.

I was wont her to behold
And clasp in armes twain.
And now with sighes manifold
Farewell my joy and welcome pain!

Ah methinks that could I yet
(As would to God I might!)
There would no joy compare with it
Unto my heart to make it light.

Henry VIII.

To NORA BARNACLE   MS. Cornell

3 August 1904   *60 Shelbourne Road*

Dear Nora Will you be 'let out' tonight at 8.30 ? I hope you will because I have been in such a whirl of trouble that I want to forget everything in your arms. So come if you can. In virtue of apostolic powers vested in me by His Holiness Pope Pius the Tenth I hereby give you permission to come without skirts to receive the Papal Benediction which I shall be pleased to give you Yours in the Agonising Jew

VINCENZO VANNUTELLI[1]
(Cardinal Deacon)

To NORA BARNACLE   MS. Cornell

[*About 13 August 1904*]   [*Dublin*]

My dear Nora You will find a sketch in this by me ('Stephen Daedalus') which may interest you.[2] I believe there was hardly a thought in my head all day but one.   JAJ

---

[1] Vincenzo Vannutelli (1836–1930), a well-known Cardinal of the Catholic Church. He came close to being elected Pope in the papal election of 1903.
[2] 'The Sisters', *Irish Homestead* (Dublin), x. 33 (13 August 1904), 676–7.

To Nora Barnacle   MS. Cornell

15 August 1904   *60 Shelbourne Road*

My dear Nora It has just struck one. I came in at half past eleven. Since then I have been sitting in an easy chair like a fool. I could do nothing. I hear nothing but your voice. I am like a fool hearing you call me 'Dear'. I offended two men today by leaving them coolly. I wanted to hear your voice, not theirs.[1]

When I am with you I leave aside my contemptuous suspicious nature. I wish I felt your head over my shoulder now. I think I will go to bed.

I have been a half-hour writing this thing. Will you write something to me? I hope you will. How am I to sign myself? I won't sign anything at all, because I don't know what to sign myself.

To Nora Barnacle   MS. Cornell

29 August 1904   *60 Shelbourne Road*

My dear Nora I have just finished my midnight dinner for which I had no appetite. When I was half way through it I discovered I was eating it out of my fingers. I felt sick just as I did last night. I am much distressed. Excuse this dreadful pen and this awful paper.

I may have pained you tonight by what I said but surely it is well that you should know my mind on most things? My mind rejects the whole present social order and Christianity—home, the recognised virtues, classes of life, and religious doctrines. How could I like the idea of home? My home was simply a middle-class affair ruined by spendthrift habits which I have inherited. My mother was slowly killed, I think, by my father's ill-treatment, by years of trouble, and by my cynical frankness of conduct. When I looked on her face as she lay in her coffin— a face grey and wasted with cancer—I understood that I was looking on the face of a victim and I cursed the system which had made her a victim. We were seventeen in family. My brothers and sisters are nothing to me. One brother alone is capable of understanding me.

Six years ago I left the Catholic Church, hating it most fervently. I found it impossible for me to remain in it on account of the impulses of my nature. I made secret war upon it when I was a student and declined to accept the positions it offered me. By doing this I made myself a

[1]   Because your voice was at my side
               I gave him pain. . . .
               Chamber Music, xvii

beggar but I retained my pride. Now I make open war upon it by what I write and say and do. I cannot enter the social order except as a vagabond. I started to study medicine three times, law once, music once. A week ago I was arranging to go away as a travelling actor. I could put no energy into the plan because you kept pulling me by the elbow. The actual difficulties of my life are incredible but I despise them.

When you went in tonight I wandered along towards Grafton St where I stood for a long time leaning against a lamp-post, smoking. The street was full of a life which I have poured a stream of my youth upon. While I stood there I thought of a few sentences I wrote some years ago when I lived in Paris—these sentences which follow—'They pass in twos and threes amid the life of the boulevard, walking like people who have leisure in a place lit up for them. They are in the pastry cook's, chattering, crushing little fabrics of pastry, or seated silently at tables by the café door, or descending from carriages with a busy stir of garments soft as the voice of the adulterer. They pass in an air of perfumes. Under the perfumes their bodies have a warm humid smell'—[1]

While I was repeating this to myself I knew that that life was still waiting for me if I chose to enter it. It could not give me perhaps the intoxication it had once given but it was still there and now that I am wiser and more controllable·it was safe. It would ask no questions, expect nothing from me but a few moments of my life, leaving the rest free, and would promise me pleasure in return. I thought of all this and without regret I rejected it. It was useless for me; it could not give me what I wanted.

You have misunderstood, I think, some passages in a letter I wrote you and I have noticed a certain shyness in your manner as if the recollection of that night troubled you. I however consider it a kind of sacrament and the recollection of it fills me with amazed joy. You will perhaps not understand at once why it is that I honour you so much on account of it as you do not know much of my mind. But at the same time it was a sacrament which left in me a final sense of sorrow and degradation—sorrow because I saw in you an extraordinary, melancholy tenderness which had chosen that sacrament as a compromise, and degradation because I understood that in your eyes I was inferior to a convention of our present society.

I spoke to you satirically tonight but I was speaking of the world not of you. I am an enemy of the ignobleness and slavishness of people but not of you. Can you not see the simplicity which is at the back of all my

[1] The passage comprises all except the last sentence of an epiphany (MS. Cornell) of Parisian *poules*. It is adapted in *Ulysses*, pp. 52–3 (42).

disguises? We all wear masks. Certain people who know that we are much together often insult me about you. I listen to them calmly, disdaining to answer them but their least word tumbles my heart about like a bird in a storm.

It is not pleasant for me that I have to go to bed now remembering the last look of your eyes—a look of tired indifference—remembering the torture in your voice the other night. No human being has ever stood so close to my soul as you stand, it seems, and yet you can treat my words with painful rudeness ('I know what is talking now' you said). When I was younger I had a friend[1] to whom I gave myself freely—in a way more than I give to you and in a way less. He was Irish, that is to say, he was false to me.

I have not said a quarter of what I want to say but it is great labour writing with this cursed pen. I don't know what you will think of this letter. Please write to me, won't you? Believe me, my dear Nora, I honour you very much but I want more than your caresses. You have left me again in an anguish of doubt.   JAJ

To Nora Barnacle   MS. Private

[*About 1 September 1904*]   *7 S. Peter's Terrace, Cabra, Dublin*

Sweetheart I am in such high good humour this morning that I insist on writing to you whether you like it or not. I have no further news for you except that I told my sister about you last night. It was very amusing. I am going out in half an hour to see Palmieri[2] who wants me to study music and I shall be passing your windows. I wonder will you be there. I also wonder if you are there will I be able to see you. Probably not.

What a lovely morning! That skull, I am glad to say, didn't come to torment me last night. How I hate God and death! How I like Nora! Of course you are shocked at these words, pious creature that you are.

I got up early this morning to finish a story I was writing. When I had written a page I decided I would write a letter to you instead. Besides, I thought you disliked Monday and a letter from me might put you in better spirits. When I am happy I have an insane wish to tell it to everyone I meet but I would be much happier if you gave me one of those chirruping kisses you are fond of giving me. They remind me of canaries singing.

[1] J. F. Byrne.
[2] Benedetto Palmieri (1863–1918?) was the best voice teacher in Dublin. A Neapolitan by birth, he taught at the Dublin Academy of Music from 1900 to 1914. He offered to train Joyce for three years free of charge in return for a share of his concert earnings for ten years. Joyce declined.

I hope you haven't that horrible pain this morning. Go out and see old Sigerson and get him to prescribe for you. You will be sorry to hear that my grand-aunt[1] is dying of stupidity. Please remember that I have *thirteen* letters of yours at present.

Be sure you give that dragoon's stays to Miss Murphy—and I think you might also make her a present of the dragoon's entire uniform. Why do you wear these cursed things? Did you ever see the men that go round with Guinness's cars, dressed in enormous frieze overcoats? Are you trying to make yourself like one of them?

But you are so obstinate, it is useless for me to talk. I must tell you about my nice brother, Stannie. He is sitting at the table $\frac{1}{2}$-dressed reading a book and talking softly to himself 'Curse this fellow'—the writer of the book—'Who in the devil's name said this book was good' 'The stupid fuzzy-headed fool!' 'I wonder are the English the stupidest race on God's earth' 'Curse this English fool' etc etc

Adieu, my dear simple-minded, excitable, deep-voiced, sleepy, impatient Nora. A hundred thousand kisses.   Jim

To Nora Barnacle   MS. Cornell

10 September 1904   *The Tower, Sandycove*[2]

My dear, dear Nora I suppose you have been very much upset since last night. I will not speak of myself for I feel as if I had acted very cruelly. In a way I have no right to expect that you should regard me as anything more than the rest of men—in fact in view of my own life I have no right at all to expect it. But yet I seemed to have expected it if only because I myself had never regarded anyone as I regarded you. There is something also a little devilish in me that makes me delight in breaking down people's ideas of me and proving to them that I am really selfish, proud, cunning and regardless of others. I am sorry that my attempt last night to act according to what I believed to be right should have

---

[1] Probably Mrs Callanan, of 15 Usher's Island, an aunt of Joyce's mother, who is a model for Miss Morkan in 'The Dead'.

[2] Joyce left 60 Shelbourne Road about 1 September; he stayed a few nights with friends and relatives, then on 9 September was taken into the Martello tower by Oliver St John Gogarty, who had leased it on 17 August 1904. (See also Oliver Gogarty, 'The Tower: Fact and Fiction', *Irish Times*, 16 June 1962, p. 11.) The arrangement, as two letters from Gogarty to G. N. A. Bell of July 1904 make clear, was that Joyce should do the tower housekeeping in return for bed and (presumably) board; he would thus be enabled to finish his novel in about a year's time. (Ulick O'Connor, *The Times I've Seen: Oliver St. John Gogarty* [New York, 1964], p. 82.) Besides this helpmeet, Gogarty had a guest in the tower, Samuel Chenevix Trench, who called himself Diarmuid Trench. Joyce used the tower as the setting for the first episode of *Ulysses*, and allowed Gogarty to be his principal model for Mulligan, and Trench his principal model for Haines.

given you so much pain but I do not see how I could have acted otherwise. I wrote you a long letter explaining as well as I could how I felt
that night and it seemed to me that you were putting aside what I said
and treating me as if I were simply a casual comrade in lust. You will
perhaps object to the brutality of my words but, believe me, to treat me
as that is, so far as my attitude towards you is concerned, to dishonour
me. Surely to God you are a woman and can understand what I say!
I know that you have acted very nobly and very generously to me but
try and answer my frankness with like frankness. Above all do not go
about brooding as it will make you ill and you know that you are in
delicate health. Perhaps you will be able to send me even a line tonight
to say that you can forgive me for all the pain I have caused you.   JIM

To JAMES S. STARKEY[1]   MS. S. Illinois (Feinberg)

15 September 1904   *7 S. Peter's Terrace, Cabra, Dublin*

Dear Starkey   My trunk will be called for at the Tower tomorrow
(Saturday) between 9 and 12.[2] Kindly put into it—a pair of black boots,
a pair of brown boots, a blue peaked cap, a black cloth cap, a black felt
hat, a raincoat and the MS of my verses[3] which are in a roll on the shelf
to the right as you enter. Also see that your host[4] has not abstracted
the twelfth chapter of my novel[5] from my trunk. May I ask you to see
that any letters coming to the Tower for me are redirected to my
address at once? Please rope the trunk as it has no lock. Faithfully
Yours   JAS A JOYCE

To NORA BARNACLE   MS. Cornell

16 September 1904   *103 North Strand Road, Fairview*[6]

Dearest Nora—Letter-writing is becoming almost impossible between
us. How I detest these cold written words! I thought I should not mind
not seeing you today but I find that the hours spin out very long. My

[1] James S. Starkey (1879–1958), Irish poet, founder and editor of the *Dublin Magazine*.
He wrote under the pseudonym of Seumas O'Sullivan.
[2] Joyce was ousted from the Martello tower by Oliver St John Gogarty, probably on
15 September 1904. Gogarty tells the story, no doubt with some embellishment, in
It Isn't This Time of Year at All! (London, 1954), pp. 76–9. For Joyce's view of the
incident, see p. 67.
[3] Later *Chamber Music*.   [4] Gogarty.   [5] *Stephen Hero*.
[6] After leaving the Martello tower, Joyce stayed for a few days with his uncle and
aunt, William (1858–1912) and Josephine Murray (1862–1924), before returning to his
family's house. The Murrays lived at this address in Fairview, a part of Dublin.

brain seems to be very empty now. When I was waiting for you last
night I was even more restless. It seemed to me that I was fighting a
battle with every religious and social force in Ireland for you and that I
had nothing to rely on but myself. There is no life here—no naturalness
or honesty. People live together in the same houses all their lives and at
the end they are as far apart as ever. Are you sure you are not under any
misapprehension about me? Remember that any question you ask me I
shall answer honourably and truly. But if you have nothing to ask I shall
understand you also. The fact that you can choose to stand beside me in
this way in my hazardous life fills me with great pride and joy. I hope
you are not breaking all before you today. Perhaps you will relieve the
slowness of tomorrow morning by letting me have a letter. It is only a
week ago, you said, since we had our famous interview about the letters
but is it not through such things that we have approached so closely to
each other? Allow me, dearest Nora, to tell you how much I desire that
you should share any happiness that may be mine and to assure you of
my great respect for that love of yours which it is my wish to deserve
and to answer.   JIM

To NORA BARNACLE   MS. Cornell

19 September 1904   *103 North Strand Road, Fairview*

Carissima It was only when I had left you some time that the connection
between my question 'Are your people wealthy?' and your uneasiness
afterwards struck me. My object, however, was to find out whether with
me you would be deprived of comforts which you have been accustomed
to at home. After thinking a good while I found a solution for your
other question—this, that you were undecided whether I should be
living in or out of the college. I slept very, very badly last night, waking
four times. You ask me why I don't love you, but surely you must
believe I am very fond of you and if to desire to possess a person wholly,
to admire and honour that person deeply, and to seek to secure that
person's happiness in every way is to 'love' then perhaps my affection
for you is a kind of love. I will tell you this that your soul seems to me to
be the most beautiful and simple soul in the world and it may be because
I am so conscious of this when I look at you that my love or affection for
you loses much of its violence.

I intended to tell you that if you receive the least hint of any act on
the part of your people you must leave the Hotel at once and send a
telegram to me (at *this* address) to say where I can see you. Your people

cannot of course prevent you from going if you wish but they can make things unpleasant for you. I have to meet my father today and shall probably stay in his house until I leave Ireland so if you write write there. The address is 7 S. Peter's Terrace, Cabra, Dublin. Adieu then, dear Nora, till tomorrow evening.   JIM

To NORA BARNACLE   MS. Cornell

[26 September 1904][1]   *7 S. Peter's Terrace, Cabra, Dublin*

My dearest Nora   I must tell you how desolate I have felt since last night. I was thinking, with my usual way of regarding things, that I had a cold but I am sure it is more than a physical ailment. How little words are necessary between us! We seem to know each other though we say nothing almost for hours. I often wonder do you realise thoroughly what you are about to do. I think so little of myself when I am with you that I often doubt if you do realise it. The mere recollection of you overpowers me with some kind of dull slumber. The energy which is required for carrying on conversations seems to have left me lately and I find myself constantly slipping into silence. In a way it seems to me a pity that we do not say more to each other and yet I know how futile it is for me to remonstrate either with you or with myself for I know that when I meet you next our lips will become mute. You see how I begin to babble in these letters. And yet why should I be ashamed of words? Why should I not call you what in my heart I continually call you? What is it that prevents me unless it be that no word is tender enough to be your name?[2]   JIM

   Write if you can find time.

To NORA BARNACLE   MS. Cornell

29 September 1904 Michaelmas Day   7 S. Peter's Terrace, Cabra, Dublin

My dearest Nora   I have written to those people in London stating *your* willingness to accept their offer.[3] I do not like the notion of London and

---

[1] The reference to Joyce's cold in this letter and in one from Nora Barnacle of 26 September makes this date fairly certain.

[2] In Joyce's story 'The Dead', Gabriel Conroy remembers having written to Gretta before they were married, 'Why is it that words like these seem to me so dull and cold? Is it because there is no word tender enough to be your name?'

[3] Evidently an offer of a job, perhaps from the Berlitz School in London.

I am sure you won't like it either but at the same time it is on the road to Paris and it is perhaps better than Amsterdam. Besides I may have some business to do in London which can be best done personally. Still I am very sorry we must begin in London. Perhaps I may be sent direct to Paris, I hope I will.

I was speaking afterwards to Mr Cosgrave and I discover that I have unintentionally wronged him. He appears to have believed what he said to you. Consequently I did not report your advice to him about the way he carries his head. Mr Cosgrave is what is called a 'solid' man and he always looks at things from the most sensible point of view.

Sometimes this adventure of ours strikes me as almost amusing. It amuses me to think of the effect the news of it will cause in my circle. However, when we are once safely settled in the Latin quarter they can talk as much as they like.

I do not like the prospect of spending today without seeing you—last night hardly counts. I hope you are happier in your mind now that the boat is really beginning to whistle for us. You asked me to write you a long letter but really I hate writing—it is such an unsatisfactory way of saying things. At the same time remember that I expect you to write if you can at all. I discover now reading this letter that I have said nothing in it. However I may as well send it since it may relieve the dulness of your evening.

The sun is shining coldly through the trees in the garden here. The gentleman in the chapel has just rung the Angelus. My brother is grinning at me from the other side of the table. Now make yourself a picture of me if you can. Adieu donc, ma chérie,   JIM

To GEORGE RUSSELL   MS. Cornell

4 October 1904   *7 S. Peter's Terrace, Cabra, Dublin*

Dear Mr Russell Since I saw you last I have received a telegram asking me to go to Switzerland by the end of the week. I am, as you may imagine, very much pressed for money. I am sure that if you can you will assist me. I gave Mr Norman[1] my third story 'After the Race' today and I think he will pay me for it tomorrow. But the mere fare to Switzerland is a considerable thing and this is why I have again to ask you to help me. Faithfully Yours   JAS A JOYCE

[1] Harry Felix Norman (1868–1947) was editor of the *Irish Homestead* from about 1899 to 1905.

To George Roberts   MS. Yale

5 October 1904   *7 S. Peter's Terrace, Cabra, Dublin*

Dear Roberts: I received another telegram telling me to start for
Zurich in Switzerland on Saturday. The cheapest fare is £3 . 15 . 0.

$$£3 . 15 . 0$$
$$\underline{\qquad\qquad 2}$$
$$£7 . 10 . 0$$

I am counting for £1 between you and Ryan.[1] That is not exorbitant, I
think, as it is my last. May I count on you for this *early* on Friday?
Answer kindly. I may call   [Unsigned]

To James S. Starkey   MS. S. Illinois (Feinberg)

[8 October 1904]   *Dublin*

Dear Starkey I am going tonight. I shall call here in twenty minutes. As
you cannot give me money will you do this for me:[2] Make up a parcel of—
    1 toothbrush and powder
    1 nail brush
    1 pair of black boots and any coat and vest you have to spare
These will be very useful. If you are not here meet me outside Davy
Byrne's with the parcel at 10 past 7. I have absolutely no boots   J A J.

To George Roberts   MS. S. Illinois (Feinberg)

[8 October 1904]   *[Dublin]*

Dear Roberts: For God's sake give that 10/– to bearer or meet me at
North Wall boat at 9 o'c[lock].   J A J

---

[1] Frederick Ryan (1874–1913), co-editor of the review *Dana*, was the author of a play,
The Laying of the Foundations, and the editor of Mustapha Kemal Pasha's *Egypt*.
[2] Starkey's father kept a pharmacist's shop.

Part II
POLA, ROME, TRIESTE
1904–1915

Pola, Rome, Trieste (1904–1915)

When Joyce arrived with Nora Barnacle in Zurich on 11 October 1904, he learned to his dismay that the Berlitz School had no place for him and was unaware of his application. The director sent him on to Trieste, where, it developed, there was no vacancy either. He finally managed to be sent to the Berlitz School in Pola, the naval port of the Austro-Hungarian empire. In this out-of-the-way place he stayed until March 1905, when he was transferred to Trieste.

Joyce was restless in Pola and even more restless in Trieste. His teaching was arduous and long; he maintained his independence of it by studying Italian and German and by writing. He brought *Stephen Hero* from Chapter XII to Chapter XXIV and wrote most of the stories of *Dubliners* during his first year abroad. On 27 July 1905 Nora Barnacle Joyce gave birth to their first child, Giorgio. Soon afterwards, alarmed by the duties of fatherhood, Joyce persuaded his brother Stanislaus to come from Dublin and join him as a teacher of English. Stanislaus arrived in October, and helped to give his brother's life more stability. But the stability itself became trying, and after almost a year of it Joyce snatched at an opportunity to become a correspondent in a Roman bank. He left for Rome with his wife and son at the end of July 1906.

Rome did not prove to his taste at all. The job at the bank was dull and demanding; the city displeased him; and he suffered the luckless experience of having a publisher, Grant Richards, contract for *Dubliners* and then fearfully refuse to publish it. Elkin Mathews's agreement to publish *Chamber Music* (in 1907) was only a little consoling. Though Joyce's life became in Rome more disordered than before, he read a good deal, wrote two more stories for *Dubliners*, planned 'The Dead' and another story, 'Ulysses', which eventually became the novel, and in general brought his relation to contemporary literature and to his native country into focus. He saw more clearly the possibilities of the modern idiom, and the feelings of bitterness towards his country which had driven him away from her were somewhat mitigated by his sense of irrevocable attachment to Ireland in exile.

In February 1907 Joyce abruptly gave notice to the bank and, after some random consideration of jobs elsewhere, returned in March to Trieste. During the summer he contracted rheumatic fever, and was himself a patient in the hospital at the time that his second child, Lucia Anna, was born there on 26 July. He wrote 'The Dead' while convalescing, and after that began to reconstruct *Stephen Hero* as *A Portrait of the Artist as a Young Man*. He gave up teaching at the Berlitz School and depended upon private lessons, which paid him better and bound him less.

Joyce had often considered returning to Ireland, and in 1909 he took Giorgio with him for a visit. Soon after his arrival he found himself almost shattered by a conversation with an old friend, Vincent Cosgrave; Cosgrave told Joyce (falsely, as it soon appeared) that he had shared Nora Barnacle's affections with Joyce during that summer of courtship in 1904. While Cosgrave's boast was exploded, it heightened Joyce's sense of himself as betrayed, if not by his wife, at any rate by his friends. The theme of betrayal is strong in the last chapter of *A Portrait of the Artist*, in *Exiles*, and in *Ulysses*.

Joyce returned to Trieste, taking with him his sister Eva so as to relieve the poverty of his father's household in Dublin and to give Nora Joyce company. But he had scarcely arrived when a chance remark of Eva's, about the lack of any regular cinema in Dublin, spurred him to enlist support from some Triestine cinema owners. Commissioned by them, he went back to Ireland in September to find a suitable hall. He carried out his mission and the Cinematograph Volta opened in December 1909. At the same time he found a Dublin publisher, Maunsel & Company, that was willing to publish *Dubliners*, and he signed a contract for it with George Roberts, the managing director.

Early in January 1910 Joyce went back to Trieste, bringing with him this time another sister, Eileen. The Volta did badly and had to be sold at a loss. Roberts delayed the publication of *Dubliners* on various pretexts, in spite of Joyce's desperate importunacy. Joyce thought of becoming a teacher of English in an Italian high school, and passed the examinations at Padua in April 1912 only to discover that his Irish degree was not acceptable. In July he allowed his wife, who had long wished to see her family in Galway, to return there with Lucia; but when she failed to write him promptly he took Giorgio and followed her. He hoped to settle the matter of *Dubliners* once and for all; Roberts, however, engaged in a series of delaying and harassing tactics, inspired in part by malice, and these ended in his refusal to publish the book and in the printer's refusal to let Joyce buy the printed sheets. Joyce returned to Trieste and never allowed himself to go to Ireland again.

In the following year, 1913, Joyce at last flushed the support he needed. W. B. Yeats, to whom he had written of his difficulties in finding a publisher, brought him into communication with the American poet Ezra Pound. Pound quickly interested Dora Marsden, editor of the *Egoist*, in serializing *A Portrait of the Artist* in her review, and it appeared there from 2 February 1914 to 1 September 1915. Grant Richards meanwhile, whose conscience had long bothered him about *Dubliners*, agreed in January 1914 to publish it, and did so on 15 June 1914. By November 1913 Joyce had begun to write *Exiles*, and in March 1914 he started *Ulysses*.

The outbreak of the first World War did not at first affect Joyce or his brother much. Joyce continued to give private lessons and to teach classes at a commercial high school in Trieste. But in January 1915 Stanislaus Joyce was interned, and after the Italian declaration of war in May of that year Joyce knew he had better leave. With the help of friends he secured permission to go to Switzerland, on condition that he promise to take no part in the war. At the end of June 1915 he and his family were allowed to leave by train for Zurich.

To Stanislaus Joyce   MS. Cornell

11 October 1904   *Gasthaus Hoffnung, Lagerstrasse,*[1]
                                              Zürich, Switzerland

Dear Stannie We arrived here safely this morning and shall probably
stay at this address. I have not yet gone to the Berlitz School but am
going there in a half an hour. Douce was in Spain on holidays but
Rivière[2] was very kind (soixante francs) and wanted me to go back at
3.30 to meet the son of the richest banker in Zürich. Nora, however, felt
naturally very lonely whenever I was away and besides her boot was
pinching her.[3] So I let the matter rest. Write here and give me detailed
accounts of *all* the news. Devan[4] came on the boat afterwards and
caught us together so perhaps it is public property now. She has written
to her mother from Paris a delightfully vague postcard. Has she been
advertised for in the papers in Dublin? If anything has come for me
send it on here. I met Curran and Murnaghan[5] in Paris but really feared
to do anything so hardy.[6] If any money comes for me between this and
Saturday wire it on here. I hope you sent the key to Rivière.[7] I called to
see Symons but failed.   JIM

  Send on my B.A. certificate and registration for me.

Part to be detached.[8]

  Go about the highways of the city but not to any of my touched
friends and make up £1 before Saturday which send me on that day
without fail. Say nothing of this to Pappie. Finalement, elle n'est pas
encore vierge; elle est *touchée*.   JIM

  [1] An error for 16 Reitergasse.
  [2] Dr Joseph Rivière (1859–1946), founder of the Institut Physicothérapique in Paris;
Joyce had met him in 1902.
  [3] A euphemism for menstruation.
  [4] Thomas Devin (c. 1868–1937), a friend of Joyce's father. He was an official in the
Dublin Corporation, but because of some disagreement with the Town Clerk was
banished from the City Hall to the City Cleansing Department. He is at the latter office
in *Ulysses*, p. 325 (252): 'From its sluice in Wood quay wall under Tom Devan's office
Poddle river hung out in fealty a tongue of liquid sewage.'
  [5] James Murnaghan (b. 1881), a fellow student of Joyce at University College, Dublin:
he became a judge of the Supreme Court.
  [6] Joyce did not want them to know he was running off with Nora Barnacle.
  [7] The key to his trunk, which had been sent after him by Stanislaus Joyce.
  [8] This part of the letter was cut off by Stanislaus Joyce, so he could show the rest of it
to his family.

To Stanislaus Joyce   MS. Cornell

31 October 1904   *Via Giulia 2, s. piano, Pola, Austria*

Dear Stannie The school in Trieste and the school here in Pola are the private property of Signor Artifoni,[1] who manages the Trieste school through Signor Bertelli.[2] When I was told to leave I spent days looking for a post as English correspondent in a commercial house. We had a terrible time for some days, I of course borrowing *in Trieste* right left and centre. I succeeded however in getting one tuition and could have done well in private lessons if I had had money to keep me alive. However the proprietor of the two schools happened to come to Trieste on business and I went to see him. By good luck he is a socialist like myself and explained to me that it would be necessary for me to sign all papers as for married people. He offered me then a post in Pola and I accepted. I left Trieste by the first boat on Saturday morning and as you will see my entrance into Pola was signalised by the enclosed magnificent notice.[3] You will find Pola on the Adriatic coast down towards Turkey. It is a large naval station of Austria and was yesterday en fête during the unveiling of a monument to the Empress Elizabeth.[4]

As I had at least four addresses in Trieste, my correspondence is very complicated. I have not yet received the certificates you sent to Switzerland but a friend of mine in Zürich sends on anything that goes there for me. Please send me on at once the number of the 'Irish Homestead' which contains my 'After the Race'. My trunk which I left in Zürich is to arrive here tomorrow or next day. Send on the key at once.

Settled here in a furnished room and kitchen, surrounded by pots, pans and kettles. The school is just across the road. Please send on at once a long and documented letter containing all the news as it is nearly a month since I left Ireland and I have had none yet. I have

---

[1] Almidano Artifoni, whose euphonious name Joyce appropriated for Stephen's Italian teacher in *A Portrait of the Artist* and *Ulysses*.

[2] Giuseppe Bertelli was sub-director of the Berlitz School in Trieste.

[3] The *Giornaletto di Pola* for 31 October 1904 carried the following 'Notice' in Italian:

'The Berlitz School begs to inform those [naval] officers and imperial and royal employees who could not enroll as pupils in English because the times desired were already taken, that yesterday evening the second English teacher arrived,

James A. Joyce B.A.

Bachelor of Arts Mod. Lit.

'One may therefore enroll for English lessons on any day for any hour between 9 and 12.   The Management.'

(The phrase 'imperial and royal' was a customary one under the Austro-Hungarian dual monarchy.)

[4] Wife of Emperor Francis Joseph; she was assassinated 10 September 1898.

finished (in Zürich) chap. XII and have written part of a new story 'Christmas Eve'.[1] If you meet any of the mystics or Byrne or Curran you can be airily happy. Tell Pappie I shall write in a day or so, as I want him to do a thing for Dr Rivière.   JIM

To JOHN STANISLAUS JOYCE   MS. Cornell

10 November 1904   *Via Giulia 2, II° piano, Pola, Austria*

Dear Pappie I am safely settled here after a good deal of wandering and a good deal of trouble. I am unable to tell you what I want you to do for Rivière till I get my trunk from Switzerland tomorrow. This is a new school here and nearly all my pupils are officers in the Austrian navy. This is the principal naval station on the Adriatic and there are ten or twelve men-o'-war always in the harbour. The town itself is very small. They speak three languages here—Italian, German (the official language) and Slav. The Italian they speak is however very corrupt. I am going to exchange exchange [sic] lessons with the German teacher here as I wish to speak it also. There are not more than three or four English people in the town and all are 'lions'. I sent you an advt from the 'Giornaletto' and I had another one—a huge thing—in which I am billed as 'dottore in filosofia'—Doctor of Philosophy—the Italian degree answering to mine. I shall send you a picture-card of Pola one of these days. It would be quite easy for Stannie to get a position in a Berlitz school in Europe if he cared to take it as they cannot get English teachers to come abroad: If he considers it tell him consult me as I now know the way these Berlitz schools are worked. He would not have to pay any fee. The weather is good summer here but I am pestered with mosquitoes all night. There was a little disturbance here after the Innsbrück [sic] riots[2] but not much. I could have started in Trieste by myself as I had two tuitions but I preferred to come on here for the present. A Berlitz teacher is not allowed to give private lessons. Stannie tells me that the 'Speaker' has printed another poem of mine (and wrongly)[3] and when I get my trunk I intend to send off more. I am

[1] A story Joyce never completed. Edited by John J. Slocum and Herbert Cahoon, it appears in *A James Joyce Miscellany: Third Series*, ed. Marvin Magalaner (Carbondale, Illinois, 1962), pp. 3–7.

[2] The riots in Innsbruck were directed against Italian law students, many of them from Trieste, who had special classes conducted in Italian. They lasted from 3 to 8 November 1904.

[3] In the *Speaker*, n.s. XI. 262 (8 October 1904), 36, the poem afterwards included in *Chamber Music* as VI, was printed under the title 'A Wish'. Lines 2 and 3 were transposed.

enclosing a letter for Stannie. Please give it to him. I hope you are still
in good health. Addio.   Jim

P.S. A letter will be read with pleasure.

To Stanislaus Joyce   MS. Cornell

19 November 1904   *Via Giulia 2, II, Pola, Austria*

Dear Stannie About Russell:[1] I have written to my printer in Dublin
and am to release my 'Holy Office' in a week.[2] I shall send the money
order to you with a list of addresses. You can deliver many in person.
But first of all I hope you have gone to the 'Homestead' and found out
if he[3] will pay me now for a new story 'Xmas Eve.' Kindly send me on a
copy of the 'Speaker', which contains my last poem[4] and also a copy of
the no which contains my other poem.[5] Also send me address of
'Harper's' and of 'Westminster Gazette'. If you can send a copy or so
of the latter so much the better.

   I have heard from Symons that Grant Richards has become bankrupt
for an immense amount of money and consequently I have written for

   [1] Stanislaus Joyce wrote his brother of an encounter with George Russell, who
expressed indignation at the elopement of Joyce with Nora Barnacle. Russell said Joyce
had behaved caddishly and added that a touch of starvation would do him good. 'Some
weeks later,' writes Stanislaus, 'I received a telegram from my brother telling me that he
had found a position as a teacher in a Berlitz School in Pola. I waited until late that
night—it must have been long past midnight—and then went to Russell's house to break
the news to him. . . . "My brother has wired to me," said I, "that he has obtained a
position in a school." "I am very glad to hear it," said Russell, looking at me suspiciously.
"I am sure you are," I replied bitterly, "that's why I came to tell you. I knew you'd be
delighted; but I'm afraid that 'touch of starvation' must wait a little while longer." '
When Russell attempted to explain his position, Stanislaus broke in, ' "It's a pity you
didn't say to my brother himself while he was here all you said to me about him."
"I would have done so, if I had thought of it," said Russell airily. Again, I forestalled
another torrent of words. "I didn't say you wouldn't," I interrupted, "I said you didn't.
That was all." I bade him goodnight and left him still talking in the little bit of garden
in front of his house.' Stanislaus Joyce, 'Early Memories of James Joyce', *Listener* xli.
1061 (26 May 1949), 896.
   Joyce's reply was in 'The Holy Office', where a description of Russell culminates a list
of unnamed reprehensible writers:

> Or him who once when snug abed
> Saw Jesus Christ without his head
> And tried so hard to win for us
> The long-lost works of Eschylus.
> (*Critical Writings*, p. 151)

   [2] Joyce was too optimistic. His broadside was not released until June 1905.
   [3] H. F. Norman. He declined to take any more stories.
   [4] 'I would in that sweet bosom be', *Chamber Music*, vi. See p. 42n.
   [5] 'O Sweetheart, hear you', *Chamber Music*, xviii, in the *Speaker*, n.s. x. 252 (30 July
1904), 408.

the return of the MS.[1] No key arrived with B A certificate. By the way you might send on the others. Tell Aunt Josephine to let me know her address. I am fairly fixed here £2 a week for sixteen hours weekly.

I have not written much of the novel—only the end of the 11th [sic] chapter in Zürich. I have written about half of 'Xmas Eve' and about five long pages of 'Esthetic Philosophy'.[2] I am at present reading some Italian translations of Lassalle[3] but it is difficult to get to the bottom of a science like political science through pamphlets of too vivid actuality. I think then that after a short course in Aristotle I will shut up the books and examine for myself in a cafe. By the way Nora makes my cigarettes for me by machine: 70 of good Turkish tobacco cost me about 8d. She is still very well and wishes to be remembered to you. She is however interested to know what went on in the Hotel.[4] Do you know nothing? As for the comments of 'Irish Ireland'—she seems to have as high an opinion of them as I have. She wonders how you can live at home and often asks me to help you to go abroad.

I have read Moore's 'Untilled Field' in Tauchnitz.[5] Damned stupid. A woman alludes to her husband in the confession-box as 'Ned'. Ned thinks &c! A lady who has been living for three years on the line between Bray and Dublin is told by her husband that there is a meeting in Dublin at which he must be present. She looks up the table to see the hours of the trains. This on DW and WR[6] where the trains go regularly: this after three years. Isn't it rather stupid of Moore. And the punctuation! Madonna!

I am going to buy Henry James's 'Madonna of the Future' today. I am afraid I cannot finish my novel for a long time. I am discontented with a great deal of it and yet how is Stephen's nature to be expressed otherwise. Eh? I am getting rather stout and mannish.

I really can't write. Nora is trying on a pair of drawers at the wardrobe
Excuse me   Jim

---

[1] Of *Chamber Music*. Joyce had submitted it to the publisher Grant Richards (1872–1948) with Arthur Symons's recommendation. The letters from Richards to Joyce are included in an essay by Robert Scholes, 'Grant Richards to James Joyce', *Studies in Bibliography* xvi (1963), 139–60.

[2] Published in *Critical Writings*, pp. 146–8. Most of these notes were eventually incorporated into *A Portrait of the Artist*, Chapter V.

[3] Ferdinand Lassalle (1825–64), German socialist, whose biography was adapted by George Meredith in *The Tragic Comedians* (1880).

[4] Finn's Hotel, where she had been employed.

[5] George Moore, *The Untilled Field*, was published in Irish in 1902 and in English in 1903. A continental edition by Tauchnitz had just appeared in 1904. The story to which Joyce alludes is 'The Wild Goose', especially pp. 364–6 of the London 1903 edition.

[6] The Dublin, Wicklow, and Wexford Railway.

To STANISLAUS JOYCE   MS. Cornell

3 December 1904   *Via Giulia 2, II, Pola, Austria*

Dear Stannie I have not yet received the papers you were to despatch to
me and I shall be glad if you will also send the old 'Speaker' as Nora has
lost the one I gave her. Have you any news of Grant Richards or of the
'Venture'.[1] I have written to Baillie but no reply. I am half way through
Chap XIII and if you like will send you Chaps XII and XIII before
Xmas for your opinion. What of H J have you read? I have read
'Madonna of the Future' and found it very pleasant reading. I am
reading the Souvenirs of Renan. Damme if I understand him. 'Un Celte,
mêlé de Gascon, mâtiné de Lappon' 'un prêtre manqué'.[2] He professes
romanticism, love for Brittany, affection for old masters, regret at
having to abandon dear old Grandmother Church—I fancy his life of
Jesus must be very maudlin stuff. No wonder Huysmans[3] calls him a
comedian. Have you any news from the Hotel.

Nora's father is a baker. They are seven in family. Papa had a shop
but drank all the buns and loaves like a man. The mother's family are
'toney' and (by the way, do you ever see Paddy Lee?) intervened.
Sequestration of Papa. Uncle Michael[4] supports Mrs and the children,
while Papa bakes and drinks in a distant part of Connacht. Uncle M is
very rich. Papa is treated very contemptuously by the family. Nora says
her mother would not lie with him. Nora has not lived at home but
with her grandmother who has left her some money.

She has told me something of her youth, and admits the gentle art of
self-satisfaction. She has had many love-affairs, one when quite young
with a boy who died. She was laid up at news of his death. Her uncles
are worthy men as you shall hear. When she was sixteen a curate in
Galway took a liking to her: tea at the presbytery, little chats,
familiarity. He was a nice young man with black curly hairs on his head.
One night at tea he took her on his lap and said he liked her, she was a
nice little girl. Then he put his hand up under her dress which was

---

[1] *The Venture, An Annual of Art and Literature*, edited by John Baillie, was published
in London in November 1904. It contained two poems afterwards included in *Chamber
Music*, xii, 'What counsel has the hooded moon', and xxvi, 'Thou leanest to the shell of
night'.

[2] Renan calls himself, 'A Celt, mixed with Gascon, crossed with Lapp', 'a half-frocked
priest'.

[3] Joris-Karl Huysmans (1848–1907), the French novelist of Dutch extraction, who
became a devout Catholic. He strongly disapproved of Renan.

[4] Michael Healy (1862–1935), Nora Barnacle's maternal uncle, was afterwards H.M.
Inspector of Customs and Receiver of Wrecks at Galway City. He and Joyce became
good friends.

shortish. She however, I understand, broke away. Afterwards he told her to say in confession it was a man not a priest did 'that' to her. Useful difference. She used to go with Mulvey (he was a Protestant) and walk about the roads with him at time[s].[1] Says she didn't love him and simply went to pass the time. She was opposed at home and this made her persist. Her uncle[2] got on the track. Every night he would be at home before her. 'Well, my girl, out again with your Protestant.' Forbade her to go any more. She went. When she came home uncle was there before her. Her mother was ordered out of the room (Papa of course was away) and uncle proceeded to thrash her with a big walking-stick. She fell on the floor fainting and clinging about his knees. At this time she was nineteen! Pretty little story, eh?

With regard to the Holy Office you may imagine I have not much money to spare. They have sent me a bill for 10s/6d but [if you l]ook among my papers I [am sure] you will find a bill for 7/6 [and you] ought to be able to raise [that much] now since there is money [coming].[3] I think the Holy Office is so clever that I shall however send you next week an order for 2s/- leaving you to get the rest.

I should like you to study by yourself or with Cosgrave some mid-wifery and embryology and to send me the results of your study.[4] I sent a picture card to May and if you like I will send you one too. As for our way of living. We get out of bed at nine and Nora makes chocolate. At midday we have lunch which we (or rather she) buys, cooks (soup, meat, potatoes and something else) in a locanda opposite. At four o'clock we have chocolate and at eight o'clock dinner which Nora cooks. The[n] [we go] to the Caffé Miramar w[here we read] the 'Figaro' of Paris and we [come] back about midnight. Eyers,[5] [the] other English teacher, is a lovely pianist and we sometimes have music. He too, though very unripe, is falling under the Daedalean spell, I fancy. I have got some-what fat and am going to the dentist next week. I shall spend the 'Speaker' cheque on my teeth and I hope in six months to have all my teeth settled. Do you ever see Dana[6] and did they print my obscene song 'Bid adieu'? I read Nora Chap XI which she thought remarkable

---

[1] Mulvey is mentioned among Molly Bloom's sweethearts in her monologue in *Ulysses*.

[2] Not Michael Healy but another uncle, Thomas Healy.

[3] The paper is torn; the bracketed words are conjectural.

[4] Nora Barnacle Joyce was now pregnant.

[5] H. J. Eyers had come to Pola only shortly before Joyce. He eventually left the school and went to Spain.

[6] *Dana*, a review edited by John Eglinton (W. K. Magee) and Frederick Ryan, published in Dublin from May 1904 to April 1905. Joyce's poem, 'My love is in a light attire', *Chamber Music*, vii, appeared in the August issue, but 'Bid adieu', *Chamber Music*, xi, was never published there.

but she cares nothing for my art. Ask hairy Jaysus[1] what am I to do?
He ought to know.   JIM

To NORA BARNACLE JOYCE[2]   MS. Cornell

[? December 1904]   Caffè Miramar, Pola, Austria

Dear Nora For God's sake do not let us be any way unhappy tonight.
If there is anything wrong please tell me. I am beginning to tremble
already and if you do not soon look at me as you used I shall have to run
up and down the café. Nothing you can do will annoy me tonight. I will
not be made unhappy by anything. When we go home I will kiss you a
hundred times. Has this fellow[3] annoyed you or did I annoy you by
stopping away?   JIM

To STANISLAUS JOYCE   MS. Cornell

28 December 1904   Via Giulia 2, II, Pola, Austria

Dear Stannie Please send me the 'Irish Homestead' containing my
story and the Xmas no. At the end of the week I send you Chaps XII.
XIII. XIV. I am now at Chap XV. and have begun the Italian version of
'Mildred Lawson'.[4] I wish you to write at once about these chapters.
You may lend them to Cosgrave or to Curran as you please but to no-
one else. You may read them to Aunt Josephine. Say I write to her
tomorrow.

   You are perhaps surprised to receive such bare letters from me but I
find I have not much to report. The weather is bitterly cold and we have
no stove. I write chiefly in the cafés. Fräulein Globocnik,[5] the secretary
of the school, has a piano and invites us for some evening[s]. She is a
melancholy little Androgyne and very sentimental with me. I daresay

---

[1] Francis Sheehy-Skeffington, who had grown a beard in protest against shaving.
Skeffington (he had not yet married and combined his own name with that of his wife)
had annoyed Joyce by refusing to give him financial help for his departure with Nora
Barnacle, and by disapproving of the elopement altogether. In a letter of 6 October 1904,
now at Cornell, Skeffington warned Joyce that the welfare of his 'companion', Nora
Barnacle, was 'probably much more doubtful' than his own. Since Skeffington was an
ardent feminist, he would be an appropriate 'expert' for Stanislaus Joyce to consult on
the behaviour of women.
   [2] Joyce must have passed this note to his wife under the table at the café.
   [3] Possibly Eyers, the other English teacher at the Berlitz School. See letter of 12 July
1905, p. 63.
   [4] The first story in George Moore, Celibates: Three Short Stories (London, 1895).
Some pages of it, translated by Joyce, are at Cornell.
   [5] Amalija Globocnik, who was friendly with the Joyces in Pola and in Trieste later.
Joyce's consistent misspelling of her name as 'Globonik' has been corrected.

there is something in me which interests women. I desire more money and liberty than I have at present and for this reason I am working at the novel and at the translation.

You notice a fall in my spirits. This is not quite well expressed by you. My new relation has made me a somewhat grave person and I have got out of the way of dissertations. I drink little or nothing, smoke vastly, sing rarely. I have become very excitable. Nora says I have a saint's face. Myself I think I have the face of a debauchee. But I am no longer so—at least I think I am not.

One night I had a severe cramp in my stomach and Nora prayed 'O my God, take away Jim's pain.' The other evening we went to a bioscope. There were a series of pictures about betrayed Gretchen. In the third last [act] Lothario throws her into the river and rushes off, followed by rabble. Nora said 'O, policeman, catch him'.

We have had quarrels—funny affairs. Nora says they were lovers' quarrels and says I am very childish. She says I have a beautiful character. She calls me simple-minded Jim. Complimenti, Signor!

Our house is unhealthy and I am looking for new quarters. Nora has conceived, I think, and I wish her to live as healthily as possible. My child, if I have one, will of course not be baptised but will be registered in my name. I do not like talking of this subject yet.

I am not much changed in appearance: a little stouter, new brown clothes, a slight moustache, and a loose scarlet tie. My voice has disimproved greatly for want of practice and from too much smoking as well as from chronic cold. I shall go to an oculist next month to get pincenez glasses which I can use on occasions as my sight is lamentable.

I don't think I have many spiritual moments to chronicle. I do not believe I shall write any more songs. You might look up every English review for the past year and see if there is an article on D'Annunzio's 'Figlia di Jorio'.[1] If there is not I would prepare an article. I expect your reply to my 'Speaker' postcard this week. If you could get a key for my trunk in Duke St I wish you would as I never received the key you sent. I have also lost that old 'Speaker' which I should like to have.

You must be contented with this letter and write fully, as I am now going home. It is very late and it is a cold walk.   JIM

Caffé Miramar.

                                                                    NORA JOYCE

Im sorry they[2] are not natural   NORA x x x x x

Best wishes for New Year   x x x x x

---

[1] Gabriele D'Annunzio, *La Figlia di Iorio*, *Tragedia pastorale*, was published in Milan in 1904.

[2] That is, the kisses (denoted by x's).

To Mrs William Murray[1]   MS. National Library

31 December 1904, New Year's Eve   *Via Giulia 2, Pola, Austria*

Dear Aunt Josephine: A thousand apologies for my usual impoliteness and a thousand best wishes to you and Uncle Willie for the New Year. My letters to Stannie will have shown you how very busy I am at all kinds of drudgery and how difficult it is for me to write long letters. Add to this my lovely laziness of temper. My publisher has smashed, my cheques go astray, you may have heard. Have you read 'After the Race'?[2] I send Chaps XII, XIII, XIV tonight or tomorrow. The money here is all irregular for some weeks and I have not been able to send them off. It is probable that I shall leave this address next week as the house is unhealthy and I want as much health as possible for Nora.

By the way, if the request does not revolt your delicacy you might write to Signora Joyce at this address (letters will be sent on). She is away from all women except a little Fräulein and is of course adorably stupid on these points. You might write some kind of a generalising 'Don't-be-alarmed-my-dear' letter as my own steely cheerfulness in what does not afflict me personally is in need of some feminine supplement.

Stannie writes to me that Alice[3] has had to undergo some operation. I hope it has been successful. He sends me also a diverting account of some mourners near the Cattlemarket. I am trying to move on to Italy as soon as possible as I hate this Catholic country with its hundred races and thousand languages, governed by a parliament which can transact no business and sits for a week at the most and by the most physically corrupt royal house in Europe. Pola is a back-of-God-speed place—a naval Siberia—37 men o'war in the harbour, swarming with faded uniforms. Istria is a long boring place wedged into the Adriatic peopled by ignorant Slavs who wear little red caps and colossal breeches.

I shall be glad to hear from you any news you may have—that is if my lax manners have not displeased you too much. I have nothing to relate about myself except that though I am often quickly disillusioned I have not been able to discover any falsehood in this nature which had the courage to trust me. It was this night three months that we left the North Wall. Strange to say I have not yet left her on the street, as many wise men said I would. In conclusion I spit upon the image of the tenth Pius. Faithfully yours   JAS A. JOYCE

[1] Wife of Joyce's maternal uncle. See p. 29n.
[2] A story in *Dubliners*.
[3] A daughter of Mrs Murray.

To STANISLAUS JOYCE   MS. Cornell

13 January 1905   *7 Via Medolino, Pola, Austria*

Dear Stannie I received your tardy letter with its budget of Cabra news. I enclose Chaps XII. XIII. XIV. I have finished Chap. XV[1] and am now at Chap XVI. Send me all documents dealing with University College period from your diary &c. I should also like a translation (18/6ᵈ) Scott Library of Strauss's Life of Jesus.[2] I am ordering Renan.[3] I want a long critical letter on these chapters. You may lend them as I said. Tell Curran I shall shortly send him a complete MS copy of my verses. I am waiting for the papers. I have written to 'Speaker' again and shall write also to Grant Richards and Baillie. This is our new room—very cosy stove and writing-desk. Return these chapters as early as you can. I shall not send others till the college episode is complete. Tell me about my literary friends—the theatre &c. I have no time to write you more now as I am hurrying back to a lesson. Nora has written to Aunt Josephine and again wishes to salute you. What the devil are you doing with yourself. Nora curls my hair up with a tongs—it is now properly *en brosse*. I look a very pretty man—O that nice old Henry James! Have you read his review on Baudelaire?[4] It is damn funny. JIM

To STANISLAUS JOYCE   MS. Cornell

19 January 1905   *7 Via Medolino, 1°. Pola, Austria*

Dear Stannie I send you the fourth story of 'Dubliners'—'Hallow Eve' —which I want you to offer at once to the Editor of the Irish Homestead.[5] Perhaps they are annoyed with me and won't honour me by printing any more. In case it is accepted I enclose a receipt—you can receive the money yourself and post it to me. Say you will be glad to be paid as soon as convenient. The 'Irish Independent' is really awful— I could not read any of the Celtic Christines[6] except the verse which

---

[1] The manuscript of *Stephen Hero* lacks the first part of this chapter, which describes Stephen Daedalus at the university.

[2] David Friedrich Strauss, *The Life of Jesus* (1835; English translation by George Eliot, 1840).

[3] Ernest Renan, *Life of Jesus* [1863], translated with introduction by William C. Hutchinson (London, n.d.). See II, 117–18.

[4] James's essay on Baudelaire, included in his *French Poets and Novelists* (London, 1878), takes the view that Baudelaire's 'evil' is only the 'nasty'.

[5] The story was not accepted. It first appeared in print, under the title 'Clay', in *Dubliners*.

[6] The Christmas number of the *Irish Homestead* was entitled *A Celtic Christmas*.

seemed to be almost unbearably bad except Collumb's[1] piece which wasn't too bad, I thought. But ask the good young gentlemen can they beat 'Hallow Eve'. I have written to Grant Richards and have sent a song 'Bid adieu' to Harper's. Is there any news of Irish Voices?—try and see O'Donoghue.[2] Have any of the volumes of Roberts'[3] press appeared and are they still disposed to print me. I expect you to write to me much oftener than you do. You know I have no-one to talk to. Nora, of course, doesn't care a rambling damn about art. When she read 'Mildred Lawson' she said Moore didn't know how to finish a story—when she saw me copy Epiphanies into my novel she asked would all that paper be wasted—which made me think of Heine.[4] She wants me to hurry up the novel and get rich and go to live in Paris. Paris and Zurich she likes very much but Pola is a queer old place. You are not to give my address to anyone without first asking my leave— this is why I want you to *receive* the money from the Homestead.[5] *What* is wrong with all these Irish writers[6]—what the blazes are they always snivelling about? Isn't it funny to read Roberts' poems about a mother pressing a baby to her breast? O, blind, snivelling, nose-dropping, calumniated Christ wherefore were these young men begotten?   Jim

To Stanislaus Joyce   MS. Cornell

7 February 1905   *7 Via Medolino, Pola, Austria*

Dear Stannie   Your card announcing your receipt of my story relieves me greatly. I expect a dilated reference thereto. I have also received birthday honours from you, Charlie and Aunt J—thanks. On the 2nd

---

[1] Padraic Colum (1881–1972), the Irish writer, had a poem, 'Cradle Song', in *A Celtic Christmas* (*Irish Homestead*, 3 December 1904). He signed it Padraic Mac Cormac Colm, this being one of several variant spellings of his last name.

[2] David James O'Donoghue (1866–1917), Irish biographer and from 1909 until his death Librarian of University College, Dublin. He compiled *The Poets of Ireland, A Biographical Dictionary* in 1892, and in a revised edition of 1912 (p. 219) made a brief favourable mention of Joyce's *Chamber Music*. O'Donoghue also wrote lives of William Carleton and James Clarence Mangan.

Irish Voices was probably an anthology of Irish poets to be issued in connection with the elaborate Irish exhibit at the St Louis Exposition in 1904. O'Donoghue was apparently to be editor, and Joyce hoped to be represented in it. But, so far as can be ascertained, the book was never published.

[3] George Roberts. See p. 23.

[4] Heinrich Heine (1797–1856), the German poet, had a mistress, Eugénie Mirat ('Mathilde'), who later became his wife. She was an almost uneducated shop-assistant, but he remained devoted to her until his death.

[5] Joyce was evidently embarrassed to be in Pola.

[6] Joyce had in mind the group of poets who clustered around George Russell, including Padraic Colum, Eva Gore-Booth, Thomas Keohler, Alice Milligan, Susan Mitchell, Seumas O'Sullivan, George Roberts, and Ella Young. Russell published a book of selections from their verse under the title *New Songs* (Dublin and London, 1904).

Nora, Eyers, Fräulein Globocnik and I went by a little steamer to the
island of Brioni (famous for cheese). Every tiny feast is a holiday in this
country. It seems a long two years since I was in Paris.

Your criticism of my novel is always interesting. The sentence 'to
sustain in person &c' is not legitimate if the phrase, 'and to protect
thereby' is between commas but is legitimate if the phrase is in brackets.[1]
I shall change the verb however. Mrs Riordan who has left the house in
Bray returns you have forgotten, to the Xmas dinner-table in Dublin.[2]
The immateriality of Isabel[3] is intended. The effect of the prose piece
'The spell of arms' is to mark the precise point between boyhood
(pueritia) and adolescence (adulescentia)—17 years.[4] Is it possible you
remark no change? Again, no old toothless Irishman would say 'Divil an
elephant': he would say 'divil elephant'[5] Nora says 'Divil up I'll get till
you come back'. Naïf sequence! Your criticism of the two aposopeias[6] is
quite just but I think full dress is not always necessary. Stephen's
change of mind is not effected by that sight as you seem to think, but it
is that small event so regarded which expresses the change. His first
skin falls. Fulham[7] is not old Sheehy—he comes in later.[8] Are my
documents on the road?

The elaborate intentions of your antepenultimate and penultimate
frigidities are a compliment. But you are not careful or just. Curran, in
my opinion, behaved to me in a generous fashion: Cosgrave, whom you
must recognise as a torpid animal once for all, was, so far as I can
remember, guilty of no duplicity towards me.[9] Do you think I am saying
what is true? You are harsh with Nora because she has an untrained

[1] Neither phrase is in the surviving manuscript.

[2] The Christmas dinner takes place in Bray, not Dublin, in *A Portrait of the Artist*.
Joyce evidently intended at first that Stephen should be a little older when it occurred.
In *Ulysses* Mrs Riordan is said to have left the Dedalus household on 29 December 1891.

[3] Stephen's sister. Joyce is referring to a lost part of the manuscript of *Stephen Hero*,
probably in Chapter XIII or XIV.

[4] *Stephen Hero*, p. 237 (a fragment probably from Chapter XIII). Joyce eventually
placed this passage, originally an epiphany, at the end of *A Portrait of the Artist*, where
it signalizes the change from adolescence to young manhood.

[5] 'He seen the pictures on the walls and began pesterin' his mother for fourpence to see
th' elephants. But sure when he got in an' all divil elephant was in it.' *Stephen Hero*,
p. 243 (probably Chapter XIII).

[6] There are several aposiopeses in the pages of *Stephen Hero* to which Joyce is referring,
but the ones meant are probably on a lost page just preceding the extant section of the
manuscript and the set piece, 'The spell of arms and voices'.

[7] Mr Fulham makes his pompous appearance in the Mullingar pages of *Stephen Hero*.

[8] David Sheehy (1844–1932), M.P. (Nationalist) for South Galway (1885–90) and for
South Meath (1903–18). He had a hospitable house to which James and Stanislaus Joyce
often went in the evening. He is a model for 'Mr Daniel' in Chapters XVI and XVII of
Stephen Hero.

[9] Stanislaus Joyce knew, as his brother did not then know, of an effort by Vincent
Cosgrave to take Nora Barnacle away from James. Having been sworn by Cosgrave to
secrecy, he evidently referred only obliquely to Cosgrave's 'treachery'.

mind. She is learning French at present—very slowly. Her disposition, as I see it, is much nobler than my own, her love also is greater than mine for her. I admire her and I love her and I trust her—I cannot tell how much. I trust her. So enough.

You might amplify the allusion you make to Finn's Hotel as she wants to know what went on there. I sent a song 'Bid adieu' to Harper's but it was returned. I wrote to Baillie of the Venture twice but no answer. I wrote to Grant Richards (who, Symons wrote to me, was bankrupt) and he answers:—I must apologise for not having sooner answered your letter with reference to the MS of your verses. I regret to say that it is not at present possible for me to make any arrangements for the publication of the book: but I may say that I admire the work exceedingly and if you would leave the matter open for a few weeks it is possible that I might then be able to make you some offer. The MS, I regret to say, has by some mistake been packed up with some furniture of mine that has been warehoused and it is not easy for me at the moment to get at it, so that in any case I shall be glad if you can leave the whole question over for a short time—You might find out [if] he is really in business still and also get me the address of the English Ill. Magazine.[1]

Is Skeffington still registrar? Is Maggie Sheehy[2] married? I wrote postcard once to May—why did she never answer me? Are the 'girls' 'snotty' about Nora? Look through the reviews to see if 'La Figlia di Jorio'[3] has been reviewed. I want to write an article to get money. There is an anxiety at the back of my mind[4] for which I want to be ready materially. I wish some damn fool would print my verses. I intend to dedicate 'Dubliners' to you—do you mind—because you seem to find the stories to your taste. Do you think they are good? or are they only as good as the stories in French daily papers. You must know that I can't answer such questions in my worse than solitude of the intellect. It is fine spring weather here. I wish I could get to Italy by summer. An Austrian officer and his mistress live in the next room. She is pretty and cheerful: they laugh at night and chase each other about the room. I am 'working in' Hairy Jaysus at present.[5] Do you not think the search for heroics damn vulgar—and yet how are we to describe Ibsen? I have

---

[1] *English Illustrated Magazine.*

[2] Margaret Sheehy, a daughter of David Sheehy, was married in 1907 to Frank Culhane.

[3] See p. 48n.   [4] Possibly a concern for his wife's health.

[5] In Chapter XVI of *Stephen Hero*, p. 39, Joyce writes of 'Hairy Jaysus' (Skeffington): 'For instance there was a serious young feminist named McCann—a blunt brisk figure, wearing a Cavalier beard and shooting-suit, and a steadfast reader of the *Review of Reviews*. The students of the college did not understand what manner of ideas he favoured and they considered that they rewarded his originality sufficiently by calling him "Knickerbockers".' He is identified as 'Hairy Jaysus' on p. 113. See above, p. 47.

written some fine critical sentences lately.[1] They have discovered a novel of Disraeli's.[2]

I find your letters dull only when you write about Nora or Henry James but no doubt both of these subjects bore you as you have no special affinity for either of them. No damn nonsense about writing short letters in future. I write short letters because I have a lot to do. I have English to teach, German to learn (I have learnt a good deal) a novel to translate, a novel to write besides letters and stories, marketing to do—Jaysus. I think I'm a hell of an industrious chap lately. And then Nora! So no more bile beans, brother John,[3] and please smile your citron smile.

I have finished Chap XV and Chap XVI and am now at Chap XVII. I was examined by the doctor of the Naval Hospital here last week and I now wear pince-nez glasses on a string for reading. My number is very strong—could you find out what is Pappie's. As soon as I get money I shall have my teeth set right by a very good dentist here. I shall then feel better able for my adventures. I am anxious to know if you think my writing has suffered any change. My life is far less even than formerly in spite of its regularity. I reach prostrating depths of impersonality (multiply 9[4] by 17—the no of weeks) but on the other hand I reach levels of great satisfaction. I am sure however that the whole structure of heroism is, and always was, a damned lie and that there cannot be any substitute for the individual passion as the motive power of everything—art and philosophy included. For this reason Hairy Jaysus seems to be the bloodiest impostor of all I have met.[5] Tell him, if you meet him, that I am about to produce a baboon baby by sitting for six hours on a jug full of soda water and ask him will he be godfather.   JIM

To STANISLAUS JOYCE   MS. Cornell

28 February 1905   *7 Via Medolino, Pola, Austria*

Dear Stannie Why do you put a note of exclamation after the sentence

---

[1] In Chapters XV and XVI of *Stephen Hero*.

[2] 'An Unfinished Novel' by Benjamin Disraeli was published in the *Times* (London) on 20, 21, and 23 January 1905.

[3] Stanislaus Joyce's premature sobriety of temperament was a family joke. James referred to entries in Stanislaus's diary as 'Bile Beans', and remembered the epithet in 'A Painful Case', where 'the headline of an advertisement for *Bile Beans* had been pasted on to the first sheet' of Mr Duffy's little sheaf of papers. Another brother, George, had nicknamed Stanislaus 'Brother John'.

[4] Probably nine hours, his working day.

[5] Skeffington had probably defended the notion that the individual should sacrifice himself for the sake of the group.

about Doran's article? It seems to me a strange subject: I should like to read the article. Your mention of Ibsen leads me to enclose you this cutting from a Trieste paper. I wish I knew enough Danish to read the volumes. What kind is the article on Ibsen in T P?[1] I notice that articles on Ibsen have very attractive titles. On what authority did you write to me 'All they said at Finn's Hotel was that Miss Barnacle had gone away'? Is Mrs Wright a fixture there. (This is putrid ink) Your compliment (Coppée[2] and myself) is rather chilly: but I have not my instruments with me (as you know) or I should not be forced to apply to others for help. I thought Curran knew the proposed length of the opus—what is this about care or cure? I have read Renan's 'Life of Jesus' (I asked you to send me Strauss):[3] it is a model of good writing in many ways: the temper is delightful. The narrative of the death I may perhaps translate for you. He calls John the Baptist the absinthe of the divine feast. I have read the Sorrows of Satan,[4] A Difficult Matter (Mrs Lovett Cameron)[5] The Sea Wolves (Max Pemberton)[6] Resurrection[7] and Tales (Tolstoy) Good Mrs Hypocrite (Rita)[8] Tragedy of Korosko (Conan Doyle)[9] Visits of Elizabeth (Elinor Glyn)[10] and Ziska.[11] I feel that I should be a man of letters but damn it I haven't the occasion yet. You have nothing to do—why don't you write full letters? I am getting some stories of Jakobsen[12] (in German) and the Feast at Solhoug[13] (also in German) to read. I have progressed a great deal in German. Read *Siren Voices*[14] and report. 'There would be' (il y aurait) tell the torpid one[15] is not an inversion. Tell him also that I am going to write a 'Dubliner' on him. Where is 'Hallow Eve' at present? Take it to the I.H.[16] again and kiss Russell from me. You might send me some report of modern English literature. Why doesn't Aunt Josephine write? I have sent you all information I have about the cheque and expect your reply to cross this.

[1] 'Henrik Ibsen', *T.P.'s Weekly* (ed. Thomas Power O'Connor), v. 117 (3 February 1905), 140–1.

[2] François Coppée (1842–1908), the French writer. Stanislaus Joyce's letter comparing his brother's work to that of Coppée has not survived.

[3] See p. 50

[4] By Marie Corelli (London, 1895). Referred to in *Ulysses*, p. 235 (184).

[5] Mrs Lovett Cameron, *A Difficult Matter* (London, 1898).

[6] Sir Max Pemberton, *The Sea Wolves* (London, 1894).

[7] Count Leo Tolstoy, *Resurrection*, translated by Louise Maude (New York, 1900).

[8] Rita (Mrs Desmond Humphreys), *Good Mrs Hypocrite* (London, 1899).

[9] Arthur Conan Doyle, *The Tragedy of Korosko, etc.* (London, 1898).

[10] Elinor Glyn, *Visits of Elizabeth* (London, 1900).

[11] Marie Corelli, *Ziska, The Problem of a Wicked Soul* (London, 1897).

[12] Jens Peter Jacobsen (1847–85), Danish novelist; his book of stories *Mogens* (1882) is probably meant.

[13] Henrik Ibsen, *The Feast at Solhoug* (1855).

[14] A translation of Jacobsen, *Niels Lyhne* (London, 1896).

[15] Cosgrave. See page 52.   [16] *Irish Homestead.*

It seems to me that what astonishes most people in the length of the novel is the extraordinary energy in the writer and his extraordinary patience. It would be easy for me to do short novels if I chose but what I want to wear away in this novel cannot be worn away except by constant dropping. Gogarty used to pipe '63' in treble when I told him the number of the chapters. I am not quite satisfied with the title 'Stephen Hero'[1] and am thinking of restoring the original title of the article 'A Portrait of the Artist' or perhaps better 'Chapters in the Life of a Young Man'. If I had a phonograph or a clever stenographist I could *certainly* write any of the novels I have read lately in seven or eight hours.

Your satirical surprise at my proposed 'dedication' of 'Dubliners' to you arises, I imagine from an exaggerated notion you have of my indifference to the encouragement I receive. It is difficult for anyone at my age to be indifferent. I am not likely to die of bashfulness but neither am I prepared to be crucified to attest the perfection of my art. I dislike to hear of any stray heroics on the prowl for me.

I think that by the time my novel is finished I shall be a good German and Danish scholar and, if Brandes[2] is alive, I shall send it to him. I have come to accept my present situation as a voluntary exile—is it not so? This seems to me important both because I am likely to generate out of it a sufficiently personal future to satisfy Curran's heart and also because it supplies me with the note on which I propose to bring my novel to a close.

I suppose you will receive this letter on Saturday or Sunday. Address your next letter to the Trieste school, Via S. Nicolo, 32, as I am transferred there. I leave Pola on Sunday morning for Trieste, but if any letters from you are on the way they will follow me. I shall see at once about your entering the Berlitz School. Here are some particulars: England, Ireland and Scotland are controlled from *London*. France, Spain, Portugal and, I think, Germany are controlled from *Paris*. Austria-Hungary, Italy, Switzerland, Turkey, Greece, Egypt are controlled from *Vienna*. You should apply to these centres according to where you want to go. This is not a good time as all posts are usually full but there may be vacancies. In September you would have no difficulty. If it is your intention to wait till September enter at once and pass the Matric. Exam. of the Royal University, as a University

---

[1] When 'A Portrait of the Artist' was rejected by the review *Dana* (see p. 4), Joyce decided on his birthday, 2 February 1904, to rewrite it as *Stephen Hero*, after the ballad of 'Turpin Hero'. Stanislaus Joyce said that both titles had been suggested to his brother by him.

[2] Georg Brandes (1842–1927), the Danish critic and friend of Ibsen.

certificate would be very useful to you. Collect besides all your other certificates and your birth-certificate. If you decide to go you must study colloquial French as you will then be able to pass anywhere in the continent except of course with the common people. If you want to go before September write and let me know and I will see if there are at present any vacancies under the control of the Vienna office. An agent would charge you three guineas, but if you go to an agent send me his name first and I will tell you if you can trust him. The following from experience: grow a moustache, pretend to know everything, and dress magnificently. If you do this you will get on better. What country do you want to go to? I will tell you where you will have most to do. You can easily live on half the pay you receive in France, Italy or Germany, but this place is very dear. Answer this letter as quickly and as fully as you can. I have suffered a good deal from the lack of the papers I asked you for. ~~Faithfully Yours~~[1] Jaysus! amn't I stupid to write that.   JIM

To STANISLAUS JOYCE   MS. Cornell

15 March 1905   *Piazza Ponterosso 3, III, Trieste, Austria*

Dear Stannie My memory has got so damn bad that I forgot to enclose you the cutting from a Trieste paper about the publication of Ibsen's letters under the editorship of his son, Sigurd: here it is. Hauptmann's last play 'Elga' was produced the night before last in Berlin. In D'Annunzio's new play 'The Light under the Bushel'[2] his son is an actor. I have read in the *Figaro* of the divorce of the Irish Joan of Arc from her husband.[3] Pius the Tenth, I suppose, will alter Catholic regulations to suit the case: an Italian comment says Irish genius is not domestic. Poor little U.I.: indignant little chap.[4] What in my letter did Pappie find lunatic? Damn you, I don't want 'Hallow Eve' back again. Sell it to Mighty AUM,[5] and forward the money. Renan is a good writer but he makes me think of a Parisian gentleman who said to me one night in great flurry at parting time, 'Alors, monsieur, au plaisir. Ici je prendrai tramway mais d'abord faut que je prenne water-closet'. Your account of your own boredom often amuses me. What is this I hear about Charlie and philosophy? I am not letting my beard grow.

---

[1] Crossed out by Joyce.   [2] Gabriele D'Annunzio, *La Fiaccola sotto il moggio* (1905).

[3] Maud Gonne and her husband, Major John MacBride, were in fact separated, not divorced.

[4] Arthur Griffith (1872–1922), editor of the nationalist weekly, the *United Irishman*, later *Sinn Féin*, and a strong defender of Maud Gonne. Joyce and he were acquainted.

[5] George Russell, with a slap at his study of Indian philosophy, in which the Sanskrit word *aum* stands for creation, being, dissolution, and ultimate reality.

Nora sings sometimes when she is dressing—is that what you mean? At
present she is licking jam off a piece of paper. She is very well, wears a
veil now and looks very pretty. Just now she came in and said 'The
landlady has her hen laying out there. O, *he*'s after laying a lovely egg.'
Jaysus! O Jaysus! By the bye—in case I forget it—do not omit to slap
Skeffington three times smartly on the bottom when you meet him next
and say you 'My brother that *was* in Po-là is going to send you your
two guineas, he says'.

I have been reading 'Confidence',[1] 'Monsieur Bergeret à Paris' by
Anatole France and 'Peter Simple' by Capt. Marryat: and I prefer the
last of the three. It seems to me much better than most of the modern
scamped adventure-stories. 'Confidence' is almost readable on account
of its inoffensiveness but it is neither delicate nor rich enough for my
taste and I found it in no way interesting. Anatole France has a very
high reputation but silence is my comment after reading two books—
perhaps his worst. He is an intellectual socialist, I understand. In 'Elga'
Hauptmann again uses the mechanism of a dream or vision.[2] He is a
very beautiful type of civilisation, in my opinion, and I wish I had
leisure enough to interpret him. I have read (in German) a play by
Hejermans—Ahasver[3] but it is nothing, I have read H. J. consecutively
and am now hesitating between De Amicis,[4] A. France and Maupassant
for a plunge. I think I shall take De Amicis. Would you be surprised if
I wrote a very good English grammar some day? I have been sending
you and Aunt J some picture postcards. It is a rather pretty game,
don't you think?

I have finished Chapters XV. XVI. XVII. XVIII and will send them
if you like. The U. College episode will take about ten chapters and I
thought of keeping all till it was ended. On the other hand that is a hell
of a time for you to wait. I have received your letter which interested
me very much but if you knew what the feuilletons and short sketches
in French papers [are] you would understand my embarrassment.[5] Is
Starkey's book[6] any good? I think Gogarty must use a typewriter: I do

[1] By Henry James (1879).   [2] As in his *Hanneles Himmelfahrt* (1894).

[3] Hermann Heijermans (1864–1924), the Dutch dramatist and novelist. *Ahasuerus*
(1893) was his first successful play; it described the plight of Jews in Russia during the
pogrom in 1890. The Wandering Jew lends his name as the title but does not appear in
the play; possibly Joyce found here a hint for *Ulysses*, where also an analogy is asserted
although the title character never appears.

[4] Edmondo de Amicis (1846–1908), Italian novelist and essayist in the tradition of
Manzoni.

[5] Stanislaus Joyce must have suggested that his brother write, or translate some of
Dubliners or the epiphanies, for the French press.

[6] James S. Starkey ('Seumas O'Sullivan'), *The Twilight People* (Dublin, March 1905).
See p. 29.

not think he could write consecutively enough for an article without some mechanical aid. I have become very cautious with money. Lothair[1] bought a jewel cross for his wife which cost him £10,000: this I can understand. One evening he 'threw the cabman a sovereign'—this I cannot understand. He cannot have had a very fine conscience on some points. You would smile to see me holding for a lower price in goloshes or reckoning a waiter's bill after him. Nora is looking at 'T.P.'s Weekly' and asks 'Is this the Ibsen you know?' I believe that Ibsen and Hauptmann separate from the herd of writers because of their political aptitude—eh?   JIM

Nora says I am to tell you she is axing at you!

To STANISLAUS JOYCE   MS. Cornell

4 April 1905   *Piazza Ponterosso 3, III, Trieste, Austria*

Dear Stannie While I was attending the Greek mass here last Sunday it seemed to me that my story *The Sisters* was rather remarkable. The Greek mass is strange. The altar is not visible but at times the priest opens the gates and shows himself. He opens and shuts them about six times. For the Gospel he comes out of a side gate and comes down into the chapel and reads out of a book. For the elevation he does the same. At the end when he has blessed the people he shuts the gates: a boy comes running down the side of the chapel with a large tray full of little lumps of bread. The priest comes after him and distributes the lumps to scrambling believers. Damn droll! The Greek priest has been taking a great eyeful out of me: two haruspices.[2]

I have now finished another chapter and am at Chapter XX. This is a terrible opus: I wonder how I have the patience to write it. Do you think other people will have the patience to read it? The other English teacher here said to me last night as he looked at my suit 'I often notice that eccentric people have very little taste: they wear anything. I give you a tip. If you have no taste you go in for grey. Stick to grey. Doesn't matter what kind—always looks gentlemanly'. Now, this seems to me on mature reflection a bloody awful position for me to be in. Some day I shall clout my pupils about the head, I fear, and stalk out.

I wish you would send me the key of my trunk as I want to sell it and buy a valise. A trunk here is a third passenger to pay for. My trunk from London to Trieste cost me about £1. If you do not dispose of

---

[1] The title character in Benjamin Disraeli, *Lothair* (1870).
[2] The priest and himself.

'Hallow Eve' at once, send the MS back as I shall send it to the London 'Daily Mail.' Get me *at once* a copy of the will of Catherine Healy[1]— born Mortimer—who was married to——Healy and died in Abbeygate St, Galway, in the year 1895, 6 or 7. Read the will yourself and send me a copy at once. You can get the will in the Record Office of the Four Courts in Dublin. Also find out if Nora can get her birth certificate by writing to the Registrar General's office as we may want it. If you see Cosgrave tell him that he is in my novel under the name of Lynch. Address your next letter to Berlitz School 32 Via S. Nicolo as I leave here on Sunday.

I have received your letter. I see three London papers regularly so some of it was not news but I am damn glad to get letters. While I was reading it in the school, one of my pupils passed through, a vulgar little Hungarian, saying flatly 'Good morning, sar' to which I replied with intention 'The divil bite your bottom'. Honestly it is awful! Send that will on AT ONCE and the key. 'Sometime fornicator . . . spiritual love' O, fie! fie! is that one for me? How did Buckley kill the Russian general?[2] I have now finished Chaps XV, XVI, XVII, XVIII, XIX and XX and am now at Chap XXI. Why don't you send me back my chapters? My health is not very good. I do not like *Confidence*: it bores me dreadfully and *Peter Simple* doesn't. Read the end of Chap XVII: I think it is well written. O blast Kincora![3] Nora is reading the slip by fits and starts to a tune of 'Old Tom Gregory, Has a big menagerie', which seems to me what old Thornton would have called a *double entente*.   JIM

Nora says she hopes you're well and have a nice girl. JAYSOOS!

To STANISLAUS JOYCE   MS. Cornell

[*? 2 or 3 May 1905*]   *Via S. Nicolo 30, II°, Trieste, Austria*

Dear Stannie   I have read in the 'Standard' of London that Grant Richards is bankrupt for £53,100–0–0. What do you think I ought to do? I want my verses to be published in the autumn. I have finished Chaps XV. XVI. XVII. XVIII. XIX. XX and XXI. I am now at Chap

---

[1] Nora Joyce's maternal grandmother, by whom she had been brought up. Joyce had the vain hope that his wife had been left money which she could now claim. Actually Mrs Healy died intestate.

[2] In a famous story of Joyce's father, Buckley shot the Russian general in the anus. Joyce is making an earthy retort to his brother's reproach of inconsistency. For Joyce's later version of Buckley's exploit, see *Finnegans Wake*, pp. 346–53.

[3] *Kincora*, Lady Gregory's play about Brian Boru, had been produced for the first time at the Abbey Theatre on 25 March 1905.

XXII. I would write another 'Dubliner' if I knew definitely the result of 'Hallow Eve'. I do not think I can write any more verse. I have great difficulty getting a room as the landladies shunt us as soon as they perceive Nora's state: but I don't care a rambling curse of Christ what any one does or what happens. I can't write any more now because Nora is dabbing me with inky paper.

I have been waiting for a letter confirming your news of E.H.[1] Nora is positive that you are making a mistake. As you may have heard I am entering for a missing letter puzzle in 'Ideas'. There are to be 48 words in batches of six. As yet 42 words have appeared and I have solved all. I am waiting for the last six. The prize is £250. I shall send you a sealed and registered letter containing a copy of my answers. You are *not* to open the letter but keep it carefully. In case I solve all or nearly all I shall also seal and register my letter to the paper so that if they do not give me a prize I can take an action against them.

My entering for this competition has kept me a very long time on Chapter XXII but you may expect to receive the chapters of the University College episode in a few weeks. I have written to Grant Richards asking for my manuscript and if he is done for I shall send a copy of the verses to John Lane as I want them published by the end of the year. I am writing (imagine!) a summary of English literature for a Berlitz Book for the Japanese: five or six pages. The German teacher here is going to Japan.

You must be surprised to get such bald letters from me but then you see that I am very busy. Skeffington, poor youth, is in a bad way. What surprises me is that these wise ones should have said that there is money in my novel. I hardly believe there is. It is a mistake for you to imagine that my political opinions are those of a universal lover: but they are those of a socialistic artist. I cannot tell you how strange I feel sometimes in my attempt to live a more civilised life than my contemporaries. But why should I have brought Nora to a priest or a lawyer to make her swear away her life to me? And why should I superimpose on my child the very troublesome burden of belief which my father and mother superimposed on me? Some people would answer that while professing to be a socialist I am trying to make money: but this is not quite true at least as they mean it. If I made a fortune it is by no means certain that I would keep it. What I wish to do is to secure a competence on which I can rely, and why I expect to have this is because I cannot believe that any State requires my energy for the work I am at present engaged in.

[1] Possibly someone of the Healy family. See p. 60.

If you look back on my relations with friends and relatives you will
see that it was a youthfully exaggerated feeling of this maldisposition of
affairs which urged me to pounce upon the falsehood in their attitude
towards me as an excuse for escape. The English teacher here says I
think of nothing but eating: and in reality I do not eat much at all. He
says I will die of a brain disease: whereas in spite of the afflicting
delicacy of that organism it does not seem to me to be diseased in any
way. He says I will die a Catholic because I am always moping in and
out of the Greek Churches and am a believer at heart: whereas in my
opinion I am incapable of belief of any kind.

Have you ever reflected what an important sea the Mediterranean is?
In the canal here the boats are lined along the quays. They are the same
old galley-looking affairs which were in use during the Middle Age. The
men row the row-boats from the standing posture. Inside the great
bosom of the prow every sailing ship has an image of some saviour,
Saint Nicholas or the Madonna or Jesus walking on the waters. Perhaps
the Baltic will replace the Mediterranean but till now importance seems
to have been in the direct ratio of nearness to the Mediterranean.

I have sent in solutions of the puzzle—all correct but owing to
distance and time a day late. I have finished the 'history of Eng.
Literature' for this German chap. I did not write because I was
expecting a letter from you. I am reading Ecclesiastical History in the
intervals of teaching. I am thinking of studying grammar. I think it
would be a better whetstone for youth than geometry. I have written to
Grant Richards and expect a reply. In my history of literature I have
given the highest palms to Shakespeare, Wordsworth and Shelley. Have
you read Turgénieff's 'Lear of the Steppes.' He does many things well
and is useful technically but in European literature he has not so high
a place as you seem to think he has.   JIM

To STANISLAUS JOYCE (Postcard)   MS. Cornell

Postmark 11 June 1905   *Via S. Nicolo 30, II°, Trieste*

Put copies of 'Holy Office' into different envelopes and deliver with the
flaps closed, and addressed upon all interested. Do not omit Skeffington
and Cousins.[1] You will find addresses in directory. Byrne, Ellwood[2] and

---

[1] James Henry Cousins (1873–1956), Irish poet and Theosophist, afterwards active in
the Theosophical movement in India. Joyce had visited Cousins and his wife, and stayed
with them for two days, in September 1904.

[2] See p. 21n.

Cosgrave also. The 'Leprechaun'[1] disturbed my peace. I am studying
Danish again with constancy. Do you know that Ibsen's married life
ended by his leaving his wife?[2] He is a curious lyrical poet. I think
Wordsworth of all English men of letters best deserves your word
'genius'. Read his poem to his lost son in 'Excursion' I think which
begins 'Where art thou my beloved son.'[3] I am now definitely studying
for the theatre. Sinico,[4] a maestro here, tells me that after two years
I can do so. My voice is extremely high: he says it has a very beautiful
timbre. I shall report on success of my verses with Lane. I changed the
last couplet of 'Though I thy Mithridates were'[5] and I have omitted
the words 'To Nora' from the first poem.[6] Write long letters. Was going
to Venice this morning but it began to rain.   JIM

To STANISLAUS JOYCE   MS. Cornell

12 July 1905   *Via S. Nicolò 30, II°, Trieste, Austria*

Dear Stannie I send you tomorrow the fifth story of 'Dubliners' that is,
'The Boarding-House'. You are to dispose of it if you can to an English
or American paper. I have a copy by me. I have also written the sixth
story 'Counterparts' and shall send it to you on Saturday if I have made
a copy by then. It is my intention to complete 'Dubliners' by the end of
the year and to follow it by a book 'Provincials'. I am uncommonly well
pleased with these stories. There is a neat phrase of five words in *The
Boarding-House*: find it.[7] John Lane has refused my verses and I have
offered them to Elkin Mathews. You will recieve a volley of correspondence from me within the next week or so of which this letter is the first.

I expect you have received by now the postcard I sent you on
Saturday last, asking you to come here to Trieste as I wanted to speak
to you on a serious matter. I have thought since that it might be too
difficult for you to manage that and so I am going to discuss affairs by
letter. You are to consider all that I write as intended solely for yourself
and Aunt Josephine, and I shall be anxiously waiting for your replies.

[1] *The Lepracaun*, a Dublin monthly of a nationalist outlook, began publication in May
1905 and continued until June 1914. Joyce was disturbed by a poem, 'The Lepracaun',
which was signed merely *Joyce*, in the first issue. The author was not James Joyce but
Robert Dwyer Joyce.
[2] A false rumour.   [3] From 'The Affliction of Margaret'.
[4] Giuseppe Sinico (1836–1907), Triestine operatic composer, choirmaster, and author
of a vocal method. Joyce took lessons in singing from him.
[5] *Chamber Music*, xxvii.
[6] 'He who hath glory lost', xxi. The order of the poems was subsequently altered.
[7] Possibly, as Robert Martin Adams suggests, the description of Polly Mooney as
'like a little perverse madonna'.

You will remember the circumstances in which I left Ireland nine months ago. Like everything else that I have done in my life it was an experiment. I can hardly say with truth that it was an experiment which has failed seeing that in those nine months I have begotten a child, written 500 pages of my novel, written 3 of my stories, learned German and Danish fairly well, besides discharging the intolerable (to me) duties of my position and swindling two tailors. I believe, besides, that I write much better now than when I was in Dublin and the incident in Chap. XXIII (?)[1] where Stephen makes 'love' to Emma Clery I consider a remarkable piece of writing. Add to this that I have eaten and drunk enough to live upon, secured glasses and a watch, and am having my teeth attended to at last. I do not think that I have wasted my time but even if I had done so it would not affect what I am about to explain.

I must, first of all, tell you that Trieste is the rudest place I have ever been in. It is hardly possible to exaggerate the incivility of the people. The girls and women are so rude to Nora that she is afraid to go out in the street. Nora can speak about thirty words of Triestine dialect (I tried and failed to teach her French) and so whenever she goes out I must accompany her and I have often to spend an afternoon looking for a very simple thing at a reasonable price. I must tell you also that as soon as she began to be any way noticeable we were turned out of our lodgings. This happened three times until I conceived the daring plan of living in the house next the school and astonishing the landlady by the glamour of that wonderful establishment. This ruse has succeeded so far but we are still in imminent danger of being put out. The director of the school and the sub-director (a vegetarian, and a German) have both wives but—no children. The director when he saw Nora said he thought I must be stark mad. The sub-director is also appalled. He has written in German and published at his own expense a 'booklet of spring flowers' in which there is a poem which begins

'In drinking I did never lag'

and another (a pure feat of the imagination in the circumstances) which begins:

> 'O, can there be for mother's heart
> A fairer poem
> Than when her child after many an effort
> Lisps the first word.'

You will see from this what an interesting atmosphere I breathe but—

---

[1] Actually Chapter XXIV of *Stephen Hero*.

to go on. Nora is almost always complaining. She can eat very few of the sloppy Italian dishes and whatever she eats gives her a pain in her chest. She drinks beer but the least thing is enough to make her sick. In Pola during the winter she suffered dreadfully from the cold and now (the thermometer being at 100° F or so) she lies nearly all day on the bed powerless with fatigue. The Trieste people are great 'stylists' in dress, often starving themselves in order to be able to flaunt good dresses on the pier and she with her distorted body (Eheu! peccatum?) and her short four crown skirt and hair done over the ears is always nudged at and sniggered at. I was thinking lately of renting a quarter (that is, two or three rooms and a kitchen) but a house-agent told me that it was very difficult to get into a quarter in Trieste if you have children. We have kitchen utensils here in the bedroom but we never use them as Nora does not like to cook in other people's kitchens. So we dine out and lunch out with the result that I am continually borrowing money from the director and the other English 'professor' and paying it back the next day. Trieste is not very cheap and the difficulties of an English teacher living with a woman on a salary fit for a navvy or a stoker and expected to keep up a 'gentlemanly' appearance and to ease his intellectual heart by occasional visits to a theatre or a bookshop are very great. Having heard the first part of the story you can understand that the régime of these schools is a reign of terror and that I should be in a much more terrorised position were it not that many of my pupils (noblemen and signori and editors and rich people) have praised me highly to the director[1] who being a socialist is very sensible of my deservingness in consequence. As it is I cannot look for a position in another school or, indeed, for any position. He gave me to understand one day very pointedly that whenever he found a teacher trying to get a post elsewhere he packed him off. He locked up my BA certificate in his safe where he said he had the certificates of the other 'professors' (a lie, of course, since I am the only qualified teacher here so far as Austrian law goes—being a doctor[2]) and informed me that whereas his copy of my contract was stamped my copy of his contract was unstamped. The slightest disapproval on the part of my genteel pupils would be sufficient to obtain for me dismissal and with my 'immorality' belled about the town I should find it next to impossible to get anything to do here. There is no hope of advancement and a continual fear of collapse. This is the economic position.

[1] Artifoni.
[2] Joyce considered his university degree to be the equivalent of the continental doctorate, but it was not.

The moral position is not very re-assuring. Reserving my own case for the present I must tell you some more things about Nora. I am afraid that she is not of a very robust constitution. In fact she is not in good health. But more than this I am afraid that she is one of those plants which cannot be safely transplanted. She is continually crying. I do not believe that she wants to have anything more to say to her people but I am quite sure (it is her own statement) that she cannot live this life with me much longer. She has nobody to talk to but me and, heroics left aside, this is not good for a woman. Sometimes when we are out together (with the other English 'professor') she does not speak a word during the whole evening. She seems to me to be in danger of falling into a melancholy mood which would certainly injure her health very much. I do not know what strange morose creature she will bring forth after all her tears and I am even beginning to reconsider the appositeness of the names I had chosen ('George' and 'Lucy'). She is also sensitive and in Pola I had once to turn the English teacher, a thoughtless young chap named Eyers, out of the room (much as I dislike such an office) for making her cry. I asked her today would she like to rear a child for me and she said very convincingly that she would, but, in my present uncertain position I would not like to encumber her with a family. Her knowledge of even ordinary affairs is very small and she cries because she cannot make the clothes for the child even after Aunt Josephine has sent her the patterns and I have bought the stuff for her. I have no time or patience now for theories as to what the State should do in such cases but I am simply trying to do what I think is best.

I think it is best for people to be happy and honestly I can see no prospect of her being happy if she continues to live this life here. You know, of course, what a high esteem I have for her and you know how quietly she gave our friends the lie on the night when she came with us to the North Wall. I think that her health and happiness would be much improved if she were to live a life more suited to her temperament and I don't think it right that even I should complain if the untoward phenomenon of 'love' should cause disturbance, even in so egoistically regulated a life as mine. The child is an unforgettable part of the problem. I suppose you know that Nora is incapable of any of the deceits which pass for current morality and the fact she is unhappy here is explained when you consider that she is really very helpless and unable to cope with any kind of difficulties. I do not know exactly the attitude of your mind towards her or towards the child which will be hers and mine but I think that in most essential things you share my opinions. As a matter of fact I know very little about women and you, probably, know less and I think you ought to submit this part of the case to Aunt Josephine who knows more than either of us. One of the English teachers said that she was not worthy of me and I am sure this would be many people's verdict but it requires such a hell of a lot of self-stultification to enter into the mood which produces such a verdict that I am afraid I am not equal to the task. After all, it is only Skeffington, and fellows like him, who think that woman is man's equal. Cosgrave, too, said I would never make anything of her, but it seems to me that in many points in which Cosgrave and I are deficient she does not require any making at all. I have certainly submitted myself more to her than I have ever done to anybody and I do not believe I would have begun this letter but that she encouraged me. Her effect on me has so far been to destroy (or rather to weaken) a great part of my natural cheerfulness and irresponsibility but I don't think this effect would be lasting in other circumstances. With one entire side of my nature she has no sympathy and will never have any and yet once, when we were both passing through an evening of horrible melancholy, she quoted (or rather misquoted) a poem of mine which begins 'O, sweetheart, hear you your lover's tale'.[1] That made me think for the first time in nine months that I was a genuine poet. Sometimes she is very happy and cheerful and I, who grow less and less romantic, do not desire any such ending for our love-affair as a douche in the Serpentine.[2] At the same time I want to avoid as far as is humanly possible any such apparition in our lives as that abominable spectre which Aunt Josephine calls 'mutual tolerance'. In fact, now that I am well on in my letter I feel full of hope again and, it seems to me, that if we can both allow for each other's temperaments, we may live happily. But this present absurd life is no longer possible for either of us.

[Sheet missing here]

my writing does not excuse him,[3] in my opinion, for having behaved towards me treacherously. I often think to myself that, in spite of the seeming acuteness of my writing, I may fail in life through being too ingenuous, and certainly I made a mistake in thinking that, with an Irish friendship aiding me, I could carry through my general indictment or survey of the island successfully. The very degrading and unsatisfactory nature of my exile angers me and I do not see why I should continue to drag it out with a view to returning 'some day' with money

---

[1] *Chamber Music*, xviii.

[2] The allusion is to Harriet Shelley's suicide in the Serpentine in 1816.

[3] Oliver St John Gogarty, whose treachery lay in his having evicted Joyce from the Martello tower.

in my pocket and convincing the men of letters that, after all, I was a person of talent. After a great dealing [sic] of hunting and searching I have thought of [a] plan which might be adopted as a temporary solution of the question and I am now going to set it out to you.

It is now the month of July and next month the interesting event is to take place. From now to next Easter I could save perhaps twenty pounds, at least twelve. I can offer my thirty-three poems and my nine stories broadcast. My verses may be accepted by a publisher and when *Dubliners* is complete I intend to offer it to Heinemann, who, I am sure, will take it. Independently of this I could send home to you a certain fraction of my salary every month and by next Easter I am sure that I could have twenty pounds in Ireland besides the prospect of my verses and stories and novel selling. It would be possible for you to save, at least, the same sum in the same time and with the two we might take a small cottage[1] outside Dublin in the suburbs, furnish it and pay the rent for a half-year in advance. I simply suggest this as an experiment which need not continue longer than twelve months if it were found to be unsuccessful.

This suggestion, however, I am very reluctant to make for many reasons. First of all, it involves a serious infringement of your liberty but on the other [hand] I do not see that you would suffer very much economically since everything could be yours. You cannot tell when you may be forced to 'compromise' your liberty as I have been forced and certainly if you *did* entertain the idea of leaving Ireland and living in a Berlitz School on the continent you may entertain this idea. If you had a job of thirty shillings a week and we had put our saved sums together I think we could give my proposal a year's trial. The second reason why I am reluctant to make this proposal is that I am uncertain whether you would like it or not. Not that I imagine that the atmosphere of our suppositious [sic] cottage could by any vagaries on the part of the two arrivals from Trieste become more unpleasant to you than the atmosphere you are at present breathing, but I am quite in the dark as to the attitude of your mind towards me and 'my companion'.[2] By the way, is there no method you can suggest of annihilating Hairy Jaysus? Isn't he an insufferable object! The third reason why I am reluctant to propose this is that I have proposed so many things which are now considered

---

[1] '... a roseschelle cottage by the sea for nothing for ever....' *Finnegans Wake*, p. 179. Bloom also wishes 'to purchase by probate treaty in fee simple a thatched bungalowshaped 2 storey dwellinghouse of southerly aspect, surmounted by vane and lightning conductor....' *Ulysses*, pp. 837–8 (712).

[2] Francis Sheehy-Skeffington ('Hairy Jaysus') had so described Nora Barnacle when he heard of Joyce's plan to leave Dublin with her. See p. 47n. He may have been alluding to *Chamber Music*, xxi.

follies of mine and done so few of them that I am beginning to think it is not right for me to expect people to help me out in my notions since I have become a settled person. However, in spite of my reluctance, I have made the proposal and there's an end of it. I shall expect your reply and if you think well of it I can send you my first instalment at the beginning of August. I hope your letter will not delay in coming.

Kindly believe that if there is anything abnormally unpleasant to you in this confession and letter it arises from my foolishness which is now to be reckoned one of my permanent assets. It is possible that my idea is really a terrible one but my mind's eye is so distracted after nine months of my present life that I am unable to see things with my former precision. Of one thing, however, I am made aware from the obscure depths of my consciousness and that is, whether my present life end this way or another way, it will end shortly: and that will be a great relief to everybody concerned.   JIM

To STANISLAUS JOYCE (Fragment of a letter)   MS. Cornell

19 July 1905   [*Trieste*]

[1] and tomorrow (Monday) for example in this torrid weather I have to give eight lessons during which I must keep continually on the alert and interested. Many of the frigidities of *The Boarding-House* and *Counterparts* were written while the sweat streamed down my face on to the handkerchief which protected my collar. I have had only two swims because it is far out to the baths and I very seldom have more than two hours free at any time.

I will confess to you in confidence that I should very much like to eat a slice of boiled leg of mutton with turnips and carrots. Also desirables are a slice of corned beef and cabbage, a sizeable beefsteak prepared on a gridiron, and (excuse the hierarchy) an intelligent supra-burgher like yourself to share the meal. Nora desires to see a kettle on the side of a fire and, though my desire is perhaps a passing one, I fear that hers is permanent. But I will not dilate on this point because it is possible that a letter of yours, on its way here now, I hope, will be so full of sensible statements that I shall have to obliterate corned beef and boiled leg of mutton from the bill of fare indefinitely.

The director told me yesterday that as soon as the other English 'professor' went away he would raise my salary. This, you will see, would help me greatly in carrying out my designs. If you agree, you are to

---

[1] The surviving part of the manuscript begins here.

dispose of my verses and stories broadcast. I am so far away that I can do little or nothing but you are on the spot. Nine stories and twenty verses should yield at the lowest ten pounds and I can easily send you another ten pounds: that makes £20. I am now beginning to be afraid that some such move must be made. Nora seems to me to be in very poor health. All yesterday and the day before she has been laid up with neuralgia and pains and today she seems to be dropping down with weakness. It is very difficult for either of us to enjoy life in these circumstances.

The preface to *The Vicar of Wakefield* which I read yesterday gave me a moment of doubt as to the excellence of my literary manners. It seems so improbable that Hardy, for example, will be spoken of in two hundred years. And yet when I arrived at page two of the narrative I saw the extreme putridity of the social system out of which Goldsmith had reared his flower. Is it possible that, after all, men of letters are no more than entertainers? These discouraging reflections arise perhaps from my surroundings. The stories in *Dubliners* seem to be indisputably well done but, after all, perhaps many people could do them as well. I am not rewarded by any feeling of having overcome difficulties. Maupassant writes very well, of course, but I am afraid that his moral sense is rather obtuse. The Dublin papers will object to my stories as to a caricature of Dublin life. Do you think there is any truth in this? At times the spirit directing my pen seems to me so plainly mischievous that I am almost prepared to let the Dublin critics have their way. All these pros and cons I must for the nonce lock up in my bosom. Of course do not think that I consider contemporary Irish writing anything but ill-written, morally obtuse formless caricature.

The struggle against conventions in which I am at present involved was not entered into by me so much as a protest against these conventions as with the intention of living in conformity with my moral nature. There are some people in Ireland who would call my moral nature oblique, people who think that the whole duty of man consists in paying one's debts; but in this case Irish opinion is certainly only the caricature of the opinion of any European tribunal. To be judged properly I should not be judged by 12 burghers taken at haphazard, judging under the dictation of a hidebound bureaucrat, in accordance with the evidence of policeman but by some jury composed partly of those of my own class and of my own age presided over by a judge who had solemnly forsworn all English legal methods. But why insist on this point? I do so only because my present lamentable circumstances seem to constitute a certain reproach against me.   Jim

P.S. I have just received a postcard from Heinemann declining my verses.

To Stanislaus Joyce (Telegram) MS. Cornell

[*27 July 1905*] [*Trieste*]

Son born Jim[1]

To Stanislaus Joyce MS. Cornell

29 July 1905 *Via S. Nicolò 30, II°, Trieste, Austria*

Dear Stannie The child was born on Thursday last the 27th July at nine o'clock in the evening. It was almost by accident I was in the city that day as I had had the intention of going away to a bathing-place. When I came back from the café at three o'clock I found Nora in pain. I had no notion it was for birth but when it continued for a long time I went to the landlady[2] and told her. She sent for her midwife and then there was proper confusion if you like. The room was all pulled about. Nora had hardly anything made not expecting the event till the end of August. However, our landlady is a Jewess and gave us everything we wanted. I told her to get everything that was wanted and gave her all the money I could lay hands on. Then I went for Dr Sinigaglia[3] who is one of my pupils. He came at once and returned in time to help Nora to give birth to the child. He says I must have miscalculated the time as it is a perfectly normal child. The people here made me go in to dinner with them and at about nine in came the old aunt Jewess smiling and nodding 'Xe un bel maschio, Signore'.[4] So then I knew an heir was born.

It was not very pleasant for me—the six hours—but it must have been a damn sight worse for Nora. But Dr Sinigaglia told me she was very brave and hardly uttered a cry, only clapped her hands when she heard it was a boy. She is very well. The child appears to have inherited his grandfather's and father's voices. He has dark blue eyes. He has a great taste for music because while I was nursing him yesterday he eyed me with great fixity as I whistled several operatic airs for him. Nora gives him her own milk.

I wonder would you mind applying to the much lamented Curran. I am in a slight fix, as you may suppose. I hardly like to do this but

[1] The telegram is in Joyce's handwriting and is evidently the copy of it which he kept. The original received in Dublin has not survived.
[2] Signora Moise Canarutto.
[3] Dr Gilberto Senigaglia (1872–1919). [4] 'It's a fine boy, sir.'

perhaps he will allow me to 'borrow' a pound from him. It's very expensive for me and I was quite unprepared. Many thanks for your telegram in reply. I am expecting a letter from you and a parcel, long overdue. I enclose a fortune[1] which a white mouse picked for me this morning. I intended it for the child but it seems applicable to myself. Please attend to the material side of this letter. I hope that you are all delighted now that you have all been made uncles and aunts of.   JIM

To STANISLAUS JOYCE (Postcard)   MS. Cornell

1 September 1905   *Via S. Nicolò 30, II°, Trieste, Austria*

Dear Stannie   Thanks for your prompt return of the story with appendage. I send you by this post the eighth story '*Ivy Day in the Committee-Room*' which I hope you will return as promptly. I would be glad to have detailed account of your interview with Koehler [sic].[2] The child has no name yet—I am waiting for funds. I do not want so much as you think but a little would do no harm. If *Dubliners* is published next spring I hope to be able to help you to get out of your swamp. Do you think it will make money? Nora is writing today to Aunt Josephine. I would be glad of some news of your house generally. Do you think an English publisher will take *Dubliners*? Is it not possible for a few persons of character and culture to make Dublin a capital such as Christiania has become? Is Cosgrave going to become a dispensary doctor by sacerdotal favour? Are you going to become a despised clerk? I hope to be able to prevent this—but what about myself?   JIM

To STANISLAUS JOYCE   MS. Cornell

18 [September] 1905[3] Sunday night   *Via S. Nicolò 30, II°, Trieste*

Dear Stannie   I am surprised that you have not written to me as you said you would or sent back my manuscript. I must ask you to exert your imagination a little with regard to me. My average number of lessons (and what lessons!) per day will now be from 8 to 10 and I am trying to finish *Dubliners*. So if you and Aunt Josephine are piqued by my not writing you must not forget these facts. I really wish you would answer me promptly, money or no money.

   I am much obliged for your careful criticisms of my stories. Your

---

[1] This has been lost.
[2] Thomas Goodwin Keohler (1874–1942), a poet and Theosophist. (He changed his name afterwards to Keller.)
[3] Joyce gives the date inaccurately as 18 *August* 1905.

comparison of them with certain others is somewhat dazzling. The authors you mention have such immense reputations that I am afraid you may be wrong. Lermontoff says, apropros of the Confessions of Rousseau, that they were vitiated by the fact that Rousseau read them to his friends.[1] I hardly think, arguing from the conditions in which they are written, that these stories can be superlatively good. I wish I could talk to you fully on this as on many other subjects. Your remark that *Counterparts* shows a Russian ability in taking the reader for an intracranial journey set me thinking what on earth people mean when they talk of 'Russian'. You probably mean a certain scrupulous brute force in writing and, from the few Russians I have read, this does not seem to be eminently Russian. The chief thing I find in nearly all Russians is a scrupulous instinct for caste. Of course, I don't agree with you about Turgénieff. He does not seem to me to be very much superior to Korolenko (have you read any of his?) or Lermontoff. He is a little dull (not clever) and at times theatrical. I think many admire him because he is 'gentlemanly' just as they admire Gorky because he is 'ungentlemanly'. Talking of Gorky what do you think of him? He has a great name with Italians. As for Tolstoy I disagree with you altogether. Tolstoy is a magnificent writer. He is never dull, never stupid, never tired, never pedantic, never theatrical! He is head and shoulders over the others. I don't take him very seriously as a Christian saint. I think he has a very genuine spiritual nature but I suspect that he speaks the very best Russian with a St Petersburg accent and remembers the Christian name of his great-great-grandfather (this, I find, is at the bottom of the essentially feudal art of Russia). I see that he wrote a 13 column letter to *The Times* of London attacking governments. Even the English 'liberal' papers are indignant. Not merely does he attack armaments, he even alludes to the Tsar as a 'weak-minded Hussar officer, standing below the intellectual level of most of his subjects, grossly superstitious and of coarse tastes'. The English liberals are shocked: they would call him vulgar but that they know he is a prince. A writer in the *Illustrated London News* sneers at Tolstoy for not understanding WAR. 'Poor dear man!' he says. Now, damn it, I'm rather good-tempered but this is a little bit too much. Did you ever hear such impudence? Do they think the author of *Resurrection* and *Anna Karénin* is a fool? Does this impudent, dishonourable journalist think he is the equal of Tolstoy, physically, intellectually, artistically or morally? The thing is absurd. But when you think of it, it's cursedly annoying also. Perhaps that

---

[1] Mikhail Yurevitch Lermontov, *A Hero of Our Own Times*, tr. Eden and Cedar Paul (London: The World's Classics, 1958), p. 98.

journalist will undertake to revise Tolstoy more fully—novels, stories, plays and all. I agree with you, however, about Maupassant. He is an excellent writer. His tales are sometimes a little slipshod but that was hardly to be avoided, given the circumstances of his life.

To return to myself. Do you think it is likely an English publisher will publish *Dubliners*? Mr T. Fisher Unwin, who 'regretted &c . . .' my verses has an advertisement in today's *Daily Mail* for Florence Warden's new thrilling story *The House by the River*. The advertisement begins with a quotation from some sensitive reviewer 'Up and down your spine' in moderate capitals. I am sure that in 'private life', as they say of the lady highkickers, Mr T. Fisher Unwin is a most 'cultured' person. Sometimes I ask myself, when similar enormities reach me, is it worth while conquering this. On the other hand, as perhaps Mr Magee and Mr Gogarty are beginning to suspect, my nature is artistic and I cannot be happy so long as I try to stifle it. You did not seem to take my statement—viz, that my present absurd life is no longer possible for me —very seriously. Therefore I repeat the remark: and I may also remind you that I have a habit (an inconvenient one for myself, it seems) of following up a conviction by an act. If I once convince myself that this kind of life is suicidal to my soul, I will make everything and everybody stand out of my way as I did before now. However I am doing what I can to live without causing unhappiness to the few people for whom I have affection.

The child has got no name yet, though he will be two months old on Thursday next. He is very fat and very quiet. I don't know who he's like. He's rather like that pudgy person of two years old who frowns at the camera in my first photograph but he has the 'companion's' eyes. How is that brisk idiot,[1] by the way? He seems to be very healthy in spite of his paternal inheritance. I think a child should be allowed to take his father's or mother's name at will on coming of age. Paternity is a legal fiction.[2] Wouldn't it be awful if I had to hawk my son from one beggarly lodgings to another, from land to land? I mean, of course, for his sake. I hope to Christ he won't have to make allowances for me when he begins to think.

I send you the ninth story of *Dubliners*, namely *An Encounter* which might bear the dedication to the author of *The Voyage of the Ophir*.[3]

---

[1] Francis Sheehy-Skeffington. See p. 47n.

[2] 'Paternity may be a legal fiction,' says Stephen Dedalus in *Ulysses*, p. 266 (207).

[3] George Meredith's royalist poem, which celebrated the voyage round the empire taken by the Prince and Princess of Wales in 1901. By a complicated chain of association, Joyce related this obsequious gesture by an able writer to the kind of homosexual temper that English public-school education was apt to produce.

(Return it at once.) You overrate this writer greatly, I think. Do you remember how I shocked you by deriving him from Lytton and Disraeli. I should have been sent to school in France. I don't like to think of some prose which I have written. But, instead, I was taught by Father Tommy Meagher[1] and Ruskin.

Have you heard of the earthquake in Calabria? I enriched the fund for the sufferers by a crown. Some phenomena of nature terrify me. It is strange that a person can be morally intrepid, as I certainly am, and abjectly cowardly in the physical sense. Some nights I look at my girl's arms with pity and think that perhaps my politeness is also a form of physical cowardice. How I would like, if only I could secure a footing, to plunge any young people I knew into a bath of spontaneous happiness. I would like to see a lot of different young natures tumbling over each other. This desire however may be egoistic. It is quite certain that in the past, for example with the 'companion' and with Gogarty and Byrne, I behaved as I did (to G's and B's astonishment, unselfishly) because my own nature would have been offended had I behaved otherwise. By the way, how is May?   JIM

P.S. No letter again today. What's up now?

To STANISLAUS JOYCE   MS. Cornell

[About 24 September 1905]   *Via S. Nicolò 30, II°, Trieste, Austria*

Dear Stannie Please send me the information I ask you for as follows:
The Sisters: Can a priest be buried in a habit?
Ivy Day in the Committee Room—Are Aungier St and Wicklow in the Royal Exchange Ward? Can a municipal election take place in October?
A Painful Case—Are the police at Sydney Parade of the *D* division?[2] Would the city ambulance be called out to Sydney Parade for an accident? Would an accident at Sydney Parade be treated at Vincent's Hospital?[3]
After the Race—Are the police supplied with provisions by government or by private contracts?[4]
Kindly answer these questions as quickly as possible. I sent my story *The Clay* (which I had slightly rewritten) to *The LITERARY World*

---

[1] Rev. Thomas Maher, S.J. (1859–1917), a master at Belvedere College from 1894 to 1897, is probably meant. Joyce's spelling of his name is influenced by Thomas Francis Meagher (1823–67), the patriot and writer.

[2] In the published story Joyce did not specify the division.

[3] Joyce changed the text to read the City of Dublin Hospital.

[4] This detail does not appear in the published story.

but the cursedly stupid ape that conducts that journal neither acknowledged it nor sent it back. This kind of thing is maddening. Am I an imbecile or are these people imbeciles. That journalist that wrote so superiorly about Tolstoy is (thank the devil) dead and, I hope, damned. By the Lord Christ I must get rid of some of these Jewish bowels I have in me yet. I went out yesterday for a walk in a big wood outside Trieste. The damned monotonous summer was over and the rain and soft air made me think of the beautiful (I am serious) climate of Ireland. I hate a damn silly sun that makes men into butter. I sat down miles away from everybody on a bench surrounded by tall trees. The Bora (the Trieste Wind) was ro-aring through the tops of the trees. I sniffed up all the fragrance of the earth and offered up the following prayer (not identical with that which Renan offered upon the Acropolis)[1]

O Vague Something behind Everything!

For the love of the Lord Christ change my curse-o'-God state of affairs. Give me for Christ' sake a pen and an ink-bottle and some peace of mind and then, by the crucified Jaysus, if I don't sharpen that little pen and dip it into fermented ink and write tiny little sentences about the people who betrayed me send me to hell. After all, there are many ways of betraying people. It wasn't only the Galilean suffered that. Whoever the hell you are, I inform you that this [is] a poor comedy you expect me to play and I'm damned to hell if I'll play it for you. What do you mean by urging me to be forbearing? For your sake I refrained from taking a little black fellow from Bristol by the nape of the neck and hurling him into the street when he spat some of his hatched venom at me. But my heroic nature urged me to do this because he was smaller than I. For your sake, I allowed a cyclist to use towards me his ignoble and cowardly manners, pretending to see nothing, pretending that he was my equal. I sorrowfully confess to you, old chap, that I was a damn fool. But if you only grant me that thing I ask you for I will go to Paris where, I believe, there is a person by the name of Anatole France much admired by a Celtic philologist by the name of Goodbetterbest[2] and I'll say to him 'Respected master, is this pen pointed enough?' Amen.

---

[1] In Ernest Renan, *Souvenirs d'enfance et de jeunesse* (1883), Chapter II is his 'Prière sur l'Acropole'. It begins, 'O nobleness! O pure and genuine beauty! Goddess whose cult denotes reason and wisdom. . . .'

[2] Richard Irvine Best (1872–1959) was Assistant Director of the National Library of Ireland 1904–23, and Director 1924–40. His translation of H. d'Arbois de Jubainville, *The Irish Mythological Cycle*, was published in Dublin and London in 1903, and the same year he founded (with John Strachan and Kuno Meyer) the School of Irish Learning in Dublin, of which he remained honorary secretary until its dissolution in 1924. He takes a prominent part under his own name (which is mocked) in the *Scylla and Charybdis* episode of *Ulysses*.

It is possible that the delusion I have with regard to my power to write will be killed by adverse circumstances. But the delusion which will never leave me is that I am an artist by temperament. Newman and Renan, for example, are excellent writers but they seem to have very little of the temperament I mean. Whereas Rimbaud, who is hardly a writer at all, has it. Of course Renan is an artist and must have the temperament but it is balanced by the temperament of a philo[lo]gist. Newman must have it too but balanced by the temperament of a theologian. I am neither *savant* nor saint. Grant Richards wrote to me, saying how much he admired *Chamber Music* but adding that, with the present public taste, he could not take more than part of the risk.[1] I wrote back thanking him (I daresay he has no money himself) and saying I had no money. I wrote to Heinemann telling him about *Dubliners* and asking would he read it and consider it. I shall send you on Wednesday or Thursday the tenth story *A Mother* and the book will be finished by the first of November. You might let me know what you think of it as I intend to dedicate it to you. You are a long time sitting on my novel. I wish you'd say what you think of it. The only book I know like it is Lermontoff's *Hero of Our Days*. Of course mine is much longer and Lermontoff's hero is an aristocrat and a tired man and a brave animal. But there is a likeness in the aim and title and at times in the acid treatment. Lermontoff describes at the end of the book a duel between the hero and G—, in which G— is shot and falls over a precipice in the Caucasus. The original of G—, stung by the satire of the writer, challenged Lermontoff to a duel. The duel was fought on the brink of a precipice in the Caucasus as described in the book. Lermontoff was shot dead and rolled over the precipice. You can imagine the thought that came into my mind.[2] The book impressed me very much. It is much more interesting than any of Turgénieff's.

Will you read some English 'realists' I see mentioned in the papers and see what they are like—Gissing, Arthur Morrison and a man named Keary.[3] I can read very little and am as dumb as a stockfish. But really I think that the two last stories I sent you are very good. Perhaps they will be refused by Heinemann. The order of the stories is as follows. *The Sisters, An Encounter* and another story[4] which are stories of my childhood: *The Boarding-House, After the Race* and *Eveline*, which are stories of adolescence: *The Clay, Counterparts,* and *A Painful Case*

---

[1] Richards's letter, which Joyce summarizes accurately, was dated 21 September 1905.

[2] That is, of his own quarrel with Gogarty.

[3] Charles Francis Keary (1848–1917). His book, *'Twixt Dog and Wolf* (London, 1901), is probably meant.

[4] 'Araby'.

which are stories of mature life: *Ivy Day in the Committee Room, A Mother* and the last story of the book[1] which are stories of public life in Dublin. When you remember that Dublin has been a capital for thousands of years, that it is the 'second' city of the British Empire, that it is nearly three times as big as Venice it seems strange that no artist has given it to the world. I read that silly, wretched book of Moore's 'The Untilled Field' which the Americans found so remarkable for its 'craftsmanship'. O, dear me! It is very dull and flat, indeed: and ill written.   JIM

PS No letter from you again today. I will fall in love with you if you keep on dodging the post like this much longer. What in the name of God are you at? If you don't answer at once, by God, I'll go to Dublin at once and get my manuscripts. Are you at 'biz'? An old man, hatless, stockingless and shirtless, a pilgrim, passed my window now on his way to the Holy Land. Two little Triestines went into a hallway and laughed till they beat each other. Funny world!

To GRANT RICHARDS   MS. Harvard

15 October 1905   *Via S. Nicolò 30, II°, Trieste, Austria*

Dear Mr Grant Richards Mr Symons wrote to me saying that Messrs Constable & Co, to whom he had spoken of me, had invited me to send them the MSS of my two books. Accordingly I made a copy of *Chamber Music* and sent it to them today. I am not sure whether you will think this act of mine discourteous but I hardly know what to do. I think you had better keep my verses as it is most probable that Messrs Constable & Co will refuse the book.

The second book which I have ready is called *Dubliners*. It is a collection of twelve short stories. It is possible that you would consider it to be of a commercial nature. I would gladly submit it to you before sending it to Messrs Constable and, if you could promise to publish it soon, I would gladly agree. Unfortunately I am in such circumstances that it is necessary for me to have either of the books published as soon as possible.

I do not think that any writer has yet presented Dublin to the world. It has been a capital of Europe for thousands of years, it is supposed to be the second city of the British Empire and it is nearly three times as big as Venice. Moreover, on account of many circumstances which I

---

[1] 'Grace.' Joyce had not yet thought of writing 'Two Gallants', 'A Little Cloud', or 'The Dead'.

cannot detail here, the expression 'Dubliner' seems to me to have some meaning and I doubt whether the same can be said for such words as 'Londoner' and 'Parisian' both of which have been used by writers as titles. From time to time I see in publishers' lists announcements of books on Irish subjects, so that I think people might be willing to pay for the special odour of corruption which, I hope, floats over my stories.

Faithfully yours   JAS A JOYCE[1]

To STANISLAUS JOYCE   MS. Cornell

[*16 October 1905*]   *Via S. Nicolò 30, II°, Trieste, Austria*

Dear Stannie I enquired today about the Hamburg route. Hamburg-Trieste, third class (via Leipsic-Dresden-Vienna) is 77 crowns. The train journey is 36 hours. The sea voyage London-Hamburg is nearly 20 hours so I am not much inclined to advise you to come that way; I am not sure even if it is the cheapest route. Try what it costs via Ostend. The sea trip is only a few hours. The railway would be Ostend-Brussels (or Luxembourg)-Monaco-Villach-Trieste. In any case tell the clerk you want to travel over German railways as they are much cheaper. Nora wants you to bring her some Indian tea in one of your pockets. The only tea here is Russian. You will be just in time for the new wine and roast chestnuts and you will be able to decide perhaps as to what language your eldest nephew Georgie speaks. I shall expect your telegram on Thursday and I hope also to have an answer to my postcard. After a month perhaps we could rent a small quarter. You have 40 and I have 45 crowns a week: that is 85 crowns (£3-11-0) and we might get a piano also. The director has offered to give me some furniture. He is very friendly with me because one of my pupils—Count Sordina has praised me very highly and brought several real live ladies and gentlemen of his acquaintance to the school.

I wrote yesterday to Constable promising to send them *Chamber Music* in a day or two and *Dubliners* in a week or so. I sent Symons a copy of *The Holy Office* which I hope he will distribute among his friends. I am copying out the eleventh story *Araby*, but I hardly think it will be worth while sending it to you as, I hope, you will be here so soon. I need hardly say how glad I will be to see you.

[1] Richards replied on 18 October 1905, 'Of course I cannot for a moment complain of your having sent your manuscript to Messrs. Constable, and I hope for your sake that that firm will decide to publish the poems. . . . If they do not, then I shall still hope that we may be able to do something with them here. It will give me great pleasure to have the opportunity of reading "Dubliners".'

I advise you to show these letters to Pappie as he may be able to help you. As for leaving the children in the lurch—what can you do in Dublin? You say you have been looking for a *job* (9 hours a day) at 15ˢ/– a week. This job is 33ˢ/– for 6 hours a day. Besides if my books are published I may be able to help you and Charlie to something definite. But what use is it to talk of the future. I have many other points connected with it to discuss with you.

This day twelvemonths I was in Paris after *touching* Dr Rivière successfully. We drove from the Gare S. Lazare to the Gare de l'Est in an open carriage. I will be in Paris again I am sure and in Dublin too. I am sure you will be glad to see Georgie. He is damnably fat and long and healthy—I suppose because Nora nurses him herself. He has a pair of big dark blue eyes which he doesn't get from me. Thanks be to the Lord Jaysus no gospeller has put his dirty face within the bawl of an ass of him yet.   JIM

Bring the tea in a loose package for fear of the Custom-House officials.

To MRS WILLIAM MURRAY   MS. Cornell

4 December 1905   *Via S. Nicolò 30, II°, Trieste, Austria*

Dear Aunt Josephine   I have been a very long time answering your letters but I have been very busy. Yesterday I sent my book *Dubliners* to a publisher. It contains twelve stories, all of which you have read except the third story *Araby* and the last one *Grace*. I have also been deterred from writing by the knowledge that voluminous correspondence was taking place between Stannie and some person or persons unknown and I was waiting until I was [sure] I would find disengaged ears. Moreover I have very little news to send you. I imagine you must be tired hearing my explicit or implicit complaints about my present life and therefore I shall not trouble you with many in this letter. You are not to argue from this that I am in the least resigned. In fact I am simply waiting for a little financial change which will enable me to change my life. At the latest it will come at the end of two years but even if it does not come I shall do the best I can. I have hesitated before telling you that I imagine the present relations between Nora and myself are about to suffer some alteration. I do so now only because I have reflected that you [are] a person who is not likely to discuss the matter with others. It is possible that I am partly to blame if such a change as I think I foresee takes place but it will hardly take place through my fault alone. I daresay I am a difficult person for any woman to put up with but on the other hand I have no intention of changing. Nora does not seem to make much difference between me and the rest of the men she has known and I can hardly believe that she is justified in this. I am not a very domestic animal—after all, I suppose I am an artist—and sometimes when I think of the free and happy life which I have (or had) every talent to live I am in a fit of despair. At the same time I do not wish to rival the atrocities of the average husband and I shall wait till I see my way more clearly. I suppose you will shake your head now over my coldness of heart which is probably only an unjust name for a certain perspicacity of temper or mind. I am not sure that the thousands of households which are with difficulty held together by memories of dead sentiments have much right to reproach me with inhumanity. To tell the truth in spite of my apparent selfishness I am a little weary of making allowances for people.

Perhaps you can send me a *critique* from a Dublin paper on Moore's novel[1] in which Father O. Gogarty appears. I hope you are in good health.   JIM

To GRANT RICHARDS   MS. Harvard

5 May 1906   *Via Giovanni Boccaccio 1, II, Trieste, Austria*

Dear Mr Grant Richards, I am sorry you do not tell me why the printer, who seems to be the barometer of English opinion, refuses to print *Two Gallants* and makes marks in the margin of *Counterparts*.[2] Is it the small gold coin in the former story or the code of honour which the two gallants live by which shocks him? I see nothing which should shock him in either of these things. His idea of gallantry has grown up in him (probably) during the reading of the novels of the elder Dumas and during the performance of romantic plays which presented to him

[1] George Moore, *The Lake* (London, 1905).

[2] Richards had written Joyce on 23 April, 'I am sorry, but I am afraid we cannot publish "The Two Gallants" as it stands; indeed, the printers, to whom it was sent before I read it myself, say that they won't print it. You see that there are still limitations imposed on the English publisher! I am therefore sending it back to you to ask you either to suppress it, or, better, to modify it in such a way as to enable it to pass. Perhaps you can see your way to do this at once.

'The same thing has to be done with two passages marked in blue pencil on page 15 of "Counterparts".

'Also—you will think I am very troublesome, but I don't want the critics to come down on your book like a cart load of bricks—I want you to give me a word that we can use instead of "bloody" in the story "Grace".'

Joyce replied on 26 April (I, 60–1) that he would change nothing, regardless of the printer's point of view. On 1 May Richards answered that the printer's opinion might be valueless in itself, but was indicative of the probable opinion of an 'inconveniently large section of the general public'.

cavaliers and ladies in full dress. But I am sure he is willing to modify his fantastic views. I would strongly recommend to him the chapters wherein Ferrero[1] examines the moral code of the soldier and (incidentally) of the gallant. But it would be useless for I am sure that in his heart of hearts he is a militarist.

He has marked three passages in *Counterparts*:

'a man with two establishments to keep up, of course he couldn't. . . .'
'Farrington said he wouldn't mind having the far one and began to smile at her. . . .'
'She continued to cast bold glances at him and changed the position of her legs often; and when she was going out she brushed against his chair and said "Pardon!" in a Cockney accent.'[2]

His marking of the first passage makes me think that there is priestly blood in him: the scent for immoral allusions is certainly very keen here. To me this passage seems as childlike as the reports of divorce cases in *The Standard*. Or is it possible that this same printer (or maybe some near relative of his) will read (nay more, actually collaborate in) that solemn journal which tells its readers not merely that Mrs So and So misconducted herself with Captain So and So but even how often she misconducted herself with him! The word 'establishment' is surely as inoffensive as the word 'misconducted.'

It is easier to understand why he has marked the second passage, and evident why he has marked the third. But I would refer him again to that respectable organ the reporters of which are allowed to speak of such intimate things as even I, a poor artist, have but dared to suggest. O one-eyed printer! Why has he descended with his blue pencil, full of the Holy Ghost, upon these passages and allowed his companions to set up in type reports of divorce cases, and ragging cases and cases of criminal assault—reports, moreover, which are to be read by an 'inconveniently large section of the general public.'

There remains his final objection to the word 'bloody'. I cannot know, of course, from what he derives the word or whether, in his plain blunt way, he accepts it as it stands. In the latter case his objection is absurd and in the former case (if he follows the only derivation I have heard for

[1] Guglielmo Ferrero (1871–1942), Italian historian and antifascist social critic. In *L'Europa giovane* (Milan, 1898), pp. 163–70, Ferrero finds a secret alliance between Puritanism, sexual aberration, and military destructiveness, using Bismarck as his example.

[2] When *Dubliners* was finally published by Grant Richards, in 1914, Joyce omitted the first two passages and, after prefacing the third with two new sentences, modified it to read, 'She glanced at him once or twice and, when the party was leaving the rooms, she brushed against his chair and said "O, pardon!" in a London accent.'

it) it is strange that he should object more strongly to a profane use of the Virgin than to a profane use of the name of God. Where is his English Protestantism? I myself can bear witness that I have seen in modern English print such expressions as 'by God' and 'damn'. Some cunning Jesuit must have tempted our stout Protestant from the path of righteousness that he defends the honour of the Virgin with such virgin ardour.

As for my part and share in the book I have already told all I have to tell. My intention was to write a chapter of the moral history of my country and I chose Dublin for the scene because that city seemed to me the centre of paralysis. I have tried to present it to the indifferent public under four of its aspects: childhood, adolescence, maturity and public life. The stories are arranged in this order. I have written it for the most part in a style of scrupulous meanness and with the conviction that he is a very bold man who dares to alter in the presentment, still more to deform, whatever he has seen and heard. I cannot do any more than this. I cannot alter what I have written. All these objections of which the printer is now the mouthpiece arose in my mind when I was writing the book, both as to the themes of the stories and their manner of treatment. Had I listened to them I would not have written the book. I have come to the conclusion that I cannot write without offending people. The printer denounces *Two Gallants* and *Counterparts*. A Dubliner would denounce *Ivy Day in the Committee-Room*. The more subtle inquisitor will denounce *An Encounter*, the enormity of which the printer cannot see because he is, as I said, a plain blunt man. The Irish priest will denounce *The Sisters*. The Irish boarding-house keeper will denounce *The Boarding-House*. Do not let the printer imagine, for goodness' sake, that he is going to have all the barking to himself.

I can see plainly that there are two sides to the matter but unfortunately I can occupy only one of them. I will not fall into the error of suggesting to you which side you should occupy but it seems to me that you credit the printer with too infallible a knowledge of the future. I know very little of the state of English literature at present nor do I know whether it deserves or not the eminence which it occupies as the laughing-stock of Europe. But I suspect that it will follow the other countries of Europe as it did in Chaucer's time. You have opportunities to observe the phenomenon at close range. Do you think that *The Second Mrs Tanqueray*[1] would not have been denounced by a manager of the middle Victorian period, or that a publisher of that period would

---

[1] A play (1893) about a man who marries a 'notorious' woman, by Sir Arthur Wing Pinero.

not have rejected a book by George Moore or Thomas Hardy? And if a change is to take place I do not see why it should not begin now.

You tell me in conclusion that I am endangering my future and your reputation. I have shown you earlier in the letter the frivolity of the printer's objections and I do not see how the publication of *Dubliners* as it now stands in manuscript could possibly be considered an outrage on public morality. I am willing to believe that when you advise me not to persist in the publication of stories such as those you have returned to me you do so with a kind intention towards me: and I am sure you will think me wrong-headed in persisting. But if the art were any other, if I were a painter and my book were a picture you would be less ready to condemn me for wrong-headedness if I refused to alter certain details. These details may now seem to you unimportant but if I took them away *Dubliners* would seem to me like an egg without salt. In fact, I am somewhat curious to know what, if these and similar points have been condemned, has been admired in the book at all.

I see now that my letter is becoming nearly as long as my book. I have touched on every point you raise in order to give you reason for the faith that is in me. I have not, however, said what a disappointment it would be to me if you were unable to share my views. I do not speak so much of a material as of a moral disappointment. But I think I could more easily reconcile myself to such a disappointment than to the thousand little regrets and self-reproaches which would certainly make me their prey afterwards. Believe me, dear Mr Grant Richards, Faithfully yours   JAS A JOYCE

To GRANT RICHARDS   MS. Harvard

31 May 1906   *Via Giovanni Boccaccio 1, II°, Trieste, Austria*

Dear Mr Grant Richards, I am sorry that in reply to my letter you have written one of so generalising a character.[1] I do not see how you can

---

[1] Richards had replied on 10 May, 'If I had written your stories I should certainly wish to be able to afford your attitude; but as I stand on the publisher's side, I feel most distinctly that for more than one reason you cannot afford it.... You won't get a publisher—a real publisher—to issue it as it stands. ... After all, remember, it is only words and sentences that have to be altered; and it seems to me that the man who cannot convey his meaning by more than one set of words and sentences has not yet realized the possibilities of the English language. That is not your case.

'The man who read your stories for us was a man whose work you are likely to know, Filson Young.... I can tell you that he thoroughly agrees with me about the impossibility of publishing the work as it is. But he is very anxious, as I am, that the book should not pass from our list.'

Alexander Bell Filson Young (1878–1932), Irish writer on many subjects, had published several books with Grant Richards, including *Ireland at the Cross Roads* (London, 1903).

expect me to agree with you about the impossibility of publishing the book as it is. Your statement that no publisher could issue such a book seems to me somewhat categorical. You must not imagine that the attitude I have taken up is in the least heroic. The fact is I cannot see much reason in your complaints.

You complain of *Two Gallants*, of a passage in *Counterparts* and of the word 'bloody' in *Grace*. Are these the only things that prevent you from publishing the book? To begin at the end: the word 'bloody' occurs in that story twice in the following passage:

> —At dinner, you know. Then he has a bloody big bowl of cabbage before him on the table and a bloody big spoon like a shovel etc . . .

This I could alter, if you insist. I see no reason for doing so but if this point alone prevented the book from being published I could put another word instead of 'bloody': But this word occurs elsewhere in the book, in *Ivy Day in the Committee-Room*, in *The Boarding-House*, in *Two Gallants*:

—'And one night man, she brought me two bloody fine cigars &c'—
Two Gallants

—'Here's this fellow come to the throne after his bloody owl' mother keeping him out of it till the man was grey . . . &c'—
Ivy Day in the Committee-Room

—'if any fellow tried that sort of game on with his sister he'd bloody well put his teeth down his throat, so he would' &c
The Boarding-House

The first passage I could alter. The second passage (with infinite regret) I could alter by omitting the word simply.[1] But the third passage I absolutely could not alter. Read *The Boarding-House* yourself and tell me frankly what you think. The word, the exact expression I have used, is in my opinion the one expression in the English language which can create on the reader the effect which I wish to create. Surely you can see this for yourself? And if the word appears once in the book it may as well appear three times. Is it not ridiculous that my book cannot be published because it contains this one word which is neither indecent nor blasphemous?

The objections raised against *Counterparts* seem to me equally trivial. Is it possible that at this age of the world in the country which the

---

[1] Joyce altered the passage in 'Ivy Day' to read, 'Here's this chap come to the throne after his old mother keeping him out of it till the man was grey.' He did not change the other passages.

ingenuous Latins are fond of calling 'the home of liberty' an allusion to 'two establishments' cannot appear in print or that I cannot write the phrase 'she changed the position of her legs often'? To invoke the name of Areopagitica in this connection would be to render the artist as absurd as the printer.

You say it is a small thing I am asked to do, to efface a word here and there. But do you not see clearly that in a short story above all such effacement may be fatal. You cannot say that the phrases objected to are gratuitous and impossible to print and at the same time approve of the tenor of the book. Granted this latter as legitimate I cannot see how anyone can consider these minute and necessary details illegitimate. I must say that these objections seem to me illogical. Why do you not object to the theme of *An Encounter*, to the passage 'he stood up slowly saying that he had to leave us for a few moments &c . . .'? Why do you not object to the theme of *The Boarding-House*? Why do you omit to censure the allusions to the Royal Family, to the Holy Ghost, to the Dublin Police, to the Lord Mayor of Dublin, to the cities of the plain, to the Irish Parliamentary Party &c? As I told you in my last letter I cannot understand what has been admired in the book at all if these passages have been condemned. What would remain of the book if I had to efface everything which might give offence? The title, perhaps?

You must allow me to say that I think you are unduly timid. There is nothing 'impossible' in the book, in my opinion. You will not be prosecuted for publishing it. The worst that will happen, I suppose, is that some critic will allude to me as the 'Irish Zola'! But even such a display of the critical intellect should not be sufficiently terrible to deter you from bringing out the book. I am not, as you may suppose, an extremely business-like person but I confess I am puzzled to know why all these objections were not raised at first. When the contract was signed I thought everything was over: but now I find I must plunge into a correspondence which, I am afraid, tends only to agitate my nerves.

The appeal to my pocket has not much weight with me. Of course I would gladly see the book in print and of course I would like to make money by it. But, on the other hand, I have very little intention of prostituting whatever talent I may have to the public. (This letter is not for publication). I am not an emissary from a War Office testing a new explosive or an eminent doctor praising a new medicine or a sporting cyclist riding a new make of bicycle or a renowned tenor singing a song by a new composer: and therefore the appeal to my pocket does not touch me as deeply as it otherwise might. You say you will be sorry if the book must pass from your list. I will be extremely sorry. But what can I do? I have thought the matter over and looked over the book again and I think you are making much ado about nothing. Kindly do not misread this as a rebuke to you but put the emphasis on the last word. For, I assure you, not the least unfortunate effect of this tardy correspondence is that it has brought my own writing into disfavour with myself. Act, however, as you think best. I have done my part. Believe me, dear Mr Grant Richards, Faithfully yours   Jas A Joyce[1]

To Grant Richards   MS. N.Y. Public Library (Berg)

20 May 1906   *Via Giovanni Boccaccio 1, Trieste*

Dear Mr Grant Richards: You say that the difficulties between us have narrowed themselves down. If this be true it is I who have narrowed them. If you will recall your first letter you will see that on your side they have broadened a little. While I have made concessions as to the alteration of a word in three of the stories you are simply allowing me to use it in a story where, not having noticed it until I pointed it out to you, you had not objected to it. Moreover you now say that you wish to leave out altogether the story 'An Encounter'. You said nothing of this in your first letter and it was I, again, who pointed out to you the 'enormity' in it. It is true that you concede one of the disputed passages in 'Counterparts' but, inasmuch as you say you have no feeling on the subject, I suppose the concession costs you much less than those I have made cost me.

I mention these facts in order that you may see that I have tried to meet your objections. We are agreed now about 'Grace', 'Ivy Day in the Committee-Room' and 'The Boarding-House'. There remain only the second passage in 'Counterparts' and the story 'Two Gallants'. I invite you to read the former story again. The incident described is (in my opinion, if that counts for anything) essential. It occurs at a vital part of the story and, if it is taken out, the effect at the end is (in my opinion) lost. However (you see that it is really I who narrow the difficulties between us) if you can point out to me expressly any word or phrase which I can alter without omitting the incident, much as I dislike to do so, I will try again to meet you.

I have agreed to omit the troublesome word in 'Two Gallants'. To

[1] On 16 May Richards replied that his firm was particularly liable to attack (presumably because of his recent bankruptcy). Since Joyce was willing to delete the word 'bloody' from three stories, he was willing to allow it in 'The Boarding-House'. He insisted that the phrase in 'Counterparts', 'she changed the position of her legs often', be removed. Finally, he asked that 'An Encounter' and 'Two Gallants' be omitted.

omit the story from the book would really be disastrous. It is one of the most important stories in the book. I would rather sacrifice *five* of the other stories (which I could name) than this one. It is the story (after 'Ivy Day in the Committee-Room') which pleases me most. I have shown you that I can concede something to your fears. But you cannot really expect me to mutilate my work!

You state your objection to 'An Encounter' (an objection I was imprudent enough to provoke) so mildly that I imagine this will not be one of our difficulties. In all seriousness I would urge the interference of the printer as soon as possible if my book is not to dwindle into a pamphlet, for each bout of letters, as it brings some little concession from my side, brings also some little new demand from yours. And as I have told you all along I am convinced that your fears are exaggerated. Many of the passages and phrases over which we are now disputing escaped you: it was I who showed them to you. And do you think that what escaped you (whose business it is to look for such things in the books you consider) will be surely detected by a public which reads the books for quite another reason?

I regret very much that the interview you suggested earlier in the correspondence is impossible. I believe that in an interview I could much more easily defeat whatever influences you in holding your present position. As for the disastrous effect the book would have if published in its present form it seems to me such a result is more likely to hit me than you. Critics (I think) are fonder of attacking writers than publishers; and, I assure you their attacks on me would in no way hasten my death. Moreover, from the point of view of financial success it seems to me more than probable than [sic] an attack, even a fierce and organised attack, on the book by the press would have the effect of interesting the public in it to much better purpose than the tired chorus of imprimaturs with which the critical body greets the appearance of every book which is not dangerous to faith or morals.

You cannot see anything impossible and unreasonable in my position. I have explained and argued everything at full length and, when argument and explanation were unavailing, I have perforce granted what you asked, and even what you didn't ask, me to grant. The points on which I have not yielded are the points which rivet the book together. If I eliminate them what becomes of the chapter of the moral history of my country? I fight to retain them because I believe that in composing my chapter of moral history in exactly the way I have composed it I have taken the first step towards the spiritual liberation of my country. Reflect for a moment on the history of the literature of Ireland as it

stands at present written in the English language before you condemn
this genial illusion of mine which, after all, has at least served me in the
office of a candlestick during the writing of the book. Believe me, dear
Mr Grant Richards,   Faithfully yours,   JAS A JOYCE

To GRANT RICHARDS   MS. N.Y. Public Library (Berg)

23 June 1906   *Via Giovanni Boccaccio 1, Trieste*

Dear Mr Grant Richards: I have received the manuscript safely. For
the next few days I shall be engaged on a translation but during next
week I shall read over the whole book and try to do what I can with it.
I shall delete the word 'bloody' wherever it occurs except in one passage
in 'The Boarding-House'. I shall modify the passage in 'Counterparts'
as best I can since you object to it so strongly. These are operations
which I dislike from the bottom of my heart and I am only conceding so
much to your objections in order that 'Two Gallants' may be included.
If you cannot see your way to publish it I will have only wasted my time
for nothing. As for the fourteenth story 'A Little Cloud' I do not expect
you will find anything in it to object to. In any case I will send it back
with the others, as you direct me.

    Some of my suggestions may have seemed to you rather farcical: and
I suppose it would be useless for me to suggest that you should find
another printer. I would prefer a person who was dumb from his birth,
or, if none such can be found, a person who will not 'argue the point.'
But let that pass.

    Your suggestion that those concerned in the publishing of *Dubliners*
may be prosecuted for indecency is in my opinion an extraordinary
contribution to the discussion. I know that some amazing imbecilities
have been perpetrated in England but I really cannot see how any
civilised tribunal could listen for two minutes to such an accusation
against my book. I care little or nothing whether what I write is
indecent or not but, if I understand the meaning of words, I have
written nothing whatever indecent in *Dubliners*.

    I send you a Dublin paper by this post. It is the leading satirical
paper of the Celtic nations, corresponding to *Punch* or *Pasquino*. I send
it to you that you may see how witty the Irish are as all the world knows.
The style of the caricaturist will show you how artistic they are: and
you will see for yourself that the Irish are the most spiritual race on the
face of the earth. Perhaps this may reconcile you to *Dubliners*. It is not
my fault that the odour of ashpits and old weeds and offal hangs

round my stories. I seriously believe that you will retard the course of civilisation in Ireland by preventing the Irish people from having one good look at themselves in my nicely polished looking-glass.

Believe me, dear Mr Grant Richards,   Faithfully yours,

JAS A JOYCE

To STANISLAUS JOYCE (Postcard)   MS. Cornell

Postmark 31 July 1906 9.30 a.m.   *Between Ancona and Foligno*

Arrived safely in Ancona.[1] Filthy hole: like rotten cabbage. Thrice swindled. All night on deck. G.[2] very good. More from Rome.   JIM

To STANISLAUS JOYCE (Postcard)   MS. Cornell

Postmark 31 July 1906 Tues. 9.30 p.m.   *presso Signora Dufour*
                                                                       Via Frattina 52, II, Rome

Arrived safely: but very tired. Write to this address. Hesitate to give my impression of Rome lest my interview with the bank-manager might change it. Terrorised by the bank, while looking for it I found this on a wall 'In this house Percy Bysshe Shelley wrote *The Cenci* and *Prometheus Unbound*'. I think you would like Rome more than I. The Tiber frightens me.   JIM

To STANISLAUS JOYCE (Postcard)   MS. Cornell

2 August 1906   *presso Signora Dufour, 52 Via Frattina, Rome*

Dear Stannie,   The bank interview went off all right yesterday. My hours are $8\frac{1}{2}$ to 12 and 2 to $7\frac{1}{2}$, damn long. Have not much to do yet. I was paid 65 lire for the journey and got an advance of 100 lire, so that for the present I seem safe. I lost my way twice here. The streets are very confusing. Many things are cheaper than in Trieste but I expect to lose money for the first week or two. Last night we heard a band in the Piazza Colonna play a selection from *Siegfried*. Very fine. Romans are excruciatingly well-mannered. Send on the news.   JIM

[1] Joyce and his family on their way to Rome had taken a train from Trieste to Fiume, and a night boat from there to Ancona.
[2] His son, Giorgio.

To STANISLAUS JOYCE   MS. Cornell

7 August 1906 11 a.m.   *52 Via Frattina, II° p, Rome*

Dear Stannie As for the passage we were not sick. Going from Fiume to
Ancona we slept all three the night on deck. Georgie held out bravely
until he came to within a few miles of Rome: then he began to get
restless. The voyage and the knocking about didn't do him the least
harm.

Fiume is a clean asphalted town with a very modern go-ahead air. It
is, for its size, far finer than Trieste. As for Ancona I cannot think of it
without repugnance. There is something Irish in its bleak gaunt
beggarly ugliness. The money-changer swindled me out of 2 lire, the
cabman out of half-a lira, and the railway official out of three lire. But
I was in such a hurry that I could not protest. We had to drive about
three miles from the pier to the train. Such a panorama of houses!

There is nothing special to relate concerning my interview with the
bank manager, who by the way, is consul for Austria-Hungary. He
wanted to know was my father alive, my age, was Harrington[1] a friend
of our family. I am at present in the Italian correspondence department,
hours, $8\frac{1}{2}$ to 12 and 2 to $7\frac{1}{2}$. The work is very easy and mechanical. The
atmosphere seems to me a little more antipathetic than that of the B.S.[2]
There are fifty to sixty employees in the bank.

I have seen S. Peter's, the Pincio, Forum, Colisseum [sic]. The
Vatican is closed on Sundays, my only free day. S. Peter's did not seem
to me much bigger than S. Paul's in London. The dome from inside does
not give the same impression of height. S. Peter is buried in the middle
of the church. The Pincio is a fine garden overlooking one gate of the
city. I expected to hear great music at the mass in S. Peter's but it was
nothing much. However it was a side-altar high mass. The church has
about twenty altars. The neighbourhood of the Colisseum is like an old
cemetery with broken columns of temples and slabs. You know the
Colisseum from pictures. While we were in the middle of it, looking at it
all round gravely from a sense of duty, I heard a voice from London on
one of the lowest gallery [sic] say:
—The Colisseum—
Almost at once two young men in serge suits and straw hats appeared
in an embrasure. They leaned on the parapet and then a second voice
from the same city clove the calm evening, saying:

[1] Joyce had sent the bank a copy of a letter of recommendation from T. C. Harrington,
Lord Mayor of Dublin.
[2] Berlitz School.

—Whowail stands the Colisseum Rawhm shall stand

When falls the Colisseum Rawhm sh'll fall

And when Rawhm falls the world sh'll fall—[1]

but adding cheerfully:

—Kemlong, 'ere's the way aht—

Besides that, a man pestered me to buy 50 postcards. I told him I was
not the Kaiser but he plied me with broken Cockney to buy them for
half a franc. And moreover, hardly am I inside the building when an
alert person approaches and says:

—Guide, sir?—

Add to this a party of Murrican gorls in charge of an old dame who
asserts that she doesn't believe a word of it. It is a relief not to understand the language sometimes. But enough now of stupid monuments.

The first thing I look for in a city is the café. Rome has one café and
that one is not as good as any of the best in Trieste. This is a damn bore
for me. It has however countless little coffee-bars. I am forced to go to a
little Greek restaurant,[2] frequented by Amiel, Thackeray, Byron, Ibsen
and Co; bill of fare in English, $1\frac{1}{2}$ for a coffee, pot of tea 6 cups 6d,
Daily Mail, N.Y. Herald, Journal. So you must read the papers for me
as I needn't say the *D.M.* and *N.Y.H.* are empty until Wyndham[3]
comes back when I may find something better. You may pay the baker.
His bill should be five or six crowns. Send its amt to me if it appears to
you excessive. But if not pay him in two instalments. Tell the tailors my
address is Edinburgh or Glasgow. You can give my address and compliments to the doctors. You enclose one (not two) postcards: from the
daughter.[4] About paying F.[5] rent. Let him speak first. Then you might
say: I cannot pay my brother's debts but I will pay for 1 month's
occupancy of my room at the full rent. Don't do this, however, before
asking time to write to me. Before entering Canarutto's cousin's, go to
Can.[6] and ask him has the furniture been sold. Explain to him that he
promised to sell it for a good price and remind him that I paid him 120
crowns and that it would be unfair to refund me none of it. Give my
address and compliments to Scholz[7] and tell him to write me what he
wants me to do. Ask him was he paid for the translation. I think 30

---

[1] Byron, *Childe Harold's Pilgrimage,* IV, cxlv.

[2] Evidently the Caffè Greco.

[3] An Anglo-Irish acquaintance of Joyce in Rome, and possibly his landlord. See p. 97.

[4] Unidentified.

[5] Francini Bruni. His family and the Joyces shared a flat at Via Giovanni Boccaccio 1[II]
in Trieste, from 24 February to 30 July 1906, when the Joyces departed for Rome.

[6] Moise Canarutto, Joyce's landlord at Via San Nicolò 30 in Trieste.

[7] Like Joyce, Scholz taught at the Berlitz School; they had collaborated on a
translation, presumably from German to English.

crowns was absurd for that work and kindly say so to A[1] when he gives you the proofs to correct. I have now only 100 lire left. However I know the place a little better now. It is a trifle dearer. I think it is better for us to make no move till the two months are over. Then, if you like, I can move you here. Any news from G.R.?[2] Send on whatever letters come from Dublin and date your letters to me.

Literally every man in Rome speaks to and laughs at Georgie. They make presents of biscuits, fruit &c. I don't believe he has cried once. When he goes into an 'echoy' place he shouts: in the Colisseum and in S. Peter's. The landlady is very fond of him: very nice person, as Maria[3] would say. Kindly answer my letters by return of post until we get more settled.   JIM

To Stanislaus Joyce   MS. Cornell

[*About 12 August 1906*]   *Via Frattina 52, II°, Rome*

Dear Stannie,   I sent you today *Sinn Fein* with two marked paragraphs.[4] I asked you to date your letters in order to see how many hours they took to come. I received a copy of the *Independent* some days ago but did not observe the notice[5] I see marked in the copy you forward. I suppose it is by the merest chance I learn this. Who knows what else has taken place in Dublin?

I was coming home to lunch from the bank when I met Nora in the street, holding out a paper and saying 'Guess the latest, guess who's married!'[6] I could think of nobody but the recently vested Charlie who, I perceive, is making great use of the suit and collars I sent him.[7] When she showed me the paper first I thought it was a practical joke, as I imagined Gogarty either in New York or on his way to Italy and have been reading the columns of the *Tribuna* as I promised in search of his advertisement.[8] However I suppose it is true. I see that it must be a sign of progress and of experience to feel one's illusions fall from one, one by

---

[1] Artifoni.   [2] Grant Richards.
[3] In Joyce's story 'Clay'. She was modelled in part on one of his mother's relatives.
[4] Evidently 'Dialogue of the Day' in *Sinn Féin*, 4 August 1906, signed Shangonagh. It is a parody of Francis Sheehy-Skeffington's weekly commentary, *Dialogues of the Day* (published in 1906–7), and alludes to Thomas M. Kettle's impending victory in the Parliamentary by-election in East Tyrone on 25 August 1906.
[5] An announcement of Kettle's election.
[6] Oliver St John Gogarty and Martha Dwane of Letterfrack, Co. Galway, were married on 1 August 1906.
[7] Charles Joyce began studying for the priesthood but did not finish.
[8] Gogarty had written on 14 June 1906 (II, 140–1) offering to meet Joyce in Rome. Joyce must have replied by promising to watch the *Tribuna* of Rome for an announcement by Gogarty of his arrival.

one. This particular loss, seemingly more of yours than of mine, is hardly suitable for discussion in letters. I disagree with you, however, when you say it would not have happened had I remained in Dublin. My feelings are double: first, I am puzzled to know whether he was in New York at all or not and why he wrote to me: and, secondly, I am curious to know how he looked in a tall silk. I fancy when he emerged from the church door his agile eye went right and left a little anxiously in search of a certain lean myopic face in the crowd but he will rapidly grow out of that remaining sensibility. However to be charitable I suppose we had better wish Mr and Mrs Ignatius Gallaher[1] health and long life.

You have often shown opposition to my socialistic tendencies. But can you not see plainly from facts like these that a deferrment of the emancipation of the proletariat, a reaction to clericalism or aristocracy or bourgeoisism would mean a revulsion to tyrannies of all kinds. Gogarty would jump into the Liffey to save a man's life[2] but he seems to have little hesitation in condemning generations to servitude. Perhaps it is a case which the piping poets should solemnise.[3] For my part I believe that to establish the church in full power again in Europe would mean a renewal of the Inquisition—though, of course, the Jesuits tell us that the Dominicans never broke men on the wheel or tortured them on the rack.

Do you think I should write to G.R.?[4] I am thinking of rewriting *A Painful Case* so you might send me the MS along with the book of notes I had in Paris and the Latin quotations from the prophecies of the Abbot Joachim of Flora.[5] This is a cursed pen but it is Sunday and every place is shut. Have you been to Can.?[6] Pay no more debts without first telling me. By the way do you think you could send me any money. Whatever you send I can send you back at the end of the month and we could make the same arrangement for next month as I shall not be properly fixed until 18th Oct. Even if they send me away then I shall

---

[1] Joyce is quoting here, with slight variation, Little Chandler's toast to Gallaher's future nuptials in 'A Little Cloud'. Gogarty was probably one of the models for the man-of-the-world Ignatius Gallaher in that story, as later for Robert Hand in *Exiles*.

[2] Gogarty rescued drowning men from the Liffey on three occasions, in 1898, 1899 and 1901.

[3]
> Nor have I known a love whose praise
> Our piping poets solemnise. . . .
> *Chamber Music*, xxvii

[4] Grant Richards.

[5] Joyce did not make use of the Abbot Joachim in 'A Painful Case', but he refers to him in the *Proteus* episode of *Ulysses*, p. 49 (39–40), as well as in the 1904 sketch, 'A Portrait of the Artist'.

[6] Canarutto.

have 315 lire in my pocket or if they keep me 250. To account for my straitened state:

skirt (Nora)	—9 lire
blouse "	—8 "
" "	—9.50
combs	—2.0
shirt (self)	—3.50
hat (self)	—5.0
hand. and collars	—2.0

I have paid the rent here in full and have 52 lire left but it will not last me till the end of the month. It is useless trying to write with this pen.

JIM

Posted 3.30 p.m. Sunday say when arrived.

To Stanislaus Joyce   MS. Cornell

Postmark 16 August 1906   *Via Frattina 52, II, Rome*

Urgent

Dear Stannie The substance of the present is financial. It is Thursday morning the 16th and I have 25 lire. In my list I forgot to include bonnet for Georgie 3 lire but the real reason the money goes so quickly is that we eat enormously. Nora is getting much healthier looking. Here is her usual dinner—two slices of roastbeef, 2 polpetti, a tomato stuffed with rice, part of a salad and a half-litre of wine. We buy the meat cooked and then take it to a little wine-shop where we are supplied with plates &c. I think the only thing to be done is this: to ask A.[1] for a week's salary in advance and to send it to me. Remember that on Monday morning I shall have *no* money so that if you have not sent on some already you must telegraph it. The fifty lire you lend me this month I shall send you back on the 1st Oct with 50 of my own to put in the bank.

I am reading *The Picture of Dorian Grey* [sic][2] in Italian. U.I.[3] arrived with notice of G's[4] posad[5] (marriage). What am I to do about G.R.? Yesterday we went to the cemetery. Pay no more bills: and please attend to this letter at once or I shall find myself once again in the sitting posture.

JIM

---

[1] Artifoni.
[2] Oscar Wilde, *Doriano Gray dipinto* (Palermo, 1906).
[3] *United Irishman.*   [4] Gogarty's.   [5] *Posadh*, Irish for 'marriage'.

To Stanislaus Joyce   MS. Cornell

Postmark 19 August 1906   *Via Frattina 52, II, Rome*

Dear Stannie Your wire arrived at 6. I asked you to wire before lunch
so that I might have it early, as I feared the P.O. here might be shut.
I received 31.40 lire. I suppose it cost you the difference between that
and 40.0 to wire it. I wired you at 8.45 a.m. When did you get it? I shall
leave discussion of money matters until arrival of your letter which I
expect tomorrow.

No advt from Gogarty. I suppose his writing to me was some drunken
freak. I suppose he wouldn't dare present me to his wife. Or does the
poor mother accompany them on the honeymoon? I suspect she is not a
tocharless[1] lass. I set the fashion, it seems. W. B. Yeats ought to hurry
up and marry Lady Gregory—to kill talk: and Colm ought to propose
to his roselike Miss Esposito.[2] I have just finished *Dorian Grey* [sic].
Some chapters are like Huysmans,[3] catalogued atrocities, lists of
perfumes and instruments. The central idea is fantastic. Dorian is
exquisitely beautiful and becomes awfully wicked: but never ages. His
portrait ages. I can imagine the capital which Wilde's prosecuting
counsel made out of certain parts of it. It is not very difficult to read
between the lines. Wilde seems to have had some good intentions in
writing it—some wish to put himself before the world—but the book is
rather crowded with lies and epigrams. If he had had the courage to
develop the allusions in the book it might have been better. I suspect he
has done this in some privately-printed books. Like his Irish imitator:[4]

> Quite the reverse is
> The style of his verses.

Can you tell me what is a cure for dreaming? I am troubled every
night by horrible and terrifying dreams: death, corpses, assassinations
in which I take an unpleasantly prominent part. As for my health I eat
well. Last night we ate an entire roast chicken and a plateful of ham,
bread and wine—and went to bed hungry.

I am going to take lessons in Danish from the 1st Sept. I have met a
Dane here—one Pedersen—and, as he can't talk Italian we mumble

---

[1] 'Dowryless' (from *tochar*, Irish for 'dowry').

[2] In a notebook which he kept late in 1904, Joyce entered a remark which he had
evidently heard, 'Miss Esposito, I never see a rose but I think of you.' Herbert Gorman,
James Joyce (London, 1941; New York, 1939), p. 135. Evidently it was Padraic
Colum who had made the remark, to Vera, one of the two daughters of Michele Esposito.

[3] Joris-Karl Huysmans, *A Rebours* (Paris, 1884).

[4] Gogarty, who in 1903 went up to Oxford from Trinity College, Dublin, intending to
win the Newdigate Prize as Wilde had done; he came second instead.

German mixed with Danish at each other. I wonder when learning it is it necessary to keep a good-sized potato in each cheek. You said it was like a nigger speaking German but it is more like Mr O'Connell (Bill)[1] speaking Dutch.

I cannot write to G.R. until I know whether this will be my address next month. Wyndham said 'for the month of August'.[2] Hard work in the bank. On Friday I did not get out till about 8.30. The correspondence reaches about 200 to 250 letters a day. The latest news is that the seat is out of my trousers.

How the devil did you think the news about Kettle would interest me.[3] But I would like to see a copy of *Dialogues of the Day*.[4] I have written three paragraphs to add to *A Painful Case*, but I don't know if I can rewrite it. I would like also to rewrite *After the Race* but if G.R. sent me the proofs I would pass the book as it is. The chase of perfection is very unprofitable.

Send me on the news. Today I discovered a photograph of Billy Walsh[5] exposed in a prominent street. Would you like to see some copies of *L'Asino*—the Italian anti-clerical newspaper.[6] I absorbed the attention of the three clerks in my office a few days ago by a socialistic outburst. One of them is a German and he was ridiculing Lombrosianism[7] and antimilitarism. He said when children cried they 'should be caned', favoured corporal punishment in schools, conscription, religion &c. I think he was surprised not to find an ally in an Inglese. Item: English and Americans abroad talk at the top of their voices.

Nora has a talent for blowing soap-bubbles. While I was wading through a chapter of *Dorian Gray* a few days ago she and Georgie were blowing bubbles on the floor out of a basin of suds. She can make them as big as a football. Georgie is a great favourite with everyone here. All the people we frequent know his name. He has added to his vocabulary 'O Gesù Mio' 'Brutto, brutto, brutto' and cleans out his ear when told to do so. Also when we go to the band in Piazza Colonna he beats time

---

[1] Joyce's grand-uncle, William O'Connell, who lived for a time with the Joyce family. He is a model for Uncle Charles, who is described in detail at the beginning of Chapter II of *A Portrait of the Artist*.

[2] Apparently Joyce had sublet a flat from Wyndham.

[3] Kettle's election. Joyce did not believe (see pp. 124–5) that the Irish problem would be solved by parliamentary means.

[4] See p. 93n.

[5] William John Walsh (1841–1921), Archbishop of Dublin and Primate of Ireland from 1885 to his death. Simon Dedalus refers to him in *A Portrait of the Artist* as 'Billy with the lip'.

[6] *L'Asino* ('The Ass'), a satirical weekly, socialist in outlook, published in Rome from 1892 to 1925.

[7] That is, theories of humane treatment of the criminal, as evolved by Cesare Lombroso (1836–1909), the celebrated Italian criminologist.

to the music, amusing the 'smiling Romans' thereby very much. He wears a long mayoral chain with little medals round his neck. By the way, if you come to Rome before Xmas, I will buy a goose for 3 lire and have it cooked where we go for dinner. Have you seen that there is a split in the socialistic camp here between Ferri[1] and your friend Labriola?[2] Only that money is so 'skinty' (a word of Alice's making)[3] I would have bought *Rosa Bernd*[4] today. If you buy *The Lake*[5] you might send it to me. Unfortunately all the English libraries are shut now or I would join one. I think I will learn Danish rapidly with this Pedersen chap. In one restaurant we go to Georgie sits sedately at the top of the table in a little high chair of his own and announces to the restaurant the arrival of each of our dishes by shouting 'Ettero, Ettero'.[6] When we were in S. Peter's he began to shout 'Iga, Iga'[7] immediately when the lazy whores of priests began to chant. Would you like any picture postcards of Rome?   JIM

Nora says she is asking for you. If there is anything interesting (Ferrero[8] etc) in the *Piccolo della Sera*, you might send it.

To STANISLAUS JOYCE   MS. Cornell

31 August 1906   *Via Frattina 52, II, Rome*

Dear Stannie, I have had no letter from you for nearly a fortnight so I suppose you are in great difficulties or else that you sent me money which was robbed in the post. In the latter case I hope you have the registration receipt. Today I received Lire 50 for I had to borrow L 100 here ten days ago. I have now 85 lire and must pay my landlady 35 and nearly 5 more for expenses. If you cannot do something at once to help me over this month I do not see how I can live. I cannot ask for an advance here as they told me the last time they were making an exception in my case as it was the first month. Indeed I hope I have not injured my position already by asking for an advance. There are two great patches on the seat of my trousers so that I cannot leave off my coat in the office and sit stewing for hours. Some nights I do not get

---

[1] Enrico Ferri (1856–1929), editor of the socialist newspaper *Avanti!* from 1904. In the Socialist Party Congress at Rome in 1906, Ferri was the representative of the Integralists, standing between the socialist revolutionaries and the Reformists. He left the party in 1911.

[2] Arturo Labriola (1873–1959), Neapolitan socialist.

[3] Joyce's cousin Alice Murray, a daughter of William and Josephine Murray.

[4] By Gerhard Hauptmann.   [5] See p. 81n.

[6] 'Eccolo, Eccolo' ('Here it is, here it is').

[7] Possibly 'Viva, viva'.   [8] See p. 82n.

away till 8 or even 8.30 and, really, to have one's mind in a turmoil about money as well as to live this way is not pleasant. I would not mind the discomfort if I saw some means of getting over the month. Is it possible A[1] would not give you any advance?

I wrote to Grant Richards a week ago: no answer, of course. I have some loose sheets in my pocket about 5 pages to add to *A Painful Case* but I am not strenuous enough to continue in the face of such continual discouragement. Aunt J sent me papers: no letter. *The Irish Catholic* and *Dialogues of the Day*. Unluckily I lost the latter in the street. I shall send you the next copy: it is very 'brilliant'. Three pages of puff by F.S.S.[2] at the end: full of thick typed catch phrases such as 'this novelty in Irish journalism' 'order at once' 'absolutely unique'. An advt appears for some booklet by (very big letters) Thomas Kettle, M.P. A column of the *Irish Catholic* is devoted to a series of letters between Dr Delany[3] and J. M. O'Sullivan M.A.: philosophical student at Bonn.[4] They are all in the public eye and favour: even Dr O. S. Jesus Gogarty. And here am I (whom their writings and lives nauseate to the point of vomiting) writing away letters for ten hours a day like the blue devil on the offchance of pleasing three bad-tempered bankers and inducing them to let me retain my position while (as a luxury) I am allowed to haggle for two years with the same publisher, trying to induce him to publish a book for which he has an intense admiration. Orco Dio![5]

I bought and read *The Lake*: and will send it when I know where to send it so that you may tell me what you think of it. The *Times* calls it a prose poem. You know the plot. She writes long letters to Father Oliver Gogarty about Wagner and the Ring and Bayreuth (memories of my youth!) and about Italy where everyone is so happy (! ! ! ! ! ! ! ! ! ! ! ! ! ! !) and where they drink nice wine and not that horrid black porter (O poor Lady Ardilaun[6] over whose lily-like hand he lingered some years back): and then she goes (in all senses of the word) with a literary man named Ellis—one of Moore's literary men, you can imagine what, silent second cousin of that terribly knowing fellow, Harding[7]—and Father Oliver Gogarty goes out to the lake to plunge in by moonlight, before which

---

[1] Artifoni.   [2] Francis Sheehy-Skeffington.

[3] Rev. William Delany, S.J. (1835–1924), was president of University College, Dublin, 1883–8 and 1897–1909. Delany had objected to Joyce's paper on 'Drama and Life', and had supported the editor of *St. Stephen's* in rejecting 'The Day of the Rabblement'.

[4] John Marcus O'Sullivan (1881–1948), a fellow student of Joyce at University College, Dublin, where he later became professor of modern history. He was elected to the Dail in 1923 and held several ministerial posts in the government. He and Delany discussed the question of coeducation in the college.

[5] 'Ogre God', a Triestine oath, slightly euphemistic for 'Porco Dio' ('Pig God').

[6] Of the Guinness family, which continues to make porter.

[7] The spokesman for the author in several of Moore's early novels.

the moon shines opportunely on 'firm erect frame and grey buttocks': and on the steamer he reflects that every man has a lake in his heart and must ungird his loins for the crossing. Preface written in French to a French friend[1] who cannot read or write English (intelligent artist, however, no doubt) and George Moore, out of George Henry Moore and a Ballyglass lady, explains that he only does it 'because, *cher ami* (dear friend), you cannot read me in my own language' Eh?

I like the notion of the Holy Ghost being in the ink-bottle. We go to a little wine-shop opposite the house at night and the proprietor who is delighted with Georgie invited us to dinner some nights ago: sardines, roast veal and tomatoes, salad, a huge English pudding, melons in rum, wine and cognac and cigars. The pudding was the gift of an old priest from Sicily—Padre Michele! though I have made open confession of my 'heresies', but I think, really, he meant nothing ill by his mess of pottage—which was excellent. He said he was an old man and thought sometimes of buying a revolver to protect himself from assault at night in the streets and asked me did I approve of that. Have you ever reflected how 'humble' is the utterance of Renan 'very few people have the right to abandon Catholicism'. What do those gentlemen in Ireland want a new University for?[2] The one they have is quite good enough for them—both in 'saince and in art'. But you must read 'Dialogues of the Day'.

Georgie can understand everything almost that is said to him and imitates every sound he hears—clocks, vendors, singing—etc. Today while Nora and he were passing through a narrow street some hoarse whore of an Italian driving a cart at breakneck speed and flourishing his whip, caught him right under the eye: and he has a long weal across his cheek and nose. Pleasant, isn't it? It puts my teeth on edge to write of it.

I must end now as I have no more time. Scholz wrote me an insolent postcard in French which made me laugh: it was so German. However, I will do what he wants me to do.[3] Oblige me by replying to this at once as you know my position.

I don't wish to 'sponge' on you but only to ask you to try and help me over this month: as, otherwise, it will be a poor look-out for me. Already

---

[1] Edouard Dujardin (1861–1949), French novelist and man of letters.

[2] There was considerable agitation in Dublin at this time for a more equitable balance between Trinity College, Dublin, which was predominantly Protestant, and University College, Dublin, predominantly Catholic. As a result, University College was made, in 1909, a part of a National University, with a much larger government subsidy and a more ambitious educational programme.

[3] Scholz wished Joyce to investigate the possibility of his being transferred to the Berlitz School in Rome.

the moon is threatening to shine upon my grey buttocks and I wish some-one would send me a pair of Father Oliver's small-clothes that he hid among the bulrushes. And if it so happens that you are in difficulties yourself write to me *at once*.   JIM

To STANISLAUS JOYCE   MS. Cornell

6 September 1906   *Via Frattina 52, II, Rome*

Dear Stannie, Last night a man came to take lessons from me and I asked him to pay in advance. He gave me 20 Lire so that with economy I can live until Monday morning. I had given up all idea of the advt as two days had intervened. He wants 30 lessons. I said I would give them for Lire 50 and he agreed: so that he owes me Lire 30. But, of course, I cannot know when he will pay. It was certainly providential. This is the second advt I answered in the *Tribuna*. The first got me the position in the bank: the second a providential pupil. He takes lessons every evening. I get out of the bank usually about 7.30 or 7.45: sometimes later. Then I have his lesson from 8 to 9 so that for this month my time-table is rather full. But I don't care so long as I can get to the 30th safely. I expect you will be able to raise something for me today and then this fellow may give me the other 30 Lire soon.

As for the trousers remember that I am sitting for $9\frac{1}{2}$ hours daily on an uncushioned, straw-bottomed chair and the stuff was always thin. Anyway the fact remains that I have two great patches on the seat and have to wear my 'tail-coat' constantly. Not a word or sign from Grant Richards. I will wait till Sunday and then write to him again. The reason I sent you *Avanti* was that it contained an article either of Lombroso or of Gorki. Maybe I sent you the wrong copy. I also sent you a copy of *L'Asino*.[1] As soon as I have a little money in my pocket I shall send you *The Lake*. You seem to be annoyed about Kettle. The reason I was not interested[2] is because I take no interest in parliamentarianism as I suppose, you know. However, I have asked Aunt J— to send me a copy of *The Nationist*—if it still exists. As for a possible friendship with Kettle it seems to me my influence on male friends is provocative. They find it hard to understand me, and difficult to get on with me even when they seem well-equipped for these tasks. On the other hand two ill-equipped women, to wit, Aunt Josephine and Nora, seem to be able to get at my point of view, and if they do not get on with me as well as they might they certainly manage to preserve a certain loyalty which is

[1] See p. 97.   [2] See letter of 19 August 1906, p. 97.

very commendable and pleasing. Of course I am not speaking of you. On all subjects—except socialism (for which you care nothing) and painting (of which I know nothing)—we have the same or like opinions.

I have never doubted that you have a talent for the latter art. But an appreciable change in our fortunes is necessary before you can develop it. It is too early to despair of such a change. Lately I found I was wishing myself at a seaside place in England or Ireland: rashers and eggs in the morning, the English variety of sunshine, a beefsteak with boiled potatoes and onions, a pier at night or a beach and cigarettes. By the way I forgot to tell you about the pension. One man wanted Lire 150 a month for only lunch and dinner for Nora and myself, exclusive of breakfast or supper. Lire 50 goes for my room, candles and washing so that I would have just 50 Lire left for clothing for three people and— evantualities.

Enclosed please find article by Ibsen—or rather excerpt. I have just received your remittance which will be wonderfully useful to me. I send you *The Lake*: send me your opinion of it. This morning in the bank that German clerk informed us what his wife should be: she should be able to cook well, to sew, to housekeep, and to play at least one musical instrument. I suppose they're all like that in Deutschland. I know it's very hard on me to listen to that kind of talk. Besides that, he is always teaching the other (ignorant) Italian clerk (and me) Latin and philosophy. He has been to some university where, he says, *der Professer* [sic] 'lectured' in Latin: and all the *studenten* spoke Latin. Greek too. Even the atmosphere of the BS[1] was better than this. However—

I don't quite agree with you about the U.I.[2] In my opinion, it is the only newspaper of any pretensions in Ireland. I believe that its policy would benefit Ireland very much. Of course so far as any intellectual interest is concerned it is hopelessly deaf. But even that deafness is preferable to the alertness of *Dialogues of the Day*. A clerk in this office has just come back, without one finger, after four weeks' sick leave. His face is studded with pimples and he has a pen behind his ear. Here is the German. They shake hands and laugh. Every one looks at the fingerless clerk with astonishment. He is very ugly, a Swiss, and has a voice like a rusty saw. Here is another Italian clerk: who says: O, long life, here you are. Même jeu (as G.M.[3] would say). Two phrases in Italian madden me. One is: di' un po' (I say). Every clerk who wanders in here from another writing-box comes in with a sodden preoccupied

---

[1] Berlitz School.   [2] *United Irishman.*
[3] George Moore. Joyce is referring to the preface (written in French) to *The Lake*. See pp. 81, 98.

air, goes over to some colleague and murmurs di' un po': and then halts
to remember what he has to say. The other phrase is *Signore*. Every
wretched scribbler, every—but why make a catalogue?—is a signore if
he works with a pen or employs an assistant. Canarutto told me his
cousin, your landlord, was (with many a significant nod) a signore. But
yet, you seem unable to share my detestation of the stupid, dishonest,
tyrannical and cowardly burgher class. The people are brutalised and
cunning. But at least they are capable of some honesty in these
countries: or, at least, they will move because it is their interest to do
so. I am a stranger to them, and a prey for them often: but, in the sense
of the word as I use it now, I am not an enemy of the people. Many
thanks for your prompt reply and await your letter.   JIM

To STANISLAUS JOYCE   MS. Cornell

[? 12 September 1906]   *Via Frattina 52, II°, Rome*

Dear Stannie I received yr. letter with enclosures. It is well you told me
who the silhouette was for I'm damned if I would have known otherwise.
It has the very artistic (I believe) merit of not resembling the original.
Of Gogarty's card I can make nothing.[1] I don't understand why he
desires that we should exchange short notes at long distances and at
different angles to the equator. What does he mean by 'acquiring the
villa villa for the natives'? Why does he expect I am going back to my,
to my land? What news does he want and what is the 'valuable' news he
has? The underlining of 'Mr' beneath the portrait of that handsome
person, Paul Verlaine, caused a smile to appear upon the face of the
dutiful employee of Messrs Nast Kolb and Schumacher but he became
serious when he perceived that the card came from 'S James's Hotel;
Paris'. By the way, talking of faces I will send you a picture postcard of
Guglielmo Ferrero and you will admit that there is some hope for me.
You would think he was a terrified Y.M.C.A. man with an inaudible
voice. He wears spectacles, is delicate-looking and, altogether, is the
type you would expect to find in some quiet nook in the Coffee-Palace
nibbling a bun hastily and apologetically between the hours of half-past
twelve and one.

I am changed in the bank from the correspondence to the reception
room. It is a good thing the salaam has gone out of fashion here. I am
with the banker's two sons and another man. Have a desk and lamp all

[1] This card, sent by Gogarty from Paris where he had gone on his honeymoon, has
not survived.

to my own self and not at all so much to do. I have to receive visitors who come with letters of credit cheques &c. Today I had the honour of cashing a cheque for 8 guineas issued by the *Freeman* of Dublin and handing 200 and odd lire to their Roman correspondent, one Mr P. J. Connellan, if you remember reading any of his articles concerning our holy father the pope and the blessed virgin mary and jesus christ and god almighty and the holy ghost and saint joseph. (Excuse this experiment. I wanted to see who would look funniest. I think saint joseph wins with jesus christ a good second) I can see the papers here too, that is, some of them. *Daily Mail* and *Figaro*. On the whole it is a change for the better and it looks as if they intended to keep me.

I have waited another day and there is no letter from you or paper from Dublin. As I told you I have a lesson every evening and the money my pupil gave me will carry me on till the 20th, I think. I asked him if he could find me another pupil as there are unfortunately 30 days in this month. I will ask him again tonight. After the 1st of Oct I think we shall eat in the house as the weather will be getting too cool for Georgie to go out. Rome certainly is not cheap. A lira goes a very short way indeed here. Wyndham ought to be back from Naples in a day or so and I ought to have an answer from Grant Richards in the morning. The mention of his name brings back to me my early youth.

On Saturday last I went up to the headquarters of the black lice[1] to find out if they had chosen their general. A carman told [me] they had elected a German[2] and were now at their pranzo.[3] Unfortunately I have not bought the *Avanti* these few nights. I would like to read an article on the subject. The Very Rev. Fr. Devitt S.J.[4] came to Rome—to help in the kitchen I suppose. The next thing we will hear will be the emperor William's enrolment in the brown scapular.[5] There was a thunderstorm here yesterday evening and seeing my agitation the banker's son was kind enough to close the shutters. A man was struck dead on the road outside the gate of S. Pancras. About Georgie I was in the bank at the time and Nora could do nothing.[6] There was a notice on the wall 'Drive Slowly' but no policeman of course. The next day I saw one of these glorious creatures cross-examining a poor little old woman, driver of a

---

[1] The Jesuits.

[2] Francis Xavier Wernz (1842–1914) was elected general of the Jesuits in 1906, and remained in this office until his death.

[3] 'Dinner' (Italian).

[4] Rev. Matthew Devitt, S.J. (1834?–1932), was Rector of Clongowes (1891–1900), and later became Professor of Moral Theology and Canon Law at Milltown Park, Dublin.

[5] The Carmelites.

[6] Stanislaus Joyce had asked why his brother did not call the police when Giorgio's face was struck with a whip. See p. 100.

little ass-cart because she hadn't her name on the shaft. He wrote a terrible lot in a little notebook and the little woman smiled timidly all over her shrivelled face and still the pencil went on and the red cock's comb in the policeman's hat bobbed. Here they dress carabinieri like stage flunkeys. They must look esthetic when they run after a mad horse. The weal has disappeared.

I think it would be safer for you to send me some money on Saturday. I will send you L50.0.0 on the 1st October: that will leave me 200 Lire. I must pay 45 to the landlady and 10 for trousers so that I will have about L140 left for the month. Every month I will send you at least L50, if the eating-at-home plan succeeds, perhaps L70. You can add, I expect, the difference between that and 100, so that we may always have something to fall back on. I read an article lately about Gissing.[1] The writer denied the stories of abject poverty. Gissing, after his first book, had always enough to live on, he said. I read an allusion in *The Tribune* which gave me some anxiety. It spoke of a series the 'X' series of booklets the publication of which was 'begun by the late firm of Grant Richards'. Now does *late* refer to the firm of Grant Richards, bankrupt, or to that of E. Grant Richards?[2] Explain to Scholz that I live two miles from the Berlitz School, that I go to the office at $8\frac{1}{2}$ in the morning and get out at 8 in the evening with an hour for lunch and that I have an English lesson every evening from 8.30 to 9.30: so that it is out of my power at present to go there and interview the director on his behalf. Is there any news of Bertelli?[3] Did you approach Canarutto again. Do so, if only to annoy him. Pay no bills whatsoever of mine. If you have not signed any documents they cannot make you. Say you paid me 22 lire a week for your board and lodgings. But I think you can be trusted not to be swindled out of money.   [Unsigned][4]

To STANISLAUS JOYCE   MS. Cornell

18[–20] September 1906   *Via Frattina 52, II°, Rome*

Dear Stannie *Tuesday* I wired you today at lunch-time and am awaiting your reply. My funds are now 8d. If nothing comes I shall have to ask my pupil to lend me a lira as I am hungry. I have had no breakfast and

---

[1] George Gissing (1857–1903), the English novelist.

[2] Richards had adopted the name of his wife, E. Grant Richards, for his reconstituted firm.

[3] The sub-director of the Berlitz School in Trieste had gone off with some of the school's money.

[4] Stanislaus Joyce has written, at the end of the letter, 'Rec'd 15 Sept. '06.'

read no papers for five days past but I could not spin out the money longer.

I received a postcard from Grant Richards 'I am sorry for the delay in writing to you definitely about *Dubliners*. I hope to do so within a very few days'.[1] He is a damned hopeful man anyway. Do you remember his postcard of two years ago about *Chamber Music*. He said: 'I shall hope to write to you very soon on the subject'? There's hopefulness for you.

I can write no more now because I am too busy thinking about the telegram and the chances of getting something to eat.

Wednesday I received your telegram last night and your remittance today. Thanks. I had to borrow 5 Lire from my pupil last night on the strength of your telegram. As to my finances I have exactly 20 lire out of which I must pay this evening five to my pupil. I cannot wriggle beyond Sunday morning on this. If you can manage to send anything by wire then I can send you even Lire 100 on the first of October. That would leave me 150 L. 40 to the landlady, 10 trousers. However make the best suggestion you can. The least I will send you is Lire 50 and whatever remains over from your suit you can put in the bank.

Why do you disapprove of my taking another pupil—if I can get one? My leisure is of little use to me and I want money. You cannot imagine I want to continue writing at present. I have written quite enough and before I do any more in that line I must see some reason why—I am not a literary Jesus Christ. However I shall hope that Mr Grant Richards shall perhaps also hope within a very few years to be able to see his way to make some communication to me regarding the unfortunately delayed MS which he admires so profoundly.

What the devil do you expect I would write to Gogarty? I asked you to explain 'Am I to acquire a villa for the natives?' You know I am getting a little stupid: I don't understand it. If I were sure that Mr Grant Richards would really hope to be able to print *Dubliners* I might have some reason to use Gogarty as an agent in advance. But really I believe *Dubliners* will only see the light when too late to give its author any pleasure.

Yerra, what's good in the end of *The Lake*? I see nothing. And what is to be said about the 'lithery' man, Ellis, and all the talk about pictures and music. Now, tell the God's truth, isn't it *bloody* tiresome? To me it is. As for 'Rev Oliver Gogarty' I think that may either have been laughingly suggested by O. St Jesus for his greater glory or hawk-eyedly intended by Moore to put O. Jesus in an *embarras*. If the latter O St Jesus has risen nobly to the situation.[2] I have violated the sanctity

---

[1] Richards's postcard was dated 14 September.   [2] By marrying.

of this office by laughing. I remembered Moore's legend about Mrs Craigie.[1] Thanks be to Christ they amuse us anyhow. *Re* Joycetown: there is I am sure some place of that name in the neighbourhood he writes of.

Thursday I find that instead of continuing this letter I must end it as I began. This is Thursday noon—a holiday here. I can live through today, tomorrow and the greater part of Saturday but cannot go beyond that. Let me explain. I got your 20 crowns yesterday morning: and had three in my pocket remaining from the night before $= 23$. Out of that I paid away 5 that I had borrowed from my pupil and 2 that I had borrowed from the landlady for the telegram $23 - 7 = 16$. Yesterday $5\frac{1}{2}$: $16 - 5\frac{1}{2} = 10\frac{1}{2}$. Today $5\frac{1}{2} = 10\frac{1}{2} - 5\frac{1}{2} = 5$. Tomorrow I must manage on 4, and that will leave 1 lira for a small lunch on Saturday morning. Now is that plain. Consequently unless you can telegraph money early on Saturday I have no means of living. You asked me to tell you how I stand. That is how I stand. As for my drinking I have rather too much to do. Last night when Nora went out to change the gold piece the landlady told her it was false. I was giving the lesson at the time and sent her with it back to the P.O. It turned out to be good French money but the suspense and toil of talking made me so sick that I couldn't eat my dinner. So that's how I stand. Kindly, if you possibly can, wire me money early on Saturday. You may rely on me for the 1st of October.

I sent you the telegram because I had no idea that money was on its way to me and saw no means of getting any.   [Unsigned]

To STANISLAUS JOYCE (Postcard)   MS. Cornell

Postmark 22 September 1906   *Via Frattina 52, II, Rome*

Dear Stannie,   Received your wire but have not yet cashed it. The official would not accept my documents, wanted a 'passport'. Finally I got annoyed and said 'By Jesus, Rossini was right when he took off his hat to the Spaniard, saying "You save me from the shame of being the last in Europe".['] The official, astounded at this, invited me to come back and repeat it! The which I declined. How I detest these insolent whores of the bureaucracy [sic]. How do the people permit such arrogance. They are all the same. I must however try to save myself these scenes. I have lost two hours and my dinner. By the way, I presume you have sent me something by post: as this will only carry me

---

[1] George Moore used to boast a good deal of his affair with Mrs Pearl Craigie, the novelist who wrote under the name of John Oliver Hobbes. No one in Dublin believed that his relations with her were more than literary.

to Monday morning. I wish I was not so weak physically sometimes. I have more need of a lictor than Renan.   JIM

Do not overlook the pith of this card.

To STANISLAUS JOYCE   MS. Cornell

25 September 1906   *Via Frattina 52, II, Rome*

Dear Stannie, At present Monday morning I am anxiously waiting for a remittance from you. My assets are two centesimi as yesterday I had to get shaved and to pay a laundry bill and to buy medicine for Georgie who has a bad cold on his chest. I wrote yesterday again to G.R. a pressing letter asking him to reply by return of post. I sent you yesterday the U.I. with an article by Gogarty of which I hope you will appreciate the full flavour.[1] The part about the chummies is particularly rich.[2] I am delighted to see that this is only an instalment. Aunt J has left off sending me Skeffington's paper[3] or writing at all. I must be a very insensible person. Yesterday I went to see the Forum. I sat down on a stone bench overlooking the ruins. It was hot and sunny. Carriages full of tourists, postcard sellers, medal sellers, photograph sellers. I was so moved that I almost fell asleep and had to rise brusquely. I looked at the stone bench ruefully but it was too hard and the grass near the Colosseum was too far. So I went home sadly. Rome reminds me of a man who lives by exhibiting to travellers his grandmother's corpse. Isn't it strange that O.G. should be anathemising ugly England just

---

[1] Oliver Gogarty wrote the first of three articles on 'Ugly England' in *Sinn Féin*, 15 September 1906. The others appeared on 24 November and 1 December 1906. He signed them all 'O.G.'

[2] Gogarty's final paragraph said of the English common man, 'In his righteousness he has called out with holy horror against the immorality of the French nation, rejoicing meanwhile like the publican that his own house is clean. When the facts of the case are only too clear to anyone who has the unblinded eye to see them, that it is this English monster that demands and supports whatever indecencies Paris can produce. He cries out again at the godlessness of the foreign Governments regarding their treatment of those women who associate with their soldiers and he points to his own forbearance, when all the time, for anyone who cares to buy it, he has published a book—too sordid and too lost to see his own hypocrisy—wherein are statistics to prove, if any proof were needed, that his own army is rottener and more immoral than any or all of the armies in Europe put together. And also as he remains with his eyes devoutly lifted he cannot perceive that at his very feet in India are slave-compounds, where women are incarcerated with more than the horrors of a harem to be debauched at the good pleasure of the Army, a body of men who, as their own statistics show, are already more than half leprous from venereal excess. So concentrated are Sludge's thoughts on prayer that he never has time to realise the fact, however he may denounce it in others, that his Army at home is in a condition so immoral as not to leave even room for such hesitation as that which preceded the destruction of Sodom.'

[3] *Dialogues of the Day.* See p. 93n.

when I wanted to be in an English watering-place. As for the eating houses which must be erected for Sludge:[1] O.G. should travel a little in beautiful Italy and artistic France. Mrs G mustn't have been very entertaining while in England since O.G. found time to write those two columns. I notice by the way that Colm isn't earning his money lately. At any rate he hasn't contributed any peatballs to the U.I. for a long time. On the way home from the Forum being very tired I went into a Dominican church where I found a comfortable straw chair. I watched two nuns at confession. Confession over confessor and penitents left the church in the direction of the cloister. But the nuns came back very shortly and knelt down beside me. Then vespers began. Then there was the rosary. Then there was a sermon. The gentleman who delivered this addressed most of his remarks to me—God knows why. I suppose I looked pious. I didn't wait for benediction. While listening to the service a most keen regret seized me that I could not gain for myself from historical study an accurate appreciation of an order like the Dominicans. I think my policy of substracting oneself and one's progeny from the church is too slow. I don't believe the church has suffered vitally from the number of her apostates. An order like this couldn't support their immense church with rent &c on the obolos of the religious but parsimonious Italian. And the same, I expect, in France. They must have vast landed estates under various names, and invested moneys. This is one reason why they oppose the quite unheretical theory of socialism because they know that one of its items is expropriation.

I received today in the nick of time your remittance of 17 Lire. The only fear I have now is that they won't pay me on the 29th. With this money I can get along till Thursday evg. Kindly let me know how much I am to send you back on the 1st and in what manner. I will wait to see if I am to be continued here and if so I will go to the B.S.[2] about you. Do you think I should waste 2 lire on buying a book of Gissing's—or ought I buy a volume of Bret Harte.[3] I have often confessed to you surprise that there should be anything exceptional in my writing and it is only at moments when I leave down somebody else's book that it seems to me not so unlikely after all. Sometimes thinking of Ireland it seems to me that I have been unnecessarily harsh. I have reproduced (in

---

[1] Gogarty calls the English common man by the name of 'Sludge' instead of 'John Bull'. He complains of the inordinate English esurience, and says their 'only gospel is the news of dinner'.

[2] Berlitz School.

[3] This was evidently Bret Harte's *Gabriel Conroy* (Boston and New York, 1903), which provided Joyce with a name for the hero of 'The Dead', and influenced his description of the snow in that story. See Gerhard Friedrich, 'Bret Harte as a Source for James Joyce's "The Dead" ', *Philological Quarterly*, xxxii. 4 (October, 1954), 442–4.

Dubliners at least) none of the attraction of the city for I have never
felt at my ease in any city since I left it except in Paris. I have not
reproduced its ingenuous insularity and its hospitality. The latter
'virtue' so far as I can see does not exist elsewhere in Europe. I have
not been just to its beauty: for it is more beautiful naturally in my
opinion than what I have seen of England, Switzerland, France,
Austria or Italy. And yet I know how useless these reflections are. For
were I to rewrite the book as G.R. suggests 'in another sense' (where the
hell does he get the meaningless phrases he uses) I am sure I should find
again what you call the Holy Ghost sitting in the ink-bottle and the
perverse devil of my literary conscience sitting on the hump of my pen.
And after all *Two Gallants*—with the Sunday crowds and the harp in
Kildare street and Lenehan—is an Irish landscape. The fuss made
about Gorky, I think, is due to the fact that he was the first of his class
to enter the domain of European literature. I, not having Gorky's claim,
have a more modest end. Ibsen ibself seems to have disclaimed some of
the rumorosity attaching to *A Doll's House*. He said testily to one
Italian interviewer, if you can believe the I.I.[1] 'But you people can't
understand it properly. You should have been in Norway when the Paris
fashion journals first began to be on sale in Christiania'. This is really my
reason for constantly plaguing reluctant relatives at home to send me
papers or cuttings from them. I wish there was an Irish Club here. I am
sure there are ten times as many Irish and American-Irish here than
Scandinavians. By the way, how did stupid old Âibsen make out the bit
here? Teaching is impossible: he must have been in some German office.

In my opinion Griffith's speech at the meeting of the National Council
justifies the existence of his paper.[2] He, probably, has to lease out his
columns to scribblers like Gogarty and Colm, and virgin martyrs like
his sub-editor. But, so far as my knowledge of Irish affairs goes, he was
the first person in Ireland to revive the separatist idea on modern lines
nine years ago. He wants the creation of an Irish consular service
abroad, and of an Irish bank at home. What I don't understand is that
while apparently he does the talking and the thinking two or three
fatheads like Martyn and Sweetman[3] don't begin either of the schemes.

---

[1] *Irish Independent*. Ibsen had died on 23 May 1906.

[2] Arthur Griffith, editor of *Sinn Féin*, gave the principal speech at the second annual
convention of the National Council in the Rotunda in Dublin early in September 1906.
He moved for a boycott of certain British goods, for a scheme of primary and secondary
education conducted on national principles, and for the creation of a national banking
system and a national civil service.

[3] Edward Martyn (1859–1923), the playwright, was re-elected president of the
National Council, and John Sweetman (1844–1937?), Chairman of the Meath County
Council (1902–8) and a former M.P., was elected a vice-president along with Griffith.

He said in one of his articles that it cost a Danish merchant less to send butter to Christiania and then by sea to London than it costs an Irish merchant to send his from Mullingar to Dublin. A great deal of his programme perhaps is absurd but at least it tries to inaugurate some commercial life for Ireland and to tell you the truth once or twice in Trieste I felt myself humiliated when I heard the little Galatti girl sneering at my impoverished country. You may remember that on my arrival in Trieste I actually 'took some steps' to secure an agency for Foxford tweeds there. What I object to most of all in his paper is that it is educating the people of Ireland on the old pap of racial hatred whereas anyone can see that if the Irish question exists, it exists for the Irish proletariat chiefly. I have expressed myself badly, I fear, but perhaps you will be able to get at what I mean. A Belfast linen company does a great deal of business in Rome through this bank. On the whole I don't think it fair to compare him with a stupid mountebank like Knickerbockers.[1]

Georgie's cold seems to be better. He can walk across the room by himself now and he has two new teeth. Certainly Rome must be very healthy. It is now noon and I am quite hungry. Last night, for example, for dinner I had soup, spaghetti al sugo, half a beefsteak, bread and cheese, grapes and a half litre of wine. The wine here is like water, poor stuff, in my opinion! The fruit is very dear. The stupid foreigners that come here in swarms put up the price of everything. Twenty years ago, I hear, it was much cheaper.   JIM

To STANISLAUS JOYCE (Postcard)   MS. Cornell

Postmark 30 September 1906   *Via Frattina 52, II°, Rome*

I am sending you 60 Lire, and will write to you fully on this absorbing question tomorrow. Cannot send it today as the P.O. is closed. Have not replied to G.R.[2] but have written the whole account to Arthur Symons. I shall hope to write[3] to G.R. when Symons answers. Tomorrow I am

---

[1] Francis Sheehy-Skeffington.

[2] Grant Richards wrote Joyce on 24 September that he could not publish *Dubliners*: 'You have certainly gone a good way to meet our objections to it—objections based on other people's prejudices and not on our own, as I have tried to make clear to you—but it still remains of a kind that would not, I think, be successful, that would prejudice the majority of its readers against its publisher, and would stand in the way of your gaining success with any future work.' He urged Joyce to send him the manuscript of his first novel, promising a decision within a fortnight of its arrival. If that were published. *Dubliners* might follow it.

[3] A phrase used by Richards.

going to interview an international jurist. Have been to the English consul who gave me the address of their adviser.

Georgie, I fear, has an attack of bronchitis. If not better tomorrow I will call in a doctor. What about the Celtic Fringe now? Only once more, love. Give it up, Jimmy, old boy.[1]   [Unsigned]

New item. The landlady has just raised the rent of our room. How thoughtful!

P.P.S. I have a new story for Dubliners in my head. It deals with Mr Hunter.[2]

To STANISLAUS JOYCE   MS. Cornell

4 October 1906   *Via Frattina 52, II°, Rome*

Dear Stannie, I sent you on Monday 53 Lire and the sending of it cost nearly another lira to say nothing of the fact that I had to go in and out of about ten cafés, to get gold and silver, as there is an intelligent rule here in the P.O. which prohibits the payment of international M.O.'s in paper. Georgie seems better at last. His medicines and doses went up to about 5 lire and I bought a bottle of some tonic for Nora. The landlady very kindly has raised my rent to 40 lire and my pupil has gone away until December next. I had also to pay him 11 lire that I borrowed from him and as he seemed a decent little fellow[3] (he is a nephew of the Abruzzese painter, Michetti.[4] Francini'll tell you who he is) I asked him to dine with us on Michaelmas evg. We had a roast duck.

Now about G.R. I have not replied to his letter. I wrote to Symons narrating the case from the beginning and asking for his advice. I went also to Wyndham. Early in the conversation, talking of nothing in particular, he told me that he and his wife neither visited nor received visits. His wife who is English is very exclusive and won't know any English people she meets abroad. Her grandfather was an admiral. She knows, he told me, many of the aristocracy of Rome and now they don't

---

[1] Joyce is probably replying to some encouraging phrases of Stanislaus Joyce in a letter from his brother that has not survived. Stanislaus may well have told him how dismayed the Celtic Fringe, that is, the fashionable writers in Dublin, would be when *Dubliners* appeared. 'Only once more, love', would refer primarily to his sending out *Dubliners* to still another publisher, and 'Give it up, Jimmy', would be Joyce's disheartened rejoinder.

[2] The story was to be entitled 'Ulysses'. Joyce never wrote it, but, as he frequently said in later life, his book *Ulysses* had its beginnings in Rome. Alfred H. Hunter was a Dubliner, rumoured to be Jewish and to have an unfaithful wife.

[3] This man's name was Terzini. See p. 118.

[4] Francesco Paolo Michetti (1851–1929), a famous Italian painter. His painting, *La Figlia di Iorio*, inspired D'Annunzio's play of the same name. See also p. 48.

go to the Embassy any more. He hates Rome and is *very* fond of Naples:
but he prefers Booloinsoormer. He made some courageous attempts to
pronounce the names of one or two of the principal streets in this city
where he has lived for eighteen years. He always tells the Romans to
their face what *he* thinks of them and he says the Italians are *most*
ungrateful. I will *find* them out, he says. He says that talking of Ald.
Kelly and the Union Jack,[1] the Irish are really *very* disloyal, *very*
disloyal. He has a Union Jack furled in his hall. He hangs it out on all
his Majesty's or her Majesty's feast-days. Some people ask him why he
doesn't hang it out on the Italian King's feast-day. But you won't catch
him doing that, he says. I argued with him politely for an hour and a
quarter. He offered me neither a cigarette, nor a biscuit nor a glass of
wine nor yet a glass of water. At the door he told me the Italians were
quite uncivilised. I would find them out. I at once found out a trattoria
where I commanded a *quite* uncivilised youth to bring me instantly a
quarter of wine and cast proudly on the table three halfpence. The
youth murmured his thanks and some *quite* uncivilised men saluted me
humbly as I strode out of the shop. I refrained from telling them to their
faces what *I* thought of them but as I strode homeward I came carefully
to the conclusion that Wyndham is probably the most *stupid, prosy,
old,* bastard at present living in this city.

I went to the English consul, who gave me the address of an international jurist, Mr St Lo Malet. This latter read all the letters and the
contract and I expect will send me his bill. He discovered some dis-
crepancies. First GR says 'I read the book myself on behalf of this
house': later 'the man who read your book for us was Filson Young'. He
says an agreement like mine is considered only a personal contract.
He advised me to try to come to terms on letter 11 and not to go to law
(Letter 11 is the letter with which G.R. returned the MS) as lawsuits
are long, and costly and as other publishers would then be reluctant to
publish me. I said I had tried to come to terms on letter 11 unsuccessfully. I told him I had written to Symons and he advised me to wait for
Symons' answer before doing anything. He gave me the address of *The
Incorporated Soc. of Authors.* He distrusts the word Incorporated which
he says probably means that they are slow to move. In one way he says
my case is strong since G.R. has broken the contract. But he says the
assessment of damages would be very difficult. G.R. has constantly
disparaged the book commercially. The contract gave me nothing on

[1] On 24 September 1906 Alderman Thomas Kelly pulled down the Union Jack from
the SS. *Shamrock* lying at the Custom House in Dublin and threw it in the Liffey. The
incident is reported in the *Evening Herald* (Dublin) of that date.

the 1st 500 and G.R. could maintain that it was unlikely my book would reach even that limit. I might be awarded £5–0–0 damages or enough money to enable me to bring out the book myself. What do you think of his opinion? I am still waiting for S to answer and have not replied to G.R.

I replied today to Gogarty's card: felicitated him on his good news whatever it might be and reminding him that the last night I met him in Nassau Street he had also good news which he asked me to go and hear. I sent him no news of my own and said I saw little profit in our exchanging any more curt notes. I regret to see he has not continued his *Ugly England* yet. I would fain hear more about the slattern comediennes—renegade artist that I am. Starkey writes two little immortal things in *Sinn Féin* about a Fiddler and (damme if I can think of the other) a Piper, I think.[1] AE ought now to write some little immortal dreamy thing about a Trombonist or, better, a Triangle-Player. I wish some unkind person would publish a book about the venereal condition of the Irish; since they pride themselves so much on their immunity. It must be rather worse than England, I think. I know very little of the subject but it seems to me to be a disease like any other disease, caused by anti-hygienic conditions. I don't see where the judgment of God comes into it nor do I see what the word 'excess'[2] means in this connection. Perhaps Gogarty has some meaning of his own for this word. I would prefer the unscientific expression 'venereal ill-luck'. Am I the only honest person that has come out of Ireland in our time? How dusty their phrases are!

Georgie now walks about all the day by himself. He doesn't seem to be so fat as he was but I suppose his cold accounts for that. He has not been out for ten days. He has a huge appetite. He makes nothing of a handful of grapes. As it is too cold in the evening now we have our dinner sent to the house. I am looking out for a little quarter and will get some furniture on hire as it is stupid to continue paying this rent for such a room as ours. I will try for one near the Pantheon where the streets are wooden as the late King is buried there. I wish they had buried a few more monarchs or emperors in the neighbourhood as the cobbled streets are fearfully noisy. Rome must have been a fine city in the time of Caesar. I believe it was chiefly on one or two hills: the interspaces being used as military exercise-grounds, market-places &c. The forum must have been a magnificent square. But the papal Rome is like the Coombe[3] or old Trieste and the new Ludovisi quarter is like any

---

[1] Seumas O'Sullivan, 'A Piper' and 'A Fiddler', in *Sinn Féin*, 22 September 1906. They are included in *The Poems of Seumas O'Sullivan* (Boston, 1923).

[2] Gogarty's word; see p. 108n.

[3] An old and poor section of Dublin, named from a street, the Coombe, which runs northwest from St Patrick's Cathedral.

secondary quarter of a fine metropolis. Not as fine as Pembroke township,[1] for example. I wish I knew something of Latin or Roman History.
But it's not worth while beginning now. So let the ruins rot. Two things
are excellent in Rome: air and water.   JIM

PS I refrain from intruding the Lsd question until I write you on
Sunday. I want you to get your wind again.   JIM

To STANISLAUS JOYCE   MS. Cornell

[9 October 1906]   Via Frattina 52, II°, Rome

Dear Stannie,   Symons wrote to me:[2]

I am glad to hear from you again. When I named you to Grant
Richards it was before his failure: I should hardly have done it since.
Still, as he has apparently begun to print yr. book I would be inclined to
give in to him as far as you can without vitally damaging your work. If
he signed an agreement to publish the 12 stories why not hold him to
that? and you could hold over the other two stories for another book
later. The great thing is to get published so that people may have a
chance of reading you. I will write a line to G.R. advising him not to lose
yr. book. I hope you will arrange it between you. Now as to yr. poems,
I feel almost sure that I can get Elkin Mathews to print them in his
shilling *Garland* series. You would get little money from him but I think
it would be worth your while to take what he offered—probably a small
royalty after expenses are covered. He did for me a little set of translations from Baudelaire's 'Petits Poèmes en Prose'. The cost was
£14–14–0 and it is now nearly covered when my royalty will begin. Tell
me if I may write and advise him to take the book. If it comes out I will
give it the best review I can in the 'Saturday' or 'Athenaeum' and I
will get one or two other people to give it proper notices. I hope you are
getting on well in Rome. Let me have a line promptly about the poems.

I answered, accepting his offer about the verses and am waiting a few
days more to see if G.R. will write. Tell me what arrangement you
propose for the verses. I will follow it perfunctorily as I take very little
interest in the publication of the verses. I see no reason however why
I should refuse to publish them—do you? And I would be glad if they
antedated *Dubliners*. I suppose they have some merit! and perhaps, if
they sold, I might make ten or twenty pounds out of them next year.

---

[1] This part of Dublin comprises Baggotrath, Donnybrook, Irishtown, Merrion,
Ringsend, and Sandymount.

[2] Symons's letter, dated 2 October 1906, is now at Cornell.

Is my attitude on the point the sign of a blunted or of a more developed mind? Tell me ought I retain the name.[1] I don't like it much. By the way can you account for the friendly tone of S's letter? The last dealing I had with him was when I served a copy of *The Holy Office* upon him. I connect it in some way with G's[2] letters. I suppose I will soon have a letter from some of the others. Symons, however, has a smart English business-like way of doing things which is highly satisfactory.

Yesterday being the anniversary of the day of my espousal and of the day of the gladness of my heart, we went out into the country and ate and drank the greater portion of several larders. Here is the full and exact list of what we ate yesterday.

10.30 a.m.	Ham, bread and butter, coffee
1.30 p.m.	Soup, roast lamb and potatoes, bread and wine
4.– p.m.	Beef-stew, bread and wine
6.– p.m.	Roast veal, bread, gorgonzola cheese and wine
8.30 p.m.	Roast veal, bread and grapes and vermouth
9.30 p.m.	Veal cutlets, bread, salad, grapes and wine

There is literally no end to our appetites. I don't believe I ever was in better health except for the sedentary life I lead. I stand fascinated before the windows of grocers' shops. My salary, I am afraid will not be sufficient to feed me in the winter. I am teaching the woman who cooks for us to cook in the English fashion. She made tripe for us the other night with onions and white sauce.

> Dear Stannie
>
> I hope you are very well I am sure you would be glad to see Georgie now he is well able to run about he is able to say a lot he has a good appetite he has eight teeth and also sings when we ask him where is Stannie he beats his chest and says non c'e piu[3]   Nora

You will see from this interpolated letter the gigantic strides which Nora has made towards culture and emancipation. The evening before last I found her stitching together skins of apples. She also asked me some time ago 'Is Jesus and God the same?' and asked me to teach her geography! Do you notice how women when they write disregard stops and capital letters?[4]

I finished Hauptmann's *Rosa Bernd* on Sunday. I wonder if he acts well. His plays, when read, leave an unsatisfying impression on the

---

[1] That is, *Chamber Music.*   [2] Gogarty's.   [3] 'He's not here any more.'
[4] A female trait memorialized by Molly Bloom's soliloquy.

reader. Yet he must have the sense of the stage well developed in him by now. He never, in his later plays at least, tries for a curtain so that the ends of his acts seem ruptures of a scene. His characters appear to be more highly vivified by their creator than Ibsen's do but also they are less under control. He has a difficulty in subordinating them to the action of his drama. He deals with life quite differently, more frankly in certain points (this play opens with Rosa and her lover emerging one after the other from opposite sides of a bush, looking at each other first and then laughing) but also so broadly that my personal conscience is seldom touched. His way of treating such types as Arnold Kramer and Rosa Bernd is, however, altogether to my taste. His temperament has a little of Rimbaud in it. Like him, too, I suppose somebody else will be his future.[1] But, after all, he has written two or three master-pieces— 'a little immortal thing'[2] like *The Weavers*, for example. I have found nothing of the charlatan in him yet.

I am following with interest the struggle between the various socialist parties here at the Congress. Labriola[3] spoke yesterday, the paper says, with extraordinarily rapid eloquence for two hours and a half. He reminds me somewhat of Griffith. He attacked the intellectuals and the parliamentary socialists. He belongs or is leader of the sindacalists. They are trades-unionists or rather trade-unionists with a definite anti-social programme. Their weapons are unions and strikes. They decline to interfere in politics or religion or legal questions. They do not desire the conquest of public powers which, they say, only serve in the end to support the middle-class government. They assert that they are the true socialists because they wish the future social order to proceed equally from the overthrow of the entire present social organisation and from the automatic emergence of the proletariat in trades-unions and guilds and the like. Their objection to parliamentarianism seems to me well-founded but if, as all classes of socialists agree, a general European war, an international war, has become an impossibility I do not see how a general international strike or even a general national strike is a possibility. The Italian army is not directed against the Austrian army so much as against the Italian people. Of course, the sindacalists are anti-militarists but I don't see how that saves them from the logical conclusion of revolution in a conscriptive country like this. It is strange

---

[1] Joyce is alluding to the famous and dubious final sentence of Arthur Symons's essay on Rimbaud in *The Symbolist Movement in Literature* (1899): 'Even in literature he had his future; but his future was Verlaine.'

[2] An ironic quotation of a phrase of Yeats.

[3] Arturo Labriola's party lost out to a combination of the Reformists and Integralists at the Socialist Congress.

that Italian socialism in its latest stage should approach so closely the
English variety.

After the preceding exordium I approach the question of my finances.
At present I possess 28½ lire (9 Oct. 12 o'c) (You have not yet acknowledged receipt of the 53 lire I sent you at 7 p.m. on 1st Oct) You can
easily make up the bill for yourself: Landlady 54, you 54: Terzini my
pupil 11, books 2, medicines 5, collars and ties 2, trousers 12, the dinner
to Terzini (he will take more lessons in December) 10, haircutting and
shave, 1, postage 1, = 180. That means that in 10 days counting the last
day of September we spent 70 lire. This appears very high. Take out of
it however 9½ lire spent on Sunday and you have 60 lire for 9 days, that
is, 6½ lire per day. The fact remains that we consumed that amt in food.
My breakfast coffee and milk and bread and butter costs 2½, Nora's and
the child's together, 5½ = .80c.

Lunch, soup for the child, and our two lunches with	
bread and wine	1.90
Grapes afterwards and the waiter	.30
Cigarettes, matches & papers	.20
My coffee at 2.45	.15
Nora's and the child's at 5 o'c	.55
Two sandwiches for us at 7 o'c	.20
Dinner for the three, waiter & grapes after (1½d + 2d. = 35c)	2.40

If you add that up you will see that it is 6 L.30c. I cannot explain how
we consume so much but the fact is so. The three of us have enormous
appetites. The little things they bring on a plate don't satisfy us. The
price of the dinner, 2.05c may seem to you high but it includes a litre of
wine, 80c and Georgie's soup 15c and bread 15c = L1 – 10: that leaves
95c for Nora's meat and vegetables and mine or less than 4½d each.
I eat a sandwich at 7 o'c when I get out as I am too hungry to wait till
dinner-time 9 o'c. At lunch we take only half a litre and a flask of
mineral water so it comes a few pence less. But I am tired of writing this
long explanation. This fact remains that on Sunday morning I shall
have need of money. I watch the papers every day in search of an advt
for English lessons but have not found any yet. As I told you my pupil
has gone away. If you are well dressed and have paid off yr. loan you
might ask Artifoni for another which, of course, you can pay off in full
on the 1st of Nov. I owe you still about 40 lire, but if you got an advance
of 40 lire from Artifoni I could send you 60 Lire on the 1st Nov, and
would then owe you only 20 Lire. Next month I shall make a different
arrangement, and if we can once get on our feet I will take a little

quarter and furnish it as, with waiters etc this dining and eating bits in the street is not very satisfactory. Write fully on receipt of this what you can do, so that you may relieve my anxiety. Wyndham, of course, is off. I hope you will not think this letter unreasonable (the latter part of it). If you calculate yourself you will see what a small margin it leaves, and remember that keen questioner Mr M. D. Berlitz who asks some-where abruptly 'How long can we resist the desire for food?'   Jim

To Stanislaus Joyce   MS. Cornell

18 October 1906   *Via Frattina 52, II°, Rome*

Dear Stannie, On receipt of your postcard I went to Wyndham's house three times without seeing him and left a note for him to call next day. I asked him for money. He has none: but he said he would try to get me some and call back that evg at 7 o'c. I waited until nearly nine then I called to his house twice unsuccessfully. I had no money so I borrowed a couple of lire from my landlady and we dined. Today Wyndham wrote saying he was very (no awfully) sorry he couldn't get me the money. Having no money or way of getting it I went to the English consul and after interviewing him extracted 50 lire from him. I had asked W— for 50 L, my idea being to send you 20 to enable you to get a suit at once. If, however, I sent you 20 now it would not reach you till Friday evg. and you are paid on Saturday morning. Besides that, there would be a lira wasted in my sending it and a half lira wasted in yr sending me back same on Saturday. However, if any thing has gone wrong write to me or wire as I have now more than L 45. I hope Saturday will see you with a suit. A— is not worth much when he can't work his wife to the extent of a suit of clothes. I don't understand your excessive sensibility. For my part I would much prefer to be ill dressed than to be hungry or in danger of being so. Why do you think of going back to Dublin? Your position from the 1st of Nov will be better than mine. You have 160 Cor. = 165 lire a month and I suppose you make 10 more on extra lessons, 175. Trieste is, as you can see, cheaper than Rome. And you have one person to support as against my two and $\frac{1}{2}$. Moreover, you are on perfectly firm ground as a teacher there while I am constantly making the most absurd mistakes here, knowing damn all about banking business. Besides, I presume Ar—[1] doesn't receive people like the Russian ambassador or Cardinal Vanutelli or such 'big pots' in his school but they come *here* to criticise *my* wearing apparel. And, in any case understanding as you must the sympathy of an English consul and

------

[1] Artifoni.

an Irish bastard you will perhaps realise that I am hardly in a better position than you myself. However I trust we will be all right from the 1st of Nov. I will send you then enough money to buy a few ties and gloves and linen so that you may satisfy those vulgar sons of whores. And if you are in need of money to eat let me know *at once*.

Symons sends me the following letter:

My dear Symons,

I am very much obliged to you for drawing my attention to Mr Joyce's work and feel sure from what you tell me of its quality that it will be a great acquisition to my Vigo series. So will you please put me into communication with Mr Joyce or arrange with him for me to see his MS. Faithfully yours,   ELKIN MATHEWS

and asks me will I send Mathews the MS. I wrote today to E.M. saying S— had sent me the letter and adding that I was re-arranging the verses but would send the MS in a few days. I do not understand your arrangement: write it out clearly again. Why do you allude to hexameter in 'Sleep Now'? ∪—∪(∪) is the foot used. Do you mean 'All day' and 'I hear' to precede 'Sleep now'? That arrangement would be rather jolty, I think. Or do you mean me to end on 'I hear?' I understand that arrangement better: namely: 'Sleep now' 'All day' and 'I hear'.[1] Also do you mean me to include the Cabra poem?[2] Can I use it here or must I publish it in a book by itself as, of course, my dancing days are over.

I wrote to Grant R— to know had he decided to refuse definitely my concessions: namely deletion of 'bloody' from 3 stories and deletion of paragraph in 'Counterparts' against inclusion of *Two Gallants* and *A Little Cloud*. If he refuses that, I will hold him to his 1st letter, in which he asked for deletion of *Two Gallants*, deletion of paragraph in *Counterparts* and deletion of 'bloody' in *Grace*. I will hold over *Two Gallants* and *A Little Cloud* and retain 'bloody' in *Ivy Day in the Committee Room*. If he does not agree to that I will write to the Society of Authors to institute proceedings against him.

As you may have seen a Russian general has been following his wife and wife's lover all over the world with intent to shoot them. Many eminent persons were consulted as to whether this was right of the said general. Among them was Father Bernard Vaughan.[3] He said, 'If it were

---

[1] This was the arrangement that was finally adopted; *Chamber Music*, xxxiv–xxxvi.

[2] This poem, 'Cabra', was given the new title of 'Ruminants' in 1919. Later it was greatly altered and became 'Tilly', the first poem in *Pomes Penyeach*.

[3] Rev. Bernard Vaughan, S.J. (1847–1922), was widely known for his sermons. Stanislaus Joyce says Vaughan was the model for Father Purdon in Joyce's story 'Grace'. See also *The Dublin Diary of Stanislaus Joyce*, ed. George Harris Healey (London and Ithaca, New York, 1962), p. 78.

my case I would simply "chuck" the woman'. I suppose he was mis-reported by a reporter with a sense for verse. Fr. B.V. is the most diverting public figure in England at present. I never see his name but I expect some enormity.

Does Aunt Josephine write to you? She never writes to me and sends *Sinn Féin* at long intervals. Is there nobody in Ireland who will think it worth his or her while to make a bundle of any old papers that are lying about his or her house and send them to me? I suppose everyone is disillusioned about me now—myself included. The reason I dislike *Chamber Music* as a title is that it is too complacent. I should prefer a title which to a certain extent repudiated the book without altogether disparaging it. It is impossible for me to write anything in my present circumstances. I wrote some notes for *A Painful Case* but I hardly think the subject is worth treating at much length. The fact is, my imagina-tion is starved at present. I went through my entire book of verses mentally on receipt of Symons' letter and they nearly all seemed to me poor and trivial: some phrases and lines pleased me and no more. A page of *A Little Cloud* gives me more pleasure than all my verses. I am glad the verses are to be published because they are a record of my past but I regret that years are going over and that I cannot follow the road of speculation which often opens before me. I think I have unlearned a great deal but I am sure I have also a great deal to learn. Your opinion of me seems to be steadily rising again: but, after all, to say that I am not a vulgar mountebank like most of the 'artists' of Ireland is little. What really is the point is: whether it is possible for me to combine the exercise of my art with a reasonably happy life. However, as I have not yet reached the age at which I— wrote *Catilina*,[1] the point need not be solved offhand. I bought *Hedda Gabler* today for fivepence—Gosse's trans. The translation seems to me wretchedly bad and the intro-duction idiotic. I wonder do these chaps know the language he writes in at all. I believe Ibsen scandalised Danish critics by his use of Norwegian idioms. My friend Pedersen pointed out locutions to me in *Bygmester Solness*[2] and said solemnly in that mellifluous tongue of his '*Det er ikke jodt dansk. Man sijer det ikke i Köbenhavn*'.[3] You should hear him pronounce the last word: it takes him about half a minute. I fancy I's attitude towards litherathure and socialism somewhat resembled mine. Pedersen did not know the meaning of a few expressions. I doubt, however, that he ever fell so low as to chronicle the psychology of

[1] Joyce was mistaken, since Ibsen wrote *Catalina* when he was twenty-one.
[2] Ibsen's *The Master Builder*.
[3] 'It is not good Danish. One doesn't say it in Copenhagen.'

Lenehan and Farrington. I suppose you read that as a result of the
socialist congress the two sub-editors of the *Avanti* resigned. Ferri
replaced them by Cicotti, formerly editor of the *Lavoratore* of Trieste
and—Labriola,[1] who is to be the German correspondent of the paper.
The funny part is that the two who resigned are members of the party
of which L is the head. Labriola is a person who interests me very much.

What do you consider weak in my letter to O.G.?[2] It definitely closes
the correspondence I should think. When he wrote to me from New
York it was you, not I, that wished he should get a cordial answer from
me. Mrs Francini, on hearing the letter, said with emotion 'Poverino!'[3]
but O.G.'s request was that I should forget the past: a feat beyond my
power. I forgive readily enough. The other night, about ten days ago,
we went into the wineshop over the way where I told you we dined once.
The man has started a restaurant but we don't frequent it as the prices
are a little too high for us. I was reading the *Avanti* and between whiles
casting about for a remark to make. Pace (the propr.) and his two
nephews one of whom is a complete bowsy, a Roman Lenehan,[4] were
eating at a table hard by. Pace is a wineshopkeeper by night and a clerk
in the Ministry of Finance by day. Finally, I said something about the
congress. Pace nodded his head (his mouth being full). The bowsy
watched me until he saw my head bend again on the paper: then he
leaned over his plate and asked huskily 'Zio, è socialista il Signor
Giacomo?'[5] Pace, having eaten what was in his mouth, glanced at me
and upcurled his lower lip and answered 'È un po' di tutto'.[6] Bowsy
smiled huskily and the other nephew coughed a laugh as he, smiling
too, helped his relatives to some salad. This I perceived through my
forehead very accurately, but it had not the least effect upon what the
poetical and mystical Swede[7] would call 'my interiors'.

On receipt of your next letter I will write to you my plans for the
month of November which I hope you will think reasonable. Nora is
going to arrange with the woman to cook in the house after the first. I
am sure that by doing so, in three months, we should have saved enough
to pay the first instalment on *everything* necessary for a quarter. Then
if you will come here I think we, with our united salaries, ought to be
able to have some comfort. Furniture is very cheap here, strange to say.
We would have more than 100 lire a week between us. Let me know if
you think well of this. We could be in a quarter by 1st of Feb or at
latest the 1st of March. I hope you will manage on Saturday to get your

[1] See pp. 98, 117.   [2] Oliver St John Gogarty. See p. 114.
[3] 'Poor chap.'   [4] A sponger in Joyce's story 'Two Gallants'.
[5] 'Uncle, is Mr James a socialist?'
[6] 'He's a little of everything.'   [7] Emanuel Swedenborg.

suit and, if you should be short of money for food, I will send you what
I can.   JIM

To STANISLAUS JOYCE   MS. Cornell

6 November 1906   *Via Frattina 52, II°, Rome*

Dear Stannie, It would have been useless to have made that suggestion
to Pace. I never go there at all. I might have gone on eating in the other
trattoria and then at the end of the month I might have asked for
credit for a week or so. But that would mean L 40 or L 50 out of my
pocket on the 1st. So I gave Nora L 50 to see if we could live a fortnight
on it. Four days have now passed and she has 25 lire left. But, she has
also bought oil and lamp-oil and coal and candles—all of which will
reduce our landlady's bill on the 1st of Dec. (This month it was L 52.–)
and she has three quarters of a bag of coal left, a big bag of coffee, a
good deal of sugar and five litres of wine. Had we gone on living out we
would have spent L 6.– at least per day: and would now have the L 25.0,
which we have,—and nothing else. So I think we have begun at last.
The only thing is the plan is risky for, if I cannot get a pupil before the
end of the month we have nowhere to get credit. But I prefer even to
risk this as I am determined to save money.

I sent my verses to Elkin Mathews, telling him they had been for two
years in bond and requesting an early decision. He writes, saying it
could not be published this side of Xmas but that as soon as he has got
some pressing WORK off his hands he will turn to and examine it. The
Soc. of Authors wants £1–1–0 subscription. The barrister[1] advised me
not to go on with the case for reason before explained to you. I thanked
him and asked him what his fee was and he said £1–0–0. So I paid 10 L
and said I would give him the rest on the 1st of December. I also gave
him *Two Gallants* to read. He said he read it with great interest and
pleasure but thought it would read better in French or Italian. He has
promised to examine all my future contracts, advises me to wait until
my verses are published and then to send *Dubliners* to some publisher
accompanied by a bundle of press notices.

I have read Gissing's *Demos: A Story of English Socialism*.[2] Why are
English novels so terribly boring? I think G. has little merit. The
socialist in this is first a worker, and then inherits a fortune, jilts his
first girl, marries a lydy, becomes a big employer and takes to drink.
You know the kind of story. There is a clergyman in it with searching

[1] St Lo Malet. See p. 113.   [2] George Gissing, *Demos* (London, 1886).

eyes and a deep voice who makes all the socialists wince under his firm
gaze. I am going to read another book of his. Then I will try Arthur
Morrison and Hardy: and finally Thackeray. Without boasting I think
I have little or nothing to learn from English novelists.

I have written to A.J.[1] asking her to send me *By the Stream of
Kilmeen* [sic] a book of stories by Seamas O'Kelly—you remember him.
He was in the degree class with me.[2] I also asked her to try to lay hands
on any old editions of Kickham, Griffin, Carleton, H. J. Smyth &c,
Banim[3] and to send me a Xmas present made up of tram-tickets, advts,
handbills, posters, papers, programmes &c. I would like to have a map
of Dublin on my wall. I suppose I am becoming something of a maniac.
I am writing to her today to know how you spell Miss McCleod's (?)
Reel.[4] I have also added in the story *The Clay* the name of Maria's
laundry, the *Dublin by Lamplight Laundry*: it is such a gentle way of
putting it.[5] I expect there will be no holding the Marquis of Lorne
whenever he sees my book.[6]

I suppose you read about Skeff and his papa-in-law?[7] They harangued
student Dublin from a car outside the University Buildings and U.
Coll., because *God Save the King* was played on the organ. 'There was a
lady in the vehicle,' the paper says. David said he was proud that day
of Nationalist Dublin. I am glad you have a suit at last. Did Bertelli
never write after that time? Item. A lamp chimney here costs one lira!

I am still suffering from this indigestion. The druggist gave me last
night a box of rhubarb pills and told me I should see a doctor if it did
not get better. It is about four or five days since I had the pleasure of
defecating. I believe this is the result of my sedentary life. I was always
accustomed to walking a good deal.

You ask me what I would substitute for parliamentary agitation in

[1] Mrs William Murray (Aunt Josephine).
[2] Joyce was confusing Seamas O'Kelly (1881–1918), who had no connection with
University College, Dublin, and Seamus O'Kelly, his fellow student. The former O'Kelly
had just published *By the Stream of Killmeen* (Dublin and London, October 1906). He
wrote plays and a novel as well as stories, and was prominent in the nationalist movement.
Joyce wrote a footnote for Herbert Gorman, *James Joyce*, p. 181, testifying to his 'great
admiration for another story of O'Kelly, "The Weaver's Grave" '.
[3] Charles Joseph Kickham (1826–82), Irish novelist and poet. Gerald Griffin (1803–40),
Irish novelist and dramatist. William Carleton (1794–1869), Irish novelist and story
writer. Perhaps Patrick James Smyth (1826–85), Irish patriot and a member of the
Young Ireland group. He was not a writer, however. John Banim (1798–1842), Irish
novelist.
[4] This detail, probably intended for 'The Dead', was not used.
[5] The allusion is explained on p. 130.
[6] Joyce's uncle, John Murray (d. 1911), who was supposed to resemble the statesman
the Marquess of Lorne (1845–1914). See p. 130. Murray was a model for Joe Donnelly
in 'Clay'.
[7] Francis Sheehy-Skeffington and David Sheehy.

Ireland. I think the *Sinn Fein* policy would be more effective. Of course I see that its success would be to substitute Irish for English capital but no-one, I suppose, denies that capitalism is a stage of progress. The Irish proletariat has yet to be created. A feudal peasantry exists, scraping the soil but this would with a national revival or with a definite preponderance of England surely disappear. I quite agree with you that Griffith is afraid of the priests—and he has every reason to be so. But, possibly, they are also a little afraid of him too. After all, he is holding out some secular liberty to the people and the Church doesn't approve of that. I quite see, of course, that the Church is still, as it was in the time of Adrian IV, the enemy of Ireland: but, I think, her time is almost up. For either *Sinn Fein* or Imperialism will conquer the present Ireland. If the Irish programme did not insist on the Irish language I suppose I could call myself a nationalist. As it is, I am content to recognise myself an exile: and, prophetically, a repudiated one. You complain of Griffith's using Gogarty & Co. How do you expect him to fill his paper: he can't write it all himself. The part he does write, at least, has some intelligence and directness about it. As for O.G. I am waiting for the *S.F.* policy to make headway in the hope that he will join it for no doubt whatever exists in my mind but that, if he gets the chance and the moment comes, he will play the part of MacNally and Reynolds.[1] I do not say this out of spleen. It is my final view of his character: a very native Irish growth, and if I begin to write my novel again it is in this way I shall treat them. If it is not far-fetched to say that my action, and that of men like Ibsen &c, is a virtual intellectual strike I would call such people as Gogarty and Yeats and Colm the blacklegs of literature. Because they have tried to substitute us, to serve the old idols at a lower rate when we refused to do so for a higher.

Of course you find my socialism thin. It is so and unsteady and ill-informed. You are wrong, however, in supposing that the intellectuals taught Labriola socialism. Intellectualism, instead, is a partial development, an alloy of sociological liberalism, of the original socialism which was really nothing but the manifesto of a class. Ferri, for example, seems a more intellectual and capable person than Labriola. But the latter contends that interest in psychiatry and criminology and litera-ture and religion are beside the question. He wishes to hasten *directly* the emergence of the proletariat. And to do this he would include in his

---

[1] Leonard MacNally (1752–1820) and Thomas Reynolds (1771–1832) were informers, notorious for having betrayed the United Irishmen. MacNally also betrayed Robert Emmet. In *Ulysses*, p. 15 (14), Stephen refers to Mulligan, modelled mostly on Gogarty, as Ireland's 'gay betrayer'.

ranks Catholics and Jews, liberals and conservatives. We were speculat-
ing one day at Barcola[1] how much was spent in military and naval
defence by England. The revenue income is £141,000,000-0-0 and the
amount spent on army and navy is 66 millions: 47%. The revenue of
Italy is 1700 million lire and of this 400 millions is spent on army and
navy: 23%. England however has a vast territory to protect and, at
least, possesses a powerful empire. Italy against the outlay of $\frac{1}{4}$ of her
revenue has an impoverished illiterate population, medieval sanitation,
a terrible accumulation of taxes, and an army and navy which would
probably fetch a few hundred pounds in a lottery. Of course, all this
money does not go into the warchest. Japan, the first naval power in
the world, I presume, in point of efficiency, spends three million pounds
per annum on her fleet. Italy spends more than twice as much.

Do you think there would be any use in my writing to Charlie? I
wanted him to make some inquiries for me. What is their address? I
wrote to A. J. at 4 Northbrook &c—was that right? A letter from Soc.
of Authors this morning saying they have to consider the claims of
older members &c &c. I am waiting to hear from Symons! I want an
English dictionary badly. I don't know how I could correct proofs at
present.

Georgie is very well and fat. He spends his day pulling about papers
clothes and shoes. He is cursed frequently by both his parents for
mislaying the comb and the sponge or the towel or my hat or shoes: and
when asked where it is he points to the ceiling or the window and says
'là!' The other evg I began to talk to Nora about something serious (! ! !):
but he wouldn't allow it. He made such a noise that we had to stop and
talk to *him*. His latest phrases are 'Bua! (brucia!)' 'Lalia! (Giornale
d'Italia)' 'Abace! (In braccia)' and 'Ata! (In terra).' The two last he
alternates very frequently. He also says 'Appetito!' and 'Addio!' The
papers I put aside for you he usually tears up.

I shall let you know in a few days how we are getting on with our new
arrangement. Do you ever read the *Daily Mail*. A fellow named Edgar
Wallace writes in it sometimes a farcical column: it is very funny. I am
labouring at the end of *Demos*. Gissing's effort to be just to his socialist
protagonist is very distressing. I read that a Dublin solicitor was found
poisoned in London when he was about to be struck off the rolls. The
bottle bore the label *Starkie's Medical Hall*.[2] No wonder, begod, if it
was as bad as his verses.

[1] A seaside suburb of Trieste, noted for its swimming establishment, rowing clubs, and
wineshops.
[2] See p. 33.

I wish someone was here to talk to me about Dublin. I forget half the things I wanted to do. The two worst stories are *After the Race* and *A Painful Case*. When I have done reading the authors I said do you think I ought to read the Russians seriously or the Danish writers? Write a long letter.   JIM

Another purgative on Friday cost me L1.–! The box of pills cost 80c–! Viva l'Italia! Avanti Savoia!

To STANISLAUS JOYCE   MS. Cornell

13 November 1906   *Via Frattina 52, II°, Rome*

Dear Stannie, I have been expecting a letter from you this long time. I have had no reply either from Aunt J or from Symons. There was a Jewish divorce case on last week in Dublin which would have interested me very much but of course nobody thought of sending me a paper.[1] I have received *Sinn Féin* and *The Leprechaun*. The editor[2] of S.F alludes to the British army as the only mercenary army in Europe. I suppose he prefers the conscription system because it is French. Irish intellectuals are very tiresome. Italy, at least, has two things to balance its miserable poverty and mismanagement: a lively intellectual movement and a good climate. Ireland is Italy without these two. I see that the Irish National Theatre season is on at present: a triple bill of which the good Lady Gregory supplies two items.[3] A play by a man named William Boyle[4] makes the dramatic critic of S.F. think of Ibsen. I am reading another book by Gissing *The Crown of Life*.[5] Here are two samples of his way of writing ' 'Arry, in fact, to use a coarse but expressive phrase, was a hopeless blackguard' 'When he left, which he did later in the day (to catch a train) the conversation resumed its usual course &c'. His books remind me of what Effore calls *Pastefazoi*.[6] I perceive that my first opinion of him was founded on pure good nature, nothing else. After all, I can read anything. I am reading every day the *feuilleton* in the Daily Mail the name of which is *The Swelling of Jordan*. I see that John Dillon[7] at the Galway election alluded to Capt. Shawe Taylor[8] as a bastard *and* a blackguard. Note the discrimination. I thought of

---

[1] See p. 132n.
[2] Arthur Griffith.   [3] *The Gaol Gate* and *The Canavans*.
[4] This play, *The Mineral Workers*, was presented at the Abbey Theatre on 20 October 1906.
[5] Published in 1899.   [6] 'Noodles and beans', a favourite Triestine dish.
[7] John Dillon (1851–1927), Irish politician, Member of Parliament for East Mayo from 1885 to 1918.
[8] Captain John Shawe-Taylor (1866–1911) was the Revolutionist candidate at the Galway City election in 1906. He was beaten by Dillon, the Nationalist candidate.

beginning my story *Ulysses*: but I have too many cares at present. Ferrero devotes a chapter in his history of Rome[1] to the Odes of Horace: so, perhaps, poets should be let live. In his book *Young Europe*[2] which I have just read he says there are three great classes of emigrants: the (I forget the word:[3] it means conquering, imposing their own language, &c), the English: the adhesive (forming a little group with national traditions and sympathies) the Chinese and the Irish!!!!: the diffusive (entering into the new society and forming part of it) the Germans. He has a fine chapter on Antisemitism. By the way, Brandes is a Jew. He says that Karl Marx has the apocalyptic imagination and makes Armageddon a war between capital and labour. The most arrogant statement made by Israel so far, he says, not excluding the gospel of Jesus is Marx's proclamation that socialism is the fulfilment of a natural law. In considering Jews he slips in Jesus between Lassalle and Lombroso: the latter too (Ferrero's father-in-law) is a Jew.[4]

We got notice yesterday. So I have to look for another room. To-morrow my money will be all gone. I am relying on a pupil who begins lessons tonight. He is taking 10 lessons for 20 lire. I have made out a receipt but perhaps he will have no money with him (he does not come again till Saturday) or will not like to pay in advance. I cannot press him as he is a friend of a clerk in the bank who recommended him to me. I will find it very hard to get a room such as we want. I must be out by the end of the month: and I will have also to pay the *Caparra*.[5] I answered two advts for lessons. One of them I missed by a post; the advertiser wrote to thank me and said he had just given his word. If I went to the café I should have seen the paper in time but I wait to read it in the bank. To economise we have given up drinking wine at lunch. But even then we would not live on Lire 25 a week. I gave Nora first L 50 and then L 20 and on that we have managed 15 days only: that is, about L 32 a week. We have still left coal and a little oil and sugar and coffee: and owe nothing. But the position is again exciting. You can see how impossible it is for me to write or do anything in such circumstances. I had about 82 lire over clear: I gave 10 to the barrister and around 70 to Nora. The other two I spent partly on—cakes! (I did so to test the truth of one of Ferrero's statements about English and Italian cakes and biscuits). I will wait until tonight before posting this.

Last night I went into an evangelical hall. The minister was English. Is it affectation or impotence of the English that they can make no

---

[1] Guglielmo Ferrero published his *Grandezza e decadenza di Roma* in five volumes in Milan from 1902 to 1907.

[2] *L'Europa giovane* (Milan, 1897).   [3] Ferrero's word is *plasmativa*, p. 116.

[4] Ibid., pp. 78–80, 358–62, 374–82, 409–13.   [5] 'Deposit.'

attempt to pronounce any language but their own. He spoke fluently
and correctly enough but it had no resemblance to Italian in sound. I
can easily distinguish the English accent, talking Italian. Candidly, I
don't know whether they assume it or not. Their accent speaking
English (particularly that of the women) is very pleasant and modulated
compared with the Irish or American accent or the Scotch accent. The
American accent is really bloody fearful to listen to. By the way, one of
the little illusions which gladden the heart of the staff of *Sinn Féin* is
that the English don't know how to pronounce their own language.
When an English tourist meets *Che Buono*[1] the latter sneers at him
because he says 'Haw, I cawn't heawh wot youah saying', but he forgets
his compatriot, who in Dick Sheehy's story, after ranging the hotel
burst in on the dinner-table, holding up his trousers and asked earnestly
'For the love o' Jaysus, gintlemin, will ye tell us where's the con-
vaynience'. By the way, they are still at the 'venereal excess' cry in Sinn
Féin.[2] Why does nobody compile statistics of 'venereal excess' from
Dublin hospitals. What is 'venereal excess'? Perhaps Mr Skeffington-
Sheehy could write something on the subject, being, as J.J.B.[3] puts it 'a
pure man'. 'Infant Jesus, meek and mild, Pity me a little child. Make me
humble as thou art, And with Thy love inflame my heart'. Anyway my
opinion is that if I put down a bucket into my own soul's well, sexual
department, I draw up Griffith's and Ibsen's and Skeffington's and
Bernard Vaughan's and St. Aloysius' and Shelley's and Renan's water
along with my own. And I am going to do that in my novel (inter alia)
and plank the bucket down before the shades and substances above
mentioned to see how they like it: and if they don't like it I can't help
them. I am nauseated by their lying drivel about pure men and pure
women and spiritual love and love for ever: blatant lying in the face of
the truth. I don't know much about the 'saince' of the subject but I
presume there are very few mortals in Europe who are not in danger of
waking some morning and finding themselves syphilitic. The Irish
consider England a sink: but, if cleanliness be important in this matter,
what is Ireland? Perhaps my view of life is too cynical but it seems to
me that a lot of this talk about love is nonsense. A woman's love is
always maternal and egoistic. A man, on the contrary, side by side with
his extraordinary cerebral sexualism and bodily fervour (from which

[1] William Bulfin (1862–1910), an Irish author who, after living for many years in
Argentina, returned to Ireland in 1902. He used the pseudonym of 'Che Buono' in
publishing his *Rambles in Eirinn* in *Sinn Féin* during 1906, but his own name appears
on the title page of the book made from these articles (Dublin, 1907).

[2] See p.108 n.

[3] J. F. Byrne is meant, though the middle initial is wrong.

women are normally free) possesses a fund of genuine affection for the
'beloved' or 'once beloved' object. I am no friend of tyranny, as you
know, but if many husbands are brutal the atmosphere in which they
live (vide Counterparts) is brutal and few wives and homes can satisfy
the desire for happiness. In fact, it is useless to talk about this any
further. I am going to lunch.

Have just received your letter. Facts are, as you surmise. We have
now Tuesday 13th 4 o'clock less than 3 lire. Tonight at 8 o'clock my
pupil comes. I shall try him but may fail. If I fail I am in the usual fix.
You ask me to scan verses. What verses? Whose verses? You ask me to
explain 'the Marquis of Lorne'.[1] Uncle John; who was considered like
the Marquis of Lorne is the person alluded to. The meaning of *Dublin
by Lamplight Laundry*? That is the name of the laundry at Ballsbridge,
of which the story treats. It is run by a society of Protestant spinsters,
widows, and childless women—I expect—as a Magdalen's home. The
phrase *Dublin by Lamplight* means that Dublin by lamplight is a
wicked place full of wicked and lost women whom a kindly committee
gathers together for the good work of washing my dirty shirts. I like the
phrase because 'it is a gentle way of putting it'. Now I have explained.
Please explain you what means 'I shall take my time about answering'
re Aunt J's letter.

I was today in the *Biblioteca Vittorio Emanuele,* looking up the
account of the Vatican Council of 1870 which declared the infallibility
of the Pope. Had not time to finish. Before the final proclamation many
of the clerics left Rome as a protest. At the proclamation when the
dogma was read out the Pope said 'Is that all right, gents?'. All the
gents said 'Placet' but two said 'Non placet'. But the Pope 'You be
damned! Kissmearse! I'm infallible!'. The two were, according to one
account, the bishops of Capuzzo[2] and Little Rock, according to another
account, the bishops of Ajaccio and Little Rock. I looked up MacHale's
life. He was bishop of Tuam and of somewhere else in *partibus*. They say
nothing of his having voted at the Vatican Council. I shall continue
there tomorrow and rewrite that part of the story.[3] *Grace* takes place in

---

[1] See p. 124.

[2] A humorous play on the diocese of Caiazzo and 'capuzo', which in Triestine dialect
means 'cabbage'.

[3] The discussion of the Vatican Council in Joyce's story 'Grace' is purposely and
amusingly confused. Only two delegates to the Council, Bishop Aloisio Riccio of Caiazzo
and Bishop Edward Fitzgerald of Arkansas, voted on the final ballot against making
papal infallibility a dogma. But on earlier ballots there was more opposition. Dr John
MacHale (1791–1881), Archbishop of Tuam in Ireland (known as 'John of Tuam'),
spoke in his leonine manner against papal infallibility, and voted against it at an earlier
stage but he submitted after the majority voted in favour.

1901 or 2, therefore Kernan at that time 1870 would have been about twenty-five. He would have been born in 1848 and would have been only 6 years of age at time of the proclamation of the Immaculate Conception dogma 1854. I want now an account of the unveiling of Smith O'Brien's statue[1] to see if MacHale was there. I can get all the dictionaries I want in the Bib. Vitt. Eman. (blast the long name) including a dict of English slang. What a pity I am so handicapped. Eglinton was sure I would come back begging to Dublin and J.J.B. that I would become a drunkard and Cosgrave that I would become a nymphomaniac.[2] Alas, gentlemen, I have become a bank clerk, and, now that I think of it, bad as it is, it's more than either of my three prophets could do.[3]

How do you like the name for the story about Hunter? I am very pleased with your admiration for Swift. I suppose I shall get interested in him some day. But I prefer people who are alive. Sometimes when I am on the track of some idea and am about to burst into speech I hear a voice 'Signor Joyce, scriva a questo signore, in francese, dicendogli che abbiamo venduto ventimila peseta————'[4] You remember the book I spoke to you of one day in the Park into which I was going to put William Dara[5] and Lady Belvedere.[6] Even then I was on the track of writing a chapter of Irish history. I wish I had a map of Dublin and views and Gilbert's history.[7] But nobody, except you, seems to take me seriously. I paid Shelley's granddaughter or grand-niece £10–0–0 the other day. Her name is Nora. She is left-handed. This is the way Leonardo wrote his notes, I am afraid—not left-handed, of course, but in this jerky way. I would like to write *The Last Supper* about Joe

---

[1] William Smith O'Brien (1803–64), Irish patriot. In 'Grace' Joyce eventually used the unveiling not of O'Brien's statue but of Sir John Gray's. Gray (1816–75) was a newspaper publisher and the organizer of Dublin's water supply.

[2] Cosgrave's slip for 'satyr'.

[3] The part of the sentence beginning 'and, now' was an afterthought inserted by Joyce in the margin.

[4] 'Mr Joyce, write to this gentleman in French, telling him we have sold twenty thousand pesetas. . . .'

[5] Pseudonym used by William Byrne (1874–1933) in his book of poems, *A Light on the Broom* (Dublin, 1901). He later became Professor of English at University College, Galway (1917–33).

[6] Mary Countess of Belvedere, wife of the first earl, was accused in 1743 of having committed adultery with her husband's brother. The letters purporting to prove her guilt were probably forged, but Lady Belvedere was persuaded to say she was guilty so as to be divorced from her debauched husband. When she did so, however, the earl did not divorce her, but cruelly imprisoned her in a house in Gaulstown, County Westmeath. There she continued to protest her innocence until her death more than thirty years later. Joyce has Father Conmee brood on these events in the *Wandering Rocks* episode of *Ulysses*.

[7] John Thomas Gilbert, *A History of the City of Dublin*, 3 vols. (Dublin, 1861), or its one-volume edition (London, 1903).

MacKernan[1]—ought I? Mother said I was a 'mocker'. Am I? It is now 6 o'clock. At 8 o'clock I will try the pupil. Write soon.   Jim

I got 20 lire from my pupil, so that I can manage until Saturday. But while I am looking for another pupil you had better try to send me some. Remember I have to live and get a room.

[Postscript at head of letter]

I think the respondent is old Harris,[2] the jeweller, of Nassau Street, from whose grandson Sinclair[3] I raised 10/– at the time of my hegira. By the bye, about the money I got on the 1st of Nov. L50 to Eng Consul, L52 for landlady, L70 to Nora, L10 to barrister, L30 to lunchman, L30 for Nora's and Georgie's clothes and hat and boots—that makes L245.—.

To Stanislaus Joyce   MS. Cornell

20 November 1906   *Via Frattina 52, II, Rome*

Dear Stannie, *Monday.* Thanks for your remittance which I received today when my funds were at zero. An advt which I answered in the *Tribuna* has brought me some money. I have been appointed 'professor' in an Ecole de Langues (which is an offshoot at low prices of the B.S.). I go there when I am finished at the bank and as I am paid L 1 per lesson it will bring me about L 10 per week. Tonight I leave the bank at 7 o'c: and then have lessons in the *Ecole* from 7.15 to 10.15. Tomorrow I have my private pupil from 7.30 to 8.30 at home and have then 1 lesson in the Ecole from 9 to 10. Between these two I make about L 14 per week more. I began in the school on Saturday and next Saturday shall probably receive 10 Lire from it. Your 20 Lire will last me till Saturday but I am afraid you will have to send some more as I shall have to pay the Caparra for a room. This will positively be the last month in which I shall have to bother you. Let each of us then save as much as he can. I can save Lire 100.— per month. I see nothing for it but to try to save money. I wrote to John Long, offering him *Dubliners.*

---

[1] The son of Joyce's landlady at 60 Shelbourne Road, Dublin.

[2] The divorce suit to which Joyce refers was heard in Dublin on 5–8 November 1906. Kathleen Hynes Harris petitioned for divorce from her husband, Morris Harris, on grounds of cruelty and misconduct. Harris was eighty-five, his wife much younger. Though of different religions, they had been married by a priest; Archbishop William Walsh had granted a dispensation for the purpose because of a 'very serious circumstance', not specified. Later they had been married also by a rabbi. The jury found Harris guilty of cruelty but disagreed on adultery, and a verdict was granted of divorce *a mensa et thoro*, with costs.

[3] Either William or Henry Sinclair.

I send you the *U.I. Leprechaun* and *Giornale d'Italia.* Yesterday another bomb went off in S Peter's. Strange to say I went there in the afternoon without knowing of its having happened. I had intended going to the morning service (and would consequently have been in the church at the time of the explosion) but that I waited in for a letter from you. Things are beginning to be pretty lively here. I saw no precautions taken in the church in the afternoon but perhaps these things are not visible. Cardinal Rampolla[1] in the procession passed me at an arm's length unprotected so far as I could see. He is a tall strong man with a truculent face. At the close of the service a priest came out on a high balcony under the dome and exhibited the sacred relics, the lance, the piece of the cross, and the towel of Veronica. This he did by marching from one end to the other of the balcony with each relic in turn and holding it over the parapet at each end while a bell rang and the procession knelt in the centre of the nave. The upper part of the dome was rather dark and the towel looked rather like a thing out of Tussaud's. The choir was very good but some of rev. gents have voices like crows. While one was cawing a young ecclesiastical student beside me (who had pointed out Rampolla to me) laughed out loud and made signs of anguish with his mouth. A peasant women with a kerchief on her head gave milk to a child during the vespers. Rampolla is like Father Murray[2] without the lower jowl: or like Father Brennan:[3] wore a red berretta stuck anyhow on his head. It's a bloody funny church, no doubt.

Tuesday

I expected a letter from you today. I received yesterday *By the Stream of Killmeen* by Seumas O'Kelly, and have read three stories of it. If you like I will send it to you afterwards. A good deal of publishing appears to be going on in Dublin at present. I would like to read more of the books, even Heblon's *Study in Blue*[4] though, as W Archer says I know it's not good for me. With great difficulty I finished Gissing's *The Crown of Life*, this crown being love according to G.G. What irritates me most in him is when he begins to write eloquently about nature. Like William Buckley,[5] the Irish novelist, who writes in *Sinn Féin*, he makes 'nature' very tiresome. A reviewer in *Sinn Féin* said that S O'K's story 'The Land of Loneliness' was worthy of Tourgénieff. The stories I have read

---

[1] Mariano Rampolla del Tindaro (1843–1913), Italian cardinal and papal secretary of state from 1887 to 1903. He almost became pope after Leo XIII.

[2] Canon Joseph Murray, parish priest of Glasthule and Dalkey.

[3] Rev. Joseph Brennan of the parish of St Joseph, Dublin.

[4] Heblon (pseudonym of Joseph K. O'Connor), *Studies in Blue* (Dublin, 1903).

[5] A writer from Cork; he published *Cambia Carty and Other Stories* (Dublin: Maunsel, 1907).

were about beautiful, pure faithful Connacht girls and lithe, broad-shouldered open-faced young Connacht men, and I read them without blinking, patiently trying to see whether the writer was trying to express something he had understood. I always conclude by saying to myself without anger something like this 'Well, there's no doubt they are very romantic young people: at first they come as a relief, then they tire. Maybe, begod, people like that are to be found by the Stream of Killmeen only none of them has come under my observation, as the deceased gent in Norway remarked.[']

I doubt if S O'K would judge my stories so urbanely, however. I wonder does his book sell. Nora, who read *Hedda Gabler* with interest twice before forgetting it, considers his stories tiresome rubbish.

The *École* is not chic. Last night one of my classes numbered nearly a dozen pupils. One of them was a lovely boor: elderly, red swollen face, sidelong glance. He made fun openly of my writing on the board, perhaps thinking I 'had no Italian', and of me as a 'professore'. Some of the pupils laughed. A rather fat girl came to my rescue by explaining everything to him over again in Italian. He wanted to know why I didn't explain in Italian. She told him it was the 'metodo'. Then he said something which made the class laugh. I was frightfully polite to him and, though I was tired, did my best to make him understand. When he was going away he told me he quite understood that I was prevented by the metodo from doing as he wished but that what he wanted etc etc. The Ecole, in fact, is bowsy. It has no books or illustrations. The pupils, I think, pay 50 c– a head for a lesson. However . . . !

Publisher's announcements are becoming worse. Really they are intolerable. Read the D.M.[1] suppl. 'Books' Renan was right when he said we were marching towards universal Americanism. I suppose you read about Caruso[2] being arrested in the monkey-house at New York for indecent behaviour towards a young lady. By the way is 'Lily is a lady' a song or a cant. I wonder they don't arrest the monkeys in New York. It took three N.Y. policemen to arrest Caruso. His impresario ridicules the charge and says Caruso has to answer shoals of 'offers' from N.Y. women of the upper classes. The papers are indignant. Do Americans know how they are regarded in Europe?

I hear a report that there was a third bomb thrown today in the Piazza di Spagna. I hardly think these can be the work of anarchists. They are very clumsily made and do no damage. It may be a trick of the police to justify them in making arrests on suspicion as the King of Greece is to be here in a few days. I hope to Jesus he won't pass by this

[1] *Daily Mail.*   [2] Enrico Caruso (1873–1921), the Italian tenor.

building during his visit as there might be a serious explosion. It is pleasant to reflect that in the event of rupture between Italy and Austria I have my office in the Austrian Consulate. I discover that I have nothing further to say now. I expected a letter from you today

I shall keep this open till 8 o'clock this evg. I have two lessons tonight. JIM

By the way of the 4 advts I answered in the *Tribuna*, one got me this position in the bank, one got me Terzini, one got me a letter of apology and regret, a miss of L 130.–, and one got me a professorship in the *École de Langues*!

Dear Stannie[1] I hope you are well you ought to tell Jim not to be doing so much as he doesnt have a minute to himself Georgie is very well thanks of all your kind inquiries for me Kisses from GEORGIE x x x x x x x x x

I hope your foot is better [Unsigned]

To STANISLAUS JOYCE MS. Cornell

Postmark 3 December 1906 Sunday noon *Via Frattina 52, II°, Rome*

Dear Stannie, I think we shall have to go to a hotel. I cannot get a room. They want 70 and 80 Lire a month for rooms, don't want couples or children, don't want to give the use of a kitchen. I went to agents put an advt in the paper, walked miles: no use. This city, I confess, beats me. If anyone asks you how I like how I like [sic] tell them I think it is the stupidest old whore of a town ever I was in. This country irks me beyond measure: perhaps I should say only this city. But the system of life must be the same everywhere. Of course, your prosy old friend H.J.[2] and other respectables like to write about Italy and Italians and subtle Romans. I have seen a lot of Romans now and if anyone asks you what I think of them you may say that so far as I can see their chief preoccupation in life is the condition (to judge from their speech) broken, swollen etc of their *coglioni* and their chief pastime and joke the breaking of wind rereward. This kind of mechanical obscenity is damnably tiresome. However, it is an expletive which I am reserving for the day when I leave the eternal city as my farewell and adieu to it.[3]

If the word vulgar has any meaning I think the European palm must go to Italy. After all, Germany has something under her uniforms. An Italian carabiniere with his absurd high hat or a Papal Swiss might be

---

[1] From Nora Joyce.   [2] Henry James.
[3] Bloom makes use of the same expletive at the end of the *Sirens* episode of *Ulysses*.

the symbol of this tawdry civilisation. As for Rossini's statement[1] it is probably not quite accurate as he forgot Turkey and Portugal. But I am discontented with everything and everybody at present—no wonder.

Aunt J writes a brief letter, half of which is about MacCormack's[2] voice and Caruso's trial.[3] I am afraid I shall have to give it up, the time is out of joint. 'We done our best, the dear knows!'

I have discontinued reading the D.M. supplement. So long as there was mystery and money in it I read but now the love interest has begun. The last sentence I read in it ran 'So he kissed away the tears and after that there was nothing more but the great glow of love—"I don't even know your name, he whispered." ' I am reading *Life's Little Ironies* by Hardy.[4] It is a late book of his. O.G.,[5] I understand, writes in Sinn Féin under the name of 'Mettus Curtius', the gent who leaped into the chasm in the forum, I think. Explain how it is that while Byrne and Pappie and Mrs Cosgrave formed a true opinion of O.G. I, with more opportunity, formed an untrue one. Send me an account of the last supper: it will amuse me even if I never write the story. Write to me also about Hunter. How can I do anything in my present condition? Last week I 'worked' 12 hours a day. This should be enough to satisfy even my dreamy Irish friends. How Starkey would laugh and how Roberts would giggle if they knew that after my day's 'wurruk' I go and speak for two hours about the pen, the blackboard and inkstand for $9\frac{1}{2}$d per hour!

It is now Friday and I have not yet got a room! One of Hardy's stories[6] is about a man in 1804 who saw 'Boney' and an adjutant taking notes on the coast of Devon, I think. The story made me think of Meredith's poem beginning 'Cannon his voice'.[7] I suppose it is because I never played football or was treated only slightly to your captain of fifty's regime[8] that I can't turn out that kind of poetry. I suppose the hero's valet is really his panegyrist poet. The other stories—wait now: here are the names 'The Son's Veto' 'A Case of Conscience' 'Two Ambitions' 'A Fiddler of Reels' 'The Melancholy Hussar' 'To Please his Wife' 'On the Western Circuit' 'A Tradition'. One or two are like the 'Boney' one. Others are about hard-working parson's sons, one is

---

[1] See p. 107.   [2] John McCormack (1884–1945), the Irish tenor.
[3] See p. 134.   [4] Thomas Hardy, *Life's Little Ironies* (1894).
[5] Oliver St John Gogarty. An article signed Mettus Curtius appeared in *Sinn Féin* on 10 November 1906. Entitled 'On Keeping Shop', it referred mockingly to 'our' glorious army.
[6] 'A Tradition of 1804'.
[7] George Meredith's poem 'Napoléon' begins:
                    Cannon his name,
                    Cannon his voice, he came. . . .
[8] Homosexuality, associated by Joyce with public-school education. See p. 73.

about a marvellous country fiddler, and the rest are about 'mésalliances' (!). One story[1] is about a lawyer on the circuit who seduces a servant, then receives letters from her so beautifully written that he decides to marry her. The letters are written by the servant's mistress who is in love with the lawyer. After the marriage (servant is accompanied to London by mistress) husband says fondly 'Now, dear J.K.–S–&c, will you write a little note to my dear sister, A.B X. etc and send her a piece of the wedding-cake.[2] One of those nice little letters you know so well how to write, love'. Exit of servant wife. She goes out and sits at a table somewhere and, I suppose, writes something like this 'Dear Mrs X— I enclose a piece of wedding-cake.' Enter husband—lawyer, genial. Genially he says 'Well, love, how have you written' and then the whole discovery is found out. Servant-wife blows her nose in the letter and lawyer confronts the mistress. She confesses. Then they talk a page or so of copybook talk (as distinguished from servant's ditto). She weeps but he is stern. Is this as near as T.H. can get to life, I wonder? O my poor fledglings, poor Corley, poor Ignatius Gallaher![3] (The banker is rather polite to me but I can't help wondering why he is always running in and out of the room. I suppose he makes money on every run) What is wrong with these English writers is that they always keep beating about the bush.

John Long answered my note today and asks me to send MS for his consideration at the same time asking who had accepted and then declined to publish the book. I wrote telling him and promising the MS in a few days. I wonder is there any chance of his taking it? What kind of 'work' does he bring out? I suppose he is no relative of the J.L. who kept the public-house at the corner of Duke Street and was a friend of our grandfather's. I will send the MS as soon as I get settled. It is now Friday evg and I have found no room yet. The old Bethelemites must have been like these Italian bastards. I feel for poor old Joseph.

Last night we were put out of our room. I had lessons from 7 to 10 after the bank. Nora was waiting for me for two hours first in a cinematograph and then in a restaurant. I ate a big dinner being very hungry and at half past eleven left the restaurant with the holy family. It was raining so to protect Nora's hat and the child I got a car and we drove to a hotel some distance away where I had heard the tariff was moderate. It was full (at least, the porter said so) and we had to drive on further to another one. Here we found a room for the night. The evening cost me

---

[1] 'On the Western Circuit'.
[2] Joyce invents the detail of the wedding cake.
[3] Corley is a character in 'Two Gallants', and Gallaher in 'A Little Cloud'.

9 Lire! Today I am again seeking a room. Address your letters meanwhile c/o Nast, Kolb & Schumacher, Rome. I send you S.F. with a
column of O.G.'s stupid drivel.[1] I see he has advanced from 'le petty
mere' as far as 'le bête noir'. This he learned I suppose from the stolidly
one-languaged Sludge.[2] What a pleasant time I am having.   Jim

To Stanislaus Joyce   MS. Cornell

7 December 1906 Tuesday evg   *Rome*

Dear Stannie, Since Saturday last we have slept in the hotel but I think
this is our last night there. After immense difficulty I have succeeded in
getting a room and, if all goes well, we move in there tomorrow evening.
This pleasant interlude has cost me about L25.— I spent all Sunday
going up and down staircases and Nora and Georgie went about during
the day, as witness a letter[3] enclosed which an usher of the bank brought
me in yesterday evening. Happily it was enclosed in an envelope. Item:
a case for Mr Thomas Hardy.[4]

Tomorrow night I will go over my MS and send it to John Long.
There is a publisher in London, name of Sisley, Ltd. He publishes
'daring' work. I saw a review in the heel of a D.M. column of a book by
E. Temple Thurston, called 'The Realist'. It was very daring and
unpleasant, D.M. said, but showed unmistakeable talent. I have
ordered it from England: it is a book of short stories. Do you think I did
right? I was going to read Hardy through but I have changed over to
Octave Mirbeau[5] instead. I have ordered a Danish Berlitz book from
Berlin. It will be published in January. In six months I ought to be able
to read the Danish writers. I would like to read some of those at whom
Ibsen hints in The Master Builder. One is named Nansen,[6] I think. I
wish I could go to Denmark. Ferrero says that Abo, Stockholm and
Copenhagen are the finest cities in Europe.[7] G.M. has re-written *The*

---

[1] Gogarty's second article on 'Ugly England' appeared in *Sinn Féin* on 24 November
1906. It is chiefly an attack upon the Jews; he speaks of 'England becoming Jewry'.
In *Ulysses* this is the point of view of Haines and of Mr Deasy, and Stephen (like Joyce)
regards it as 'drivel'.

[2] That is, from the Englishmen, here viewed collectively, who taught Gogarty at
Oxford. For Sludge, see p. 109n.

[3] Presumably an ungrammatical complaint from Nora Joyce.

[4] Joyce refers to Hardy's story about the servant girl who could not write letters. See
p. 137.

[5] Octave Mirbeau (1850–1917), French novelist and playwright. See p. 140.

[6] Peter Nansen (1861–1918), Danish novelist and publisher. His writings are elegant
in style, rather cynical and daring in content. Ibsen is much more likely to have had in
mind Knut Hamsun (1859–1952), the Norwegian novelist.

[7] In *L'Europa giovane*, p. 213. See above p. 128.

Lake. D.M. praises his artistic conscience. 'Very few writers &c.' The Maunsel Press has emitted some booklets, also: poems of Ella Young:[1] and a young gentleman whom you may remember standing white-faced outside McGarvey's has published verses in praise of, I think, the Sacred Heart.[2]

Wed. morn. I am sitting in the office. The winter has begun. There are no stoves, fires or pipes. My hands are cold. I blow my nose every three minutes. I have just read an advt in the paper wanted a manager for some place, salary L100 a month. What a beautiful country! Your friend H.J. ought to get a running kick in the arse for writing his tea-slop about it. I am damnably sick of Italy, Italian and Italians, outrageously, illogically sick. Every time a pupil asks me how I like Rome I vent some sneering remark. I hate to think that Italians ever did anything in the way of art. But I suppose they did. What did they do but illustrate a page or so of the New Testament![3] They themselves think they have a monopoly in the line. I am dead tired of their bello and bellezza. A clerk here is named (he is round, bald, fat, voiceless) Bartoluzzi. You pronounce by inflating both cheeks and prolonging the u. Every time I pass him I repeat his name to myself and translate 'Good day, little bits of Barto'. Another is named Simonetti: They are all little bits of something or other, I think. This is my first experience of clerks: but do they all talk for 5 minutes about the position &c of a penwiper? I think the Irish are the most civilised people in Europe, be Jesus Christ I do: anyway they are the least burocratic [sic]. From the foregoing drivel you can judge the state of my mind in this country where 'they drink nice wine not horrid black porter.'[4] Useless: too cold: stick hands in pocket.

Thurs. morn. We are in our new quarters. Expected a letter from you this morning here (bank). (Address at end of letter) Today after lunch I shall go over my MS for John Long.

Frid morn No letter from you yet. Our room is quite small: one bed: we sleep 'lying opposed in opposite directions, the head of one towards the tail of the other'.[5] Blasphemed often while correcting MS. Stories dreadfully dull. When I get home at 10 o'clock after the bank and school

[1] Ella Young (1873–1956), *Poems* (Tower Press Series, Dublin: Maunsel, 1906). Her later books, *The Rose of Heaven* (Dublin, 1920) and *Celtic Wonder Tales* (Dublin, 1923), were both illustrated by Maud Gonne.

[2] Cathal McGarvey's tobacco shop, An Stad ('The Stop'), was in North Frederick Street. It was a nationalist meeting-place in the early years of this century. The pale-faced young poet may have been John Burke, a solicitor.

[3] This sentence was inserted in the margin as an afterthought.

[4] Quoted from George Moore. See p. 99.

[5] In the *Ithaca* episode of *Ulysses*, Leopold and Molly Bloom are similarly oriented.

and have taken my dinner I am so tired that I can barely skim over the
Avanti or a page of a novel before my eyelids are heavy with the sleep
men have named etc.[1] To make up I get up about 7 o'c and go out and
read in a café. I am reading *Sebastien Roch* by Mirbeau.[2] The beginning
deals with life in a Jesuit college. It must be difficult to succeed in
France where nearly everyone writes well. I should like to read Zola but
have not the heart to attack his twenty volume history of France. Who
called Moore the English Zola? I wonder: he must have had large
powers of comparison. I think I will read Mirbeau and Hardy together
alternately. What are you doing in this line at present? It is a very dark
cloudy day, drizzling rain. I wish some power would lift me as far as, say,
Talbot Street and let me walk about for an hour or so and then lift me
back again. My imagination is so weak that I am afraid all the things I
was going to write about have become uncapturable images. It is 9.30.
I would like to go asleep at present. My glasses annoy me. They are
crooked and there is a flaw in both of the glasses. It is a bloody nuisance
to have to carry bits of glass in your eye. A moment ago I was leaning
my head upon my hand and writing when the banker rushed past me.
He said something to me which I did not catch. I jumped up and went
to his desk obediently: I had not heard what he said. He repeated it,
however, smiling, it was 'Diritto, Signor Joyce. Non è bello così.'[3] They
are a funny lot, these bankers. There are four in all, two brothers
Schumacher and father and son Nast-Kolb, also a younger one. One of
them is like Ben Jonson with a big belly, walks sideways, wears a cap on
his head, blinks his eyes. The brother is a little man white-haired with a
pen behind his ear. These are the Schumacher brothers. One of them is
(the elder) is [sic] consul for Austria-Hungary. The other family
consists of father, who is very old, and bandy legged, with thick white
eyebrows. Every morning he patters in here, stops, looks about him,
says good-morning, and patters out again. The son, the brisk person, is
like Curran in manner and complexion. Yesterday they put down
carpets here: everyone said they were beautiful (How I hate that word).
I suppose it would be the height of impudence if I said I think they
are somewhat 'common' people. Anyway they talked a lot about the
carpet.

Letter just received. What I have told you about rooms is painfully

---

[1] 'Among pale eyelids heavy with the sleep/Men have named beauty.' W. B. Yeats,
'To the Secret Rose'.

[2] *Sebastien Roch* (1890), a novel which bitterly attacks the Jesuit school at Vannes
which Mirbeau attended as a boy. Joyce must have seen similarities to his own autobiographical novel.

[3] 'Sit up, Mr Joyce. That doesn't look well.'

correct. I don't know why we were given notice by the landlady nor do I know whether it was the reason you suggest.[1] I don't know anything except that I suppose I ought to cease grumbling and take up the white man's burden. Do you imagine you are corresponding with the indifferential calculus that you object to my vituperation on Italy and Rome. What the hell else would I do? If you had to traipse about a city, accompanied by a plaintive woman with infant (also plaintive), run up stairs, ring a bell, 'Chi c'è?' 'Camera' 'Chi c'è?' 'Camera!'[2] No go: room too small or too dear: won't have children, single man only, no kitchen. 'Arrivederla!' Down again. Rush off: give a lesson for 9½d, rush back to bank, etc etc. Am sending MS to John Long by same post. Didn't change anything. No pen, no ink, no table, no room, no time, no quiet, no inclination. Never mind, it will be back in a week or so. Only I stuck in 'bloody' before the late lamented.[3] How I should enjoy a night on Venetian waters with Miss Farchi's[4] romance and reality. The Italian imagination is like a cinematograph, observe the style of my letter. Wurruk is more dissipating than dissipation. Thanks for Whitman's poems. What long flowing lines he writes. Kick in the arse for the following. G.K.C: G.B.S: S.L: H.J: G.R.[5] Kicks in the arse all round, in fact. Write at once. Sent paper Sunday. Not surprised: Italian Post. Write. Via Monte Brianzo 51 IV° Rome   JIM

Tomorrow is a holiday![6]
  „   „   „   „   „
  „   „   „   „   „ !

Deo Gratias!
  „   „   !
  „   „   !

To STANISLAUS JOYCE   MS. Cornell

Postmark 10 January 1907   *Via Monte Brianzo 51, IV°, Rome*

Dear Stannie I have been so busy these days (and am so still) that I had no time to write. You appear to be exasperated at my financial distress. No wonder.

I am sending you *The Realist*[7] and O'Kelly's book, a story of which he

---

[1] Stanislaus Joyce had evidently proposed his brother's drunkenness as the reason.
[2] 'Who's there?' 'Room!'   [3] Queen Victoria. See p. 85n.
[4] A teacher of Italian in Trieste.
[5] G. K. Chesterton, George Bernard Shaw, Sidney Lee, Henry James, Grant Richards.
[6] Immaculate Conception Day.   [7] See p. 138.

is dramatising in *Sinn Féin*.[1] Also a paper called *The Republic*.[2] You
will notice that Cruise O'Brien's 'boy' is auditor of U.C. Debating
Society.[3] There is a Welshman who is teacher in the school. He dined
with us on New Years Eve and with him a lady manicurist. She invited
us to dinner for New Year's Day. She is young, lives alone, has a
beautiful quarter: long dress, nervous. She has manicured the King of
England. (*We* never say the 'King') All men are dolls or puppets, I
think, except the English. My hatred of Italy and Italians is on the
increase.

I had to suspend this letter for three or four days. I have not a
moment to myself all day. I have read *Tales of Mean Streets* by Morrison[4]
and *Plain Tales from the Hills*.[5] I suppose, after all, there must be some
merit in my writing. No word from Long or Mathews. If I knew Ireland
as well as R.K. seems to know India I fancy I could write something
good. But it is becoming a mist in my brain rapidly. I have the idea of
three or four little immortal stories in my head but I am *too cold* to
write them. Besides, where's the good. Ibsen, of course, may have liked
that kind of sport.[6] But then he never broke with his set. I mean,
imagine Roberts or Fay,[7] with an allowance from the Irish Republic
moving round Europe with correspondence tied at his heels like a goat's
tether and you have H.I.[8] In the same circumstances perhaps I too
would be an egoarch.

Anyhow I shall never be a model bank clerk. Everyone complains of
my writing. I would tell you also a story of a letter I wrote in Italian but
that it is *too bloody long to tell*. No more at present: rushing off to
WORK. [Scene: draughty little stone-flagged room, chest of drawers to
left, on which are the remains of lunch, in the centre, a small table on
which are *writing materials* (*He* never forgot them) and a saltcellar: in
the background, small-sized bed. A young man with snivelling nose sits
at the little table: on the bed sit a madonna and plaintive infant. It is a
January day.][9] Title of above: *The Anarchist*.

---

[1] *His Father's Son*, a play in three acts by Seamas O'Kelly, was serialized in *Sinn Féin*,
in the issues of 15, 22, 29 December 1906 and 5 and 12 January 1907.

[2] A nationalist weekly published in Belfast from 13 December 1906 to 16 May 1907.

[3] Francis Cruise O'Brien (1885–1927), son of J. Cruise O'Brien, was related by
marriage to the Sheehy family. Three years younger than Joyce, he was one of the ablest
students at University College, Dublin, in the years following Joyce's graduation. He was
prominent in nationalist politics and afterwards became a leader-writer for the *Freeman's
Journal* and then for the *Irish Independent*.

[4] Arthur Morrison, *Tales of Mean Streets* (London, 1894).

[5] By Rudyard Kipling (London, 1887).

[6] That is, total absorption in his work regardless of his environment.

[7] W. G. Fay, rather than his brother Frank, is probably meant.

[8] Henrik Ibsen.   [9] Joyce's square brackets.

I am stealing another moment to tell you that Aunt J— has written to me. The news is that O.G.'s mother is 'beastly dead'[1] and that O.G. is very rich. I wonder was this the valuable news O.G. had in mind. I suppose he will write again after a decent interval. But I fear nothing short of £150 a year, free of duty, would be of any use to me. The other day I was thinking about my novel. How long am I at it now? Is there any use continuing it? Everyone appears to think I am behaving very well better than they expected. But it's not pleasant behaving well to please people. I understand Nora is about to have another child. Certainly Georgie is the most successful thing connected with me. But he's only a small part mine. I think he rather likes me, however. When I come to eat he pulls over the chair and says 'Se' (sede). I bought him a rocking-hoss the night of the Epiphany. 4 L. Are you annoyed?

Next bout. They are celebrating this week in Sylvester's Church the union of the rites. Every morning a different rite. I should *love* to go. But I might as well be in Cabra for all I see of anything Coptic, Greek, Chaldean &c. Excuse the way I scrawl. Any minute the banker [breaks off]

To STANISLAUS JOYCE   MS. Cornell

[*?1 February 1907*][2]   *Via Monte Brianzo 51, IV°, Rome*

Dear Stannie, I read in the D.M. under the heading 'Riot in a Dublin Theatre' that a 'clerk' named Patrick Columb[3] and someone else were put up at the Police Courts for disorderly conduct in the Abbey Theatre at a performance of Synge's new play 'The Playboy of the Western World'. The story, I believe, is of a self-accused parricide with whom all the girls of a district FALL IN LOVE. The clerk P.C. said (he was fined 40s or 14 days) that nothing would deter him from protesting against such a slander on Ireland. There was also booing at certain strong expressions in the play. The evening ended in confusion. A

---

[1] Joyce is quoting a remark that Oliver St John Gogarty had evidently made about the death of Joyce's own mother. In *Ulysses*, p. 8 (8), Stephen Dedalus reproaches Mulligan for having said, 'O, it's only Dedalus whose mother is beastly dead.'

[2] Several riots occurred at the Abbey Theatre during the first run of *The Playboy of the Western World*, but the one referred to in this letter took place on Tuesday night, 29 January. The Northern Police Court proceedings were held the following morning. English newspapers took two days to come to Rome, so the date of this letter can be conjectured.

[3] Not the poet Padraic Colum, as Joyce assumed, but his father. The younger Padraic Colum wrote a letter to the press defending his father's action, and refused Lady Gregory's offer to pay the fine.

Trinity college youth created another row by singing 'God save the King'. W.B.Y.[1] gave evidence and said he could not hear one word of the play. When the police were first called in it was he and L.G.[2] who asked them to withdraw. They had decided, on account of the organised opposition, to run the play for a week longer than they had first intended. He would send free tickets to any who had been prevented from hearing the play. It was Synge's masterpiece, he said: an example of the exaggeration of art (I am glad he has got a phrase to add to that priceless one of Saint Booooof about style).[3] Synge was interviewed and said he claimed the right as an artist, to choose whatever subject he wished! I am waiting for the Dublin papers. Columb must either have been forsaken by Kelly[4] or have returned to his office since he is called a clerk. I suspect Synge's naggin is on the increase.[5] I knew, before now, that there was a schism in the theatre: as all of Columb's plays have been given by the 'Irish Theatre'[6] and the reviews of Yeats and Lady Gregory and Miss H O R N Y M A N's[7] productions which have appeared lately in Sinn Féin have been hostile. Yeats says the Irish obeyed great leaders in the past but now they obey ignorant committees. I believe Columb and the Irish Theatre will beat Y and L.G. and Miss H: which will please me greatly, as Yeats cannot well hawk his theatre over to London. However I am sure that many of the hermetists don't know which to choose. It is lucky for O.G. that his mourning allows him to wait a little longer. Synge will probably be condemned from the pulpit, as a heretic: which would be dreadful: so that Stiffbreeches[8] and Ryan[9] really *ought* to start another paper in defence of free thought, just for a week or so. I'm sure Ryan is the man for it. I suppose *Sinn Féin* and *The Leader* will find out *all* about Synge's life in Paris: which will be nice for Lady G and Miss H. And as for pore old A.E. I suppose he is nibbling cabbages up in Rathgar in quite an excited frame of mind at the amount of heresy which is rife in Dublin. Starkie writes a poem in *Sinn Féin* about the world-fruit withering on the tree and there being none to pluck it. But enough now of the mummers. That Southern X

[1] W. B. Yeats.

[2] Lady Gregory.

[3] Yeats was fond of Charles-Augustin Sainte-Beuve's remark, 'There is nothing immortal in literature except style.'

[4] Thomas F. Kelly, an American millionaire and the younger Colum's patron.

[5] Joyce had written in his broadside 'The Holy Office' of John Millington Synge as 'him who sober all the day/Mixes a naggin in his play'. The implication in this letter is that Synge is drinking too much.

[6] A rival to the Abbey Theatre in Dublin.

[7] Annie E. Horniman, the principal backer of the Abbey Theatre.

[8] W. K. Magee (John Eglinton).

[9] Frederick Ryan, editor with Magee of *Dana* in 1904–5. See p. 33n., p. 46n.

chap, SEÑOR Bulfin,[1] who is I am assured an Irishman, has a letter in Sinn Féin, ridiculing a Union Jack regatta in Galway. Two columns are consumed by his account of the talk of the classes. Ex: 'Nice weather' 'O, chawming' 'Chawming regatta', 'O, rawtha' 'Funny how little interest the country takes in these kind of things' 'Quite too awfully funny, doncherknow!' He makes great fun of the shake-hands over a five-bar gate and the [breaks off]

To STANISLAUS JOYCE   MS. Cornell

6 February 1907   [*Rome*]

I received and signed Mathews' agreement, as I told you. I wrote also to Long, as I told you, but that son of a bitch hasn't answered me yet. So I wrote to him peremptorily the day before yesterday. *Ulysses* never got any forrader than the title. I have other titles, e.g. *The Last Supper*, *The Dead*, *The Street*, *Vengeance*, *At Bay*: all of which stories I could write if circumstances were favourable. I wrote to Berlin some days ago for the Danish Berlitz Book which has just appeared. The news here is that we leave our present quarters on the 15th and go to live in the Corso, where Nora found a room. I expect she will be satisfied for a week or so. She is, as Reynolds's Newspaper would say, *enceinte*. Georgie is weaned. We eat lunch in the house and dine in a trattoria in the night. I took Nora and Georgie to a comic opera on Sunday 'Le Carnet du Diable'. I was very bored by the end. It was very silly and musicless. The *artistes* had no voices: but just one topnote or so. Georgie crowed now and again and when he did an idiot in front of us turned round angrily and said 'Sh!' I suppose he was afraid of missing some priceless sentence of the dialogue.

I read a few volumes of G de M.[2] lately for amusement and was amused by the same. Now I am on to Anatole France again. But if I want real esthetic satisfaction I must wait till the MS of *Dubliners* returns to me once more to roost. I have divided my papers, sending you *Independent* and *Mail* and Connellan[3] the others. By the way, the old servant in our place because we are leaving will not call me in the morning as she used to. Formerly she used to backbite her mistress to Nora: and she got a New Year's gift from Nora. She passes the door a dozen times in the morning without knocking. Isn't stupidity of that

---

[1] William Bulfin had visited the Martello tower in Sandycove when Joyce and Gogarty were living there in September 1904, and describes the encounter in *Rambles in Eirinn*, pp. 322–4.

[2] Guy de Maupassant.   [3] See p. 104.

kind distressing? I could tell you another pretty story about women.[1]
If you can spare the time you might just run over to London and kick
John Long's long arse for a few minutes or so, will you? He hasn't
answered me yet. Symons wrote me another card a day or two ago,
asking had I come to terms with Mathews and repeating that he would
do all he could for the book when it came out.[2] I mustn't forget to
dedicate it to O.G. or perhaps to the memory of his mother. Do you
remember my parody of Leo XIII's prayer after mass?[3] It has come into
my mind just now and made me laugh. Baby,[4] Poppie,[5] Pappie and
Charlie sent me picture postcards on my birthday! ! ! The postcards are
all coloured green, dark sea, sage, emerald, cabbage &c. In the school
here there is another Dubliner teaching, named Craig. He is another
Mug Ryan in appearance, tries very hard to conceal the drap in his
accent, comes from Kingstown. Has an irritatingly slow way of talking,
looking at the ground, appearing to meditate before he emits a word. I
suppose you saw old Cusack is dead.[6] I have given up reading *Avanti* but
enclose paragraph for Artifoni.[7] It was too dull for me. Kindly write soon
and long. About the money I find it difficult to do more than pull along.
Remember there are three people now. And I suppose it will be worse
when there are four but however.... I suppose I shall make a few shillings
out of the verses.   JIM

To STANISLAUS JOYCE   MS. Cornell

11 February 1907   *Via Monte Brianzo 51, IV°, Rome*

Dear Stannie I sent you yesterday copies of the F.J.[8] containing fuller

---

[1] Joyce is quoting a favourite ballad of his, 'The Yellow Ale', in which the speaker dies
because of his wife's infidelity. The song ends, 'And but that my own little mother was a
woman/I could tell you another pretty story about women.'

[2] Symons's postcard, now at Cornell, is dated 26 January 1907.

[3] This prayer, which Pope Leo XIII in 1884 ordered to be said kneeling after the
celebration of Low Mass, ended with the following words: 'Holy Michael the Archangel,
defend us in the day of battle; be our safeguard against the wickedness and snares of the
devil. May God restrain him, we humbly pray, and do thou, prince of the heavenly hosts,
by the power of God thrust down to hell Satan and with him all wicked spirits who
wander through the world for the ruin of souls. Amen.' Cf. *Ulysses*, p. 559 (427): 'And
snares of the poxfiend ... Thrust syphilis down to hell and with him those other licensed
spirits.'

[4] Joyce's sister Mabel (1893–1911), the tenth and last child in the family.

[5] Joyce's sister Margaret (1884–1964), the second child.

[6] Michael Cusack (1847–1907), founder of the Gaelic Athletic Association (1884) and a
model for the militant nationalist whom Joyce calls 'the Citizen' in the *Cyclops* episode
of *Ulysses*. Cusack used to refer to himself as 'Citizen Cusack'.

[7] He was a socialist and therefore interested in this socialist newspaper.

[8] *Freeman's Journal* (Dublin).

accounts of the Abbey riots. The debate[1] must have been very funny.
Our old friends Skeff. and Dick Sheehy seem to have just been taking
a walk round themselves since October 1904.[2] I read Sheehan's with
pleasure and surprise. I would like, however, to hear the phrases which
drove out the ladies with expressions of pain on their faces.[3] The pulpit
Irishman is a good fellow to the stage Irishman.[4] I see that Synge uses
the word 'bloody' frequently, and the great phrase was 'if all the girls in
Mayo were standing before me in their shifts',[5] wonderful vision. Yeats
is a tiresome idiot: he is quite out of touch with the Irish people, to
whom he appeals as the author of 'Countess Cathleen'.[6] Synge is better
at least he can set them by the ears. One writer speaks of Synge and his
master Zola(!) so I suppose when *Dubliners* appears they will speak of
me and my master Synge. Of course just the very week I wanted it most
Aunt J did not send *Sinn Féin*. As I told you before I think the Abbey
Theatre is ruined. It is supported by the stalls, that is to say, Stephen
Gwynn, Lord X, Lady Gregory etc who are dying to relieve the monotony
of Dublin life. About Synge himself I cannot speak. I have read only
one play of his *Riders to the Sea*, which made Yeats first think of the
Greeks (who are always with us)[7] and then of the early plays of the most
Belgian of Shakespeares.[8] Synge asked me to read it in Paris and when I

---

[1] A debate on the merits of *The Playboy of the Western World* was held at the Abbey
Theatre on 4 February 1907.

[2] In the *Freeman's Journal* of 5 February 1907, Francis Sheehy-Skeffington is quoted
as saying at the debate that he was both for and against. 'The play was bad, the organised
disturbance was worse, the methods [the police] employed to quell that disturbance were
worst of all.' Richard Sheehy declared, 'The play was rightly condemned as a slander on
Irishmen and Irishwomen. An audience of self-respecting Irishmen had a perfect right
to proceed to any extremity.'

[3] Daniel T. Sheehan (whom Joyce had known at University College) spoke, as a
peasant now working for a medical degree in Dublin, to defend Synge's play. He said,
in part: 'Mr. Synge had drawn attention to a particular form of marriage law which,
though not confined to Ireland, was very common in Ireland. It was with a fine woman
like Pegeen Mike and a tubercule Koch's disease man like Shaun Keogh—and the point
of view was not the murder at all, but when the artist appears in Ireland who was not
afraid of life and his nature, the women of Ireland would receive him.' The newspaper
reports that 'At this stage in the speech many ladies, whose countenances plainly
indicated intense feelings of astonishment and pain, rose and left the place. Many men
also retired.' An earlier phrase of Sheehan's about Irishwomen was 'lost in the noise'.

[4] Sheehan also said he came 'to object to the pulpit Irishman, just as they objected to
the stage Irishman'.

[5] This phrase, which does not appear in the published play, is mentioned in the same
issue of the *Freeman's Journal* as one that was 'struck out'.

[6] Joyce misread the account. What Yeats said was, 'The author of "Kathleen-ni-
Houlihan" appeals to you.' Unlike his earlier play, *The Countess Cathleen*, this one was
very popular with the nationalists, and his mentioning it brought cheers.

[7] Joyce had been especially scornful of the Greek dramatists in his early paper, 'Drama
and Life'.

[8] Maurice Maeterlinck (1862–1949). Octave Mirbeau, reviewing Maeterlinck's first
play, *La Princesse Maleine* (1889), in *Le Figaro*, labelled him 'le Shakespeare belge', and
the description clung.

told him what I thought of it and expounded a long critical attack on the catastrophe as he used it he did not pay the least attention to what I said. So perhaps his later work has merit. If Synge really knows and understands the Irish peasant, the backbone of the nation, he might make a duodecimo Björnsen.[1] Colm is out of the question and Russell and Coosins.[2] Sheehan seems to be a little different from the other young men with ideas in Ireland. I suspect he must have got a high place in all his exams and so can afford to treat the church on equal terms. This whole affair has upset me. I feel like a man in a house who hears a row in the street and voices he knows shouting but can't get out to see what the hell is going on. It has put me off the story I was 'going to write'—to wit, *The Dead.* John Long has not even answered my second letter. What am I to do?

I am reading at present some of the old Italian story-tellers, such as Sermini,[3] Doni[4] etc and also Anatole France. I wonder how he got his name. Crainquebille,[5] of course, is very fine and parts or rather phrases of his other books. However I mustn't complain since he suggested *Ivy Day in the Committee-Room*, and has now suggested another story *The Dead.*[6] It is strange where you get ideas for stories. Stupid little Woodman[7] gave me *The Boarding-House*, Ferrero *The Two Gallants.* Others I thought of myself or heard of. I have some kind of thing stirring in my head at present, but winter is my close season.

I expected a letter from you today, but none came. No papers from Aunt J——. I received a letter from Pappie the day before yesterday, in which he asked me for a £1.–/–/. I wrote, re-iterating what I had said about Charlie and one of the children[8] and saying that I could not send anything before the end of the month. The fact is I have little or no money this month. Nora being tired of our room took another one so that I am under double rent. On Friday we change and I must pay fresh rent L35.–. Moreover, relying on Padre Michele's word when he promised a rich private pupil, I chucked the school. P.M. came to the bank about ten days ago and asked me what I wanted for a private

[1] Björnstjerne Björnson (1832–1910), Norwegian writer, always overshadowed by Ibsen.

[2] A purposeful misspelling of the name of James H. Cousins.

[3] Gentile Sermini, Italian writer of novellas, who was born in the fourteenth century and lived into the fifteenth.

[4] Antonio Francesco Doni (1513–74), Italian writer of novellas.

[5] Anatole France, *L'Affaire Crainquebille* (Paris, 1901). France's real name was Jacques Anatole Thibault.

[6] Possibly by the story 'Le Procurateur de Judée', in which also the focus of attention is upon the dead man who never appears.

[7] Identified by Stanislaus Joyce as a Cockney schoolteacher who was teaching English as the Berlitz School in Trieste when his brother was first transferred there.

[8] He had probably suggested that his brother Charles and one of his sisters be sent to Trieste to join him.

lesson. I said $2\frac{1}{2}$ frs. Since then he has not appeared, so that I am in a beautiful stew. I am determined, however, that this borrowing shall not go on next month: as I intend to have a little liberty for myself both to read, write and rest. This month I am also without my pupil's money as he will not pay again, owing to holidays intervening, until exactly the 1st of March. However, I have new hat and boots and vests and socks and a Danish Book and Georgie has a new coat and hat and I gave a dinner. Now when you get this you will have to send me 10 crowns. I don't even know my future address, except that it is in the Corso! Write a short letter on good *thick* note-paper and place the note inside, addressing it to me c/o Messrs Nast Kolb & Schumacher, Via S. Claudio, Rome. I shall send you a card during the week telling you what else I shall want. You said you could give me 20 lire this month if I gave you proper notice. I shall probably want 30, as you see, I am unforseenly without the school. I daresay you are tired of these letters. I am too. Next month I shall adopt a different plan. I suppose I may rely, then, on your sending me 10 crowns by return of post. If you cannot send it I give up the problem. I might also mention the expenses incidental to my son and heir who has to have a new sheet and breaks panes of window and drinking vessels rather freely.

I must break off this letter now as I am not very well. All this trouble and bustle always finds its way into the bosom of my stomach. I was going to squander a lira on the *Dusk of the Gods*[1] tonight but am afraid that, in my present pendulous mood, I couldn't stand in the gallery for 3 hours. Let me hear from you to the above effect *by return* and advise me what I am to do to get back my MS from Long. My last bout with the law cost me 30 frs and Grant Richards nothing.   Jim

To Stanislaus Joyce (Postcard)   MS. Cornell

Postmark 14 February 1907   *Via Monte Brianzo 51, IV°, Rome*

Dear Stannie I expect you have my letter this morning and hope you will answer it by return of post. I have no idea how we are to finish the month unless you can help me. What you send I will pay you back punctually on the first as then, besides my pay, I will have 40 lire, 20 from my old pupil and 20 from a new one who is to begin then. I went to the *Dusk of the Gods*. Beside me in the gallery was an elderly man who smelt of garlic. He said it was a colossal opera and that it required great voices. He had heard it in Hamburg. He spoke a few words to me

---

[1] Richard Wagner's opera, *Götterdämmerung*.

in English, such as, very cold, very good and beautiful. Before me was another man who said Wagner's music was splendid but intended only for Germans. It was all intellect: no heart. Every time the horn motive sounded my garlicy friend twisted to me and said confidently: Adesso viene Sigfrido.[1] He yawned much during the third act and went away before the last scene. When Brunnhilde brought on the horse, the latter, being unable to sing, evacuated: whereat the funny Italian disyllable flew from end to end of the gallery. There were many spectators who followed the opera with scores and librettos. On the stairs coming away and in the street I heard many people hum correctly and incorrectly the nine notes of the funeral motive. Nothing in the opera moved me. I have heard the funeral march often before. Only when Siegfried dies I responded from the crown of my head to his cry 'O sposa sacra.' I suppose there are a few men from time to time who really feel an impulse towards Gawd.   [Unsigned]

To STANISLAUS JOYCE   MS. Cornell

16 February 1907   *Via Monte Brianzo 51, IV, Rome*

Dear Stannie, Nothing happened.[2] I understood that A.[3] promised me I could go back whenever I liked; otherwise I should not have given notice. Kindly state in what condition the school is. Could I not return to Trieste and give private lessons? It is a pleasant state of mind to be in. I suppose I have made a *coglioneria*.[4] You may imagine the state of my nerves. Who knows how this will end. For my part I have one life. I have felt lately that is slipping from me 'like water from a muslin bag'. Coppinger is a 'Merrion Square Surgeon'.[5] Synge is a storm centre: but I have done nothing. John Long has not answered me. I wrote him an insolent letter today: so I suppose I will never see the MS of *Dubliners* again. I would like to be in Trieste again not for the sake of the school but because I should sometimes have opportunity of meeting somebody who shared to a certain extent, my temperament. I am fond of Georgie, of course, but I fear (funny, just as I wrote the word two Americans ejaculated it opposite me) I fear that my spiritual barque is on the rocks. There is some element of sanity in this last mad performance of mine, I am sure. I feel somehow that I am what Pappie said I wasn't a

---

[1] 'Now Siegfried is coming.'

[2] Stanislaus Joyce evidently suspected that his brother had had some kind of trouble at the bank.

[3] Artifoni.   [4] 'A ball-up.'

[5] Charles Coppinger, M.D., of 17 Merrion Square North. His name was apparently mentioned in connection with the Abbey Theatre riots.

gentleman. But that is *balls*, as Rudolph Ellwood would say. Anyway I am a fish out of water. I would like to go back to Trieste because I remember some nights walking along the streets in the summer and thinking over some of the phrases in my stories. I have just been listening to Americans discussing Giordano Bruno in honour of whom there is a procession here tomorrow.[1] They seem to know something of him but I dislike the accent.

I will write you more fully on receipt of your letter. At present, I am too disturbed to write a long letter. Your *coglionato*[2] brother   Jim

To Stanislaus Joyce   MS. Cornell

[? *1 March 1907*]   *Via Monte Brianzo 51, IV°, Rome*

Dear Stannie, This letter I shall probably put aside once or twice in order to dispatch postcards to you. I shall also steer clear of any financial details at least until I have got the other thing off my chest first. I may say however that I would hardly have taken the step I took had I not relied on A's promise as a certainty: and moreover I understood from your letters that you had a great deal more to do than you could find time for. But let us 'hasten away' from that deplorable aspect of the case.

I have come to the conclusion that it is about time I made up my mind whether I am to become a writer or a patient Cousins. I foresee that I shall have to do other work as well but to continue as I am at present would certainly mean my mental extinction. It is months since I have written a line and even reading tires me. The interest I took in socialism and the rest has left me. I have gradually slid down until I have ceased to take any interest in any subject. I look at God and his theatre through the eyes of my fellow-clerks so that nothing surprises, moves, excites or disgusts me. Nothing of my former mind seems to have remained except a heightened emotiveness which satisfies itself in the sixty-miles-an-hour pathos of some cinematograph or before some crude Italian gazette-picture. Yet I have certain ideas I would like to give form to: not as a doctrine but as the continuation of the expression of myself which I now see I began in *Chamber Music*. These ideas or instincts or intuitions or impulses may be purely personal. I have no

---

[1] Giordano Bruno (c. 1548–1600) had been burned at the stake for his heretical philosophy on 17 February 1600. At the end of the nineteenth century he was rehabilitated, a statue was erected in the Campo de' Fiori in 1889, and an annual procession took place on his deathday.

[2] 'Balled-up', rather than the usual meaning, 'duped'.

wish to codify myself as anarchist or socialist or reactionary. The
spectacle of the procession in honour of the Nolan[1] left me quite cold. I
understand that anti-clerical history probably contains a large percentage of lies but this is not enough to drive me back howling to my gods.
This state of indifference ought to indicate artistic inclination, but it
doesn't. Because I take about a fortnight to read a small book. I was
about two days making up my mind to go and see the *Dusk of the
Gods*. I weighed the cold, the distance, the crush, discomfort &c.
Finally I went and tried to interest myself but was considerably bored.

The fault, I believe, is more mine than Wagner's but at the same time
I cannot help wondering what relation music like this can possibly have
to the gentlemen I was with in the gallery. By the way both the banker
and his brother seem to be well educated yet I have never heard them
discuss anything except the whereabouts of the 'blaues Heft' (the book
in which the exit of bonds is noted) and of the 'rotes Heft' (the book in
which the entry of same is noted). I have been trying to read Carducci's[2]
verses, induced by the fact that he died unfortified by the rites of R.C.C.
But not only does it not interest me: it even seems to me false and
exaggerated. I dislike Italian verse. I find Italian men lacking in delicacy
and virility. They are intelligent as a rule and clever but babyish. Of
delicacy neither their men nor their women have a scrap. I don't so
much object to its absence in the latter. The day of Bruno's memorial
procession I was standing among the crowd waiting for the cortege to
appear. It was a murky day and, being Sunday, I had not washed. I was
wearing a white felt hat, faded by reason of heavy rains. Scholz's five
crown cloak hung bawways[3] on me. My boots, being Sunday, were
coated with a week's dirt and I was in need of a shave. In fact, I was a
horrible example of free thought.[4] Near me were two good-looking
young women, females, of the people, that is. They were in charge of an
elderly woman and a middle-aged man. They were low-sized and quince-
coloured in the face with amiable dog's eyes. One of them had a trinket
on a long chain and this she constantly raised slowly to her lips and
rested it there, slowly parting them, all the time gazing tranquilly about
her. I watched her do this for quite a long time until I perceived that the
trinket was a miniature revolver! I tried to explain my sensation to one
or two Italians, narrating the fact as best I could. They saw nothing

---

[1] Giordano Bruno was born in Nola. Joyce had referred to him without further
explanation as 'the Nolan' in his early essay, 'The Day of the Rabblement'.
[2] Giosuè Carducci (1836–1907), the Italian poet.
[3] Irish expression meaning 'arseways'.
[4] 'You behold in me, Stephen said with grim displeasure, a horrible example of free
thought.' *Ulysses*, p. 23 (20).

strange in it or typical or significant. One of them told me that many Italian women wear a cazzo as a trinket and after that they talked to their heart's content about cazzo and Co—a topic which, in my opinion, it requires a great deal of talent or else a great deal of courage to render in any way interesting. When I enter the bank in the morning I wait for someone to announce something about either his cazzo, culo or coglioni.[1] This usually happens before a quarter to nine.

I received yesterday a letter from John Long in which he said that his reader had advised not to print the book and &c &c.[2] So *Dubliners* is once again roosting on my shelf. By the same post I received from Elkin Mathews the proofs of *Chamber Music*. It is a slim book and on the frontispiece is an open pianner! Shall I send you the proofs to correct. I don't know whether the order is correct. I don't like the book but wish it were published and be damned to it. However, it is a young man's book. I felt like that. It is not a book of love-verses at all, I perceive. But some of them are pretty enough to be put to music. I hope some-one will do so, someone that knows old English music such as I like. Besides they are not pretentious and have a certain grace. I will keep a copy myself and (so far as I can remember) at the top of each page I will put an address, or a street so that when I open the book I can revisit the places where I wrote the different songs.

I am sorry you have not written about the Abbey Street row.

I leave here for an unknown destination either the 15th or 30th of next month. I have written to various agencies and advts in different parts of Italy and France. But I would like to get out of Italy, if possible. I laughed at Eglinton and his cake but I fear I have eaten nearly all mine: still his must be a trifle stale by this. I would like to live in a warm town by the sea where I could write and think at leisure. Marseilles is not a tourist place but a port like Trieste and I chose it because it is cheap to get at, lively, good climate and must be cheaper than Rome. Besides the Italian colony there is 100,000. I detest office work. I would prefer even work in a shipping office at a harbour where I could go in and out. After all I must be worth something, even commercially. I know three languages[3] very well and two others[4] passably well and with Greenham and Sanguinetti[5] and here in Rome I have had 'experience' and I have written for 'Fortn. Review' 'Sat. Review' 'Speaker' *ETC*.

---

[1] Slang for 'penis, anus or testicles'.
[2] Long's letter of rejection, dated 21 February 1907, is at Cornell.
[3] English, Italian, and French.   [4] German and Danish.
[5] A Triestine business firm for which Joyce had evidently done some correspondence. Richard Greenham, an Englishman who lived in Milan in his later years, does not recall Joyce's work for him, and presumably it was of short duration.

I sent you today one of the proofs of the verses to see if the order is correct. The other I have corrected and sent back. I have answered several advts and hope to be able to get some position in which I can find the heart to go on with my writing. It seems to me better to try that line as it might bring me money. As for Nora and Georgie it seems to me easy to exaggerate. I suppose it will hardly come to starvation point. You seem to imagine that I should settle down to make myself a *carriera* here, beginning at 250 frs a month and ending 20 years hence at 450 frs a month, with all the accompaniments of such a *carriera*, a quarter, a servant, children at school, a small bank a/c and a great fear of everything in me. This is what I *should* do but I doubt very much if I *will* ever do it. We will see. Whatever happens it will hardly come to me as a surprise. I have changed a few verses in *Chamber Music* and have, that is, allowed my later self to interrupt the music, perhaps improving the poem as in the case of the Mithridates one.[1] But the verses are not worth talking about: and I begin to think neither are the stories.

[Unsigned]

To MARGARET JOYCE   MS. Cornell

8 December 1908   *Via S. Caterina 1, I°p°, Trieste (Austria)*

Dear Poppie Thanks for sending on the music. I have seen your letter to Stannie and his reply which is enclosed with this. I have an idea which you will tell me if you like. I will send Georgie among you for six weeks or so next summer in charge of Stannie if you think such a proposal would have the effect desired.[2] Neither he nor Stannie would be any expense as (if we can manage the thing at all) we shall pay all expenses of travelling and board with you. Perhaps he might be a good influence in your household and I fancy all of you would be glad to make his acquaintance. He could go about the end of July and come back to Trieste about the end of August or first of September. If you like the idea and think it likely to do good I shall write to Pappie myself.

I suppose you will think this a hare-brained idea like all the others I have had hitherto but if you walk round it for about a quarter of an hour and look at it from all sides it will begin to look right enough.

I will send him very gladly if that will make yiz all happy and loving. I told him I was going to and he has been canvassing all the people in the house for a valise to put his clothes in and go to 'Dubirino'.

[1] *Chamber Music*, xxvii.
[2] Margaret Joyce had urged her brother to try to reconcile John Joyce to his mésalliance.

Thank you, I feel a little better of the rheumatism and am now more like a capital S than a capital Z. Hoping this will find you as it leaves me at present, thank God, I am, dear sister, your Most Affectionate Brother   Jim

To G. Molyneux Palmer[1]   MS. National Library

19 July 1909   *Via Vincenzo Scussa 8, Trieste*

Dear Mr Palmer: I received safely your other three songs for which I thank you very much and beg you kindly to excuse me for not writing sooner. However, I was rather busy with rehearsals of a concert at which I had to sing in the quintette from the *Master Singers*. Do you understand the infatuation of people for this opera? I think it is pretentious stuff.

The second three songs please me better than the first five. The setting of the first is very delicate and the effect is finely sustained in the third. The rendering of 'Play on, invisible harps &c' follows the change of the verse splendidly. All the persons to whom I showed your music think it very distinguished.

I am going to Ireland this week and shall try to bring your songs under the notice of someone in Dublin who may bring them out. If you should happen to be in Ireland during the month of August I should be glad to meet you. My address is: 44 Fontenoy Street, Dublin.

There is no likelihood of my writing any more verse unless something unforeseen happens to my brain. I have written a book of stories called *Dubliners* and am in treaty with a publisher about it. Besides that I am at work on a novel *A Portrait of the Artist* at which I have been engaged now for six years. When (or rather *if*) either of these sees the light you may be sure I shall not fail to send you a copy of it.

I hope you may set all of *Chamber Music* in time. This was indeed partly my idea in writing it. The book is in fact a suite of songs and if I were a musician I suppose I should have set them to music myself. The central song is XIV after which the movement is all downwards until XXXIV which is vitally the end of the book, XXXV and XXXVI are tailpieces just as I and III are preludes. With kind regards

James Joyce

[1] Geoffrey Molyneux Palmer (1882–1961), an English organist and composer who came to live in Ireland.

To NORA BARNACLE JOYCE (Postcard)   MS. Cornell

Postmark 29 July 1909   *44 Fontenoy Street, Dublin*

We arrived safely here tonight.[1]

The first thing I saw on the pier at Kingstown was Gogarty's fat back but I avoided him.

All are delighted with Georgie, specially Pappie.

Write to one of the girls giving her directions about him.

With love to Lucia   JIM

To STANISLAUS JOYCE   MS. Cornell

4 August 1909   *44 Fontenoy Street, Dublin*

Dear Stannie, The article on Don Carlos[2] was not inserted.

Mr and Mrs Skeffington met me and invited me to their house: I did not go.

Russell and McGee[3] came up to me in the street and were very friendly. I went to see Curran and found him looking ugly and disposed to be unfriendly. Kettle is in the country. I have written to him asking him to make an appointment with me. Have got the list of Intermediate Board and will make application in due time.[4]

Maunsel and Co = Geo. Roberts and Maunsel Hone. From what I learn Roberts is the person Hone being an Oxford insipid. I called to see Hone: he was in Belfast. I met Roberts in the street and smoothed him down standing him a drink (I took lithia).[5] He is very self-important. I am to meet both of them to know their verdict on Monday next.

Have written to the Glasgow branch of Dun's Review, but got no answer. Best is away: so is Cousins. Here are some opinions of my appearance.

> *Aunt J*—lost all boyishness
> *Cosgrave*—in splendid health
> *Eglinton*—looking very ecclesiastical
> *Gogarty*—Jaysus, man, you're in phthisis.

[1] Joyce and his son George went to Dublin in late July 1909, remaining until 9 September.

[2] Don Carlos (1848–1909), pretender to the Spanish throne, died at Varese, Italy, on 18 July, and Joyce evidently wrote an article about him.

[3] W. K. Magee.

[4] Joyce had probably intended to apply for an appointment as examiner in foreign languages for the Intermediate Examinations, which were given to students in secondary schools throughout Ireland.

[5] A mineral water.

O'Leary Curtis[1]—much more mature
Sheehan[2]—very thin
Eileen[3]—very foreign-looking
Keohler—You look 35
Mrs Skeff[4]—Not a bit changed
Skeff—Somewhat blasé.
Everybody—Melancholy
Russell—Like a man of business.

Gogarty met me on Merrion Sq. I passed him. He ran after me and took me by the arm and made a long speech and was very confused. He asked me to go to his house. I went. He made me go in and rambled on. To everything I said 'You have your life. Leave me to mine'[.] He invited me to go down to Enniskerry in his motor and lunch with him and wife. I declined. I was very quiet and sober. He offered me grog, wine, coffee, tea: but I took nothing. In the end he said, blushing 'Well do you really want me to go to hell and be damned'. I said 'I bear you no illwill. I believe you have some points of good nature. You and I of 6 years ago are both dead. But I must write as I have felt'. He said 'I don't care a damn what you say of me so long as it is literature'. I said 'Do you mean that?' He said 'I do. Honest to Jaysus. Now will you shake hands with me at least?' I said 'I will: on that understanding'.

Byrne I have not seen.
Arthur Symons has G.P.I.![5]
Synge is said to have been syphilitic, poor man.[6]
Tell Nora to write to me   JIM

To NORA BARNACLE JOYCE   MS. Cornell

6 August 1909   *44 Fontenoy Street, Dublin*

Nora I am not going to Galway nor is Georgie.

I am going to throw up the business I came for and which I hoped would have bettered my position.

I have been frank in what I have told you of myself. You have not been so with me.

---

[1] William O'Leary Curtis (d. late 1920s), a Dublin journalist, is mentioned in Joyce's broadside, 'The Holy Office'.
[2] See p. 147n.
[3] Eileen Joyce (1889–1963), later Mrs Frantisek Schaurek.
[4] Hanna (Mrs Francis) Sheehy-Skeffington (1877–1946).
[5] General paralysis of the insane. Symons suffered a severe mental collapse in 1908.
[6] A false report, probably caused by the secrecy attending Synge's last illness.

At the time when I used to meet you at the corner of Merrion Square and walk out with you and feel your hand touch me in the dark and hear your voice (O, Nora! I will never hear that music again because I can never believe again) at the time I used to meet you, *every second night* you kept an appointment with a friend of mine outside the Museum, you went with him along the same streets, down by the canal, past the 'house with the upstairs in it', down to the bank of the Dodder. You stood with him: he put his arm round you and you lifted your face and kissed him. What else did you do together? And the next night you met *me*!

I have heard this only an hour ago from his lips.[1] My eyes are full of tears, tears of sorrow and mortification. My heart is full of bitterness and despair. I can see nothing but your face as it was then raised to meet another's. O, Nora, pity me for what I suffer now. I shall cry for days. My faith in that face I loved is broken. O, Nora, Nora have pity for my poor wretched love. I cannot call you any dear name because tonight I have learnt that the only being I believed in was not loyal to me.

O Nora is all to be over between us?

Write to me, Nora, for the sake of my dead love. I am tortured by memories.

Write to me, Nora, I loved you only: and you have broken my faith in you.

O, Nora, I am unhappy. I am crying for my poor unhappy love.

Write to me, Nora.   JIM

To NORA BARNACLE JOYCE   MS. Cornell

7 August 1909   *44 Fontenoy Street*

It is half past six in the morning and I am writing in the cold. I have hardly slept all night.

Is Georgie my son? The first night I slept with you in Zurich was October 11th and he was born July 27th. That is nine months and 16 days. I remember that there was very little blood that night. Were you fucked by anyone before you came to me? You told me that a gentleman named Holohan (a good Catholic, of course, who makes his Easter duty regularly) wanted to fuck you when you were in that hotel, using what they call a 'French letter[']. Did he do so? Or did you allow him only to fondle you and feel you with his hands?

---

[1] Vincent Cosgrave. His claim was false, as Joyce soon discovered.

Tell me. When you were in that field near the Dodder (on the nights when I was *not* there) with that other (a 'friend' of mine) were you lying down when you kissed? Did you place your hand on him as you did on me in the dark and did you say to him as you did to me 'What is it, dear?' One day I went up and down the streets of Dublin hearing nothing but those words, saying them over and over again to myself and standing still to hear better the voice of my love.

What is to become of my love, now? How am I to drive away the face which will come now between our lips? Every second night along the same streets!

I have been a fool. I thought that all the time you gave yourself only to me and you were dividing your body between me and another. In Dublin here the rumour here is circulated that I have taken the leavings of others. Perhaps they laugh when they see me parading '*my*' son in the streets.

O Nora! Nora! Nora! I am speaking now to the girl I loved, who had red-brown hair and sauntered over to me and took me so easily into her arms and made me a man.

I will leave for Trieste as soon as Stannie sends me the money, and then we can arrange what is best to do.

O, Nora, is there any hope yet of my happiness? Or is my life to be broken? They say here that I am in consumption. If I could forget my books and my children and forget that the girl I loved was false to me and remember her only as I saw her with the eyes of my boyish love I would go out of life content. How old and miserable I feel!   JIM

To STANISLAUS JOYCE (Postcard)   MS. Cornell

8 August 1909   *44 Fontenoy Street, Dublin*

Dear Stannie My business here is ended. As soon as you have collected the money send it on at once so that I may leave with as little delay as possible.   JIM

To NORA BARNACLE JOYCE   MS. Cornell

19 August 1909   *44 Fontenoy Street, Dublin*

My darling I am terribly upset that you haven't written. Are you ill?

I have spoken of this affair to an old friend of mine, Byrne, and he took your part splendidly and says it is all a 'blasted lie'.

What a worthless fellow I am! But after this I will be worthy of your love, dearest.

I sent you three enormous bags of shell cocoa today. Tell me if you get them right.

My sister Poppie goes away tomorrow.

Today I signed a contract for publication of *Dubliners*.

Excuse me to Stannie for not writing to him.

My sweet noble Nora, I ask you to forgive me for my contemptible conduct but they maddened me, darling between them.[1] We will defeat their cowardly plot, love. Forgive me, sweetheart, won't you?

Just say a word to me, dearest, a word of denial and O I shall be so transported with happiness!

Are you well, my darling? You are not fretting, are you? Don't read over those horrible letters I wrote. I was out of my mind with rage at the time.

I must go down now all the way to the G.P.O. to post this as the post has gone here: it is after one at night.

Good night 'my precious'!

No man, I believe, can ever be worthy of a woman's love.

My darling, forgive me. I love you and that is why I was so maddened only to think of you and that common dishonourable wretch.

Nora darling, I apologise to you humbly. Take me again to your arms. Make me worthy of you.

I will conquer yet and then you will be at my side.

Good night 'my dearest' 'my precious'. A whole life is opening for us now. It has been a bitter experience and our love will now be sweeter.

Give me your lips, my love.

> 'My kiss will give peace now
> And quiet to your heart.
> Sleep on in peace now,
> O you unquiet heart'[2]

JIM

To NORA BARNACLE JOYCE   MS. Cornell

21 August 1909   *44 Fontenoy Street, Dublin*

My dear little Nora I *think* you are in love with me, are you not? I like to think of you reading my verses (though it took you five years to find

[1] Byrne suggested to Joyce that Cosgrave and Gogarty were in cahoots to break up Joyce's marriage. See p. 163.
[2] *Chamber Music*, xxxiv.

them out). When I wrote them I was a strange lonely boy, walking about by myself at night and thinking that some day a girl would love me. But I never could speak to the girls I used to meet at houses. Their false manners checked me at once. Then you came to me. You were not in a sense the girl for whom I had dreamed and written the verses you find now so enchanting. She was perhaps (as I saw her in my imagination) a girl fashioned into a curious grave beauty by the culture of generations before her, the woman for whom I wrote poems like 'Gentle lady' or 'Thou leanest to the shell of night'. But then I saw that the beauty of your soul outshone that of my verses. There was something in you higher than anything I had put into them. And so for this reason the book of verses is for you. It holds the desire of my youth and you, darling, were the fulfilment of that desire.

Have I been cruel to you? One cruelty at least I have not been guilty of. I have not killed the warm impulsive life-giving love of your rich nature. Look now, dearest, into the deeps of your own heart and tell me that living beside me you have not seen your heart aging and hardening. No, you are capable of deeper finer feeling now than then. Tell me, my own little Nora, that my companionship was good for you and I will freely tell you all that your companionship has meant to me.

Do you know what a pearl is and what an opal is? My soul when you came sauntering to me first through those sweet summer evenings was beautiful but with the pale passionless beauty of a pearl. Your love has passed through me and now I feel my mind something like an opal, that is, full of strange uncertain hues and colours, of warm lights and quick shadows and of broken music.

I am so agitated, Nora dear, about how I am to get together money to bring over Eva[1] and myself and also to go to Galway to see your people. I wrote today to your mother but really I don't want to go. They will speak of you and of things unknown to me. I dread to be shown even a picture of you as a girl for I shall think 'I did not know her then nor she me. When she sauntered to mass in the morning she gave her long glances sometimes to some boy along the road. To others but not to me'.

I will ask you, my darling, to be patient with me. I am absurdly jealous of the past.

Be happy, my simple-hearted Nora, till I come. Tell Stannie to send me a whole lot of money and quickly so that we may meet soon. Do you remember the day I asked you indifferently 'Where will I meet you this

---

[1] Eva Mary Joyce was the eighth child in John Stanislaus Joyce's family, born 26 October 1891 and died 25 November 1957.

evening?' and you said without thinking 'Where will you meet me, is it? You'll meet me in bed, I suppose'.

Magari! magari![1]   JIM

To STANISLAUS JOYCE   MS. Cornell

21 August 1909   *44 Fontenoy Street, Dublin*

Dear Stannie The contract with Maunsel was stamped yesterday in the Stamp Office and the book will come out probably in March. The price is 3/6 nett. I am applying for the examinership as soon as the other certificates come. Kettle was most friendly to me but I received no invitation to Sheehy's[2] though they must know I am in Dublin. In the new National University there will be no chair of Italian only a lecture-ship in 'commercial Italian'! at £100 a year for lectures a few times in the week in the evenings. I could get it but would be ill-advised to take it. I have written to Synge's brother to know definitely about the play. I also went to the Abbey Theatre and they showed me the costumes used and are giving me the music of the Keen.[3] The manager is reserving a seat for me for the first performance of *Blanco Posnet*. I have had cards printed with the indication 'P.d.S.–, Trieste' and tomorrow am going to see the Manager of the Midland Rwy. I shall say I am on the Italian press and am writing a series of articles on Ireland and try to get a pass to Galway. Poppie went away yesterday to Kilkenny and will not be seen again until she goes to New Zealand.[4] I sent Nora a stone of shell cocoa. Pay the duty on it which cannot be high and see that Nora takes it *every morning* and *evening*. Kettle marries Mary Sheehy[5] on the 8 Sept. Kathleen[6] marries Cruise O'Brien. Skeffington has a son two months old. Caruso sang here yesterday. Neither Irish Times, Express, or Mail would allow me to interview him though at the Corinthian Club dinner he spoke to the toast in Italian and his reply was translated. An Italian Opera Co is playing here[7] (Aida Gonzaga[8] of 'I Puritani' last

[1] An Italian expression meaning 'I would it were so.'
[2] David Sheehy.   [3] In *Riders to the Sea*.
[4] Margaret Joyce was admitted to the Sisters of Mercy; she was sent to New Zealand, where she gave piano lessons in the convent.
[5] A daughter of David Sheehy. She was a model for Emma Clery in *Stephen Hero* and *A Portrait of the Artist*, though Joyce invented most of the romantic episodes in his novels. Stanislaus Joyce says she inspired two poems in *Chamber Music*, xii and xxv. In later life Mrs Kettle was surprised to learn that Joyce had a liking for her, and she can remember no signs of it.
[6] Kathleen Sheehy, another daughter of David Sheehy.
[7] Cavaliere F. Castellano's Italian Grand Opera Company at the Gaiety Theatre.
[8] Unidentified opera singer.

autumn) is in it [)] but I have been too distracted to go to it. I told the story of this miserable blackmail to Byrne and his opinion is that Gogarty and the other[1] are in collusion. He was very kind to me in the matter. He says that the other's price is half a crown. I liked very much his attitude. I think he is in love himself.

However—we will kill that too like the rheumatism. Eva must come back with me. It means the future happiness of my house: and Nora expects her to come. I rely on you to do all you can to that end and we shall have a fine winter of it.

Nora writes warmly of your kindness to her. Try to cheer her up now and we will put things right. Thanks: and if that was those bowsies' object thay have done just the contrary of what they intended   JIM

To NORA BARNACLE JOYCE   MS. Cornell

22 August 1909   *44 Fontenoy Street, Dublin*

Dear love How sick, sick, sick I am of Dublin! It is the city of failure, of rancour and of unhappiness. I long to be out of it.

I think always of you. When I go to bed at night it is a kind of torture for me. I will not write on this page what fills my mind, the very madness of desire. I see you in a hundred poses, grotesque, shameful, virginal, languorous. Give yourself to me, dearest, all, all when we meet. All that is holy, hidden from others, you must give to me freely. I wish to be lord of your body and soul.

There is a letter which I dare not be the first to write and which yet I hope every day you may write to me. A letter for my eyes only. Perhaps you will write it to me and perhaps it will calm the anguish of my longing.

What can come between us now? We have suffered and been tried. Every veil of shame or diffidence seems to have fallen from us. Will we not see in each other's eyes the hours and hours of happiness that are waiting for us?

Adorn your body for me, dearest. Be beautiful and happy and loving and provoking, full of memories, full of cravings, when we meet. Do you remember the three adjectives I have used in *The Dead* in speaking of your body. They are these: 'musical and strange and perfumed'.

My jealousy is still smouldering in my heart. Your love for me must be fierce and violent to make me forget *utterly*.

[1] Vincent Cosgrave.

Do not let me ever lose the love I have for you now, Nora. If we could go on together through life in that way how happy we should be. Let me love you, Nora. Do not kill my love.

I am bringing you a little present. It is all my own idea and I have had great trouble in getting it done as I wished. But it will always remind you of this time.

Write to me, dearest, and think of me.

What is a week or ten days to all the time of joy before us!   Jim

To Nora Barnacle Joyce (Illustrated letter card[1])   MS. Cornell

26 August 1909   *4 Bowling Green, Galway*

My dear little runaway Nora   I am writing this to you sitting at the kitchen table in your mother's house! ! I have been here all day talking with her and I see that she is my darling's mother and I like her very much. She sang for me *The Lass of Aughrim*[2] but she does not like to sing me the last verses in which the lovers exchange their tokens. I shall stay in Galway overnight.

How strange life is, my dear love? To think of my being here! I went round to the house in Augustine Street where you lived with your grandmother and in the morning I am going to visit it pretending I want to buy it in order to see the room you slept in.

[1] The illustrations are of Galway places: St Ignatius Church, the Claddagh, Salthill, Claddagh Church (interior), and Menlo Castle.

[2] Joyce had first heard this ballad or part of it from Nora Joyce. It impressed him so much that he made the ending of 'The Dead' turn upon it. The words tell how a woman who has been seduced and abandoned by Lord Gregory comes in the rain, their baby in her arms, to beg for admission to his house. Three of the verses run approximately as follows:

> If you'll be the lass of Aughrim
> As I am taking you mean to be
> Tell me the first token
> That passed between you and me.
>
> O don't you remember
> That night on yon lean hill
> When we both met together
> Which I am sorry now to tell.
>
> The rain falls on my yellow locks
> And the dew it wets my skin;
> My babe lies cold within my arms;
> Lord Gregory, let me in.

The late Donagh MacDonagh pointed out that this is a variant of 'The Lass of Roch Royal', No. 76 in F. J. Child, *The English and Scottish Popular Ballads* (New York, 1957), ii, 213–26.

I have asked them for photographs of you as a girl but they have none.

Who knows, darling, but next year you and I may come here. You will take me from place to place and the image of your girlhood will purify again my life.   JIM

To NORA BARNACLE JOYCE   MS. Cornell

31 August 1909   *44 Fontenoy Street, Dublin*

My darling It is now nearly two in the morning. My hands are shivering with cold for I have had to go out to bring home my sisters from a party: and now I must walk down to the G.P.O. But I do not want my love to be without her letter in the morning.

The ornament I had made expressly for you is now safe in my pocket. I show it to everyone so that everyone may know I love you, Nora dear, and think of you, darling, and wish to honour you.

I was singing an hour ago your song *The Lass of Aughrim*. The tears come into my eyes and my voice trembles with emotion when I sing that lovely air. It was worth coming to Ireland to have got it from your poor kind mother—of whom I am *very* fond, Nora dear.

It is perhaps in art, Nora dearest, that you and I will find a solace for our own love. I would wish you to be surrounded by everything that is fine and beautiful and noble in art. You are not, as you say, a poor uneducated girl. You are my bride, darling, and all I can give you of pleasure and joy in this life I wish to give you.

Nora darling, let our love as it is now never end. You understand now your strange erring wilful jealous lover, do you not, dearest? You will try to hold him in all his wandering moods, will you not, dearest? He loves you, believe that always. He has never had a particle of love for anyone but you. It is you who have opened a deep chasm in his life.

Every coarse word in speech offends me now for I feel that it would offend you. When I was courting you (and you were only nineteen, darling, how I love to think of that!) it was the same. You have been to my young manhood what the idea of the Blessed Virgin was to my boy-hood.

O tell me, my sweet love, that you are satisfied with me now. One word of praise from you fills me with joy, a soft rose-like joy.[1]

Our children (much as I love them) must not come between us. If they

---

[1] Compare *A Portrait of the Artist as a Young Man*, p. 177 (172–3).

are good and noble-natured it is because of *us*, dear. We met and joined our bodies and souls freely and nobly and our children are the fruit of our bodies.

Good night, my dearest girl, my little Galway bride, my tender love from Ireland.

How I would love to surprise you sleeping now! There is a place I would like to kiss you now, a *strange* place, Nora. Not on the lips, Nora. Do you know where?

Good night, beloved!   JIM

To NORA BARNACLE JOYCE   MS. Cornell

2 [September] 1909[1]   *44 Fontenoy Street, Dublin*

Dear Nora I have had no letter from you today and hope you have not written any to me addressed to Galway. I forgot to tell you not to.

I am in a wretched state of confusion and weakness on account of doing what I told you. When I woke up this morning and remembered the letter I wrote you last night[2] I felt disgusted with myself. However if you read through all my letters from the beginning you will be able to form some idea of what I feel towards you.

I have not enjoyed one day of my holidays. Your mother remarked my habit of sighing and said I would break my heart by it. I suppose it must be bad for me.

I hope you take that cocoa every day and are getting a *little* fatter on it. I suppose you know why I hope that.

I am worried to death about you, myself, the return journey and Eva. I hope Stannie will wire me enough for both of us.

Dublin is a detestable city and the people are most repulsive to me. I can eat nothing I am so agitated.

When is this cursed thing going to end? When am I going to start? My brain is empty. I can write nothing to you tonight.

Nora, my 'true love', you must really take me in hand. Why have you allowed me to get into this state? Will you, dearest, take me as I am with my sins and follies and shelter me from misery. If you do not I feel my life will go to pieces. Tonight I have an idea madder than usual. I feel I would like to be flogged by you. I would like to see your eyes blazing with anger.

I wonder is there some madness in me. Or is love madness? One moment I see you like a virgin or madonna the next moment I see you

---

[1] Misdated 2 *October* 1909 by Joyce.   [2] This letter has not survived.

shameless, insolent, half naked and obscene! What do you think of me at all? Are you disgusted with me?

I remember the first night in Pola when in the tumult of our embraces you used a certain word. It was a word of provocation, of invitation and I can see your face over me (you were *over* me that night) as you murmured it. There was madness in *your* eyes too and as for me if hell had been waiting for me the moment after I could not have held back from you.

Are you too, then, like me, one moment high as the stars, the next lower than the lowest wretches?

I have *enormous* belief in the power of a simple honourable soul. You are that, are you not, Nora?

I want you to say to yourself: Jim, the poor fellow I love, is coming back. He is a poor weak impulsive man and he prays to me to defend him and make him strong.

I gave others my pride and joy. To you I give my sin, my folly, my weakness and sadness.   JIM

To NORA BARNACLE JOYCE   MS. Cornell

3 September 1909   *44 Fontenoy Street, Dublin*

My true love Your present is lying before me on the table as I write, ready. I will now describe it to you. It is a flat square case of brown leather with two narrow golden borders. When you press a spring it opens and the case itself inside is cushioned with soft orange-coloured silk. A small square card lies in the case and on the card there is written in golden ink the name *Nora* and under that the dates *1904–1909*. Under the card is the ornament itself. There are five little cubes like dice (one for each of the five years we have been away) made of yellowish ivory which is more than a hundred years old. These are drilled through and strung together on a thin gold fetter chain the links of which are like small safety pins so that the whole string forms a necklet and the clasp is at the back beside the middle dice. In the centre of the chain in the front and forming part of the chain itself (*not* hanging from it like a pendant) there is a small tablet also of yellowish ivory which is drilled through like the dice and is about the size of a small domino piece. This tablet has on both sides an inscription and the letters are engraved into it. The letters themselves were selected from an old book of types and are in the fourteenth century style and very beautiful and ornamental. There are three words engraved on the face

of the tablet, two above and one underneath, and on the reverse of the
tablet there are four words engraved, two above and two below. The
inscription (when both sides are read) is the last line of one of the early
songs in my book of verses,[1] one which has also been set to music: and
the line is therefore engraved three words on the face and four on the
back. On the face the words are *Love is unhappy* and the words on the
back are *When Love is away*. The five dice mean the five years of trial
and misunderstanding, and the tablet which unites the chain tells of the
strange sadness we felt and our suffering when we were divided.

That is my present, Nora. I thought over it a long time and saw every
part of it done to my liking.

Save me, my *true* love! Save me from the badness of the world and of
my own heart!   Jim

To Nora Barnacle Joyce   MS. Cornell

5 September 1909   *44 Fontenoy Street, Dublin*

My dearest girl Tomorrow night (Tuesday) if I get money wired for I
hope to leave here with Eva and Georgie.

Now I have some news for you, my darling. My good friend Kettle is
to be married on Wednesday and tonight I had a conversation of four
hours with him. He is the best friend I have in Ireland, I think, and he
has done me great services here. He and his wife are coming to Trieste
to spend a day or two there during their honeymoon and I am sure that
you, my darling, will help me to give them a good welcome. Put the
house in order and be sure the piano is not lifted and see that your
dresses are right. Get the carpenter to deliver that table and stools. He
is a very good-hearted fellow and I am sure you will like his wife.
Unfortunately I have no money to make them a present. But I will send
on a copy of *Chamber Music* from London.[2] Tell Stannie to take it to my
binder and have it done exactly like the one for Schott[3] and at once so
that it will be ready when they come. We will try to entertain them the
best way we can and I am sure that my warm-hearted girl will be glad to
give pleasure to two people who are at the entrance of their life together.
Will you not, dearest?

[1] *Chamber Music*, ix.

[2] A grateful allusion to Kettle's complimentary review of this book in the *Freeman's
Journal*, 1 June 1907.

[3] Probably Enrico Schott, a patron of music then living in Trieste, and a friend of
Ettore Schmitz. Schott was responsible for bringing Gustav Mahler to Trieste to conduct
concerts in 1904 and 1906. Perhaps Joyce hoped that Schott would have some of the
lyrics of *Chamber Music* set to music and sung.

And now about ourselves. My darling, tonight I was in the Gresham Hotel and was introduced to about twenty people and to all of them the same story was told: that I was going to be the great writer of the future in my country. All the noise and flattery around me hardly moved me. I thought I heard my country calling to me or her eyes being turned towards me expectantly. But O, my love, there was something else I thought of. I thought of one who held me in her hand like a pebble, from whose love and in whose company I have still to learn the secrets of life. I thought of you, dearest, you are more to me than the world.

Guide me, my saint, my angel. Lead me forward. Everything that is noble and exalted and deep and true and moving in what I write comes, I believe, from you. O take me into your soul of souls and then I will become indeed the poet of my race. I feel this, Nora, as I write it. My body soon will penetrate into yours, O that my soul could too! O that I could nestle in your womb like a child born of your flesh and blood, be fed by your blood, sleep in the warm secret gloom of your body!

My holy love, my darling Nora, O can it be that we are now about to enter the heaven of our life?

O, how I long to feel your body mingled with mine, to see you faint and faint and faint under my kiss!

Goodnight, goodnight, goodnight!   JIM

To Nora Barnacle Joyce   MS. Cornell

7 September 1909   *44 Fontenoy Street, Dublin*

My little silent Nora Days and days have passed without a letter from you but I suppose you thought I would have left before now. We leave tomorrow night. By the end of the week or by Sunday we will be together, I hope.

Now, my darling Nora, I want you to read over and over all I have written to you. Some of it is ugly, obscene and bestial, some of it is pure and holy and spiritual: all of it is myself. And I think you see now what I feel towards you. You will not quarrel with me any more, will you, dear? You will keep my love always alive. I am tired tonight, my dearest, and I would like to sleep in your arms, not to do anything to you but just to sleep, sleep, sleep in your arms.

What a holiday! I have not enjoyed myself in the least. My nerves are in a dreadful state from worry of all kinds. Will you nurse me when I go back to you?

I hope you take that cocoa every day and I hope that little body of you[rs] (or rather *certain* parts of it) are getting a little fuller. I am laughing at this moment as I think of those little girl's breasts of yours. You are a ridiculous person, Nora! Remember you are now twenty-four and your eldest child is four. Damn it, Nora, you must try to live up to your reputation and cease to be the little curious Galway girl you are and become a full happy loving woman.

And yet how tender my heart becomes when I think of your slight shoulders and girlish limbs. What a rogue you are! Was it to look like a girl you cut away the hair between your legs? I wish you would wear black underclothes. I wish you would study how to please me, to provoke my desire of you. And you will, dearest, and we will be happy now, I feel.

How long the journey will be going back but O how glorious will be the first kiss between us. Do not cry, dear, when you see me. I want to see your eyes beautiful and aglow. What will you say to me first, I wonder?

La nostra bella Trieste! I have often said that angrily but tonight I feel it true. I long to see the lights twinkling along the *riva* as the train passes Miramar.[1] After all, Nora, it is the city which has sheltered us. I came back to it jaded and moneyless after my folly in Rome and now again after this absence.

You love me, do you not? You will take me now into your bosom and shelter me and perhaps pity me for my sins and follies and lead me like a child.

> I would in that sweet bosom be
> (O sweet it is and fair it is!)
> Where no rude wind might visit me.
> Because of sad austerities
> I would in that sweet bosom be.
>
> I would be ever in that heart
> (O soft I knock and soft entreat her!)
> Where only peace might be my part.
> Austerities were all the sweeter
> So I were ever in that heart.[2]

JIM

---

[1] Miramare is a white marble castle near Trieste, built in the Norman style by the Archduke Maximilian in 1854–6.

[2] *Chamber Music*, vi.

To Nora Barnacle Joyce   MS. Cornell

7 September 1909   *44 Fontenoy Street, Dublin*

Dearest Tomorrow night we leave. At the last moment I have managed
everything and Eva is coming. Prepare for us.

I was trying to recall your face but could only see your eyes. I want
you to look your best for me when I come. Have you any nice clothes
now? Is your hair a good colour or is it full of cinders? You have no
right to be ugly and slovenly at your age and I hope now you will pay
me the compliment of looking well.

I am excited all day. Love is a cursed nuisance especially when
coupled with lust also. It is terribly provoking to think that you are
lying waiting for me at this moment at the other end of Europe while I
am here. I am *not* in a *nice* mood just now.

Let me talk of your present. Do you like the idea? Or do you think it
as mad as myself? Has your mother or sister written to you about me?
I rather fancy they liked me. How stupid I am asking you questions you
have no time to answer!

Keep that piano and get a camp bed for Eva and Georgie. Be sure
and have a fine warm dinner or supper or breakfast for us when we
arrive. You will, won't you? You will let me feel from the first moment
I put my foot inside my house that I am going to be happy in every way.
Don't begin to tell me stories about debts we owe. I will ask you, darling,
to be as kind to me as you can be as I am dreadfully nervous from all the
worry and *pensieri* I have had, very very nervous indeed. How strange it
will be when I first catch sight of you! To think of you waiting, waiting
there for me to come back!

I hope you will like my sister Eva. People say it is unwise to bring a
sister into the house but you asked me to, dear. You will be kind to her,
I am sure, my good-hearted little Nora. And perhaps in two years' time
your sister Dilly will come to stay with us for a few months.

My darling, I have such a lot to tell you and will tell it to you every
night in the intervals of doing something else. What a moment that is,
dear! A brief madness or heaven. I know I lose my reason for the time it
lasts. At first how cold you were, Nora, do you remember? You are a
strange little person. And sometimes you are *very* warm indeed.

Have some appearance of money when I go back. Will you make me a
nice cup of black coffee in a nice small cup? Ask that snivelling girl
Globocnik how to do it. Make a good salad, will you? Another thing
don't bring onions or garlic into the house. You will think I am going to

have a child. It is not that but I don't know what to do I am so upset and excited.

My dear, dear, dear little Nora goodbye now for tonight. I wrote you every night. Now I am not *too* bad: and I am bringing you my gift. O, Lord, how excited I am!   JIM

To STANISLAUS JOYCE (Telegram)   MS. Cornell

12 September 1909   *Milan*

Domattina otto Pennilesse[1]

To NORA BARNACLE JOYCE (Postcard)   MS. Cornell

20 October 1909   *[Paris]*

[No salutation]

Reached here today and leave tonight for London.[2] Tell Stannie to call on *Latzer*[3] Via Veneziani, 2, II° to whom I wrote telling him my brother could give the lessons in my absence. Am rushing for train and fear I may miss it. Don't fret   JIM

To NORA BARNACLE JOYCE   MS. Cornell

[? 25 October 1909]   *44 Fontenoy Street, Dublin*

My poor little lonely Nora I let so many days go by without writing because only a few minutes before I left Trieste you called me an imbecile because I came home late after being so busy all day. But now I am sorry for you. Please, Nora, do not say these things to me any more. You know I love you. Busy as I am ever since I came I think all day of what presents I can bring you. I am trying to buy for you a splendid set of sable furs, cap, stole, and muff. Would you like that?

I feel the day all wasted here among the common Dublin people whom I hate and despise. My only consolation is to speak about you to my sisters whenever I can as I used to do to your sister Dilly. It is very cruel for us to be separated. Do you think now of the words on your ivory necklet? I have three distinct images of you always in my heart this

---

[1] 'Tomorrow morning at eight. Penniless.' The last word is mock-Italian.

[2] Joyce was on his way back to Dublin, this time alone, to start the first regular Dublin cinema, the Cinematograph Volta. His Triestine partners were to follow him as soon as he had completed preliminary arrangements.

[3] Possibly Paolo Latzer (1892–1956), whose family had come to Trieste from Graz a few years before.

time. First, as I saw you the instant I arrived. I see you in the corridor, looking young and girlish in your grey dress and blue blouse and hear your strange cry of welcome. Second, I see you as you came to me that night when I lay asleep on the bed, your hair loose about you and the blue ribbons in your chemise. Lastly, I see you on the platform at the station the moment after I said goodbye to you, half turning away your head in grief with such a strange posture of helplessness.

You dear strange little girl! And yet you write to ask if I am tired of you! I shall never be tired of you, dearest, if you will only be a *little* more polite[.] I cannot write you so often this time as I [am] dreadfully busy from morning to night. Do not fret, darling. If you do you will ruin my chances of doing anything. After this I hope we shall have many many many long years of happiness together.

My dear true good little Nora do not write again doubtfully of me. You are my only love. You have me completely in your power. I *know* and *feel* that if I am to write anything fine or noble in the future I shall do so only by listening at the doors of your heart.

What nice talks we had together this time, had we not, Nora? Well, we will again, dear. Coraggio! Please write me a nice letter, dear, and tell me you are happy.

Tell my handsome little son that I will come to kiss him some night when he is fast asleep and not to fret for me and that I hope he is better and tell that comical daughter of mine that I would send her a doll but that 'l'uomo non ha messo la testa ancora'.[1]

Now, my little bad-tempered bad-mannered splendid little girl, promise me not to cry but to give me courage to go on with my work here. I wish you would go to Madame Butterfly and think of me when you hear the words 'Un bel di'[2]   JIM

Keep my letters to yourself, dear. They are written for you.

To Nora Barnacle Joyce   MS. Cornell

27 October 1909   *44 Fontenoy Street, Dublin*

My darling Tonight the old fever of love has begun to wake again in me. I am a shell of a man: my soul is in Trieste. You alone know me and love me. I have been at the theatre with my father and sister—a wretched play,[3] a disgusting audience. I felt (as I always feel) a stranger in my own

---

[1] 'The man hasn't put the head on it yet.'   [2] In Act II.
[3] Either *Sweet Lavender* at the Gaiety Theatre or *The Still Alarm* at the Queen's Theatre.

country. Yet if you had been beside you [sic] I could have spoken into your ears the hatred and scorn I felt burning in my heart. Perhaps you would have rebuked me but you would also have understood me. I felt proud to think that my son—mine and yours, that handsome dear little boy you gave me, Nora—will always be a foreigner in Ireland, a man speaking another language and bred in a different tradition.

I loathe Ireland and the Irish. They themselves stare at me in the street though I was born among them. Perhaps they read my hatred of them in my eyes. I see nothing on every side of me but the image of the adulterous priest and his servants and of sly deceitful women. It is not good for me to come here or to be here. Perhaps if you were with me I would not suffer so much. Yet sometimes when that horrible story[1] of your girlhood crosses my mind the doubt assails me that even you are secretly against me. A few days before I left Trieste I was walking with you in the Via Stadion (it was the day we bought the glassjar for the conserva).[2] A priest passed us and I said to you 'Do you not find a kind of repulsion or disgust at the sight of one of those men?' You answered a little shortly and drily 'No, I don't'. You see, I remember all these small things. Your reply hurt me and silenced me. It and other similar things you have said to me linger a long time in my mind. Are you with me, Nora, or are you secretly against me?

I am a jealous, lonely, dissatisfied, proud man. Why are you not more patient with me and kinder with me? The night we went to *Madame Butterfly* together you treated me most rudely. I simply wanted to hear that beautiful delicate music in your company. I wanted to feel your soul swaying with languor and longing as mine did when she sings the romance of her hope in the second act *Un bel dì*: 'One day, one day, we shall see a spire of smoke rising on the furthest verge of the sea: and then the ship appears'. I am a little disappointed in you. Then another night I came home to your bed from the café and I began to tell you of all I hoped to do, and to write, in the future and of those boundless ambitions which are really the leading forces in my life. You would not listen to me. It was very late I know and of course you were tired out after the day. But a man whose brain is on fire with hope and trust in himself *must* tell someone of what he feels. Whom should I tell but you?

I love you deeply and truly, Nora. I feel worthy of you now. There is not a particle of my love that is not yours. In spite of these things which blacken my mind against you I think of you always at your best. If you would only let me I would speak to you of everything in my mind but

[1] See p. 45.   [2] 'Marmalade.'

sometimes I fancy from your look that you would only be bored by me. Anyhow, Nora, I love you. I cannot live without you. I would like to give you everything that is mine, any knowledge I have (little as it is) any emotions I myself feel or have felt, any likes or dislikes I have, any hopes I have or remorse. I would like to go through life side by side with you, telling you more and more until we grew to be one being together until the hour should come for us to die. Even now the tears rush to my eyes and sobs choke my throat as I write this. Nora, we have only one short life in which to love. O my darling be only a little kinder to me, bear with me a little even if I am inconsiderate and unmanageable and believe me we will be happy together. Let me love you in my own way. Let me have your heart always close to mine to hear every throb of my life, every sorrow, every joy.

Do you remember that Sunday evening coming back from *Werther*[1] when the echo of the sad deathlike music was still playing in our memories that, lying on the bed in our room, I tried to say to you those verses I like so much of the *Connacht Love Song* which begin

> 'It is far and it is far
> To Connemara where you are'[2]

Do you remember that I could not finish the verses? The immense emotion of tender worship for your image which broke out in my voice as I repeated the lines was too much for me. My love for you is really a kind of adoration.

Now, dearest, I want us to be happy. Try to get yourself into better health while I am away and please obey me in the small things I ask you to do. First, to eat as much as you can so that you may become more like a woman than the dear awkward-looking simple slender little girl you are. If that cocoa is out get Stannie to send an order for more: the cost is 5s/6d. In the meantime drink plenty of the other cocoa and chocolate. Pay some off the bill to your dressmaker. I sent you today two books of patterns to choose from. On Saturday I send you seven or eight yards of Donegal tweed to have a new dress made from. I have been inquiring about a set of furs for you and if my business turns out well here I will simply smother you in furs and dresses and cloaks of all kinds. I have some very fine furs in my mind for you.

[1] Jules Massenet, *Werther* (1892).
[2] Actually the 'Mayo Love Song', words by Alice L. Milligan, music by C. Milligan Fox. It is included in Charlotte Milligan Fox, *Four Irish Songs* (Dublin: Maunsel, n.d. but about 1909). The two lines that follow those quoted by Joyce are:
> To where its purple glens enfold you
> As glooming heavens that hold a star . . .

Write now, my dear love, and tell me you are doing what I ask. Tell me you are happy because you see that I love you and am true to you and think of you. I am true to you, Nora, and I think of you all day and always.

Goodnight, darling. Be happy for this short time we are divided, and whenever you think of me give a kiss to my image in Georgie.

Addio, mia *cara* Nora!   JIM

To NORA BARNACLE JOYCE   MS. Cornell

1 November 1909   *44 Fontenoy Street, Dublin*

My dear little Butterfly I got your letter this evening and am glad you like that photograph of your unworthy lover taken in all his warpaint. I hope you got my little present of gloves safely. I sent them just as I sent you my first present five years ago—from the 'Ship.' The nicest pair is that one of reindeer skin: it is lined with its own skin, simply turned inside out and should be warm, nearly as warm as certain districts of your body, Butterfly. Twelve yards (not eleven as I wrote) of tweed were sent you from Donegal. I would like the coat of your dress to reach nearly the base of the skirt and to be collared, belted and cuffed with dark blue *leather* and lined with bronze or dark blue satin. If this affair comes off and I am continued beyond the fifth of November and receive fresh money I hope to send you a splendid set of furs which I am selecting specially. They are grey squirrel. There would be a grey squirrel cap with violets at the side and a long broad flat stole of grey squirrel and a beige granny muff of the same on a steel chain, both lined with violet satin. Would you like that, dear? I hope I may be able to get it for you. I am also getting ready a special Xmas present for you. I have bought specially cut sheets of parchment and am copying out on them all my book of verses in indelible Indian ink. Then I will get them bound in a curious way I like myself and this book will last hundreds of years. I will burn all the other MSS of my verses and you will then have the only one in existence. It is very hard to copy on parchment but I work at it hoping it will give pleasure to the woman I love.

It is two o'clock at night. I have been copying here alone in the kitchen since they all went to bed and now I am writing to you. I wish I could look up and encounter those dog's eyes of yours. I will try to deserve the trust they have in me.

Do not fret, little Butterfly. Here are a few lines of verse written four hundred years ago by a poet who was a friend of Shakespeare's:

Tears kill the heart, believe.
O strive not to be excellent in woe
Which only breeds your beauty's overthrow.[1]

You are a sad little person and I am a devillishly melancholy fellow myself so that ours is a rather mournful love I fancy. Do not cry about that tiresome young gentleman in the photograph. He is not worth it, dear.

It is very good of you to enquire about that damned dirty affair of mine.[2] It is no worse anyhow. I was alarmed at your silence first. I feared you had something wrong. But you are all right, are you not, dearest? Thank God! Poor little Nora, how bad I am to you!

Never mind Eva but you might see that Stannie looks after himself. I hope he is better now. Addio, Giorgino e Lucetta! Vengo subito![3] And addio, Nora mia!   JIM

To NORA BARNACLE JOYCE   MS. Cornell

18 November 1909   *44 Fontenoy Street, Dublin*

[No salutation]

I dare not address you tonight by any familiar name.

All day, since I read your letter this morning, I have felt like a mongrel dog that has received a lash across the eyes. I have been awake now for two whole days and I wandered about the streets like some filthy cur whose mistress had cut him with her whip and hunted him from her door.

You write like a queen. As long as I live I shall always remember the quiet dignity of that letter, its sadness and scorn, and the utter humiliation it caused me.

I have lost your esteem. I have worn down your love. Leave me then. Take away your children from me to save them from the curse of my presence. Let me sink back again into the mire I came from. Forget me and my empty words. Go back to your own life and let me go alone to my ruin. It is wrong for you to live with a vile beast like me or to allow your children to be touched by my hands.

Act bravely as you have always done. If you decide to leave me in disgust I will bear it like a man, knowing that I deserve it a thousand times over, and will allow you two thirds of my income.

---

[1] From John Dowland, 'I saw my lady weep', in his *Second Booke of Songs or Ayres* (1600).

[2] A minor complaint probably contracted from a prostitute.

[3] 'I'm coming at once.'

I begin to see it now. I have killed your love. I have filled you with disgust and scorn for me. Leave me now to the things and companions I was so fond of. I will not complain. I have no right to complain or to raise my eyes to you any more. I have utterly degraded myself in your sight.

Leave me. It is a degradation and a shame for you to live with a low wretch like me. Act bravely and leave me. You have given me the finest things in this world but you were only casting pearls before swine.

If you leave me I shall live for ever with your memory, holier than God to me. I shall pray to your name.

Nora, remember something good of the poor wretch who dishonoured you with his love. Think that your lips have kissed him and your hair has fallen over him and that your arms have held him to you.

I will not sign my name because it is the name you called me when you loved me and honoured me and gave me your young tender soul to wound and betray.

To NORA BARNACLE JOYCE   MS. Cornell

19 November 1909   *44 Fontenoy Street, Dublin*

[No salutation]

I received two very kind letters from her today so that perhaps after all she still cares for me. Last night I was in a state of utter despair when I wrote to her. Her slightest word has an enormous power over me. She asks me to try to forget the ignorant Galway girl that came across my life and says I am too kind to her. Foolish good-hearted girl! Does she not see what a worthless treacherous fool I am? Her love for me perhaps blinds her to it.

I shall never forget how her short letter to me yesterday cut me to the quick. I felt that I had tried her goodness too far and that at last she had turned on me with quiet scorn.

Today I went to the hotel where she lived when I first met her. I halted in the dingy doorway before going in I was so excited. I have not told them my name but I have an impression that they know who I am. Tonight I was sitting at the table in the dining-room at the end of the hall with two Italians at dinner. I ate nothing. A pale-faced girl waited at table, perhaps her successor.

The place is very Irish. I have lived so long abroad and in so many countries that I can feel at once the voice of Ireland in anything. The disorder of the table was Irish, the wonder on the faces also, the curious-looking eyes of the woman herself and her waitress. A strange land this is to me though I was born in it and bear one of its old names.

I have been in the room where she passed so often, with a strange dream of love in her young heart. My God, my eyes are full of tears! Why do I cry? I cry because it is so sad to think of her moving about that room, eating little, simply dressed, simple-mannered and watchful, and carrying always with her in her secret heart the little flame which burns up the souls and bodies of men.

I cry too with pity for her that she should have chosen such poor ignoble love as mine: and with pity for myself that I was not worthy to be loved by her.

A strange land, a strange house, strange eyes and the shadow of a strange, strange girl standing silently by the fire, or gazing out of the window across the misty College park. What a mysterious beauty clothes every place where she has lived!

Twice while I was writing these sentences tonight the sobs gathered quickly in my throat and broke from my lips.

I have loved in her the image of the beauty of the world, the mystery and beauty of life itself, the beauty and doom of the race of whom I am a child, the images of spiritual purity and pity which I believed in as a boy.

Her soul! Her name! Her eyes! They seem to me like strange beautiful blue wild-flowers growing in some tangled, rain-drenched hedge.[1] And I have felt her soul tremble beside mine, and have spoken her name softly to the night, and have wept to see the beauty of the world passing like a dream behind her eyes.   [Unsigned]

To Nora Barnacle Joyce   MS. Cornell

22 November 1909   *44 Fontenoy Street, Dublin*

Dearest Your telegram lay on my heart that night. When I wrote you those last letters I was in utter despair. I thought I had lost your love and esteem—as I well deserved to do. Your letter to me this morning is very kind but I am waiting for the letter you probably wrote after sending the telegram.

I hardly dare to be anyway familiar with you yet, dear, until you give me leave again. I feel I ought not to, though your letter is written in your old familiar roguish way. I mean, when you say what you will do to me if I disobey you in a certain matter.[2]

---

[1] In Act I of *Exiles*, Robert Hand calls Bertha, 'A wild flower blooming in a hedge.'
[2] Compare Martha Clifford's letter in *Ulysses*, p. 95 (77–8).

I will venture to say just one thing. You say you want my sister to bring you across some underlinen. Please don't, dear. I don't like anyone, even a woman or a girl, to see things belonging to you. I wish you were more particular in leaving certain clothes of yours about, I mean, when they have come from the wash. O, I wish that you kept all those things *secret, secret, secret*. I wish you had a great store of all kinds of underclothes, in all delicate shades, stored away in a great perfumed press.

How wretched it is to be away from you! Have you taken your poor lover to your heart again? I shall long for your letter and yet I thank you for your kind good telegram.

Do not ask me to write a long letter now, dearest. What I have written above has saddened me a little. I am tired of sending words to you. Our lips together, our arms interwoven, our eyes swooning in the sad joy of possession, would please me more.

Pardon me, dearest. I intended to be more reserved. Yet I must long and long and long for you.   Jim

---

To Nora Barnacle Joyce   MS. Cornell

27 November 1909 Saturday evg.   [*Dublin*]

Dearest Nora I leave tonight in a moment for Belfast[1] and must miss your letter tonight. Tomorrow I come back and will write again. Dream of me Your lover   Jim

---

To Nora Barnacle Joyce   MS. Cornell

2 December 1909   *44 Fontenoy Street, Dublin*

My darling I ought to begin by begging your pardon, perhaps, for the extraordinary letter I wrote you last night.[2] While I was writing it your letter was lying in front of me and my eyes were fixed, as they are even now, on a certain word in it. There is something obscene and lecherous in the very look of the letters. The sound of it too is like the act itself, brief, brutal, irresistible and devilish.

Darling, do not be offended at what I wrote. You thank me for the beautiful name I gave you. Yes, dear, it is a nice name 'My beautiful wild flower of the hedges! My dark-blue, rain-drenched flower!'. You see I am a little of a poet still. I am giving you a lovely book for a present too: and it is a poet's present for the woman he loves. But, side

---

[1] The partners were also considering new cinemas in Belfast and Cork.
[2] Joyce's letter of 1 December 1909 has not survived.

by side and inside this spiritual love I have for you there is also a wild
beast-like craving for every inch of your body, for every secret and
shameful part of it, for every odour and act of it. My love for you allows
me to pray to the spirit of eternal beauty and tenderness mirrored in
your eyes or to fling you down under me on that soft belly of yours and
fuck you up behind, like a hog riding a sow, glorying in the very stink
and sweat that rises from your arse, glorying in the open shame of your
upturned dress and white girlish drawers and in the confusion of your
flushed cheeks and tangled hair. It allows me to burst into tears of pity
and love at some slight word, to tremble with love for you at the sound-
ing of some chord or cadence of music or to lie heads and tails with you
feeling your fingers fondling and tickling my ballocks or stuck up in me
behind and your hot lips sucking off my cock while my head is wedged
in between your fat thighs, my hands clutching the round cushions of
your bum and my tongue licking ravenously up your rank red cunt. I
have taught you almost to swoon at the hearing of my voice singing or
murmuring to your soul the passion and sorrow and mystery of life and
at the same time have taught you to make filthy signs to me with your
lips and tongue, to provoke me by obscene touches and noises, and even
to do in my presence the most shameful and filthy act of the body.
You remember the day you pulled up your clothes and let me lie under
you looking up at you while you did it? Then you were ashamed even to
meet my eyes.

You are mine, darling, mine! I love you. All I have written above is
only a moment or two of brutal madness. The last drop of seed has
hardly been squirted up your cunt before it is over and my true love
for you, the love of my verses, the love of my eyes for your strange luring
eyes, comes blowing over my soul like a wind of spices. My prick is still
hot and stiff and quivering from the last brutal drive it has given you
when a faint hymn is heard rising in tender pitiful worship of you from
the dim cloisters of my heart.

Nora, my faithful darling, my sweet-eyed blackguard schoolgirl, be
my whore, my mistress, as much as you like (my little frigging mistress!
my little fucking whore!) you are always my beautiful wild flower of the
hedges, my dark-blue rain-drenched flower.   JIM

To NORA BARNACLE JOYCE   MS. Cornell

3 December 1909   *44 Fontenoy Street, Dublin*

My darling little convent-girl, There is some star too near the earth for
I am still in a fever-fit of animal desire. Today I stopped short often in

the street with an exclamation whenever I thought of the letters I wrote you last night and the night before. They must read awful in the cold light of day. Perhaps their coarseness has disgusted you. I know you are a much finer nature than your extraordinary lover and though it was you yourself, you hot little girl, who first wrote to me saying that you were longing to be fucked by me yet I suppose the wild filth and obscenity of my reply went beyond all bounds of modesty. When I got your express letter this morning and saw how careful you are of your worthless Jim I felt ashamed of what I had written. Yet now, night, secret sinful night, has come down again on the world and I am alone again writing to you and your letter is again folded before me on the table. Do not ask me to go to bed, dear. Let me write to you, dear.

As you know, dearest, I never use obscene phrases in speaking. You have never heard me, have you, utter an unfit word before others. When men tell in my presence here filthy or lecherous stories I hardly smile. Yet you seem to turn me into a beast. It was you yourself, you naughty shameless girl who first led the way. It was not I who first touched you long ago down at Ringsend. It was you who slid your hand down down inside my trousers and pulled my shirt softly aside and touched my prick with your long tickling fingers and gradually took it all, fat and stiff as it was, into your hand and frigged me slowly until I came off through your fingers, all the time bending over me and gazing at me out of your quiet saintlike eyes. It was your lips too which first uttered an obscene word. I remember *well* that night in bed in Pola. Tired of lying under a man one night you tore off your chemise violently and got on top of me to ride me naked. You stuck my prick into your cunt and began to ride me up and down. Perhaps the horn I had was not big enough for you for I remember that you bent down to my face and murmured tenderly 'Fuck up, love! fuck up, love!'

Nora dear, I am dying all day to ask you one or two questions. Let me, dear, for I have told you *every*thing I ever did and so I can ask you in turn. I wonder will you answer them. When that person[1] whose heart I long to stop with the click of a revolver put his hand or hands under your skirts did he only tickle you outside or did he put his finger or fingers up into you? If he did, did they go up far enough to touch that little cock at the end of your cunt? Did he touch you behind? Was he a long time tickling you and did you come? Did he ask you to touch him and did you do so? If you did not touch him did he come against you and did you feel it?

Another question, Nora. I know that I was the first man that blocked

[1] Vincent Cosgrave.

you but did any man ever frig you? Did that boy[1] you were fond of ever
do it? Tell me now, Nora, truth for truth, honesty for honesty. When
you were with him in the dark at night did your fingers *never, never*
unbutton his trousers and slip inside like mice? Did you ever frig him,
dear, tell me truly or anyone else? Did you *never never, never* feel a
man's or a boy's prick in your fingers until you unbuttoned me? If you
are not offended do not be afraid to tell me the truth. Darling, darling,
tonight I have such a wild lust for your body that if you were here
beside me and even if you told me with your own lips that half the red-
headed louts in the county Galway had had a fuck at you before me I
would still rush at you with desire.

God Almighty, what kind of language is this I am writing to my
proud blue-eyed queen! Will she refuse to answer my coarse insulting
questions? I know I am risking a good deal in writing this way, but if
she loves me really she will feel that I am mad with lust and that I must
be told all.

Sweetheart, answer me. Even if I learn that you too have sinned
perhaps it would bind me even closer to you. In any case I love you. I
have written and said things to you that my pride would *never again*
allow me to say to any woman.

My darling Nora, I am panting with eagerness to get your replies to
these filthy letters of mine. I write to you openly because I feel now that
I can keep my word with you.

Don't be angry, dear, dear, Nora, my little wild-flower of the hedges.
I love your body, long for it, dream of it.

Speak to me, dear lips that I have kissed in tears. If this filth I have
written insults you bring me to my senses again with the lash as you
have done before. God help me!

I love you, Nora, and it seems that this too is part of my love. Forgive
me! forgive me!   JIM

To NORA BARNACLE JOYCE   MS. Cornell

6 December 1909   *44 Fontenoy Street, Dublin*

Noretta mia! I got your pitiful letter this evening telling me you were
going about without underclothes. I did not get 200 crowns on the 25th
but only 50 crowns and 50 again on the 1st. Enough about money. I
send you a little banknote and hope you may be able to buy a pretty
frilly pair of drawers at least for yourself out of it and will send you

---

[1] Michael Bodkin. See p. 201n.

more when I am paid again. I would like you to wear drawers with three or four frills one over the other at the knees and up the thighs and great crimson bows in them, I mean not schoolgirls' drawers with a thin shabby lace border, tight round the legs and so thin that the flesh shows between them but women's (or if you prefer the word) ladies' drawers with a full loose bottom and wide legs, all frills and lace and ribbons, and heavy with perfume so that whenever you show them, whether in pulling up your clothes hastily to do something or in cuddling yourself up prettily to be blocked, I can see only a swelling mass of white stuff and frills and so that when I bend down over you to open them and give you a burning lustful kiss on your naughty bare bum I can smell the perfume of your drawers as well as the warm odour of your cunt and the heavy smell of your behind.

Have I shocked you by the dirty things I wrote to you. You think perhaps that my love is a filthy thing. It is, darling, at some moments. I dream of you in filthy poses sometimes. I imagine things so *very* dirty that I will not write them until I see how you write yourself. The smallest things give me a great cockstand—a whorish movement of your mouth, a little brown stain on the seat of your white drawers, a sudden dirty word spluttered out by your wet lips, a sudden immodest noise made by you behind and then a bad smell slowly curling up out of your backside. At such moments I feel mad to do it in some filthy way, to feel your hot lecherous lips sucking away at me, to fuck between your two rosy-tipped bubbies, to come on your face and squirt it over your hot cheeks and eyes, to stick it up between the cheeks of your rump and bugger you.

Basta per stasera![1]

I hope you got my telegram and *understood* it.

Goodbye, my darling whom I am trying to degrade and deprave. How on God's earth can you possibly love a thing like me?

O, I am so anxious to get your reply, darling!   JIM

To NORA BARNACLE JOYCE   MS. Cornell

8 December 1909   *44 Fontenoy Street, Dublin*

My sweet little whorish Nora I did as you told me, you dirty little girl, and pulled myself off twice when I read your letter. I am delighted to see that you do like being fucked arseways. Yes, now I can remember that night when I fucked you for so long backwards. It was the dirtiest

[1] 'Enough for this evening!'

fucking I ever gave you, darling. My prick was stuck up in you for hours, fucking in and out under your upturned rump. I felt your fat sweaty buttocks under my belly and saw your flushed face and mad eyes. At every fuck I gave you your shameless tongue came bursting out through your lips and if I gave you a bigger stronger fuck than usual fat dirty farts came spluttering out of your backside. You had an arse full of farts that night, darling, and I fucked them out of you, big fat fellows, long windy ones, quick little merry cracks and a lot of tiny little naughty farties ending in a long gush from your hole. It is wonderful to fuck a farting woman when every fuck drives one out of her. I think I would know Nora's fart anywhere. I think I could pick hers out in a roomful of farting women. It is a rather girlish noise not like the wet windy fart which I imagine fat wives have. It is sudden and dry and dirty like what a bold girl would let off in fun in a school dormitory at night. I hope Nora will let off no end of her farts in my face so that I may know their smell also.

You say when I go back you will suck me off and you want me to lick your cunt, you little depraved blackguard. I hope you will surprise me some time when I am asleep dressed, steal over to me with a whore's glow in your slumbrous eyes, gently undo button after button in the fly of my trousers and gently take out your lover's fat mickey, lap it up in your moist mouth and suck away at it till it gets fatter and stiffer and comes off in your mouth. Sometime too I shall surprise you asleep, lift up your skirts and open your hot drawers gently, then lie down gently by you and begin to lick lazily round your bush. You will begin to stir uneasily then I will lick the lips of my darling's cunt. You will begin to groan and grunt and sigh and fart with lust in your sleep. Then I will lick up faster and faster like a ravenous dog until your cunt is a mass of slime and your body wriggling wildly.

Goodnight, my little farting Nora, my dirty little fuckbird! There is *one lovely word*, darling, you have underlined to make me pull myself off better. Write me more about that and yourself, sweetly, *dirtier*, dirtier.

JIM

To NORA BARNACLE JOYCE   MS. Cornell

9 December 1909   *44 Fontenoy Street, Dublin*

My sweet naughty little fuckbird, Here is another note to buy pretty drawers or stockings or garters. Buy whorish drawers, love, and be sure you sprinkle the legs of them with some nice scent and also discolour them just a little behind.

You seem anxious to know how I received your letter which you say is worse than mine. How is it worse than mine, love? Yes, it is worse in one part or two. I mean the part where you say what you will do with your tongue (I don't mean sucking me off) and in that lovely word you write so big and underline, you little blackguard. It is thrilling to hear that word (and one or two others you have not written) on a girl's lips. But I wish you spoke of yourself and not of me. Write me a long long letter, full of that and other things, about yourself, darling. You know now how to give me a cockstand. Tell me the smallest things about yourself so long as they are obscene and secret and filthy. Write nothing else. Let every sentence be full of dirty immodest words and sounds. They are all lovely to hear and to see on paper even but the dirtiest are the most beautiful.

The two parts of your body which do dirty things are the loveliest to me. I prefer your arse, darling, to your bubbies because it does such a dirty thing. I love your cunt not so much because it is the part I block but because it does another dirty thing. I could lie frigging all day looking at the *divine* word you wrote and at the thing you said you would do with your tongue. I wish I could hear your lips spluttering those heavenly exciting filthy words, see your mouth making dirty sounds and noises, feel your body wriggling under me, hear and smell the dirty fat girlish farts going pop pop out of your pretty bare girlish bum and *fuck fuck fuck fuck* my naughty little hot fuckbird's cunt for ever.

I am happy now, because my little whore tells me she wants me to roger her arseways and wants me to fuck her mouth and wants to unbutton me and pull out my mickey and suck it off like a teat. *More* and *dirtier* than this she wants to do, my little naked fucker, my naughty wriggling little frigger, my sweet dirty little farter.

Goodnight, my little cuntie I am going to lie down and pull at myself till I come. Write more and dirtier, darling. Tickle your little cockey while you write to make you say worse and worse. Write the dirty words big and underline them and kiss them and hold them for a moment to your sweet hot cunt, darling, and also pull up your dress a moment and hold them in under your dear little farting bum. Do *more* if you wish and send the letter then to me, my darling brown-arsed fuckbird.   JIM

To NORA BARNACLE JOYCE   MS. Cornell

10 December 1909   *44 Fontenoy Street, Dublin*

Dearest I am awfully disappointed by your letter tonight. All day I was planning to get together the little note I enclose and wondering what you would write to me.

I wired you *Be careful.* I meant be careful to keep my letters secret, be careful to let nobody see your excitement and be careful not to (I am half ashamed to write it now). I was afraid, Nora, you might get so hot that you would give yourself to somebody.

Buy something nice with this note, dearest. I shall be dreadfully miserable if these last letters of ours come to an end. I am exhausted with this business here. Last night I was not in bed till near five between letters and advertisements and telegrams.

Your letter is so cold I have no heart to write you like before. I have gazed a long time at your other letters and kissed certain words in them, one of them over and over again.

Perhaps tomorrow you will write again. Good night, dearest.   JIM

To NORA BARNACLE JOYCE   MS. Cornell

11 December 1909   *44 Fontenoy Street, Dublin*

My dearest Nora   No letter from you again tonight. You have not answered.

The four Italians have left Finn's Hotel and live now over the show. I paid about £20 to your late mistress, returning good for evil. Before I left the hotel I told the waitress who I was and asked her to let me see the room you slept in. She brought me upstairs and took me to it. You can imagine my excited appearance and manner. I saw my love's room, her bed, the four little walls within which she dreamed of my eyes and voice, the little curtains she pulled aside in the morning to look out at the grey sky of Dublin, the poor modest silly things on the walls over which her glance travelled while she undressed her fair young body at night.

Ah not lust, dearest, not the wild brutal madness I have written to you these last days and nights, not the wild beast-like desire for your body, dearest, is what drew me to you then and holds me to you now. No, dearest, not that at all but a most tender, adoring, pitiful love for your youth and girlhood and weakness. O the sweet pain you have brought into my heart! O the mystery your voice speaks to me of!

Tonight I will not write to you as I have done before. All men are brutes, dearest, but at least in me there is also something higher at times. Yes, I too have felt at moments the burning in my soul of that pure and sacred fire which burns for ever on the altar of my love's heart.

I could have knelt by that little bed and abandoned myself to a flood of
tears. The tears were besieging my eyes as I stood looking at it. I could
have knelt and prayed there as the three kings from the East knelt and
prayed before the manger in which Jesus lay. They had travelled over
deserts and seas and brought their gifts and wisdom and royal trains to
kneel before a little new-born child and I had brought my errors and
follies and sins and wondering and longing to lay them at the little bed
in which a young girl had dreamed of me.

Dearest, I am so sorry I have not even a poor five lire note to send you
tonight but on Monday I will send you one. I leave for Cork tomorrow
morning but I would prefer to be going westward, toward those strange
places whose names thrill me on your lips, Oughterard, Clare-Galway,
Coleraine, Oranmore, towards those wild fields of Connacht in which
God made to grow 'my beautiful wild flower of the hedges, my dark-blue
rain-drenched flower'.   JIM

To NORA BARNACLE JOYCE (Fragment of a letter)   MS. Cornell

[? *13 December 1909*]   [*Dublin*]

go to others? You can give me all and more than they can. Do you
believe in my love at last, dearest? Ah, do, Nora! Why everyone who
has ever seen me can read it in my eyes when I speak of you. As your
mother says 'they light up like candles in my head'

The time will fly now, my darling, until your loving tender arms
encircle me. I will never leave you again. Not only do I want your body
(as you know) but I want also your company. My darling, I suppose that
compared with your splendid generous love for me my love for you looks
very poor and threadbare. But it is the best I can give you, my own dear
sweetheart. Take it, my love, save me and shelter me. I am your child as
I told you and you must be severe with me, my little mother. Punish me
as much as you like. I would be delighted to feel my flesh tingling under
your hand. Do you know what I mean, Nora dear? I wish you would
smack me or flog me even. Not in play, dear, in earnest and on my naked
flesh. I wish you were strong, *strong*, dear, and had a big full proud
bosom and big fat thighs. I would love to be whipped by you, Nora love!
I would love to have done something to displease you, something trivial
even, perhaps one of my rather dirty habits that make you laugh: and
then to hear you call me into your room and then to find you sitting in
an armchair with your fat thighs far apart and your face deep red with
anger and a cane in your hand. To see you point to what I had done and

then with a movement of rage pull me towards you and throw me face downwards across your lap. Then to feel your hands tearing down my trousers and inside clothes and turning up my shirt, to be struggling in your strong arms and in your lap, to feel you bending down (like an angry nurse whipping a child's bottom) until your big full bubbies almost touched me and to feel you flog, flog, flog me viciously on my naked quivering flesh!! Pardon me, dear, if this is silly. I began this letter so quietly and yet I *must* end it in my own mad fashion.

Are you offended by my horrible shameless writing, dear? I expect some of the filthy things I wrote made you blush. Are you offended because I said I loved to look at the brown stain that comes behind on your girlish white drawers?[1] I suppose you think me a filthy wretch. How will you answer those letters? I hope and hope you *too* will write me letters even madder and dirtier than mine to you.

You can if you only wish to, Nora, for I must tell you also that [breaks off]

To NORA BARNACLE JOYCE   MS. Cornell

15 December 1909   *44 Fontenoy Street, Dublin*

Dearest No letter! only a short rude one from Stannie. For God's sake let me be spared any of the old trouble or I shall end in a madhouse. Try, dear, till your lover comes back to make things run smoothly. I can write no more. What does he fight with me for? I am doing my best for you all. Please, dear, give him plenty to eat and let him be comfortable. Don't bother him about debts: and for God's sake don't bother me about them. I sent you pictures. Get him to put them up in the kitchen, the big one opposite the fire. Put up well.

No letter! Now I am sure my girlie is offended at my filthy words. Are you offended, dear, at what I said about your drawers? That is all nonsense, darling. I know they are as spotless as your heart. I know I could lick them all over, frills, legs and bottom. Only I love in my dirty way to think that in a certain part they are soiled. It is all non-sense, too, dear, about buggering you. It is only the dirty sound of the word I like, the idea of a shy beautiful young girl like Nora pulling up her clothes behind and revealing her sweet white girlish drawers in order to excite the dirty fellow she is so fond of; and then letting him stick his dirty red lumpy pole in through the split of her drawers and up up up in the darling little hole between her plump fresh buttocks.

[1] Compare *Ulysses*, pp. 929–30 (780–1).

Darling, I came off just now in my trousers so that I am utterly played out. I cannot go to the G.P.O. though I have three letters to post.

To bed—to bed!

Goodnight, Nora mia!   Jim

To Nora Barnacle Joyce   MS. Cornell

16 December 1909   *44 Fontenoy Street, Dublin*

My sweet darling girl At last you write to me! You must have given that naughty little cunt of yours a most ferocious frigging to write me such a disjointed letter. As for me, darling, I am so played out that you would have to lick me for a good hour before I could get a horn stiff enough even to put into you, to say nothing of blocking you. I have done so much and so often that I am afraid to look to see how that thing I had is after all I have done to myself. Darling, please don't fuck me too much when I go back. Fuck all you can out of me for the first night or so but make me get myself cured. The fucking must all be done by you, darling, as I am so small and soft now that no girl in Europe except yourself would waste her time trying the job. Fuck me, darling, in as many new ways as your lust will suggest. Fuck me dressed in your full outdoor costume with your hat and veil on, your face flushed with the cold and wind and rain and your boots muddy, either straddling across my legs when I am sitting in a chair and riding me up and down with the frills of your drawers showing and my cock sticking up stiff in your cunt or riding me over the back of the sofa. Fuck me naked with your hat and stockings on *only* flat on the floor with a crimson flower in your hole behind, riding me like a man with your thighs between mine and your rump very fat. Fuck me in your dressing gown (I hope you have that nice one) with nothing on under it, opening it suddenly and showing me your belly and thighs and back and pulling me on top of you on the kitchen table. Fuck me into you arseways, lying on your face on the bed, with your hair flying loose naked but with a lovely scented pair of pink drawers opened shamelessly behind and half slipping down over your peeping bum. Fuck me if you can squatting in the closet, with your clothes up, grunting like a young sow doing her dung, and a big fat dirty snaking thing coming slowly out of your backside. Fuck me on the stairs in the dark, like a nursery-maid fucking her soldier, unbuttoning his trousers gently and slipping her hand in his fly and fiddling with his shirt and feeling it getting wet and then pulling it gently up and fiddling with his two bursting balls and at last pulling out boldly the mickey she loves to handle and frigging it for him softly, murmuring into his ear dirty words and dirty stories that other girls told her and dirty things she said, and all the time pissing her drawers with pleasure and letting off soft warm quiet little farts behind until her own girlish cockey is as stiff as his and suddenly sticking him up in her and riding him.

Basta! Basta per Dio!

I have come now and the foolery is over. Now for your questions!

We are not open yet. I send you some posters. We hope to open on the 20th or 21st. Count 14 days from that and 3½ days for the voyage and I am in Trieste.

Get ready. Put some warm-brown-linoleum on the kitchen and hang a pair of red common curtains on the windows at night. Get some kind of a cheap common comfortable armchair for your lazy lover. Do this above all, darling, as I shall not quit that kitchen for a whole week after I arrive, reading, lolling, smoking, and watching you get ready the meals and *talking, talking, talking, talking* to you. O how supremely happy I shall be! ! God in heaven, I shall be happy there! I figlioli, il fuoco, una buona mangiata, un caffè nero, un Brasil,[1] il Piccolo della Sera, e Nora, Nora mia, Norina, Noretta, Norella, Noruccia ecc ecc . . .

Eva and Eileen must sleep together. Get some place for Georgie. I wish Nora and I had two beds for night-work. I am keeping and shall keep my promise, love. Time fly on, fly on quickly! ! I want to go back to my love, my life, my star, my little strange-eyed Ireland!

A hundred thousand kisses, darling!   Jim

To Nora Barnacle Joyce   MS. Cornell

20 December 1909   *44 Fontenoy Street, Dublin*

My sweet naughty girl I got your hot letter tonight and have been trying to picture you frigging your cunt in the closet. How do you do it ? Do you stand against the wall with your hand tickling up under your clothes or do you squat down on the hole with your skirts up and your hand hard at work in through the slit of your drawers ? Does it give you the horn now to shit ? I wonder how you can do it. Do you come in the act of shitting or do you frig yourself off first and then shit ? It must be a fearfully lecherous thing to see a girl with her clothes up frigging furiously at her cunt, to see her pretty white drawers pulled open behind and her bum sticking out and a fat brown thing stuck half-way out of her hole. You say you will shit your drawers, dear, and let me fuck you

---

[1] 'The children, a fire, a good dinner, a black coffee, a Brazil' (cigar).

then. I would like to hear you shit them, dear, first and then fuck you.
Some night when we are somewhere in the dark and talking dirty and
you feel your shite ready to fall put your arms round my neck in shame
and shit it down softly. The sound will madden me and when I pull up
your dress

No use continuing! You can guess why!

The cinematograph opened today. I leave for Trieste on Sunday
2 January. I hope you have done what I said about the kitchen,
linoleum and armchair and curtains. By the way don't be sewing those
drawers before anybody. Is your dress made. I hope so—with a long
coat, belted and cuffed with leather etc. How I am to manage Eileen's
fare I don't know. For God's sake arrange that you and I can have a
comfortable bed. I have no great wish to do anything to you, dear. All
I want is your company. You may rest easy about my going with—.[1]
You understand. That won't happen, dear.

O, I am hungry now. The day I arrive get Eva to make one of the
threepenny puddings and make some kind of vanilla sauce without
wine. I would like roast beef[,] rice-soup, capuzzi garbi,[2] mashed
potatoes, pudding and black coffee. *No, no* I would like stracotto di
maccheroni,[3] a mixed salad, stewed prunes, torroni,[4] tea and presnitz.[5]
Or *no* I would like stewed eels or polenta[6] with . . .

Excuse me, dear, I am *hungry* tonight.

Nora darling, I hope we will pass a happy year together. Am writing
Stannie tomorrow about cinematograph.

I am so glad I am now in sight of Miramar. The only thing I hope is
that I haven't brought on that cursed thing again by what I did. *Pray*
for me, dearest.

Addio, addio, addio, addio!   JIM

To NORA BARNACLE JOYCE   MS. Cornell

22 December 1909   *44 Fontenoy Street, Dublin*

My dearest Nora I send you by this post registered, express and insured
a Christmas present.[7] It is the best thing (but very poor after all) that
I am able to offer you in return for your sincere and true and faithful
love. I have thought every detail of it when lying awake at night or
racing on cars around Dublin and I think it has come out nice in the

---

[1] The word 'whores' is omitted by Joyce.   [2] 'Sauerkraut.'
[3] 'Pot roast with macaroni.'   [4] 'Nougats.'
[5] A Triestine pastry, baked at Easter.   [6] A corn-meal dish.
[7] The bound manuscript book of *Chamber Music*.

end. But even if it brought only one quick flush of pleasure to your cheek when you first see it or made your true tender loving heart give one quick bound of joy I would feel *well, well, well* repaid for my pains.

Perhaps this book I send you now will outlive both you and me. Perhaps the fingers of some young man or young girl (our children's children) may turn over its parchment leaves reverently when the two lovers whose initials are interlaced on the cover have long vanished from the earth. Nothing will remain then, dearest, of our poor human passion-driven bodies and who can say where the souls that looked on each other through their eyes will then be. I would pray that my soul be scattered in the wind if God would but let me blow softly for ever about one strange lonely dark-blue rain-drenched flower in a wild hedge at Aughrim or Oranmore. Jim

To Nora Barnacle Joyce   MS. Cornell

23 December 1909   *44 Fontenoy Street, Dublin*

My dearest Nora By the time you get this you will have received my present and my letter and will have passed your Christmas. Now I want you to get ready for my coming. If nothing extra turns up I leave Ireland on Saturday 1 January at 9.20 p.m. with Eileen, though how or where I am to get the money I don't know. I hope you have put the posters in the kitchen. I intend to paper it week by week with the programmes. If you could get a few yards of linoleum or even an old carpet and any kind of a brokendown *comfortable* cheap armchair for the kitchen and a cheap common pair of red curtains I think I would be very comfortable there. Is it at all possible for us to have a bed more? Perhaps Francini would sell us his by the month. I sent you every penny I could spare, dearest, but now I am stranded as the present I gave you, you little nuisance, cost me a terrible lot of soldi. But don't think I am sorry, darling. I am delighted to have given you something so fine and beautiful. Now, darling, urge on Stannie to help me to get back promptly with Eileen and then we will begin our life together once more. O how I shall enjoy the journey back! Every station will be bringing me nearer to my soul's peace. O how I shall feel when I see the castle of Miramar among the trees and the long yellow quays of Trieste! Why is it I am destined to look so many times in my life with eyes of longing on Trieste? Darling, when I go back now I want you always to be patient with me. You will find, dear, that *I am not a bad man*. I am a poor impulsive sinful generous selfish jealous dissatisfied kind-natured poet but I am not a bad deceitful person. Try to shelter me, dearest, from the storms of the world. I love you (do you believe it now, darling?) and O I am so tired after all I have done here that I think when I reach Via Scussa I will just creep into bed, kiss you tenderly on the forehead, curl myself up in the blankets and sleep, sleep, sleep.

Darling, I am so glad you like my picture as a child. I was a fierce-looking infant, was I not? And really, dear, I am just as big a child now as I was then. The foolishest things are always coming into my head. You know the picture of the man with his finger up in the *Piccolo della Sera* which you say is 'Jim making some new suggestion'.[1] I am *sure*, darling, in your heart of hearts you must think I am a poor silly boy. You proud little ignorant saucy dear warm-hearted girl how is it that I cannot impress you with my magnificent poses as I do other people? You see through me, you cunning little blue-eyed rogue, and smile to yourself knowing that I am an impostor and still you love me.

Dearest, there is one part of your letter I hardly like to allude to.[2] I have no right whatsoever to do so and I recognise that you are free to act as you wish. I will not ask you to remember our children. But remember that we loved each other truly as boy and girl almost in that heavenly summer five years ago in Dublin. Darling, I am a sad-hearted person in reality and O I believe that if such a thing as you seem to be thinking of took place I could not live. No, dear, I am too jealous, too proud, too sad, too lonely! I would not go on living, I think. Even now I feel my heart so quiet and sorrowful at the thought that I can only stare at the words I am writing. How sad life is, from one disillusion to another!

JIM

To NORA BARNACLE JOYCE   MS. Cornell

24 December 1909 Xmas eve   *44 Fontenoy Street, Dublin*

My darling Nora I have just wired you the beautiful motive from the last act of the opera you like so much *Werther*: 'Nel lieto dì pensa a me'.[3] And as it was too late to wire you money I paid £1 to my partner here Rebez and got him to wire to Caris[4] in Trieste to pay Signora Joyce immediately 24 crowns. I hope you will have a merry Xmas, darling.

---

[1] A billboard on the roof of the *Piccolo* building showed the upper half of a big man with hand held high and index finger extended, signalling passers-by to use a particular brand of paper for rolling their cigarettes.

[2] Nora Joyce threatened to leave him.

[3] 'Think of me that happy day.' Jules Massenet, *Werther*.

[4] Giuseppe Caris, one of Joyce's partners in the Volta.

Now, dearest, I expect Stannie will wire me all he can for the 1st so that I can start.

Darling, I am in a most dreadful state of excitement at present. All day I have been in the middle of the bustling Xmas crowd down at the cinematograph. There was a young constable there on special duty. When it was over I took him upstairs to give him a drink and found he was from Galway and his sisters were at the Presentation Convent with you. He was amazed to hear where Nora Barnacle had ended. He said he remembered you in Galway, a handsome girl with curls and a proud walk. My God, Nora, how I suffered! Yet I could not stop talking to him. He seems a fine courteous-mannered young man. I wondered did my darling, my love, my dearest, my queen ever turn her young eyes towards him. I *had* to speak to him because he came from Galway but O how I suffered, darling. I am dreadfully excited. I don't know what I am writing. Nora, I want to go back to you. Forget everybody but me, darling. I am sure there are finer fellows in Galway than your poor lover but O, darling, one day[1] you will see that I will be something in my country. How excited and restless I feel! I enclose his sister's names. I saw that he was astonished at how you had ended. But, O God, would I not give you all the Kingdoms of this world if I only could. O, darling, I am so jealous of the past and yet I bite my nails with excitement whenever I see anybody from the strange dying western city in which my love, my beautiful wild flower of the hedges, passed her young laughing girlish years. Nora dearest, why are you not here to comfort me? I must end this letter I am so dreadfully excited. You love me, do you not, my dearest bride? O, how you have twisted me round your heart! Be happy, my love! My little mother, take me into the dark sanctuary of your womb. Shelter me, dear, from harm! I am too childish and impulsive to live alone. Help me, dear, pray for me! Love me! Think of me! I am so helpless tonight, helpless, helpless!   Jim

A million kisses to my darling dew-laden western flower, a million million kisses to my dear Nora of the curls.   Jim

Your mother sent that present and I wrote to thank her.

To Nora Barnacle Joyce (Postcard)   MS. Cornell

[*26 December 1909*] *S. Stephen's Day*   *44 Fontenoy Street, Dublin*

Dearest I got your letter (a very scatter-brained one too) this morning and the wedding-card you enclose. Don't send any present for me. Keep

---

[1] An allusion to the aria, 'Un bel dì', in Puccini's *Madama Butterfly*, Act II.

all you can. Ask Stannie to wire me what he can next week. Hope you got safely my present and telegram and the £1 I sent you through Caris. Hope to start this day week. Thanks for your good wishes for Xmas and I hope you got over it fairly well. Tell G. and L. that I am coming soon and to keep their noses clean. I hope they had a pleasant time. Addio,

JIM

Keep a little torrone and mandorlato[1] for Eileen.

To STANISLAUS JOYCE   MS. Cornell

12 January 1911   *Via della Barriera Vecchia 32, III, Trieste*

[No salutation]

Dr Paul Marquardt, Acquedotto 16, offers you a lesson between 7 and 9 p.m., four pupils and asks you to call.

I take the opportunity of letting you know (as you have no doubt heard) that I am about to leave Trieste. Your friend Miss O'Brien (of London) has made copious apologies to me (whether for herself alone or for other I am not concerned to know) and I learn that your charges express tearful compunction. I intend to do what Parnell was advised to do on a similar occasion: clear out, the conflict[2] being beneath my dignity, and leave you and the *cattolicissime*[3] to make what you can of the city discovered by my courage (and Nora's) seven years ago, whither you and they came in obedience to my summons, from your ignorant and famine-stricken and treacherous country. My irregularities can easily be made the excuse of your conduct. A final attempt at regularity will be made by me in the sale of my effects, half of which will be paid in by me to your account in a Trieste bank where it can be drawn on or left to rot according to the dictates of your conscience.

I hope that your mind will be properly benefitted by the barter you have made of me and mine against the aforesaid Cockney virgin and comfortress of the afflicted and the preoccupied Christographer of the Via dell'Olmo (on whom the editor of the *Fortnightly Review* will shortly wait in person) and that, when I have left the field, you and your sisters will be able, with the meagre means at your disposal, to carry on the tradition I leave behind me in honour of my name and my country.

JIM

[1] Christmas candies made of almond paste.
[2] The cause of this dispute between the two brothers is not known.
[3] Eileen and Eva Joyce are meant. The word means 'hyper-Catholics'.

To Stanislaus Joyce (Postcard)   MS. Cornell

22 January 1911   *Barriera Vecchia 32, III*

It may interest you to hear that *Dubliners*, announced for publication
for the third time yesterday 20 January, is again postponed *sine die* and
without a word of explanation. I know the name and tradition of my
country too well to be surprised at receiving three scrawled lines in
return for five years of constant service to my art and constant waiting
and indifference and disloyalty in return for the 150,000 francs of continental money which I have deflected into the pockets of hungry Irishmen and women[1] since they drove me out of their hospitable bog six
years ago.   Jim

To the Editor[2]   MS. Cornell

17 August 1911   *Via della Barriera Vecchia 32, III,*
                                                          Trieste (Austria)

Sir May I ask you to publish this letter which throws some light on the
present conditions of authorship in England and Ireland?

Nearly six years ago Mr Grant Richards,[3] publisher, of London
signed a contract with me for the publication of a book of stories
written by me, entitled *Dubliners*. Some ten months later he wrote
asking me to omit one of the stories and passages in others which, as he
said, his printer refused to set up. I declined to do either and a correspondence began between Mr Grant Richards and myself which lasted
more than three months. I went to an international jurist in Rome
(where I lived then) and was advised to omit. I declined to do so and the
MS was returned to me, the publisher refusing to publish notwith-
standing his pledged printed word, the contract remaining in my
possession.

---

[1] Presumably through his agency for Irish tweeds and his connection with the Volta.

[2] Joyce sent copies of this letter to many newspapers; it was published in full in *Sinn
Féin* on 2 September 1911 and, with the controversial passage omitted, in the *Northern
Whig* (Belfast) on 26 August 1911.

[3] Richards, to whom Joyce sent a copy of this letter, replied amicably on 28 August
1911,

'Dear Mr Joyce, I am, naturally, interested in the letter which you are sending to the
press and of which you have been kind enough to send me a copy. I don't think you quite
realize a publisher's difficulties. But still. . . .

I have often thought of your work and if at any time you care, in spite of what has
passed, to let me see anything else on which you may have been engaged, I hope you will
not hesitate. Sincerely yours,   Grant Richards'

Six months afterwards a Mr Hone wrote to me from Marseilles to ask me to submit the MS to Messrs Maunsel, publishers, of Dublin. I did so: and after about a year, in July 1909, Messrs Maunsel signed a contract with me for the publication of the book on or before 1 September 1910. In December 1909 Messrs Maunsel's manager begged me to alter a passage in one of the stories, *Ivy Day in the Committee Room*, wherein some reference was made to Edward VII. I agreed to do so, much against my will, and altered one or two phrases. Messrs Maunsel continually postponed the date of publication and in the end wrote, asking me to omit the passage or to change it radically. I declined to do either, pointing out that Mr Grant Richards of London had raised no objection to the passage when Edward VII was alive and that I could not see why an Irish publisher should raise an objection to it when Edward VII had passed into history. I suggested arbitration or a deletion of the passage with a prefatory note of explanation by me but Messrs Maunsel would agree to neither. As Mr Hone (who had written to me in the first instance) disclaimed all responsibility in the matter and any connection with the firm I took the opinion of a solicitor in Dublin who advised me to omit the passage, informing me that as I had no domicile in the United Kingdom I could not sue Messrs Maunsel for breach of contract unless I paid £100 into court and that, even if I paid £100 into court and sued them, I should have no chance of getting a verdict in my favour from a Dublin jury if the passage in dispute could be taken as offensive in any way to the late king. I wrote then to the present king, George V, enclosing a printed proof of the story with the passage therein marked and begging him to inform me whether in his view the passage (certain allusions made by a person of the story in the idiom of his social class) should be withheld from publication as offensive to the memory of his father. His Majesty's private secretary sent me this reply:

Buckingham Palace

The private secretary is commanded to acknowledge the receipt of Mr James Joyce's letter of the 1 instant and to inform him that it is inconsistent with rule for His Majesty to express his opinion in such cases. The enclosures are returned herewith   11 August 1911

Here is the passage in dispute:

—But look here, John,—said Mr O'Connor.—Why should we welcome the king of England? Didn't Parnell himself... ?—

—Parnell,—said Mr Henchy,—is dead. Now, here's the way I look at it. Here's this chap come to the throne after his old mother keeping

him out of it till the man was grey[1]. He's a jolly fine decent fellow, if
you ask me, and no damn nonsense about him. He just says to himself:—*The old one never went to see these wild Irish. By Christ, I'll go
myself and see what they're like.*—And are we going to insult the man
when he comes over here on a friendly visit? Eh? Isn't that right,
Crofton?—

Mr Crofton nodded his head.

—But after all now,—said Mr Lyons, argumentatively,—King
Edward's life, you know, is not the very . . .—

—Let bygones be bygones.—said Mr Henchy—I admire the man
personally. He's just an ordinary knockabout like you and me. He's
fond of his glass of grog and he's a bit of a rake, perhaps, and he's a
good sportsman. Damn it, can't we Irish play fair?—[2]

I wrote this book seven years ago and, as I cannot see in any quarter
a chance that my rights will be protected, I hereby give Messrs Maunsel
publicly permission to publish this story with what changes or deletions
they may please to make and shall hope that what they may publish
may resemble that to the writing of which I gave thought and time.
Their attitude as an Irish publishing firm may be judged by Irish public
opinion. I, as a writer, protest against the systems (legal, social and
ceremonious) which have brought me to this pass. Thanking you for
your courtesy, I am, Sir, Your obedient servant   James Joyce

To Nora Barnacle Joyce (Postcard)   MS. Cornell

[*12 July 1912*]   *Via della Barriera Vecchia 32, III,*
                                          Trieste (Austria)

Dear Nora Having left me five days without a word of news you scribble
your signature with a number of others on a postcard. Not one word of
the places in Dublin where I met you and which have so many memories
for us both! Since you left I have been in a state of dull anger. I
consider the whole affair wrong and unjust.

I can neither sleep nor think. I have still the pain in my side. Last
night I was afraid to lie down. I thought I would die in sleep. I wakened
Georgie three times for fear of being alone.

It is a monstrous thing to say that you seem to forget me in five days
and to forget the beautiful days of our love.

---

[1] In the story as it was finally published, another sentence was introduced here: 'He's
a man of the world, and he means well by us.'

[2] Joyce has pasted this whole quotation from the story in *printed* form on the second
page of his letter.

I leave Trieste tonight as I am afraid to stay here—afraid of myself.
I shall arrive in Dublin on Monday. If you have forgotten I have not. I
shall go *alone* to meet and walk with the image of her whom I remember.

You can write or wire to me in Dublin to my sister's address.

What are Dublin and Galway compared with our memories?   JIM

To STANISLAUS JOYCE   MS. Cornell

Postmark 7 August 1912   *4 Bowling Green, Galway (Ireland)*

Dear Stannie The story about the flat is this. I received on 24 Feb
notice. That was unpleasant but valid. I then with Nora went about
looking for a flat and visited thirty. The house agent *himself* stopped me
in via Bellini and asked me had I found a flat. I said no. He said the
matter would be smoothed over, to leave it to him, that he did not want
me to leave as he did not know what kind of people might come into the
flat, that Picciola was very fond of me and intended to take English
lessons from me during the winter and that if any repairs were necessary
he even believed that Picciola would pay for them! ! ! Similar conversations took place 4 times. I told the porter and every one who visited the
flat that I was remaining. When I paid the last quarter I asked had he
spoken to Picciola. He said he would see in a few days and repeated the
story about English lessons. I consider (and will contest by force and by
law) that this is a verbal revocation of the notice. On the strength of it
I left Trieste. I have written the whole story to Picciola himself and say,
if he will not have me in the house, I shall vacate the flat for the 24 Feb
or 24 November: For the 24 Aug. no.[1] The house agent did a *nice* thing
to rescind the contract with the incoming tenant. Tell him to sign a
contract with nobody. He has played a double game (as I told Picciola
who is a pig, in any case) and has only himself to blame. But for his
intervention I should have found a flat. I have also written to Eileen to
explain the matter to Serravallo. If in spite of that Picciola insists on
putting me and my family on the street I promise you you will see some
fun in the house. If he does so he is an inhuman person and I will treat
him as such. I am however almost sure that he will agree to my proposal.
In the meantime if you have nothing better to do call again on the
houseagent and let him know that I intend to remain in that house
after the 24 Aug and that if anything bad happens the result will lie at
his door. Take possession of the house till I return. Don't let my debts

[1] Moving day in Trieste was 24 August, so a landlord, wishing to change tenants,
would insist on this date.

trouble you. Tell them I am away and will return in the month of September. They would get the same answer at Economo's[1] door and would salute and go away. Fano[2] perhaps would be nasty not the others. Have just finished second article on Aran and will send. Send on at once twelve copies of P.d.S with 1st article.[3] I went to Clifden on Monday to interview Marconi or see station.[4] Could do neither and am waiting reply from Marconi House London. Wrote to Roberts 4 times and at last got enclosed.[5] Have written a letter to Hone calling on him to see that I am acted loyally by. Immediately I hear will write. Call to the pharmacy and see that my letter to P———[6] is forwarded at once. Tell Bartoli I have a lot of news *re* transatlantic scheme[7] and to see my second article on Aran. I think since I have come so far I had better stay a little longer if possible. Nora's uncle[8] feeds us in great style and I row and cycle and drive a good deal. I cycled to Oughterard on Sunday and visited the graveyard of *The Dead*.[9] It is exactly as I imagined it and one of the headstones was to J. Joyce. Do you like 1st article? I send you news of Skeffington and of O.G. Have got a view of Killala for Sordina.[10] Price[11] writes me a letter every day. He has a cure for the foot and mouth disease which is devastating Irish cattle. Styrian oxen suffer from it and are cured but 2000 Irish beasts have been killed. He writes (like you) 'Be energetic. Drop your lethargy. Forget Leinster for Ulster.[12] Remember that Sir John Blackwood died in the act of putting on his

---

[1] Baron Leonida Economo (1874–1952) was one of the richest men in Trieste.

[2] Giuseppe Fano, owner of an office-supply store, and a creditor of Joyce.

[3] 'La Città delle Tribù: Ricordi Italiani in un Porto Irlandese' ('The City of the Tribes: Italian Echoes in an Irish Port') was published in the *Piccolo della Sera* on 11 August 1912, and 'Il Miraggio del Pescatore di Aran. La Valvola dell'Inghilterra in Caso di Guerra' ('The Mirage of the Fisherman of Aran. England's Safety Valve in Case of War') on 5 September 1912. Both may be read in translation in *Critical Writings*.

[4] The Marconi station was built at Clifden in 1910.

[5] Roberts's letter has not survived.

[6] Picciola.

[7] A plan for constructing a new transatlantic port at Galway City.   [8] Michael Healy.

[9] Nora Joyce had known a young man, Michael Bodkin, in Galway, and her account of him gave Joyce some of the details for Michael Furey in 'The Dead'. Bodkin also had died young and was buried in the graveyard near Oughterard.

[10] Count Francesco Sordina was interested in French Revolutionary and Napoleonic history. Joyce had evidently talked with him about Killala, in County Mayo, which was the landing place of eleven hundred French troops on 22 August 1798. Theirs was the third French expedition mounted against Ireland in three years. After some early successes they were forced by Lord Lieutenant Cornwallis to surrender on 9 September. The French were allowed to return to France, while the United Irishmen who had come with them were sentenced to death.

[11] Henry N. Blackwood Price, a model for Mr Deasy in *Ulysses*, was assistant manager of the Eastern Telegraph Company in Trieste.

[12] That is, forget Joyce's problems in Dublin (in the province of Leinster) for those of Price, an Ulsterman.

topboots in order to go to Dublin to vote against the Union.[1] You will get your name up if you write this up'. I cannot do so. I have written the whole thing to W. Field M P (pres. of Irish Cattle Traders Society) who of course never answered.[2] I am writing to explain to Price. Do you think he is right or I. I wanted Field who is in the line to take it up not I myself. I think Price ought to look for a cure for the foot and mouth disease of Anna Blackwood Price.

Remembrances from all. Write a card to Nora's uncle. Please look cheerful and write to   JIM

To NORA BARNACLE JOYCE   MS. Cornell

[21 August 1912]   *[Dublin]*

My dear Nora I saw Lidwell[3] today and after an hour obtained from him the enclosed letter. I took it to Roberts. Roberts said it was no good and that it should have been addressed to him. I asked Lidwell to write it to Roberts. Lidwell refused and said that I not Roberts was his client. I went to Roberts and told him this. Roberts said that Lidwell should write him a long letter on the whole case saying what I could do, as he could not endanger the firm. I said I would sign an agreement to pay him £60 (sixty pounds) the cost of a 1st edition if the book was seized by the Crown. He said that was no use and asked could I get two securities for £1000 (a thousand pounds) each—in all £2000 (two thousand pounds = 50,000 francs) to indemnify the firm for loss over publishing my book. I said that no person admired me so much as that and in any case it could never be proved that the loss (if any) of the firm was due to my book. He said then that he would act on his solicitor's advice and not publish the book.

I went then into the backroom of the office and sitting at the table, thinking of the book I have written, the child which I have carried for years and years in the womb of the imagination[4] as you carried in your

---

[1] In *Ulysses* Mr Deasy asserts that Sir John Blackwood (1722–99) voted *for* the Union. Blackwood was an Ulster M.P. from 1761 to his death, and was noted as an opponent of the Union of England and Ireland. It is possible, but most unlikely, that Price, who was descended from Blackwood, knew of some unrecorded family tradition about a last-minute switch in his ancestor's opinions. See Robert Martin Adams, *Surface and Symbol* (New York, 1962), pp. 20–2.

[2] On 17 August 1912 William Field sent a letter to the *Evening Telegraph* (Dublin), enclosing one from Price which was dated 13 August 1912 from Styria, Austria. The newspaper published both letters on 18 August. Most of Price's letter is quoted in Ellmann, *James Joyce* (New York and London, 1959), pp. 336–7. It is parodied in *Ulysses*, pp. 40–1 (32–3).

[3] John G. Lidwell (d. 1919), a solicitor, was a friend of Joyce's father.

[4] 'In the virgin womb of the imagination the word was made flesh.' *A Portrait of the Artist*, p. 221 (217).

womb the children you love, and of how I had fed it day after day out of my brain and my memory, wrote him the enclosed letter.[1] He said he will send it tonight to his solicitor in London and let me know.

I am like a man walking in his sleep. I don't know what is going on in Trieste. Stannie has not sent me what I asked him for. Eva and Florrie would have nothing to eat but for me. Stannie has sent them nothing and Charlie nothing and me nothing. I don't know where my desk and table and MSS and books will end. You are away in Galway. I don't know how we can get back to Trieste or what we shall find there. I don't know what to do about my diploma or my book. My father says that Roberts will have a new objection even after my letter. The town is beginning to fill and I should like to forget all and be here with you and take you about during the Horse Show. Pover'a me![2] [sic]

This is my holiday.

Give my regards to Mr Healy. Tell him I have not a moment to write. Give a kiss to Giorgio and Lucia.

I hope you liked the verses. I spoke of you today to my aunt and told her of you—how you sit at the opera with the grey ribbon in your hair, listening to music, and observed by men,—and of many other things (even very intimate things) between us.

I told you of my grief at Galway Races. I feel it still. I hope that the day may come when I shall be able to give you the fame of being beside me when I have entered into my Kingdom.

Be happy, dear, and eat and sleep. You can sleep now. Your tormentor is away   JIM

[Enclosure to above letter]

From JOHN G. LIDWELL (Copy)

[*21 August 1912*]

Dear Sir,

Re '*Dubliners.*'

Referring to our correspondence concerning the stories 'Ivy Day in the Committee Room' and 'An Encounter.' As the passages you have shown me are not likely to be taken serious notice of by the Advisers of the Crown, they would not interfere with the publication, nor do I consider a conviction could be easily obtained. Yours faithfully,

JOHN LIDWELL

---

[1] See II, 309–10.   [2] A slip for *Povero me* ('Poor me').

To NORA BARNACLE JOYCE   MS. Cornell

[Postmark 22 August 1912]   *[Dublin]*

My dear distant Nora I saw Roberts today and we spoke of the binding
&c of my book so that a ray of hope has sprung out of the clouds. He
told me to call back tomorrow at 12.

I have taken a double-bedded room at 21 Richmond Place on the
North Circular Road and I am foolish enough to hope that you and I
may be able to spend some happy days after all this trouble. How I
should love to go about with you during Horse Show Week and have
money to take you here and there. I can get passes for the theatres. Be
sure to have nice petticoats and stockings. You can have your hair
dressed here. Have you the grey ribbon I like so much? Would you come
up tomorrow? I am afraid to ask because Stannie has not written to me
and my money is almost at an end. Perhaps he will write tomorrow. I
have passed a terribly exciting week over my book. Roberts spoke to me
today of my novel, and asked me to finish it. Would you like to come to
the theatre with me and have supper together afterwards? I hope you
are as plump as you were? Is your tight naughty lilac blouse clean? I
hope you clean your teeth. If you don't look well I will send you back to
Galway. Be sure not to break your hats especially the high one. I have a
nice room in the front with two beds. If all goes well could we not pass a
few days in each other's company. I should like to show you many places
in Dublin that are mentioned in my book. I wish you were here. You
have become a part of myself—one flesh. When we go back to Trieste
will you read if I give you books? Then we could speak together. Nobody
loves you as I do and I should love to read the different poets and dramatists and novelists with you as your guide. I will give you only what is
finest and best in writing. Poor Jim! He is always planning and planning!

I hope I shall have good news tomorrow. If only my book is published
then I will plunge into my novel and finish it.

The *Abbey Theatre* will be open and they will give plays of Yeats and
Synge. You have a right to be there because you are my bride: and I am
one of the writers of this generation who are perhaps creating at last a
conscience in the soul of this wretched race.[1] Addio!   JIM

(Write as usual to Todd Burns[2] not to my address)

[1] Stephen Dedalus writes in his diary at the end of *A Portrait of the Artist*: 'Welcome,
O life! I go to encounter for the millionth time the reality of experience and to forge in
the smithy of my soul the uncreated conscience of my race.'
[2] Todd, Burns & Co., cloth merchants and tailors, 17, 18, and 47 Mary Street, Dublin,
where May Joyce was employed.

To Stanislaus Joyce   MS. Cornell

23 August 1912   [*Dublin*]

Dear Stannie I spent yesterday with Roberts discussing binding, paper, advertisement &c of the book.

This morning I called and received the enclosed letter. Roberts was not there as he had arranged. After having received it I sat for an hour in a sofa in Lidwell's office thinking if I would buy a revolver and put some daylight into my publisher. I showed the letter to Lidwell who said I had been badly treated but that I could do nothing and the publishers were quite right as what he had seen of the book was objectionable.

Then I went to Pappie who told me to put the letter in my pocket, buck up, take back the MSS and find another publisher. Then I went to May who said quietly 'O well, you expected that, didn't you?'

I went to Roberts and spoke to him from three to five. My defense was:

i) A railway co. is mentioned once and then exonerated from all blame by two witnesses, jury and coroner.

ii) Public houses are mentioned in four stories out of 15. In 3 of these stories the names are fictitious. In the 4th the names are real because the persons walk from place to place (*Counterparts*)

iii) Nothing happens in the public houses. People drink.

iv) I offered to take a car and go with Roberts, proofs in hand, to the 3 or 4 publicans really named and to the secretary of the railway co. He refused.

v) I said the publicans would be glad of the advertisement.

vi) I said that I would put fictitious names for the few real ones but added that by so doing the selling value in Dublin of the book would go down.

vii) I said that even if they took action for libel against Maunsel that the jury would be a long time before awarding damages on such a plea.

viii) I said that his legal adviser was a fool to advise him to sue me. If he sued me (even if I lived in Dublin) a jury would say he had the MS for 10 months and I was not liable for his error in judgment. But if he sued me in Trieste I would hold the whip and would laugh him out of court.

ix) I suggested that his lawyer encouraged correspondence and litigation for his own profit.

Exhausted I stopped. Roberts walked about, noted on a paper and said he would write again to London and let me know on Monday.

No letter letter [sic] has reached me from you and no remittance. I am therefore helpless and newsless. However, I presume you will write tomorrow morning.

I will fight to the last inch with every weapon in my power.[1]   JIM

To MRS WILLIAM MURRAY   MS. National Library

9 December 1912   *Via Donato Bramante 4, Trieste*

Dear Aunt Josephine: I am very sorry to hear of Uncle Willie's death though from what you told me I knew it was a matter of some months only. It is a very sad collapse and I do not know enough of the end to write you more fully. We had many wild nights together, many arguments. He was the only member of my mother's family who seemed to take any pride out of my existence: and I can still remember the tone of his voice when he spoke of 'my nephew'. After all he was a man, like us all or like many of us, worthy of a better life than he had assigned him.

If you have time to write me afterwards I shall be very glad to hear from you and will certainly answer: though, to tell the truth, I dislike to see the Dublin postmark as all the envelopes contain sad news of death, poverty or failure of some kind. If I had known in time I should have sent a wreath in my name and in that of my children but I received a card (or rather Eileen received it) only on Thursday night. I telegraphed lest you might think I had known before then.

Nora begs me to send you her condolence. I renew my own to you and yours. I hope at least that he did not suffer much towards the end. While I was writing this letter many memories came into my mind. Nearly all are pleasant memories: and these are perhaps the best legacy that one can leave to others. And so I take leave of him with pity and regret.

If you will send me a copy of a photograph of his I shall be very glad indeed to have that reminder of a good-hearted and lively companion of my youth. Believe me, dear Aunt Josephine, Yours very sincerely,

JIM

To W. B. YEATS   MS. Yeats

25 December 1912   *Via Donato Bramante 4, II, Trieste (Austria)*

Dear Yeats I have sent the set of proofs of my unfortunate book *Dubliners* to a publisher: Martin Secker, 5 John Street, Adelphi. You would do me a great service if you could intervene in its favour and, I

[1] But Roberts refused to publish *Dubliners*.

hope, some service also to the literature of our country. As you will easily understand it is very difficult for a person living so far away to push on these matters and my book seems to be pursued by a strange ill-luck. If you can do anything in the matter I am sure you will.

Wishing you the compliments of the season Sincerely yours

JAMES JOYCE

To STANISLAUS JOYCE   MS. Cornell

9 September 1913   *Via Montfort 4*[1]

Dear Stannie I present the enclosed lines[2] to your young friends of the *Rowing Club* if they want them for a dinner programme or some such thing—with the rheumatic chamber poet's (or pot's) compliments. *Quid si prisca redit Venus?*[3] Perhaps you may like them.   JIM

P.S. $16 + 10 = 26$.[4]

To GRANT RICHARDS   MS. N.Y. Public Library (Berg)

23 November 1913   *Via Donato Bramante 4, Trieste*

Dear Sir I sent you two years ago a copy of a letter which I sent to the press concerning my book *Dubliners*. Since then the book has had a still more eventful career. It was printed completely and the entire edition of 1000 copies was burned by the publisher. A complete set of printed proofs is in my possession. In view of the very strange history of the book—its acceptance and refusal by two houses, my letter to the present king, his reply, my letter to the press, my negotiations with the second publisher—negotiations which ended in malicious burning of the whole first edition—and furthermore in view of the fact that Dublin, of which the book treats so uncompromisingly, is at present the centre

---

[1] Joyce was writing from the flat of Ettore Schmitz (see p. 275n.).

[2] 'Watching the Needleboats at San Sabba', later included in *Pomes Penyeach*. Joyce had seen his brother Stanislaus take part in a race of needleboats (racing shells) at San Sabba, near Trieste. As the scullers pulled towards shore, they began to sing an aria sung by Johnson in the last act of Giacomo Puccini's *La Fanciulla del West*. Joyce's poem played on the lines:

> Aspetterà ch'io torni,
> E passeranno i giorni e passeranno i giorni
> ed io non tornerò ed io non tornerò.

('She will await my return,/And days will pass and days will pass/and I will not return and I will not return.')

[3] 'What if the old love should return?' That is, what if he should begin to write poetry again? The line is taken from Horace, *Carmina* III.9.17.

[4] Austrian crowns borrowed from or by Stanislaus Joyce.

of general interest, I think that perhaps the time has come for my luckless book to appear.

I have written a preface[1] narrating objectively its history and as there are 100 orders ready for it in this city I am prepared, if need be, to contribute towards the expenses of publication—expenses which I presume will be lighter as the book will be set up from printed proofs.

Awaiting your prompt reply I am, dear sir Yours sincerely

JAMES JOYCE

30 November 1913

A CURIOUS HISTORY[2]

The following letter, which was the history of a book of stories, was sent by me to the Press of the United Kingdom two years ago. It was published by two newspapers so far as I know: *Sinn Fein* (Dublin) and the *Northern Whig* (Belfast).

[There follows Joyce's letter to the press of 17 August 1911][3]

I waited nine months after the publication of this letter. Then I went to Ireland and entered into negotiations with Messrs Maunsel. They asked me to omit from the collection the story 'An Encounter', passages in 'Two Gallants', 'The Boarding House', 'A Painful Case', and to change everywhere through the book the name of restaurants, cakeshops, railway stations, public houses, laundries, bars and other places of business. After having argued against their point of view day after day for six weeks and having laid the matter before two solicitors (who, while they informed me that the publishing firm had made a breach of contract, refused to take up my case or to allow their names to be associated with it in any way.) I consented in despair to all these changes on condition that the book were brought out without delay and the original text were restored in future editions, if such were called for. Then Messrs Maunsel asked me to pay into their bank £1000 as security, or to find two sureties of £500 each. I declined to do either; and they then wrote to me, informing me that they would not publish the book, altered or unaltered, and that if I did not make them an offer

[1] The preface was 'A Curious History'.
[2] First published in the *Egoist* (London), I. 2 (15 January 1914), 26–7. Ezra Pound prefixed the following note:
'The following statement having been received by me from an author of known and notable talents, and the state of the case being now, so far as I know, precisely what it was at the date of his last letter (November 30th), I have thought it more appropriate to print his communication entire rather than to indulge in my usual biweekly comment upon books published during the fortnight.
'Mr. Joyce's statement is as follows:'
[3] See pp. 197–9.

to cover their losses on printing it they would sue me to recover the same. I offered to pay sixty per cent of the cost of printing the first edition of one thousand copies if the edition were made over to my order. This offer was accepted, and I arranged with my brother in Dublin to publish and sell the book for me. On the morrow when the draft and agreement were to be signed the publishers informed me that the matter was at an end because the printer refused to hand over the copies. I then went to the printer. His foreman told me that the printer had decided to forego all claim to the money due to him. I asked whether the printer would hand over the complete edition to a London or continental firm or to my brother or to me if he were fully indemnified. He said that the copies would never leave his printing house, and that the type had been broken up and that the entire edition of one thousand copies would be burnt the next day. I left Ireland the next day, bringing with me a printed copy of the book which I had obtained from the publisher.   James Joyce

Via Donato Bramante 4, II, Trieste, Austria

To Stanislaus Joyce (Postcard)[1]   MS. Mrs Nelly Joyce

16 June 1915[2]   *Via Donato Bramante 4, II, Trieste*

Lieber Stannie: Wir sind noch hier und bei guter Gesundheit. Ich hoffe dass Du bist es auch. Falls wir reisen ab ich werde Dir schreiben. Hab' kein Angst für uns. Bis jetzt hat man uns immer gut behandelt. Ich habe etwas geschrieben. Die erste Episode meines neues Roman "Ulysses" ist geschrieben. Die erste Teil, die Telemachie, besteht aus vier Episoden: die zweite von fünfzehn, dass ist, Ulysses Wandlungen: und die dritte, Ulysses Heimkehr, von andre drei Episoden.[3] Lebwohl.   Jim
Absender: James Joyce[4]

---

[1] Stanislaus had been arrested as an enemy alien in January 1915, and was now interned as a prisoner of war in Schloss Kirchberg an der Wild in lower Austria, about seventy-five miles north of Vienna.

[2] The date was the eleventh anniversary of 'Bloomsday', when the events of *Ulysses* supposedly took place.

[3] Joyce soon changed this plan to make the first part consist of three episodes, the second part of twelve, and the third of three.

[4] (Translation)

'Dear Stannie: We are still here and in good health. I hope you are the same. If we leave I will write you. Don't worry about us. Up to now we've been well treated. I have written something. The first episode of my new novel *Ulysses* is written. The first part, the Telemachiad, consists of four episodes: the second of fifteen, that is, Ulysses' wanderings: and the third, Ulysses' return home, of three more episodes. Best wishes.   Jim
Sender: James Joyce'

Part III

ZURICH, TRIESTE

1915–1920

Zurich, Trieste (1915–1920)

After a rather frightening journey as enemy aliens through Austria, Joyce and his family arrived in Zurich on 30 June 1915. Without particularly meaning to settle in that city, they remained there during the war and for almost a year after the Armistice. The problems of living arranged themselves more easily this time. Through Triestine connections Joyce secured some language pupils and made some new friends, such as Ottocaro Weiss, Edmund Brauchbar, Victor Sax, and Georges Borach. Money began to flow towards him with less obstruction than in the past. Nora Joyce's uncle, Michael Healy, gave some to tide them over their initial expenses in Switzerland. Then Ezra Pound contrived, with the help of Yeats and the acquiescence of Edmund Gosse, a grant for Joyce from the Royal Literary Fund. This was supplemented by a small subsidy from the Society of Authors, and then by a more official benefaction, a Civil List grant awarded Joyce by the Prime Minister in August 1916.

More important than these were gifts from two other persons. Harriet Shaw Weaver, touched by Joyce's situation and convinced of his genius, began to send him money, anonymously at first, on 22 February 1917, and eventually attempted to give him a permanent endowment by gifts of stock. Edith Rockefeller McCormick, a wealthy American patron of the arts and of psychoanalysis then living in Zurich, gave Joyce a substantial monthly stipend from March 1918 through September 1919. He received other gifts and some royalties as well, so that, after reaching Zurich in poverty, Joyce by the end of his stay had capital as well as income. In these four years he subtly changed social position.

While in Zurich Joyce consolidated his role as a new force in modern literature. Although he still experienced difficulties in publishing his books, these were much less serious than heretofore. The serial publication in the *Egoist* of *A Portrait of the Artist as a Young Man* was concluded in September 1915. When James B. Pinker, who began acting as Joyce's agent in that same year, could not place the book anywhere, Miss Weaver formed the Egoist Press to make a first venture into book publishing. A new problem arose when no English printer was willing to risk setting the book in type. Then B. W. Huebsch in New York courageously interposed and published *A Portrait* in the last days of 1916. At the same time he imported sheets of *Dubliners* from

Grant Richards and brought out the first American edition of that book as well. Now Miss Weaver was able to publish an English edition of *A Portrait*, using American sheets, in 1917.

These two books, and the enthusiastic reviews they elicited in both countries, awoke interest in Joyce's work on *Ulysses*. Ezra Pound suggested to Margaret Anderson and Jane Heap, the editors of the *Little Review* in New York, that they begin serial publication of the book, and they eagerly agreed. Instalments appeared there from March 1918 until September–December 1920, by which time more than thirteen of the eighteen chapters had been published. Meanwhile Miss Weaver brought out a much smaller portion of the book in five issues of the *Egoist* during 1919. Joyce succeeded also in having *Exiles* published by Richards and Huebsch simultaneously in May 1918, and on 7 August 1919 he realized a more intimate ambition when the play was produced in Munich in German translation. Though it lasted only one performance, the indignation it stirred up among the critics and theatregoers made Joyce hope for more success in the future.

His stay in Zurich was marked by a great exfoliation of Joyce's creative powers. His talent grew in confidence and extravagance, dazzling and sometimes even disquieting his friends. A change came concomitantly in his relations with Ireland; these grew less tense now that he was assured of an international audience. He could more easily give expression to that fascination he had always felt with the life of Dublin, especially the classless, almost anarchic life of the streets, the cemetery, the public houses, the library steps. The conception of Leopold Bloom as his hero for the book liberated him, for Bloom could be an unembittered, comic witness of what Stephen Dedalus, because of his thwarted ambitions and blocked ideals, observed with such resentment and anger. The conception of a modern Odyssey gratified Joyce's love of scholarship; it enabled him to speculate ingeniously about the origins of Greek and Semitic civilisations, about the naturalistic basis for Ulysses' semi-mythical wanderings, about the theme of the oneness of all ages which had always attracted him. He began his systematic attacks upon conventional English, building the language afresh by fragmenting its sentences, compounding its old words into new ones, parodying its standard styles, and in general dosing English prose with slang, archaisms, the rhythms of learned texts strangely mingled with those of ordinary speech, and a compressed poetry. Behind him Zurich, suddenly confronted by this and other manifestations of a revolutionary spirit, sat like some austere grandmother, long since inured and indifferent to the babbling of unfamiliar progeny.

Joyce's temperament was one that led easily to altercations. In Dublin he had quarrelled with Oliver St John Gogarty, then with Vincent Cosgrave, and finally with George Roberts, while from Rome and Trieste he had fought vainly against Grant Richards. In Zurich he found a grander adversary in the British Empire. This battle began modestly enough in April 1918, when Joyce and an English actor, Claud W. Sykes, established a theatrical company they called the English Players. Joyce fell into a minor dispute with Henry Carr, an employee of the British Consulate General in Zurich who was one of the company's actors; when the Consul-General showed no sympathy he presented his case to the British Minister to Berne and finally, through Ezra Pound, to the Foreign Office. On the local level, he waged two lawsuits against Carr, winning one on 15 October 1918 and losing the other on 11 February 1919. He summarized this artist's war against official society in an open letter in late April 1919, just as he had done in August 1911 in his dispute with Roberts over *Dubliners*.

Although the dispute with the British Consulate General was enlivening, Joyce's last three years in Zurich were blurred and distressed by the eye trouble which up to now had been minor. In February and March 1917 he suffered an attack of glaucoma; it appeared to abate under treatment, but on 18 August he suffered a new attack so severe that he had to undergo an iridectomy six days later. This was the first of what proved to be a series of eleven eye operations during the next fifteen years. On 12 October 1917 he went to Locarno to recuperate in the milder climate of Italian Switzerland, but, not finding the atmosphere congenial, he returned to Zurich in January 1918.

At the end of 1918 a half-comic, half-pathetic note was introduced into his life by his meeting with a young and pretty Swiss woman named Martha Fleischmann. The affair never became more than preliminary, a matter mostly of looking and letter-writing, at once naughty and operatic. As if to avoid compromising himself, Joyce wrote his letters to Martha Fleischmann with Greek 'e's' (ϵ), just as Bloom did to Martha Clifford in *Ulysses*. This clandestine interlude persisted until 2 February 1919, after which Fräulein Fleischmann went to an asylum, her 'guardian' (actually her lover) made a fuss, and Joyce retreated from the affair as timidly as he had entered it.

When war ended Joyce lingered in Zurich before returning to his furniture and books in Trieste. His sister Eileen Schaurek and her husband went back to Trieste first, at the end of 1918, and his brother Stanislaus, released after four years of internment, soon followed them. Joyce left Zurich in mid-October 1919, the more reluctantly because he had struck up a close friendship with an English painter, Frank Budgen, who sympathized with his literary experiments and encouraged them. In Trieste Joyce felt his old friends were changed, and his brother was less attentive; no doubt he was himself less casual and informal in manner than before the war. He was reinstated in his old position as a teacher at the commercial high school in Trieste, which was now being transformed into a university. The whole city was low-spirited, suffering from the loss of the maritime eminence it had enjoyed under Austria. During the spring of 1920 Joyce began to contemplate the possibility of going away at least for a holiday.

Ezra Pound, who was then travelling in Italy, helped to bring him to a decision. He persuaded Joyce to meet him on 8 June 1920 at Sirmione, on Lago di Garda, and made clear that the best base of operations from which to arrange to publish *Ulysses* would be Paris. He promised to prepare the ground there by encouraging his many friends to translate Joyce's books into French, arrange for the production of *Exiles*, and find a suitable flat. With these inducements the Joyces left Trieste for good and arrived, on 8 July 1920, in Paris.

30 June 1915   *Reinhardstrasse 7, Zurich VIII (Switzerland)*

Dear Sir I am obliged by your favour of 26 instant and return you duly filled up under separate registered cover the printed form which you forwarded me.

At the outbreak of war I was in Trieste where I have lived for the last eleven years. My income there was derived from two sources: i) my position in the Higher School of Commerce ii) private lessons. After the outbreak of war I was confirmed in my position by the Austrian Ministry of Public Instruction, Vienna, from whom I held and hold it. The school however closed in spring, nearly all the professors having been called up as officers of the reserve. My second source of income in normal times, viz., private lessons, produced very little in the first months and nothing at all in the next months owing to the critical conditions of the city. In these circumstances I lived with great difficulty and was obliged to recur to the assistance of friends, as stated under.

When, one month after the Italian declaration of war, the military authorities decided on the partial evacuation of the city I asked for, and obtained at once, a safe conduct for myself, my wife and children to the Swiss frontier. I have been here one month now. I received from a relative of my wife's a small sum of money, £15, of which some remains. In order to leave Trieste I effected a loan on my furniture and this sum went for trainfare (owing to the fact that the railways of Trentino and South Tyrol were in our war zone we were obliged to come by a circuitous route) and clothing.

I receive nothing in the way of royalties. My contributions to reviews etc were made twelve years ago. From my first publisher and from my second I did not receive any money for royalties, the sale in both cases being below the required number. In the case of my second publisher I bought and paid for at trade prices 120 copies of my book as a condition of publication. For my contributions to reviews in the current year, *The Smart Set* and *The Egoist*, I received no payment.

I enclose a medical certificate which attests my state of health and shall be much obliged if you will kindly return it to me under registered cover when it has been examined. In present circumstances in this country where I may have to remain for some time it seems very difficult to obtain any work of the kind which I do. My literary work during the last eleven years has produced nothing. On the contrary my second book *Dubliners* cost me a considerable sum of money owing to the eight years of litigation which preceded its publication. I have tried to obtain an engagement with several schools here but have not succeeded.

I trust that I have given you a clear statement of the facts of the case. I am writing to my friends Mr W B Yeats and Mr Ezra Pound who, I am sure, will corroborate me in my statements. I am, dear Sir, Sincerely yours   JAMES JOYCE

Debts contracted in the course of the war.
    i) to Baron Ambrogio Ralli, Palazzo Ralli, Trieste, Austria,
          Crowns/Austrian/300.–
    ii) to Gioacchino Veneziani Esq. Murano, Venice, Italy,
          Crowns/Austrian/250.–
              Cr. A. 550.–

Enclosure
1 Medical Certificate

To MICHAEL HEALY[1]   MS. National Library

2 November 1915   *Kreuzstrasse 19, Zurich*

My dear Mr Healy: I received the day before yesterday your kind letter and this morning your Money Order (£9) for which I thank you most sincerely. It is most welcome and useful. Nora has bought a lot of flannels and other clothes which the children need in this climate and a hat which she finally selected from the few hundred which were shown to her. We are now fairly well fortified against the cold. As for myself I am to be seen in a shellcocoa-coloured[2] overcoat which an absent-minded German left behind him and I bought for eleven francs. Of his moral character I know nothing. But I am sure that he has (or had) uncommonly short arms. I presume the overcoat is mine now since I paid for it to his late landlady but I feel, as Mr R. G. Knowles[3] used to sing,

> "I'm only airing it for him:
> It doesn't belong to me."

---

[1] Nora Joyce's uncle (see p. 45n.) entered the Customs and Excise Service in 1883 and served in Galway until 1916 when he was transferred to Dublin. In 1922 he retired and lived in Galway.

[2] Joyce used this invented epithet, of the tide, in *Ulysses*.

[3] R. G. Knowles (1858–1919), music-hall comedian.

I was introduced to the millionaire I wrote you of some days ago. He told me that his daughter is rather ill and asked me to give him my address as he says he wishes to speak with me about my play of which he has heard. I was also introduced to the president of the Russian Club here who talks of translating it into Russian and producing it. Besides I have written to Geneva to see if it can go on there in a French version. I also met the chief actor here who presented me to the director of the Zurich Stadttheater and, through another friend, I got an introduction to a solicitor here whose father is director of the Stadttheater in Bern. My poor shoes are nearly worn out after it all, as you can imagine; but I hope something will come out of it all. Immediately I have any good news I shall let you know. I hope you managed to get that copy of *The New Age*. I hear now that there is a long article[1] about me and the play, the name of which by the way is *Exiles*, in a Chicago review called *Drama* but I have not seen it yet.

I thank you for your inquiries about my brother. He sent me his photograph last week. He has a long full beard and looks like the late Duke of Devonshire. He tells me that he sprained his wrist, playing tennis, but is now better. If you send him a postcard with greetings from Galway I am sure he will answer you. His address is:

> Stanislaus Joyce
> (Internierter britischer Staatsangehöriger)
> Schloss Grossan bei Raabs
> Nieder Österreich

My sister[2] was when I last heard from her well and still in Prague. I believe her husband has been exonerated from military service much to her (and I fancy his) relief. I forget whether I thanked you for having verified the quotation about our excellent friend Bombados.[3] If I did not I do so now. I shall correct it on the proof—if I ever see one. I am sorry to hear you have so much to do. However, as you say, it is a good thing to be alive in such times. I had letters from Trieste on Saturday. So far as my flat is concerned it seems to be as I left it but life is certainly pleasanter here just at present. Today is the feast of S. Justin Martyr, patron of Trieste, and I shall perhaps eat a cheap small pudding somewhere in his honour for the many years I lived in his city. As for the future it is useless to speculate. If I could find out in the meantime who is the patron of men of letters I should try to remind him that

---

[1] By Ezra Pound. Actually it did not appear until February 1916.
[2] Mrs Eileen Joyce Schaurek.
[3] See *A Portrait of the Artist as a Young Man*, Chap. III.

I exist: but I understand that the last saint who held that position resigned in despair and no other will take the portfolio.

In conclusion I thank you very sincerely for your great kindness and also for your kind and encouraging message to me. You may be sure that I will continue to do all that I can. Nora Giorgio and Lucia send you all their warm regards with which I include mine also. With renewed thanks to you Sincerely yours   JAMES JOYCE

To EMMA CUZZI[1]   MS. Brocchi

7 December 1915   *Kreuzstrasse 19, III, Zurigo VIII, Svizzera*

Gentilissima signorina Tante grazie delle due stampe del bassorilievo[2] che cercavo, come sa, da un pezzo. Una, quella non rimodernata, farò incorniciare in una cornice ellitica che farò poi 'sporcare' in celeste e grigio (uso Silvestri)[3] per creare l'illusione del 'gran ponte del cielo'[4] attorno alla figura dell'artefice. Eppoi sono superstizioso. Chi sa se l'advento in casa mia di quel tale non mi recherà una lieta notizia? Se così è sia doppiamente lodato il suo cortese pensiero.

Saluti cordiali a Lei ed alla sua famiglia   JAMES JOYCE[5]

To W. B. YEATS   MS. Yeats

14 September 1916   *Seefeldstrasse 54, parterre rechts, Zurich VIII*

Dear Yeats: Ezra Pound writes to me telling me of your kindness in writing a letter of recommendation on my behalf as a result of which a royal bounty has been granted to me (£100).[6] I need scarcely say how acceptable this money is to me at such a time and in such circumstances

---

[1] Emma Cuzzi (1896–1958), later Signora Aganippo Brocchi, had been a pupil of Joyce in Trieste.

[2] A bas-relief at the Villa Albani in Rome. It represents Daedalus completing a second wing for Icarus, who stands in front of the first and holds up the other so his father can work on it.

[3] Tullio Silvestri, a Triestine painter and a friend of Joyce.

[4] A phrase from Puccini's *Madama Butterfly*, Act II, scene ii.

[5] (Translation)

'Dear Miss Cuzzi, Many thanks for the two prints of the bas-relief which I had been looking for, as you know, for a good while. I shall have the un-retouched one framed in an oval frame which I shall then have stained in sky-blue and grey (Silvestri style) to create the illusion of the "great bridge of the sky" around the image of the artificer. Besides, I am superstitious. Who knows if the coming into my house of this man will not bring me good news? If this should happen may your kind thought be doubly praised. Best regards to you and your family   James Joyce'

[6] A Civil List grant.

but, apart from its usefulness, it is very encouraging as a sign of recognition and I am very grateful to you for your friendly and valuable support. I hope that now at last matters may begin to go a little more smoothly for me for, to tell the truth, it is very tiresome to wait and hope for so many years. It seems that my novel will really come out this autumn in New York and London. I am sending the typescript of my play *Exiles* (which has already been rejected in Zurich, Berne, Turin and by the Stage Society in London) to Pound who says that Mr Knoblauch[1] will read it. Besides this I am writing a book *Ulysses* which however will not be finished for some years. Possibly the novel and play will engage the attention of my six or seven readers (7 copies of *Dubliners* were sold in the last six months) until it is ready. Pound speaks of offering the play to some new review *Seven Arts*, that is, if it is not accepted by *Drama* (Chicago) where it is being read, I believe. Mr Archer too said he would read it.

I hope your own affairs prosper well and that your health is good. I have been away so many years that I know little or nothing about what is published in England. I saw some time before I left Trieste the Italian version of *Countess Cathleen* in a bookshop and I must say that the few passages which I read I did not like. It is, I think, a great pity that my friend Vidacovich's version was not published. His rendering of many parts (especially of the song *Impetuous heart*) was excellent. I do not know where he is now (in Rome, I think) or what became of the translation we made together of Synge's *Riders to the Sea*. I read it one night to Mrs Sainati, a very original actress, and her husband took away the *copione* to read it again. Vidacovich also tried his hand with me on a version of my story *Ivy Day in the Committee Room* for the *Nuova Antologia* but the attempt was a dismal failure.

I have every reason to be grateful to the many friends who have helped me since I came here and I can never thank you enough for having brought me into relations with your friend Ezra Pound who is indeed a wonder worker.

With very many thanks again and all good wishes Sincerely yours
JAMES JOYCE

To MRS THOMAS KETTLE[2]   MS. Texas

25 September 1916   *Seefeldstrasse 54, rechts, Zurich*

Dear Mrs Kettle: I have read this morning, with deep regret in the

---

[1] Edward Knoblock (1874–1935), American dramatist who lived mostly in England.
[2] *Née* Mary Sheehy; see p. 162n.

Times that my old school fellow and fellow student Lieutenant Kettle has been killed in action. I hope you will not deem it a stranger's intrusion on your grief if I beg you to accept from me a word of sincere condolence. I remember very gratefully his benevolent and courteous friendliness to me when I was in Ireland seven years ago.

May I ask you also to convey to your sisters (whose addresses I do not know) my sympathy with them in the losses they have suffered? I am grieved to hear that so many misfortunes have fallen on your family in these evil days.

Believe me to be, dear Mrs Kettle, very sincerely yours

JAMES JOYCE

To HARRIET SHAW WEAVER   MS. British Museum

8 November 1916   *Seefeldstrasse 54, parterre rechts, Zurich VIII*

Dear Miss Weaver: Thanks for your two letters. I shall be obliged if you will forward a copy of *Chamber Music* to Mr Huebsch and also the press notices which I enclose. I agree to your proposal of an article with a woodcut but fear that your readers have already had enough of me. In any case tomorrow I shall send photographs, one for the *Egoist* and one for Mr Huebsch. As regards the 'biographical items' which he requires will you kindly refer him to "Who's Who?" (1916) and forward him also a copy of *The Egoist* (15 January 1914)? I send also some account of my books on the enclosed slip[1] as I suppose that is what he means. With kind regards sincerely yours   JAMES JOYCE

Chamber Music: Some of these verses were printed in the *Saturday Review* and *Speaker* (London) and in Dane? (Dana?) (Dublin). Mr Symons arranged for their publication by Mr Matthews.

Dubliners: Mr Norman, editor of the *Irish Homestead*? (Dublin) agreed to take stories from me but after the second story he told me that his readers had complained. The other stories I wrote in Austria.

A Portrait of the Artist as a Young Man: I began this novel in notes before I left Ireland and finished it in Trieste in 1914. Before I left I offered an introductory chapter to Mr Magee (John Eglinton) and Mr Ryan, editors of *Dana*. It was refused.

[1] The list that follows is from Miss Weaver's copy of Joyce's notes.

Exiles: (a play) I wrote this in Trieste 1914–1915. (v. *Drama* Chicago Febry 1916.

Ulysses: I began this in Rome six years [ago] (or seven) and am writing it now. I hope to finish it in 1918.

Address: I have lived in Trieste since 1904—except for a stay of one year in Rome. I left it in July 1915 when the Austrian authorities gave me at my request a permit (for my family and myself) to the Austro-Swiss frontier. Since then I have lived in Zurich.

Irish Literary Theatre. I refused to sign the letter of protest against *Countess Cathleen* when I was an undergraduate. I was the only student who refused his signature. Some years later I made the acquaintance of Mr Yeats. He invited me to write a play for his theatre and I promised to do so in ten years. I met Synge in Paris in 1902 (where I went to study medicine). He gave me *Riders to the Sea* to read and after his death I translated it into Italian (for Mr Sainati ?). I also translated Mr Yeats' *Countess Cathleen* but the project failed as we had translated the first version and Mr Yeats did not wish that version to be offered to the Italian publisher.

Ezra Pound.   Mr Pound wrote to me in Trieste in 1913, offering me his help. He brought the MSS of my novel to *The Egoist* where it was published serially (from February 1914 to September 1915). He also arranged for the publication in America and England. He has written many articles (all most friendly and appreciative) about me in English and American papers. But for his friendly help and the enterprise of Miss Weaver, editor of *The Egoist*, in accepting *A Portrait of the Artist* after it had been refused by all publishers, my novel would still be unpublished.

Early Publications (1) "Parnell" a pamphlet written when I was nine years old (in 1891) on Parnell's death. It was printed and circulated in Dublin. I do not know if any copy is to be found today. (2) An article on Ibsen in the *Fortnightly Review* written when I was seventeen. Ibsen was so kind as to send me a message of thanks for it. (3) *The Day of* [the] *Rabblement* (a pamphlet on the Irish Literary Theatre). This was written for the

University Review but refused insertion by the censor
as was also an essay on co-education by my fellow
student, the late Mr Skeffington. We published the
essays together in pamphlet form.

To [Harriet Shaw Weaver]   MS. British Museum

6 March 1917   *Seefeldstrasse 73, Zurich VIII*

Dear Sir (or Madam): Messrs Black, Monro, Saw and Co wrote to me
on 22 February that they have been instructed by you to forward me on
1 May, August, September and February cheques for £50, making a
total of £200. They add that you are an admirer of my writing and
desire to be anonymous.[1] First of all I will ask you to forgive my delay
in answering. Since 4 February I have been laid up with a painful and
dangerous illness of the eyes (rheumatic iritis). As it is the fifth attack
which I have had and was complicated with synechia it was quite impossible for me to write until today.

I am deeply touched by your generosity. I scarcely know what to say.
It has given me the greatest encouragement and, coming at such a time
as the present, relieves my mind of many worries. Allow me to express
my sincerest gratitude both for the munificence of your gift and for the
delicacy of its giving. I hope that the future may justify in some measure
an act so noble and considerate.

I should like to make some poor return and am therefore writing to
the publishers of my books asking them to send me copies so that I may
beg you to accept them from me with a dedication.

As soon as I am cured I shall continue to write a novel at which I am
working *Ulysses*. I have written also a play *Exiles* and if it is published
this year I shall send it to you.

Once more I ask you to accept my deepest thanks and to believe that I
am most gratefully and sincerely yours   James Joyce

To Ezra Pound[2]

9 April 1917   *Seefeldstrasse 73, Zurich VIII*

Dear Pound: Many thanks for yours of 26th ult. which arrived only
this morning. Owing to the delay and the fact that I have nothing ready,
I am sending you an accompanying note, as you wish. I sent three pieces

[1] Miss Weaver disclosed her identity as patron only in July 1919. See p. 240.
[2] From a typewritten copy.

of verse in December, I think, to *Poetry* (Chicago) through my agent, but heard nothing more of them. If they have not been and will not be published, would you take them in reversion? As regards stories I have none. I have some prose sketches, as I told you, but they are locked up in my desk in Trieste. As regards excerpts from *Ulysses*, the only thing I could send would be the Hamlet chapter, or part of it—which, however, would suffer by excision. If there is anything else I could do—perhaps a simple translation or review—will you tell me? I shall be glad to do it, though I am quite sure that, with your usual friendliness, you exaggerate the value of my poor signature as a 'draw'. I have been thinking all day what I could do or write. Perhaps there is something if I could only think of it. Unfortunately, I have very little imagination. I am also a very bad critic. For instance, some time ago a person gave me a two-volume novel to read, *Joseph Vance*.[1] I read it at intervals for some time, till I discovered that I had been reading the second volume instead of the first. And if I am a bad reader I am a most tiresome writer—to myself, at least. It exhausts me before I end it. I wonder if you will like the book I am writing? I am doing it, as Aristotle would say, by different means in different parts. Strange to say, in spite of my illness I have written enough lately.

As regards my novel, it seems that it has now come to a standstill. I did not see any review in the *New Statesman*. Mr Boyd[2] sent me a notice from the *New York Sun*, about 2,000 words, by Mr Huneker,[3] very favourable. Miss Weaver sent me also other American notices but they seem to have fallen out of the envelope somewhere on the way. By the way, I think you ought to type your letters to me without cancellings of any kind. Perhaps that delayed your last letter.

As I wrote you, the Stage Society wishes to reconsider my play, *Exiles*. I shall ask my agent[4] to submit it also for publication in London and New York this autumn. I wish I could hear of a good dramatic agent in America who would take it up. Perhaps it would be more successful than *A Portrait of the Artist*. I send you a limerick thereon:

> There once was a lounger named Stephen
> Whose youth was most odd and uneven.
> > He throve on the smell
> > Of a horrible hell
> That a Hottentot wouldn't believe in.

[1] William De Morgan, *Joseph Vance* (New York, 1906).
[2] Ernest Boyd (1887–1946), American critic born in Dublin, author of *Ireland's Literary Renaissance* (New York, 1922).
[3] James Gibbons Huneker (1860–1921), American essayist and critic of the arts.
[4] James Brand Pinker (1863–1922).

In spite of the efforts of the critics of the *Times* and *Manchester Guardian* to galvanize the book into life, it has collapsed or is about to collapse—possibly for lack of inverted commas.[1] I should like to hear what Yeats says about *Exiles*.

I am rather tired for I have been correcting misprints in my novel. There are nearly four hundred. No revise was sent to me. This in view of a possible second edition during the century. The announcement on the last page of *The Egoist* is a pious exaggeration—so Miss Weaver writes.

In any case I am better. Please write to me about your review. I shall go on writing, thanks to the kindness of my unknown friend and also of Mr Quinn.[2]

I hope you are well. My wife and noisy children thank you for your good wishes. From me, *ogni bene!* [Sincerely yours   JAMES JOYCE]

To EZRA POUND   MS. New York Public Library (Manuscript)

20 August 1917   *Seefeldstrasse 73, Zurich VIII*

Dear Pound: I have just wired you: Cable Quinn confirm or remit you telegraphically nothing here remitting. You wrote on 17 July you had a letter from him to say he had sent me an advance on the MS of my play. I take it that letter from New York must have been dated 8 July or thereabouts. It is now 20 August. No money has arrived here and on inquiry at the telegraph office I hear that none has arrived there either. There must be some miscarriage or mistake which had better be cleared up. I remit you 6/- cable expenses. If insufficient be sure to deduct the rest from what is remitted for me.

Am sorry to hear you have been so overworked. As regards myself I am sorry to say that my health has again taken a bad turn. On Saturday when walking in the street I got suddenly a violent Hexenschuss which incapacitated me from moving for about twenty minutes. I managed to crawl into a tram and get home. It got better in the evening but next day I had symptoms of glaucoma again—slightly better today. To-morrow morning I am going to the Augenklinik. This climate is impossible for me so that, operated or not, I want to go away next month. I am advised to go to Italian Switzerland. There are other reasons also for going. It will be, I fear, very difficult to keep these rooms heated during the bad Zurich winter and it becomes more and more difficult to get different articles of food so that I think my best plan is to move into

---

[1] Joyce used dashes instead of the usual inverted commas in the dialogue of *A Portrait*.
[2] John Quinn (1870–1924), New York lawyer and patron of the arts.

some cheap pension down there. I shall do this if Mr Quinn's money arrives and if there is a prospect that your suggestion of some months ago will become a fact; I mean about *Ulysses*. You suggested that it could appear serially in *Egoist* and *Little Review* and thus bring me double fees. I am prepared to consign it serially from 1 January next, instalments of about 6000 words. It will be necessary for me to replace in some way the lessons I forfeit by going away from here. The subvention I receive from my unknown and generous benefactor is now 350 instead of 420 frs a month owing to rate of change—equivalent in purchasing value to 250 frs in normal times. It is most useful of course and but for it I should be in the poorhouse but I need to supplement it. Let me know whether this plan of yours is still feasible. I hope it is.

My agent has considerable difficulty with Mr Richards about the publication of my play. He (Mr R.) disposed of the remainder of *Dubliners* as waste paper in America and is now bringing back his own copies to save trouble of having a new edition brought out. Mr Archer wrote you sent him copy of my novel. He says he cannot read it: too depressing. He can read only detective stories, he says. Is he ill?

Shall finish now. Please do not be alarmed about me. My sight is a little weak today but I shall get over it as I got over other things. I did not receive your verses or those of Mr Eliot nor even my own

With kindest regards Sincerely yours   JAMES JOYCE

To EZRA POUND   MS. Yale

[*22 October 1917*]   *Pension Villa Rossa, Locarno, Switzerland*

Dear Pound: I came here a few days ago but was so busy looking after luggage etc that I could not write. It is useless to go into the subject of my physical and financial collapse in August. As regards the former what is done is done. I cannot see very well even yet but the sight gets better. About the latter I owe you and Miss Weaver very much for your prompt kindness.[1] But for you I should have been derelict. I notice that you blame yourself for having misled me. The stupidity, however, is at my end. I am glad *Ulysses* is to appear in both reviews[2] from March on and now that I can read and write again I shall get to

[1] They helped persuade Edward Marsh to pay for the eye operation.
[2] The *Little Review* and the *Egoist*, though publication in the latter was delayed.

work. I hope you will both like it. I send you a copy of *Marzocco* with an article by Mr Diego Angeli.[1] The Manager of Messrs Cres and Co spoke to me about a French translation of my novel (to be published in the course of the present century) and Dostoyevsky's daughter was here yesterday. She has read Mr Angeli's article and wants a copy of the book. She will have to print one for herself, I fear. My wife told me you are bringing out a book with an essay in it about the novel. It may interest therefore to hear that after the first edition had been sold out and the book reviewed in eight countries the printers wrote asking the writer to delete and alter passages in it and refused to print even the second edition. I believe Miss Weaver has found some printer in the country who will do it, he says. I am now correcting proofs of *Exiles*. Yeats wrote to me about it but he seems to have forgotten what it is about.[2] In any case he says his theatre is passing through a crisis. The actors he has now cannot even play low comedy. In the hope that things may have improved I am writing to him again about [it] rather pressingly. I am also going to write to Mr Martyn[3] though I do not know him. If their theatre has no actors to play it surely they could be trained. If not what are they doing on the stage? I shall write also to Mr Sturge Moore who, you said, liked it and to Mr Archer again and to Mr Grein[4] and possibly to Mr Short,[5] Mr Barker[6] and Mr Symons. In fact, as usual, I shall write a great number of letters to a great number of people.

I got copies of *Little Review* with your amusing and highspirited lines.[7] The review looks more prosperous since you took over the European editorship.

I hope Mrs Pound and yourself are quite well. This letter, tardy as it is, is not very long or even complete but sometimes I find it difficult to keep my eyes open—like the readers of my masterpieces.

I have the impression that I am forgetting to tell you many things. No doubt I shall remember them five minutes after having posted this letter. I got Mr Eliot's verses[8] only this morning.

Accept my very sincere thanks however lamely expressed, for having helped me at such a difficult moment. Yours very gratefully

James Joyce

[1] Diego Angeli, 'Un Romanzo di Gesuiti' (review of *A Portrait*), *Il Marzocco* (Florence) xxii. 32 (12 August 1917), 2–3. A translation by Joyce of this article appeared in the *Egoist* v. 2 (February 1918), 30.

[2] Yeats's letter is in II, 405.   [3] Edward Martyn.

[4] J. T. Grein (1862–1935), founder of the Independent Theatre of London in 1891, and a prominent playwright, theatre critic, and manager.

[5] Probably Clement Shorter (1857–1926), the English critic.   [6] H. Granville Barker.

[7] Ezra Pound, '*L'Homme moyen sensuel*', *Little Review* iv. 5 (September 1917), 8–16.

[8] T. S. Eliot, *Prufrock and Other Observations* (London, 1917).

To Edouard Dujardin[1]   MS. S. Illinois (Feinberg)

10 November 1917   *Pension Daheim, Locarno*

Monsieur: Votre fils au consulat français de Zurich m'a donné votre
adresse. J'écris pour vous prier de vouloir bien me dire où je pourrais
obtenir un exemplaire de votre roman *Les Lauriers Sont Coupés*.
J'avais l'édition originale mais elle se trouve maintenant en Autriche
d'où, étant sujet britannique, il ne m'est pas très facile de la ravoir.[2]
J'ai demandé chez les libraires de Zurich et d'ici mais inutilement.
J'espère que vous me pardonnerez la liberté que je prends mais j'ai, je
crois, deux excuses valides étant un sincère admirateur de votre œuvre
si personelle et si indépendante et étant en même temps un humble
vigneron dans la vigne du seigneur.

Agréez, Monsieur, l'assurance de ma très haute considération

James Joyce[3]

To Fanny Guillermet[4]   MS. Yale

5 September 1918   *Universitätsstrasse 38, Zurich*

Dear Miss Guillermet: Since you write English so well I suppose I can
answer also in English. I hope you have now received safely the books I
sent you registered, your own novel and my play signed. I read your
novel with much interest though I do not like the epistolary form in
which you have written it. It is seductive but has the inevitable draw-
back that one can see only from one angle. The inclusion also in some of
the letters of literal transcripts from 'l'autre' is a device, necessary no
doubt, which dissatisfies. The only successful attempt in that line which
I have read is Merimée's *Abbé Aubain* where the last letter completely

---

[1] Joyce always insisted that he had drawn the technique of the *monologue intérieur*
from Dujardin's novel, *Les Lauriers sont coupés* (Paris, 1887), and after *Ulysses* was
published he helped Dujardin achieve belated recognition for his literary innovation.
This letter, written while *Ulysses* was still in a fairly early stage, helps to confirm
Joyce's debt.

[2] Joyce bought *Les Lauriers sont coupés* in a railway kiosk in France in 1903.

[3] (Translation)

'Sir: Your son in the French Consulate at Zurich has given me your address. I write
to ask if you would be so kind as to tell me where I might obtain a copy of your novel,
Les Lauriers sont coupés. I used to have the first edition but it is now in Austria whence,
being a British subject, I cannot easily have it again. I have asked the booksellers in
Zurich and here for it but in vain. I hope you will forgive me for taking this liberty
but I have, I think, two valid excuses, for I am a sincere admirer of your work, so
personal, so independent, and also am a humble labourer in the vineyard of the Lord.
Sincerely yours   James Joyce'

[4] A Swiss writer, who had reviewed *A Portrait of the Artist* for the *Journal de Genève*.

turns the scales the other way. But every form of art has its limitations and it is better to judge a book by what it achieves within its limits.

Your book reminded me somewhat of Amiel who, I imagine, must be a favourite with you. What tiresome critics call the 'plot' seems to [me] to be suffused by a sentiment very rare in French literature. I mean the Huguenot strain which is apparent for example in Mr Gide's *La Porte Etroite* a book with which yours seems to me to have some analogy. Perhaps you will think this judgment fantastic but you must allow for the fact that after all I am a foreigner.

I suppose you yourself (for more reasons than one) are displeased by the end of the book. Artistically however it seems to me a completion rather than an interruption. I am sorry I cannot keep the novel as you have no other copy but 'épuisé' is a very pleasing word to a writer's ears.

I send you some more notices of my *Portrait* which may interest you but like most writers (and mothers?) I am thinking chiefly of my latest work. After your rather scathing attack on my 'manque de goût' I am waiting with some trepidation for your criticism. As I seldom read papers I shall be very much obliged if you will send me *three* copies of the issue in which it is published, one for myself and one each for my English and American publishers.

I envy anyone who writes in French not so much because I envy the resources of that language (whose function I find to be for the most part a standard of moderation and criticism rather than one of innovation) but on account of the public to which one can appeal. Writing in English is the most ingenious torture ever devised for sins committed in previous lives. The English reading public explains the reason why.
Sincerely yours   JAMES JOYCE

To SIR HORACE RUMBOLD Bart.[1]   TS. Cornell

30 November 1918   *Universitätsstrasse 29, 3, Zurich*

His Excellency
sir Horace Rumbold, Bart,
H.M. British Minister,
BERNE

Sir I beg leave to bring the following facts to Your Excellency's notice.
On the 1 May 1918 I went to the British consulate, Zurich, to collect

[1] Sir Horace George Montagu Rumbold (1869–1941), British diplomat, Minister to Berne from 1916 to 1918, and Minister to Warsaw in 1919–20. (This letter is taken from a typewritten copy.)

25 francs due to the 'English Players'[1] by an employee of the consulate, Mr Henry Carr, on tickets sold to and unpaid by him for the production by the 'English Players' on the 29 April 1918 of 'The Importance of being Earnest' in which Mr Carr, at the invitation of the producer for the 'English Players', Mr Claud Sykes, had played a part. Mr Carr declined to pay this sum, demanded from me 150 francs[2] in addition to the sum he had already received and when I declined to pay this sum, on the instruction of Mr Sykes, informed me that he would organise a boycott of all our future productions, called me in the presence of witnesses 'a cad and a swindler' and threatened to 'wring my neck the next time he met me in the street'. I replied 'That is not language that should be used in a government office' and thereupon left the office.

On the 1 May 1918 I wrote a registered letter to Mr Consul Bennett[3] here complaining of this treatment and demanding an apology from Mr Carr. No answer was returned.

I then placed the matter in a solicitor's hands and passed Mr Carr's threat of assault over to the Zurich police. On the advice of the lawyer of the British consulate, Dr George Wettstein, Mr Carr advanced his claim to 475 francs and claimed that the British consulate is extra-territorial. The Swiss political department, appealed to by my solicitor, Dr Conrad Bloch, disallowed this latter claim.

Since the 1 May 1918 the 'English Players' have given or are about to give eight public performances of English plays, alone or in conjunction with Italian and French companies, largely and generously supported by the American colony and by Swiss and others interested in English literature. The plays given include works by Browning, Wilde, Synge, Houghton, Mr Shaw and sir James Barrie. The boycott threatened by Mr Carr exists for since the 1 May 1918 Mr Consul Bennett has not been present at any performance and, at the instigation of Mr Carr, has done all in his power to malign and counteract our efforts.

In July 1918 when I lay dangerously ill and in danger of blindness Mr

---

[1] The English Players were a group of actors organized by Joyce and Claud W. Sykes in Zurich in the spring of 1918. Their first production was Wilde's *The Importance of Being Earnest*, on 29 April at the Theater zur Kaufleuten on Pelikanstrasse. Joyce was in charge of the business arrangements. He got along badly with Henry Carr, a young employee of the British Consulate, who was playing the role of Algernon Moncrieff, and perhaps took some pleasure in giving Carr the lesser remuneration of ten francs, which was for amateurs, instead of thirty, which professional actors in the company received. Carr was piqued and, when Joyce came to the Consulate the next day to collect money for tickets which he had sold, threatened to throw him downstairs.

[2] Carr claimed the cost of a new suit, which he said he had bought specially to wear in the play.

[3] Andrew Percy Bennett (1866–1943) was British Acting Consul-General in Zurich from 1899 to 1918. He became Minister to Panama, 1919–23, and to Costa Rica, 1920–3.

Consul Bennett wrote me a registered letter inviting me to compound a felony with him and threatening to penalise me if I refused to do so.[1] Of this document I declined in courteous terms to take service.

On the 15 October 1918 the Swiss court gave judgment in my favour, ruled out the counterclaim of 475 francs advanced by Dr Wettstein on behalf of his client and condemned Mr Carr to pay the sum due and all costs. A copy of this judgment is enclosed.

The 'English Players' is the only enterprise in Switzerland which has done anything for English dramatic literature. The expenses incurred by Mr Sykes and myself amount to U[2] 10,000 franc We have not received any subsidy and our balancesheet shows a large deficit in spite of our moral success. What we have done cost us enormous work under enormous difficulties and, at Mr Sykes request I enclose a letter from the prime minister, Mr Lloyd George [that] recognises the merits of our efforts.

I believe that Your Excellency will hold, as I hold, that it is no part of the duties of consular officials, as set forth in the acting instructions issued by the foreign office, to commit or to aid and abet blackmail and assault or to organise a calumnious boycott of English literature or to invite British subjects to compound felony and threaten to penalise them if they decline to do so.

As Mr Consul Bennett has shown tacit and open approval of the aforesaid acts of blackmail and assault and attempted felony and has not replied to my grave charge against an employee of his office I appeal, as one of His Majesty's subjects and as a man of letters whom His Majesty has honoured by a munificence in recognition of services rendered to English literature, to Your Excellency the official representative of His Majesty in this country, and crave from Your Excellency that protection and redress from the insult of violence which are the right and the privilege of the least of His Majesty's subjects. I am, Your Excellency's obedient servant   JAMES JOYCE

To [MARTHA FLEISCHMANN][3]   MS. Straumann

[? *Early December 1918*]   [*Zurich*]

Vous n'êtes pas fâchée alors.

[1] The felony was presumably perjury, that is, breaking a promise he had made to the Austrian authorities in Trieste to remain neutral in the war.

[2] Ungefähr ('approximately').

[3] This and the three letters that follow were written by Joyce to Martha Fleischmann, a young woman who lived near him in Zurich. He aspired to a romantic attachment with her. The survival of this correspondence is due to Heinrich Straumann, Professor of English in the University of Zurich, who purchased the letters from Fräulein

J'avais de la fièvre hier soir, en attendant votre signe.

Mais pourquoi ne voulez-vous pas m'écrire même une parole—votre nom? Et pourquoi fermez-vous toujours les stores de la fenêtre? Je veux vous voir.

Je ne sais pas ce que vous pensez de moi.

Comme je vous ai déjà dit nous nous sommes vus et—parlés—mais vous m'avez oublié.

Voulez-vous que je vous dise quelque chose?

Ma première impression de vous.

Voilà.

Vous étiez vétue de noir avec un gros chapeau aux ailes flottantes. La couleur vous allait très bien. Et j'ai pensé: un joli animal.

Parce qu'il y avait quelque chose de franc et presque d'impudique dans votre allure. Puis, en vous regardant, j'ai observé la mollesse des traits reguliers et la douceur des yeux. Et j'ai pensé: une juive. Si je me suis trompé il ne faut pas vous offenser. Jésus Christ a pris son corps humain: dans le ventre d'une femme juive.

J'ai pensé souvent à vous et après, quand je vous ai reconnue à la fenêtre je vous regardais dans une espèce de fascination dont je ne peux me libérer.

Il se peut que tout ça vous laisse indifférente.

Il se peut que je vous semble ridicule.

J'accepte votre jugement.

Mais hier soir vous m'avez fait un signe et mon cœur a sauté de joie.

Je ne sais pas votre âge.

Moi, je suis vieux—et je me sens plus vieux encore.

Peutêtre ai-je trop vécu.

J'ai 35 ans.[1] C'est l'âge que Shakespeare a eu quand il a conçu sa douleureuse passion pour la 'dame noire.' C'est l'âge que le Dante a eu quand il est entré dans la nuit de son être.

Je ne sais pas ce qui arrive en moi.

Est-il possible qu'une personne éprouve sentiments commes les miens et que l'autre ne les éprouve point?

Je ne sais pas ce que je veux.

Je voudrais vous parler.

Je me figure un soir brumeux. J'attends—et je vous vois vous approcher

Fleischmann's sister. His account of the incident may be read in *Letters of James Joyce*, II, 426–31.

This letter (which like the others is given in the original spelling) was probably the second that Joyce wrote, since in it he mentions another. He did not yet know Martha Fleischmann's name.

[1] A romantic computation: Joyce was nearly thirty-seven.

de moi, vétue de noir, jeune, étrange et douce. Je vous regarde dans les yeux et mes yeux vous disent que je suis un pauvre chercheur dans ce monde, que je ne comprends rien de ma destinée ni de celle des autres, que j'ai vécu et péché et crée, que je m'en irai, un jour, n'ayant rien compris, dans l'obscurité qui nous a enfantés tous.

Comprennez-vous peutêtre le mystère de votre corps quand vous vous regardez dans la glace, d'où est venue la lumière fauve de vos yeux; le teint de votre chevelure?

Comme vous étiez gracieuse, hier soir, assise à la table, rêveuse et puis, soudainement, levant ma lettre à la lumière.

Quel est votre nom?

Pensez vous, quelquefois, à moi?

Ecrivez-moi un mot à l'adresse que je vous donne.

Vous pouvez m'écrire aussi en allemand. Je le comprends très bien.

Dites-moi quelque chose de vous-même.

Oui, écrivez-moi demain.

Je crois que vous êtes bonne.[1] . . .[2]

---

[1] Here the edge of the paper is torn off.

[2] (The translations of this and the following letters were made by Christopher Middleton and appear here by his permission.)

    'Then you are not annoyed.

I had a fever yesterday evening, waiting for a sign from you.

But why do you not want to write even one word to me—your name? And why do you always close your shutters? I want to see you.

I do not know what you think of me.

As I have already told you, we met—and talked together—but you have forgotten me.

Would you like me to tell you something?

My first impression of you.

Here it is.

You were dressed in black, wearing a big hat with waving feathers. The colour suited you very well. And I thought: a pretty animal.

Because there was something frank and almost shameless in your allure. Then, as I watched you, I noticed the softness and the regularity of your features, and the gentleness of your eyes. And I thought: a Jewess. If I am wrong, you must not be offended. Jesus Christ put on his human body: in the womb of a Jewish woman.

I thought of you often, and later, when I recognised you at the window, I watched you with a kind of fascination from which I cannot free myself.

It may be all this leaves you indifferent.

It may be I seem ridiculous to you. I accept your judgment.

But yesterday evening you gave me a sign, and my heart leapt for joy.

I do not know your age.

As for me, I am old—and feel even older than I am.

Perhaps I have lived too long.

I am 35. It is the age at which Shakespeare conceived his dolorous passion for the "dark lady". It is the age at which Dante entered the night of his being.

I do not know what is happening in me.

Is it possible for one person to have feelings like mine, and for the other not to have them at all?

I do not know what I want.

I would like to talk to you.

To Martha Fleischmann   MS. Straumann

[? December 1918]   *[Zurich]*

Qu'y a-t-il?

Vous ne m'avez pas salué!

Je descends avec cette lettre a la porte.

Ai-je offensée?

Mais comment?

Je vous prie de m'envoyer un mot toute de suite. Voilà une enveloppe déja préparée. Jetez-la à la boite et mettez un seul mot dedans.

Etes-vous fâchée? *Oui* ou *non*.

Je ne comprends rien.

Pour l'amour de Dieu envoyez-moi un mot.

La belle nuit que je vais passer![1]

To Martha Fleischmann   MS. Straumann

[9 December 1918][2]   *[Zurich]*

Arme liebe Marthe

I imagine a misty evening to myself. I am waiting—and I see you coming towards me, dressed in black, young, strange, and gentle. I look into your eyes, and my eyes tell you that I am a poor seeker in this world, that I understand nothing of my destiny, nor of the destinies of others, that I have lived and sinned and created, and that one day I shall leave, having understood nothing in the darkness which gave birth to both of us. Perhaps you understand the mystery of your body when you look at yourself in the mirror, where the wild light in your eyes comes from: the colour of your hair?

How graceful you were yesterday evening, as you sat at the table, in a dream, then suddenly lifted my letter up to the light.

What is your name?

Do you think of me sometimes?

Write to me at the address I give you.

You can write to me in German too. I understand it very well.

Tell me something about yourself.

Yes, write to me tomorrow.

I think that you are good. . . .'

[1] (Translation)

'What is the matter?

You gave me no sign of greeting!

I am going to take this letter to the door.

Have I offended?

But how?

I beg you to send me a line immediately. Here is an envelope all ready. Put it in the letter-box and write just one word in it. Are you angry? *Yes* or *no*.

I understand nothing.

For the love of God send me a line.

A fine night I'm going to spend!'

[2] A copy of *Chamber Music*, belonging to Professor Straumann, is inscribed by Joyce

Was haben Sie gehabt?

Ich bin noch unsicher aber glaube dass ich Sie gesehen habe heute abend.

Ich hatte Angst Ihnen zu schreiben weil ich wusste nicht wer bei Ihnen war und dachte dass meine Briefe in die Hände von fremde Leute kommen könnten.

Jedes Abend habe ich geschaut.

Ich habe mir sogar Vorwürfe gemacht weil ich dachte dass vielleicht Ihre Krankheit in Folge einer Erkältung am jenem letzten Abend war. Dann dachte ich, ich wurde Ihnen trotzdem schreiben und mit der Name einer Freundin schreiben!

Je continue en français parce que l'allemand ne me va pas.

Si vous avez beaucoup souffert en ces jours, moi, j'ai souffert aussi.

Il me semblait que l'unique rayon de lumière qui dans ces dernières années ait percé l'obscurité de ma vie, s'était éteinte.

J'étais même imbécile!

Chaque matin j'ouvrais, j'ouvrais le journal et j'avais peur de lire votre nom parmi les annonces des morts! Je l'ouvrais toujours avec angoisse, très, très lentement.

Je pensais: elle s'en ira—elle qui m'a regardé avec pitié—peutêtre avec tendresse.

La maladie change beaucoup.

Elle nous conduit quelquefois jusqu'au seuil de la mort: et nous voyons les choses autrement.

Vous n'avez pas peur de la mort—moi, si!

Vous avez pensé peutêtre que votre sentiment pour moi était une folie; vous avez entrevu les ombres de l'au delà.

Eh bien! Ce sont les ombres menteuses!

Je voudrais vous envoyer des fleurs mais j'ai peur.

J'attendrai encore. Peutêtre ce n'était pas vous que j'ai vue?

J'ai vu mon livre de poésies dans votre main.

Est-ce que vous avez compris?

J'ai écrit quelque chose pendant votre maladie—quelque chose de très amer qui a blessé beaucoup mes amis

Oui, j'ai souffert aussi.

J'hésite encore avant de vous envoyer cette lettre

Si elle tombe dans les mains d'une autre personne???

---

to Martha Fleischmann with this date. He probably left the book for her himself and wrote this letter on the same day. The inscription uses Greek 'e's' in Martha Fleischmann's name but normal ones in Joyce's own signature, as if he recognized the futility of disguising his name in his own book.

11 heures

Je vais jeter cette lettre à la boîte.

Je ne peux plus attendre!   J.[1]

To MARTHA FLEISCHMANN   MS. Straumann

[*2 February 1919*]   [*Zurich*]

Nach langes Erwarten sah ich gestern abend Dein Gesicht, aber so blass, so müde und so traurig!

Der erste Gruss an diesem Tag kam von Dir—durch die Nacht

Und durch die Nacht der Bitterkeit meiner Seele fielen die Küsse Deiner Lippen über meinen Herz—weich wie Rosenblätter, sanft wie Tau.

---

[1] (Translation)
'Poor dear Marthe

What has been the matter with you?

I am still not sure, but I think I saw you this evening.

I was afraid to write to you, since I did not know who was with you, and thought my letters might fall into the hands of strangers.

I have watched for you every evening.

I even reproached myself because I thought your illness might perhaps be due to a cold caught that last evening.

Then I thought I would write to you anyhow, and write under the name of a girlfriend!

I'll continue in French because German does not suit me.

If you have suffered much during these days, I too have suffered.

It seemed that the sole ray of light which in all these last years has pierced the darkness of my life had been put out.

I was even out of my mind!

Every morning I opened, opened the paper and was afraid I might read your name in the death announcements! I would open it always in anguish, very, *very* slowly.

I thought: she will go away—she who has looked at me with pity—perhaps with tenderness.

Illness changes things.

It takes us sometimes up to the threshold of death: and we see things differently.

You are not afraid of death—but I am!

Perhaps you thought your feeling for me was madness; you have glimpsed the shades of the beyond.

Ah well! Those shades are deceivers!

I would like to send you flowers, but I am afraid.

I shall go on waiting. Perhaps it was not you I saw?

I saw my book of poems in your hand.

You understood it?

I wrote something while you were ill—something very bitter which has wounded my friends deeply.

Yes, I have suffered too.

I am still hesitant about sending you this letter

If it were to fall into someone else's hands???

11 o'clock

I am going out to post this letter.

I cannot wait any longer!   J.'

'O rosa mistica, ora pro me!'[1]   J.

Maria Lichtmesse 1919.[2]

To FRANK BUDGEN[3]   MS. Yale

19 June 1919   *Zurich*

Dear Budgen: Are you still there? I sent on your dream book and hope
it reached you, but if it did not, well, no matter, let it go.[4] The news?
Paul Suter[5] brought your sketch here and I must really thank you for it
as it seems to my barbarian eye a delicate and provocative object. Paul
was with us at the Pfauen Restaurant where we did honour to the
golden wine named by him who writes 'The Archiduchessa' because:

(suppressed by Censor)[6]

Other news? Mr Gschwind who 'looks after the dibs' embezzled 1,000
francs of the company's money and there is open war. Colum writes
to me from New York that a sympathy movement for me has begun
there and they are cabling me 11,000 francs in support of my case and
project. I hear there are to be thunderbolt articles in the Press. I sent
off the statement to London to my agent who is reluctant to circulate
it and also to the Foreign Office and to the chief two delegates of the
Irish-American mission in Paris. Pound writes disapproving of the
Sirens, then modifying his disapproval and protesting against the close
and against 'obsession' and wanting to know whether Bloom

(prolonged cheers from all parts of the house)

could not be relegated to the background and Stephen Telemachus
brought forward.

The chapter of the *Cyclops* is being lovingly moulded in the way you

[1] From the Litany of Loreto, which however has 'ora pro nobis' instead of 'ora pro me'.
'Mistica' should be 'mystica'.

[2] (Translation)
'After long waiting I saw yesterday evening your face, but so pale, so tired, and so
sad!
Today the first greeting came from you—through the night
And through the night of the bitterness of my soul the kisses of your lips fell upon my
heart—soft as rosepetals, gentle as dew.
"O rosa mistica, ora pro me!"   J.
Candlemas 1919'

[3] Frank Budgen (1882–1971), English artist and writer, was a close friend of Joyce in
Zurich and in later life.

[4] This is a quotation from a poem called 'At the Gates of Sleep' by Frank Budgen
which he sent with the 'dream book'.

[5] Paul Suter (b. 1895), brother of the sculptor August Suter, a friend of Frank Budgen.

[6] Joyce's parenthesis. See p. 244.

know. The Fenian is accompanied by a wolfhound who speaks (or curses) in Irish. He unburdens his soul about the Saxo-Angles in the best Fenian style and with colossal vituperativeness alluding to their standard industry. The epic proceeds explanatorily 'He spoke of the English, a noble race, rulers of the waves, who sit on thrones of alabaster, silent as the deathless gods'.

Private Enclosed find playbill.

This morning a threatening violent letter from the Vormund.[1] The sister has been dying. M—[2] in a madhouse or Nervenanstalt but now back again threatening suicide. Gave him all my correspondence. Violent gestures towards me. I did not even know she was back nor have I seen her since the feast of candles.[3] Well, I got up and went to the Lion's Den. Long interview wherein I displayed all that suave human diplomacy, that goodness of heart, that understanding of others, that timidity which yet is courage, those shining qualities of heart and head which have so often . . . Result, stasis: Waffenstillstand.

Mem. No allusion to this in your reply which I expect confidently twenty years after.   J.J.

To Frank Budgen   MS. Yale

11 July 1919   *Universitätsstrasse 29, Zurich*

Dear Budgen: What the hell kind of an address is this? And are you there? And are you coming back to Z.? I send you enclosed description of pictures which have been offered me for sale, prices marked on back. The daubs[4] are here in Z. If you can sell any of them you get 5% or 10%. I forget which. The whole lot would bring a commission of 30,000 frs. I think. Write and be damned to the waste of ink. Am taking P.S.'s[5] verses now to the Zürcher Post. Am sending you a photo of myself. Portrait of wife[6] framed and up. Sir Whorearse Rumphole has been 'gently removed' from Berne. Lord Acton in charge. 5000 frs cabled from U.S.A. for my cause. Everyone beginning to be on the move here. I have offered to finance the E.P.[7] After prolonged deliberations they very kindly and most considerately consented to accept 10,000 francs of my dirty money in consideration of my former good behaviour

---

[1] Rudolf Hiltpold, Martha Fleischmann's lover, though he professed to be her *Vormund* or guardian.
[2] Martha Fleischmann.   [3] 2 February 1919.
[4] The 'daubs' in question were old master pictures smuggled, Frank Budgen thought, out of Austria. The project here referred to came to nothing.
[5] Paul Suter.   [6] Painted by Frank Budgen.   [7] English Players.

and unstained character. Am arranging a concert of Irish traditional and modern music for the Tonhalle with Milner as singer.

Arrivederci presto, pittore bevitore.[1]   J.J.

P.S. An interpellation will be made in the U.S. Senate regarding the past official conduct of Mr Consul Bennett who is at present in a part of the world where the U.S.A. are interested. My agent refuses to circulate my statement in merry England.

To Harriet Shaw Weaver   MS. British Museum

20 July 1919   *Universitätsstrasse 29, Zurich*

Dear Miss Weaver: I have delayed my reply to your letter because I hoped to have had either a telegram or a letter from your solicitors but, as neither has come and as I am in a state of perplexity, I am writing to you now. You have probably discovered by now that I am a very stupid person—a fact which I should have preferred to conceal. I was misled by certain statements or allusions in the last letter your solicitors sent me as well as by my own misinterpretation of what I mistook for a hint as to the name of my benefactress.[2] If you know in what complete ignorance I live of events and persons in London you will perhaps be inclined to forgive my stupidity. I seldom see a paper or a book and am not in correspondence with anyone there apart from formal letters and (now rather rare) letters from Mr Pound. There is no reason why I should withdraw the phrases to which you allude but there is every reason why I should apply and do apply the contrary epithets to myself.

I have felt during these last days of waiting an added sense of perplexity due to the fact that at the moment when I have the very great pleasure of knowing that it is you who have aided and are aiding me so munificently you write me that the last episode sent[3] seems to you to show a weakening or diffusion of some sort. Since the receipt of your letter I have read this chapter again several times. It took me five months to write it and always when I have finished an episode my mind lapses into a state of blank apathy out of which it seems that neither I nor the wretched book will ever more emerge. Mr Pound wrote to me rather hastily in disapproval but I think that his disapproval is based on grounds which are not legitimate and is due chiefly to the varied interests of his admirable and energetic artistic life. Mr Brock[4] also wrote to me begging me to explain to him the method (or methods) of

---

[1] 'Let us meet soon, painter tippler.'
[2] Joyce had guessed that his patron was Lady Cunard.
[3] The *Sirens*.   [4] A. Clutton Brock (1868–1924), English critic.

the madness but these methods are so manifold, varying as they do from one hour of the day to another, from one organ of the body to another, from episode to episode, that, much as I appreciate his critical patience I could not attempt to reply. I must ask you to add to the great favours which you have given me also that of long suffering. If the *Sirens* have been found so unsatisfactory I have little hope that the *Cyclops* or later the *Circe* episode will be approved of: and, moreover, it is impossible for me to write these episodes quickly. The elements needed will fuse only after a prolonged existence together. I confess that it is an extremely tiresome book but it is the only book which I am able to write at present.

During these last two years when I have received your gifts I have always had the foreboding (now proved false) that each episode of the book as it advanced would alienate gradually the sympathy of the person who was helping me. The word *scorching* transmitted to me by your solicitors in reply to my tentative inquiry has a peculiar significance for my superstitious mind not so much because of any quality or merit in the writing itself as for the fact that the progress of the book is in fact like the progress of some sandblast. As soon as I mention or include any person in it I hear of his or her death or departure or misfortune: and each successive episode, dealing with some province of artistic culture (rhetoric or music or dialectic), leaves behind it a burnt up field. Since I wrote the *Sirens* I find it impossible to listen to music of any kind.

I have tried to express my gratitude to you but I cannot do so. As you are the person who introduced my book *A Portrait of the Artist as a Young Man* to the 'notice' of the public I shall feel very thankful to you if you will accept from me the MS of that book. It is in Trieste and, as soon as circumstances there are more favourable, I shall get it and forward it to you.

You have given me most generous and timely help. I wish I could feel myself worthy of it either as a poet or as a human being. All I can do is to thank you. Very sincerely yours   JAMES JOYCE

To HARRIET SHAW WEAVER   MS. British Museum

6 August 1919   *Universitätsstrasse 29, Zurich*

Dear Miss Weaver: I have once again to thank for your gift of £100 sent to me by your solicitors pending the completion of the settlement and for your long expected letter. I am infinitely relieved by it. Perhaps

I ought not to say any more on the subject of the *Sirens* but the passages
you allude to were not intended by me as recitative. There is in the
episode only one example of recitative, on page 12 in preface to the song.
They are all the eight regular parts of a *fuga per canonem*: and I did not
know in what other way to describe the seductions of music beyond
which Ulysses travels. I understand that you may begin to regard the
various styles of the episodes with dismay and prefer the initial style
much as the wanderer did who longed for the rock of Ithaca. But in the
compass of one day to compress all these wanderings and clothe them
in the form of this day is for me possible only by such variation which,
I beg you to believe, is not capricious.

In confirmation of what I said in my last letter I enclose a cutting
from a Dublin paper, just received, announcing the death of one of the
figures in the episode.[1]

It will perhaps interest you to know that my play *Exiles* will be produced for the first time tomorrow night in Munich at the Muenchner
Schauspielhaus. I have received many telegrams inviting me to be
present but I shall not be there to see it. I mention this because I
remember that after its publication I received from you, to my considerable surprise, a message of very appreciative praise. I am sending you a
copy of the translation published here in Zurich a few months ago as I
think you may wish to have it also.

The questions raised in a former letter of yours are not pressing but,
while I thank Miss Marsden[2] for the compliment she pays me, I should
prefer to see my book priced at 3/– which is about its value, I think.

With many thanks for your generosity to me and for the great interest
you take in my writing and with many kind regards gratefully and
sincerely yours   James Joyce

To G. Herbert Thring[3]   TS. Texas

21 September 1919   *Zurich*

Dear Sir, My attention has been drawn to a letter recently written by
your Society to Mr Curti,[4] Solicitor, of Zurich. As the partner of Mr
Sykes I should like to bring a few facts to your notice.

---

[1] The cutting reported the death of J. G. Lidwell, solicitor, at his residence in
Kingstown.

[2] Dora Marsden (1882–1960), a close friend of Miss Weaver, was editor of the *Egoist*
from January to June 1914. She devoted her later years to writing on metaphysical
problems.

[3] From a typed copy. George Herbert Thring (1859–1941) was secretary of the Incorporated Society of Authors, Playwrights and Composers from 1892 to 1930. He wrote
The Marketing of Literary Property (London, 1933).

[4] Probably Arthur Curti (1872–1942), a lawyer in Zurich, expert in English law.

Mr Sykes and I founded the English Players company in Zurich in April 1918 for the production of plays in the English language. The company produced plays in English in spite of difficulty, boycott and financial loss, and was the only enterprise of the kind in Switzerland during the war. It was impossible for Mr Sykes to obtain in some cases the consent of the dramatists owing to the postal delays, censorship and frequent and prolonged closure of frontiers, although every effort was made to avoid what might have seemed an infringement of literary courtesy. Mr Sykes was in direct communication with Mr Edward Martyn, who gave him permission to produce *The Heather Field*, with Mr Meyer, agent of the late Stanley Houghton, who gave him permission to produce *Hindle Wakes*, and with Mr Robert Ross (deceased) and Mr Samuel French with regard to the production of Wilde's *The Importance of Being Earnest*. He has asked Mr Curti therefore to let him know the names of the authors who are claiming fees.[1] The question of the production on the Continent of Europe of plays in the English language seems, moreover, to be an exceptional case not foreseen in the clauses of the Berne convention. Mr Sykes was legally advised on this subject at the outset that such productions were free.

The aims and achievements of the company are such, I believe, as will be approved of by the members of your Society, and, owing to Mr Sykes' energy and persistance, the prospects financially and artistically are now much brighter.

My name as a writer will perhaps not be unknown to you, and I am indebted to your Society for generous and timely aid in the past. I trust that the proposal which Mr Curti is forwarding you on our behalf will meet with your approval and put an end to any misunderstanding which may have arisen. I am, dear Sir, Sincerely yours,   JAMES JOYCE

To FRANK BUDGEN   MS. Yale

[*December 1919*]   *Via Sanità 2, Trieste*

Dear Budgen: I enclose two letters, underlining two significant passages. As regards the letter from S[2] if you are manager of the E.P. at present the only message I wish you to convey is one of my regret for the constant trouble he encounters, which I hope he will succeed in over-

---

[1] Thring was acting on behalf of Bernard Shaw, whose play *Mrs. Warren's Profession* had been presented by the English Players on 30 September 1918 and on a number of occasions thereafter. They also gave *The Dark Lady of the Sonnets*.

[2] Claud W. Sykes, founder (with Joyce) of the English Players.

coming. Personally, however, I cannot attend to this matter in the present disturbed state of my domestic economy. I wrote twice to the secretary of the authors' union. They don't want letters. They want cash. So do I—and badly. I may say that if I had in my pocket the money I gave the E.P. lately = about 10,000 lire at present exchange I would be better off. This for yourself however. I beg you to give my regards to Mr S and Mrs S with apologies for my silence—understandable in present circumstances. I hope he will write no more petulant letters to me who am in no way to blame.

As regards W[1] he seems to be threatening libel proceedings by his letter in which case possibly yourself, Hummel[2] and I will be led forth shackled 'for they were malefactors'. Since I came here I wrote a long letter to Mrs M, asking her very urgently to consider the 'advisability of the revivability' of her aid. That distinguished lady never answered. W pretends he did not know my address here—another piece of fooling. He forgets only what he dislikes to remember, viz., that he promised me as a gift DOKTOR JUNG'S (prolonged general universal applause) Wandlungen der LIBIDO (shouts *Hear! Hear!* from a raughty tinker and an Irishman in the gallery). For God's sake give those louts the go by. As for Mr Garryowen's[3] poetic lecture I am glad I was not there. Pound wrote 'enthusing' about the Cyclops episode and thereafter less heatedly telling me that Quinn is no monk, he, (Q,) having bought £300 worth of pictures from Wyndham Lewis—unpaid for. Miss Weaver writes saying that after a perusal of it she found it hard to keep from interlarding her speech with I's[4] favourite adjective. By the way did you get the sealed packet, the bottle of wine, etc. There are in Mr Owen's room about 40 or 50 copies of *Verbannte*. Could you remove them to your studio and sell them (for yourself I mean) whenever anyone comes in and drink my health—in Her Most Excellent Excellency's the Archduchess's most excellent piss (Pardon! Fendant de Valais). Only please keep ten copies of the stage edition and five copies of the other. Also if Mrs M doesn't reply within a month I shall take back the MS.

No chance of a flat here. The town is full of rumours of my success

---

[1] Ottocaro Weiss (1896–1971), a good friend of Joyce in Zurich, but out of favour because Joyce unjustly suspected him of having caused Mrs Edith Rockefeller McCormick to discontinue her allowance of 1000 Swiss francs a month. Weiss's letter denying blame is the one Joyce chooses to misconstrue here. In Paris a few years later, Ettore Schmitz attempted to reconcile the two men, and they met without rancor, Joyce having more or less decided that his suspicions had been unfounded. For a fuller account, see Ellmann, *James Joyce*, pp. 405–8, 411, 468–9, 473–4, 476–9, 481–3.

[2] Daniel Hummel (b. 1895), a friend of Budgen in Zurich.

[3] The name of the dog in the *Cyclops* episode of *Ulysses*.

[4] The unnamed narrator of the *Cyclops* episode.

(financial chiefly) in foreign parts so that I avoid all contact with people. Need I tell you what a great privation it is to me to have not here within earshot your ever patient and friendly self? I hope you will let me know in advance what you are going to do, if staying there or moving south. I have not written a word of *Nausikaa* beyond notation of flappers' atrocities and general plan of the specially new fizzing style (Patent No. 7728. S.P. E.P. B.P. L.P.). My regards to Paul Suter and Danni Hummel. Next time I shall send you a letter for Miss Herter.[1] Your pictures have now reached Chiasso only! Seemingly they are being admired *en route*. Please write as soon as possible. It is quite easy as I now find if you once sit down. How are you progressing artistically? This letter is full of materiality. So am I—alas! A very hearty handshake.

James Joyce

To Frank Budgen   MS. Yale

3 January 1920   *Via Sanità 2, Trieste*

Dear Budgen: I hope you are alive, well and sold something in Basel. Your pictures came all right and are up, machine arrived broken, books safe: total cost about 400 francs! The situation here is highly unpleasant. No flat or sign of one. I have refused lessons up to the present but am appointed to the school again—it is now a commercial university. One hour a day. For six weeks after my arrival I neither read nor wrote nor spoke. But as it cannot go on so I started *Nausikaa* and have written less than half. Perhaps I can finish it for February 2. No reply from Mrs M. It seems that gentility cannot be acquired in a single generation. Quinn replied after a month offering 700 frs down on account of *Ulysses* MS. I did not answer. He now offers 1500 frs down, without naming the ultimate sum. I shall write to Mrs M to know if she wants it. Miss Weaver sent me her photo with a melancholy letter about her age—43. I heard nothing more from Sykes—thank God—or the English foulplayers but people tell me they still perform. Lenassi[2] was here twice smelling around—God knows for what. Weiss I met on New Year's day in the street. He approached smiling (I suppose at my disreputable get-up) and saluted. I replied. We now cook for ourselves in this household. Till yesterday I was paying about 35 lire a day to my brother-in-

---

[1] On the staff of the British Consulate in Zurich. She typed the *Cyclops* episode with the help of Budgen's dictation.

[2] A Triestine whom Joyce had known in Zurich, where he was suspected of being an espionage agent.

law. Now I pay him half rent, gas, coal and we pig for ourselves. Jolly!
Apart from this is the damnable boredom. Not a soul to talk to about
Bloom. Lent the chapter to one or two people but they know as much
about it as the parliamentary side of my arse. My brother [knows]
something but he thinks it a joke, besides he was four years in prison
[?], has a devil of a lot to do and likes a gay elegant life in his own set.
O shite and onions! When is this bloody state of affairs going to end.
Have you the copies of *Verbannte*? If so sell them (if anyone will take
'em) and keep the cash for yourself. I suppose P.S.[1] is now married.
Give him my best wishes. Are you staying on in Zurich? Is there any
God's chance of your coming here for a week. I doubt if I can raise the
whole lot. I could put you up however for that length of time and feed
but there is the bloody fare. I might be able to go halves in it. Perhaps
next month? *Nausikaa* will be finished, I hope. To abandon the book
now would be madness. First half of *Cyclops* appeared in November
with excision of the erection allusion. Do you ever see Siegfried Lang?[2]
I wish he would send me back *registered* my novel. The copy is not mine
but dedicated. On receipt of this approach an inkbottle with intention.
I know it is a bore but I should like to hear your views and plans. By the
way do you or did you know any Weavers in St Ives. I ask because Miss
W sent me a snapshot taken there. *Verbannte* appears to have gone
under in Germany. Writing *Ulysses* is a tough job enough without all
this trouble. The prospect of starting lessons next month is damn
pleasant. Winter here is mild enough and will soon be over. Plenty of
good opera but I never go. (Can't because 'somebody' either sold or
pawned my dress suit and it costs about 600 lire to buy one.) Perhaps if
I had my own flat it might not be so bad. (I may remark that the greater
part of the furniture here is mine.) Doing any kind of business upsets
me. Schlie (Mrs Piazza's man) is here. A decent kind of fellow—not a
psychoanalyst. Had a card from Ruggiero.[3] Thank him if you see him. I
wish you a happy New Year and hope to see you soon. As for travelling,
being ex-british consul you should find no difficulties, I suppose—but I
daresay I am selfish as usual in suggesting such a troublesome and (to
you) unprofitable move. In any case please write by return. *Nausikaa* is
written in a namby-pamby jammy marmalady drawersy (alto là!) style
with effects of incense, mariolatry, masturbation, stewed cockles,
painter's palette, chitchat, circumlocutions, etc etc. Not so long as the
others.

Arrivederci ben presto.   JAMES JOYCE

---

[1] Paul Suter.   [2] A Swiss poet.
[3] Paul Ruggiero (b. 1887), a bank employee in Zurich and a lifelong friend of Joyce.

To Mrs William Murray (Postcard)   MS. National Library

5 January 1920   *Via Sanità 2, Trieste*

Thanks for card received. Will you please send me a bundle of other
novelettes and any penny hymnbook you can find as I need them? All
are well here except myself. Another thing I wanted to know is whether
there are trees (and of what kind) behind the Star of the Sea church in
Sandymount visible from the shore and also whether there are steps
leading down at the side of it from Leahy's terrace. If you can find out
these facts for me quickly I shall be glad.

Renewed wishes for 1920 from all here.   Jim

To Harriet Shaw Weaver   MS. British Museum

6 January 1920   *Via Sanità 2, Trieste*

Dear Miss Weaver: Many thanks indeed for your kind thought of sending me your photographs at Christmas. I am very glad to have them. I
am sorry however that my silly verses caused you some moments of de-
pression. They are not worth so much. I wonder then what kind of
impression my tiresome interminable unexhil[ar]ating book *Ulysses*
makes on you! I notice that the snapshot you sent is from Saint Ives.
May I ask if you come from there? I have heard very much about it from
a friend of mine, a painter.[1] I have been inquiring about the best way to
send the MS[2] as the postal service in this annexed zone is not very good.
I think my brother-in-law (who is cashier of the CzecoSlovak bank
here)[3] can arrange to have it sent with their mail in four different send-
ings. If this cannot be done I shall send it (also in four lots) by post. Of
course if all or any of it goes astray I shall write it out again for you but
it would be better for you to have the original. The 'original' original I
tore up and threw in to the stove about eight years ago in a fit of rage
on account of the trouble over *Dubliners*. The charred remains of the
MS were rescued by a family fire brigade and tied up in an old sheet
where they remained for some months. I then sorted them out and pieced
them together as best I could and the present MS is the result.

The copies of the novel sent to Messrs Bemporad have arrived but
those for Messrs Schimpff have not yet come. I fancy that many could
be sold here but perhaps the exchange, so unfavourable to Italian
buyers, will be an obstacle. Unfortunately I have not yet found a flat

---

[1] Frank Budgen.   [2] Of *A Portrait of the Artist as a Young Man.*
[3] Frantisek Schaurek.

and have not as much quiet and freedom as I should like. I am working at the *Nausikaa* episode. It is very consoling to me that you consider me a writer because every time I sit down with a pen in my hand I have to persuade myself (and others) of the fact. However I hope to finish this episode during January.

I ought to return your kindness in sending me your photographs but, except for a few snapshots, I have no photograph of myself made between the year 1904 when I left Ireland and 1915 when I left Austria. I have however another made in Zurich for Mr Huebsch and one taken in Paris but do not wish to inflict them on you unless you would like to have them. I believe the photograph taken in Zurich is good but the others are not. Your photographs are excellent, I think. But when I sent a photograph some years ago to Mr Pound he wrote me a letter in alarm (wellfounded, as it came out afterwards) about the pathological condition of the eyes.

I renew my good wishes to you for 1920 and hope to complete my book during the year. With sincerest thanks and regards   JAMES JOYCE

To MRS WILLIAM MURRAY   MS. National Library

[*February 1920*]   *Via Sanità 2, Trieste*

Dear Aunt Josephine: I hope you are well and that the operation you spoke of went off successfully. Thanks for the journals. I want that information about the Star of the Sea Church, has it ivy on its seafront, are there trees in Leahy's terrace at the side or near, if so, what, are there steps leading down to the beach? I also want all the information you can give, tittletattle, facts etc about Hollis Street maternity hospital. Two chapters of my book[1] remain unfinished till I have these so I shall feel very grateful if you will sacrifice a few hours of your time for me and write me a long letter with details. My novel is translated into Swedish. The Italian translation of *Exiles* comes out in April. The American censor burned all the copies of last issue of *Little Review* on account of instalment of my book *Ulysses*.   JIM

To HARRIET SHAW WEAVER   MS. British Museum

25 February 1920   *Via Sanità 2, Trieste*

Dear Miss Weaver: I am sending this registered because several letters sent by me (including two to you) went astray it seems and also a few

---

[1] *Nausikaa* and *Oxen of the Sun.*

and some books addressed to me here. For the present it is better to
register letters here as there is a great deal of confusion. About three
weeks ago I sent the *Nausikaa* episode in duplicate to Mr Pound. If he
has not sent it on to you will you please write to him for it. I heard from
him this morning much to my relief for I feared that too had gone
astray and the prospect of doing it all over again was not pleasant. A
Mr Heaf or Heap of the *Little Review*[1] wrote to me a very friendly and
complimentary letter in which he said that the U.S.A. censor had
burned the entire May issue and threatened to cancel their licence if
they continue to publish *Ulysses*. This is the second time I have had the
pleasure of being burned while on earth so that I hope I shall pass
through the fires of purgatory as quickly as my patron S. Aloysius. I am
working now on the *Oxen of the Sun* the most difficult episode in an
odyssey, I think, both to interpret and to execute.

I am sending you under separate cover a snapshot taken in 1913 by
my brother-in-law and if I can find it I shall also send one taken in 1903
in Paris.[2] A painter in Zurich[3] has a halfdone portrait of me which his
friends call 'Herr Satan'.

Exiles will come out in an Italian version next month in Milan the
translator being Mr Linati who finds that book more suited to introduce my writings than the novel or the stories. Perhaps it is just as well
that the letter in which I gave you several addresses here of booksellers
did not reach you. I think any copies sent here would be wasted.
Yesterday the English pound was at 62 with the result that the single
copy of my novel at present here was priced at 24 lire. A 9/– book would
sell for 36 lire. French novels cost 20 lire. So that Italians are now
reading only the Italian novels priced at 4.5 lire.

I was interested to read what you told me in your last letter as I
myself started to study medicine three times, in Dublin, Paris and again
in Dublin. I would have been even more disastrous to society at large
than I am in my present state had I continued. Perhaps I should have
continued in spite of certain very adverse circumstances but for the
fact that both in Ireland and in France chemistry is in the first year's
course. I never could learn it or understand in the least what it is about.

Mr Huebsch writes rather urgently about *Ulysses*. I shall tell him
that it may be finished for publication late in autumn but without
engagement on my side. If the type for the first half were set early in
summer I could perhaps revise it then. I do not know whether they have

---

[1] Jane Heap (d. 1964), co-editor (with Margaret Anderson) of the *Little Review*.

[2] The photograph, actually dated 1902, is reproduced in *Letters* II, between pp. 56 and
57.

[3] Frank Budgen.

my complete typescript in New York. It would be creating trouble to set from the *Little Review*, as many passages are omitted and hopelessly mixed. With kind regards sincerely yours   JAMES JOYCE

To FRANK BUDGEN   MS. Yale

15 March 1920   *Via Sanità 2, Trieste*

Dear Budgen: On receipt let me know express or by wire if you can come to Trieste at the beginning of April. This would not prevent you going to England in summer. Perhaps I too might go to Cornwall and then Ireland. My plan is this. Sell off what you can and don't want. If you can put 300 frs in your pocket, outside fare, you get 1000 lire on arrival here owing to exchange. I will have a room ready for you. *Re* studio I think you could have Silvestri's.[1] I can introduce you to many of your craft here. I can get you lessons here, not tiresome, at 6 or 7 lire an hour. You will learn Italian. You will see the Mediterranean. You will surely find something to paint in this colourfull place. Food is not so dear. You will see ME. You will hear (till you get sick) the bloody Oxen of the bloody Sun. If you want to scut there are always boats to take you by long sea or trains and we can raise the fare. If you want a job in a shipping office here you can probably get one. If you decide lose no time. Sell off. Buchmann will perhaps advance you somewhat (say 200 frs) on a picture, seascape, to be painted here = 600 lire. Go, if you decide, to Italian consulate. Call yourself painter, coming here to paint. I will work this end here and have your permission wired.

Where is my bloody watch, you bloody lousy robber that I trusted with the confiding beauty of my angelic nature. Where are Tripcovich's packet of Godforsaken goodfornothing letters about LUV?[2] Where are the copies of that splendid masterpiece *Verbannte*

by

JAMES JOYCE

Answer at once   J.J.

P.S. My brother says he can get you lessons at *10 lire* an hour. A friend of his is head of the Strangers' Movement Dept at the Governatorato here so that all is clear.

BE ENERGETIC.

[1] Tullio Silvestri.

[2] During the First World War Count Mario Tripcovich, a friend of Joyce in Trieste, was separated from his fiancée, Silvia Mordo, who had gone with her family to Italy. Since they could not correspond directly because of wartime censorship, they sent their letters to Joyce in Zurich; he in turn made abstracts and forwarded them to the parted lovers.

To FRANK BUDGEN   MS. Yale

20 March 1920   *Via Sanità 2, Trieste*

Dear Budgen: Just got your letter of 23 but I hope your decision is not
final. 1st. The passport difficulty is not a difficulty at all, I think,
because probably on consignment of your F.O. pass they can issue you
a consular pass. 2nd. As regards going to England how does the Trieste
plan interfere with that. It is quite on the cards that I shall be going
there or thereward provisionally about June or July. 3rd. The exchange
rates are against you in England and in your favour here. That is for
27 or 30 francs you get 100 lire. Life is cheaper here than in Switzerland.
4th. Apart from me surely you have something to gain by a visit, even
if brief, to this part of the world and is it not in your interest to see
certain things both here and in Venice. A Greek friend of mine Sofiano-
pulos was going to Zurich. I asked him to see you and explain verbally
the situation. If you consent to sacrifice 3 hours of the day you can
earn 150 to 200 lire per week. As a matter of fact I had (or have) two
pupils hanging over for you contingent on your arrival. I give no lessons.
My brother is full up and has constantly to decline offers. If you saw
your way clear at all I believe a visit here might do you good. I understand that Switzerland is now impossible and perhaps you want to
settle down in England but before abandoning Europe, it would do you
no harm to see this part of it. So I send this off in the hope that it may
lead you to modify your programme when and if Mr Ballocks (pardon
Bollag) comes up to the scratch.

Sykes wrote me from Milan suggesting he would come here to discuss
the E.P. but as I saw no use in it I let him proceed to Genoa. As regards
watch books packet that depends on your final decision. I thought if
you came you could bring the MS of *Ulysses*. My regards to the Suters
and to Hummel when you see him.

Am working hard at *Oxen of the Sun*, the idea being the crime committed against fecundity by sterilizing the act of coition. Scene, lying-
in hospital. Technique: a nineparted episode without divisions introduced by a Sallustian-Tacitean prelude (the unfertilized ovum), then
by way of earliest English alliterative and monosyllabic and Anglo-
Saxon ('Before born the babe had bliss. Within the womb he won
worship.' 'Bloom dull dreamy heard: in held hat stony staring') then
by way of Mandeville ('there came forth a scholar of medicine that men
clepen etc') then Malory's *Morte d'Arthur* ('but that franklin Lenehan
was prompt ever to pour them so that at the least way mirth should not

lack'), then the Elizabethan chronicle style ('about that present time young Stephen filled all cups'), then a passage solemn, as of Milton, Taylor, Hooker, followed by a choppy Latin-gossipy bit, style of Burton-Browne, then a passage Bunyanesque ('the reason was that in the way he fell in with a certain whore whose name she said is Bird in the Hand') after a diarystyle bit Pepys-Evelyn ('Bloom sitting snug with a party of wags, among them Dixon jun., Ja. Lynch, Doc. Madden and Stephen D. for a languor he had before and was now better, he having dreamed tonight a strange fancy and Mistress Purefoy there to be delivered, poor body, two days past her time and the midwives hard put to it, God send her quick issue') and so on through Defoe-Swift and Steele-Addison-Sterne and Landor-Pater-Newman until it ends in a frightful jumble of Pidgin English, nigger English, Cockney, Irish, Bowery slang and broken doggerel. This progression is also linked back at each part subtly with some foregoing episode of the day and, besides this, with the natural stages of development in the embryo and the periods of faunal evolution in general. The double-thudding Anglo-Saxon motive recurs from time to time ('Loth to move from Horne's house') to give the sense of the hoofs of oxen. Bloom is the spermatozoon, the hospital the womb, the nurse the ovum, Stephen the embryo.

How's that for high?

Well, get hold of a pen now and tell me what you think of doing? I hope you will come for a time anyway. Spring here is very pleasant. Opera continues also after Easter. *Sigfrido* with one of the greatest Italian tenors Bassi. Arrivederci—e presto   JAMES JOYCE

To EZRA POUND   MS. Yale

5 June 1920   *Via Sanità 2, III, Trieste*

Dear Pound: I went to the station this morning to start at 7:30. On my arrival there I was told that a passenger train which had left some hours before had collided with another, result as per enclosed cutting. Luckily I was not on it. I was also told that the 7:30 express Trieste–Paris is now off owing to strike. There are two trains between T and Desenzano, viz: one at 11:30 A.M. reaching there about the witching hour of midnight. The other at 5, travelling (or crawling) all night and reaching there about 6 next morning. This train is impossible for me.

Now it is my intention to travel over that line en route for England

and Ireland as soon as possible but I think it is unprofitable to go now. I suppose after 12 June you will go to London. In that case we shall meet then, I hope. My only reason for accepting your kind invitation to Sirmione[1] was to meet you. But still it would be a big expense for you. And also for me if I travelled secondclass. You may judge of the state of the railway here by second cutting.

My reasons for travelling north are these. I am in need of a long holiday (by this I don't mean abandonment of *Ulysses* but quiet in which to finish it) away from here. Without saying anything about this city (*de mortuis nil nisi bonum*)[2] my own position for the past seven months has been very unpleasant. I live in a flat with eleven other people and have had great difficulty in securing time and peace enough to write those two chapters. The second reason is: clothes. I have none and can't buy any. The other members of the family are still provided with decent clothes bought in Switzerland. I wear my son's boots (which are two sizes too large) and his castoff suit which is too narrow in the shoulders, other articles belong or belonged to my brother and to my brother-in-law. I shall not be able to buy anything here. A suit of clothes, they tell me, costs 600–800 francs. A shirt costs 35 francs. I can just live with what I have but no more. Since I came here I suppose I have not exchanged 100 words with anybody. I spend the greater part of my time sprawled across two beds surrounded by mountains of notes. I leave the house at 12:22 and walk the same distance along the same streets buy the Daily Mail which my brother and wife read and return. Idem in the evening. I was once inveigled into a theatre. I was once invited to a public dinner, as professor of the Scuola Superiore here, and next day received from them a request to subscribe 20,000 or 10,000 or even 5000 lire of Italian war loan. I must buy clothes so I think I ought to go to Dublin to buy them.

Thirdly, my two children have not slept in a bed since we came. They repose on hard sofas and the climate here is very trying in July–September.

Fourthly, the rate of exchange is readjusting itself. While the pound (I mean the other pound, the English not the American one) stood at 100 or 90 I could fight the prices here because my money was in English currency. Today the pound is at 62 and my brother-in-law (who is cashier of a bank here) says it is gravitating towards a lower price owing to certain trade manoeuvres or nobody could buy at such high figures.

[1] Joyce's regular misspelling of this place as 'Sermione' has been corrected.

[2] Trieste had been favoured by the Austro-Hungarian empire as its only important merchant port; now, under Italy, the city had no such importance and seemed inert.

If it reaches 50 I cannot swim any more but disappear under the surface.
If I went to Switzerland I could not keep myself and family there: besides
I dislike returning to places. Prices here are from 8 to 10 times what
they were in 1914.

I could give lessons here (most people expected it of me) but I will not.
I have a position in that school which the government has now raised to
the rank of a university. My pay is about 3/– an hour for 6 hours a week.
This I shall resign as it wastes my time and my nerves.

I cannot find a flat here. To find one you must hold in the right hand
a check for 20,000 or 30,000 lire as keymoney.

So I propose to pass three months in Ireland in order to write *Circe*
and the close of the book. I should return here with my family in
October (if anyone finds a flat for us in the meantime) or, if not, without
them in order to write the end of it.

Financially my position is that I shall receive on 25 June (£62–10–0)[1]
and if my New York publisher advances (£25). I presume that by the
time this £87 is finished I shall [be] within measurable distance of 25
September when I get another £62–10–0. My wife and children could
stay in Galway. I too there or in Dublin. The disturbed state of Ireland
is of course a reason for not going. There may be other reasons. But I
could not go to an English seaside town as it would be too dear. If I
manage to do this and if you are in London at the end of June there are,
I suppose, several things I could do such as seeing my agent. What do
you think of this plan? I must finish my book in quiet even if I sell off
the furniture I have here.

I hope you received safely *The Oxen of the Sun* and have sent it off to
London and New York. I was bringing down another copy this morning.
The worst of it is I fear that Linati may come down on you. I wrote him
yesterday express that I should be in Sirmione tonight and mentioned
your suggestion of our meeting!

Have you seen *Poesia* or shall I send it?[2]

I hope Mrs Pound is still well. It is a pity that I cannot see my way to
go now but perhaps it is better so if I can manage the other and in that
case we can meet more comfortably.

Let me know as soon as possible about the safe arrival of chapter.

With many regrets and regards sincerely yours   JAMES JOYCE

P.S. This is a very poetical epistle. Do not imagine that it is a subtly

---

[1] The income on a gift from Harriet Shaw Weaver.

[2] Joyce's poem, 'A Memory of the Players in a Mirror at Midnight', was published in
Poesia (Milan) I. 1 (April 1920), 27.

worded request for secondhand clothing. It should be read in the evening when the lakewater[1] is lapping and very rhythmically.

To Mrs William Murray (Postcard)   MS. National Library

17 June 1920   *Via Sanità 2, III, Trieste*

Dear Aunt Josephine: Thanks for letter to which I shall reply more fully. As regards the gazette or police news or whatever the devil it is it was always on sale in low newsagents. You must be misinformed unless it is a brandnew regulation. Well, can you obtain for me *Reynold's* or *Lloyd's Weekly News* or *News of the World* for the weeks ending? Keep them till my next card when I shall tell you where to send them either to Paris or to London. We leave here, I expect, in a fortnight but I must remain a week or so between Paris and London. More anon. Thanks.

Jim

[1] An allusion to the line in Yeats's 'The Lake Isle of Innisfree',

I hear lake water lapping in low sounds by the shore,

and to the Lago di Garda near which, at Sirmione, Pound was sojourning.

Part IV

PARIS

1920–1939

Paris (1920–1939)

To live in Pola had been embarrassing for Joyce, to live in Rome irritating, to live in Trieste quaint but inconvenient. After those cities Zurich had been at least safe and unavoidable. To live in Paris came for a time suspiciously close to being pleasant. A pervasive enthusiasm for artistic change predisposed many Frenchmen to welcome him. Then too, the city was full of expatriates and visitors, some of them happily Irish, and most of them also ready to be attracted by original endeavour. Joyce complained outwardly, but inwardly approved his new situation. Though he shunned public life, there was some satisfaction in knowing that he was a point of civic interest, to be gestured at or whispered about as he stepped elegantly down the street. He sheltered himself behind silence on literary matters, a silence that became formidable, and behind a porous candour about his personal problems of money, children, and health. So he rebuffed with the one and absorbed with the other.

Thanks to Ezra Pound and to Pound's friends, Joyce found an audience ready for him. There was immediate talk of translating his books, of producing *Exiles* on the French stage, of writing articles about him. One admirer lent him a flat free of charge for the summer and early fall, another gave him an extra bed and a writing table, a third furnished a warm overcoat. Secretly encouraged, Joyce applied himself to both his literary task of finishing *Ulysses* and his practical one of having it published under suitable auspices. All attempts to find a publisher in England or the United States proved unavailing, but his meeting with Sylvia Beach on 11 July 1920, three days after his arrival in Paris, led ultimately to a solution. Miss Beach, an American woman, timidly offered, in April 1921, to publish *Ulysses* herself under the imprint of her Paris bookshop, Shakespeare and Company. Joyce at once consented.

Miss Beach was aided by her friend Adrienne Monnier, whose bookshop, the Maison des Amis des Livres, was on the rue de l'Odéon across from her own. They waged a literary campaign for Joyce which lasted for more than a year before *Ulysses* was in print. They enlisted the support of virtually everyone who ventured into their street, particularly of Valery Larbaud, whose reputation as a writer, translator, and critic of taste and talent was already secure. Larbaud gave a public lecture on

Ulysses at Mlle Monnier's bookshop on 7 December 1921, two months
before publication, and his knowledgeable endorsement encouraged a
flow of advance subscriptions to Shakespeare and Company.

Ulysses appeared at last on Joyce's fortieth birthday, 2 February 1922.
He was greatly agitated by the event and determined that publication
in Paris should not retard the acceptance of his book in England and
the United States. At first he suspected a boycott by reviewers; when
articles began to appear, he followed them with nervous passion, thanked
the critics by letter, thought up devices to keep the book before the
public, coaxed his friends and badgered acquaintances into helping it.
The greatness of *Ulysses* would have established itself, but Joyce felt
compelled to accelerate its recognition whenever, wherever he could.

During this period his home life remained unsettled. After leaving
the flat which had been loaned to him until November 1920, he allowed
himself to drift without conviction from one makeshift arrangement to
another, as if reluctant to commit himself to anything permanent. Nora
Joyce's temper was frayed by this haphazard life, and she felt too little
interest in *Ulysses* to read it. Against her husband's wishes she took her
children to see her family in Galway on 1 April 1922. This visit turned
out to be ill-timed, for the Irish Civil War flamed up in the west of
Ireland; they had to leave at once and return to Paris. The effect of this
incident was to make Joyce even more dependent upon his wife's
adherence than in the past, and he was gratified when she concessively
agreed to read some of *Ulysses* a few months later. His relations with
Nora were often tense during the rest of his life, but she never again
seriously considered leaving him. The couple went so far as to be
legally married in London on 4 July 1931, though this ceremony was
chiefly to secure his family in their rights to his property.

The subject of the book that was to follow *Ulysses* had probably
begun to grow in Joyce's mind before *Ulysses* was finished, since one of
the first things he did was to sort out unused notes left from the earlier
book. On 10 March 1923, a month after he had done this, he began to
write *Finnegans Wake*. The title was confided to his wife and to no
one else; it referred both to the hod carrier of the ballad, who was
miraculously resurrected by the whisky at his wake, and to the tough,
vegetable recurrence of human life and misbehaviour. The book was to
combine the affirmation of life, which he had always defined as the
central function of literature, with the scepticism about particular
living beings which had always been natural to him. It was to be alternately lyrical and combative or satirical, and always comic. To avoid
and transcend a 'goahead plot', it was to be based upon a theory of

cyclical recurrence which insisted on the typical character of every particular, whether person or incident.

Joyce must have known from the start that his new book would not be easy to read, for he intended it to be a night view of man's life, as *Ulysses* had been a day view. He would use the techniques of the dream, since in dreams all ages become one, attempts at concealment fail to convince, social and conventional barriers disappear. 'Wideawake language' and 'cutandry' grammar would not serve him; to represent night accurately Joyce thought he must descend to the makinghouse of language below the conscious choice of settled words. He determined upon the pun, often multilingual, as a linguistic mixture which could suggest the nighttime merging of the particular and the typical, of the struggle for expression and the forms of speech. As in his other books, the immediate focus would be on a family as the basic human group, and the flux of history would coalesce momentarily in the lives of the Earwicker family at Chapelizod near Dublin.

The composition of *Finnegans Wake* was harassed by two major impediments. The first was Joyce's eye trouble, which began again on his arrival in Paris. He suffered from a painful inflammation of the iris, and his vision was blurred by the formation of successive cataracts. The result was that he submitted to a series of ten operations in addition to the one he had already undergone in Zurich. These took place on 3, 15?, and 28 April 1923, 10 June 1924, 29 November 1924, 15? April 1925, 8 December 1925, 12 December 1925, June 1926, and 15 May 1930. The last of these, the only one performed by Professor Alfred Vogt of Zurich, proved fairly successful; but Joyce continued to have severe eye attacks and was never free of anxiety on the score of possible future operations.

The second major trouble was the response of his friends to *Finnegans Wake*. Some parts of the book came into existence easily and were published in preliminary form in magazines: in Ford Madox Ford's *transatlantic review* (April 1924), T. S. Eliot's *Criterion* (July 1925), Adrienne Monnier's *Navire d'argent* (October 1925), Ernest Walsh's *This Quarter* (Autumn–Winter 1925–1926), and then in Eugene and Maria Jolas's *transition* (April 1927—April–May 1938). As the first of these appeared, Joyce's friends waited indulgently for the clarity to come. But when the book gave evidence of being written throughout in 'no language', they exchanged questioning looks and slowly began to express their doubts to Joyce himself. His brother denounced the 'drivelling rigmarole' as early as 1924, Ezra Pound wrote on 1 November 1926 that he could make nothing of the new work, Miss Weaver wondered on 4 February 1927 if he were not wasting his genius,

Wyndham Lewis published an attack on all Joyce's writings later in this year.

Joyce was not so indifferent as might be supposed; he wrote hurt letters asking for encouragement and, with more vigour, sought new supporters. He worked into his fable, 'The Ondt and the Gracehoper', afterwards pp. 414–19 of *Finnegans Wake*, a defence of his book against Lewis; he sampled Pound's judgment in other literary matters in order to point out several obvious lapses of taste; he instructed Miss Weaver both by letter and personally in his method and purpose; he published, on 7 July 1927, *Pomes Penyeach*, a collection of his later verse, as evidence that he could be grammatically sane if he chose. In May 1929 a group of his friends, marshalled by him, published a defence of his book entitled, with mock modesty that was like pretentiousness, *Our Exagmination round his Factification for Incamination of Work in Progress*. In July of this year he formally proposed to James Stephens, his fellow Dubliner, that Stephens complete the book for him, but Stephens conceived the tactful reply that, though he was willing to try, he was sure Joyce would finish it himself. He added that *Anna Livia Plurabelle*, which had been published in book form in 1928, was 'the greatest prose ever written by a man'.

The result of these tearings and mendings was a realignment of Joyce's acquaintance. His relationship with Miss Weaver was the least strained; but that with Pound became merely polite, and that with Lewis was now mutually distrustful. Even Sylvia Beach seems to have secretly flagged in her literary loyalty. A group of new friends, readier for innovation, offered a more unqualified allegiance; these were Eugene and Maria Jolas, Paul and Lucy Léon, Stuart and Moune Gilbert, Samuel Beckett, Louis Gillet, Nino Frank, and others for short periods.

In a mood of self-commiseration, Joyce fled his own affairs to embrace the cause of an Irish-French opera singer, John Sullivan, whose immense tenor voice astounded him and whose failure to secure engagements worthy of his talent seemed a parallel of his own plight. He was convinced that established cliques were working against Sullivan as against himself, and threw himself fanatically into securing Sullivan adequate recognition. This campaign began in November 1929, and did not taper off until after 1931. It gradually became clear to Joyce, as it was already to Sullivan, that the voice was losing some of its quality, but Joyce obstinately continued to work up interest in his friend.

He was recalled from his 'Sullivanizing' of the early 'thirties by some unexpected incidents in his family. The first was the marriage of his son

George, on 10 December 1931, to Helen Kastor Fleischman. Next came his father's death in Dublin on 29 December 1931, a great grief which however was lightened somewhat for Joyce by the birth of his grandson, Stephen James Joyce, on 15 February 1932. But the principal family trouble came from his daughter, Lucia, who in 1932 showed signs of the schizophrenia which had presumably begun during her girlhood, but had been dismissed by her parents as childish eccentricity. The next seven years of Joyce's life were pervaded by a frantic and unhappily futile effort to cure her by every means known to medicine as well as by simples of his own devising. He felt in some sense responsible for her condition, and refused to accept any diagnosis which did not promise hope. It seemed to him that her mind was like his own, and he tried to find evidence in her writing and in her drawing of unrecognised talent. Lucia spent long and short periods in sanitariums and mental hospitals, between which she would return to stay with her parents until some incident occurred which made it necessary she be sent away again. Joyce found doctors to give her glandular treatments, others to inject sea water, others to try psychotherapy; he sent her on visits to friends in Switzerland, England, and even Ireland. The last in 1935 was disastrous: she grew worse rather than better. He placed her next in the care of Miss Weaver and a nurse in England, with a doctor attempting a new cure; when this failed, he brought her to France, where she stayed with Mrs Jolas; ultimately even Joyce conceded she must be put into a *maison de santé* near Paris. There he continued to visit her, he wrote letters to her, he refused to give up hope that she was getting better. Some of his friends felt he was too zealous in her behalf, but his family feeling had always been intense and now found full and open expression.

During the nineteen-thirties Joyce moved forward by fits and starts with *Finnegans Wake*. The outlines of the book were clear to him, but the interconnections had to be worded, the new linguistic medium had to be consistent and of one piece, and a few chapters were still to be written. At last after sixteen years he completed the book in 1938, and it was published on 4 May 1939.

The response to *Finnegans Wake* discontented him, and when war was declared in September he saw it as a force which might push his book into oblivion. A fresher anxiety was for Lucia, who had to be moved with the other occupants of her *maison de santé* to safer quarters at Pornichet near La Baule. Joyce and his wife made sure of her transfer by going there in September 1939. They returned to Paris in October, to find that George's wife had suffered a breakdown. They felt compelled to take charge of Stephen Joyce by sending him to Mrs

Jolas's Ecole Bilingue, which had been moved from Neuilly to a village
near Vichy called Saint-Gérand-le-Puy in what was later Unoccupied
France. Joyce and his wife decided to follow their grandson there.
After nineteen years in Paris they left the city and reached St Gérand
on 24 December 1939. Their affairs were in dismal confusion.

12 July 1920   *rue de l'Université, 9, Paris*

Dear Miss Weaver: I arrived here with my family three days ago. My intention is to remain here three months in order to write the last adventure *Circe* in peace (?) and also the first episode of the close. For this purpose I brought with me a recast of my notes and MS and also an extract of insertions for the first half of the book in case it be set up during my stay here. The book contains (unfortunately) one episode more than you suppose in your last letter. I am very tired of it and so is everybody else.

Mr Pound wrote to me urgently from Sirmione (lake of Garda) that in spite of my dread of thunderstorms and detestation of travelling I went there bringing my son with me to act as a lightning conductor. I remained two days there and it was arranged when I explained my general position and wishes that I should follow him on to Paris. I returned to Trieste but I did not believe that I should ever succeed in wheeling the caravan of my family out of it—or if I did that I should ever succeed in reaching Paris. For this reason I thought it better to wait before writing to you and have delayed also a few days since I came here because even then I was by no means sure that I could find rooms here. These have been found and it seems that my address will be rue de l'Assomption, 5, I, Passy, Paris. But I am not there yet so for a few days more will you please address letters to me c/o Mr Ezra Pound, Hotel Elysée, rue de Beaune 9, Paris?

I hope you duly received *Oxen of the Sun* which Mr Pound sent you on from Italy. Mr Froment Fels,[1] editor of *L'Action*, wishes to begin the serial publication of the French translation[2] (to be made by Mme Ludmilla Savitsky who has an article on Mr Aldington in the last issue of the *Anglo-French Review*) in the next number, to be preceded by a translation of Mr Pound's article on me in his last book *Instigations*. He also wishes to draw up a contract for the publication of the novel in book form when the serial publication is complete. You may remember that he wrote to me about this a year and a half ago in Zurich. Mr Lugne Poe,[3] formerly manager of the *Odéon* and now of the *Théâtre de*

---

[1] A slip for Florent Fels.   [2] Of *A Portrait of the Artist as a Young Man*.
[3] Aurélien-Marie Lugné-Poë (1869–1940), French actor and producer, founded the Théâtre de l'Œuvre in Paris in 1893.

l'Oeuvre, has taken *Exiles* to consider it for production. A translator for this has also been found and, I believe, a publisher. You would greatly oblige me if you could send me on a copy of *Exiles* for the translator and place the amount to debit of my next account. Also if it is not too much trouble I should like three copies of the *Egoist* (15 January 1913?),[1] the number which contained the story of *Dubliners* as there is someone here also who wished or wishes to translate some of the stories.

I hope that all this will lead to something practical. It is all due to Mr Pound's energy.

I hope also that I shall be able to finish the twelfth adventure[2] at my ease. Like its fellows it presents for me great technical difficulties and for the reader something worse. A great part of the nostos or close was written several years ago and the style is quite plain. The whole book, I hope (if I can return to Trieste provisionally or temporarily in October) will be finished about December after which I shall sleep for six months. With kind regards sincerely yours   JAMES JOYCE

To FRANK BUDGEN   MS. Yale

27 July 1920   *rue de l'Assomption 5, Passy, Paris*

Dear Budgen: Glad to hear from you as I wrote you several times in vain. Possibly letters miscarried. Am writing Rösi Suter[3] by this post. I remain at above address till October at least. Have a small flat partly furnished which a friend put at my disposal. Try to arrange to stop a few days in Paris. If you like I could find you a cheap room in a small hotel down here unless you want to put up at the Ritz. If it costs you, say, 5 frs Swiss a day there, the exchange being 240, you would have 12 frs a day here and you can live well inside that. Besides I want to hear you on the *Oxen* episode and want to bore the life out of you about *Circe* which is half written. The *Portrait* is being translated into French and perhaps the play will be put on at *L'Oeuvre*. Trieste was a very bad mark but I did two big chapters in it all the same. *Circe* is the last adventure, thank God. Hope you get something out of M'Cormick Stiftung.[4] Just mention my name. Get your passport made out also at French Consulate for sojourn of 3 months here, though I believe you can stop 12 days without it. Still it is better, and get the British one marked for stay or travelling to France and England. The French will do this for you if you

---

[1] Actually 15 January 1914.   [2] *Circe*.
[3] A sister of August and Paul Suter.
[4] A fund set up by Mrs McCormick to aid artists in financial straits. The Stiftung bought two of Frank Budgen's pictures.

say you were a British consular employee and the British will do it for
you if you just say that you are coming to visit me. When travelling you
get into those waggons, called railway coaches, which are behind the
locomotive. This is done by opening a door and gently projecting into
the compartment yourself and your valise. A man in an office will give
you a piece of cardboard in exchange for some money. By looking at it
attentively you will see the word *Paris* printed on it which is the name
of this stop. There are seats for you to sit on in the carriage but you
must not get out of it while it is moving as you might in that case be
left behind. Now, may the almighty God bless you and enable you to
carry out all these instructions of mine to you this afternoon. Saying
which I hereby take you by the hand and remain, dear sir, most expectantly yours.   J.J.

P.S. Drop a card in reply. Leave the packet with one of the 99 Suters,
also I suppose the copies of *Verbannte*. Auf wiedersehen!

To Stanislaus Joyce   MS. Cornell

Postmark 29 August 1920   *rue de l'Assomption 5, Passy, Paris*

Dear Stannie: I had a letter yesterday from Miss Weaver, saying that
she has made me a further gift of £2000 (two thousand). Will send you
particulars later. Will you ask Frank to telephone to those sons of
bitches at the Adriatica[1] (the man's name is Bruna) who have bungled
the sending of my case of books which I gave them on the 30 June? I am
much inconvenienced by their cursed mumchanciness. Giorgio has been
offered a position here in an American Trust Agency which would
develop into a secretaryship and travellership for same. The salary
would be about 200 frs (French) a month to begin with. Lucia has
become Napoleon-mad, a fact you may inform Sordina of.[2] Quinn sent
3500 francs. Huebsch is crying off *Ulysses*. Miss Weaver writes nobody
will print it. So it will be printed, it seems, in Paris and bear Mr John
Rodker's imprint as English printer.[3] Eliot, Wyndham Lewis, Rodker
and their wives keep moving between London, Paris and the country.
Dinners and lunches are the order of the day.[4] An admirer of mine, an

[1] The Società Adriatica di Spedizione, headed by Leopoldo Popper, father of Amalia
(see II, 262).
[2] See p. 201n.
[3] John Rodker (1894–1955), English poet, novelist, and publisher.
[4] Wyndham Lewis describes in *Blasting and Bombardiering* how Joyce insisted upon
paying for all the meals, cabs, and tips during the meetings that they and Eliot had
in Paris.

American officer,[1] presents me with an army overcoat. Budgen was here a week, gone to London. Also Mrs Sykes: and her husband is coming. What about *Little Reviews* etc?

I enclose cutting of Lord French's latest speech—delivered in Dublin. He has left Ireland which, being an Irishman, he refuses to annihilate.[2] Sir Horace Rumbold, has been unanimously chosen as First Emperor of Ireland. Please hang the Union Jack out of the scullery window at the exact instant when he ascends his ancestral throne of alabaster.[3] If a man named Buckley[4] calls, asking to see His Majesty, he is on no account to be admitted. By Order   JAMES

(Heb. Vat. Terg. Ex. Lut. Hosp. Litt. Angl. Pon. Max.)[5]

P.S. Ask Frank to ask that Hungarian in his bank the Magyar for Mr e.g. *Mr* Joseph Smith.[6]

To ALESSANDRO FRANCINI BRUNI   MS. S. Illinois (Croessmann)

[? *8 September 1920*]   *rue de l'Assomption 5, Parigi, XVI*

Caro Francini: Un maledetto contrattempo intralcia il mio lavoro. La cassa di libri (peso ca. 40 chili, quadrata segni 'J.J. 38'[7] spedita da Trieste, 29.vi.920, dalla Società Adriatica (A. Bruna), Piazza delle Poste) non si trova più! Ti prego passa dai miei verso le 13.30 quando troverai tutt'e due in casa. Domanda se sanno qualcosa. Se non forse tu potresti da parte tua—tuo padre non è o non era impiegato alla ferrovia. Da parte mia il Ministero degli Esteri (francese) dove c'è un segretario che ammira i miei scritti farà il possibile per rintracciarla lungo le linee francesi. Ma certo l'incaglio dev'essere in quel bel paese dove l'ano

---

[1] William Aspenwall Bradley.

[2] John Denton Pinkstone, 1st Earl of Ypres, Lord French (1852–1925), field marshal, was appointed Lord-Lieutenant of Ireland in 1918, a post which he held until 30 April 1921 after the passage of the Government of Ireland Act. He took part in an All-Ireland conference on 24 August 1920, and the *Irish Times* of the following day quotes him as having proposed a resolution, 'That this Conference records its conviction that the policy of the Government in Ireland is inevitably leading to civil war, and it is of paramount importance that immediate steps be taken to secure peace in Ireland.' His speech was a forceful statement of the same position.

[3] Joyce is alluding to the imagery of the *Circe* episode of *Ulysses*, where Bloom is crowned 'emperor president and king chairman'. The 'thrones of alabaster' are identified as water-closets in the *Cyclops* episode, p. 422 (325).

[4] See p. 60n.

[5] Hebraeus Vaticanus Tergestis Exul Lutetiae Hospes Litterarum Anglicarum Pontifex Maximus, or Vatican Jew, Exile from Trieste, Guest of Paris, High Priest of English Letters.

[6] This would be Smith *úr*. Joyce was trying to represent Bloom's Hungarian grandfather.

[7] Joyce's initials and age.

suona.[1] Puoi immaginarti il mio stato d'anima [sic] dopo sette anni di lavoro e quale. Tutti s'aspettano la chiusa delle avventure. Ho già scritto l'episodio di *Circe* un sei volte. Credo sia la cosa più forte ch'io abbia scritto malgrado la mia espulsione in circostanze note alla dea che mi protegge.

Ti mando alcuni giornali. Mio fratello può averli per un giorno ma non più, prego, perchè diventano stantii. Passali al Benco. Spedii diversa roba al Buttana. Non so se ne fece uso o no.

Avrai inteso mio nuovo colpo di fortuna? Cosa c'è col tuo libretto?

Dunque, caro Franzin,[2] te prego, dai domanda a lori se i sa andove ze sta roba parchè mi go mandasto da un zerto sior Driatiko che ze proprio rente alla posta granda sta cassa el mi ga dito che i sui omini i la mandaria cul[3] caro e che iera pulido proprio ma esso i me dise che qualchedun le ga menà in condoto e ga messo sora non so che cossa o che i ga sbregà cul fero cossa so mi, ma sior Driatico ga firmato mona de ostia[4] che lu ga zercà così e colà in ogni buso cul lume e no ze gnanca rimasta la spusa, arra.

Una streta de man del tuo

JACOMO DEL OIO
sudito botanico

P.S. Cassa no iera ciavada[5] con ciave ma iera soltanto roba de ciodi che go comperasto da un taliano che se ciama el sior Greinitz Neffen[6] cul sara do letere e trentoto che go copià drio l'Aufgabe de mio fio che studia per ritmetico.   J.J.[7]

---

[1] Joyce, amused by the Italian nationalism of Triestines who had lived so long under Austrian rule, parodies here the familiar identification of Italy as '[il] bel Paese là dove'l sì suona' ('The beautiful land where the *sì* rings out') (*Inferno*, XXXIII, l. 80).

[2] From this point Joyce writes in a corrupt Triestine dialect, the kind a Triestine would use in mimicking the way a Slovene speaks the dialect. So Adriatica becomes Driatika, the Triestine 'un italian' becomes 'un taliano', and articles are omitted before nouns.

[3] A blend of 'col' ('with the') and 'cul' ('arse').

[4] A blasphemous vulgarism, for which 'son of a bitch' is a weak equivalent.

[5] A play on 'fucked' and 'locked'.

[6] A mocking reference to the Italian nationalism of Triestines with un-Italian names. Greinitz Neffen (Nephews) was a tool and hardware firm with its main office in Graz, Austria. Its Triestine branch had just been taken over by an Italian corporation following the First World War.

[7] (Translation)
'Dear Francini: A damned mishap is holding up my work. The case of books (weight c. 40 kilos, square, stamped "J.J. 38" sent from Trieste, 29 June 1920, from the Società Adriatica (A. Bruna), Piazza delle Poste) is not to be found! Please drop in on my relatives about 1:30 p.m. when you will find both at home. Ask if they know anything. If not perhaps you could yourself [do something]—is not or was not your father a railway employee. For my part, the Ministry of Foreign Affairs (French) where there is a secretary who admires my writings will do what is possible to trace them along the French railways. But certainly the hitch must be in that beautiful country where the arse is sounded. But imagine my state of mind after seven years of

To CARLO LINATI[1]

21 September 1920   *rue de l'Assomption 5, Parigi XVI*

Caro Signor Linati: Riguardo alla proposta del sig. Dessy visto l'enorme
mole e la più che enorme complessità del mio maledettissimo romanzac-
cione credo sia meglio mandargliene una specie di sunto—chiave—
scheletro—schema (per uso puramente domestico). Forse che Lei ha il
testo la mia idea apparirà più chiara. Se no, scriva al Rodker che Le
farà avere gli altri esemplari. Ho indicato soltanto 'Schlagworte' [sic][2]
nel mio schema ma credo che capirà lo stesso. È l'epopea di due razze
(Israele–Irlanda) e nel melemimo tempo il ciclo del corpo umano ed
anche una storiella di una giornata (vita). La figura di Ulisse mi ha
sempre affascinato sin da ragazzo. Cominciai a scrivere una novella per
Dubliners 15 anni fa ma smisi. Sette anni lavoro ora a questo libro—
accidenti! È una specie di enciclopedia anche. La mia intenzione è di
rendere il mito *sub specie temporis nostri* non soltando ma permettendo
che ogni avventura (cioè ogni ora, ogni organo, ogni arte connessi ed
immedesimati nello schema somatico del tutto) condizionasse anzi
creasse la sua propria tecnica. Ogni avventura è per così dire una persona
benchè composta di persone—come favella l'Aquinate degli angelici
eserciti. Nessuno stampatore inglese ha voluto stamparne una parola.
In America la rivista è stata soppressa quattro volte. Ora, ho inteso, si
prepara un grande movimento contro la sua pubblicazione da parte di
puritani, imperialisti inglesi, repubblicani irlandesi e cattolici—che
alleanza! Io merito il premio Nobel per la pace, per diamine!

Dunque se crede faccia prima l'articolo a cui accenna, poi scelga

---

work, and what work. Everyone is waiting for the end of the adventures. I have
already written the *Circe* episode some six times. I think it is the strongest thing I have
written in spite of my expulsion in circumstances known to the goddess who protects
me.

I am sending you some newspapers. My brother can have them for a day but no
longer please since they get stale. Pass them on to Benco. I sent several things to
Buttana. I don't know if he made use of them or not.

Have you heard of my new stroke of luck? What about your libretto?

So, dear Franzin, come on and please ask them if they know where this stuff is
because I sent it through a certain Mister Driatiko who is near the main post office and
he told me that his men would send it by cart and everything would have gone all right
but now they say that someone took it to the lavatory and put I don't know what on it
or that they have torn it up with an iron or what do I know, but Mister Driatico signed
himself son of a bitch that he has searched up and down in every hole with a light and
not even the stink of it is left, arrah.

A handshake from   Giacomo of the Oil, botanic subject
P.S. The box was not locked with a key but only nailed with nails I bought from an
Italian who is named Mr Greinitz Neffen with only two letters and thirty-eight that I
copied from the homework of my son who is studying to be an arithmetician.   J.J.'
[1] From a photostat.   [2] 'Catchwords' (German).

qualche capitolo non troppo irto di difficoltà ed une parte potrebbe apparire nel numero successivo.

Un grave contrattempo ritarda la signora *Circe*. Spedii a Trieste al 29 giugno una cassa di libri ecc per il mio lavoro qui a Parigi. Mai arrivata! Telegrafai, scrissi, riscrissi. Niente. Con tutto ciò faccio l'impossibile. Saluti cordiali   James Joyce

P.S. Da, che fogli sconsi che ho scelti per lo schema—veramente degni del libraccio stesso! La prego, di rimandermeli—'per l'onor della famiglia'   J.J.[1]

To Frank Budgen   MS. Yale

Michaelmas 1920   *rue de l'Assomption 5, Passy, Paris*

Dear Budgen: Have met Sargent[2] several times and dined. He is held up here for a week. The stories he tells me of mob manners in London are almost incredible. Have worked some of it into *Circe* which by the way is a dreadful performance. It gets wilder and worse and more involved but I suppose it will all work out. Thanks for the papers you send

---

[1] (Translation)
'Dear Mr Linati: As to Mr Dessy's suggestion I think that in view of the enormous bulk and the more than enormous complexity of my damned monster-novel it would be better to send him a sort of summary—key—skeleton—scheme (for home use only). Perhaps when you have the text my idea will appear clearer to you. Otherwise write to Rodker and ask him to let you have the other copies. I have given only 'Schlagworte' in my scheme but I think you will understand it all the same. It is the epic of two races (Israel–Ireland) and at the same time the cycle of the human body as well as a little story of a day (life). The character of Ulysses has fascinated me ever since boyhood. I started writing a short story for *Dubliners* fifteen years ago but gave it up. For seven years I have been working at this book—blast it! It is also a kind of encyclopaedia. My intention is not only to render the myth *sub specie temporis nostri* but also to allow each adventure (that is, every hour, every organ, every art being interconnected and interrelated in the somatic scheme of the whole) to condition and even to create its own technique. Each adventure is so to speak one person although it is composed of persons—as Aquinas relates of the heavenly hosts. No English printer wanted to print a word of it. In America the review was suppressed four times. Now, as I hear, a great movement is being prepared against the publication on behalf of puritans, English imperialists, Irish republicans and Catholics—what an alliance! Golly, I deserve the Nobel peace prize.
Well, if you think so, write first the article you suggested, then you will have to choose some chapter not too bristling with difficulties and part of it could appear in the next issue.
A serious mischance has delayed Madam *Circe*. On 29 June I dispatched from Trieste a case of books etc. for my work here to Paris. It never came! I wired, wrote, wrote again. Nothing. All the same I am doing the impossible. Cordial greetings
James Joyce
P.S. Heavens, what disgusting sheets of paper I have chosen for the schema—really worthy of the horrible book itself! Please send them back to me—"for the honour of the family"   J.J.'
[2] Louis Sargent, a British painter and a friend of Frank Budgen.

which, though very onesided, are most useful. Tomorrow I send you another 10 francs. I see there is or was a paper by Lord Alfred Douglas *Plain English*. Can you lay hold of any copies? In fact anything in that line will be useful. I am sorry you do not think your ideas on Circe worth sending. As I told you a catchword is enough to set me off. *Moly* is a nut to crack. My latest is this. Moly is the gift of Hermes, god of public ways, and is the invisible influence (prayer, chance, agility, *presence of mind*, power of recuperation) which saves in case of accident. This would cover immunity from syphilis ($\sigma\acute{v}$ $\phi\iota\lambda os$ = swine-love?). Hermes is the god of signposts: i.e. he is, specially for a traveller like Ulysses, the point at which roads parallel merge and roads contrary also. He is an accident of providence. In this special case his plant may be said to have many leaves, indifference due to masturbation, pessimism congenital, a sense of the ridiculous, sudden fastidiousness in some detail, experience. It is the only occasion on which Ulysses is not helped by Minerva but by her male counterpart or inferior.

Curious that Sargent should be an authority on animals. His character also, it seems to me, may have been like his namesake in the Nestor episode—the schoolboy? written before I had heard of him.

Huebsch my New York publisher is here. They say *Ulysses* will come out first in a private edition of 1000 copies at 150 frs each!

Are you strong on costume? I want to make *Circe* a costume episode also. Bloom for instance appears in five or six different suits. What a book!

I hope you are working well. Got notice to quit this matchbox and am running about looking for a flat. Hell! I must get *Circe* finished and *Eumeus* under way before I move anywhere.

Mind those Yahoos!   J.J.

To Frank Budgen   MS. Yale

24 October 1920   *rue de l'Assomption 5, Paris XVI*

Dear Budgen: Excuse delay in writing and this scrawl. Flat hunting every blessed day with no result. Must leave here on Friday or Saturday. A dreadful job and of course *Circe* put aside completely. Sargent is comfortably settled for little or nothing and suggested I go there or thereabouts. But *Exiles* is accepted by Lugné-Poë and already translated and is to be put on in December. The novel more or less the same and to go away now would be to mar any chances I have here. I perceive the editor

of B of F¹ (a Jew by his name) has been up before the beak and fined so
whatever else in that way you send had better be enclosed in a copy
of the *Christian Hero* or some such paper. I hope you are working and
progressing. I don't want to move anywhere till *Circe* is finished. If
you see the October *Dial* in any reading room you will find a long film
about me. I observe a furtive attempt to run a certain Mr Marcel
Proust of here against the signatory of this letter. I have read some
pages of his. I cannot see any special talent but I am a bad critic.
Still I think a fall of mine would not altogether disappoint some
admirers. It seems to me I have made a bad impression here. I am too
preoccupied (Bloomesque word) to rectify it.

The problems raised in *Circe* (of good taste, tact, technique, etc.) are
taking up all my time. In order to solve them I must be delivered of all
other cares.

Write if you get this in spite of railway strike. Sincerely yours

JAMES JOYCE

P.S. Last night I thought of an *Entr'acte* for Ulysses in middle of book
after 9th episode *Scylla & Charybdis*.² Short with absolutely no relation
to what precedes or follows like a pause in the action of a play. It would
have to be balanced by a *matutine* (very short) before the opening and
a *nocturne* (also short) after the end. What? I agree about the explanation of syphilis. I always thought the etymology was syn philein (together with loving, connected with it) but a man named Bradley says
the other. Moly could also be absinthe the cerebral impotentising (!!)
drink or chastity. Damn Homer, Ulysses, Bloom and all the rest.

To JOHN MCCORMACK   MS. McCormack

8 December 1920   *Boulevard Raspail 5, Paris*

Dear MacCormack: In the general confusion the other afternoon I had
not an opportunity to tell you how delighted we were by your singing,
especially the aria from *Don Giovanni*. I have lived in Italy practically
ever since we last met but no Italian lyrical tenor that I know (Bonci³
possibly excepted) could do such a feat of breathing and phrasing—to
say nothing of the beauty of tone in which, I am glad to see, Roscommon

---

¹ *Bits of Fun*, a comic weekly of a highly 'spicy' nature; Joyce made use of it in
writing the *Circe* episode of *Ulysses*.

² This was not added, nor were the matutine and nocturne mentioned in the lines
below.

³ Alessandro Bonci (b. 1870), Italian tenor.

can leave the peninsula a fair distance behind. We are all going to hear you again next Tuesday and I am sure you will have another big success.

Di nuovo tanti mirallegri ed una stretta di mano cordialissima.[1]
Sincerely yours   JAMES JOYCE

To FRANK BUDGEN   MS. Yale

10 December 1920   *Boulevard Raspail 5, Paris*

Dear Budgen: An eye attack was hanging on and off for a fortnight owing to cold and damp of the hotel so we took this flat for six months. It has about 100 electric lamps and gas stoves but how I am going to pay for it damn me if I know. I am looking for lessons. Anyhow we are in it and if any wad of money turns up for me perhaps you would like to take a trip across here for a few days. Of course if it would be unpleasant for you, say so out. I could fix you at this end and we could have a few days 'rest' from our labours. Do you find these latitudes (London must be worse) dreadful to live in? But for creature comforts it would be hell. Thanks for the papers. Now I want you to do another favour for me and in a great hurry. The whirligig movement in *Circe* is on the refrain *My Girl's a Yorkshire* etc, but to unify the action the preceding *pas seul* of S.D. which I intended to balance on the gramophone of the opposite kip should be on the air of that same ditty played on Mrs Cohen's pianola with lights. I enclose 10 francs. Will you be so kind as to apply to any vendor (a big one) of musichall airs. It was popular between 1904 and 1908. I want words and music. I have a piano here and telephone (Saxe 34-33). I hope to finish Circe before Christmas. By the way is it not extraordinary the way I enter a city barefoot and end up in a luxurious flat. Still, I am tired of it. Giorgio is employed on trial—no salary yet but it is experience and he could make a career if we stay on. My mood grows bitterer on account of Trieste and other things. At first I had not thought of the slaughter of the suitors as in Ulysses' character. Now I see it can be there too. I am going to leave the last word with Molly Bloom—the final episode *Penelope* being written through her thoughts and body Poldy being then asleep. *Eumeus* you know so there remains only to think out *Ithaca* in the way I suggest.

What is Paul Suter's address. I am going to send him a little Christmas reminder (a portrait of Verlaine—not the usual one) in memory of our Pfauennights.[2] I have not heard from Sargent but will write him

---

[1] 'Again many congratulations and a very cordial handshake.'
[2] Nights at the Pfauen café in Zurich.

one of these days. Do you keep up your acquaintance with Pound? I hope so.

What about yourself? What are you doing? I hope you have done more than I have who have been botching and patching that bloody old Circe since last June. The *Nausikaa* case comes on next Monday. Are you still in Sargent's flat? Now that I have one of my own I don't spend much in 'buses. In fact I rarely leave the house.

A point about Ulysses (Bloom). He romances about Ithaca (Oi want teh gow beck teh the Mawl Enn Rowd, s'elp me!) and when he gets back it gives him the pip. I mention this because you in your absence from England seemed to have forgotten the human atmosphere and I the atmospheric conditions of these zones.

Can you tell a poor hardworking man where is the ideal climate inhabited by the ideal humans? Address answers (enclosing 5/–P.O.) to:
sincerely yours   JAMES JOYCE

To ETTORE SCHMITZ[1]   MS. Fonda Savio

5 January 1921   *5 Boulevard Raspail, Parigi VII*

Caro Signor Schmitz: L'episodio di *Circe* fu finito tempo fa ma quattro dattilografe rifiutarono di copiarlo. Finalmente si pressentò una quinta la quale, però, lavora molto lentamente sicchè il lavoro non sarà pronto prima della fine di questo mese. Mi si dice conterrà 170 pagine forma commerciale. L'episodio di *Eumeo* il quale è quasi finito sarà pronto anche verso la fine del mese.

Secondo il piano stabilito dal mio avvocato a Nuova York 'Ulisse' escirà colà verso il 15 giugno p. v. in un'edizione privata e limitata a 1500 esemplari dei quali 750 per l'Europa. Il prezzo sarà di $12.50 risp. 4 sterline l'esemplare. Percepisco mille sterline come 'tacitazione'.[2] Contemporaneamente però si preparano articoli ed articoletti per sfondare la citadella non so con quale risultato e poco m'importa.

Ora l'importante: non posso muovermi da qui (come credevo di poter fare) prima di maggio. Infatti da mesi e mesi non vado a letto prima delle 2 o 3 di mattina, lavorando senza tregua. Avrò presto esaurito gli appunti che portai qui con me per scriver questi due episodi.[3] C'è a

---

[1] Ettore Schmitz (1861–1928) wrote novels and stories under the pseudonym of Italo Svevo. He and his wife, Livia, took lessons in English from Joyce in Trieste.

[2] This arrangement fell through.

[3] The rest of this paragraph is written in a style that mimics what the Triestines called 'austriacan'—that blend of 'austriaco' (Austrian) and 'italian' (Italian) which the Austrian authorities in Trieste had developed in writing bureaucratic Italian.

Trieste, nel quartiere di mio cognato, l'immobile segnato col numero politico e tavolare di via Sanità, 2, e precisamente situato al terzo piano del suddetto immobile nella camera da letto attualmente occupata da mio fratello, a ridosso dell'immobile in parole e prospettante i prostriboli di pubblica insicurezza,[1] una mappa di tela cerata legata con un nastro elastico di colore addome di suora di carità, avente le dimensioni approssimative d'un 95 cm. per cm. 70. In codesta mappa riposi i segni simbolici dei languidi lampi che talvolta balenarono nell'alma mia.

Il peso lordo, senza tara, è stimato a chilogrammi 4.78. Avendo bisogno urgente di questi appunti per l'ultimazione del mio lavoro letterario intitolato 'Ulisse' ossia 'Sua Mare Grega',[2] rivolgo codesta istanza a Lei, colendissimo collega, pregandoLa di farmi sapere se qualcuno della Sua famiglia si propone di recarsi prossimamente a Parigi, nel quale caso sarei gratissimo se la persona di cui sopra vorebbe avere la squisitezza di portarmi la mappa indicata a tergo.

Dunque, caro signor Schmitz,[3] se ghe xe qualchedun di sua famiglia che viaggia per ste parti la mi faria un regalo portando quel fagotto che no xe pesante gnanca per sogno perchè, la mi capissi, xe pien de carte che mi go scritto pulido cola pena e qualchevolta anche col bleistiff[4] quando no iera pena. Ma ocio a no sbregar el lastico, perchè allora nasserà confusion fra le carte. El meio saria de cior na valigia che si pol serar cola ciave che nissun pol verzer. Ne ghe xe tante di ste trappole da vender da Greinitz Neffen rente del Piccolo che paga mio fradel el professor della Berlitz Cul.[5] Ogni modo la me scriva un per de parole, dai, come la magnemo. Revoltella[6] me gha scritto disendo che xe muli da saminar per zinque fliche[7] ognidun e dopo i xe dotori de Revoltella e che mi vegno là da qui [?] per dar lori l'aufgabe[8] par inglese a zinque fliche, ma nongo risposto parchè iera una monada e po la marca mi vegnaria costar cola carta tre fliche come che xe ogi [?] coi bori e mi avanzaria do fliche per cior el treno e magnar e bever tre giorni, cossa la vol che sia.

---

[1] A play on *pubblica sicurezza* (police).

[2] Literally, 'His Greek mother', and so a comic glance at Homer, but the Triestine epithet means, 'His whore of a mother'.

[3] The rest of this paragraph is in Triestine dialect.

[4] The usual Italian mispronunciation of the German word for pencil, *Bleistift*.

[5] A play on 'school' and 'cul' ('arse').

[6] The Scuola Superiore di Commercio Revoltella, a commercial high school in Trieste, then in process of becoming the University of Trieste. Joyce taught there from about 1913 to 1915 and again in 1920.

[7] 'Flica', a slang word meaning ten *soldi*, but no longer used at the time of this letter. Joyce uses it humorously to mean 'lira'.

[8] German for 'lesson'.

Saluti cordiali e scusi se il mio cervelletto esaurito si diverte un pochino ogni tanto. Mi scriva presto, prego.   James Joyce[1]

To Frank Budgen   MS. Yale

[*28 February 1921*]   *Boulevard Raspail 5, Paris*

Dear Budgen: First of all many happy returns of your birthday[2] and secondly my regards and apologies to Mr and Mrs Sargent for not

---

[1] (Translation)

'Dear Mr Schmitz: The *Circe* episode was finished some time ago, but four typists refused to copy it. Finally a fifth turned up; she is very slow, however, so that the work will not be finished before the end of this month. I am told it will contain 170 pages, commercial size. The *Eumeus* episode, which is almost finished, will also be ready around the end of the month.

According to the plan arranged by my lawyer in New York, *Ulysses* will appear there around 15 June next in a private edition limited to 1500 copies, of which 750 will be for Europe. The price will be $12.50 or 4 pounds sterling per copy. I am to receive 1000 pounds as "payoff". At the same time, however, articles long and short are being prepared in order to storm the citadel, with what effect I don't know and don't much care.

Now for the important matter: I cannot leave here (as I had hoped to) before May. As a matter of fact, for months and months I have not gone to bed before 2 or 3 in the morning, working without respite. I shall soon have used up the notes I brought with me here so as to write these two episodes. There is in Trieste in the quarter of my brother-in-law in the building bearing the political and registry number 2 of Via Sanità and located precisely on the third floor of the said building in the bedroom presently occupied by my brother, in the rear of the building in question, facing the brothels of public insecurity, an oilcloth briefcase fastened with a rubber band having the colour of a nun's belly and with the approximate dimensions of 95 cm. by 70 cm. In this briefcase I have lodged the written symbols of the languid sparks which flashed at times across my soul.

The gross weight without tare is estimated at 4.78 kilograms. Having urgent need of these notes for the last incident in my literary work entitled *Ulysses* or "His Whore of a Mother", I address this petition to you, most honourable colleague, begging you to let me know if any member of your family intends to come to Paris in the near future, in which case I should be most grateful if the above-mentioned person would have the kindness to bring me the briefcase specified on the back of this sheet.

So, dear Signor Schmitz, if there is someone in your family who is travelling this way, he would do me a great favor by bringing me this bundle, which is not at all heavy since, you understand, it is full of papers which I have written carefully with a pen and at times with a bleistiff when I had no pen. But be careful not to break the rubber band because then the papers will fall into disorder. The best thing would be to take a suitcase which can be locked with a key so nobody can open it. There are many such traps on sale at Greinitz Neffen, next to the *Piccolo*, for [one of] which my brother the Professor at the Berlitz Cul will pay. At any rate write me a few words. How are you getting along? Revoltella has written me saying that there are boyos to be examined at five fliche each after which they will be Revoltella doctors and that I should come from here to give them English lessons at 5 fliche, but I haven't answered because the postage stamps and stationery, the way money is today, will cost me three fliche and I will be left with two fliche to take the train and eat and drink for three days, isn't that something to think about.

Cordial greetings and excuse if my little worn-out brain amuses itself a little every so often. Write me soon, please.   James Joyce'

[2] Frank Budgen was born 1 March 1882.

having acknowledged safe receipt of the book sent me. What a time! A rent (£300) which keeps me in continual fever, running about here and there mortgaging my income in advance. Then up every night till 3 or even later writing. *Circe* is finished long ago, also *Eumeus* and I am writing *Ithaca*. I have dreadful worries about a typist. Four declined to do *Circe*, at last one admirer(ess) volunteered. She started but when she had done 100 pp her father got a seizure in the street (a Circean episode) and now my MS is written out in fair hand by someone who passes it to someone else who sends it to be typed. I sent *Eumeus* to a third typist. A hysterical letter from the translatress of the *Portrait*.[1] No word, or syllable of word, from Pound. Or fair Trieste where I wrote asking for the forwarding of certain MSS. I had a letter from a Mr Valery Larbaud (French translator of S. Butler and novelist) says he has read *Ulysses* and is raving mad over it, that Bloom is as immortal as Falstaff (except that he has some few more years to live—Editor) and that the book is as great as Rabelais (Merde de bon Dieu et foutre de nom de nom!—comment of Monsieur François). I shall send both chapters as soon as possible. I suppose you are in a hard way. Have you tried that article I suggested? Or have you anything else literary? If Lewis has any influence etc shall I write to him, but you must tell me his address. Let me know. Pound has left London for good. What is wrong with him I don't know. Hummel was here a few times lately and we go to him next Sunday.

I suffer from frightful attacks of neuralgia. Sargent told me you feel twinges of rheumatism. Beware of it. Some determined effort should be made to right affairs generally but all I can do is to slave along at Bloom, curse him.

I am writing *Ithaca* in the form of a mathematical catechism. All events are resolved into their cosmic physical, psychical etc. equivalents, e.g. Bloom jumping down the area, drawing water from the tap, the micturition in the garden, the cone of incense, lighted candle and statue so that not only will the reader know everything and know it in the baldest coldest way, but Bloom and Stephen thereby become heavenly bodies, wanderers like the stars at which they gaze.

The last word (human, all too human) is left to Penelope. This is the indispensable countersign to Bloom's passport to eternity. I mean the last episode *Penelope*.

Now, dear friend, being some twentyeight days older than you, I take the liberty of suggesting that some kind of end be put to this tomfool existence we are both leading. Mine is more absurd than yours. Let me

---

[1] Ludmila Savitsky.

know what exactly you are doing and how you are getting on, if you have sold anything or are travelling for soap. O, my prophetic soul, when I put soap in Ulysses' pocket. I am heaping all kinds of lies in to the mouth of that sailorman in *Eumeus* which will make you laugh.

At one time I thought the slaughter of the suitors un-Ulyssean. In my present frame of mind, I have modified my opinion.

Schluss. Prosit! And to our next meeting with song and dance as in 1919 of blastedly expensive memory.

ad multos annos!   JAMES JOYCE

P.S. If you or Sargent can pick up any handbook *cheap* on Freemasonry or any ragged, dirty, smudged, torn, defiled, effaced, dogeared, coverless, undated, anonymous misprinted book on mathematics, or algebra or trig. or Eucl. from a cart for 1d or at most $2\frac{1}{4}$d tant mieux.   J.J.

To ALESSANDRO FRANCINI BRUNI   MS. S. Illinois (Croessmann)

7 June 1921   *71 rue du Cardinal Lemoine, Vᵉ, Parigi*

Caro Francini: Suppongo che quell'articolo nell'*E.N.*[1] sia opera tua. Grazie. La chiusa è bella. Eccomi di nuovo sloggiato (e Silvestri che vuol mandarmi una tela sua dove ha la testa? Avessi una casa mia ben volentieri ci metterei i suoi quadri nonchè certi ammenicoli lasciati costì)—il quinto sloggio in 11 mesi. Il quartiere Boulevard Raspail mi costava la bellezza di 2000 lire al mese. Questo invece non mi costa niente. Il romanziere francese Valery Larbaud è fuori della grazia di Dio causa il mio *Ulisse* che proclama la più vasta ed umana opera scritta in Europa dopo Rabelais. Prescindendo da questo (del quale giudicherà l'avvenire) ha saputo corroborare il suo parere coi fatti. Avendo avuto qualche sentore dei miei grovigli fece arredare di nuovo il suo appartamento e me lo mise a disposizione per i mesi estivi. È qualche cosa d'incredibile. Dietro il Panthéon a 10 minuti dal Lussemburgo una specie di piccolo parco, al quale si accede attraverso due cancelli, silenzio assoluto, grandi alberi, uccelli (non di quei che intendi tu, veh!)[2] pare di essere a 100 chilometri da Parigi. Il mobiglio è delizioso. Egli ed il primo attore del teatro *Vieux Colombier* hanno ideato una specie d'ammobiliamento fantastico eppure comodissimo. È possibile ch'io valga qualche cosa? Chi l'avrebbe detto dopo la mia ultima esperienza a Trieste? Larbaud dice che il solo episodio di *Circe* basterebbe per fare la rinomanza di uno scrittore francese per la vita.

---

[1] *Era Nuova*, a Triestine daily newspaper which was published between 1919 and 1923.
[2] 'Uccello' in Italian means not only 'bird', but also, vulgarly, 'penis'.

Ma o! ed a! ed ahime! ed oibo! che libro! L'episodio d'*Itaca* adesso
tutto geometria, algebra e matematica e dopo *Penelope* finalmente!
Potessi tuffare la mia testa in un mare di ghiaccio! È già sotto i torchi il
libro ed aspetto le prime bozze domani l'altro. Sarà pubblicato però
appena in ottobre o novembre. Trattandosi di tre edizioni costose
bisogna evitare i refusi. I colori della legatura (scelti da me) saranno
lettere bianche in campo azzurro—la bandiera greca quantunque
realmente d'origine bavarese ed importata colla dinastia. Eppure in certo
qual modo simboleggiano bene il mito—le isole bianche sparse nel mare.

Quanto al lato materiale credo se l'edizione va bene (le sottoscrizioni
vengono ogni giorno—oggi 3 dall'Australia) riceverò qualcosa fra
100.000 e 150.000. Ma non è questo che mi preoccupa. Nessuna somma
potrà mai pagarmi il lavoro e lo sciupìo .. Si potrebbe scrivere qualcosa
di veramente comico sui sottoscriventi di questo mio libraccio—un
figlio o nipote di Bela Kun, il ministro della guerra britannico Winston
Churchill, un vescovo anglicano ed un capo del movimento rivoluzion-
ario irlandese.[1] Son diventato un monumento—anzi vespasiano![2]

Giorgio è a Zurigo per le sue vacanze. Ordinerò il libro di Papini[3] ma
non prometto di leggerlo per il momento. Salutami Benco e Silvestri
pittore-speditore.

Bien d'amitiés à Madame et à Daniele[4] . . . Una stretta di mano

JAMES JOYCE[5]

[1] Probably Desmond Fitzgerald (1889–1947), Irish politician. He was Minister for
Publicity from 1918 to 1922, for External Affairs from 1922 to 1927, and for Defence
from 1927 to 1932.

[2] A 'vespasian' is a urinal, so named in honour of the Roman emperor who taxed them.

[3] Giovanni Papini (1881–1956), Italian writer. The book was probably his *Storia di
Cristo* (1921).

[4] Francini's son. The ellipsis following is Joyce's.

[5] (Translation)
'Dear Francini: I suppose this article in the *Era Nuova* is your work. Thank you.
The close is fine. Here I am, forced to move again (and Silvestri, who wants to send me
one of his paintings, where does he abide? If I had a house of my own I should be very
glad to put his pictures there, as well as some knick-knacks left behind)—my fifth
move in eleven months. The flat on the Boulevard Raspail cost me a good 2000 lire a
month. But this one costs me nothing. The French novelist Valery Larbaud is beside
himself on account of my *Ulysses* which he proclaims the vastest and most human
work written in Europe since Rabelais. Apart from that (which the future will settle)
he has known how to corroborate his opinion with deeds. Having had some indication
of my mix-up he had his flat redecorated and put it at my disposition for the summer
months. It is unbelievable. Behind the Pantheon, ten minutes from the Luxembourg,
a kind of little park, with access through two barred gates, absolute silence, great
trees, birds (not, mind you, the sort you're thinking of!), like being a hundred kilo-
meters from Paris. The furnishings are tasteful. He and the principal actor of the Vieux
Colombier theatre have designed a kind of furniture which is fantastical but very
comfortable. Is it possible that I am worth something? Who would have said so after
my last experience in Trieste? Larbaud says that a single episode, *Circe*, would suffice
to make the fame of a French writer for life. But oh! and ah! and alas! and ugh! what a

To Frank Budgen   MS. Yale

[Late June 1921]   *71, rue du Cardinal Lemoine, Vᵉ, Paris*

Dear Budgen: Have you seen Lewis? If nothing has come out of the
Lady Cunard suggestion the Ellerman line is still open. The friend I
spoke of is here. Write to me. *Ithaca* is giving me fearful trouble.
Corrected the first batch of proofs today up to Stephen on the strand[1]
which I read out to you on a memorable night in Zurich (Universitätsstrasse 29) with mirthful comments.[2] Hummel and Giorgio left for
Zurich on the 4th. In the words of the Cyclops narrator the curse of my
deaf and dumb arse light sideways on Bloom and all his blooms and
blossoms. I'll break the back of *Ithaca* tomorrow so 'elp me fucking
Chroist. Write by return   JJ

P.S. There is an article about me in *Today*[3] but I haven't seen it, the
rlwy strike (for which *YOU*[4] are responsible) seems to have disorganised
the parcels bloody post again. (English undefiled!)

To Harriet Shaw Weaver   MS. British Museum

24 June 1921   *71, rue du Cardinal Lemoine, Paris V*

Dear Miss Weaver: Apparently we were both alarmed and then relieved for different reasons. I can only repeat that I am glad it is not any
trouble of your own and as for myself having been asked what I have

---

book! The episode of *Ithaca* now is all geometry, algebra, and mathematics, and then
finally *Penelope*! I'd like to dip my head in a sea of ice! The book is already in press
and I expect the first proofs day after tomorrow. It will be published only in October or
November. Three expensive editions being involved, misprints have to be avoided. The
colours of the binding (chosen by me) will be white letters on a blue field—the Greek
flag though really of Bavarian origin and imported with the dynasty. Yet in a special
way they symbolize the myth well—the white islands scattered over the sea.

On the material side I think if the edition goes well (subscriptions come every day—
three today from Australia) I will receive between 100,000 and 150,000 [lire]. But that
is not what concerns me. No sum of money could compensate me for my toil and
trouble . . Something really comic could be written about the subscribers to my tome—
a son or nephew of Bela Kun, the British Minister of War Winston Churchill, an
Anglican bishop and a leader of the Irish revolutionary movement. I have become a
monument—no, a vespasian.

Giorgio is in Zurich for his holidays. I will order Papini's book but I don't promise
to read it for the moment. Greet Benco and Silvestri the painter-shipper.

Good wishes to your wife and to Daniele . . . A handshake   James Joyce'

[1] The *Proteus* episode.

[2] Described in the second chapter of Budgen's book, *James Joyce and the Making of
'Ulysses'* (London, 1934, reissued, Bloomington, Ind., 1961; 2nd. ed., London, 1972).

[3] The leading article, probably by Holbrook Jackson, in *To-Day* (London) VIII. 46
(June 1921), [133]–4.

[4] Budgen was a onetime socialist.

to say why sentence of death should not be passed upon me I should like to rectify a few mistakes.

A nice collection could be made of legends about me. Here are some. My family in Dublin believe that I enriched myself in Switzerland during the war by espionage work for one or both combatants. Triestines, seeing me emerge from my relative's house occupied by my furniture for about twenty minutes every day and walk to the same point the G.P.O. and back (I was writing *Nausikaa* and *The Oxen of the Sun* in a dreadful atmosphere) circulated the rumour, now firmly believed, that I am a cocaine victim. The general rumour in Dublin was (till the prospectus of *Ulysses* stopped it) that I could write no more, had broken down and was dying in New York. A man from Liverpool told me he had heard that I was the owner of several cinema theatres all over Switzerland. In America there appear to be or have been two versions: one that I was almost blind, emaciated and consumptive, the other that I am an austere mixture of the Dalai Lama and sir Rabindranath Tagore. Mr Pound described me as a dour Aberdeen minister. Mr Lewis[1] told me he was told that I was a crazy fellow who always carried four watches and rarely spoke except to ask my neighbour what o'clock it was. Mr Yeats seemed to have described me to Mr Pound as a kind of Dick Swiveller. What the numerous (and useless) people to whom I have been introduced here think I don't know. My habit of addressing people whom I have just met for the first time as 'Monsieur' earned for me the reputation of a *tout petit bourgeois* while others consider what I intend for politeness as most offensive. I suppose I now have the reputation of being an incurable dipsomaniac. One woman here originated the rumour that I am extremely lazy and will never do or finish anything. (I calculate that I must have spent nearly 20,000 hours in writing *Ulysses*). A batch of people in Zurich persuaded themselves that I was gradually going mad and actually endeavoured to induce me to enter a sanatorium where a certain Doctor Jung (the Swiss Tweedledum who is not to be confused with the Viennese Tweedledee, Dr Freud) amuses himself at the expense (in every sense of the word) of ladies and gentlemen who are troubled with bees in their bonnets.

I mention all these views not to speak about myself or my critics but to show you how conflicting they all are. The truth probably is that I am a quite commonplace person undeserving of so much imaginative painting. There is a further opinion that I am a crafty simulating and dissimulating Ulysses-like type, a 'jejune jesuit', selfish and cynical. There is some truth in this, I suppose: but it is by no means all of me

[1] Wyndham Lewis.

(nor was it of Ulysses) and it has been my habit to apply this alleged quality to safeguard my poor creations for on the other side, as I stated in a former letter, I removed so much of any natural wit I had that but for your intuitive help I should be destitute.

I cannot understand the part of your letter about a new circle of friends here. Most of the people to whom Mr Pound introduced me on my arrival here struck me as being, as the elder Mr Dedalus would have phrased it, 'as I roved out one fine May morning'. The director of *L'Oeuvre* theatre who was so enthusiastic about *Exiles* and bombarded me with telegrams has just written a most insolent letter in slang to say that he was not such a fool as to put on the piece and lose 15,000 francs. My consolation is that I win a box of preserved apricots —a bet I made with Mr Pound (who was optimistic) after a cursory inspection of the director aforesaid. I signed a letter giving him *carte blanche* to do what he liked with the play, adapt it, put it on, take it off, lock it up etc knowing that if I refused to sign in a week it would have been said that I was an impossible person, that I was introduced to the great actor Lugne-Poe and given a great opportunity and would not take it. I have been a year in Paris and in that time not a word about me has appeared in any French periodical. Six or seven people are supposed to be translating *Dubliners* in different parts of France. The novel[1] is translated and presented but I can get no reply from the publishers (?) about it though I have written four times asking even for the return of the typescript. I never go to any of the various weekly reunions as it is a waste of time for me at present to be cooped up in overcrowded rooms listening to gossip about absent artists and replying to enthusiastic expressions about my (unread) masterpiece with a polite amused reflective smile. The only person who knows anything worth mentioning about the book or did or tried to do anything about it is Mr Valery Larbaud. He is now in England. Would you like him to visit you before he returns?

To return however to the indictment. What Mr Lewis and Mr McAlmon[2] told you is, I am sure, right but at the same time you may have misunderstood what they said. I do not attach the same importance to the "excess" mentioned as you do and as Mr Lewis does, apparently. And yet you are both probably right. This is another reason why your letter relieved me. I suppose you will think me an indifferent kind of rascal. Perhaps I am. Mr Lewis was very agreeable, in spite of my deplorable ignorance of his art, even offering to instruct me in the art of the Chinese of which I know as much as the man in the moon. He

---

[1] *A Portrait of the Artist.*   [2] That is, Robert McAlmon. See p. 289.

told me he finds life in London very depressing. There is a curious kind of honour-code among men which obliges them to assist one another and not hinder the free action of one another and remain together for mutual protection with the result that very often they waken up the next morning sitting in the same ditch.

This letter begins to remind me of a preface by Mr George Bernard Shaw. It does not seem to be a reply to your letter after all. I hate pose of any kind and so I could not [write] a highflown epistle about nerve tension and relaxation, or asceticism the cause and the effect of excess etc etc. You have already one proof of my intense stupidity. Here now is an example of my emptiness. I have not read a work of literature for several years. My head is full of pebbles and rubbish and broken matches and bits of glass picked up 'most everywhere. The task I set myself technically in writing a book from eighteen different points of view and in as many styles, all apparently unknown or undiscovered by my fellow tradesmen, that and the nature of the legend chosen would be enough to upset anyone's mental balance. I want to finish the book and try to settle my entangled material affairs definitely one way or the other (somebody here said of me 'They call him a poet. He appears to be interested chiefly in mattresses') And in fact, I was. After that I want a good long rest in which to forget *Ulysses* completely.

I forgot to tell you another thing. I don't even know Greek though I am spoken of as erudite. My father wanted me to take Greek as third language my mother German and my friends Irish. Result, I took Italian. I spoke or used to speak modern Greek not too badly (I speak four or five languages fluently enough) and have spent a great deal of time with Greeks of all kinds from noblemen down to onionsellers, chiefly the latter. I am superstitious about them. They bring me luck.

I now end this long rambling shambling speech, having said nothing of the darker aspects of my detestable character. I suppose the law should take its course with me because it must now seem to you a waste of rope to accomplish the dissolution of a person who has now dissolved visibly and possesses scarcely as much 'pendibility' as an uninhabited dressing gown. With kindest regards gratefully and sincerely yours   JAMES JOYCE

To FRANK BUDGEN   MS. Yale

16 August 1921   [*71, rue du Cardinal Lemoine, Paris*]

Dear Budgen: Thanks for your letter. First of all send me that *Sieges of*

Gibraltar and also Conan Doyle's *History of South African War* published by same house Nelson in their cheap collection. By the way please be sure to send these by *book post* registered and express. Parcels of books sent as parcels take 6 weeks! Incredible but true. As regards that 60 pp book would it be too much to suggest to you the following: get an exercise book and detach the leaves of it. If you read rapidly through the book again you could jot down on the sheets anything *in the words of the book* you think interesting and a quick sketch of those views (not artistic I am *not* an artist) this plan you might follow with the other books and then simply put the sheets in an envelope and send them on to me.

Penelope is the clou[1] of the book. The first sentence contains 2500 words. There are eight sentences in the episode. It begins and ends with the female word *yes*. It turns like the huge earth ball slowly surely and evenly round and round spinning, its four cardinal points being the female breasts, arse, womb and cunt expressed by the words *because*, *bottom* (in all senses bottom button, bottom of the class, bottom of the sea, bottom of his heart), *woman, yes*. Though probably more obscene than any preceding episode it seems to me to be perfectly sane full amoral fertilisable untrustworthy engaging shrewd limited prudent indifferent *Weib. Ich bin der* [sic] *Fleisch der stets bejaht.*[2]

Enclosed 20 francs about 8/6. More will follow. Send on that letter.

J.J.

Molly Bloom was born 1871.

To Mrs WILLIAM MURRAY   MS. National Library

14 October 1921   *9, rue de l'Université. Paris VII*

Dear Aunt Josephine: Thanks for prompt reply to my letter. *Ulysses*, a huge book of about 800 pages, about 11 inches by 7, ought to be out in about three weeks or so. The cheapest copies cost £3 each, the dearest £7 each. I shall send you one. I get very few free copies they are so dear.

I want all the information, gossip or anything you remember about the Powells—chiefly the mother and daughters. Were any of them born abroad? When did Mrs Powell die. I never heard of a 3rd brother, only Gus and Charley. The women were Mrs Gallaher, Mrs Clinch, Mrs Russell. Where did they live before marriage? When did the major, if that was his rank, die? Also any information you have about the Dillons

---

[1] French for 'star turn', or topper.
[2] 'woman. I am the flesh that always affirms.' Joyce is playing on Mephistopheles' identification of himself in Goethe's *Faust*, Act I: 'I am the spirit that always denies.'

(Mat Dillon and his bevy of daughters, Tiny, Floey, Atty, Sara, Nannie and *Mamie*, especially the last, the cigarette smoker and Spanish type). Get an ordinary sheet of foolscap and a pencil and scribble any God damn drivel you may remember about these people.

Can you ask anybody to call at 81 Summerhill and ask what is my father's address. He wrote to Lucia a month or so ago a rather amusing letter in copperplate handwriting. If he goes out with a man to protect him I think he is quite right, to judge by the papers I see, as everyone seems to carry his life in his hands in the dear old land of the shamrock. I am sorry to hear you had that tragedy in your family too. In the circumstances it may be unreasonable to trouble you—but I need all this information and quickly. If the country had not been turned into a slaughterhouse of course I should have gone there and got what I wanted. In great haste with kind regards   JIM

P.S. If you want to read *Ulysses* you had better first get or borrow from a library a translation in prose of the *Odyssey* of Homer. Also I forgot to ask what do you know about Hunter who lived in Clonliffe road and Alf Bergan[1] etc etc. I mean what has become of them. I know what the relations were there. You needn't inquire from other people. I am writing to you. If you know or remember write what you can. I don't want the help of my fellow countrymen, moral or material. Send me your full address—Ballybough?

To MRS WILLIAM MURRAY   MS. National Library

2 November 1921   *rue de l'Université 9, Paris VII*

Dear Aunt Josephine: Thanks for the information. Enclosed will explain why I am too busy to write longer today. *Ulysses* ought to be out by the 18 or 20 of this month. Two more questions. Is it possible for an ordinary person to climb over the area railings of no 7 Eccles street, either from the path or the steps, lower himself from the lowest part of the railings till his feet are within 2 feet or 3 of the ground and drop unhurt. I saw it done myself but by a man of rather athletic build. I require this information in detail in order to determine the wording of a paragraph. Secondly. Do you know anything of Mat Dillon's daughter Mamy who was in Spain? If so, please let me know. Did any of your

---

[1] Alfred Bergan (d. *c.* 1950) was at one time assistant to the sub-sheriff of Dublin, Long John Clancy, and is so identified in *Ulysses*. Later he worked as a clerk in the office of David Charles, solicitor, of Clare Street, Dublin. He was a good friend of Joyce's father.

girlfriends ever go there? Thirdly and last. Do you remember the cold
February of 1893. I think you were in Clanbrassil street. I want to know
whether the canal was frozen and if there was any skating. Kind regards

JIM

To Harriet Shaw Weaver   MS. British Museum

10 December 1921   *rue de l'Université 9, Paris VII*

Dear Miss Weaver: I enclosed [sic] the article[1] I spoke of. The biographical part of it is such a grotesque distortion of facts that I scarcely
know what to say all the more as I know the writer for the past ten
years and he must have lost his memory. You figure in it as an 'American
admirer' and I as a kind of cardinal Mezzofanti speaking '18 European
and oriental languages'! The intention of course is friendly so there the
matter ends.

The séance went very well. In the middle of the *Cyclops* episode the
light went out very much as it did for the *Cyclops* himself but the
audience was very patient. Strange to say Mr Larbaud's biographical
introduction also contained a number of misstatements though I had
answered many times the questions he asked me. Nobody seems to be
inclined to present me to the world in my unadorned prosaicness. At the
last moment he decided to cut part of the *Penelope* fragment but as he
told me so only when he was walking to the table I accepted it. I daresay what he read was bad enough in all conscience but there was no sign
of any kind of protest and had he read the few extra lines the equilib-
rium of the solar system would not have been greatly disturbed.

I ought now to attack the formidable problem of that money but I
get so many proofs (I enclose more) by two posts a day that I cannot say
much beyond this that your suggestion that it should be invested is one
that I agree with in principle. Still if that were done now I *might* possibly
run short of resources between now and the time of publication which
might be postponed so that perhaps it is best not to do so. I am sometimes tormented by the fear that the printinghouse will be burned or
some untoward event occur at the very last moment. Would you like to
see the cover of *Ulysses*? I believe there are some typist's errors in that
plan I sent you. In one of his allusions Mr Larbaud welded two episodes
together. Seemingly such an attitude is compatible with much understanding of the book and friendliness towards its writer. There are only
about 180 pages more to print I should say so that very soon these—

[1] Possibly by Silvio Benco in *Il Secolo* (Milan).

and a great many other points can be put to the test by throwing the book to the world.

I am sure that this letter is rather more puzzleheaded than usual but the printer, for some reason, sends me now proofs of *Circe*, *Eumeus* and *Penelope* at the same time without having finished the composition of the first two and I have to work on them simultaneously different as they are so that I remind myself of the man who used to play several instruments with different parts of his body.

I have heard that a parody of the book entitled *Ulysses Junior* appears in the *New York Herald*. They might have waited till the poor senior was properly 'home from the sea'. I also hear that one of the writers of the futurist group here stimulated by *Ulysses* has begun a work to be entitled *Telemachus*. I wish him joy.

With kindest regards sincerely yours   JAMES JOYCE

To HARRIET SHAW WEAVER   MS. British Museum

8 February 1922[1]   *rue de l'Université 9, Paris VII*

Dear Miss Weaver: Many thanks for your kind telegram. Two copies of *Ulysses* (nos 901 and 902) reached Paris on 2 February and two further copies (nos 251 and 252) on 5 February. One copy is on show, the other three were taken by subscribers who were leaving for different parts of the world. Since the announcement that the book was out the shop has been in a state of siege—buyers driving up two or three times a day and no copies to give them. After a great deal of telegraphing and tele-phoning it seems that 7 copies will come today and 30 tomorrow. A more nerveracking conclusion to the history of the book could scarcely have been imagined! The first 10 copies of the *edition de luxe* will not be ready before Saturday so that you will not receive your copy (no 1) before Tuesday of next week at the earliest. I am glad for my own sake (though hardly for yours) that you are advertising an English edition. I hope it will be possible in that event to correct the numerous misprints. Mr Pound says it is.

I find that I must draw on that reserve fund again to the extent of £50 as there is no money in yet and whatever comes between now and the 15 instant will be utilised for payment of a postponed draft payable on that date. I hope when in a few weeks' time I have access to some of the proceeds to reintegrate your gift.

---

[1] Misdated 8 January 1922 by Joyce. Enclosed with this letter is an obituary about J. B. Pinker, at one time Joyce's literary agent.

Thanks also for the prompt return of the *Penelope* episode (the name of which by another strange coincidence is your own). It did not arrive too late. Your description of it also coincides with my intention—if the epithet 'posthuman' were added.[1] I have rejected the usual interpretation of her as a human apparition—that aspect being better represented by Calypso, Nausikaa and Circe, to say nothing of the pseudo Homeric figures. In conception and technique I tried to depict the earth which is prehuman and presumably posthuman.

With kindest regards yours very sincerely and to the end importunately   JAMES JOYCE

To ROBERT McALMON[2]   MS. Pearson

[*March 1922*]   *rue de l'Université 9, Paris VII*

Dear McAlmon: Thanks for the ring and the ties. I don't mean you to go to Cannes to buy ties for me! God forbid. I thought you always travelled with a trunk full of them and threw out a few dozen a week but evidently I was misled by rumour.

> The press and the public misled me
> So brand it as slander and lies
> That I am the bloke with the watches
> And that you are the chap with the ties.

The ring is very nice and episcopal. I am glad you are getting on with *Ulysses* also the bleeding officers. A notice (first to appear) from *Observer* will be sent you by Miss Beach. As a result 136 orders came in one day! I hope the edition will soon be shipped off so that I may get a rest. My family go to Ireland for a few months on 1 April. Am still on the track of that flat with hopes. Pound and Shaw are in a letter fight over me. Wyndham Lewis is to arrive tonight. Laurence Vail invited me and family to his wedding breakfast tomorrow. I scarcely know him though I think they met him or her[3] somewhere.

Don't throw *Ulysses* out of the window as you threaten. Pyrrhus was killed in Argos like that. Also Socrates might be passing in the street.

[1] Miss Weaver had used the epithet 'prehuman'.

[2] Robert McAlmon (1896–1956), American short story writer, publisher in the early 1920s of Contact Editions. On 14 February 1921 he married Winifred Ellerman, better known under her *nom de plume* of Bryher, in New York City. He lived principally in Paris until 1940, when he returned to the United States. His reminiscences of Joyce and other writers are contained in *Being Geniuses Together* (London, 1938).

[3] Kay Boyle.

I envy you the sun and air and sea. It is dull and unphilosophic here. Write again when recovered from Bloomitis. Sincerely yours

JAMES JOYCE

To LADY GREGORY   TS. NY. Public Library (Berg)
(Dictated letter)[1]

8 August 1922   *9 rue de l' Université, Paris*

Dear Lady Gregory: I am recovering from a dangerous eye illness which has lasted three months and therefore am dictating this reply to your letter of July twenty seventh.

While thanking you for the friendly remembrance contained in it, and for acts of kindness in the past I shall feel very much obliged if you will omit from your forthcoming book, which I understand is largely a history of the Irish literary movement, all letters of mine and all mention of me. In doing so you will be acting strictly in accordance with the spirit of that movement, inasmuch as since the date of my letter, twenty years ago, no mention of me or of my struggles or of my writings has been made publicly by any person connected with it.

Mr. Pound has enclosed with your letter, a letter from Mr. Yeats to him in which there are several kind expressions concerning my book Ulysses. May I ask you to be kind enough to convey to Mr. Yeats, for whose writing I have always had great admiration, my thanks for his favorable opinion, which I value very highly. Believe me, dear Lady Gregory, Sincerely yours   JAMES JOYCE

To MRS WILLIAM MURRAY   MS. National Library

23 October 1922   *Hotel Suisse, Quai des Etats-Unis, Nice*

Dear Aunt Josephine: A few days before I left Paris I got a letter from you which seemed very wrathful. The facts are these. *Ulysses* was published on 2 February. When the edition was sold out Nora said she wanted to go to Ireland to see her mother. I did all I could to dissuade her but her friends here and in Ireland told her it was as simple as anything. Finally as my father also wished to see the children I let them go but made them promise to stay a week or so in London and watch. I managed to hold them up in London for ten days by means of express

---

[1] Joyce's dictated letters are printed as written, or typed, by the amanuensis, except for the correction of obvious slips.

letters and telegrams. Then they suddenly left for Ireland. They stopped a night in Dublin and Lucia kindly suggested that they should visit my father whose address she remembered. This they did and went on to Galway. In Galway my son was dogged about the streets and as he told me since he could not sleep at night with the thought that the Zulus, as he calls them, would take him out of bed and shoot him. A drunken officer swaggered up to him blocking the path and asked him 'How does it feel to be a gintleman's son?'. Meanwhile in Paris utterly exhausted as I was after eight years ceaseless labour I was on the verge of lunacy. Needless to say what I had foreseen took place and the next thing was that I got a telegram from London to say that they wanted to come back to Paris. The warehouse opposite their lodgings in Galway was seized by rebels, free state troops invaded their bedrooms and planted machine guns in the windows. They ran through the town to the station and escaped in a train lying flat on their bellies (the two females that is) amid a fusillade which continued for an hour from right and left between troops on the train and ambushes along the line. They fled through Dublin in the dark and so came back to Paris. I then sent Lucia to a summer camp on the coast of Normandy for four months and Giorgio to the Austrian Tyrol. After which I collapsed with a furious eye attack lasting until a few weeks ago—but apparently that does not interest. I am here at present in the hope of regaining my sight and my health.

The second cause of your wrath seems to be my book. I am as innocent in this case as in the former. I presented it to you seven months ago but I never heard anything more about it beyond a few words acknowledging receipt and an allusion in your last letter. The market price of the book now in London is £40 and copies signed are worth more. I mention this because Alice[1] told me you had lent it (or given?) and people in Dublin have a way of not returning books. In a few years copies of the first edition will probably be worth £100 each, so book experts say, and hence my remark. This of course has nothing to do with the contents of the book which it seems you have not read. I sent it however as I sent all my other books and at your request in a letter of a year or so ago. There is a difference between a present of a pound of chops and a present of a book like *Ulysses*. You can acknowledge receipt of the present of a pound of chops by simply nodding gratefully, supposing, that is, that you have your mouth full of as much of the chops as it will conveniently hold, but you cannot do so with a large book on account of the difficulty of fitting it into the mouth.

[1] Daughter of Mrs Murray.

The third point of wrath is the fact that no reply was made to Mabel[1] when she announced her marriage by sending a piece of weddingcake till I dictated a letter from London. That succulent morsel arrived when I was lying in a darkened room in continual pain and danger of loss of sight and continually threatened with an operation. I gave instructions that the letter be answered and our congratulations sent. This was not done. A violent and dangerous illness for months in a hotel in the centre of Paris in the middle of the intense excitement (letters, telegrams, articles) caused by the publication of *Ulysses* explains why there was some slight confusion, I suppose.

I ought not to have been obliged to write this long letter but it is better to write it than not as the letter Nora is going to write will probably not reach you before the early spring of 1931 A.D. In the meantime if you have any remarks or information to transmit to me about whatever you think I take an interest in well and good but wrathful epistles should be addressed preferably to Nora or her advisers there and here or to the president of your free fight or the leader of the irregulars or to the parish priest of Fairview or to the Sacred Heart to whom Ireland is dedicated and not to me. No doubt you will see Nora some other time when she goes to revisit her native dunghill though it is doubtful if Giorgio or Lucia will go. The air in Galway is very good but dear at the present price. The only enlivening feature of their journey appears to have been their interview with my father who amused them vastly by the virulence, variety and incandescence of curses which he bestowed on his native country and all in it—a litany to which his eldest son says *Amen* from the bottom, that is to say, the nethermost or lowest part of his heart.

Nora and Lucia are here with me and Giorgio who is in Paris will probably come down too as I think I shall take a place here for the winter. All are well as we hope you all are too.

A second edition of *Ulysses* was published on the 12 October. The entire edition of 2000 copies at £2.2.0 a copy was sold out in four days.

Kind regards and remembrances from us all.   JIM

P.S. That reminds me that in your letter you seem to assume that Nora and the children (the 'child' Giorgio is taller than his father and Lucia after her camp work could go on a circus trapeze) went to Ireland for the purpose of visiting Mr Devan[2] and the second Mrs Devan. This had not struck me till you mentioned it but you might be right for all that. They have gone out to have tea and ladies' music at a café on the

---

[1] Another daughter of Mrs Murray.
[2] Thomas Devin (see p. 40n.).

esplanade but I will ask them when they come back. I expect they will both deny it but who knows whether they will be telling the truth or not? That's the point.   J.

To Mrs William Murray   MS. National Library

10 November 1922   *Hôtel Suisse, Nice*

Dear Aunt Josephine: This is a shorter letter. I am not annoyed that you call Giorgio and Lucia children, I do so myself. I am glad to hear my book is in a press as other islanders are not like you in your indifference to its market value. You said Charley[1] was reading it and that you would tell me what he said and how he looked after reading it. Is he in the press? If so I hope he gets his meals regularly but how does he manage about shaving? I gather that you have not finished it and neither has Berty[2] but I think Nora will beat you all in the competition. She has got as far as page 27 counting the cover.

You say there is a lot of it you don't understand. I told you to read the *Odyssey* first. As you have not done so I asked my publisher to send you an article which will throw a little light on it. Then buy at once the *Adventures of Ulysses* (which is Homer's story told in simple English much abbreviated) by Charles Lamb. You can read it in a night and can buy it at Gill's or Browne and Nolan's for a couple of shillings. Then have a try at *Ulysses* again.

I asked whether you had lent it because you never wrote me a word about it and the night Alice and Katsy dined with us I asked them and understood them to say that someone in Blackrock had it. There were a couple of waiters buzzing around the table at the time so perhaps I did not catch the words accurately.

Now I hope the discourtesy involved in not visiting you and in not writing to acknowledge receipt of the wedding cake is lifted off my shoulders. There is a suggestion in your letter that all is nice and quiet now and ideal for another visit (compare enclosed remarks[3] by a good Jesuit father who never told a lie in his life) but as the last trip cost me about £200 and very nearly my eyesight too some other mug will foot the next bill. You say that most people now have got a hardening of the heart. It seems so: and a softening of the brain. When Nora's uncle heard the story of her sprawling on the floor and the rale old Irish bullets hopping off the promontory of her back he nearly fell off his chair

---

[1] One of Joyce's brothers.   [2] Bernard Murray, Mrs Murray's son.
[3] The enclosure is lost.

laughing. Yet he is one of the very few wellwishers I have in the country and would do a great deal to help me as he has often done.

We shall probably meet in London. I expect to go there in the early spring and again in the summer. That is a more sensible plan. We return to Paris on Sunday so when writing next address

12 rue de l'Odéon

Paris VI

c/o Shakespeare and Company

That address will always find me.

Send me any news you like, programmes, pawntickets, press cuttings, handbills. I like reading them.

Greetings from all here   JIM

To MRS WILLIAM MURRAY   MS. National Library

21 December 1922   *26 Avenue Charles Floquet, Paris VII*

Dear Aunt Josephine: A few lines to wish you a happy Christmas and a good New Year. I shall have to begin mine with an operation but after that I hope my sight will definitely improve. I am glad to know you are well in any case in spite of the lively atmosphere over there. I suppose you received the *Criterion* and *English Review*. The former ought to have posted you right about the book but you ought to get the other book I suggested Lamb's *Adventures of Ulysses*. I have been trying to collect my notes as well as my poor sight will allow and I find several names of people connected with the family who were of the older generation when I was a boy. I wonder if I sent you an exercise book with the names of these persons at the tops of the pages would you be kind enough (whenever you have a spare moment and anything occurs to your mind) to scribble down in pencil or pen anything noteworthy, details of dress, defects, hobbies, appearance, manner of death, voice, where they lived, etc just as you did for the questions I sent you about Major Powell—in my book Major Tweedy, Mrs Bloom's father? They all belong to a vanished world and most of them seem to have been very curious types. I am in no hurry. You could send me back the book in six months if you like but I would feel greatly obliged if you could fill in any details for me as you are the only one who is likely to know about them.

I hope this will find you in the enjoyment of a pleasant Christmas and send you kind greetings from myself and all here.   JIM

To Harriet Shaw Weaver   MS. British Museum

11 March 1923   *26 Avenue Charles Floquet, Paris VII*

Dear Miss Weaver: I am glad to hear that the recent event in your family is of a happier character. Thank you for sending the book to my brother but why are these copies unnumbered. Is that regular? I am sorry to hear that another 500 copies have been seized. I suppose this means the loss and collapse of half the whole edition.[1] Would it be too much to ask you to send me registered the copy of *La Tribuna* with the article by Mr Cecchi,[2] as I am sceptical about the arrival of another copy. I will send it back. Miss Beach tells me Mr Powys Mathers told her there was a second attack on *Ulysses* in *The Sporting Times* stating that the second edition could be bought for 10 shillings. Several readers of that admirable paper sent her Treasury notes. I continue the dionine treatment with Dr Borsch. I am sure you are blaming me for my cowardice and procrastination. I confess to the first but it is now at Dr Borsch's suggestion that I continue and although he has not increased the dose my sight has slowly improved. I had a long talk with him the other evening. He said that if I had allowed myself to be operated in May[3] in all probability I should have lost the sight of my eye completely. He said I had no glaucoma foudroyant (for which an operation is needed within twentyfour hours) and proved it by saying that I never had any tension worth speaking of since I went to him. He said too that I did well not to be operated in London, that my sight had resisted marvellously and that I am quite healthy!!! He also added that in his opinion the operation during a crisis in Zurich[4] was a mistake (though it was well done) as the exudation flowed over into the incision and reduced the vision of the eye considerably and permanently. The question is almost as complicated as *Ulysses*.

I must have expressed myself badly. I did not mean that I could supply an answer to the question of the relative merits of the two volumes. As Homer has been about 3700 years dead (he went blind from glaucoma according to one of my doctors Dr Berman[5] as iridectomy had not been thought of) we must wait till 5623 A.D. to answer it. I meant that if

---

[1] That is, of the London-Paris edition of the autumn of 1922. In all, only 500 copies of that edition were seized and confiscated by the Customs authorities at Folkestone. 'Half the whole edition' is a mistake, since that edition was of 2100, not 1000 copies.

[2] Emilio Cecchi (b. 1887), the distinguished Italian critic and short story writer, had written a brief article on *Ulysses* in the Rome newspaper, *La Tribuna*, 2 March 1923.

[3] In May 1922 Joyce had had an extremely severe eye attack in Paris.

[4] In August 1917.

[5] Dr Louis Berman (1893–1946), a well-known New York endocrinologist who examined Joyce in Paris in July 1922 at Ezra Pound's instigation.

your reading of the earlier poem has brought up any questions of structure or interpretation I shall be very glad indeed to elucidate the point raised before I forget it myself.

Yesterday I wrote two pages—the first I have written since the final *Yes* of Ulysses.[1] Having found a pen with some difficulty I copied them out in a large handwriting on a double sheet of foolscap so that I could read them. *Il lupo perde il pelo ma non il vizio*, the Italians say. The wolf may lose his skin but not his vice or the leopard cannot change his spots. With kindest regards sincerely yours   JAMES JOYCE

To HARRIET SHAW WEAVER   MS. British Museum

12 October 1923   Victoria Palace Hotel, 6, rue Blaise Desgoffe, Paris

Dear Miss Weaver: I send you express the piece so that it may reach you before the weekend. I have been a long time in the company of these old gentlemen-historians and am rather tired of them. On the other [side] I am scribbling a kind of plan of the verses which follow the prose immediately.[2] With kind regards sincerely yours   JAMES JOYCE

---

[1] Those two pages, a sketch of King Roderick O'Conor, which together with three other early sketches (on Kevin, on 'pidgin fella Berkeley', and on Tristan and Isolde) Miss Weaver typed for Joyce when he was in England in August 1923, were not used by him till 1938, when he inserted them in an amplified form at the end of Chapter 3 of Part II of *Finnegans Wake* (pp. 380–2).

[2] With this plan Joyce is glossing the poem in *Finnegans Wake*, pp. 398–9, the four stanzas of which emphasize respectively each of the Four Masters, the Franciscan monks who in 1632–6, at their monastery in Donegal, compiled the *Annals* of Ireland. The poem reads:

Anno Domini nostri sancti Jesu Christi
Nine hundred and ninetynine million pound sterling in the blueblack bowels of the bank
*   of Ulster.*
Braw bawbees and good gold pounds, galore, my girleen, a Sunday'll prank thee finely.
And no damn loutll come courting thee or by the mother of the Holy Ghost there'll be
*   murder!*

O, come all ye sweet nymphs of Dingle beach to cheer Brinabride queen from Sybil
*   surfriding*
In her curragh of shells of daughter of pearl and her silverymonnblue mantle round her.
Crown of the waters, brine on her brow, she'll dance them a jig and jilt them fairly.
Yerra, why would she bide with Sig Sloomysides or the grogram grey barnacle gander?

You won't need be lonesome, Lizzy my love, when your beau gets his glut of cold meat and
*   hot soldiering*
Nor wake in winter, window machree, but snore snug in my old Balbriggan surtout.
Wisha, won't you agree now to take me from the middle, say, of next week on, for the
*   balance of my days, for nothing (what?) as your own nursetender?*
A power of highsteppers died game right enough—but who, acushla, 'll beg coppers
*   for you?*

I tossed that one long before anyone.
It was of a wet good Friday too she was ironing and, as I'm given now to understand, she
*   was always mad gone on me.*

[On verso]

Pronoun	Evangelist		Four Masters	Ore	Evangelist Symbols	Liturgical Colours	Day	Province	Accent
A: thou:	Matthew	: Matt Gregory:	Peregrine O'Clery:	gold:	——	: blue-black:	Palm Sunday:	Ulster:	Belfast
B: she:	Mark	Marcus Lyons:	Michael O'Clery:	silver:	lion	: moonblue:	Holy Tuesday:	Munster:	Cork-Kerry
C: you:	Luke	Luke Tarpey	Farfassa O'Mulconry:	steel:	calf/ɲᴅɪᴀᵽᴅ	: red:	Spy Wed:	Leinster:	Dublin
D: I:	John	Johnny MacDougall	Peregrine O'Duignan:	iron:	eagle:	: black:	Good Friday	Connacht:	Galway-Mayo

The liturgical colours are really violet for the three Synoptic gospels and black for the Johannine[.] Marcus Lyons' day is indicated indirectly. Dougal (ᴅᴜᴅ ʒᴀʟʟ) means dark foreigner (i.e. the Dane). The apocrypha are represented by Lally and Roe and Buffler etc.[1]   J.J.

To HARRIET SHAW WEAVER   MS. British Museum

19 November 1923   *Hotel Victoria Palace, 6 rue Blaise Desgoffe,*
                                              Paris (Montparnasse)

Dear Miss Weaver: Thanks for your letter and press cuttings. I suppose you have seen Mr Eliot's article in the *Dial*.[2] I like it and it comes opportunely. I shall suggest to him when I write to thank him that in alluding to it elsewhere he use or coin some short phrase, two or three words, such as one he used in speaking to me 'two plane'. Mr Larbaud gave the reading public about six months ago the phrase 'interior monologue' (that is, in *Ulysses*). Now they want a new phrase. They cannot manage more than about one such phrase every six months—not for lack of intelligence but because they are in a hurry.

Thanks also for *Arabia Deserta*[3] and the *Querschnitt*.[4] I wish I could go away somewhere and read the former for my own pleasure but alas in spite of all I said I am working overtime again. My eye is still

---

Grand goosegreasing we had entirely with an allnight eiderdown bed picnic to follow.
By the cross of Cong, says she, rising up Saturday in the twilight from under me, Mick,
    Nick the Maggot or whatever your name is, you're the mose likable lad that's come my
    ways yet from the barony of Bohermore.
[1] The calf, which is given as the symbol for Luke, is a slip for ox, as Professor John V. Kelleher points out. Joyce's Irish is also inexact.
[2] T. S. Eliot, 'Ulysses, Order, and Myth', *Dial* LXXV. 5 (November 1923), 480–3.
[3] Charles Montagu Doughty's *Travels in Arabia Deserta* (1888) was republished in 1920–1.
[4] Several early poems of Joyce (*Chamber Music*, xii, xv, xxvi, xxix, xxxvi) had been published in *Der Querschnitt* (Frankfurt a.M.) III. 3/4 (Fall 1923), 157–9.

bandaged but gives me no trouble. I hope to be all right by the middle of the week.

I do not know how long more we shall be here. I hope not for Christmas. A certain princess Murat[1] to whom I was introduced (I had hardly shaken hands when I began to recite *Je cherche un appartement de cinq ou six pièces, trois chambres, salon, salle à manger*) promised she would find me one when she comes back from London. However I caught the cold in my eye on a wildgoose chase to Versailles on a similar errand. Nevertheless I cannot stop now for I must try to block out (roughly, at least) certain parts of the book before my next holiday. The passages typed represent twice or three times as much, the rest being already written in the sense that additions will be made all over the present text from notes to which I have now no access.

I see that you leave London on Thursday for a few months holiday in the country. I hope you will enjoy yourself there. I shall [send] on the typescript of the next piece as soon as it is done.

This muddled year is ending badly for me as my treasury is now approaching the condition of a Torricellian vacuum. I have made arrangements by which the quarterly interest which I get on 25–28 December will reach me a few days before Christmas (this independently of your solicitors) but until then there is nothing coming in except a remittance of £20 on the 6–8 December. Mr Quinn was to have sent me a cheque in settlement of the *Ulysses* MS but as you see did not do so. It is a bother that I have to write about this but, apart from the minor matters of board and lodgings, I do not wish to be in this position here at present. I delayed this letter till the last moment hoping that the money you spoke of would come by any post. I daresay your solicitors groan in spirit every time my name is mentioned but perhaps it is now possible for them to advance some of it.

I am sure you appreciate my thoughtfulness in thus adding to your worries on the eve of your departure and I know how relieved you will feel if you do not see me on the platform at the station with a barricaded eye and a long list of requests for unobtainable objects.

Such therefore is my present condition but as you say the photograph shows me in a favourable light. Mr Pound has ups and downs. He does not always look like that. Perhaps it was because he took off his glasses. The photograph[2] appeared in the *New York Times*.

I am going out with this letter to catch the mail. I hope you will not

---

[1] Princess (Marguerite) Murat (1886–1956).

[2] This photograph of Pound, John Quinn, Ford Madox Ford, and Joyce is reproduced in *Letters* III, between pp. 96 and 97.

be annoyed with me for writing it? With kindest regards sincerely yours

JAMES JOYCE

To Nora Barnacle Joyce[1]   MS. Private

[*? 5 January 1924*][2]   [*Paris*]

Dear Nora: The edition you have is full of printers' errors. Please read
it in this. I cut the pages. There is a list of mistakes at the end   JIM

To Ettore Schmitz   MS. Fonda Savio

30 January 1924   *Victoria Palace Hotel, 6 rue Blaise Desgoffe,*
                                                     Paris, rue de Rennes

Caro amico, Sono andato alla stazione ma nessun treno era in arrivo
(nemmeno ritardato) nell'ora indicatami. Ne ero molto dispiacente.
Quando ripasserà per Parigi? Non potrebbe pernottare qui?

Grazie del romanzo con la dedica.[3] Ne ho due esemplari anzi, avendo
già ordinato uno a Trieste. Sto leggendolo con molto piacere. Perchè si
dispera?[4] Deve sapere ch'è di gran lunga il suo migliore libro. Quanto
alla critica italiana non so. Ma faccia mandare degli esemplari di
stampa a

1) M. Valery Larbaud chez Nouvelle Revue Française
                      3 rue de Grenelle
                      Paris
2) M. Benjamin Crémieux chez Revue de France
                        (troverà l'indirizzo su un esemplare)
3) Mr T. S. Eliot, Editor 'Criterion'
                  9 Clarence Gate Mansions
4) Mr F. M. Ford 'The Transatlantic Review'
                27 Quai d'Anjou
                Paris

[1] Although Nora Joyce had been given copy No. 1000 of *Ulysses* (now at Buffalo), she
had never consented to read it. Joyce evidently had reason to feel she was more amenable
now.

[2] The date must be that of the fourth printing, January 1924, because this was the first
to have corrections bound in at the end.

[3] Schmitz had sent a copy of *La Coscienza di Zeno* (Bologna, 1923) with the inscription:
'27.12.23. Many thanks for your kindness. My best wishes to you and your family.
Do not get angry—please—about the papers on which I write my wishes. E.S.' The
volume is now at Buffalo.

[4] Schmitz wrote Joyce in January 1924 that he was discouraged by the reception of his
book and felt that he had again done a foolish thing, and at an age—sixty—when one
hates to cut a foolish figure.

Parlerò o scrivero in proposito con questi letterati.[1] Potrò scrivere di più quando avrò finito. Per ora due cose mi interessano: Il tema: non avrei mai pensato che il fumare potesse dominare una persona in quel modo. Secondo: il trattamento del tempo nel romanzo. L'arguzia non vi manca e vedo che l'ultimo capoverso di *Senilità* 'Si, Angiolina pensa e piange ecc . . .'[2] ha sbocciato grandemente alla chetichella.

Tanti saluti alla Signora se si trova costì. Spero avremo il piacere di veder loro fra breve.

Una stretta di mano   JAMES JOYCE

P.S. Anchè, Mr Gilbert Seldes[3] 'The Dial' (indirizzo?) *New York*'[4]

To ETTORE SCHMITZ   MS. Fonda Savio[5]

20 February 1924   *Victoria Palace Hotel, 6 rue Blaise Desgoffe,*
                                              Paris, rue de Rennes

Caro amico, Mandi i libri senz'altro. Ho già parlato di Lei a Larbaud ed a Crémieux. Faccia il mio nome scrivendo a Seldes ed a Eliot. Mandi

---

[1] Joyce was as good as his word; he succeeded in stirring up Larbaud and Crémieux in particular, and the result of their advocacy was that Schmitz, until then snubbed by Italian critics, began to receive serious consideration.

[2] The last sentence in *As a Man Grows Older* says, 'Yes Angiolina thinks and sometimes cries, thinks as though the secret of the universe had been explained to her or the secret of her own existence, and is sad as though in all the whole world she could not find one solitary *deo gratias*.'

[3] Gilbert Seldes (b. 1890), American writer and editor.

[4] (Translation)

'Dear friend: I went to the station, but no train was due (nor any overdue), for the hour which had been indicated. I was very sorry. When will you be coming through Paris again? Could you not spend the night here?

Thank you for the novel with the inscription. I now have two copies, having already ordered one in Trieste. I am in the process of reading it with great pleasure. Why are you discouraged? You must know that it is by far your best book. As far as the Italian critics are concerned, I do not know. But have review copies sent to 1) M. Valery Larbaud, c/o *Nouvelle Revue Française*, 3 rue de Grenelle, Paris; 2) M. Benjamin Crémieux, c/o *Revue de France* (you will find the address on a copy); 3) Mr T. S. Eliot, Editor *Criterion*, 9 Clarence Gate Mansions; 4) Mr F. M. Ford, *The Transatlantic Review*, 27 Quai d'Anjou, Paris. I shall speak or write to these men about the matter. I shall be able to write more when I have finished it. At the moment two things interest me. The theme: I would never have thought that smoking could dominate a person in that way. Secondly: the treatment of time in the novel. There is no absence of wit in it and I notice that the last line of *As a Man Grows Older*: "Yes, Angiolina thinks and weeps, etc . . ." has impressively developed in privacy.

Greetings to Signora Schmitz if she is there. I hope we shall have the pleasure of seeing you before long.

A handshake   James Joyce

P.S. Send a copy also to Gilbert Seldes, *The Dial* (address ?) New York'

[5] Text and translation (with slight changes) from *Inventario* II. 1 (Spring 1949), where the letters of Schmitz and Joyce are presented by Harry Levin.

anche un esemplare a Lauro di Bosis ed a Enzo Ferrieri, direttore 'Il Convegno', via S. Spirito 24, Milano.

Il suo libro sarà certo apprezzato. Chi non apprezzerà il colendissimo medico dott. Coprosich (sanctificetur nomen suum) che si lavò anche il viso? Ma con quel nome che Lei gli ha dato, avrebbe dovuto fare ben altri lavacri!

A proposito di nomi: ho dato il nome della Signora alla protagonista del libro che sto scrivendo. La preghi però di non impugnare nè armi bianche nè quelle da fuoco giacchè si tratta della Pirra irlandese (o piuttosto dublinese) la cui capigliatura è il fiume sul quale (si chiama Anna Liffey) sorge la settima città del cristianesimo le sei altre essendo Basovizza, Clapham Junction, Rena Vecia, Limehouse, S. Odorico nella valle in lacrime e San Giacomo in Monte di Pietà.[1]

Mi rimandi dopo letto il ritaglio accluso.

Saluti cordiali alla Sua Signora e a Lei stesso una stretta di mano.

JAMES JOYCE[2]

To HARRIET SHAW WEAVER   MS. British Museum

7 March 1924   [*Paris*]

Dear Miss Weaver: I have finished the Anna Livia piece. Here it is. After it I have hardly energy enough to hold the pen and as a result of work, worry, bad light, general circumstances and the rest. A few words to explain. It is a chattering dialogue across the river by two washerwomen who as night falls become a tree and a stone. The river is named Anna Liffey. Some of the words at the beginning are hybrid Danish-

---

[1] Basovizza and San Odorico are two villages near Trieste; Rena Vecia ('old arena') is a slum section in the city; San Giacomo in Monte is a working-class section. Joyce adds 'nella valle in lacrime' ('in the vale of tears') and changes 'in Monte' to 'in Monte di Pietà' ('in the pawnshop').

[2] (Translation)

'Dear friend, By all means send the books. I have already spoken to Larbaud and Crémieux about you. Use my name when you write to Seldes and Eliot. Also send a copy to Lauro de Bosis and Enzo Ferrieri, editor of *Il Convegno*, 24 via Santo Spirito, Milan.

Your book will certainly be appreciated. Who will not be able to appreciate the honourable Dr Coprosich (*sanctificetur nomen suum*) who even washed his face? With such a name he should have performed very different ablutions!

A propos of names: I have given the name of Signora Schmitz to the protagonist of the book I am writing. Ask her, however, not to take up arms, either of steel or fire, since the person involved is the Pyrrha of Ireland (or rather of Dublin) whose hair is the river beside which (her name is Anna Liffey) the seventh city of Christendom springs up, the other six being Basovizza, Clapham Junction, Rena Vecia, Limehouse, S. Odorico in the Vale of Tears and San Giacomo in Monte di Pietà.

Send back the enclosed clipping after you have read it.

Cordial greetings to your wife and a handshake to you.   James Joyce'

English. Dublin is a city founded by Vikings. The Irish name is ḃáıle-
Áťᴀ-Clıᴀť (Ballyclee) = Town of Ford of Hurdle. Her Pandora's box
contains the ills flesh is heir to. The stream is quite brown, rich in
salmon, very devious, shallow. The splitting up towards the end (seven
dams) is the city abuilding. Izzy will be later Isolde (cf. Chapelizod).

I enclose a group taken for *New York Times*.[1]

I hope you are well and that the piece will please you. With kindest
regards sincerely yours   JAMES JOYCE

To HARRIET SHAW WEAVER   MS. British Museum

30 September 1924   *Euston Hotel, London*

Dear Miss Weaver: I hope you had a smooth passage across in spite of
Patrick and are now safe and sound in the seclusion of Paris. I send you
a copy of the *Fortnightly*. As you will see he[2] has not bought a copy[3]—
or rather pretends he has not. His remarks are seriously meant. He
ought to be informed that there is now a special cheap edition 565,423
words $=8 \times 70,877\frac{7}{8} = 8$ novel lengths, slightly shopsoiled, a genuine
bargain going for 60 francs $=\frac{60}{68}=\frac{30}{43}=$ about $\frac{3}{4} \times 20/- = 15/- \div 8$ about
$1/11\frac{1}{4}$ per normal novel suitlength real continental style—you can't
beat it for the money. A few days ago he told a reporter he had made
£10,000 out of *Saint Joan* or was it out of old saint Mumpledum?

With kindest regards sincerely yours   JAMES JOYCE

To MRS WILLIAM MURRAY   MS. National Library

2 November 1924   *8 Avenue Charles Floquet, Paris VII*

Dear Aunt Josephine: On receipt of a letter from Charlie[4] last night I
wired to you to tell you how shocked we all were to hear such sudden
bad news of your health. I hope he has mislead himself about you. I had
even hoped to meet you in London a couple of weeks [ago]. I wrote to
Alice[5] and rang her up several times before we left but she was still in
Dublin. They did not tell me at the hospital (S. George's) that your
grave illness was the cause of her absence. I thought she was simply on
holidays. I do not remember you ever having been ill and I sincerely
hope your strength will carry you through this severe strain—whatever

---

[1] See note p. 298.

[2] Bernard Shaw, who refused to subscribe to *Ulysses*, ostensibly because of its high
price.

[3] Of *Ulysses*.   [4] Joyce's brother.   [5] See p. 291.

your illness is, Charlie did not say. I go to England more frequently now and I was looking forward so much to meeting you either there or in Dublin in the near future. Only yesterday morning I was going to write to you—as usual about some point in my childhood as you are one of the two persons in Ireland who could give me information about it. Charlie sent me an extremely kind message from you. I am very deeply touched that you should have considered me worthy of remembrance at such a grave hour. You attached me to you in youth by so many acts of kindness, by so much help and advice and sympathy, especially after my mother's death, that it seems to me as if your thought of me now is one of reproach. Nothing would give me greater pleasure than to talk with you over many things. I cannot employ the usual language or invoke assistance but if I am estranged in that I am still attached to you by many bonds of gratitude and affection and of respect as well. I hope these hurried words may be acceptable to you. I shall feel glad and honoured always if they are.

Nora, Giorgio and Lucia send their best wishes for your recovery. I hope you will see them as I know you would like to.

I am going to wire to Charlie to let me know how you are.

Charlie's letter is so grave that he suggests that I should write to you a word which I cannot bring myself to write. Forgive me if my reluctance to do so is wrong. But I send you this poor word of thanks and I will still hope in spite of the bad news. Very gratefully and affectionately your nephew   JIM

To HARRIET SHAW WEAVER   MS. British Museum

9 November 1924   *8 Avenue Charles Floquet, Paris VII*

Dear Miss Weaver: It was very good of you to send all those notices in the midst of your rush. How politely Brother Jonathan tries to place the blame for his blunder on your shoulders and what a nice sweet neat amiable little letter Mr Bennett sent. I wish the novel had been published without those critical remarks on its jacket.[1] The other cuttings are of a piece.

I am sorry Mr Lewis was in a bad mood. Did you mention the portrait to him? I wonder why Mr Eliot has to fly over here to see what Shaun

---

[1] Miss Weaver arranged with Jonathan Cape that he should take over the copyrights of Joyce's books and republish them. When the new edition of *A Portrait of the Artist* appeared, the jacket included an encomium from Arnold Bennett. Bennett wrote in great irritation to the *Times Literary Supplement* to say that the quotation was from his review of *Ulysses*, and that he did not admire *A Portrait of the Artist* at all.

calls the proprietoress.[1] Mr Larbaud tells me he is invited to a dinner there for that occasion consisting of steak and a pound and a half of bacon with some chops followed by beefsteak with a splendid onion and fried bacon and grilled steak.[2]

I enclose a letter which explains everything.[3] As I expected the temperature is on the rise. I am now deep in the confidence of both camps. Larbaud has now definitely broken with Fargue who is closely connected with Ippolita (M—d—e la Pr—nc—ss— d— B—st—n—.[4] I give her this name because that is the name of a lady who throws somebody or herself under an Italian goods train[5] set in motion by signor Gabriel of the Annunciation)[6] who is sentimentally championed by Larbaud who has been denounced by Miss Monnier who is helped by Miss Beach. Larbaud has been warned not to walk, run or creep through the rue de l'Odéon. Ippolita told several people that A.M. was a bookseller and A.M. told me about Ippolita and several people and V.L. told me about A.M. and Fargue and Ippolita and then we had some steak followed by fried bacon with rashers and two pounds of Ippolita which was quite tender after the goods engine followed by a splendid muddle.

My wife went to see Dr Borsch. The result: tomorrow he is not free. Tuesday is a holiday. I shall see him on Wednesday. He says he will have to make a larger operation—similar to that in Zurich. That I am highly nervous and in consequence of repeated attacks there is a great deal of secretion. He said I will get back my sight! It is very weak today so I shall not write much more.

I think that at last I have solved one—the first—of the problems presented by my book. In other words one of the partitions between two of the tunnelling parties seems to have given way.

I shall be glad to have *Penguin Island*.[7]

---

[1] Marguerite (Chapin) Caetani, Princess di Bassiano (1881–1963), was financing Eliot's review, the *Criterion*. *Finnegans Wake*, p. 406.

[2] Compare Shaun's 'stockpot dinner of a half a pound of round steak very rare' and an avalanche of other dainties in *Finnegans Wake*, p. 406.

[3] The letter was from Valery Larbaud, 6 November 1924, and said he was 'no longer on speaking terms with Miss Beach (a complicated *imbroglio* of frustrated interests)'. He continued: 'what about Morel's translation? and the part I was to play in that affair?' For Morel, see p. 307n.

[4] Princess di Bassiano.

[5] Probably the works of Joyce are meant by this metaphor of Italian goods, though he may also be glancing at Schmitz's.

[6] Gabriele D'Annunzio, here as elsewhere acknowledged by Joyce as a formative influence.

[7] Joyce had asked Miss Weaver to procure a copy of Anatole France's *Penguin Island* (1908) for him. She informed him on 7 November 1924 that she was reading it herself before sending it on.

With many thanks and kindest regards sincerely yours

JAMES JOYCE

To HARRIET SHAW WEAVER   MS. British Museum

27 January 1925   *8 Avenue Charles Floquet, Paris VII*

Dear Miss Weaver: Tomorrow I shall send you MS and typescript of the first two watches of Mr Shaun (what I read, slightly revised) and the day after MS and typescript of the rest. There is an interruption near the middle (indicated in the MS). I shall be anxious to hear what you think of it. I don't know how I managed to do so much with the operation and convalescence and holiday. I hope you will write to me about it. Miss Beach will send you a book of spirit talks with Oscar Wilde[1] which will explain one page of it. He does not like *Ulysses*. Mrs Travers Smith, the 'dear lady' of the book, is a daughter of the late professor Dowden of Trinity College, Dublin.

Here is another Borsch dialogue of yesterday.

Dr B.: How is our eye?

J.J.: *Semper idem.*

Dr B. (business): Not to me. I have still a fortnight.

J.J.: Ten days, doctor. You still think you'll win.

Dr B.: Sure I'll win.

J.J.: (baffled, beaten, vanquished, overcome, pulverised) smiles broadly

Dr B.: You'll see all right.

J.J.: It is an obstinate eye, doctor, no?

Dr B.: No fellow is any good if he's not obstinate.

J.J. (checkmated, silenced, overpowered) smiles broadly: And when do you think you can prescribe for the lenses?

Dr B.: Three weeks or a month after.

I don't know what he means. But he ought to be ambassador for the two Americas. I asked him then if the woman from Bordeaux who was operated about the same time would get her sight. She is a bad case, he said, but there is a little hope for her.

I ought to tell you a few things. The Irish alphabet (ailm, beith, coll, dair etc) is all made up of names of trees. nać (orah) is H. oyin O. Bruno Nolano (of Nola) another great southern Italian was quoted in my first pamphlet *The Day of the Rabblement*. His philosophy is a kind

---

[1] Hester Travers Smith, *Psychic Messages from Oscar Wilde* (London, 1924). Compare *Finnegans Wake*, pp. 419, 421, 422.

of dualism—every power in nature must evolve an opposite in order to realise itself and opposition brings reunion etc etc. Tristan on his first visit to Ireland turned his name inside out. The Norwegian-Danish language has neither masculine nor feminine: the two genders are common and neuter. The article follows the noun Mand*en*, hence Land*en*. Man siger at jeg er blever Konservativ (they say I am still a Tory) is the first line of a poem by Ibsen. The words expressing nightmares are from Greek, German, Irish, Japanese, Italian (my niece's childish pronunciation) and Assyrian (the stargroup called the 'gruesome hound'). I speak the latter language very fluently and have several nice volumes of it in the kitchen printed on jampots. Most coastal towns in Ireland (E) are Danish. The poor old fellows were often wreckers. In ancient Dublin there was a ceremony similar to that of the Doge wedding the Adriatic sea.

I hope this may help you. You would probably find it out if the piece were in print. It is hard to believe in typescript.

I hope you are having good weather up there after the rains and the eclipse. Will you please present my regards to Miss Marsden? I hope I may soon see her book as I heard she was having some research work done here in Paris.

Exiles will be given—they say—about the 15 February.[1] The electric light here is going out, I am afraid. I will end this letter. The light goes down, down and then up, up. With kindest regards sincerely yours

JAMES JOYCE

To HARRIET SHAW WEAVER   MS. British Museum

13 June 1925   *2 Square Robiac (192 rue de Grenelle) Paris VII*

Dear Miss Weaver: There has been so much hammering and moving going on here that I could scarcely hear my thoughts and then I have just dodged an eye attack. In fact when I was last writing to you I felt pain and rushed off to the clinic where the nurse sent me on to Dr Borsch. He said I had incipient conjunctivitis from fatigue probably. Next day it was worse nevertheless he insisted I was not to put off a theatre engagement I had accepted (Chaliapine). I went but had to leave in mid-opera. He then told me it would be nothing if I went about and amused myself! It got better but I had three or four very unpleasant days.

---

[1] The Neighborhood Playhouse in New York produced *Exiles* on 19 February 1925; it continued for 41 performances, ending 22 March.

We are settling down here slowly but there is a dreadful lot to do. The Breton girl having ordered her furniture seems to have left us in the lurch. She does not answer letters. I daresay we shall get right in time. I suppose I ought to have made this move long ago but operations held me up for one thing and I knew it needed a big sum of money and though I knew I could probably get it I could not bring myself to ask for it in bulk. But now the fat is in the fire.

I had the three living rooms which open up done in your colours, bluesea and seasand, thus, blue with yellow hangings, a neutral brown and the drawing room yellow with blue hangings. I am able to distinguish the blue from the yellow and *viceversa*.

I hope you have the *Contact* book. I put in a few puzzles more into my piece.[1] I am working hard at *Shem* and then I will give Anna Livia to the *Calendar*. Morel[2] will have to type all again as my typist is away. I have got out my sacksful of notes but can scarcely read them, the pencillings are so faint. They were written before the thunder stroke.

Tuohy[3] has now sent two telegrams, having discovered that Martinmas is not in Derbyshire, I suppose. He wants to come here to paint me. I want him to go there to paint you. You want him to stay where he is and paint himself. He certainly wants me to pose myself and he certainly wants himself to pose me for himself and certainly he does now be wanting to paint me posed by himself, himself for myself.

(With apologies to Miss Gertrude Stein)

Is it dreadfully necessary

> AND

(I mean that I pose etc) is it useful, I ask
this

> Heat!?

We all know Mercury will

> *when*

he Kan!

> but as Dante saith:
> 1 Inferno is enough

Basta, he said, *un' inferno, perbacco!*
And that bird—

> Well!

He

≡ oughter know!

(With apologies to Mr Ezra Pound)

Did Fossett change those words? They was two. Doesn't matter.

[1] 'From Work in Progress' (*Finnegans Wake*, pp. 30–4).
[2] Auguste Morel, French poet.   [3] Patrick Joseph Tuohy (1894–1930), Irish painter.

'Gromwelling' I said and what? O, ah! Bisexycle that was the bunch.[1] Hope he does, anyhow. O rats! It's just a fool thing, style. I just shoot it off like: If he aint done it, where's the use? Guess I'm through with that bunch.[2] (With apologies to Mr Robert McAlmon)
(Re-enter Hamlet)

Have you made a copy of Raymond's letter. I should like to show it to Morel.[3] Did Miss Beach send you the Hamburg paper. What a cheerful figure I must have looked at that Penman's Banquet! With kindest regards sincerely yours   JAMES JOYCE

To HARRIET SHAW WEAVER   MS. British Museum
15 August 1925   *Régina Palace Hotel & d'Angleterre, Arcachon*

Dear Miss Weaver: I left Rouen (where we were drenched for 9 days out of twelve) and stopping a night in Niort and Bordeaux reached here. Thunderstorms greeted my stay in Niort and Bordeaux. Here the weather is serene and warm. I wanted to go on to London, if possible, before going back to Paris but as *Exiles* will be put on in January or February I decided to come south now (in spite of the heat) and go to London then. The soil here is dry sand and the climate ought to improve me and I am only an hour from Dax where Dr Borsch advised me to go. I hope I can do so for a week or so before I go away. But certainly my sight is curious—even in the good eye. At Fécamp in the ninth row of the stalls I could not see the actors' faces. The morning after I came here I tried to walk down to the beach but had to come back as my sight was overclouded. It is very trying on one's nerves.

The other part of the news is. My concierge writes (without accents) that he is leaving the house. *Envoyer* he writes *envoillez*. Lest I should forget him he encloses a bill. Mr Gorman, my biographer, has been firing letters and telegrams at me. He wants to come and see me. He is in *Victoria Palace Hotel*, Paris. Mr Walsh has been holding me up with his delay in printing Shem and now the editor of the *Calendar* has written for the fourth or fifth time to know if he can announce Δ[4] for October. I think I shall say yes for I want to correct these two pieces at once and get a few minutes of torpor before the next act.

---

[1] 'gromwelled' and 'bisexcle' appear on pp. 116 and 115 respectively of *Finnegans Wake*. McAlmon probably typed the passage for Joyce, but insouciantly miscopied it.

[2] A favourite word of McAlmon, used also in the title of his book of stories, *A Hasty Bunch* (1922).

[3] Raymond, the son of a nurse at an eye clinic, in taking Joyce's dictation left out capitals and punctuation. Morel, who was translating *Ulysses* into French, was opposed to Joyce's view that a similar practice should be followed in the final episode of the book, Penelope's long unpunctuated monologue. Eventually Joyce won out.

[4] *Anna Livia Plurabelle.*

I started to read Mr Gillet's article[1] when my sight was better than it is today. I read about half and was much amused by it and gave it to my son. He gave it back saying it was not at all amusing so I then read the rest of it which, in fact, is very harsh. I think the explanation is to be found in a letter he wrote Miss Beach explaining the delay in finishing his article, his reason being 'mais je viens de subir la perte de ma mère'. He makes one or two good points which, however, I could answer. But it does not matter. It will act like the *Quarterly*, savage and tartarly.

When are you going to London. Mr Mac Cormack will surely give a concert there and I would like you to hear him. Could someone there look out for you and book a seat for you? My host here is onearmed.

Rouen is the rainiest place getting
Inside all impermeables, wetting
Damp marrow in drenched bones.
Midwinter soused us coming over Le Mans
Our inn at Niort was the Grape of Burgundy
But the winepress of the Lord thundered over that grape of Burgundy
And we left it in a hurgundy.
    (Hurry up, Joyce, it's time!)
I heard mosquitoes swarm in old Bordeaux
So many!
I had not thought the earth contained so many
    (Hurry up, Joyce, it's time)
Mr Anthologos, the local gardener,
Greycapped, with politeness full of cunning
Has made wine these fifty years
And told me in his southern French
Le petit vin is the surest drink to buy
For if 'tis bad
Vous ne l'avez pas payé
    (Hurry up, hurry up, now, now, now!)
But we shall have great times,
When we return to Clinic, that waste land
O Esculapios!
    (Shan't we? Shan't we? Shan't we?)

With kindest regards and with remembrances to Miss Marsden sincerely yours   JAMES JOYCE

[1] This article, published on 1 August 1925 in the *Revue des Deux Mondes*, by Louis Gillet (1876–1943) of the French Academy, was definitely hostile. Subsequently Gillet took a much more favourable view of Joyce's work and the two men became friendly.

To HARRIET SHAW WEAVER   MS. British Museum

22 October 1925   *2 Square Robiac, 192 rue de Grenelle, Paris VII*

Dear Miss Weaver: I have been laid up for about ten days with a lamentable sort of a cold, a dreary thing of which Paris is full. I hope you have better air up there. Now I am better but still rheumy. I detest it.

I hope you got the *Revue Nouvelle*. The Hades episode translated by Morel is to appear in the December N.R.F. Two days ago the proof of ⸦[1] arrived from Como. I corrected it, rubbed on more boot polish and sent it back express. I hope it comes out in a week or so. I ought to go into the clinic then, ought I not?

I send you some advance press opinions of Δ [2]

My father: He has gone off his head, I am afraid. He has overworked himself. Why did he not go to the bar? He speaks better than he writes.

My brother Charles: Received. Off to Carlow for a few days.

My brother Stanislaus: What are you driving at? To make the English language quite incomprehensible. Literary bolshevism. Too flabby for my taste.

Arthur Power:[3] Always glad to receive anything. Could you place enclosed MSS with your agent?

Laubenstein:[4] No acknowledgment.

E.P.: F.M.F.: E.W.: idem.[5]

Claudel (Paul): I thought I knew English until I read it.

Mrs Wallace: I don't understand a single word. What is it about?

Wallace:[6] I remembered parts I had heard from you.

Huddleston:[7] Why would the English printer not print it?

I am working at Λd still.[8] In a few days, Saturday, I think the men will have finished here. They brought some furniture for the diningroom and took it back a few days after to stuff it! I never do that when I supply prose to the public. All stuffing done on the premises.

With kindest regards from a bronchially impeded author sincerely yours   JAMES JOYCE

P.S. Please remember me to Miss Marsden. Will her book come out this season?   J.J.

---

[1] *Shem*. See p. 314n.   [2] See p. 308n.

[3] Arthur Power (b. 1891), Irish writer.

[4] Arthur Laubenstein, American organist.

[5] Ezra Pound, Ford Madox Ford, Ernest Walsh.

[6] Richard Wallace (1870–1927), an American book illustrator and advertising man in Paris. He and his wife, Lillian, were good friends of the Joyces.

[7] Sisley Huddleston (1883–1952), English journalist.

[8] The fourth watch of *Shaun*.

To Dámaso Alonso[1]   TS. Alonso

31 October 1925   *2 Square Robiac, Paris, France*

Dear Mr Alonso: Many thanks for your kind letter. As regards the
Spanish title of my novel, from what you say it seems better to use the
word Adolescente.[2] As you say the Spanish Joven is impossible. Nevertheless, I believe that the classical meaning of adolescence is a person
between the ages of seventeen and thirty-one and this would cover only
the fifth chapter of the book and represents about one fifth of the
entire period of adolescence, whereas in English at least, while the word
adolescent is quite inapplicable to the person represented in chapters 1,
2 and even 3, the term young man can be applied even to the infant on
page one, of course in joke. What is the usual description of self-
portraits made in youth used in the catalogue of your Spanish picture
galleries? The word autoritrato seems to me an insufficient description
of a picture. The title of the French translation which I sent you, in
order that you may consult it on doubtful points is taken from the
catalogue of the Louvre.

As regards your question, please refer in all cases to the French
translation.[3] I did not revise it but I helped the translator a good deal.

Page 31:[4] This is a kind of foot-stool with two ears, stuffed without
a wooden frame. The term is childish and popular. Compare the
word 'hassock'

Page 92:[5] An abbreviation of the word, made by schoolboys,
'translation'

Page 105:[6] This is a kind of sweet meat made of a soft marsh-
mellow jelly which is coated first with pink sugar and then pow-
dered, so far as I remember with cocoanut chips. It is called 'Slim

---

[1] Dámaso Alonso (b. 1898), the eminent Spanish poet and critic. He was lecturing on
Spanish language and literature at Cambridge in 1924 and 1925, and on his return to
Spain in the latter year wrote to Joyce asking for interpretations of certain passages in
A Portrait. Joyce's reply is taken from a photostat kindly supplied by Alan Cohn, who
has also furnished the information in the notes.

[2] The translation, signed by Dámaso Alonso with the pseudonym Alfonso Donado, was
published in Madrid in 1926 under the title, *El Artista adolescente (retrato)*. In a letter to
Alan Cohn the translator wrote: 'You will see we had a sort of discussion about the
Spanish title of the book. The one I chose never satisfied me. I must say I never could
find anything better.'

[3] 'In his letter', writes Dr Alonso, 'Joyce referred me to the French translation. This
I avoided as much as I could. I think my Spanish translation was closer to the original
character of the novel than the French one. There is in some respects a likeness between
Spanish and Irish people's idiosyncrasy.'

[4] 'Toasted boss.' Joyce is referring to page numbers in the Jonathan Cape edition of
A Portrait of the Artist (London, 1924).

[5] 'Trans.'   [6] 'Slim jim.'

Jim' because it is sold in strips about a foot or a foot and a half in length and an inch in breadth. It is very elastic and can be eaten by two people at the same time.

Page 119:[1] Schoolboy's abbreviation for problems set by a master to his class on the model of some theorum or problem in whatever book of Euclid's Geometry they are reading.

Page 222:[2] A euphemism used by Cranley [sic] in as much as it begins with the same letter for a product of the body the mono-syllabic term for which in English is sometimes used as an exclama-tion and sometimes as descriptive of a person whom one does not like. In the French language it is associated with Marshal Cam-bronne[3] and the French (the females at least) sometimes use a similar euphemism employing the [word] miel instead of the word used by the military commander.

Page 224:[4] He means nothing except that he affects to consider the name of the Middlesex philosopher as the name of a race horse.

Page 232:[5] Cranly misuses words. Thus he says 'let us eke go' when he means to say 'let us e'en go' that is 'let us even go'. Eke meaning also and having no sense in the phrase, whereas even or e'en is a slight adverbial embellishment. By quoting Cranly's misquotation Lynch gives the first proof of his culture. The word yellow (the second word) is his personal substitution for the more sanguine hued adjective, bloody.

Page 242:[6] A reference to Plato's theory of ideas, or more strictly speaking to Neo-Platonism, two philosophical tendencies with which the speaker at that moment is not in sympathy.

Unnumbered Page:[7] Translate this word for word. It means and is intended to mean, nothing.

---

[1] 'Sums and cuts.'   [2] 'Sugar.'

[3] Pierre Cambronne (1770–1842), a French general at Waterloo who is said to have responded to an English order for surrender, 'Merde!' ('Shit!'). Joyce made a point of almost never using vulgar words in his letters (except to his wife); hence this roundabout explanation.

[4] 'We'll have five bob each way on John Anthony Collins.' Collins (1676–1729) was an English deist.

[5] 'Let us eke go, as Cranly has it . . . Damn your yellow insolence.'

[6] In explaining *claritas* to Lynch, Stephen says that the connotation is rather vague. 'Aquinas uses a term which seems to be inexact. It baffled me for a long time. It would lead you to believe that he had in mind symbolism or idealism, the supreme quality of beauty being a light from some other world, the idea of which the matter was but the shadow, the reality of which it was but the symbol.'

[7] Probably, as Alan Cohn suggests, a reference to p. 277, where the squat student asks Cranly, 'Do you intend that now, . . . as *ipso facto* or, let us say, as so to speak?' Alonso had presumably not given the page of this quotation.

Page 285:[1] An allusion to the New Testament phrase 'The light under a bushel'.

Page 285:[2] In rowing. Compare Rower's heart. The phrase of course suggests at once a disappointment in love, but men use it without explanation somewhat coquettishly, I think.

Page 232:[3] A form of procope for 'Damn your soul'.

I hope you will let me have a copy of this Spanish version when it comes out. If you send me your copy of the English when you have finished with it I shall be very happy to sign it for you, if you would like to do so. Sincerely yours,   JAMES JOYCE

P.S. Will you please address your reply to me here in Paris and not in Arcachon.   J.J.

To HARRIET SHAW WEAVER   MS. British Museum

21 May 1926   *2 Square Robiac, 192 rue de Grenelle, Paris*

Dear Miss Weaver: Λabc[4] came back typed and Λd[5] will be here on Sunday or Monday. To what address can I send them and is the post safe. I have also to send you *Gens de Dublin*. The German version of A P O T A A A Y M[6] seems to have gone astray. I sent it to you before the Spanish one. I wish you would read through Λabcd and tell me how they interact.

Wyndham Lewis rang me up twice last week. I arranged to meet him at the clinic and we went to a café. He told me he wanted to meet me because he is to bring out a critical review (6 times yearly) *The Tyro-critic* (I hope he will correct the misspelling). It is to be all critical and philosophic and contain no creative work. But he wanted to make an exception in my case and asked me would I give him something. I said I would with great pleasure. I will tell you more about the interview when we next meet. I was much upset that day. My wife and I had a taxi collision an hour before. The front window at my side was smashed and the flying glass cut a neat design round my umbrella. I was unhurt.

If I have not filled in a gap in the typescript before sending it it

---

[1] 'Shining quietly behind a bushel of Wicklow bran.'

[2] 'When we came away father . . . asked me why I did not join a rowing club. I pretended to think it over. Told me then how he broke Pennyfeather's heart.' A rower's heart is said to be enlarged by rowing and so prone to attacks when the exercise is given up.

[3] '——Your soul!'

[4] The first three watches of *Shaun*, *Finnegans Wake*, pp. 403–554.

[5] The fourth watch of *Shaun*; see p. 310n.

[6] *A Portrait of the Artist as a Young Man.*

means that I could not think of the question to insert there. It has bothered me for some time.

I have the book now fairly well planned out in my head. I am as yet uncertain whether I shall start on the twilight games of ⌐∧ and ⊣ which will follow immediately after Δ or on K's orisons, to follow ∧d.[1] But my mind is rather exhausted for the moment.

Have you read Saint Patrice? There is a book on Bruno (though not on Nolan) by Lewis McIntyre (Macmillan). I do not know if Vico has been translated. I would not pay overmuch attention to these theories, beyond using them for all they are worth, but they have gradually forced themselves on me through circumstances of my own life. I wonder where Vico got his fear of thunderstorms. It is almost unknown to the male Italians I have met. With kindest regards sincerely yours

JAMES JOYCE

To HARRIET SHAW WEAVER   MS. British Museum

8 November 1926   *2 Square Robiac, 192 rue de Grenelle, Paris*

Dear Miss Weaver: I shall not allude to the sad subject of your letter except to say that perhaps it is enough that your sister's improvement has not been completely undone by such a sudden shock as she had. I hope she will go on as before. A good friend of mine in Trieste, count Sordina (to whom with another Greek I owe my liberation from Austria) had practically the same kind of stroke and is now out and about. He must be about sixty, if not more.

I set to work at once on your esteemed order[2] and so hard indeed that I almost stupefied myself and stopped, reclining on a sofa and reading *Gentlemen Prefer Blondes*[3] for three whole days. But this morning I started off afresh. I am putting the piece in the place of honour, namely the first pages of the book. Will try to deliver same punctual by Xmas. But cd send sample, viz. page 1, if customer so desires. The book really has no beginning or end. (Trade secret, registered at Stationers Hall) It ends in the middle of a sentence and begins in the middle of the same sentence. Your piece is the prelude to the *Contact* piece which is continued by the MS you have, the *Criterion, This Quarter* and *Navire d'Argent* where the first part of the book ends. The third part you have

---

[1] The signs have the following meanings: ⌐ *Shem,* ∧ *Shaun,* ⊣ *Isobel,* Δ *Anna Livia Plurabelle,* K *Kevin.*

[2] Miss Weaver's 'order' was for a piece to be founded on a tradition concerning what was reputed to be a giant's grave of prehistoric Britain, traces of which had been discovered near Penrith in Cumberland.

[3] By Anita Loos.

also Λabcd. I have written only a small part of the second ending with Roderick O'C.[1] The fourth will be shorter than the others.

The news is. Ernest Walsh[2] died of consumption. Antheil[3] had bad double pneumonia but got over it and is gone to Chamonix. Roth[4] issues a monthly in which he prints a garbled *Ulysses*. He sells, I am informed, over 40,000 copies a month and has already published one third of the whole work. We cabled to John Quinn's successor to enjoin him. After ten days he cabled, declining to take up the case. We are trying to stop the publication by means of friends in the Attorney General's office on other grounds. I gave Λabcd to Mr Galantière[5] to sell in the U.S.A. The Rheinverlag want to rush out next month with a translation[6] of which I verified 88 pages. They decline to let the translator come here. I informed them that the German literary press would be circularised with a disclaimer if they did. Now am waiting. Pound has gone to Rapallo and wants to bring out a review. He asked me to send him Λabcd to read. His child is here at nurse. I sent you some papers which you can perhaps send on for the files afterwards.

It is a long time or seems so since I wrote to this address. You may perhaps see me disguised as an Italian organist grinding out this prose-poem under your window maugre the prohibition on the corner. With kindest regards sincerely yours   JAMES JOYCE

P.S. *Re* sample vide above. Reply will oblige
respeakfolly yours
M. M. Inkpen & Paperasses
(Writers to the Signet)

To HARRIET SHAW WEAVER   MS. British Museum

15 November 1926

brings us back to Howth Castle & Environs. Sir Tristram, violer d'amores, had passencore rearrived on the scraggy isthmus from North Armorica to wielderfight his penisolate war; nor had stream rocks by the Oconee exaggerated themselse to Laurens County, Ga, doublin all the time; nor avoice from afire bellowsed mishe mishe to tauftauf thuartpeatrick; not yet, though venisoon after, had a Kidscad buttended a bland old isaac; not yet, though all's fair in vanessy, were sosie sesthers wroth with twone jonathan. Rot a peck of pa's malt had Shem or Shen brewed

---

[1] King Roderick O'Connor.   [2] Editor of *This Quarter*.   [3] See p. 354n.
[4] Samuel Roth.   [5] Lewis Galantière.   [6] Of *Ulysses*.

by arclight and rory end to the regginbrow was to be seen ringsome on the waterface.[1]

JAMES JOYCE

Paris. 15/xi/926

Dear Madam: Above please find prosepiece ordered in sample form. Also key to same. Hoping said sample meets with your approval

yrs trly

Jeems Jokes

Howth (pron Hoaeth) = Dan Hoved (head)
Sir Amory Tristram 1st earl of Howth changed his name to Saint
     Lawrence, b in Brittany (North Armorica)
Tristan et Iseult, passim
viola in all moods and senses
Dublin, Laurens Co, Georgia, founded by a Dubliner, Peter Sawyer, on
     r. Oconee. Its motto: Doubling all the time.
The flame of Christianity kindled by S. Patrick on Holy Saturday in
     defiance of royal orders
Mishe = I am (Irish) i.e. Christian
Tauf = baptise (German)
Thou art Peter and upon this rock etc (a pun in the original Aramaic)
Lat: Tu es Petrus et super hanc petram
Parnell ousted Isaac Butt from leadership
The venison purveyor Jacob got the blessing meant for Esau
Miss Vanhomrigh and Miss Johnson had the same christian name.
Sosie = double
Willy brewed a peck of maut
Noah planted the vine and was drunk
John Jameson is the greatest Dublin distiller
Arthur Guinness " "   "   "   brewer
Arthur Wellesley (of Dublin) fought in the Peninsular war.
rory = Irish = red
rory = Latin, roridus = dewy
at the rainbow's end are dew and the colour red
bloody end to the lie in Anglo-Irish = no lie
regginbrow = Germ regenbogen + rainbow
ringsome = Germ ringsum, around

[1] The opening of *Finnegans Wake*.

When all vegetation is covered by the flood there are now eyebrows on
the face of the Waterworld

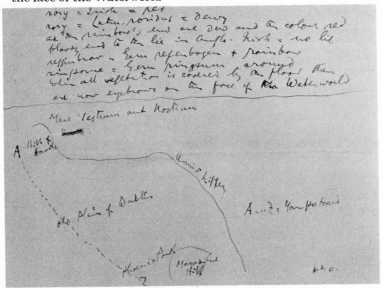

exaggerare = to mound up

themselse = another Dublin 5000 inhabitants

Isthmus of Sutton a neck of land between Howth Head and the plain

Howth = an island for old geographers

passencore = pas encore and *ricorsi storici* of Vico

rearrived = idem

wielderfight = wiederfechten = refight

bellowsed = the response of the peatfire of faith to the windy words of
the apostle

To Harriet Shaw Weaver   MS. British Museum

24 November 1926   *2 Square Robiac, 192 rue de Grenelle*

Dear Miss Weaver: The phrase about the Waterworld's face is mine
own.[1] Please correct 'Sir Tristram, violer d'amores, fr'over the short sea,
had passencore rearrived fra North Armorica on the scraggy isthmus of
Europe Minor' etc. I sent Λabcd to E.P. at his request and he has
written turning it down altogether, can make nothing of it, wading
through it for a possible joke etc. I sent you papers about the Roth
affair. I have been greatly overworked and overworried these last few

---

[1] See lines 1–2 above. In a letter of 20 November 1926 Miss Weaver asked where this
phrase had come from.

weeks and yesterday took to the sofa again. Today I restarted. One
great part of every human existence is passed in a state which cannot be
rendered sensible by the use of wideawake language, cutandry grammar
and goahead plot. I think you will like this piece better than sample.
With kindest regards sincerely yours   JAMES JOYCE

To BERNARD SHAW[1]   MS. British Museum

26 November 1926   *Paris*

Dear Sir: Allow me to offer my felicitations to you on the honour you
have received and to express my satisfaction that the award of the
Nobel prize for literature has gone once more to a distinguished fellow
townsman Sincerely yours   JAMES JOYCE

To HARRIET SHAW WEAVER   MS. British Museum

29 November 1926   *2 Square Robiac, 192 rue de Grenelle*

Madam i ave today finished the draft No 2 in nice MS of peece of prose
y^r rispected O/ to me which i will now give 1 coat of french polish to
same which will turn out A 1 as desired

   it is a very nice peece and i ope same will be found most sootable to
your bespoke in question

   i am, Madam trly y^{r}s   Ɛ (his mark)[2]

To HARRIET SHAW WEAVER   MS. British Museum

1 February 1927   *2 Square Robiac, 192 rue de Grenelle, Paris*

Dear Miss Weaver: I hope your neuralgia is now all gone, never to
return. Your letter gave me a nice little attack of brainache. I conclude
you do not like the piece I did? I have been thinking over it. It is all
right I think—the best I could do. I will gladly do another but it must
be for the second part or fourth and not till after the first week in
March or so, as the editors of *transition* liked the piece so well that they
asked me to follow it up and I agreed to finish off the part between the
end of *Contact* and *Criterion* for the second number. Part I will then
have been published. Do you not like anything I am writing. Either the
end of Part I Δ is something or I am an imbecile in my judgment of

---

[1] From a typescript made by Dan H. Laurence. He notes that this is the only
congratulatory letter about the Nobel Prize that Shaw appears to have preserved.
[2] The symbol of Shem, i.e. James.

language. I am rather discouraged about this as in such a vast and difficult enterprise I need encouragement.

It is possible Pound is right but I cannot go back. I never listened to his objections to *Ulysses* as it was being sent him once I had made up my own mind but dodged them as tactfully as I could. He understood certain aspects of that book very quickly and that was more than enough then. He makes brilliant discoveries and howling blunders. He misled me hopelessly as to the source of the first benefaction in Zurich and since then I have not relied on his perspicacity. A minute after I had made his acquaintance at Desenzano as we drove across the country by night he asked me 'Was it John Quinn then?'! My high tenor shout of 'Who?' must have been heard in Milan.

The protest[1] appears tomorrow. It has been cabled to 900 papers in U.S. I feel honoured by many of the signatures and humiliated by some, those of Gentile, Einstein and Croce especially. It is curious about them too on account of Vico. I think perhaps Pound wishes to remain in that small circle of shadow reserved for those whose signatures are 'supererogatory' and I shall write to him so. There are the reserved seats and now let us sit down in peace and wait till the band begins

> *For he's a jolly queer fellow*
> *And I'm a jolly queer fellow*
> *And Roth's bad German for yellow*
> *Which nobody can deny.*

With kindest regards sincerely yours   JAMES JOYCE

To HARRIET SHAW WEAVER   MS. British Museum

18 February 1927   *2 Square Robiac, 192 rue de Grenelle*

Dear Miss Marsden:[2] Before I write trying to explain what I am doing and why I want the case of Pound's soundness of judgment at the

---

[1] This refers to the International Protest against the unauthorised and mutilated edition of *Ulysses* published by Samuel Roth in the U.S.A.

[2] A slip for Weaver. It suggests Joyce's agitation of mind over several recent letters of Miss Weaver in which she objected to *Finnegans Wake*. On 29 January 1927 she wrote of the protest, 'I wish Mr Pound had signed it, considering that the book in question is *Ulysses* and not the present one. And perhaps when the present book is finished you will see fit to lend ear to several of your older friends (E.P. to be included in the number): but the time to talk of that matter is not yet.' Joyce was disturbed, but she held her ground. 'It seems to me you are wasting your genius,' she wrote on 4 February. 'But I daresay I am wrong and in any case you will go on with what you are doing, so why thus stupidly say anything to discourage you? I hope I shall not do so again.' He asked her to read some poems by Ralph Cheever Dunning, whom Pound was extravagantly praising, and on 11 February 1927 she agreed that the poems were disappointing.

present moment more gone into. I am glad you agree about Dunning.[1]
Some time ago Mrs Symons asked me (from her husband)[2] if I had not
written any verse since *Chamber Music* and if it would collect. I said it
would make a book half as big but I did not trust my opinion of it as I
rarely thought of verse. There are about fifteen pieces in all, I think and
I suppose someone someday will collect them. I mentioned this to Pound
and asked could I show him, say, two.[3] I left them at his hotel. A few
days after I met him and he handed me back the envelope but said
nothing. I asked him what he thought of them and he said: They belong
in the bible or the family album with the portraits. I asked: You don't
think they are worth reprinting at any time. He said: No, I don't.
Accordingly I did not write to Mrs Symons. It was only after having
read Mr Dunning's drivel which Pound defends as if it was Verlaine
that [I] thought the affair over from another angle. They are old things
but are they so bad that *Rococo*[4] is better than their poorness?

I am working on but in a grumbling quarter convinced way. I am
sorry the piece gave you no pleasure. It was hard when writing it to
keep myself at the right pitch and perhaps it suffered. Roth for one
thing but worse than that (I did not tell you before because you had
your own trouble) my brother-in-law in Trieste blew his brains out
while my sister was on her way from Ireland to Trieste. He was dead
when she was here and neither she nor my wife (she not even yet)
knew about it, only my children who are too young to understand. I had
a dreadful time playing up to them and was almost in the 'jimjams' for
about a month after. He lived, unconscious, for 26 hours after rolling
his eyes from side to side. During the war he escaped conscription by
reason of some sore which he used to provoke or aggravate in his leg.
This had nothing to do with his suicide. Having mostly recovered from
that shock I made the additions herewith[5] to your piece.

Remember me to Miss Marsden With kindest regards sincerely yours

JAMES JOYCE

P.S. John Galsworthy ⎱ signed
　　　James Stephens ⎰

[1] Ralph Cheever Dunning, English poet, had published *Hyllus, A Drama* (London,
1910), and *An Italian Tale* (Paris, 1913). The work which impressed Pound was *The
Four Winds*, published only in *Poetry* and the *transatlantic review*. Of this Pound wrote
to H. L. Mencken in February 1925, 'Dunning is 47, first case I have met where a chap
has done mediocre and submediocre stuff up to such an age, and then pulled the real
thing (Mr Eliot don't like it, but then he don't see either Yeats or Hardy); possibly
Dunning is of our generation and concealed from the young.' *Letters of Ezra Pound*,
ed. D. D. Paige (New York, 1950), p. 270.

[2] Arthur Symons.

[3] Joyce enclosed typed copies of 'A Flower Given to My Daughter' and 'On the Beach
at Fontana'.

[4] A poem in *The Four Winds*.   [5] Not included here.

To HARRIET SHAW WEAVER (Postcard)   MS. British Museum

16 April 1927   *Paris*

Dear Miss Weaver: I wish you a pleasant Easter up in the north. I finished my revision and have passed 24 hours prostrate more than the priests on Good Friday. I think I have done what I wanted to do. I am glad you liked my punctuality as an engine driver. I have taken this up because I am really one of the greatest engineers, if not the greatest, in the world besides being a musicmaker, philosophist and heaps of things. All the engines I know are wrong. Simplicity. I am making an engine with only one wheel. No spokes of course. The wheel is a perfect square. You see what I am driving at, don't you? I am awfully solemn about it, mind you, so you must not think it is a silly story about the mooks and the grapes.[1] No, it's a wheel, I tell the world. *And* it's all *square*. With kindest regards sincerely yours   JAMES JOYCE

To HARRIET SHAW WEAVER   MS. British Museum

13 May 1927   *2 Square Robiac, 192 rue de Grenelle, Paris*

Phoenix park.
   —   symbol used by Michelet to explain Vico's theory
O felix culpa! S. Augustine's famous phrase in praise of Adam's sin.
   Fortunate Fault! Without it the Redeemer wd not have been born.
   Hence also for the antecedent sin of Lucifer without which Adam wd
   not have been created or able to fall.
Ex nihilo nihil fit
Ex malo bonum fit
   Out of nothing comes nothing
     — —evil   —   good
Nicky (Old Nick, Lucifer, Satan)
Mickelmassed (Michael, his conqueror = much heaped up)
Malum in Latin means evil and apple.
Hill, rill, ones in company &c
   This rhythm occurs often
      Arthur Guinness, Sons & company, Ltd
      Awful Grimmest Sunshat Cromwelly, Looted.
     — — Sons & Company, & their carriageable tochters
Hill = ⊔
Rill = Δ

---

[1] A fable in *Finnegans Wake*.

Less be proud, be proud of them but naturally, as hill (go up it) as river
 (jump it).

Norronesen = Old Norse, warrior

Irenean = Irish born, peace (eirene)

secrest = superlative of most secret

soorcelossness = the source is not to be found any more than that of the
 Nile

Quare siles = Why are you silent

Homfrie Noanswa (Albert Nyanza)

Unde gentium festinas? Where the dickens are you hurrying from?

Livia Noanswa (Victoria Nyanza)
 the source of the Nile, later supposed to represent ⊔ + Δ
 the quarry & the silexflint suggest ⊔ silent
 undy, gentian & festy hues suggest Δ running & bubbling.

Wolken = (woollen cap of clouds (wolkin — welkin)

Frowned = He is crowned with the frown of the deaf

Audi *urio* (I long to hear)

Es *urio*   (" " " eat)

Evesdrip = wd listen to the dripping drops of his house's e(a)ve Δwater.

mous = Chaucerian form to suggest distance in time

dinn = Oriental mixture of din & djinn, the noise of an angry armed
 spirit, to suggest distance in space

bottles (battles) = the vintner's dream of Satan & Michael

far ear = far east

mous at hand = close at hand

Mark! (the King & the admonition)

His vales etc   His hill begins to be clouded over in the effort to hear

With lithpth   Δbabble

Hairfluke (Herrfluch = the curse of the Lord on you for not talking
 louder, he tries to grab her hair which he hopes to catch by a fluke

If he could bad twig her
 twig = Anglo-Irish = understand
 twig = beat with a twig.

Impalpabunt

Oculos habent et non videbunt

Aures habent et   " audient

Manus   "   "   " non palpabunt
 His ear having failed, he clutches with his hand & misses & turns
 away hopeless & unhearing (he abhears)[1]

---

[1] Joyce is here explaining the passage in *Finnegans Wake* (I.i), p. 23, which had been
published in *transition* in April:
 O foenix culprit! Ex nickylow malo comes mickelmassed bonum. Hill, rill, ones in

Mr Garnett[1] says he can only stare (a man of letters, of a literary family and a very whimsical and good writer himself) like at a cow at this. So much the worse for the cow.   J.J.

To Harriet Shaw Weaver   MS. British Museum

20 May 1927   *2 Square Robiac, 192 rue de Grenelle, Paris*

Dear Miss Weaver: I am sorry to have to trouble you with a request. I am afraid you will find it tedious but I think you ought to read the proofs of instalment 4. I send you herewith the final MS additions, and the proof should be read with *both*, my handwriting will be more familiar than my son's, the final additions are in *green* ink. I shall correct the proof from the perhaps faulty copy in Eliot Paul's[2] possession at the same time. It will be sent to you in a few days. Also if any of my additions or changes have not appeared in instalments 1, 2 and 3 I should be glad if you would indicate page and line, referring to transition.

I leave tomorrow for Holland and will send my address. Mr Donald Friede, owner of Boni and Liveright, offered me this morning $2000 down and 15% royalties to publish my new book, but I declined. As regards that book itself and its future completion I have asked Miss Beach to get into closer relations with James Stephens. I started reading one of his last books yesterday *Deirdre*. I thought he wrote *The Return of the Hero* which I liked. His *Charwoman's Daughter* is now out in French. He is a poet and Dublin born. Of course he would never take a fraction of the time or pains I take but so much the better for him and me and possibly for the book itself. If he consented to maintain three or four points which I consider essential and I showed him the threads he could finish the design. JJ and S (the colloquial Irish for John Jameson and Son's Dublin whisky) would be a nice lettering under the title. It would be a great load off my mind. I shall think this over first and wait until the opposition becomes more general and pointed.

Dulce et decorum est prope mare sedere—boglatin for it is a sweet and

---

company, billeted, less be proud of. Breast high and bestride! Only for that these will not breathe upon Norrônesen or Irenean the secrest of their soorcelossness. Quarry silex, Homfrie Noanswa! Undy gentian festyknees, Livia Noanswa? Wolkencap is on him, frowned; audiurient, he would evesdrip, were it mous at hand, were it dinn of bottles in the far ear. Murk, his vales are darkling. With lipth she lithpeth to him all to time of thuch on thuch and thow on thow. She he she ho she ha to la. Hairfluke, if he could bad twig her! Impalpabunt, he abhears.

[1] David Garnett (see p. 324n.).

[2] Elliot Paul (1891–1958), American writer and journalist, and for a time assistant editor of *transition*.

seemly thing to sit down by the sea. With kindest regards sincerely
yours   JAMES JOYCE

To SYLVIA BEACH[1]   MS. Buffalo

27 May 1927   *Grand Hotel Restaurant Victoria, La Haye*

Dear Miss Beach: I return you herewith posthaste the pomes in their
proper order with correct dates and text and an addition to face p 2
and if you fill in the titlepage it is all right but I should like to check a
final proof in bound proof. Has my brother not sent on the rest of the
MSS yet?[2] I am sorry I could not hear you.[3] There is a station (on 1950)
at Scheveningen but it seems in this season only for transmitting. There
is scarcely a soul there on account of the cold spell so we stay in the
town and tram it out: it is only about 10 minutes. Here it is very quiet
and dear but the people are very civil and obliging and not rapacious
really. It is the exchange and the small things do not hit them at all
though to us they seem terribly dear. The strand is wild and endless.
Unfortunately I had a dreadful time with a savage dog on Wednesday
25 inst. My wife and Lucia had gone for tea and I walked on a mile or so
and lay down on my overcoat reading the baedeker and trying to make
out the coastline when the brute rushed from Lord knows where at me.
I beat him off a few times. His owner ran up and his mistress and they
got him down but he slunk round when their back was turned and
attacked me again in the same way fully four times. It lasted I am sure a
quarter of an hour. In my alarm my glasses got knocked and one of the
lenses flew away in the sand. When Madame or whatever she was
finally lugged the animal away growling the owner and I went down on
her knees and after groping for a long time found the lens. I feel so
helpless with those detestable animals. Revolver? I suppose he would
have me before I made up my mind to fire. Or carry stones in my
pocket? If I could do the trick of gentleman into fox[4] I could save my
brush better.

　　　Thank Mrs Antheil for the words.[5] I shall use some of them. As
regards the rest I will explain to her in Paris. I hope Ulysses IX[6] will

---

[1] Transcription corrected with the assistance of Melissa W. Banta.

[2] Joyce sent to Stanislaus Joyce for a number of his manuscripts; he wished to present
the manuscript of *Dubliners* and that of *Stephen Hero* to Miss Beach.

[3] Miss Beach spoke on the French radio about the publication of *Ulysses* in Paris.

[4] An allusion to *Lady into Fox* (London, 1922), a novel of David Garnett (b. 1892), the
English writer.

[5] Presumably Russian words (since Mrs Antheil was from Russia), to be worked into
Finnegans Wake.

[6] The ninth printing of *Ulysses* was issued this month.

soon ascend the papal throne. His motto is to be: *Triste canis vulpibus* = This 'ere dog will worry them there foxyboys. With kindest regards sincerely yours   JAMES JOYCE

To HARRIET SHAW WEAVER   MS. British Museum

26 July 1927   *2 Square Robiac, 192 rue de Grenelle*

Dear Miss Weaver: I am glad you got the booklet[1] and did not dislike it. None of the others (Symons, Yeats, Pound, my father, brother etc) to whom I sent copies even acknowledged receipt of it. I expect Slocombe's notice in the *Herald*[2] will be the last as it was the first. Miss Beach and Miss Monnier have gone to Savoy. I did not change lawyer because a) it was nearly impossible to find one to act b) he is the most influential American in Paris[3] except the ambassador c) all the dossier is in his office in New York d) his first act when Miss Beach retired was to send her his bill for services in her mother's case e) I am not sure that I know all the facts of the case or that Miss Beach does e) [sic] his letter was so callous in any case that I thought it better not to antagonise him. Her father and sister arrive here in August. What the result will be I do not know.

It is now proposed that Miss Monnier is not to do successive editions of *Ulysse*. I understand that the N.R.F. will do them, if needed. She will do a limited semi-private edition, I think.[4]

More kilos of abuse about ⊔. Mr Shane Bullock[5] calls me a monster and Mr Ben Hecht[6] a Jack the Ripper. The review[7] has received letters from former friendly critics, Edwin Muir, [sic] deploring my collapse.

I am working night and day at a piece[8] I have to insert between the last and ⌐. It must be ready by Friday evening. I never worked against time before. It is very racking.

This house is shuttered up, ten out of twelve flats being left by absent families. I wish I saw some prospect of air and rest and relief from the

---

[1] *Pomes Penyeach* (Paris: Shakespeare and Company, 1927).

[2] George Slocombe (1894–1963), English journalist, literary critic, and writer on history and art. Joyce told Slocombe he had the 'melancholy distinction' of being the only reviewer of *Pomes Penyeach*. George Slocombe, *The Tumult and the Shouting* (New York, 1936), p. 221. The review was 'On the Left Bank', *Daily Herald* (London), 14 July 1927.

[3] Benjamin Conner (1878–1965?), an American lawyer in Paris.

[4] The first printing of *Ulysse*, 1200 copies, was issued in February 1929 by Adrienne Monnier, the second in January 1930 by J.-O. Fourcade. The third printing, also in 1930, was by her and Gallimard, and subsequent printings have been by Gallimard.

[5] Shane F. Bullock (1865–1935), Irish novelist.

[6] Ben Hecht (1894–1964), American playwright and novelist.   [7] *transition*.

[8] Chapter VI (*Finnegans Wake*, pp. 126–68). The chapter that follows is about Shem.

storms and stifling heaviness but I see none. I enclose an explanation of one of the added phrases on p. 1 of last instalment. Two of your guesses were fairly near[1] the last is off the track.[2] The piece I am hammering at ought to reveal it.[3] Please excuse this but I have Friday on the brain. With kindest regards sincerely yours   JAMES JOYCE

[Enclosure]

L'Arcs en His Cieling Flee Chinx on the Flur.[4]

1) God's in his heaven All's Right with the World
2) The Rainbow is in the sky (arc-en-ciel) the Chinese (Chinks) live tranquilly on the Chinese meadowplane (China alone almost of the old continent[s] has no record of a Deluge. Flur in this sense is German. It suggests also Flut (flood) and Fluss (river) and could even be used poetically for the expanse of a waterflood. Flee = free)
3) The ceiling of his (⊓)[5] house is in ruins for you can see the birds flying and the floor is full of cracks which you had better avoid
4) There is merriment above (larks) why should there not be high jinks below stairs?
5) The electric lamps of the gin palace are lit and the boss Roderick Rex is standing free drinks to all on the 'flure of the house'
6) He is a bit gone in the upper storey, poor jink. Let him lie as he is (Shem, Ham and Japhet)
7) The birds (doves and ravens) (cf the jinnies is a cooin her hair and the jinnies is a ravin her hair) he saved escape from his waterhouse and leave the zooless patriark alone.

To HARRIET SHAW WEAVER   MS. British Museum

14 August 1927   *2 Square Robiac, 192 rue de Grenelle, Paris*

Dear Miss Weaver: I am sorry you have bad news about illness in Miss Marsden's family but I am glad it is over. We have had a sequence of storms here and I have been dragging on from one week to the next. At last I finished the piece for t.6 and had the MS sent you in two parcels. It is better so because they have a registration book with the post

---

[1] 'Ireland's Eye' and 'Phoenix Park'.   [2] 'Dublin Bay.'
[3] Chapter VI is a series of twelve questions and answers. The answer to the first is 'Finn MacCool'. In his letter of 14 August 1927 (below) Joyce gave her a further clue.
[4] This is one of the names given to Anna Livia Plurabelle's 'mamafesta' about her husband. In *Finnegans Wake*, p. 104, it is given as 'Arcs in His Ceiling Flee Chinx on the Flur'.
[5] Symbol for Earwicker.

office at the shop. Please let me know if you get it. No 11 is Λ in his
know-all profoundly impressive role for which an 'ever devoted friend'
(so his letters are signed)[1] unrequestedly consented to pose (the appel-
lation 'darling X' has also been addressed to me who am hopelessly
given to the use of signorial titles). I wanted it as ballast and the whole
piece is to balance Λabcd more accurately. I never worked against time
in this way or in such troubling conditions. I think it is right enough.
Λ *doctus* is a bit husky beside the more melodious Shaun of the third
part but the words of Trismegistus are harsh too after the songs of
MacCormack.

As regards my going away and resting there is no prospect of that
unless I sell out more stock. The cheque I shall get in September will
be devoured by Dr Stehl, dentist, and the income tax collector and that
I receive in October will be devoured by the landlord to the extent of
nearly one half. The atmosphere here is as bad as it could be and I wish
I could get away. In fact I need months and months of rest as I am
wound up. My position is a farce. Picasso has not a higher name than I
have, I suppose, and he can get 20,000 or 30,000 francs for a few hours
work. I am not worth a penny a line and it seems I cannot even sell such
a rare book as *Dubliners* (Dublin). Of course I have turned down a
number of lecture tours in America and refused interviews.

I ought to hold on here till spring, I suppose, to see whether the
German and French translations come out and how they go if they do.
But it becomes more and more of a strain. I know if I go it will collapse.
In practically no case has any consideration shown to my work since its
appearance been uninfluenced by the general impression 'il semble avoir
très réussi' which I purposely tried to keep to set off other elements of
the case.

I am more and more aware of the indignant hostility shown to my
experiment in interpreting 'the dark night of the soul'. The personal
rancours of disappointed artists who have wasted their talents or
perhaps even their genius while I with poorer gifts and a dreadful lot of
physical and mental hardship have or seem to have done something
would not apply in your case. And this is one of the chief reasons why,
being unable to change, [I] proposed to discontinue my way of writing.
The first and third parts being done (5 years work) I could perhaps do
the second and the short fourth, but I need rest, and a lot of it. Any
duffer ought to be able to pick the threads for part 2 out of the immense
sombre *melopées*[2] of 1 and 3.

I saw A.E.'s review of P.P.[3] It is not unfriendly though I doubt if he

---

[1] Wyndham Lewis.   [2] 'Recitatives.'   [3] *Pomes Penyeach.*

can like very much verse which is not about an idea. I don't think reviews mean much always. Not a single notice appeared in the English press yet a London bookseller ordered 850 copies a few days ago and Dublin took 250. I saw orders from Naples, The Hague, Budapest etc. I suppose on certain types it will make the same impression as its author at the supper table. One lady who came to pray remained to scoff. 'He looked as if he were drowned' she remarked. *Et ça m'est parfaitement égal.*

If you consent to the proposal on page 1 will you let me know so that Messrs Monro Saw and the whole office may have an opportunity of suspending all the legal affairs in London in order to attend to me and to nobody else. Otherwise please write me a letter of any kind, ignoring the proposal most pointedly, but at least touching upon the other aspects of this missive.

As to 'Phoenix'. A viceroy who knew no Irish thought this was the word the Dublin people used and put up the monument of a phoenix in the park. The Irish was: fionn uirŝe (pron. finn ishghe = clear water) from a well of bright water there.[1]

I hope the house you are in is quieter and please tell Miss Marsden that I hope her mother will pick up after such a bout of illness as you describe. With kindest regards sincerely yours   James Joyce

P.S. Did I not acknowledge *Two Worlds*? Yes, I got it, thanks. I do not know what influence the Sacco-Vanzetti protest, if finally successful, will have, pro or con, on my case   J.J.

To Georg Goyert   MS. S. Illinois (Croessmann)

19 October 1927   *2 Square Robiac, 192 rue de Grenelle*

Dear Mr Goyert: I have not yet seen the German *Ulysses*.[2] I do not like at all the title *So Sind Sie in Dublin*.[3] It is not my point of view which would be, if at all, *So Sind Wir in Dublin*.[4] But I like neither. If 'Dubliners' is impossible what about 'In Dublin Stadt' or 'Dublin an der Liffey'?[5]

Please let me know by return Sincerely yours   James Joyce

---

[1] With this help Miss Weaver did in fact guess 'Finn's Town' and 'Finn's City' in a letter of 17 September 1927. The subject is not mentioned further in the letters that have come to light; probably Joyce did not wish her to come any closer to the right answer.

[2] Published 15 October 1927.

[3] 'What They're Like in Dublin.'   [4] 'What We're Like in Dublin.'

[5] 'In Dublin City' or 'Dublin on the Liffey'. The title Goyert eventually chose for his translation of *Dubliners*, which was published by Rhein-Verlag in Basel in 1928, was *Dublin: Novellen.*

To the EDITOR of the *Revue Nouvelle*[1]

10 February 1928   *Paris*

Cher Monsieur, La demande que vous venez de me faire au sujet d'une
contribution éventuelle de ma part à votre numéro spécial dédié à la
mémoire de Thomas Hardy me touche profondément. Je crains mal-
heureusement de manquer des titres nécessaires pour donner une
opinion qui ait une valeur quelconque sur l'œuvre de Hardy, dont j'ai
lu les romans il y a tant d'années que je préfère ne pas en faire le compte;
et en ce qui concerne son œuvre poétique, je dois vous avouer que je
l'ignore complètement. Il y aurait donc de ma part une singulière
audace à émettre le moindre jugement sur la figure vénérable qui vient de
disparaître: il vaut mieux que je laisse ce soin aux critiques de son pays.

Mais quelque diversité de jugement qui pourrait exister sur cette
œuvre (s'il en existe), il paraît par contre évident à tous que Hardy
offrait dans son attitude du poète vis-à-vis du public, un honorable
exemple de probité et d'amour-propre dont nous autres clercs avons
toujours un peu besoin, spécialement à une époque où le lecteur semble
se contenter de moins en moins de la pauvre parole écrite et où, par
conséquent, l'écrivain tend à s'occuper de plus en plus des grandes
questions qui, du reste, se règlent très bien sans son aide.

JAMES JOYCE[2]

To HARRIET SHAW WEAVER   MS. British Museum

Postmark 26 March 1928   *Hotel du Rhin & de Newhaven, Dieppe*

Ondt (Nor) = angry

[1] This letter was published in a special Thomas Hardy number of the *Revue Nouvelle*
(Paris) IV. 38–9 (January-February 1928), 61. The text is taken from there.

[2] (Translation)
'Dear Sir, The request you have just made me for a possible contribution by me to
your special issue dedicated to the memory of Thomas Hardy touches me deeply.
I fear unfortunately that I lack the necessary qualifications to give an opinion about
Hardy's work which would have any value, for I read his novels so many years ago
that I prefer not to remember how many; and as for his poetical work, I must confess
to you that I am totally ignorant of it. So it would be singularly audacious for me to
render the least judgment upon the venerable figure who has just disappeared: it is
better for me to leave this responsibility to critics of his own country.

But whatever diversity of judgment may exist about his work (if any does exist), it is
none the less evident to all that Hardy demonstrated in his attitude of the poet in
relation to his public, an honourable example of integrity and self-esteem of which we
other clerks are always a little in need, especially in a period when the reader seems to
content himself with less and less of the poor written word and when, in consequence,
the writer tends to concern himself more and more with the great questions which, for
all that, adjust themselves very well without his aid.   James Joyce'

Gracehoper = Graeshoper (Nor)

Floh = Ger. flea

Luse = O.E. louse

Bienie = Biene (Ger) bee

Vespatilla = Lat. little wasp Ital.

pupa = entom. term : = doll

pulicy = Ital. dial = pula = flea

commence insects = commit incest

everlistings = laurel bushes

harry me &c = Vico, thunderclap, marriage with auspices, burial of dead,
      providence

puce = Fr. flea

fourmish = Fr. ant

Spinner's = Ger. spider

fourmilierly = Fr. anthill

Tingsomingenting = Nor = nothing

Besterfarther = Nor grandfather
                  also conqueror

Zeuts = Zeus + Zeit (time)

myrmidins = myrmis Ger. ant

pszozlers = Pol. bee

sommerfugl = Nor butterfly

sphex = insect

Nix &c = Ger. dial. = Nothing

Pou = Fr. louse

lopp = Nor. flea

Weltall = Ger. universe

raumy = Ger. space

psyche = Gr. butterfly
            also E. gloss

laus = Ger. louse

mouche = Fr. fly

chairmanlook = Germanlooking

wetting with waps (betting, wasp, wop (Americ. slang for Italian)

sylph = entom. term

Iomio = Ital Dio mio! (he is not on the sociallist but on the egolist).

Crick = cricket

whilepaper = time also wallpaper

lustre = 5 years also chandelier

mensas & seccles (tables & settles)
            also months and siècles

ephemerids = insect living a day

the ternitary = eternity also termitary (white anthill)

cicada = Ital. kind of cricket

grillo = Ital cricket (aver grilli in capo = to have a bee in one's bonnet)

leivnits = Leibnitz also live nits i e young lice (cf ak Kant, *schoppin*hour
        etc and other philosophers)

Tossmania = Tasmania, he stands on his head to be really 'antipodal'

phthin = Gr. louse

lugly = ugly and luglio, It = July

Tournedo = tornado and tournedos (we turn our back to the wind)

tilehats = tall hats (tile, slang) also tiles from huts

Bora etc = Bora (adriatic wind)

                Aurora Borealis

tetties = It. roofs also dial. breasts

coppe = rooftiles (It. dial)

unshrinkables = pyjamas

swarming of = Ger to be enthusiastic over (i.e. himself)

monkynous = monkeynuts also the 'nous' rational intelligence cf
        monasticism

confucion of minthe, confession of mind
                'infusion de menthe'

ap*p*i = Ital. beer

Li*b*ido

cosy fond tuttes = Così fan tutte (Mozart)
                So do Ladies All.

Be jiltses etc. = By Jesus Christ
                also By Jaysus wept/Dublin accent

schneezed = Germ to sneeze in snow (Schnee)

eyeforsight = Eifersucht. Ger. jealousy

wittol = O.E.—a conniving cuckold

spizz = Ital dialect = itch

spass = Germ amusement

formicolation = Lat. ant also penis & melding [?]

amiesing = Ger. ant

faith hope & charity

Dorcu = Irish grasshoper

Dunshager = Irish anthill

odderkop = other head
                also Nor spider

myre = mire also Nor
        ant

actual   grace

sanctifying "

despair and presumption are sins against hope

$Xo\rho os^1$

Dear Miss Weaver: These few lines of explanation may be useful. I would continue but I feel rather tired this afternoon. I shall write as soon as I am really rested—if ever. With kindest regards one who hopes for grace   J.J.

[1] Joyce is explaining here a large part of the fable of the Ondt and the Gracehoper (*Finnegans Wake*, pp. 414–18), particularly the following sentences:

The Gracehoper was always jigging ajog, . . . he was always making ungraceful overtures to Floh and Luse and Bienie and Vespatilla to play pupa-pupa and pulicy-pulicy . . . and to commence insects with him, . . . ameng the everlistings . . . He would of curse melissciously, . . . lamely, harry me, marry me, bury me, bind me, till she was puce for shame and allso fourmish her in Spinner's housery at the earthsbest schoppin-hour so summery as his cottage, which was cald fourmillierly Tingsomingenting, groped up. Or, if he was always striking up funny funereels with Besterfarther Zeuts . . . attended to by . . . a myrmidins of pszozlers pszinging . . .

. . . Pou! Pschla! Pyuh! What a zeit for the Goths! vented the Ondt, who, not being a sommerfool, was thothfully making chilly spaces at hisphex affront of the icinglass of his windhame, which was cold antitopically Nixnixundnix. We shall not come to party at that lopp's, he decided possibly, for he is not on our social list . . .

The Ondt was a weltall fellow, raumybuilt and abelboobied . . . He was sair sair sullemn and chairmanlooking when he was not making spaces in his psyche, but, laus! when he wore making spaces on his ikey, he ware mouche mothst secred . . . wetting with the bimblebeaks [*First Draft* has: wetting with waps] . . . and wheer the midges to wend hemsylph . . . he wist gnit! . . . Iomio! Iomio! Crick's corbicule, which a plight! . . .

He had eaten all the whilepaper, . . . chewed up all the mensas and seccles, . . . made mundballs of the ephemerids and vorasioused most glutinously with the very timeplace in the ternitary—not too dusty a cicada of neutriment for a chittinous chip so mitey . . . He took a round stroll and he took a stroll round and he took a round strollagain till the grillies in his head and the leivnits in his hair made him thought he had the Tossmania. . . .

The Gracehoper . . . promptly tossed himself in the vico, phthin and phthir . . . [*First Draft* speaks of: a lugly tornado the Boraborryellas blasting the sheets off the coppeehouses.] Behailed His Gross the Ondt, . . . with unshrinkables farfalling from his unthinkables, swarming of himself in his sunnyroom, sated before his comfortumble phullupsuppy of a plate o'monkynous and a confucion of minthe . . . , as appi as a oneysucker or a baskerboy on the Libido, with . . . Vespatilla blowing cosy fond tutties . . . Emmet and demmet and be jiltses crazed and be jadeses whipt! schneezed the Gracehoper, aguepe with ptchjelasys and at his wittol's indts, what have eyeforsight!

The Ondt, that true and perfect host, a spiter aspinne, was making the greatest spass a body could . . . for he was spizzing all over him like thingsumanything in formicolation . . . He was ameising himself hugely at crabround and marypose, chasing Floh out of charity and tickling Luse, I hope too, and tackling Bienie, faith, as well, and jucking Vespatilla jukely by the chimiche. Never did Dorsan from Dunshanagan dance it with more devilry! The veripatetic imago of the impossible Gracehoper on his odderkop in the myre, after his thrice ephemeral journeeys, sans mantis ne shooshooe, featherweighed animule, actually and presumptuably sinctifying chronic's despair, was sufficient and probably coocoo much for his chorous of gravitates.

To HARRIET SHAW WEAVER   MS. British Museum

8 August 1928   *Hotel und Restaurant Mirabell, Salzburg*

Dear Miss Weaver: Here is a short note on p. 130 of t. 13.[1]

The Maronite (Roman Catholic) liturgy, the language of which is Syrian is at the back of it. On Good Friday the body of Jesus is un-screwed from the cross, placed in a sheet and carried to the sepulchre while girls dressed in white throw flowers at it and a great deal of incense is used. The Maronite ritual is used in Mount Lebanon. Λb departs like Osiris the body of the young god being pelted and incensed. He is seen as already a Yesterday (Gestern, Guesturning back his glance amid the wails of 'Today!' from To Morrow (to-maronite's wail etc). The apostrophe balances the hyphen Guesturn's, To-maronites.

This censing scene is led up to by:

licet ut lebanos (p. 12) = this may be used as incense (libanos is Greek for incense)

the 'libans and the sickamours and the babilonias etc' of Izzy's rambling remarks

the words 'at my frank incensive'. 'Idos be' (idos is also Greek for incense and the name of an 'artificial tongue' 'thurily' (for thoroughly)— t(h)us—t(h)uris is Latin for incense 'Weih?—Up the Shameroaugh!' Weihrauch is German for incense. Here it sounds also shamrock but means a cloudscreen or shamscreen 'licensed and censered' p. 13 etc, also 'sedro' Syriac for [word illegible].

The choir of girls splits in two: those who pronounce Oahsis and those who pronounce Oeyesis (cf Our Father who/which art etc). The Latin is 'Quasi cedrus exaltata sum in Lebanon etc' see A.P.O.T.A.A.A.Y.M. Belvedere College chapter.[2] There are in all 29 words in the threnody 6 × 4 = 24 and the final 5 = 29 (Tu autem, Domine, miserere nobis!).

This leapyear chorus is repeated lower down in imitation of the Maronite and Latin 'pax' given by embrace of arms. The girls do nothing really but turn one to another, exclaiming one another's name joyfully (Frida! Freda! etc). These are 29 words for 'Peace' taken from or modelled on the following tongues and variations (German, Dano-Norwegian, Provençal, French, Greek, French variations, Malay, Echo, Gipsy, Magyar, childrens, Armenian, Senegalese, Latin variation, Irish, Diminutive, N. Breton, S. Breton, Chinese, Pidgin, Arabic, Hebrew, Sanskrit, Hindustani and English = O for goodness sake leave

---

[1] This passage, amplified, figures on pp. 470–1 of *Finnegans Wake*.
[2] *A Portrait of the Artist as a Young Man*, chapter III.

off!). This word was actually sighed around the world in that way in 1918.

Please tell me if you like this treatment of the theme

With kindest regards sincerely yours   JAMES JOYCE

To HARRIET SHAW WEAVER (Dictated letter)   MS. British Museum

20 September 1928   *192 rue de Grenelle, Paris*

Dear Miss Weaver: We got back here a few days ago. I could not write before or even dictate because S.G.[1] was with me and part of the letter should have been about himself. We got on very well together. He has prepared an extension of his article in T-13[2] with an explanation verbatim of the paragraph about poaching and fishing. I suggested to him to do this with three color pencils using the first for the words and phrases which presented no difficulty to him; the second for those which became clearer after two or three readings or from remembrance of other parts of the text; and the third for what remained insoluble. It turned out that this last was only a small percentage and though it included things which were very obvious (for instance the word nippy which is known to three or four fifths of the population of London as a nickname for a Lyons tea shop girl and almost as current as midinette in Paris) he did not know; having lived twenty years in the East before the word got current, but I insisted on his leaving this and appealing to the reader for help. He also read me in Salzburg several chapters or rather sketches of chapters, of his exposition of Ulysses which is almost wholly technical and much more detailed than that of Jordan Smith,[3] if that is his name. I suggested to him to link it up here and there with Berard's book on the Phoenician origin of the Odyssey[4] and also with the work in progress. The translation is now finished.[5] V.L. sent me a list of difficulties which I solved for him and informed me that he would celebrate his birthday twenty ninth of August, by going off his diet of milk and rusks in favor of some wine of the country in my honor and to celebrate both events. His work is now at an end.

A.M. the translator. Had taken a good deal of license here and there, sometimes incorporating whole sentences of his own manufacture. These

---

[1] Stuart Gilbert.

[2] *transition* 13 (Summer 1928). Gilbert's article, 'Prolegomena to *Work in Progress*', was later included in *Our Exagmination*, pp. 47–75 (see p. 339).

[3] Paul Jordan-Smith, 'Ulysses', in his *On Strange Altars* (New York, 1924), pp. 14–34.

[4] Victor Bérard, *Les Phéniciens et l'Odyssée*, 2 vols. (Paris, 1902–3).

[5] The French translation of *Ulysses* by Auguste Morel and Valery Larbaud assisted by Stuart Gilbert.

were struck out. The translation is really his and has been done with
great care and devotion, but like many other people, by dint of brooding
on it he sees one aspect to the exclusion of another. In his case it is the
coarseness which excludes the others. Or perhaps I should say the
violence. I said to A.M. (the publisher)[1] about these bits 'a little too
much Madagascar here.' He is in fact a French colonial born. Perhaps
this explains it. I hope the three patch up their differences when the
work is out. SG's work was very useful but it was absolutely necessary
to have VL's final revision as he is very accurate; slow, fastidious and
rather timid. I saw, or rather was shown, the prospectus yesterday;
which A.M. brought me along with some other difficulties which I
solved much to her delight. The prospectus will be out this week and
the volume of nearly a thousand pages in December or January, which
in France, usually means June, but in this case will probably be
speeded up to mean the second of February. She is having it printed by
a very old established printer (1500 and something) at Chartres under
the shadow of the Cathedral almost. She brought me down there to see
the place which is a few miles from her place in the country, and insisted on lighting a candle for me in the Cathedral, all for good luck.
She becomes more and more superstitious, thinks that V.L. is be-
witched by L.P.F.[2] and I wish she could find out who is bewizarding me,
for I have at the present moment, and all for my own self, episcleritis,
conjunctivitis, blepharitis and a large boil on my right shoulder. So
much for candles. Besides which I am most uncommonly fatigued and it
is a physical impossibility for me to attempt revision of the piece for
T-14 which therefore will have to come out without me for they have
been ringing me up ever since I got back.

The case against Roth is up for next month. At the last moment
almost Conner's[3] partners in N.Y. cabled me that I ought to withdraw
the suit for damages as there was no copyright case and get an injunction against use of name. There never was any case on copyright and I
understood always that it was to be tried under the law of property but
as it would have been folly for me to have opposed the opinion of
American lawyers on the spot, and as on the other hand, I considered
that I held to a certain extent a position of trust, I instructed them, if
they had satisfactory means of knowing that Roth had so disposed of
all the money which he had made in America by misuse of my name and
mutilation of my text that no considerable part of it could be recovered

---

[1] Adrienne Monnier, publisher of *Ulysse*.
[2] Léon-Paul Fargue (1878–1947), the French writer.
[3] See p. 325n.

either under copyright or property laws, to press for some judgment, an injunction against further use of my name with nominal damages of one dollar, or whatever is the American equivalent for the English farthing, a judgment; that is, which when recorded, would establish a precedent in case law in favor of unprotected European writers whose cause in this matter was the same as my own. The bill of costs will now come rolling across the Atlantic. I think they were probably influenced by the number of offers which have been recently made me for the publication of W. in P. work in progress. But I had these offers made to them and through them simply in order to substantiate the claim for damages which they were advancing when the case came into court. At all events D.F.[1] has transferred his copyright of my property (and most uncommon kind of him) to me, that is part one, and Conner's partners at my instruction and at my expense, have printed and deposited at Washington, copyright dummies in my name for the fragments in T.10–12 and 13.

A.L.P.[2] has not yet arrived but I expect her every day. I promised Drinkwater[3] that I would reserve a copy for him though it is not easy to do this with such an edition. Did Miss Beach send you copies of photos he took of us and his letter in which he said that his wife, under the influence of reading me, had announced that she was terribly sick of bluggage. I think it not impossible that he may consent to do a preface for another fragment and I even thought of proposing to Gage [sic] that he ask Edgar Wallace to do one, the tortoise and the hare.

I have received three offers to give a series of lectures in Switzerland, two most urgent letters in which that extraordinary person Mr. Wilson of Willington announces his willingness to pay mine and my wife's expenses up there and back and hotel expenses and what he calls a royal welcome from the miners and for all I know a present of a few tons of coal also. He sent me some sort of a gift, I am not sure whether it is a cartridge coach [sic] or a case for cigars and cigarettes. It is rather embarrassing to reply. I also had a visit from a very high up person of the Russian Embassy here. Full of great admiration and proposing to bring me là-bas. But from all I can gather the condition of that country is dubious enough without inflicting on it the blighting influence of my one-quarteried personality.

---

[1] Donald Friede. This small edition was printed for copyright purposes. See John J. Slocum and Herbert Cahoon, *A Bibliography of James Joyce* (New Haven, Conn., 1953), pp. 41–2.

[2] *Anna Livia Plurabelle*, published as a small book by Crosby Gaige in New York in October 1928.

[3] John Drinkwater (1882–1937), English poet and playwright.

I have also bad news. Poor Italo Svevo[1] was killed on Thursday last in a motor accident. I have no details yet only a line from my brother and so I am waiting before I write to his widow. Somehow in the case of Jews I always suspect suicide though there was no reason in his case especially since he came into fame, unless his health had taken a very bad turn.[2] I was very sorry to hear of it but I think his last five or six years were fairly happy.

About fifty pages of Rebecca West's book[3] were read for me yesterday but I cannot judge until I hear the whole essay. I think that *P.P.*[4] had in her case the intended effect of blowing up some bogey bogus personality and that she is quite delighted with the explosion. It is a pity that W.L.[5] did not wait for its publication too as it would probably have much mollified his attack. By the way, have you not received any press cuttings lately about his book and can you tell me how many more books he has published since I left Paris a few months ago? There seems to be a mention of me every week in the New Statesman. The Irish Statesman, which you don't get, had an article about T-13 and some correspondence. Buck Mulligan fell out of an aeroplane with or after or before a Lady Martin. One may joke a little about it because fortunately neither the air man nor the airmaid seem to be any the worse. In fact they fell into a very shallow sea and I suppose are now merman and mermaid. The story seems rather curious but there is a comic poem about it in a Galway paper and the information comes from an allusion in a letter from my mother-in-law whose method of writing is often as cryptic as my own. The plane must have been very low but I am glad that they are both uninjured.

I have probably forgotten several things I wanted to say. I had no iritis of the eyes but the thing I told you, proceeding from outward infection it seems but it is very bothering and troublesome, and I have to go to the clinic every morning. Mrs. Bécat[6] is making [a] wonderful carpet for me representing the [Liffey] flowing through Dublin into the Irish Sea with the arms of Norway; Dublin; Ireland and my own all woven into the scheme. There is a case pending in Germany and Switzerland between Rasher of Zurich (I wish somebody would make bacon of him for he is an impossible escroc) and the Rheinverlag[7] but I need not weary you about that nor with an account of my holidays.

---

[1] Pseudonym of Ettore Schmitz; see p. 275n.   [2] Svevo did not commit suicide.
[3] *The Strange Necessity* (1928).   [4] *Pomes Penyeach.*
[5] Wyndham Lewis. This refers to his book *Time and Western Man* (1927).
[6] Adrienne Monnier's sister.
[7] Over German rights to *Exiles*, published by Rascher & Cie., Zurich, in 1919.

What are your plans for the Autumn and Winter? If my eyes do not get better to allow me to work (and what joy there will be in some quarters if they do not) I thought it would be useless for me to stay in Paris doing nothing and that I would go to Torquay but I am always making imaginary journeys. The complete eclipse of my seeing faculties so kindly predicted by A.M.'s young friend from Oxford, the ghost of Banquet [sic], I am warding off by dressing in the three colors of successive stages of cecity as the Germans divide them; namely, green Starr; that is, green blindness, or glaucoma; grey Starr; that is, cataract, and black star, that is dissolution of the retina. This therefore forms a nocturnal tri-color connected by one common color; green, with Shaun's national flag of peas, rice, egg yolk. The grey of evening balancing the gold of morning and the black of something balancing the white of something else, the egg probably. So I had a jacket made in Munich of a green stuff I bought in Salzburg and the moment I got back to Paris I bought a pair of black and grey shoes and a grey shirt; and I had a pair of grey trousers and I found a black tie and I advertised for a pair of green braces and Lucia gave me a grey silk handkerchief and the girl found a black sombrero and that completed the picture.

I will now close this letter which I ought to have written long ago. It was rather amusing to dictate it because my mind has been a stupid blank for weeks and I have the vapors; or the languors or something of that kind. So I hope it will amuse you though I really am not in such good humor as you might suppose from the few damp squibs of humor contained herein.

Just one paragraph more: What about Miss Marsden's book? Is it coming out this year or any part of it? I am glad you have had good weather but a more boring summer I never passed; with one heat wave after another in Central Europe. Pound's book of Cantos is out, a most magnificent thing in gold and scarlet at prices ranging from five to fifty pounds. Antheil[1] wrote to me he was coming to Salzburg to see Otto Kahn[2] (who by the way must have most of his time taken up dodging people who want to see him for one purpose only) but he did not come. He writes that the Cologne opera affair at which we are supposed to assist from the Royal Box is a sure thing and that he has some splendid proposals from one of the three greatest publishing combines in Europe.

With kindest regards; sincerely yours,   JAMES JOYCE

[1] George Antheil. See p. 354n.
[2] Well-known New York financier and patron of the arts.

To SIGNORA LIVIA SCHMITZ[1]   MS. Fonda Savio

24 September 1928   *Paris*

Dear Mrs Schmitz: A Trieste newspaper has been forwarded to me
from Le Havre in which there is a paragraph about the fatal accident to
poor Schmitz and the injuries to yourself.

I telegraphed you at your Trieste address although I did not know
where you then were.

We are all greatly shocked to hear of his death. A very sympathetic
notice by Madame Crémieux appeared in the Nouvelles Littéraires and
I am having a copy sent to you.

I am also asking the editor of Transition to reprint, by permission of
the same paper, Mr Nino Frank's article written when you were last
here which is the best literary portrait I can recall of my old friend. I, at
least, can see him through the lines of it.

Later on, when time and the remembrance of your own devotion to
Italo Svevo have in some way reconciled you to such a loss will you
please let me know what success he had with the English and American
publishers to whom I had recommended him?

I spoke to his German publisher in Zürich[2] in July and he told me
they would bring the book out this autumn.

I hope you have recovered from your shock and your injuries. It is
perhaps a poor, but still some consolation, to remember that our last
meetings in Paris were so pleasant to us all.

Please remember me if at any time my help can serve to keep alive
the memory of an old friend for whom I had always affection and
esteem.

To yourself, dear Mrs Schmitz, and to your daughter, all our
sympathy.

Sincerely yours   JAMES JOYCE

To HARRIET SHAW WEAVER   MS. British Museum

27 May 1929   *192 rue de Grenelle, Paris*

Dear Miss Weaver: O[3] is out today. Up till the last day I had to super-
vise it and check the references etc made by the 12 yet on opening it

---

[1] Text from Livia Veneziani Svevo, *Vita di mio marito* (Trieste, 1958), pp. 167–8.
[2] Dr Daniel Brody of Rhein-Verlag.
[3] Symbol of *Our Exagmination round his Factification for Incamination of Work in Progress* (Paris: Shakespeare and Co., 1929).

this morning I light on the word 'whoreson' classified by Jolas among the neologisms coined by W.S. in *Cymbeline*! I gave the title 'Tales Told of Shem and Shaun' to the Crosbye's[1] book. J.N.W. Sullivan having declined to do the preface I proposed to them C.K. Ogden (author in part of The Meaning of Meaning) who did a very useful introduction. Picasso was too busy painting somebody so the next aim was Brancusi. He first did a kind of a head of me which the C's didn't much like so he went on and did something like this[2]

O *please* turn over!

Of course it's not all sideways like that but those are the lines and it's signed and called Symbol of J.J. The book is out on Saturday. I consider the preface a great gain. I get on well with Brancusi (who is something of a fogey like myself) deploring modern feminine fashions, the speed of modern trains etc etc. His design of me will attract certain buyers. But I wish he or Antheil, say, could or would be as explicit as I try to be when people ask me: An' what's this here, Guvnor?

I got S.G. to write to Courtney, editor of the *Fortnightly*, reminding him of my first step in literature and proposing a chapter (Hades) for the review. Courtney died last November but the acting editor was taken by the idea and took S.G.'s article in to appear in July. This is also a nice wide breach made by the long gun [blot] you sometimes hear of.

Aldington came to see me. Des Imagistes the collection of poems published about 1500 years ago is to come out in a new form, i.e. contributions of today by the three more or less unknown contributors. I, not having any verse and not wishing to seem un-colleaguelike proposed to give him Kevin's page from Pt II. I have looked for it but can't

---

[1] Harry Crosby (1898–1929) and Caresse Crosby (1892–1970), founders of the Black Sun Press, published a fragment of *Finnegans Wake*.

[2] The drawing is copied from Joyce's version, in the papers of the late Stuart Gilbert.

find it, high or low. So could you please make me a copy when you have time therefor.

There being nothing of mine in the current no. of 'transition' I got Jolas to translate Curtius[1] article for it and put in Beckett's and the glossary part of S.G.'s.

With kindest regards

(to be continued tomorrow)

Don't fail to read special summer no tomorrow containing account of A M's picnic, E P's Dinner and a hundred other bright features.

Wenn es ist furchtbar heiss
Lesen die Jeiss![2]

Sincerely yours   JAMES JOYCE

To HARRIET SHAW WEAVER   MS. British Museum

28 May 1929   *192 rue de Grenelle, Paris*

Continuation

Lucia's disqualification for the dancing prize was received by a strong protest from a good half of the audience (*not* friends of ours) who called out repeatedly 'Nous réclamons l'irlandaise! Un peu de justice, messieurs!' She got the best notice, I think. Another Paris link has snapped, Mme Puard, my old clinic nurse, having left for a sanatorium. As regards myself, I finished the 28 days iodine treatment but have not yet been back to Dr Hartmann. I have had too much to do, being up sometimes till 1.30 fooling over old books of Euclid and algebra. I have arranged to get Faktorovitch (who helps me in these matters) to review the Crosbye's book on condition that he does not produce a mere flattery. He is a Russian (a bolshevik too and possibly a semi-official one) but I don't mind as we never talk politics and he is most obliging but chiefly he represents a class of my readers which ought to have their say, i.e. the foreignborn admirers. To succeed O I am planning X that is a book of only 4 *long* essays by 4 contributors (as yet I have found only one—Crosbye—who has a huge illustrated edition of the *Book of the Dead*, bequeathed to him by his uncle)—the subjects to be the treatment of night (cf *B* of *D* and S. John of the Cross 'Dark Night of the

---

[1] Ernst Robert Curtius, 'Technik und Thematik von James Joyce', *transition* 16–17 (June 1929), 310–25.

[2] Suggested translation: 'When the heat goes from bad to worse/Read Jerce!'

Soul'), the mechanics and chemistry, the humour and I have not yet fixed on the fourth subject. This for 1930, when I shall also, I hope, send out another fragment, this time about ⊓ with another preface, Δ and ⊏¹ having by that time passed into currency. I have also arranged for the translation into an Italian review of Beckett's article and will try to do the same for Budgen's in a Danish or Swedish one. I have also proposed to a young Dublin artist to do an illustration for the old earwig's funeral (Time, Saturn) which, as you will see, I introduced into the *Ondt and Gracehoper*. And that, I think, ends my activities for the moment. Do not blame me for all this intriguing. I have little or no support and have to defend a difficult cause, whether right or wrong I no longer know or care two straws.

As regards the dinner with E.P. and E.H.² they had a fine friendly set-to midway over G.A. whom H accuses of simulated sickness, subscription seeking, semi-blackmail and so on, P replying that H is known for his mendaciousness. The description of both seeming to suit myself rather well I got them on to another subject. P then wanted me as 'the leader of European prose' (!) to write 'an open letter' denouncing, with Roth as pretext, everything American and proposing dire retribution on U.S. ambassadors, consuls etc. H said this was moonshine as it would do me no end of harm with thousands of Americans who had supported me and support me still. Of course while I argued pro and con with P I had not for a moment the faintest intention of taking his advice. By the way he is in London. Has he been to see you? He did not go to rue de l'Odéon.

A.M. wants to get up a country picnic to celebrate Bloomsday and the French Ulysse. Two char-à-bancs full of people! I am afraid of the heatwave and storms and would much prefer a glass of milk and a bath bun like the Private Secretary who every day in every way seems to me a better and better Imitation of Christ. Pound says the most outrageously amusing things sometimes. Kicking his long legs around in the drawingroom he upset a little sacred image McGreevy (Lord knows why!) gave me at Xmas so that a thread got twisted round S. Joseph's neck, E.P. exclaiming 'Gee! I never knew that *that* blighter had been hanged too!'

Here I will stop for today because the editor of the *Revue de France* wants to see me in the next room about an article.

I hope you were not at Guildford during that last bad storm I read of. With kindest regards sincerely yours   JAMES JOYCE

---

¹ *Shem* and *Shaun*.   ² Ezra Pound and Ernest Hemingway.

To Harriet Shaw Weaver   MS. British Museum

16 July 1929   *Imperial Hotel, Torquay*

Dear Miss Weaver: Everyone seems delighted with this place—especially my wife—but the hotels are very difficult, no single rooms in the smaller ones and the prices especially for August far higher than in France. I got them to make a reduction here for a month's stay and booked a room for you at same rate from 7 to 14 August. I hope that is all right. If you have not yet written to M.S. & Co. I think the amount would have to be put up £30 from 120 to 150£. I hope this won't cause delay if they have begun.

I saw J.D., J.S. and T.S.E.[1] The first is arranging for me to be seen by some famous doctor for eyes when I return to London. J.S. is coming down here on Saturday for a weekend to talk about my book. He is going to America in a fortnight. He spoke about giving lectures. He seemed to be much impressed and moved by my proposal to hand over the work to him if I found my sight or the opposition demanded it and said I could rely on him to help me in anything. But he says I will do it and added that A.L.P. is the 'greatest prose ever written by a man'! J.D. told me at dinner he thought the last pages of it one of the greatest things in Eng. literature. I thought it better my proposal to J.S. should come now so that if I am forced to it in the end it may appear less abrupt and more spontaneous.

T.S.E most friendly. He wants his firm to publish S.G's book and to bring out an English papercover edition at 2/ of A.L.P.

Please watch T.L.S., *Spectator*, *New Statesman* and *Catholic News*.

With kindest regards sincerely yours   James Joyce

To Valery Larbaud (Dictated Letter)   TS. Bib. Municipale, Vichy

30 July 1929   *Imperial Hotel, Torquay*

Dear Larbaud: It is useless to begin an account of the half year and more I had of worry, expense and nerves in Paris. Our three visits to Hospital etc. It is all over I hope and well over, but I could not fix my mind to write. And then, I had to work literally night and day on Shem and Shaun and then I left, and here in Torquay, not seeing well I fell over a wall a week or so ago and even yet sleep badly from the pain of

[1] John Drinkwater, James Stephens, and T. S. Eliot.

my arm. Moreover though I can read with some difficulty, my sight is
much worse than it was etc. etc. Anyhow we hope Mrs Nebbia and yourself have the opposite story to tell. We return to Paris sometime in
September and I ought to go to see an oculist in Barcelona before Christmas, Borsch of Paris being dead. And do tell me when, where and how
we are likely to meet for it becomes everyday more impossible to discuss
me and what I am trying to do by letter.

First the small news, the French press on *Ulysses* was much better
than the German and A.M. hopes to arrange for an ordinary edition
in January. I suppose you heard about the commemoration lunch,
yourself, Morel and Gilbert being absent however. I was with Morel the
night before at the theatre and until one o'clock at Weber's and he promised me he would come but then sent me a telegram saying he had to
meet his pupil at a station between Paris and Vannes. I know this was
true but he could have come by straining a point. He is not well, has to
undergo operations on both legs, lest he become suddenly immobilised
and talks of retiring to his island in the Pacific Ocean! It is all rather
regrettable don't you think? He is rather sauvage but if he had come it
would perhaps have given him some satisfaction. Gide and Jaloux
couldn't come but Dujardin, Valéry, Soupault and Romains were there.
And L.P.F.[1] was beside me. By the way he spoke to me somewhat wist-
fully about you, asking me when I heard from you and so on and gave
me to understand that though you were still estranged, your public
utterances concerning him and his writing were untroubled and serenely
appreciative. Of which appreciation he expressed his appreciation.
Valéry and he wanted to make speeches but I put a veto on that. There
were no English or Americans except the kind lady who is typing this.[2]
But there were two riotous young Irishmen and one of them Beckett
whose essay you will find in the Exag[3] fell deeply under the influence of
beer, wine spirits, liqueurs, fresh air, movement and feminine society
and was ingloriously abandoned by the Wagonette in one of those
temporary palaces which are inseparably associated with the memory
of the Emperor Vespasian.[4] Before I go on, Gilbert has an article in the
current *Fortnightly*—one of the chapters of his book on my *Ulysses*—
Hades, and he wants to place another in French in a Paris review, not
the *Revue de Paris*. The chapter being that on the Wandering Rocks.
Can you suggest which Review, or do you know anyone in the *Revue de
France* for example? A third chapter will appear in October *Transition*,

---

[1] Léon-Paul Fargue.   [2] Helen Kastor Fleischman.
[3] *Our Exagmination round his Factification for Incamination of Work in Progress.*
[4] See p. 280n.

Aeolus, and a fourth he wants to place in an American or Italian monthly of the same standing. The whole book has an introduction and eighteen chapters and it ought to come out in English in the late autumn or spring if T. S. Elliot who asked to be allowed to read it for the publisher Faber and Gwyer (the *Criterion*) accepts it.

What you say about the Exag is right enough. I did stand behind those twelve Marshals more or less directing them what lines of research to follow. But up to the present though at least a hundred copies have been freely circulated to the press and press men not a single criticism has appeared. My impression is that the paper cover, the grandfather's clock on the title page and the word Exagmination itself for instance incline reviewers to regard it as a joke, though these were all my doing, but some fine morning not a hundred years from now some enterprising fellow will discover the etymological history of the orthodox word examination and begin to change his wavering mind on the subject of the book, whereupon one by one others will faintly echo in the wailful choir, 'Siccome i gru van cantando lor lai.'[1]

I hope you got T.T. of S. and S.[2] and liked the edition. What do you think of Ogden's preface and Brancusi's whirligig. From your silence I fancy that at least you find it difficult. It is, and it would be childish to deny it, but I am sending you by the next post a curious book which may or may not look to you like English at first sight and it does not come from any Black Sun magical press outside England as she is spoken, nor is it written by an escaped continentalized Dubliner inflicted with the incurable levity of youth. It is written by the right honorable Robert Bridges, Poet Laureate to His Majesty the King English now aged three score and ten (I mean R.B.) and issued from Oxford where they make the best shirts. It seems to me that it would be interesting to that imaginary Reader let us call him, the Good Terrafirmaite equally at home in Potsdam, Sacré Coeur, Maladetta and whatever is the Portuguese for Devil take the hindmost to read in the most affable of all tongues, because the most accessible, some recording by you of this curious meeting of extremes. What do you think about it? I wish I had some leisure and that both our minds were free from preoccupation to discuss with you about it. So that I hope we shall soon meet in Paris. I feel that Fargue would be interested in the conversation for his mind has been running fairly constantly in the same direction now for some years but there is in his case the almost fatal objection that he is a man of one language only, though perhaps one could discuss

---

[1] 'As the cranes go chanting their lays.' *Inferno*, Canto V, i.46.
[2] *Tales Told of Shem and Shaun* (Paris: Black Sun Press, 1929).

the advantages and disadvantages of this for all eternity. Anyhow I am now hopelessly with the goats and can only think and write capriciously. Depart from me ye bleaters, into everlasting sleep which was prepared for Academicians and their agues!

With kind regards and looking forward as well as backward to the last and next bottles of Vouvray Moncontour   Sincerely yours

JAMES JOYCE

[In Joyce's hand]

P.S. Prayer to be recited after having read the above:
    Lord, send us both the green coat and cocked hat! Amen.

(40 days indulgence)

To HARRIET SHAW WEAVER (Dictated letter)   TS. British Museum

18 March 1930   *2 Square Robiac, 192 rue de Grenelle, Paris*

Dear Miss Weaver: It is some months since you heard from me but I sent you a few messages in that time. I finished the revision of the fragment for publication last night at seven, and, I suspect, my literary career at the same time. Before I start explaining the reasons for my persistent silence I had better put in the forefront the most irksome part of this missive, namely that I must ask you to instruct Messrs Monro Saw to sell out immediately two hundred pounds of War Stock and oblige me by remitting the amount, as they are usually kind enough to do on return of the witnessed forms. I shall explain later in the letter why I need this. A state of tension, of a somewhat more acute kind than those with which you have been occasionally acquainted in the past, has developed in the last few days between the Rue de Grenelle and the Rue de l'Odeon so that I do not think it politic for me to present myself there for a week or so, the tension being chiefly at that end, until this matter is settled. The causes of this are ostensibly the fact that I have overrun my royalty account by a month or so but in reality the reason is somewhat different, for at no time in the past ten years have I ever been exact in this respect.

I will now jump into another part of the pool of despond. One of the reasons is said to be that I did not take the opportunity of accompanying Sullivan[1] to Barcelona to see the oculist he has such faith in Dr Barracquer. I had several reasons for not doing so. When he mentioned

---

[1] John Sullivan or O'Sullivan, Irish-born opera singer, and for a time leading tenor of the Paris Opéra. Joyce became his most enthusiastic admirer.

him to me several months ago I wrote to Barcelona a long letter narrating the full history of my case, and adding that my daughter had a
cast in her eye which she was rather diffident about having operated.
He replied, quoting very high fees (which I had asked about), almost
completely ignoring my case, and replying mainly to the part about
Lucia. She has since been successfully operated. It was nothing at all,
it took twenty minutes to do (Collinson did it), she came home in a
taxi and in a week both her eyes were straight, and she suffered practically nothing. In the second place I disliked the idea of going to a
country where the political dictatorship had just collapsed and I have
been told that the dictator himself is now dead. If Sullivan had been
singing in Barcelona for a few weeks, I might still have gone, but he was
only passing through it on his way to Algiers and we should have been
alone, I being almost helpless on account of my sight, had anything
occurred. While I was turning these things over in my mind Mrs
Sullivan rang me up, nominally about her daughter. I must tell you
that his daughter aged 23 was some weeks before that in a very critical
state. Neither the father nor the mother is a practical person and the
doctor they had was a thorough fool. . he had diagnosed the case as one
of appendicitis and was starving it accordingly. The mother-in-law
who lives with them then got a stroke of hemiplegia and I prevailed on
Sullivan to call in Dr Fontaine who at once brought the girl to a radio-
logist and it was found that she had tubercular peritonitis. If this
discovery had been made ten days later the case would have been hopeless. As it is, she has had five weeks of ultraviolet rays treatment and is
to be sent to Switzerland on the fifteenth of April for a six months cure
in the mountains, which it is believed will be successful. As Sullivan
was singing that night in Belgium I asked his wife to dine with us. She
told me that he was inclined to be vague and unsatisfactory in such
matters and that nobody had any influence over him except myself and
that she wished me to urge on him strongly the necessity of making all
the arrangements before he went to Algiers, as afterwards it might be
too late. I said I would do so though I did not think it necessary. She
then asked me whether we had decided to go, adding that he was not
going alone. It struck me then that it was unwise for me to travel on
this particular occasion, though she said that I was the only one of his
friends to whom he had not introduced the lady and that he probably
would not do so, but would rejoin her from Barcelona on. There is
nothing very terrible in this, tenors I believe according to the modern
Ulysses, have usually several cases of the same kind running con-
currently. The surprising thing is that in this case there is only one

and that it has been going on for twelve years. Still, not knowing
precisely what the upshot of the journey might be it seemed better to
stay in Paris and await his return to Paris, which I expect will take
place on scheduled time in spite of the hinted hints. There was finally another reason. I had lately had some gossip carried to me about Sullivan
and myself which I thought it better not to encourage, especially
since from another quarter my wife's name was involved in it too.
I am sending you however under separate cover, along with my American lawyer's letter—of which later—letters from two ladies concerning
doctors in Wiesbaden and Zurich, and I think I will try one of these—
for the moment which I don't know.

I heard from Miss Beach that you are very disturbed about the
notices in the English press concerning my oncoming blindness, I
wonder who is responsible for these. The sight of one eye becomes
slowly worse, while the sight of the other becomes slightly better. What
can possibly be the causes in my bodily condition or habits which
militate for one and against the other? Dr Fontaine is also rather
distant with me. I have the highest opinion of her and allowed her to
bring me after Borsch's death to be seen by a young French ophthalmo-
logist, Dr Hartmann, who said the only possible solution of the case
was that my eye trouble proceeded from congenital syphilis which
being curable, he said the proper thing for me was to undergo a cure of
I have forgotten what. . I told this to Dr Collinson and he dissuaded me
strongly from undergoing it. He said that at the very beginning Dr
Borsch and he had discussed this possibility and that Borsch had
excluded it categorically on account of the nature of the attacks, the
way in which they were cured and the general reactions of the eye. He
said too at any moment a skilful operation on the left eye ought to give
you normal sight, the eye ground being quite healthy, but he had
known cases in which the use of the drug in question had had a bad
effect on the optic nerve. So that ended that for me. If you knew how
highly the disease I have mentioned is respected in this country you
would understand Dr Fontaine's aloofness. Syphilis is for the French
what God Save the King is for the English, when it is mentioned tout
le monde se decouvre.

Now let me tell you what has been done in these last few months. The
second German edition of *Ulysses* came out and the third is to come out
in June. The second French edition came out and the publisher appears
to be quite happy about it. Gilbert has finished the revision of his first
proofs and his book is to come out the third week in April.[1] A L P is

---

[1] *James Joyce's* Ulysses, *A Study.*

announced to appear on May 1st. I offered H.C.E.[1] to the Fountain Press, successors to Crosby Gaige. They declined to pay the price asked, whereupon I gave it to Babou and Kahane of Paris, who will bring it out on the 12th April. Hearing this, the Fountain Press partner in Paris came to me and asked me for a fourth fragment after having just turned down the third! I gave him an evasive answer whereupon he found out Messrs Babou and Kahane and bought up half the edition in advance. Messrs Babou and Kahane *plus* Mr Adams then wrote to me via Pinker, making me an offer for an advance on the completed book and I also received a similar offer through the *Chicago Tribune* from a house in America named Selt, proposing what they called a stiff sum in advance and expressing their willingness to wait seven years for the completed manuscript. I shall return to the offer transmitted by Pinker about forty pages later on, when I get back to the rue de l'Odeon. Other things done are . . the Polish and Czech translations have been arranged. Exiles was produced in Berlin at the Deutsches Volkstheater on the 9th, they invited me to be present but I did not go. It is to be produced in Milan on the 15 April. The English translation of Dujardin's book will be published by the Mandrake Press with a preface by George Moore and a note about my connexion with the book. Two of Gilbert's chapters have appeared in French, in Echanges and the Revue de Geneve, but it is scarcely worth while sending them since the English book will be in your hands in a few weeks. I think it probable that Fourcade my French publisher will do this in French. He gave a big dinner for me some days ago, one of the best I ever saw on a table. But I was anything but a success and when I tell you that I left before the champagne you will be able to judge in what kind of a mood I was. However I sent madame a bouquet next morning and I will ask them to dine with me in a more quiet way soon.

Conner, my American lawyer in the suit against Roth, has sent me his bill for £600. I do not propose to pay this as it seems to me exorbitant for the ends gained. The Paris section of this bill of costs is £200 and the New York section £400. The publishers of HCE paid me on signing the contract fifty per cent of the whole amount, namely 25000 francs, out of which I paid 13000 francs arrears of income tax and 6500 rent and charges. I have still to pay 14000 francs arrears of income tax, but I can do this in two lots as I arranged through one of the managers of Lloyds Bank here who is a great reader of mine. I propose, however, to instruct Babou and Kahane to pay over the other £200 due on the

[1] *Haveth Childers Everywhere* (a fragment, like *Anna Livia Plurabelle*, of *Finnegans Wake*).

first of May to Conner, as these people, in addition to bungling the case, for they could have pressed for the injunction right away, have been the manipulators of the difficult question of copyright in my present work, of which more anon. Aldington has sent me a message that I am not to pay anything, as it is or ought to be a public question, in view of the judgment obtained, but I had already had copies of the injunction sent to the directors of the Pen Club and I do not know whether they have moved even so far as to publish that injunction in their journal. Aldington has been very active lately about me and has been agitating to have the ban on Ulysses lifted; so that for the settlement of the balance I shall wait on till I hear more of his plans.

When I ceased contributing to *Transition* I felt a sudden kind of drop as I was determined not to try to attack the second part in such an ill-equipped state (the revision of this last fragment has been a frightful job, extending over two months day and night sometimes till one in the morning, with seven different people helping me to do seven different parts of the labour, but of course such a condition of affairs could not possibly continue). In this frame of mind I first heard Sullivan singing and for the last four and a half months I have been working incessantly to try to get him past the Italian ring which protects the London, New York and Chicago opera houses. In temperament he is intractable, quarrelsome, disconnected, contemptuous, inclined to bullying, un-diplomatic, but on the other hand good humoured, sociable, unaffected, amusing and well-informed. He supports a family connection of eleven people and is fifty years of age. In these circumstances it was necessary for me to force the pace and I did so. I got him very fine notices in the Morning Post (twice), Daily Telegraph, Daily News, Manchester Guardian, Irish Independent, Irish Statesman, Chicago Daily Tribune, New York World, New York Sun (twice), Daily Mail, New York Times with photograph, l'Intransigeant and la Rampe of Paris. I have made a side attack on the Chicago and New York Operas. As a result I have obtained for him his first engagement in Dublin; he is to sing there on April 27th, for which he gets £120, five times as much as he draws at the Paris opera. Also Sir T. Beecham whom I got to send over two critics to hear him has promised to engage him for the English pro-duction of William Tell, probably at the same figure, and Adams, who has a finger in theatrical pies also, has promised, chiefly with an eye on my book, to arrange a series of symphonic concerts for him in the United States. All this, for a person who really exerted himself and did not know very well the milieu in which he was working, involved a tremendous amount of telephoning, writing, interviewing, newspaper

hunting, theatre-going, entertaining and being entertained. As a result
of all that and the revision of H C E , I am quite flattened out and in fact
for the last two days have been having quite a series of miniature
fainting fits, lasting only a few seconds. Sullivan, thank goodness, has
gone to Africa for a few weeks, but in any case I shall ease off when he
comes back, for I have set in motion all the machines I could think of.
I think there is more behind the state of tension I alluded to in the
beginning than my well known inability to keep accounts straight. For a
few weeks it was smilingly tolerated as a fad, but when it was seen that I
went farther and stronger, the impression was made that I had gone
slightly soft in the head. My introduction of Sullivan down there dis-
pelled that impression, thanks to his breezy French manner and general
air of having escaped from a boarding-school at the age of forty nine.
But when I again resumed the campaign, the former impression came
back. You must know that the opera in Paris is considered, not without
some reason, by the Paris intellectuals as beneath contempt and the
spectacle of the immensely illustrious author of Ulysses endeavouring to
hustle crowds of journalists and protesting admirers into that old
fashioned playhouse to hear antiquated music sung by old timer
Sullivan was too much. No doubt I may have exaggerated in my
exertions for him and perhaps made myself ridiculous in the eyes of
sober thinking people, but I do not care very much, for it is incompar-
ably the greatest human voice I have ever heard, beside which Chaliapine is braggadocio and McCormick insignificant. On one of the
evenings he sang when Miss Beach and Miss Monnier were present I
said, it may seem incautiously, when asked by the latter why I had
done all I had for a person they considered unknown, that since I had
come to Paris I had been introduced (i.e. by them) to a great number
of recognised geniuses, without specifying names, in literature, music,
painting and sculpture, and that for me all these persons were quite
sympathetic and friendly, but that they were all, for me, perhapses,
but that there was no perhaps about Sullivan's voice. I said this purposely, first because I have always insisted that I know little about
literature, less about music, nothing about painting and less than
nothing about sculpture; but I do know something about singing, I
think. And secondly because I am being continually placed in difficult
situations which I am not quick-witted enough to know how to handle
by the sudden exaltations and depressions of the Odéon Bourse, not, of
course, where I am concerned, because they have never swerved in their
loyalty to me. The second cause is this—I have spent a lot of money
and diplomatic efforts in securing for myself a copyright of Work in

Progress in the United States. I have it, but they have me too, just as I had it and they had it in the Roth case. To maintain my copyright there, I have no option. I must publish first through an American firm. Adams, who is a lawyer, knows this and Conner had told me so already. I dislike this. I have confidence in Miss Beach and I have none in Adams or in any other man publisher, for that matter, for all of them whom I have had up to the present were either incompetent or dishonest or both. But Miss Beach naturally feels that the book that she has been waiting for and has helped me so much with, is not being energetically enough given to her by me. This is not a case for energy but for prudence and some form of compromise, American wealth, law and power being what they are. The third point is my apparent indifference concerning the *Ulysses* editions, articles and publications, apart from their sales, and my inclination to cease where I am and let someone else write the rest. I cannot discuss this last point now, for these last days I am light in the head.

I do not think that if I cease working there is much point in my continuing to live in Paris. It involves continual sacrifice of capital for one thing, which up till now was covered over by an output on my part, so that I do not think I shall renew the lease of this apartment, and as for my books it is useless to transport immense loads of what I cannot read so that I think I shall keep only the signed gift books and good old dictionaries. These questions I shall now think over, having nothing else to do, as I have to decide by May. I will now end this letter and I hope it has not bored you too much. I now refer your attention to the first paragraph and if the affair can be fixed up by Monday or Tuesday (it usually takes a week) I shall be much relieved.

The general health here is good and I hope yours is, except for the lightness in my head.

With kindest regards sincerely yours   JAMES JOYCE

From JOHN SULLIVAN to JO DAVIDSON   TS. Library of Congress

23 June 1930   *Theatre National de l'Opera, 1 rue Glück, 1, Paris*

Mr John Sullivan presents his compliments and encloses herewith a copy of a challenge[1] which he is sending to the press.

[1] The challenge, which follows, was apparently written by Joyce, who probably also thought up the scheme of a vocal duel.

The version sent to the French press was a little different, but also reads as if Joyce had written it:

                                   DÉFI

      De la justice avant toute chose!

[Enclosure]

To the EDITOR 'New York Herald'   *Theatre National de l'Opera,*
                                           1 rue Gluck, 1, Paris

De la Musique avant toute chose . . .

Your musical critic Mr. Louis Schneider, in his notice of the recent performance at the Paris Opera of *Guillaume Tell*, with Mr. Lauri-Volpi in the tenor role, informs the numerous readers of your journal that this was an exceptional performance, such as only a really great artist could have given. As I have, for many years, sustained this part, notably the most difficult ever written for the tenor voice, at the National Academy of Music here, where I am to-day *titulaire du rôle,* I claim the right, under your favor, to state publicly in these columns that Mr. Lauri-Volpi, quite departing from the tradition upheld at this theatre for the last hundred years by all who have preceded him, cut out more than half of the singing part assigned to him by the composer. To be precise, all the arduous recitatives, without one exception, were suppressed. The duet with Tell in the first act was reduced to one third of its length and vocal difficulty, as was the duet with the soprano in the second act and the celebrated and trying trio which immediately follows. As if this were not enough, Mr. Lauri-Volpi most prudently avoided the perilous duel with the chorus which was written to form the climax of the whole Opera.

These being the facts, I courteously invite Mr. Lauri-Volpi to sing this part in its entirety and as it was composed by his fellow countryman Rossini and as I myself have sung it over two hundred times throughout France, Belgium, Spain and North and South America, but especially

---

Le critique musical du New York Herald à Paris, M. Louis Schneider ayant rendu compte à ses nombreux lecteurs de la représentation à l'opera du Guillaume Tell de Rossini avec M. Lauri Volpi tenant le rôle d'Arnold comme d'une représentation digne d'un grand artiste, je me permets en ma qualité de titulaire depuis des années de ce rôle à l'Académie Nationale de Musique d'affirmer que M. Volpi s'est permis de couper un peu plus de la moitié de son rôle, en supprimant les recitatifs, diminuant le trio et évitant totalement le duel perilleux contre le choeur final. En outre je défie M. Lauri Volpi de chanter ce rôle tel que son compatriote Rossini l'a écrit et comme moi-même je l'ai chanté des centaines de fois dans toutes les villes principales de la France, de la Belgique et de l'Italie même, où cet opéra enseveli à cause du manque du tenor capable de le chanter après la mort du celèbre Tamagno qui le chanta pour la dernière fois en 1889, a été ressuscité pour moi en 1922 au théâtre San Carlo à Naples, sous la direction de M. Tullio Seraphin. Je propose donc à M. Volpi de chanter ce rôle integralement sans transpositions ni coupures dans n'importe quelle salle de Paris où je pourrais le chanter aussi. Je laisse comme arbitre des deux executions M. L. Schneider lui-même auquel j'offrirai pour cette occasion un exemplaire de la partition originale de cet opéra élégamment reliée, convaincu du reste qu'un amateur de musique comme il semble l'être ne pourra trouver que fort agréable de refaire connaissance directe avec un chef d'oeuvre qu'il semble avoir en grande partie oublié.   (Signé) John Sullivan

in all the principal cities of Italy. I had, indeed, the honor of being chosen by Mr. Tullio Serafin when this Opera was revived by him at the San Carlo Theatre of Naples in 1923, after a lapse of thirty four years, during which time no tenor had been found in all Italy to sustain the part after the death of the celebrated Tamagno. If Mr. Lauri-Volpi will sing this role, without transpositions or omissions at any Paris theatre or concert hall, where I may be allowed to sing it also, I am willing to accept Mr. Louis Schneider as judge. Nay more, to facilitate him in coming to his verdict, I shall be most happy to present to him an elegantly bound edition of the operatic score, feeling sure that such an eminent musician will welcome this opportunity of becoming re-acquainted with a masterpiece which he would appear to have very successfully forgotten.

Et tout le reste est ... publicité.[1] Sincerely yours

(Signed) John Sullivan

To George Antheil[2]

7 September 1930   *Les Golf Hôtels, Etretat*

Dear Antheil: Many thanks for MS song which I sent off to Hughes.[3] I will write to you about it from Paris where I return on Wednesday. I am sending you Byron's *Cain* to look over. I think it could be the basis of a fine libretto. As you have never heard Sullivan sing in opera you cannot have an idea of the effect created by his stage presence, diction and voice combined. If you decide on the subject I suggest there is only one singer in the world capable of presenting such a figure. I wish we could talk over the idea together. [Sincerely yours   James Joyce]

To Harriet Shaw Weaver (Dictated letter)   TS. British Museum

22 November 1930   *192 rue de Grenelle, Paris VII*

Dear Miss Weaver: I enclose the final sheet of the first draft of about

[1] 'And all the rest is ... publicity'; a play on Verlaine's line, 'Et tout le reste est littérature.'

[2] George Antheil (1900–59), composer of seven symphonies and several operas, of whom Stuart Gilbert has noted: 'He is generally recognized as one of the leading figures in the world of modern music. His *ballet mécanique* (whose *première* at the Théâtre des Champs-Elysées, Paris, the writer of this note—and, I think, Joyce—attended) was certainly the outstanding event of the 1927 season. The letters to Antheil are interesting for the light they throw on Joyce's attitude to music, which (as it seemed to me) appealed to him chiefly as a vehicle for celebrating the (preferably tenor) human voice.'

[3] Herbert Hughes (1882–1937), Belfast musician and critic.

two thirds of the first section of Part II (2,200 words) which came out like drops of blood. Excuse me for not having written but I have had a dreadful amount of worry all this last month about my son's projected marriage about which my wife is extremely pessimistic and concerning which I have to proceed like an aged old rat walking over broken bottles. I had to put off my journey to Zurich five different times but am leaving tomorrow with the Gormans[1] and my wife, as he has to have his eyes seen to too. My address will be Elite Carlton Hotel, until Thursday or Friday. I shall write to you at once what Vogt says. I think the piece I sent you[2] is the gayest and lightest thing I have done in spite of the circumstances.

I enclose a letter from Antheil, I have consented to cut Byron's piece for Opera purposes and sign the cuts but no more. I suppose you saw that Mrs Snowden has induced a British Government and a Labour one at that to put up £90,000 in aid of the Beecham and Guinness syndicate. Of course I sent her off through the Paris correspondent of the Daily Herald half a ton of material about Sullivan who is at present dodging shots in Barcelona.

This will be all for to-day as H.C.E. remarks but please write to me in Zurich where I shall be glad to have a letter.

The scheme of the piece I sent you is the game we used to call Angels and Devils or colours. The Angels, girls, are grouped behind the Angel, Shawn, and the Devil has to come over three times and ask for a colour, if the colour he asks for has been chosen by any girl she has to run and he tries to catch her. As far as I have written he has come twice and been twice baffled. The piece is full of rhythms taken from English singing games. When first baffled vindictively he thinks of publishing blackmail stuff about his father, mother etc etc etc. The second time he maunders off into sentimental poetry[3] of what I actually wrote at the age of nine: 'My cot alas that dear old shady home where oft in youthful sport I played, upon thy verdant grassy fields all day or lingered for a moment in thy bosom shade etc etc etc etc.'[4] This is interrupted by a violent pang of tooth ache after which he throws a fit. When he is baffled a second time the girl angels sing a hymn of liberation around Shawn. The page enclosed is still another version of a beautiful sentence from Edgard Quinet which I already refashioned in Transition part one beginning since the days of Hiber and Hairyman etc. E.Q. says that the wild flowers on the ruins of Carthage Numancia etc. have survived the political rises and downfall of Empires. In this case the wild flowers

---

[1] Herbert Gorman (1893–1954), American novelist and Joyce's first biographer.

[2] Part II, section 1, of *Finnegans Wake*.

[3] Seemingly a word omitted. Perhaps 'bits'.   [4] *Finnegans Wake*, p. 231.

are the lilts of children. Note especially the treatment of the double rainbow in which the iritic colours are first normal and then reversed.

With kindest regards and the hope that you are not annoyed with me for my silence   Sincerely yours   James Joyce

From Lucia Joyce to Signora Livia Schmitz   MS. Fonda Savio

25 January 1931   *[Paris]*

Dear Mrs Schmitz: Giorgio duly received your kind and charming present and wrote to thank you for it though you do not seem to have got his letter, before leaving for his honeymoon in Germany. My father replied to Miss de Zoëte[1] several weeks ago. A long time ago he made it a rule that he would not write a preface to his own or another's book or notes of explanation or give an interview or deliver a lecture. He has in fact refused several times offers for highly paid lecture tours in german, english and american cities to say nothing of France. He says, morover that a preface from him would damn the book in the eyes of readers in England and America for whom he is still a pariah and by whom his present method of writing is considered 'una vera senilità.' As for the title he agrees with you that Senility is impossible. He suggests As a Man Grows Older or Goodbye, Deo Gratias. And if these titles seem far from the original he says that the cavatina in *Rigoletta* La donna è mobile is sung on the english operatic stage as Fair shines the moon tonight. He spoke to his friend Mr Ford Maddox Ford (address 32 rue de Vaugirard, Paris VIe) who has consented to do the preface but [needs] a copy of both books in english and italian before he does it. Mr Ford is perhaps the best known and most successful lecturer among english authors in the United States. He is also of a certain age himself and can write an admirable 'causerie'. My father says that if you will have three copies of Zeno and three copies of the proofs of Senilità (in english) sent to him by the publishers he will do his best to have it noticed at great length in two leading american and english papers. He will also recommend the book to his german czeck and polish publishers and show it to many influential men of letters.

My mother joins me in sending you friendly greetings and good wishes for the coming year.   Lucia Joyce

P.S. Or better he thinks Adieu Deo Gratias.

[1] Beryl de Zoëte, translator of Italo Svevo's novel *Senilità*, which was eventually published with Joyce's suggested title *As a Man Grows Older*, with a preface by Stanislaus Joyce.

To Stanislaus Joyce   MS. Cornell

18 July 1931   [*London*]

Dear Stannie: The *Piccolo* does not contain either in report or Pasini's speech any allusion to the telegram I sent that morning or to your presence among the professors or to Larbaud and Miss Monnier or to myself.[1] Whoever eventually writes the preface to *Senilità* should mention that fact.[2]

Thanks for your wire. The other branches of the family (Paris excepted) expressed consternation. I had offered my nephew George[3] who is workless £1 a week if he would help me with my notes from 2 to 5 pm every day but his stepmother (he is 21) took from him the *Exagmination* I had lent him and we were given to understand that our influence etc etc. The Press Association by the way but particularly the *Sunday Express* made a most spirited attempt at blackmail but funked it at the end, the rumour having gone around that I had come in for a big sum which would enable me to fight them for libel. The affair as you know is as clear as mock turtle.[4] Having eloped with my present wife in 1904 she with my full connivance gave the name of Miss Gretta Greene which was quite good enough for il Cav. Fabbri who married us and the last gentleman in Europe il conte Dandino who issued the legitimate certificates for the offspring, but this full connivance voided the marriage in the eyes of English law see Hargreave's[5] Laws of England page 471–2 and the second ceremony was thought advisable to secure the inheritance under will. I have a slight cough this morning so please forgive me if I now desist.

With best Xmas wishes to Mr and Mrs Joyce from Mr and Mrs Ditto MacAnaspey[6] and here's jumping that bucket as Tinker said to his gipsy[7] I remain, dear professor, matrimonially yours

Monico[8] Colesser[9]

---

[1] At a ceremony in honour of Ettore Schmitz on 26 April 1931.
[2] Stanislaus Joyce did so in the Introduction, p. xii.
[3] Son of Charles Joyce.
[4] Joyce and Nora Barnacle were married on 4 July 1931 at the Registry Office in Kensington. To avoid talk he concocted a story of a previous marriage, but the journalists and photographers gave embarrassing publicity to the ceremony.
[5] Really Halsbury's.
[6] A catch phrase of Joyce's father, meaning simply 'ditto'.
[7] Traditional gipsy marriage ceremony.
[8] See p. 396n.
[9] An absurd teacher of German at the Berlitz School in Trieste.

To HARRIET SHAW WEAVER   MS. British Museum

27 October 1931   *2 Avenue Saint Philibert, Passy, Paris*

Dear Miss Weaver: The report[1] is all right, thank goodness, so that's that.

I finished pulling together the first 8 episodes last night and as I am quite fatigued and it is a splendid day Giorgio is taking us out for a long country drive. I shall write you about the money and other things to Frodsham. To my great relief I find that much more of the book is done than I had hoped for. Souppault[2] who has been on a lecture tour in the U.S.A. told me yesterday that the government would have no chance of winning a suit against *Ulysses*. He said it is on the extension lecture programme for many universities and actually prescribed for the M.A. degree for next year in the New York university. So let them take off the ban and I suppose England will follow suit as usual a few years later. And Ireland 1000 years hence.

May I ask you to put through two telephone calls before you leave London. 1) Paddington inform. To get Botzain 3 Gloucester Terrace— of course the house not he) and find out why he sent me the hair lotion and the pommade. 2) August Milner, Wimpole Street? or thereabouts to ask him to get from Mrs Malcolm, 15 Sunderland Terrace, W2 *Music and Letters,* read it and return to me.

Please return *Four* to Léon.[3] The writer should not have used O.G.'s[4] letter in an article. The latter is a swimmer, boxer, cyclist, aviator, motorist and of course I cut a poor figure, eyeless etc. Still the world begins from an egg. Enough of them and all alien annoyances. I have a job on hand. Kindest regards sincerely yrs   JAMES JOYCE

To HARRIET SHAW WEAVER   MS. British Museum

17 December 1931   *2 Avenue S. Philibert, Passy, Paris*

Dear Miss Weaver: My American lawyers having again asked for a payment of the other 2000 $ I sent Conner the enclosed letter which please return. Miss Beach raised an objection to my sending it on account of a 'falsehood' in it which would be shown up if C. asked to see my contract with her. The 'falsehood' was in the phrase stating

---

[1] On his health.

[2] Philippe Soupault (b. 1897), French writer, a good friend of Joyce in the 1920s and '30s, who collaborated in the French translation of *Anna Livia Plurabelle*. His *Souvenirs de James Joyce* was published in Algiers in 1943.

[3] Paul Léon (1893–1942), Joyce's friend and helper, killed by the Nazis during the war.

[4] Oliver St John Gogarty.

that when I filed the suit I apparently was not the owner of the U.S.
rights. She says I was. I replied that the contract must have been
simply a putting into writing of her pre-existent intention. To which
she said I was the owner then etc. Nevertheless I sent the letter.

Souppault, who goes returns [sic] to U.S.A. in a month proposed to
put the French consul-general of N.Y. on the track of the new Roth
edition, it being a *contrefaçon* of a French printer's output just as a
falsified French perfume would be and a meeting was arranged between
him, Miss Monnier and Miss Beach Léon and myself. But Miss Monnier
then asked me to go to see her alone. She read me a letter she had
written to Paul Claudel, the ambassador, who is a lunatic catholic, she
says, and intensely annoyed by *U* (he sent back a presentation copy of
the first edition) but has lost prestige as a poet so much with the
younger generation that she thinks, with the aid of Gillet's article
which she also sent, that he will take this opportunity to rehabilitate
himself. I doubt very much that she is right. It is not an ambassador's
job though a consul might effect a seizure of the copies. Possibly Claudel
is a convert like Maritain and if so his protestant mentality would well
suit an Irish catholic element over there which is of an even worse breed.

She also told me that the N.R.F. angered at her refusal to give them
U had decided to favour Lawrence's *Lady Chatterli's* [sic] *Lover*,
which is coming out in French. I also received a letter from a man in
England who has nearly completed a long study and exegesis of this
work and has obtained opinions about it from G.B.S., A.H., O.S.,
M.M. and E.T.C. and wants an opinion from me. These are all to be
printed in front of this study and exegesis of this work. In the middle of
my own work have I got to listen to this. I read the first 2 pages of the
usual sloppy English and G.S.[1] read me a lyrical bit about nudism in
a wood and the end which is a piece of propaganda in favour of something which, outside of D.H.L.'s country at any rate, makes all the
propaganda for itself.

T.S.E. has been appointed professor at Harvard and is to leave
England next year. Good Lord! Have I to deal with those printers face
to face? Kindest regards sincerely yours   JAMES JOYCE

To T. S. ELIOT   MS. Faber

1 January 1932   *2 Avenue S. Philibert, Passy, Paris*

Dear Eliot: Excuse me if I am backward in my work and correspondence.

[1] S.G. (Stuart Gilbert) is meant.

I have been through a bad time telephoning and wiring to Dublin about my father. To my great grief he died on Tuesday. He had an intense love for me and it adds to my grief and remorse that I did not go to Dublin to see him for so many years. I kept him constantly under the illusion that I would come and was always in correspondence with him but an instinct which I believed in held me back from going, much as I longed to. *Dubliners* was banned there in 1912 on the advice of a person who was assuring me at the time of his great friendship. When my wife and children went there in 1922, against my wish, they had to flee for their lives, lying flat on the floor of a railway carriage while rival parties shot at each other across their heads and quite lately I have had experience of malignancy and treachery on the part of people to whom I had done nothing but friendly acts. I did not feel myself safe and my wife and son opposed my going.

I have been very broken down these last days and I feel that a poor heart which was true and faithful to me is no more.

I will prepare the end of Pt. I after a few days' rest.

I have heard about your Harvard appointment.[1] I offer my congratulations if the appointment is pleasant for you and I hope Mrs Eliot and yourself will have all luck and happiness this year. Sincerely yours

JAMES JOYCE

To HARRIET SHAW WEAVER   MS. British Museum

17 January 1932   *2 Avenue S. Philibert, Passy, Paris*

Dear Miss Weaver: Thanks for your message of sympathy. I spent the four days after Xmas sending messages to my father by wire and letter and by telephone to the hospital every evening. The weeks since then have been passed in prostration of mind. Gilbert came here four or five times but I could not collect my thoughts or do anything. I am thinking of abandoning work altogether and leaving the thing unfinished with blanks. Worries and jealousies and my own mistakes. Why go on writing about a place I did not dare to go to at such a moment, where not three persons know me or understand me (in the obituary notice the editor of the *Independent* raised objections to the allusion to me)? But after my experience with the blackmailers in England I had no wish to face the Irish thing. And all my family and even my Irish friends were against it. My father had an extraordinary affection for me. He was the silliest man I ever knew and yet cruelly shrewd. He

---

[1] As Charles Eliot Norton Professor.

thought and talked of me up to his last breath. I was very fond of him always, being a sinner myself, and even liked his faults. Hundreds of pages and scores of characters in my books came from him. His dry (or rather wet) wit and his expression of face convulsed me often with laughter. He kept it in old age. When he got the copy I sent him of *Tales Told* etc (so they write me) he looked a long time at Brancusi's *Portrait of J.J.*[1] and finally remarked: Jim has changed more than I thought. I got from him his portraits, a waistcoat, a good tenor voice, and an extravagant licentious disposition (out of which, however, the greater part of any talent I may have springs) but, apart from these, something else I cannot define. But if an observer thought of my father and myself and my son too physically, though we are all very different, he could perhaps define it. It is a great consolation to me to have such a good son. His grandfather was very fond of him and kept his photograph beside mine on the mantelpiece.

I knew he was old. But I thought he would live longer. It is not his death that crushed me so much but self-accusation.

Helen is not delivered yet. Since Miss Beach screamed at me as I told you and said she would give the rights to me as a Xmas present (she did not) I heard no more till she returned my last letter to Conner without comment and the enclosed.[2] An imbecile thing it is, too.

She rang me up a day or so ago in a great excitement about my 'jubilee'. People had come from Berlin where they were going to do something or other. She said she had intended to leave Paris for a holiday but if I liked she would cancel that and organise something here too. I was too dejected to make a reply.

I am glad this letter did not cause the collapse the other I wrote caused. But it tired me a little.

I hope your own news is good. With kindest regards sincerely yours

JAMES JOYCE

To the MAYOR OF FLORENCE   TS. Private

9 April 1932   *2 Avenue Saint Philibert, Passy, Paris*

Magnifico Podestà Anzitutto Le chiedo venia se non rispondo che oggi e se la mia risposta si presenta sotto questa forma agghindata e stinta ma la pregiatissima Sua lettera inoltrata da Londra mi è pervenuta con qualche ritardo ed in fatto di calligrafia sono un vero imbrattacarte. La ringrazio del cortese invito nonchè delle generose parcelle di viaggio

---

[1] See p. 340.   [2] The enclosure has not survived.

offertemi ed apprezzo altamente l'onore che un tale invito proveniente dal primo cittadino di tanta città mi conferisce.

Mi duole assai di non essere in grado di accettare e di dovere rinunciare al privilegio di parlare dinanzi ad un auditorio amichevole nella capitale toscana. Purtroppo le fate che s'inchinarono sopra la mia culla mi tolsero il dono della facondia, vanto di molti miei connazionali e mi lasciarono in sua vece una 'lingua di lana in bocca baggiana'.[1] La prego dunque di tenermi per iscusato.

Se mi è lecito proporre un altro nome credo che il mio amico, il poeta americano Ezra Pound, il quale ha tradotto in inglese le opere di un grande scrittore fiorentino, Guido Cavalcanti, potrebbe benissimo rimpiazzarmi. Il suo indirrizzo è: 12 via Marsala, Rapallo dove abita da dieci anni.

Nel mentre porgo a Lei, al chiarissimo rettore della regia Università di costì ed al comitato da Loro presieduto i miei sinceri ringraziamenti. La prego, Magnifico Podestà, di gradire i sensi dei miei piu doverosi ossequi.

JAMES JOYCE[2]

To CONSTANT HUNTINGTON[3]   TS. Yale

22 May 1932   *2 Avenue Saint Philibert, Passy, Paris*

Dear Mr Huntington   I do not think I can usefully add anything to

[1] A play on the expression, 'lingua toscana in bocca romana'—'the Tuscan tongue in a Roman mouth'—which Italians consider the perfection of their language.

[2] (Translation)

'Your Honour the Mayor: First of all I ask your pardon for not replying until today and then in this bedizened and faded form, but your most esteemed letter forwarded from London reached me after some delay and as for handwriting I am a mere scribbler. I thank you for your courteous invitation as well as the generous travelling expenses offered me and I value highly the honour that such an invitation, coming from the first citizen of such a city, confers upon me.

I regret very much being unable to accept, and having to forgo the privilege of speaking before a friendly audience in the Tuscan capital. Unfortunately the fates who bent over my cradle deprived me of the gift of eloquence—the ornament of many of my compatriots—and left me in its stead "a woollen tongue in a foolish mouth." I beg you therefore to excuse me.

If it be permissible for me to propose another name I think that my friend, the American poet Ezra Pound, who translated into English the works of a great Florentine writer, Guido Cavalcanti, might replace me excellently. His address is: 12 via Marsala, Rapallo, where he has lived for ten years.

On this occasion I offer my sincere thanks to you, to the very distinguished rector of the royal university there, and to the committee over which you preside. I beg you, Your Honour the Mayor, to accept this expression of my deepest respect.

James Joyce'

[3] Constant Huntington (d. 1962), chairman of G. P. Putnam's Sons Ltd., London. He had asked Joyce to offer some direct comment on Schmitz's book. The text of this letter is from a typewritten copy. Another copy, bearing the date 30 May 1932, is at Cornell.

what my learned friend, the professor of English at the University of Trieste[1] (see titlepage) has written in his preface to Senilita, (As) A man grows older.

With regard to the other book[2] by the author of Senilità the only things I can suggest as likely to attract the British reading public are a preface by sir J. M. Barrie, author of My Lady Nicotine, opinions of the book (to be printed on the back of its jacket) from two deservedly popular personalities of the present day, such as, the rector of Stiffkey[3] and the Princess of Wales and (on the front of the jacket) a coloured picture by a Royal Academician representing two young ladies, one fair and the other dark but both distinctly nicelooking, seated in a graceful though of course not unbecoming posture at a table on which a book stands upright, with title visible and underneath the picture three lines of simple dialogue, for example:

Ethel: Does Cyril spend too much on cigarettes!

Doris: Far too much.

Ethel: So did Percy (points)—till I gave him ZENO. Sincerely yours

JAMES JOYCE

To STUART GILBERT   MS. Gilbert

22 July 1932   *Carlton Elite Hotel, Zurich*

Dear Gilbert: I showed Beckett's acrostic[4] to Mr and Mrs Jolas.[5] The latter thought it poor, the former thinks it acid and not funny. I think it is all right—though if I may suggest anything it seems to me 'tickled to death' is better than 'giggling to death' though the 'g' is nearer 'j'.

The news about Lucia was satisfactory enough till today when she announces her arrival here with the nurse next Friday. I wish she would stay where she is. I have written to Dr Codet about her as, of course, I am nervy all the time at having taken her out of his hands on my own responsibility.

The news about my right eye is bad. I have not gone back to Vogt. He says I should have left other things aside and come to him before. How can I possibly make an engagement with him now even if he does decide to risk the two difficult operations which he fears he cannot even make?

I wrote to Faber and Faber offering to refund them the £150 advance

---

[1] Stanislaus Joyce; see p. 356n.   [2] Italo Svevo, *La Coscienza di Zeno* (1924).

[3] Rev. Harold Francis Davidson (1875–1936), Rector of Stiffkey, was tried and convicted on various charges of immoral behavior in March and July 1932.

[4] For Samuel Beckett's acrostic on Joyce, see Ellmann, *James Joyce*, pp. 714–15.

[5] The American poet Eugene Jolas (1894–1952) edited the important magazine *transition* from April 1927 to spring 1938. He and his wife Maria (b. 1895), herself a writer and teacher, were close friends of the Joyces.

on *Work in Progress* and scrap the contract. I hate to have this on my mind too. I am proposing to my 'estate agents' to pay off the whole of the lease less discount and let the flat furnished for 1 gn. a week and then sell the sticks. Off with my flat, so much for Kensington!

I am not surprised McGreevy does not want to write any more about me—especially for nothing. Why should he? Goll's article is pretty bad but Tuohy's, Colum's, Lewis's, etc. portraits are also bad. As I wrote to Miss Weaver: es tut mir leid aber es ist absolut nichts zu malen. Un chef de rayon à la Samaritaine. Vous désirez, Madame? Blancs, n'est-ce-pas? Au fond, dans le petit coin. O pardon, Monsieur le Président, je croyais que vous étiez Madame la Boulangère. Un canon? parfaitement. Suivez-moi par ici! O excusez-moi, mon petit moutard! Je t'ai fait du mal? Laisse-moi te caresser, ça passera. Merdre de merdre, c'est un bouledogue anglais! O ouch! O ouch! Comment, Monsieur le Directeur, mes huit jours? Mais je suis bouleversé. Sapristi! Je viens de renverser la Tour Eiffel des mouchoirs à 2 frs 75![1] . . . [Sincerely yours

JAMES JOYCE]

To ALFRED BERGAN[2]   MS. N.Y. Public Library (Manuscript)

5 August 1932   *Carlton Elite Hotel, Zurich*

Dear Mr Bergan: I hope this finds you in good health and that you excuse me for not having written to you before but my daughter has been rather ill and I myself am here on account of my wretched eyes. I may have to submit to two more operations, making the full dozen, or the right eye may be left to go blind—the devil or the deep sea.

It was very kind of you to act as you did about poor Pappie's will and if you will let me know the cost of the tombstone I shall send a cheque for it. The names of my parents are John Stanislaus and Mary Jane.

I wonder what became of all the signed editions of my books I sent to Pappie. Apart from any material value (the first Paris edition of *Ulysses* signed is worth about £35) I do not want them to be in the hands of strangers.

You are in this book by name[3] with so many others of Pappie's

---

[1] 'I'm sorry but there is absolutely nothing to paint. Head of the rayon department at the Samaritaine. And for you, Madam? Linens, is it? At the back, over in the corner. Oh excuse me, Mr President, I thought you were the baker's wife. A cannon? Of course. Come with me this way. Oh excuse me, little fellow! Have I hurt you? Let me rub it, it will go away. Shite, it's an English bulldog! Ouch! Ouch! My eight-day notice, you say, sir? I'm all confused. Oh, the devil! I've just knocked over the Eiffel Tower of 2-francs-75 handkerchiefs.'

[2] See p. 286n.   [3] In the *Cyclops* episode.

friends. I remember very well your singing *One of the Family* and *Sister Susie's Playing*. You always made the same mistake in one line of the latter, a mistake prompted by politeness and encouraged by conviviality, for you sang 'would make both you and I sick' instead of 'would make both me and you sick'.

My grandson Stephen was born a month after Pappie died. I wrote a little verse about it[1] and if I ever publish it I will send you a copy. No man could be worthy of such intense love as my father had for me

With many remembrances and all good wishes sincerely yours

JAMES JOYCE

To W. B. YEATS   MS. Yeats

5 October 1932   *Hôtel Metropole, Nice*

Dear Yeats: Many thanks for your letter and the kind words you use. It is now thirty years since you first held out to me your helping hand. Please convey my thanks also to Mr Shaw whom I have never met.

I hope that the Academy of Irish Letters (if that is its title) which you are both forming will have the success it aims at. My case, however, being as it was and probably will be I see no reason why my name should have arisen at all in connection with such an academy: and I feel quite clearly that I have no right whatsoever to nominate myself as a member of it.

I am returning under separate cover the rules you were good enough to send me.

I hope your health keeps good. For myself I have to go back to Zurich every three months about my eyes. Still, I work on as best I can.

With grateful remembrance   Sincerely yours   JAMES JOYCE

To HARRIET SHAW WEAVER   MS. British Museum
(Telegram sent by Paul Léon)

23 January 1933   *Paris*

Miss Weaver   74 Gloucester Place   London

If not too late please send 121 Ebury Street Pimlico London wreath two guineas sending cheque only leaves green brown but excluding ivy absolutely stop inscription to George Moore[2] from James Joyce Paris.

---

[1] 'Ecce Puer.'   [2] He died 21 January 1933.

From LUCIA JOYCE to FRANK BUDGEN   TS. Budgen

3 September 1933   *42 rue Galilée, Paris*

Dear Mr. Budgen, We are just back from Geneva and my father sends
you the following suggestions. Keep a close hold on your american
wrights. The Continental wrights he believes he can arrange for you
with the Albatross Press who have published him. For this purpose get
your publishers to send a copy[1] to his agent Pinker to be forwarded at
my father's request to Mr. Reece. Have nothing to do with Tauchnitz
but have a copy sent to Mr. Daniel Brody Rheiverlag 35 a Konigin-
strasse Munich his german publishers. He says if all the germans have
gone daffed by then a Swiss firm might do the translation. In any case
copys should go to Dr. Edward Corrody literary editor of the N Z Z[2] and
Prof. Bernard Fehr[3] of the University of Zurich 24 Eleonora Strasse
both of whom are personal friends of his. He suggests as motto for your
book these lines of Godfried Kellers Ich will spiegeln mich in jenen
Tagen, die wie Lindenwipfelwehen entflohen, wo die Silbersaiten
angeschlagen, zart doch behend gab den ersten ton.[4]

With regard to the Zunfthaus the Safran one was the Guild of dyers.
The Zimmerleuten one is now quiet chic with the french chef named
Michel who can serve you Kangaroo-schwanzsuppe[5] which is a change
from the Zurich cuisine at wartime.[6]

The frase of the latin mass which you could not read is on Ulysses
page I. The old catholics Augustiner Kirche are a good example of a
Mooks gone Gripes.[7] They separated from Rome in 71 when the
infallibility of the pope was proclaimed a Dogma but they have since

[1] Of *James Joyce and the Making of 'Ulysses'*; see p. 281n.

[2] Dr Eduard Korrodi (b. 1885), Swiss author, literary critic for the *Neue Zürcher
Zeitung*.

[3] Bernhard Fehr (1876–1938) was Professor of English at the University of Zurich
from 1927 until his death.

[4] A slightly inaccurate quotation from Gottfried Keller's poem, 'Jugendgedanken':

> Ich will spiegeln mich in jenen Tagen,
> Die wie Lindenwipfelwehn entflohn,
> Wo die Silbersaite, angeschlagen,
> Klar, doch bebend, gab den ersten Ton,
>> Der mein Leben lang,
>> Erst heut noch, widerklang,
>> Ob die Saite längst zerrissen schon. . . .

('I want to see my mirrored image in those days / Which fled like the flutterings of the
tops of lindens, / When the silver cord, struck, / Clear, yet quivering, gave its first note,
/ Which resounded all my life, even today, though the cord snapped long ago.')

[5] 'Kangaroo-tail soup.'

[6] Budgen discusses the guilds briefly in his book (p. 25), but without using the extra
details Joyce furnished him.

[7] For this fable see *Finnegans Wake*, pp. 152–9.

gone much more apart. They have abolished auricular confession they have the eucarist under two species but the faithful received the cup only at Whitsun. I see no prayers to the B V M or the saints in their prayer book and no images of her or them around the church. But most important of all they have abolished the Filioque clause in the creed concerning which there has been a schism between western and eastern christendom for over a thousand years, Rome saying that the Holy Ghost proceeds from the father and the son. Greece and Russia and the East Orthodox churches that the procession is from the father alone, ex patre without Filioque. Of course the dogmas subsequently proclaimed by Rome after the split are not recognized by the east such as the Immaculate conception. See the Mooks and the Gripes that is West and east, paragraph beginning when that Mooksius and ending Philioquus.[1] All the grotesque words in this are russian or greek for the three principal dogmas which separate Shem from Shaun. When he gets A and B on to his lap C slips off and when he has C and A he looses hold of B. My father hopes you will enjoy Ascona the most boring place in Switzerland and not fail to visit Geneva by far its most beautiful and elegant city. Sincerely yours,   LUCIA JOYCE

To T. S. ELIOT   MS. Faber

18 December 1933   *42 rue Galilée, Paris (Etoile)*

Dear Eliot: Thanks for your letter but the U.S. ban does not 'seem' to be lifted. It is lifted. I have here counsel's brief (100 printed pp) and the judge's ruling, about 12 pages. He states that his ruling is as legally valid as a decision by judge and jury, both parties having agreed to have the case tried before him alone. He orders that his ruling be filed. Three-fourths of the text was published in the N. Y. Herald Tribune of 7 December. The U.S. attorney-general, immediately after the decision, stood up and said he accepted the judge's ruling with great satisfaction and that the state would not appeal from it to a higher court. The defendant, Cerf, then said he would publish the book with an account of the proceedings (I suppose like the *édition définitive* of *Madame Bovary*) on 19 January next.

My solicitors don't understand very clearly why they were written to. No more do I. I told you I am the absolute owner of the copyright and property rights in England.

En somme, one half of the English-speaking world has given in. The

---

[1] *Finnegans Wake*, p. 156.

other half, after a few terrifying bleats from Leo Britannicus, will follow—as it always does.

I am sorry you are not coming over. Anyhow I wish you a happy Xmas and good luck in the coming year. Sincerely yours James Joyce

To Michael Healy   MS. National Library

20 December 1933   *42, rue Galilée, Paris*

My dear Mr Healy: The enclosed card, done by Lucia, is to wish you a merry Xmas and a happy New Year. I hope things will go better now after the U.S. decision. It took me about 13 years to bring it off. England will follow, as usual. Ireland scarcely matters as there is a negligible market there for anything of this kind.

I have sent you from Avignon the case of wine: Clos S. Patrice 1920. It is the oldest vineyard there and before the sojourn of the popes at Avignon what is now called *Châteauneuf du Pape* was known as *Vin de S. Patrice*. I never met an Irishman who had heard of it but I got Count O'Kelly, the Irish F.S. envoy here, and Dulanty, the High Commissioner in London, to adopt it as the wine of their legations or offices or whatever they call them. I never drink it myself as it is red and the white wine of the same *clos* is not very good.

The lees are shaken up by the voyage so the bottles should stand a few weeks in a tempered room.

I told Establet to prepay the duty and I hope he will.

Do not let Mr Greeny[1] become too affectionate with it if you invite him to taste it as I caught him several times during dinner signalling over my shoulder to an engaging young woman whom he had met in the train. Moreover, he was stopping in a hotel beside the Folies-Bergère— a nice change after the Vatican, I told him.

Well, good health to everybody, including the pope who blessed and the judges who freed my book—and ourselves. Sincerely yours

James Joyce

To Harriet Shaw Weaver   MS. British Museum

28 July 1934   *Grand Hotel Britannique, Spa, Belgique*

Dear Miss Weaver: Will you please send back the enclosed when read. I don't know what to do about the *lettrines*. I have now lost the Xmas

---

[1] A friend of Healy's from the west of Ireland.

market for the book. They meant months of work, 3 at least, apart from their value. What a softheaded idiot! If any notice of my fragment appeared in the English press in which Lucia's name is mentioned will you please send it to me. The Dutch firm was willing to do the Chaucer poem without any money from my side.

We came here a day or so ago to allow a brigade of workmen time to get in order clean, paint etc a flat which had been occupied for 20 years by the same people and to allow my wife time and space to repair her very exhausted nervous system. This place (my choice) is easily the most charming one of its kind we have ever seen but the weather is not good and, worst of all, the newsboys keep careering round the streets shouting out about 'l'Autriche'. I am afraid poor Mr Hitler-Missler will soon have few admirers in Europe apart from your nieces and my nephews, Masters W. Lewis and E. Pound.[1] My wife is making a cure of baths which, I think, will do her good. Did Léon send you a bundle of MS?[2] Indispensable for the Xmas fire.

I am still on the watch for news from the U.S. courts. I fancy they will rise on the 31 instant for the long vacation. I think the delay is a good sign.

I read of the usual terrible thunderstorms in England this summer. Thank Jupiter, we have escaped so far.

I have been working very hard and hope to get on quickly once I am in dock again.

I suppose you are as usual superior to weather conditions and in the goodest of health. With kind regards sincerely yours   JAMES JOYCE

To STANISLAUS JOYCE (Postcard)   MS. Cornell

[*Mid-August 1934*]   [*Vervins*]

Sir Arthur W.[3] was never here but the strongest of the ferruginous springs is called after him the *Duc de Fer*. We may go on to Luxembourg for a week. We are within an hour or so's train ride of Aix-la-Chapelle where Charlemagne is buried and Cologne. But I dislike going over the border even on a half-day motor coach trip. I wish everyone was as good

---

[1] The range of Pound's sympathies expanded from Mussolini to include some aspects of Hitlerism. Wyndham Lewis in 1931 published a series of articles in *Time and Tide* which were incorporated in his book *Hitler* (London, 1931). He reversed these pro-Nazi views in 1939 with two books, *The Jews, Are They Human?* (London, March 1939) and *The Hitler Cult* (London, December 1939).

[2] Of *Finnegans Wake*.

[3] Arthur Wellesley, Duke of Wellington (1769–1852), 'the Iron Duke'.

humoured and as good tempered as me and you. Don't go to Austria for your holidays whatever you do.   JIM

To GEORGE and HELEN JOYCE   MS. Kastor

28 November 1934   *Carlton Elite Hotel, Zurich*

Dear Oigroig and Neleh: Since everything's upside down I address you thusly. I have just spoken with Mrs E. Jolas of Neuilly s/ Seine who tells me she had such a nice long letter from you and that you have decided that she is to have the privilege of removing all the articles of furniture from the premises occupied by you in borough number seven of the city of Paris. She was almost frantic with delight as she babbled over the telephone, breaking into snatches of gipsy music, yodelling, clacking her heels like Argentina and cracking her fingers. It is a perfect godsend for her, poor Mrs E. Jolas. For months and months she has been going around asking everybody to give her some sort of light work such as snuffing candles or putting salt in the saltcellars, anything. But no one could help her. So she used to lie listlessly in a hammock all day and had begun to think there was no hope left. Now your wonderful letter has arrived and it has made her the happiest woman in all France today. She said to me 'Dearest J. Joyce, won't you give this little girl a great big hand?' and I replied 'Sure thing!'. You know I come of a most musical family and there is nothing I enjoy so much as running up and down six flights of stairs with a cottage piano on my shoulders. The Paris-Orleans line has run an extension up to your door and is placing 2 powerful locomotives and fourteen trucks at your disposal. Mrs E. J and myself will be as gleeful as two spoiled children. She will wear a white pinafore and a big blue sash and I cricket flannels. Have we cold feet about removals? No, sir! Do we put service before self as all good and true rotarians should? You have said it. So we're off at once.

> Goodbye, Zurich, I must leave you,
> Though it breaks my heart to shreds
>   Tat then attat.[1]
> Something tells me I am needed
> In Paree to hump the beds.
> Bump! I hear the trunks a tumbling
> And I'm frantic for the fray.

[1] Imitation of drum taps.

Farewell, *dolce far niente!*
Goodbye, Zürichsee![1]

Gruetzi, gruetzi, gruetzi mit einand![2]   Obbab[3]

(anca mi)[4]

To Alfred Bergan   MS. N.Y. Public Library (Manuscript)

20 December 1934   *Carlton Elite Hotel, Zurich*

Dear Mr Bergan, This is the only way I can invite you to drink to both our healths this Christmas so please let it pass.

We are still detained here and cannot return to Paris till after New Year. I hope you are in good health and spirits. Giorgio (my son) gave his first concert over the radio in New York a week ago[5] and he too will not be back in Paris till the Spring. MacCormack says he has a magnificent bass. How glad Pappie would have been of this. There have been voices on both sides of our family for several generations, but nobody ever really made a career out of it. McGuckin[6] used to say Pappie had the best tenor voice in Ireland in his time. You never heard him at his best. He had a voice very like that of Jean de Reszke. We used to have merry evenings in our house, used we not?

In answer to your question. No, I am not interested in Irish Sweepstake tickets. I suppose the staircases in all the hospitals in Dublin are now made of solid gold. The only decent people I ever saw at a racecourse were the horses. The late Shah of Persia when invited by King Edward to go to Goodwood replied: I know that one horse runs quicker than than [sic] another but which particular horse it is doesn't interest me.

With all good wishes to you for a merry Xmas and a happy New Year and with friendly remembrances sincerely yours   James Joyce

[1] As Stuart Gilbert points out, this is a parody of a patriotic song, 'Dolly Gray', of the same vintage as 'The Absent-Minded Beggar' referred to in *Ulysses*. The refrain ran:

> Goodbye, Dolly, I must leave you,
> Though it breaks my heart to go.
> Something tells me I am needed
> In the front to face the foe.
> Hark! I hear the bugles calling
> And I must no longer stay.
> Goodbye, Dolly, I must leave you,
> Goodbye, Dolly Gray.

[2] 'I greet you, I greet you, I greet all of you!' (In Züri Dütsch, the dialect of Zurich.)
[3] Babbo ('Daddy') reversed.   [4] 'Me [Nora Joyce] too.'
[5] For the National Broadcasting Company.
[6] Barton McGuckin (1852–1913) was the leading tenor of the Carl Rosa Opera Company. He heard John Stanislaus Joyce sing about 1875.

To LUCIA JOYCE   MS. Texas

27 April 1935   *7 rue Edmond Valentin, Paris 7ᵉ*

Cara Lucia: Ti mando qui accluse oltre 2 lire sterline. Spero che hai
ricevuto i volumi di Tolstoy. Secondo me *How Much Land Does a Man
Need* è la più grande novella che la letteratura del mondo conosce.
Amavo molto anche *Padrone e Servitore* benchè qui forse c'entri un
pochino di propaganda.

Spero che vai più piano adesso colle uova quantumque sia il cibo
classico per Pasqua. Ebbi una lettera di Helen. Sembra che siamo tutti
quanti pieni di guai. Non è colpa loro certo ma non hanno trovato quel
paese della cuccagna ch'era il lore sogno. Due piccoli dettagli sono
abbastanza divertenti se si vuole. Giorgio si lascia crescere la barba e
la tua lettera a Giorgio ha fatto un pellegrinaggio prima nel *vielgesungenes Deutschland.*[1]

Si ho letto nei giornali dell'incendio di La Plaza a Dublino.[2] La notizia
non mi ha molto commosso. Ma sembra che la signora Anna Livia non
abbia fatto il suo dovere anche se i pompieri hanno fatto il loro. Molto
fumo e poca acqua. Ma troveranno un altro edificio per continuare il
loro nobile lavoro in favore degli ospedali dublinesi ed i poveri medici,
le povere suore, i poveri ammalati ed i poveri preti consolatori di questi
ultimi. Lascia ch'io pianga.[3] È bravo, cavallo!

Ed a proposito di preti se si abbuoni alla biblioteca costì domanda
La Vita di Father Healy. Lo conobbi e credo che abbia battezzato uno
od una della mia famiglia. Era il parroco di Little Bray, frequentava
molto la corte del vicere ed era un uomo molto spiritoso.

L'angelo che regola le stagioni ha dimenticato che siamo alla vigilia
del mese di maggio perchè ci serve ogni giorno un tempo freddo, umido
ed uggioso.

Mi parli di due mascalzoni che visitano il tuo bungalow. Sono forse i
ladri che tentavano tempo fa di penetrare nel bungalow per rubare i
tesori d'arti, coffani di pezzi d'oro e stoffe preziosissime che senza dubbio
contiene. Ci sono ancora idealisti, a quanto pare, in questo mondo
cinico e spavaldo e lo sciopero dei trams ecc entra nella sua nona setti-
mana. Che fortuna per i calzolai. Non tutto il male viene per nuocere.

Dai calzolai al cuiro n'è solo un passo. Ecco perchè ti communico il

---

[1] 'Much-sung-of Germany.'

[2] A fire on 24 April that destroyed the Plaza, a building in Middle Abbey Street,
Dublin, which was the office of the Irish Hospitals Sweepstakes. At first it was reported
that the firemen were hampered by restrictions on the water supply.

[3] A line from Handel's opera *Rinaldo.*

fatto che la signora Bailly[1] è andata anche a Bray o vicino a Bray. Leggo che il consiglio municipale fa construire molte nuove case. Perbacco, si capisce!

Noi siamo abbastanza bene e speriamo che la tua salute va migliorandosi. Non cedere a momenti di malinconia. Un bel di[2] tutto si cambierà per te. E più presto di quello che non credi.

Dunque secondo te Curran è sparito. Forse si è semplicamente nascosto dietro un cespuglio. Ed hai preso il tè colla signorina Costello. Molto bene. Questo nome sembra italiano ma non lo è affatto. È una corruzione, credo, di due parole irlandesi che significano: bel piede.

Facci sapere se hai bisogna di qualche cosa, voglio dire, vestiti ecc per la stagione ventura. Il poeta Byron scrisse questi due verse a proposito:

'The English winter ending in July
To recommence in August.'

Aspettiamo sempre le tue lettere e pensiamo molto di te, sperando sempre che il tuo soggiorno costì ti faccia del bene.

Salutami la tua cugina Boschenka[3] che mi ha scritto un paio di volte e che ringrazio. Ti abbraccio   BABBO

P.S. Un certo Ulisse un dì seduto sul lido dell'isola della ninfa Calipso scrisse colla sua mazza nella rena. Mi domando se tu non abbi scritto qualle cartoline con un ombrellino giapponese imbevuto dell'acqua azzurra del golfo di Neonapoli. Ad ogni modi eccoti tre per le tue due. E bene che gli angeli ti portino questo messaggio poiche angelo in greco significa messaggero.   B.[4]

---

[1] See p. 377n.

[2] 'Un bel dì', the famous aria in Act II of Puccini's *Madama Butterfly*.

[3] Boschenka Schaurek (now Mrs Delimata), daughter of Mrs Eileen Joyce Schaurek.

[4] (Translation)

'Dear Lucia: I send you here enclosed 2 more pounds sterling. I hope you have received the volumes of Tolstoy. In my opinion *How Much Land Does a Man Need* is the greatest story that the literature of the world knows. I used to be very fond also of *Masters and Servants* even though a bit of propaganda perhaps enters into it.

I hope you are going easy now with the eggs although they are the classic food for Easter. I had a letter from Helen. It seems that we all have our troubles. It is not their fault certainly but they have not found the land of Cockaigne that was their dream. Two little details may amuse you. Giorgio has grown a beard and your letter to Giorgio made a pilgrimage first into *vielgesungenes Deutschland*.

Yes, I read in the papers about the fire in the Dublin Plaza. The news did not upset me much. But it seems to me that Dame Anna Livia did not do her duty even if the firemen did theirs. Much smoke and little water. But they will find another edifice in which to continue their noble work for the benefit of the Dublin hospitals and the poor doctors, the poor sisters, the poor sick people and the poor priests, consolers of these last. Let me weep. And cheers for the racehorse!

And talking of priests, if you subscribe to the library there ask for *The Life of Father Healy*. I knew him and I think he baptized a boy or girl in my family. He was the

To HARRIET SHAW WEAVER   MS. British Museum

1 May 1935   *7 rue Edmond Valentin, Paris 7ᵉ*

Dear Miss Weaver: I don't know whether this letter will be very legible. This morning in the street I found my sight very hazy. I made the mistake of correcting proofs for about 6 hours the other day, as I did not want to be always victimising the Jolases.

Minor matters first. I cannot or rather Léon [cannot] collect a penny from the Dutch publisher[1] who owes Lucia and myself 40,000 frs and in addition to that my American publisher seems to owe me royalties on 10,000 or 15,000 copies which he is not inclined to send over. As to the illustrations made for the U.S. edition of *Ulysses*[2] they are yours for ever and ever. Amen. If they had been signed L.J. instead of H.M.[3] people would have had a different tale to tell. I am only too painfully aware that Lucia has no future but that does not prevent me from

---

parish priest of Little Bray, used to frequent the viceroy's court and was a very witty man.

The angel who regulates the seasons has forgotten that we are on the eve of the month of May for he serves out to us every day cold, damp and cloudy weather.

You speak of two ruffians who visit your bungalow. They are perhaps the robbers who attempted some time ago to penetrate into the bungalow to steal the art treasures, caskets of gold coins and precious stuff which doubtless it contains. There are still idealists, apparently, in this cynical and rude world and the tram strike etc enters upon its ninth week. How fortunate for shoemakers. Not all ills hurt.

From shoemakers to leather is only a step. That is why I inform you that Mrs Bailly has also gone to Bray or to the neighbourhood of Bray. I read that the municipal council is building many new houses. Begob, it's understandable!

We are fairly well and hope that your health is improving. Do not give way to moments of melancholy. One fine day or other everything will change for you. And sooner than you might think.

So according to you Curran has disappeared. Perhaps he is simply hidden behind a bush. And you have had tea with Miss Costello. Very good. That name seems Italian but it is not so at all. It is a corruption, I think, of two Irish words meaning: beautiful foot.

Let us know if you need anything, that is to say, clothes etc for the coming season. The poet Byron wrote two apposite verses:

"The English winter ending in July
To recommence in August."

We always look forward to your letters and think a great deal about you, always hoping that your stay over there is doing you good.

My greetings to your cousin Boschenka who has written to me a couple of times and to whom I send thanks. I embrace you   Babbo

P.S. A certain Ulysses, seated one day on the strand of the island of the nymph Calypso, wrote with his stick on the sand. I wonder if you haven't written those cards with a Japanese parasol drenched in the blue water of the gulf of Neo Naples. Anyway here are three for your two. It's well that angels carry this message to you because in Greek angel means messenger.   B.'

[1] The Servire Press, in the Hague, which published a fragment of *Finnegans Wake* with some illustrative work by Lucia Joyce in 1934.

[2] New *de luxe* edition published by the Limited Editions Club, 1935.

[3] Henri Matisse.

seeing the difference between what is beautiful and shapely and what is ugly and shapeless. As usual I am in a minority of one. If I tell people that no tenor voice like Sullivan's has been heard in this world for 50 years or that Zaporoyetz, the Russian basso, makes Chialiapin sound like a cheap whistle or that nobody has ever written English prose that can be compared with that of a tiresome footling little Anglican parson who afterwards became a prince of the only true church[1] they listen in silence. These names mean nothing to them. And when I have stumbled out of the room no doubt they tap their foreheads and sigh.

And speaking about the bass voice in general and my son in particular he went over to America, we were told, for four months. He has been there now a year. He is at present on crutches. He sang twice over the radio to the natives who love poor old Ireland and insist that, if he is to please them, he must forget all about the unmusical countries of Europe and croon to them about *Mother Machree* and *A Little Bit of Heaven*. He has earned in all 35$. This amount he could have got in any southern French town for one performance before an audience which, however redolent of garlic, unlike the halfcastes in Covent Garden and the Metropolitan really does know the difference between a B and a bull's foot. I have sent him over tons of music. No use. They insist that he is from Erin's green isle and must sing that classical aria *Blatherskite*.

I am writing this letter because Léon tells me you were kind enough to ring him up last night for news of me. I sleep like a log, eat like a hog and people say I have *une mine superbe*. But if they could see inside the watch they would use other words. I feel like an animal which has received four thunderous mallet strokes on the top of his skull. Yet in my letters to both my children and my daughter-in-law I keep up a tone of almost gay responsibility.

As for Lucia it is not clear to me at all from your letter whether you liked her or not. And that is the only thing that matters. She did not go over to live on you as a parasite and please do not imagine that because members of my family bear my name or have some facial or vocal resemblance to me (I am not speaking of Giorgio and Lucia, of course) that there is much kinship. *Non, merci!* When I was in London in 1931 I offered my imbecile brother's idiot son a weekly salary to help me with my notes to let him know what the book is about (by the way, what is it about?) I gave him a copy of the book of essays commonly called *An Exag*. His beautiful puresouled Irish stepmother, from whose face a negro would run away in terror, threw the book in the fire and forbade him to visit me. Not one line did any of them send us after Lucia's visit

[1] Cardinal Newman.

to them. My cousin whom she also visited was over here judging cats did not think it worth her while to ring us up or to call on us. Possibly this giddy Dame is wroth with me on account of my very frigid response to her declarations of affection (utterly insincere, of course) in a taxicab here last year. She forgets or has not learnt that in this vile city wine, woman and wit are freely traded in the marketplace. Since Lucia's arrival in Ireland, apart from telegrams asking for money, we have received no news at all from my sister except a few lines sent from a hotel. Her daughters who according to Budgen are film beauty types have now taken to the pen and then there were voluminous letters from my friend Curran addressed however not to me but to my wife, the long-suffering mother, the wife of this renegade. These were not answered as my wife has made a vow to write only one letter every seventh year. But as they contained a proposal to bring Lucia to a medical gentleman who has studied psycho-analysis in the United States, I at once cabled calling that off.

After a good deal of talking I induced my wife to write to Lucia so that letters which now arrive are addressed to us both. This is a slight advance. But while I am glad in a way that Lucia is out of the dangers of Paris and especially of London every ring of the doorbell gives me an electric shock as I never know what the postman or telegraph boy is going to bring in. And if it is bad news all the blame will fall on me.

Perhaps I was too hasty in thinking you meant to throw doubt on Lucia's word. I am again in a minority of one in my opinion as everybody else apparently thinks she is crazy. She behaves like a fool very often but her mind is as clear and as unsparing as the lightning. She is a fantastic being speaking a curious abbreviated language of her own. I understand it or most of it. Before she went to London she spoke to me about you and what you had done for me. She wanted through herself to establish a final link between the dissolute being who is writing these lines and your honourable self. Then she went on to Ireland with the same idea. Whatever she may have succeeded in doing with you she will do nothing over there. How well I know the eyes with which she will be regarded! Léon is concerned for what she may do to prejudice my name there. And my wife who personally is probably worth both of her children rolled together and multiplied by three thinks that this is the chief reason for my constant state of alarm. So far as I can know myself it is not so.

So long as she was within reach I always felt I could control her—and myself. And in fact I could. But now though I have the faithful support of my wife and Léon's loyal friendship and that of some others here to say nothing of your own patience and sympathy there are moments and hours when I have nothing in my heart but rage and despair, a blind man's rage and despair.

I cannot be such an utter fool as to be inventing all this. But I can no longer control matters. On many sides I hear that I am and have been an evil influence on my children. But what are they doing away from that evil influence? On the other hand what can I honestly ask them to come back to? Paris is like myself a haughty ruin or if you like a decayed reveller. And any time I turn on the radio I hear some British politician mumbling inanities or his German cousin shouting and yelling like a madman. Perhaps Ireland and the U.S. are the safe places. And perhaps this is where the gas is really going to be turned on. Well, so be it. The motto under my coat of arms, however, is: *Mors aut honorabilis vita.*

And in addition to all this my son's Yankee Doodle doctor wants him to undergo an operation on the throat. And Mr John Allen[1] that intrepid publisher who started to print *Ulysses* last October is still at work on the title page of that work.

Here there comes the girl with two letters one from Mr Bailly[2] whose wife has also gone to Bray and the other from Lucia which I hesitate to open. So I shall arise and take them both down to Léon, if I can find a cab, that is to say, because this is a socialist holiday. However some descendant of Peter the Great may be prowling around, marauding. If there is anything in Lucia's letter I shall add a postscript.

My eyes are trebly fatigued by now as the writing of this epistle was punctuated with lachrymal stops.

What I would like to know if you are writing to me is whether you liked Lucia or not. She said she was sending me a letter she had from you but of course, scatterbrain forgot to put it in. She may be mad, of course, as all the doctors say but I do not like you to mention her in the same breath with my cousin or sister or anybody else. If she should be so mentioned then it is I who am mad. With kindest regards sincerely yours   JAMES JOYCE

To JOHN HOWLEY[3]   MS. University College, Galway

29 July 1935   *7 rue Edmond Valentin, Paris 7ᵉ*

Dear Sir: My uncle-in-law Mr Michael Healy has asked me to send

---

[1] A slip for John Lane, the Bodley Head.

[2] Réné Bailly, French industrialist. His wife was, like Mrs Joyce, from Galway City.

[3] John Howley (1866–1941), Professor of Philosophy and Librarian of University College, Galway.

you a prospectus concerning the facsimile MS edition of my booklet
Pomes Penyeach (so brought out in Paris in 1932) which I had much
pleasure in offering to your library and you the graciousness to accept.
Two other European libraries possess copies, the Bibliothèque Nationale
here and the British Museum in London. But I wished to offer a copy to
your library not only because the designer of the *lettrines* is a granddaughter of your city and the writer of the verses bears one of its tribal
names but also as a small acknowledgement of a great debt of gratitude
to Mr Healy himself for his kindness and courtesy during so many years.
Sincerely yours   JAMES JOYCE

To GEORGE JOYCE   MS. Kastor

28 October 1935   *7 rue Edmond Valentin, Parigi 7*

Caro Giorgio: Tuo nonno, quando gli si narrava un incontro come
quello tuo coll'impiegato della. N.B.C., soleva pensare alle lagrime
sparse nel grigiore dell'oliveto di Getsemani. Ma perchè proprio due
persone eleganti come tu e la mia nuora vi ostinate a voler entrare nel
palazzo del canto per la scala di servizio non mi è molto chiaro.

E non mi è molto chiaro come e cosa e quando devo scrivere. Secondo
te a macchina o forse in istampato. Secondo Helen in inglese o forse in
americano. Secondo mamma poco importa giacchè scrivo sempre 'all the
wrong things'.

> Aiutami dunque, O Musa, nitidissima Calligraphia!
> Forbisci la forma e lo stil e frena lo stilo ribelle!
> Mesci il limpido suon e distilla il liquido senso
> E sulla rena riarsa, deh!, scuoti lungo il ramo!

Ho sentito una diffusione della *Forza del Destino* con Pinza.[1] Non c'è
male, lui, voglio dire. Insomma al di sopra della media. La musica
sarebbe ideale per un numero di prestidigitatore [sic] o piuttosto di
orsacchiotti danzanti. Ho visto una pellicola irlandese *Lily of Killarney*
basata sull'opera.[2] Sta a sentire. L'azione si svolge nel 1828. Ebbene i
personaggi fumano sigarette, telefonano (in piena campagna irlandese)
cantano *Father O'Flynn* (composta 60 anni più tardi da Villiers
Stanford) il tenore canta la musica del baritono, i gendarmi sono
vestiti alla foggia delle nuove guardie irlandesi. Roba da chiodi!

---

[1] Ezio Pinza.

[2] A film version of the opera by Sir Julius Benedict, which in turn was based upon
Dion Boucicault's play *The Colleen Bawn*, itself an adaptation of Gerald Griffin's novel
The Collegians (1829).

Quei due Zukovich (?)[1] e l'altro[2] mi propongono Laughton[3] per *Ulisse* se approvo. Mi sembra troppo 'ariano'. Andrò a vedere Arliss[4] che fu, dicono, un buon Disraeli. E la tua voce che fa? E Stevie come sta. Di a Helen che siamo contenti ch'ella sta bene di nuovo e suo padre pure. Tante belle cose a tutti quanti. Ti abbraccio   Babbo[5]

To Alfred Bergan   MS. N.Y. Public Library (Manuscript)

21 December 1935   *7 rue Edmond Valentin, Paris 7ᵉ*

Dear Mr Bergan: I hope this finds you hale and hearty and as I cannot easily manage to drink to both our good lucks at this distance perhaps the enclosed may solve the problem. These are such mad times in the world that it is probably the best thing to do.

I don't suppose there is any left now of my father's friends except you and Mr Devan. If you ever see him please remember me to him.

As you will see I have changed my address here and have been busy putting new frames round the portraits of Messieurs my ancestors.

---

[1] Louis Zukofsky (b. 1904), American poet.

[2] S. J. Reisman. He and Zukofsky had done a film script of *Ulysses*.

[3] Charles Laughton (1899–1962), English actor.

[4] George Arliss (1868–1946), English Jewish actor who played the title role in the film *Disraeli* (1929).

[5] (Translation)

'Dear Giorgio: Your grandfather, when someone told him of a meeting like the one you had with that N.B.C. official, used to be reminded of the tears shed in the garden of olives of Gethsemane. But whyever two elegant people like you and my daughter-in-law persist in wanting to enter the palace of song by the service stairs is not altogether clear to me.

And how and what and when and how much I ought to write to you is not altogether clear to me either. According to you, on a typewriter or perhaps in print. According to Helen in English or perhaps in American. According to Mama it doesn't matter because I always write "all the wrong things".

Aid me then, O Muse, resplendent Calligraphia!
Supply the form and style, and curb the rebellious pen!
Pour out limpid sound and distill the liquid sense.
And over the parched sand, pray, extend your branch!

I heard a broadcast of the *Forza del Destino* with Pinza. Pretty good, I mean he was. On the whole, above average. The music would be ideal for a prestidigitator or for little dancing bears. I saw an Irish film in London *Lily of Killarney* based on the opera. Listen. The action takes place in 1828. Well, the characters smoke cigarettes, telephone (in the heart of the Irish countryside), sing *Father O'Flynn* (composed 60 years later by Villiers Stanford) the tenor sings the baritone role, the policemen are dressed after the style of the new Irish guards. Rubbish!

These two Zukovich (?) and the other are proposing Laughton for *Ulysses* if I think well. He seems too "Aryan" to me. I am going to see Arliss who was, they say, a good Disraeli. And how is your voice coming along? How is Stevie? Tell Helen we are glad she is well again and her father too. Good wishes to everybody. I embrace you

Babbo'

These worthy people are seeing quite a lot of Europe and they look at one another in a way that suggests: Where next?

I hope you will pass a very merry Christmas and that you will lift your glass to old times, as I shall do. And I wish you also good health and all happiness in the coming year. Sincerely yours   JAMES JOYCE

To HARRIET SHAW WEAVER   MS. British Museum

9 June 1936   *7 rue Edmond Valentin, Paris 7ᵉ*

Dear Miss Weaver: My brother, expelled from Italy, is due here on the 16 inst, with or without his wife and bulldog.[1] My son has to remain in bed or on a couch for 4 or 5 months. My daughter is in a madhouse where I hear she fell off a tree. I have to pay the following bills immediately if not sooner:

Dr Welti (surgeon)   6000
Dr Garnier (assistant)   1000
Dr Fawcett (assistant
   to Dr Fontaine)   500
Dr Rossi (locum of Dr
   Islandsky   1000
Dr Delmas (Keeper
   of the madhouse)   2700
= 1 month's board and 2 intemperometrical blood tests)

I paid already the American Hosp. fee and the surgeon Dr Bone who operated me.

The reason I have to pay Drs Welti and Garnier and the reason I already paid (2000 frs) to the Clinique at Asniers where my son was operated is that my son asked me to do so.

I also paid prof. Agadjarian 1700 frs.

After these payments there will remain outstanding only Dr Islandsky and whatever is still due to Dr Macdonald.

I believe I can cover most of the expenses of publication of my daughter's alphabet.[2] My idea is not to persuade her that she is a Cézanne but that on her 29th birthday in the aforesaid madhouse she may see something to persuade her that her whole past has not been a failure. The reason I keep on trying by every means to find a solution for her case (which may come at any time as it did with my eyes) is that

[1] In the end Stanislaus Joyce did not come to Paris, but he and his brother met in Switzerland in September 1936.

[2] *A Chaucer A. B. C.*, with initial letters by Lucia Joyce, was published with a preface by Louis Gillet in July 1936 by the Obelisk Press in Paris.

she may not think that she is left with a blank future as well. I am aware that I am blamed by everybody for sacrificing that precious metal money to such an extent for such a purpose when it could be all done so cheaply and quietly by locking her up in an economical mental prison for the rest of her life.

I will not do so as long as I see a single chance of hope for her recovery, nor blame her or punish her for the great crime she has committed in being a victim to one of the most elusive diseases known to man and unknown to medicine. And I imagine that if you were where she is and felt as she must you would perhaps feel some hope if you felt that you were neither abandoned nor forgotten.

Some mysterious malady has been creeping over both my children (the doctors are inclined to trace it back to our residence in Switzerland during the war) and if they have not succeeded in doing anything for themselves it is to blame, not they. My daughter's case is far the worse of the two though how my son was able to do even as much as he did with his voice in the U.S. in such a state as he was (he could not lift a cup often from the table much less control his vocal chords) is also a mystery to me.

Léon says I am to write this letter. Very rightly. I suppose. He does not wish to be blamed for having been a complacent party to my financial suicide. I like writing it just as much as you will like reading it.

For several years he has been asking me insistently to write a letter of explanation to the British Trustee, begging His Excellency to allow me, who am known to all as a wholesale squanderer, to cash some moneys, entrusted to him for the education of my children. I never met him and I don't know who he is or what he has to do with my two children and I do not intend to write him any letter black or white on the subject. Blockhead as he probably is he might well be excused for wondering why I should now be needing this money for the education of Giorgio aged 31 and father of a son aged $4\frac{1}{2}$ and Lucia aged 29.

If you have ruined yourself for me as seems highly probable why will you blame me if I ruin myself for my daughter? Of what use will any sum or provision be to her if she is allowed, by the neglect of others calling itself prudence, to fall into the abyss of insanity? It is useless to blame the doctors either.

I hate writing these letters. That is why I gave it up almost in despair. But since I have to pay these doctors somebody has to write it. With kindest regards sincerely yours   James Joyce

To Sean O'Faolain[1]   MS. Ellmann

16 July 1936   *7 rue Edmond Valentin, Paris 7ᵉ*

Dear Sir: A bird alone—a pretty grey finch at present in a cage—flew
into our flat through an open window yesterday morning. Perhaps he
was scared and sought refuge from the air squadrons then over the city
or perhaps he came from Wicklow to remind me that I had not acknowledged receipt of your book. This I do now with thanks.

I am afraid, however, that I cannot be of any real service to you. I
never write for any journal or periodical and I have not read a novel in
any language for very many years so that my opinion is quite worthless.
I buy them sometimes when [I] know the writer personally. Nevertheless, I shall take your book away with me when I go away on my holidays
next month.

It was very kind of you to send me the book. Sincerely yours

JAMES JOYCE

To Stephen Joyce   MS. Stephen Joyce

10 August 1936   *Villers s/Mer*

My dear Stevie: I sent you a little cat filled with sweets a few days ago
but perhaps you do not know the story about the cat of Beaugency.

Beaugency is a tiny old town on a bank of the Loire, France's longest
river. It is also a very wide river, for France, at least. At Beaugency it is
so wide that if you wanted to cross it from one bank to the other you
would have to take at least one thousand steps.

Long ago the people of Beaugency, when they wanted to cross it, had
to go in a boat for there was no bridge. And they could not make one
for themselves or pay anybody else to make one. So what were they to
do?

The Devil, who is always reading the newspapers, heard about this
sad state of theirs so he dressed himself and came to call on the lord
mayor of Beaugency, who was named Monsieur Alfred Byrne. This
lord mayor was very fond of dressing himself too. He wore a scarlet robe
and always had a great golden chain round his neck even when he was
fast asleep in bed with his knees in his mouth.

The devil told the lord mayor what he had read in the newspaper and
said he could make a bridge for the people of Beaugency so that they

---

[1] Sean O'Faolain (b. 1900), the Irish novelist, short-story writer, and critic, had sent
Joyce his new novel, *Bird Alone* (London and New York, 1936).

could cross the river as often as they wished. He said he could make as good a bridge as was ever made, and make it in one single night. The lord mayor asked him how much money he wanted for making such a bridge. No money at all, said the Devil, all I ask is that the first person who crosses the bridge shall belong to me. Good, said the lord mayor.

The night came down, all the people in Beaugency went to bed and slept. The morning came. And when they put their heads out of their windows they cried: O Loire, what a fine bridge! For they saw a fine strong stone bridge thrown across the wide river.

All the people ran down to the head of the bridge and looked across it. There was the devil, standing at the other side of the bridge, waiting for the first person who should cross it. But nobody dared to cross it for fear of the devil.

Then there was a sound of bugles—that was a sign for the people to be silent—and the lord mayor M. Alfred Byrne appeared in his great scarlet robe and wearing his heavy golden chain round his neck. He had a bucket of water in one hand and under his arm—the other arm—he carried a cat.

The devil stopped dancing when he saw him from the other side of the bridge and put up his long spyglass. All the people whispered to one another and the cat looked up at the lord mayor because in the town of Beaugency it was allowed that a cat should look at a lord mayor. When he was tired of looking at the lord mayor (because even a cat grows tired of looking at a lord mayor) he began to play with the lord mayor's heavy golden chain.

When the lord mayor came to the head of the bridge every man held his breath and every woman held her tongue. The lord mayor put the cat down on the bridge and, quick as a thought, splash! he emptied the whole bucket of water over it. The cat who was now between the devil and the bucket of water made up his mind quite as quickly and ran with his ears back across the bridge and into the devil's arms.

The devil was as angry as the devil himself.

Messieurs les Balgentiens, he shouted across the bridge, vous n'êtes pas de belles gens du tout! Vous n'êtes que des chats! And he said to the cat: Viens ici, mon petit chat! Tu as peur, mon petit chou-chat? Tu as froid, mon pau petit chou-chat? Viens ici, le diable t'emporte! On va se chauffer tous les deux.

And off he went with the cat.

And since that time the people of that town are called 'les chats de Beaugency'.

But the bridge is there still and there are boys walking and riding and playing upon it.

I hope you will like this story.   Nonno

P.S. The devil mostly speaks a language of his own called Bellsybabble which he makes up himself as he goes along but when he is very angry he can speak quite bad French very well though some who have heard him say that he has a strong Dublin accent.

To John Sullivan (Postcard)   MS. Texas

26 August 1936   *Elsinore, Denmark*

Greetings from the place which inspired Ambroise Thomas[1]

JAMES JOYCE

To Alfred Bergan   MS. N.Y. Public Library (Manuscript)

25 May 1937   *7 rue Edmond Valentin, Paris 7ᵉ*

Dear Mr Bergan: I am so sorry to hear your bad news that our old friend Mr Devin[2] is gone. Only on Wednesday last I gave his name to a young American writer who is doing my biography and has gone to Dublin, Mr Herbert Gorman. I told him to see you and Mr Devin as you were the only people still left (as I thought) who could remember all the pleasant nights we used to have singing. Mr Devin's song was 'O boys, keep away from the girls I say'. The moral of it fell on deaf ears in my case and I dont think it meant very much to him either. He used to play the *Intermezzo* from *Cavalleria Rusticana*—a version of his own and would have been a fine pianist if he had studied as he had a very agreeable touch on the keys. He used to collapse with laughter after a preliminary scream in a high tone at certain sallies of my father's. He must have been a fine looking fellow when he was young and he had charming manners. He comes into Ulysses under the name of 'Mr Power' and also into 'Dubliners'. I regret that my friend (who, by the way, is staying quite close to you at the Royal Hibernian Hotel) did not meet him and talk with him. He has letters to and from a number of literary people in Dublin. Many of them are very fair written too and one or two more than that but they never meant much to me personally and mean less now.

[1] The reference is to their standing joke that Ambroise Thomas's opera *Hamlet* (1868) had been Shakespeare's source for his play of the same name.
[2] See p. 40n.

The Lord knows whether you will be able to pick the Kersse-McCann story[1] out of my crazy tale. It was a great story of my fathers and I'm sure if they get a copy of *transition* in the shades his comment will be 'Well, he can't tell that story as I used to and that's one sure five!'

I hope you are well and send you all good and friendly greetings sincerely yours   James Joyce

To C. P. Curran   MS. Curran

14 July 1937   *7 rue Edmond Valentin, Paris 7*

Dear Curran: Don't be alarmed by this bloody letter and the five heads [of] France on the envelope.[2] My pen is charged with gore because the work on the proofs of Pts I & III of *W i P* is now so involved that I have to recur to my old habit of coloured inks and pencil and the stamp is intended to help les chômeurs intellectuels. In fact I am treading this winepress all alone though of the Currans there is one with me[3] and as today is S. Bastille I am sending you the twelve apostles; each of whom is named Patrick and is a bottle unto himself. Wine from the royal Pope will cross the ocean green better at present than Spanish ale[4] which is reported to be rather heady.

I was greatly pleased by your kind present but why the date 1935? For years I have been trying to get any of E.H.'s libretti[5] for pantomime. Perhaps you will find one some day. Especially *Turko the Terrible.* My father's old friend R. J. Thornton ('Tom Kernan')[6] used to tell me about Giuglini flying his big kite on Sandymount strand when he was a boy. He went mad some years later. Dubliners put him above Mario even as a tenor. Selskar Gunn[7] (without an 'e') used to come with us to the opera to hear Sullivan. He is the son of Michael Gunn.[8] The brother James was a good friend of my father's and they used to listen at the

[1] Joyce retells in *Finnegans Wake* (pp. 309–31) his father's story about a hunchbacked Norwegian captain who ordered a suit from a Dublin tailor named Kerse. When it was made, the captain complained that it did not fit, and the tailor said no one could make a suit that would fit him. Philip McCann, Joyce's godfather, was evidently the source of the story. These pages were in *transition 26* (February 1937), 35–52.

[2] The envelope had five stamps depicting Anatole France. This letter is in red ink; hence the epithet 'bloody'.

[3] Miss Elizabeth Curran (daughter) was then in Paris.

[4] A reference to Mangan's 'My Dark Rosaleen'.

[5] Edwin Hamilton (1849–1919) wrote the libretti of several pantomimes, one of them *Turko the Terrible*, mentioned in *Ulysses.*

[6] Character in *Ulysses.*

[7] Selskar Gunn (1883–1944), an authority on public health and an officer of the Rockefeller Foundation.

[8] Michael Gunn built and managed the Gaiety Theatre in Dublin.

back of the darkened theatre sometimes when Tietjens and Trebelli[1] were rehearsing. He told me his sister Haidée had drawn his attention to the many allusions to her father and mother ('Bessie Sudlow')[2] in *W. i. P.*.

Gorman and Mrs Gorman had dinner with me a few nights ago. I had not met him since his return. I asked him had anybody mentioned Sullivan. No. Or opera, No. Or singing. Not a word. Ichabod.

He said he had a grand time in Eire but at Clongowes it seems the password was 'O, breathe not his name'. Surely this was an excess of prudence on your part. However, I leave it to you, as the man with the hump said to his son.

By way of Clongowes Fr Conmee used to say my letters home were like grocer's lists. *Sono sempre quello.* For I am sending you another £2 & ten 10/– and I would like you to exhaust the amount in the purchase of all the songs available by French, Ashcroft, Wheatley and Vousden[3] and when the £2 ½ is finished let me know and I will remit more. I should like these soon. I know most of them but want them, if possible, in low keys. Who is the Val. Vousden whose name I sometimes see. A grandson? I remember the old man. The last time I saw him was making a patriarchal entry into the Black Maria outside Store Street. He had a long white beard, typifying the wisdom of the morning after.

Also at what price can I buy last year's *Dublin Directory* and *Who's Who*. If I order them from here they will charge me full rates which is absurd as old Casey[4] used to say.

Some doctors and people who saw Lucia lately agree that she is much better than 2½ years ago. What a dreadful trial to be laid on any girl's shoulders! I had arranged for her to go out on a motor ride today but there's the rain in bucketfulls! *Pas de chance!* The 26th is her birthday. Will you please send her a message (*not* a present, it's too complicated with the customs). Maison de Sante Dr Delmas, 23 rue de la Marie, Ivry s/Seine. She will be delighted to see that people remember her. I mean just a word from Mrs Curran and yourself. *Merci d'avance.*

I met Gillet for a moment in the vestibule at the opera—the ballets, it was rotten and no good, the English. I had not time to talk to him as he wanted to. He enjoyed his stay greatly and then added: I also saw

[1] Curran writes: 'Tietjens was a superb soprano. Her genius as a singer was equalled by her warm heart and both made her a Dublin idol. She sang first in Dublin in 1857 . . . and her connection with Dublin lasted 15 years and more.' When Gounod's *Faust* was first performed in Dublin (1863) Trebelli sang Siebel to Tietjens' Marguerite.

[2] Bessie Sudlow, a popular and charming actress, then Mrs Michael Gunn, played such parts as Lady Teazle and Ariel.

[3] Dublin music-hall singers.

[4] Joe Casey, Irish patriot whom Joyce met in Paris in 1902.

the president. A look of anguish and distraction came over his operatic countenance (he was to have been a deep bass, trained for the stage) and having said his line he went out into the night.

The money is in another envelope. When are you coming to Paname?[1] I want to know the exact date if possible. I want to meet you. I hope Mrs. Curran and Miss Curran are well. And also your loyal self.

Raining greetings to A.L.P. sincerely yours   JAMES JOYCE

To DAVID FLEISCHMAN[2]   MS. Fleischman

8 August 1937   *7 rue Edmond Valentin, Paris 7ᵉ*

Dear David: If your mother has had more quieting news from New York and if you can find an evening hour in this blistering heat cooled off by *imber serotinus*[3] I should be much obliged if you could do me a favour.

I have sent you registered a book[4] you certainly will have read as a young boy, probably more than once. I need to know something about it. I never read it and have nobody to read it to me and it takes too much time with all I am doing. Could you perhaps refresh your memory by a hasty glance through and then dictate to your mother (who, I hope, will buy me a bunch of new ribbons to spry up—her typewriter) an account of the plot in general as if it were a new book the tale of which you had to narrate in a book review. After that I should like you to mark with blue pencil in the margin the most important passages of the plot itself and in red pencil here and there wherever the words or dialogue seem to call for the special attention of a European. Don't care about spoiling the book. It is a cheap edition. If you can then return it to me soon I shall try to use whatever bears upon what I am doing.

Many thanks in advance but if for any reason you cannot do this it will be no great loss.

The heat is abominable. I hope you all, especially Stevie,[5] keep out of the sight of that monotonous old gasometer,[6] the sun. Sincerely yours

                                                      JAMES JOYCE

[1] Slang for 'Paris'.

[2] David Fleischman (b. 1919), George Joyce's stepson, the son of Helen Fleischman (Joyce) and Leon Fleischman.

[3] 'Evening rain', a phrase from the Vulgate, Deuteronomy 11.14.

[4] Mark Twain, *Huckleberry Finn*. There are scattered references to this book in *Finnegans Wake*. See Adaline Glasheen, *A Census of Finnegans Wake* (Evanston, Ill. and London, 1956), p. 38, and the *Finnegans Wake* holograph notebook VI. B.46 at Buffalo, which contains material based on David Fleischman's work.

[5] Stephen James Joyce.   [6] *Finnegans Wake*, pp. 95, 131.

To Frank Budgen   MS. Yale

9 September 1937   *Grand Hôtel, Dieppe*

Dear Budgen: Many thanks. Just what I want.[1] Have used a lot of it.
The encounter between my father and a tramp (the basis of my book)
actually took place at that part of the park. I went to the Br. Consulate
and with the official consulted Lloyds Register 1935. No trace of that
phantom ship.[2] Could you trace her. I hope you noted, by the way, the
tayleren's Christian name.[3] But one or two questions I mean till you
send back the book marked, which do, but registered to Paul Léon,
27 rue Casimir-Perier, Paris, 7*e*.

What is Devereux's Christian name also Sturk's?

Her name Lilia or Lilian?

Is Archer (Dangerfield) an Irishman?

In what chapter is Sturk's dream of recognition? This point is a fine
one, I think, since he saw the deed in a half dream.

Why does Archer go back to Chapelizod and put his head in the noose?

Yes. I know that sickening thud. But keep on, Bruce, saith the
spider. What is the book called? I should subscribe to the Verdant One.[4]

Sincerely yours   James Joyce

To Ezra Pound   Rachewiltz Trust

12 November 1937   *7 rue Edmond Valentin, Paris*

Dear Pound: Perhaps you have had a letter by now from Mrs Dyer.[5]
When I spoke with her some days ago she said she would write to you.
It seems she has published only 12 of the 22 Purcell sonatas (if that
is what they are) but is doing the rest and some music by Bartok. She
said she would send you 5 or 6 of them. I am supposed to go to visit
her press one of these days and I shall mention the radio. But surely she
has thought of this herself? Is any of this music vocal and for a low
voice? If so perhaps Giorgio could sing it over the radio. He will broad-

---

[1] Budgen's notes on J. Sheridan Le Fanu, *The House by the Churchyard* (1863).

[2] Joyce had been sent a throwaway which runs: 'Dublin Tenders Limited / 3 hour
coastal cruise on board / pleasure steamer / JOHN JOYCE / sailing from Victoria
Wharf, Dun Laoghaire / (weather and other circumstances permitting).' A list of sailing
dates and hours follows; the cruises took place from 17 August to 25 August 1937, and
the fares were two shillings for adults, sixpence for children. On the back of a copy he
gave Stuart Gilbert, Joyce wrote: 'This extraordinary advt reached me from Dublin.
I had it copied. Qu'est-ce que ça veut dire?' For the ship's history see *Letters* III, 404.

[3] An obscure reference to *Finnegans Wake*, p. 311.

[4] *Tit Bits*, which had a bright green cover.

[5] Mrs Louise B. M. Dyer, Australian patron of music.

cast from Poste Parisien on Tuesday next at 7.45 but of course he had to sing what they chose to start with. I shall mention this when I see her. She is a wealthy Australian who has published a large edition of Couperin's music. I tried to interest her in a performance of *Norma* at the old Roman theatre of Orange (the ideal opera for such a theatre) with a fellow countrywoman of her own, Marjorie Lawrence [(]of the Paris opera) in the name part, Sullivan as Pollione and Carducci (you may have met him at my house) to conduct. The plan fell through. I think the part was too hard for la Lawrence and in any case Mrs Dyer went to the Antipodes. So that was that.

If you wish me to try anything else for Purcell and yourself I shall do so with great animation.

Could you give me a word of introduction to Gerhart Hauptmann? When I was a boy in Dublin I made a translation (!) of his *Michael Kramer*, a play which I still admire greatly. Perhaps he would do me the honour and pleasure of signing it—his text, I mean, in book form not my well meant atrocity which some U.S. buyer obtained by stealth, I suppose, from some admiring relation of mine in the old town. He is, or was, a neighbour of yours and I think you told me you knew him. Cordialement votre JAMES JOYCE

To GEORGE and HELEN JOYCE MS. Kastor

12 January 1938 noon *Paris*

Dear Giorgio and Helen: Your N.Y. cable came this morning. We are glad to hear you are all well and hope you had not a bad crossing.[1] No specially bad weather was announced in the press. We hope, Helen, you found your father in better state and on the way to a recovery which will render an operation unnecessary. Your first letter, however, will give us fuller news and we hope better news though today's is not bad.

Nino Frank dined with us on Sunday. According to him the Luxembourg people[2] would like to engage Giorgio's voice definitely, that is, for a certain number of broadcasts each month. So he seems to have made an excellent impression. I have sent them a reminder this morning that I am still waiting for the disc. Lord Carlow[3] was here yesterday with the sheets for me to sign.[4] He got Giorgio's letter. I gave him the

[1] George and Helen Joyce went to the United States, because of her father's illness, at the end of December 1937. They returned on 26 April 1938.

[2] Radio Luxemburg.

[3] George Lionel Seymour, Viscount Carlow (1907–44), founded the Corvinus Press in 1936.

[4] The first 25 copies of *Storiella as She is Syung* were signed by Joyce in the colophon. The whole edition consisted of 175 copies.

N. Y. Herald for the B.B.C. people and sent it also to Dulanty and the
Luxembourg station. Mrs Jolas came back on Sunday. Jolas is in
Zurich. I hope the winter is not too severe over there. I have not much
news. I am rather tired as I worked very late but will add a postscript
when I come back before this is mailed. We are going to the hospital
to see Beckett.[1] I send you two bundles of papers.

P.S. 2 p.m. Siamo tornati dall'ospedale. Oramai egli è fuori di pericolo.
La stilettata era al di sopra del cuore. Questo è illeso, i polmoni anche
ma c'è una perforazione della pleura, l'involucro circondante la pleura.
La casa mia il giorno dopo la tua partenza era come la borsa, telefonate
da ogni dove. Si saprà più di quest'affare quando sarà portato al
tribunale. La polizia arrestò l'aggreditore ieri l'altro. La ferita non
lascerà tracce pregiudiziali, dice il dott. Farvert che rimpiazza la
Fontaine in quell'ospedale. Beckett l'ha scappata bella. Non avevo
torto dunque d'allarmarmi quando appresi che aveva fatto una nottata
fuori dell'albergo. Sua madre e suo fratello giunsero qui tre giorni fa col
velivolo. Ho visto lui ma non lei. Insomma di quei due spromessi sposi[2]
ambedue, cioè ed Enzo e Lucia, sono ora all'ospedale. Buona fortuna
costì Ti abbraccio   BABBO[3]

From PAUL LÉON to FRANK BUDGEN   TS. Budgen
(Largely dictated by Joyce)

?29 January 1938   *Paris*

Late spring three years ago J.J. coming back from Z'ch after a second
visit to Vogt—sight may be a little better.

[1] Samuel Beckett was gratuitously stabbed in Paris, and refused to prosecute his
assailant.
[2] A play on the Italian classic novel, Alessandro Manzoni, *I Promessi Sposi* (1825–6),
and on the fact that the young woman in the book is named Lucia. The young man is
Renzo.
[3] (Translation)
   'P.S. 2 p.m. We are back from the hospital, he is now out of danger. The stab was
above the heart; that is uninjured, and the lungs also, but there is a perforation of
the pleura, the layer of tissue surrounding the pleura. My house on the day after your
departure was like the stock exchange, telephone calls from everywhere. We will know
more about the affair when it goes to court. The police arrested the assailant the day
before yesterday. The wound will not leave any harmful aftereffects, according to
Dr Farvert who took Dr Fontaine's place at the hospital. Beckett has had a lucky
escape. I had good reason to be alarmed when I heard he had spent the night away
from his hotel. His mother and brother arrived here three days ago by airplane. I have
seen him but not her. So, as for these two unbetrothed lovers, both, to wit Enzo and
Lucia, are now in the hospital. Good luck there I embrace you   Babbo'

Concert of Volpi heard. Also much talk about a performance of William
Tell with Volpi in the part of Arnold. Conversations with Sullivan
establish that Volpi had the entire score cut by some half of it and the
key lowered by a half note. This Volpi performance is narrated with all
sorts of compliments in the N.Y. Herald (Paris edition) by their official
musical critic (M. Louis Schneider). Immediately a letter is written to
him containing a wager by Sullivan to let him and Volpi sing both the
part of Arnold in the original score in any concert hall—the arbiter to
be Mr. Schneider—and the stakes to be a copy of the original full score
nicely bound. Naturally no reply from either Schneider or Volpi (considering Schneider had written that nobody at present could sing the
part of Arnold as had been done by Volpi).

A week later—performance of Guillaume Tell with Sullivan. Sitting in
the fifth row right aisle next to the passage your obedient servant next
to him J.J. next to him, Mrs. Léon and next to her Mrs. J—somewhere
in the stalls an Irish Miss correspondent of some paper, and a gentleman
correspondent of the Neue Züricher Zeitung.

First and second act pass with great applause, J.J. being greatly
enthused. Third act where there is no Sullivan on the stage spent in the
buffet.

Fourth Act after the Aria 'Asile héréditaire' sung with great brio and
real feeling by S. applause interminable. J.J. excited to the extreme
shouts 'Bravo Sullivan—Merde pour Lauri Volpi'. The abonnés (this
being I believe a Friday) rather astonished, one of them saying: Il va
un peu fort celui-là.

Half an hour later: at the Café de la Paix. Great conversation in which
S. joins after he has changed clothes. At the moment of parting the
Neue Züricher Zeitung correspondent having been talked to all evening
about music approaches J.J. with the following words:

The Correspondent: Thank you so much for the delightful evening. I
have some pull with my paper and should you wish I could arrange for
an article or two by you to appear there about your Paris impressions:
J.J.: Many thanks but I never write for the newspapers.
The Correspondent: Oh! I see you are simply a musical critic.

Next day article in the press. M. J.J. returned from Z'ch after a
successful operation goes with friends to the Opera to hear his compatriot S. sing William Tell. Sitting in a box. After the fourth act aria

he takes off his spectacles and is heard saying 'Thank God I have recovered my eyesight'.[1]

To FERDINAND PRIOR[2]   MS. Budtz-Jørgensen

29 May 1938[3]   *7 rue Edmond Valentin, Paris 7ᵉ*

Bedste Herre: Jeg har modtaget Deres venlige Brev af 17de denne Maaned samt ved den uventede Gave 'Danske in Paris'. Bogen er yderst smukke og meget interessant for mig. Som de vistnok ved allerede er mit Fødselssted Dublin en norsk By og vi har haft et Danske komplette Hus[4] i vor Hovedstad gennem flere Aarhundreder endog efter Klontarfsslaget. Vore Dublinerne ere temmelig naesevise og betragter også idag Danskerne og Normaendene blot som Barbarer, Klosterplynderer o. s. v., men de 'sorthårige Fremmede' (som vi naevner dem 'Dubhgall') have grundlaeggede den første Byencivilisation i den grønne ø.

Jeg har uheldigvis gjørt kun et korte Besøg i Danmark to eller tre Åre siden, når jeg var, som synger min Ven Kai Friss Møller 'i Lysets Land kun seldvinbuden Gaest'.[5] Tvivlets vilde De finde mit 'Dansk' lidt traettende og måske umulig at forstå. Jeg beder om Onskyld. Jeg kjender Sproget, men har i alle Tilfaelde intet Øvelse deri her i Paris. Modtag de hjaerteligste Hilsener og med aerbødigste Tak end al mere for Deres Godhed jeg har den Aere at tegne mig Deres hengivne

JAMES JOYCE[6]

---

[1] Joyce was telescoping two incidents: (1) his taking off his bandages and crying out that he had recovered his sight; and (2) his shouting 'Bravo Sullivan—Merde pour Lauri Volpi'. By this time he apparently wished the former to be considered a journalistic invention, but his correspondence in 1930 indicates it was a carefully planned manoeuvre. See III, 198–9.

[2] Ferdinand Prior (1868–1948), Danish Consul-General in Paris from 1919 to 1933. A banker, he translated Kierkegaard into French.

[3] The texts of this letter and the following one are taken from an article by Jørgen Budtz-Jørgensen, 'To Breve paa Dansk fra James Joyce', in the Copenhagen newspaper *Nationaltidende* (12 May 1953), 8, with slight corrections based on photostatic copies of the letters. Joyce's Danish is imperfect but comprehensible.

[4] Christ Church Cathedral, much remodelled since the Danes founded it.

[5] Kai Friis Møller, *Indskrifter* (Copenhagen, 1920), p. 9. The line quoted is also the poem's title.

[6] (Translation by Jens Nyholm)

'Dear Sir: I have received your kind letter of the 17th of this month, together with the unexpected gift, *The Danes in Paris*. The book is extremely handsome and interests me very much. Perhaps you are aware that my birthplace, Dublin, is a Norwegian city and that we have had a complete Danish house in our capital for several centuries, that is, since the battle of Clontarf. Our Dubliners are rather impertinent and even today they consider the Danes and Norwegians to be just barbarians, plunderers of monasteries, etc., but the "black-haired foreigners" (as we call them, "Dubhgalls") founded the first city civilization on the green island. I have unfortunately made only

To Ferdinand Prior   MS. Budtz-Jørgensen

30 May 1938   *Paris*

P.S. Jeg har skrevet så hurtig igår iaftes at jeg har glemt at sige at jeg
har bedt Fru Jolas at hun skulde sende Dem en Exemplar af *transition*
(det toogtyvende jeg tro)[1] hvori findes et Kapitel af min nuvaerende
Vaerk (Helten er en Vikingkjaempe), hertil naevnte 'Work in Progress'
fordi det indeholder den viderunderlige Eventyr af Skraederen fra
Dublin og Sømanden fra Norge. Men Fanden alene ved hvis De vilde
kunne forstå hvad Fortaellingen mener eller overhovedet hvad betyder
dette hele Ordspindelvaev!

Engang igien mange Tak   J.J.[2]

To Daniel Brody   MS. Brody

16 June 1938 Bloomsday   *Paris*

Dear Mr Bródy: Thanks for your good wishes on this day which you
never forget. My book—on which I am working all day and all night as
well—is to be published by Faber and Faber (London) and the Viking
Press (New York). I am glad to know you are safe and well. Glad also to
be able to tell in an anniversary message that last evening my friend in
the French F.O. rang up to say that permission for H. Broch[3] to enter
France had been telegraphed to the French C.G. in Vienna. I am trying
to get two other people into America and hope I shall succeed.

With best wishes to Mrs Brody and yourself sincerely yours

JAMES JOYCE

---

one brief visit to Denmark two or three years ago, when I was, as my friend Kai Friis
Møller sings, "a self-invited guest in the land of light." Doubtless you will find my
"Danish" a bit tiring and perhaps impossible to comprehend. Please excuse it. I know
the language but have had no practice in it here in Paris. Please accept my cordial
greetings and my respectful thanks for your kindness. I have the honour to sign
myself sincerely yours   James Joyce'

[1] A slip for *transition 26* (February 1937), 109–29 (*Finnegans Wake*, pp. 309–31).

[2] (Translation)

'P.S. I wrote so hurriedly last night that I forgot to tell you I had asked Mrs Jolas
to send you a copy of *transition* (22 I think), which contains a chapter from my
present work (the hero is a Viking giant), up to now entitled *Work in Progress*, because
it contains the wonderful story of the tailor from Dublin and the sailor from Norway.
But the devil knows whether you will be able to understand what the story means or
what this entire wordspiderweb is about.

Once more, many thanks   J.J.'

[3] Hermann Broch (1886–1951), Austrian novelist and critic. He was author of *James
Joyce und die Gegenwart* (Vienna, Leipzig, Zurich, 1936). Broch and Daniel Brody were
both obliged to emigrate because of being Jewish.

To LIVIA SVEVO[1]   MS. Texas

[*1 January 1939*] *1938–39*   *Parigi*

Gentile Signora: Finalmente ho finito di finire il mio libro. Sono già tre
lustri che pettino e ripettino la chioma di Anna Livia. E ora che
s'avanzi alla ribalta. Spero che Berenice intercederà per la sua piccola
consorella affinchè trovi in questo vasto mondo, per la grazia delle dee,
'almeno un Deo Gratias qualunque'.[2]

    Buon Natale e Buon Anno a Lei ed ai Suoi   JAMES JOYCE[3]

To VISCOUNT CARLOW (Express letter)   MS. Yale

28 January 1939   *7 rue Edmond Valentin, Paris 7ᵉ*

Dear Lord Carlow: Is it quite certain that you will be in Paris on
Thursday morning next[4] and will you be passing the night of the same
day, Candlemas, here? Because, if so, and if Lady Carlow is with you
my daughter-in-law who is giving a dinner party in my honour and to
celebrate the publication of my book asks me to say that you will be
very welcome both. It is at my son's place this year 17 Villa Scheffer,
Paris XVIᵉ.

    There is another point. My book[5] is to be sent over on Wednesday by
air express but unfortunately the delivery of these parcels is never
certain because they pass through the *Douane* to collect a minimal duty
and, of course, the *douanier* can have no idea that I shall be waiting
for the wretched parcel. It might arrive at the last moment after a day
of exhaustive waiting and even that would be too late to allow of my
showing it to my daughter (who lives outside Paris) in the early afternoon. Or it might just arrive the morning after the 2nd in which case I
should feel inclined to throw it out of the window. In sum, I should like
to be sure of having it on that morning. It was only after you had rung
off that I thought of this. Of course, I don't want to interfere in any way

---

[1] Signora Schmitz had changed her name legally to Svevo.
[2] The last words of Italo Svevo's *Senilità*.
[3] (Translation)
    'Dear Signora: I have at last finished finishing my book. For three lustra I have
been combing and recombing the locks of Anna Livia. It is now time that she tread
the boards. I hope that Berenice will intercede for her little sister so that she may find
in this vast world, thanks to the gods, "at least one solitary Deo Gratias".
    Merry Christmas and Happy New Year to you and your family.   James Joyce'
[4] Joyce's fifty-seventh birthday, 2 February 1939.
[5] *Finnegans Wake*. It was not officially published until 4 May 1939, but Faber & Faber
managed to have ready an unbound copy (really a set of final proofs) from the printer,
R. MacLehose and Company, in time for Joyce's birthday.

with your plans but as you told them to me they seemed to fit in with my idea.

If you are not already in the country or at air work somewhere perhaps you could ring up Faber and Faber. The person who is [in] charge of the book there is Mr de la Mare.[1] The book is to be sent from the Glasgow printers or binders on Monday. Anyhow a telegram from you one way or another would relieve my mind.

I am still very exhausted but I shall try to be better by Thursday though I am afraid the traditional *pas seul* with high kicking effects associated with that birthday feast will be beyond my powers this year of grace.[2]

Incidentally you will discover the title of the book which my wife has kept secret for seventeen years, being the only one who knew it. I think I can see some lofty thinkers and noble livers turning away from it with a look of pained displeasure Sincerely yours　　　　JAMES JOYCE

To LIVIA SVEVO　　　　　　　　　　　　　　　　MS. Texas

[1 May 1939] Calendimaggio[3]　　　　*34 rue des Vignes, Paris, XVI*

Gentile signora: Ho ricevuto la lettera acclusa inviatami dal sig. Scarpelli.[4] C'è un equivoco. Non avevo affatto l'intenzione di criticare l'opera letteraria dell'autore ma bensì l'opera del suo legatore. Infatti i fogli volanti (è proprio il termine) del libercolo si staccavano ad uno ad uno dopo la lettura di ogni pagina. Forse il mio esemplare è eccezionale. Ma in simili circostanze come non pensare alla commedia giacosiana[5] ed alla caducità delle cose terrestri? Non ho fatto che chiamare carta carta e colla colla. La prego di rassicurarne lo scrittore. Pare che si senta offeso. Non lo è e non lo era. Ma . . . Oibo! (per non dire Uibaldo!)[6] Endove ze andado finir el morbin famoso dei terriestini?[7] No ghe ze gnente de mal, benedeto de Dio! Go ciolto un poco de zeroto da Smolars[8]

---

[1] Richard de la Mare (b. 1901), then a director and later chairman of Faber & Faber.

[2] On his birthday Joyce customarily performed a dance, which consisted mostly of remarkably high kicks.

[3] 'Kalends of May.'

[4] Ubaldo Scarpelli, author of a pamphlet on Svevo. Joyce had complained that it needed glue.

[5] Joyce alludes to Giuseppe Giacosa's comedy *Come le foglie* ('Like the leaves'), the pun being on *foglie* ('leaves') and *fogli* ('pages').

[6] The rest of the letter is in Triestine dialect.

[7] A humorous echo of a song which was sung in Trieste in the mid-nineteenth century by a Slovene streetsinger named Sonz: 'Viva Terjeste, Viva anche terjestini, Viva l'zardin publico, Viva anca bela zatà.' ('Long live Trieste, Long live the Triestines too, Long live the public garden, Long live also the beautiful city.') Joyce was acquainted with the song.

[8] A well-known stationery store in Trieste.

e adeso el se tien insieme pulido. E diga al sior Scarpelli che no stia
bazilar, che mi no go dito gnente de mal e per amirare quel bravo omo
che iera Italo Svevo semo in due, lu e mi.

Giovedì sarà pubblicado el mio libro a Londra e in Ameriga. Ze anca
la festa de Santa Moniga[1] se mi ricordo ben, al quatro. Moniga[2] son
stado mi forse (La mi scusi, siora) che go messo disdoto ani dela mia
vita a finir quel mostro de libro. Ma cossa La vol? Se nasse cussì. E,
corpo de bigoli, ne go bastanza. Co ghe digo mi!

Con doverosi ossequi mi segno devmo   JAMES JOYCE

P.S. Lingua sciolta, nevvero, signora![3]

To GEORGE ROGERS[4]   MS. Rogers

Postmark 3 August 1939   *34 rue des Vignes, Paris XVI*

Caro signor Rogers: Dunque. Giorgio è stato bocciato ingloriosamente
dalla giuria invisibile della B.B.C.[5] Quell'alto consesso promulgò il suo
verdetto, vale a dire, che la sua voce era ben al disotto del livello
richiesto e che no vedeva nemmeno perchè il suo nome dovrebbe essere
aggiunto alla lora lista per un avvenire più o meno eventuale.

[1] Saint Monica is celebrated in fact on 4 May.

[2] An allusion to a local anecdote involving a complicated play on 'monica', which in
Triestine means 'nun' but is also a slightly euphemistic variation on 'mona', meaning
'vagina' and 'stupid person'.

[3] The following translation is taken, with slight changes, from 'Carteggio . . . Svevo-
Joyce', ed. Harry Levin, *Inventario* II. 1 (Spring 1949), 136–7. The translator points out
the special Triestine expressions, *morbin* in the sense of *buon omore*, *bazilar* in the sense of
essere preoccupato. The spelling is also dialectal.

'Dear Signora: I have received the enclosed letter sent me by Signor Scarpelli.
There has been a misunderstanding. I did not at all intend to criticize the literary work
of the author, but the work of his binder. As a matter of fact the fly leaves (that is the
word) of the pamphlet came out one by one as I read each page. Perhaps my copy is
an exception. But under the circumstances how could one not think of Giacosa's
comedy and of the transitoriness of all earthly things? I have only called paper paper
and glue glue. I beg you to reassure the writer. It appears that he feels offended. He is
not and never was. But . . . Alas! (Not to say alack!) What has become of the famous
laughing spirit of the Terriestines? No harm was meant, God wot! I got a little tape at
Smolars and now the thing holds together in fine shape. And tell Signor Scarpelli not
to be upset, that I have spoken no evil and that he and I make two who admire the
splendid man that Italo Svevo was.

Thursday my book will be published in London and in America. It is also Saint
Monica's day, if I remember rightly, on the fourth. But it is I who am perhaps an ass
(forgive me, Signora), to have devoted eighteen years of my life to completing that
monster of a book. But what is one to do? One is born that way. Yet, by God, I have
had enough. And that's that!

With due respect, I am your devoted   James Joyce

P.S.—This is free language, isn't it, Signora?'

[4] George Rogers (b. 1911), Professor at the Royal Academy of Music, had offered to
introduce George Joyce to officials of the British Broadcasting Corporation.

[5] Professor Rogers says that George Joyce sang very well and was grossly undervalued.

Siccome Giorgio si mostra molto taciturno, mi rivolgo a Lei. Cosa diamine è successa a quall' nazione? Si accorse Lei di qualche cosa nell'ambiente, una stiza, un'ostilità, fretta, impreparazione ecc. Od il timor panico distrusse la sua voce totalmente o cantò davvero in modo da meritare l'opprobriosa sentenza. 'Al di sotto del livello della Granbretagna in fatto di arte canora!' Per l'ugola celeste di Santa Cecilia, per quanto affirochito sia diventato il mio proprio ruggito, non m'aspettavo mai questo calcio di ciucco! Ed il guaio è ch'egli è sempre disposto ad accettare la condamna. Sarei molto grato di un Suo breve cenno in merito. SalutandoLa cordialmente devmo

JAMES JOYCE[1]

To FRANK BUDGEN   MS. Yale

20 August 1939   *Hotel Schweizerhof, Bern*

Dear Budgen: I return your article and hope the F.R. takes it.[2] A pity you did not develop your ideas about the landscape. You ought to jot them down anyway. Ojetti's [?] article has a paragraph that bears on a page of your article, I thought, so I sent it. Perhaps you can puzzle it out from the French. 'Raggi icchese' is Italian for X-rays.

These suggestions:

(a) The expression about the pun being all right because the R.C. church is founded on it is not correct. It should be Christian church but the whole phrase should be recast out of its too 'true believer' mould.

(2) Reread the second phrase in the hagiographic triptych in Part IV (S. L. O'Toole is only adumbrated). Much more is intended in the colloquy between Berkeley the arch druid and his pidgin speech and Patrick the arch priest and his Nippon English. It is also the defence

---

[1] (Translation)
'Dear Mr Rogers: So. Giorgio has been ingloriously failed by the invisible jury of the B.B.C. That high court issued its verdict, to wit, that his voice was well below the required standard and that no one saw reason to include his name on their list for some future date.
Since Giorgio is so reticent I turn to you. What the deuce did happen at that audition? Did you feel something in the atmosphere, a row, some hostility, haste, unpreparedness etc. Or stage fright completely destroyed his voice and he really sang in a way to deserve the offensive sentence. "Below the level of Great Britain in the art of singing!" In the name of St Cecilia's heavenly ugola, even if my own lion's roar is half spent, I never expected this donkey's kick! And the trouble is that Giorgio is always inclined to accept condemnation. I should be very grateful for a short note from you about it all. With cordial greetings yours sincerely   James Joyce'
[2] Budgen's article on *Finnegans Wake* remained unpublished until 1941, when it appeared in *Horizon* (IV).

and indictment of the book itself, B's theory of colours and Patrick's practical solution of the problem. Hence the phrase in the preceding Mutt and Jeff banter 'Dies is Dorminus master' = Deus est Dominus noster plus the day is Lord over sleep, i.e. when it days.

(3) As your title begins well the article why not end well with any of the other names given by the Egyptians to their scripture? The book of the Dead is also the book of the Chapters of the Coming-Forth by Day. Good luck   JAMES JOYCE

P.S. Among another batch of reviews I got is this from London *Daily Herald* (verbatim):   5 August 39

Finnegan's Wake by J.J. (F. and F. 25/–).

An Irish stew of verbiage by the author of *Ulysses* with unexpected beauty emerging now and then from the peculiar mixture.

C'est tout.

Part V

SAINT-GÉRAND-LE-PUY, ZURICH

1939–1941

Saint-Gérand-le-Puy, Zurich (1939–1941)

The great chords of *Finnegans Wake* had been struck, even if few people heard them. Joyce's life now moved through dislocation and illness towards its end. Having resided in one city or another for fifty-seven years, he found the village life of St Gérand dull and more dull. The lack of distraction rendered more anguishing his growing recognition that even the life of his own family was out of control. His son's marriage had collapsed, and his daughter-in-law, shaken in mind for the last two years, was taken back to the United States. George Joyce stayed on in Paris, leaving his parents uncertain of his address. Lucia was off in Pornichet, too far away to visit. Only Stephen was near by at Mrs Jolas's school, and this was likely to be closed before long.

Joyce and Nora lived disconsolately at St Gérand for almost a year, from the day before Christmas 1939 until 14 December 1940, except for two months (mid-April to mid-June of 1940) when they went to nearby Vichy, which was less dreary. Any hope of waiting out the second World War as they had waited out the first waned rapidly. In May the Germans swarmed demonically into western Europe. After the fall of Paris on 14 June, a group of refugees appeared at St Gérand, including George, Samuel Beckett, and the Léons. The Germans passed through the village a few days later, but shortly withdrew and left the semblance of control of Unoccupied France to Pétain's government.

The presence of Léon pleased Joyce; he took the opportunity to check *Finnegans Wake* with him for misprints, and they made a list together. But in August and September it became clear that no one was planning to stay in St Gérand. Léon left in that month, and so did Maria Jolas at her husband's urging. Joyce had put off coming to any decision, but it seemed likely that George would be conscripted if they remained much longer, and the Vichy government was less than eager to entertain British subjects in its territory.

At the beginning of September Joyce still hesitated about where to go, but he began writing letters to Swiss mental asylums to see if he could find one suitable for Lucia. His preference for the continent over the United States focused his thoughts inevitably upon Switzerland. At first the Swiss were singularly unflattered by this decision, probably because the local officials had no notion who Joyce was. They rejected his first application on 30 September 1940. Then the most influential men in Zurich interceded on his behalf, friends offered financial guarantees, and on 29 November the Swiss relented and informed Joyce that he and his family would be admitted. With Stephen Joyce in their care, they left St Gérand on 14 December 1940 at 3 o'clock in the morning, and made their way slowly but without incident to Zurich, where they arrived on 17 December.

In Zurich Joyce stayed at a pension and lived quietly. He walked about with his grandson and told him stories; he made a few notes which unfortunately do not indicate with what sort of book he would next have boarded English literature. Depressed as he found himself, he could as always be enlivened in the evening with friends present. He wrote some letters thanking people for helping him to reach Switzerland, and his last written communication was a postcard to Stanislaus Joyce naming some people who might assist him if his wartime situation in Italy became untenable. The list, which included people in Switzerland, possibly suggests that he had begun to despair of much further communication with his brother, and perhaps of longer life.

His health had evidently been impaired at St Gérand because of an undiagnosed duodenal ulcer. He and his wife and son assumed that the sporadic pains he sometimes experienced came from nerves, as a doctor in Paris had assured them several years earlier. So at first no one was greatly concerned by the intense stomach pains he began to complain of on Friday night, 10 January 1941. But the morphine administered by a doctor who lived nearby did not alleviate them, and in the early morning Joyce was brought to a Zurich hospital. There, a perforated ulcer being suspected, an operation was performed that morning. At first it seemed to have been successful, but the next day his strength flagged and he lost consciousness. On 13 January, at 2.15 in the morning, Joyce died. He was buried two days later, after a small ceremony, in the Fluntern cemetery that overlooks the city of Zurich.

To Jacques Mercanton[1]   MS. Mercanton

9 January 1940   *Hotel de la Paix, S. Gérand-le-Puy (Allier)*[2]

Cher Monsieur Mercanton: Voila les causes de mon long silence. Ma bru,
à son tour, devenue completement folle, a été internée d'office. La malheureuse, apres avoir ruiné sa famille et son foyer et accumulé des dettes pour
un $\frac{1}{2}$ million de francs, est la plupart du temps en plein délire. Mon
fils, totalement désorienté, se trouve à Paris avec les amis. Il cherche à
s'occuper. J'ai dû prendre l'enfant à mes charges. Il est ici dans une école
et je fais un partage entre ici, Paris et La Baule où ma fille est toujours.

Vous me parlez d'un certain 'roman' que j'ai écrit. Ici personne n'a
soufflé mot de son existence. J'ai reçu encore des critiques parmi
lesquelles une 'contribution' bien bizarre vient de Helsinki où, pour de bon
et comme le prophète le previt, le Finn again wakes.[3] Il y avait une aussi
dans la revue romaine *Panorama* du 12 novembre. Puisque le livre entier
est fondé sur l'œuvre d'un penseur italien . . . ?[4] En somme, un 'fiasco'
total quant à la critique européenne jusqu'ici. Et je n'arrive pas même
à toucher mes tantièmes à cause des lois sur l'exportation du Kapital.

J'écrirai à Francini quand je retrouverai sa lettre. Va-t-il publier sa
brochure[5] dans une edition de luxe, sur Japon?

Si vous m'écrivez tapez à la machine. Si vous allez à Lausanne buvez
3 litres de Villeneuve à mes trois intentions. Cordialement votre

James Joyce[6]

---

[1] Jacques Mercanton (b. 1910), a Swiss critic, whose article on Joyce was published in
Europe (15 April 1938).

[2] The Joyces went to stay at Saint-Gérand-le-Puy on 24 December 1939, chiefly to be
near their grandson at Mrs Jolas's school there.

[3] Joyce saw the Russo-Finnish war as a confirmation of his book's title.

[4] Giambattista Vico is meant.

[5] Alessandro Francini Bruni evidently had in mind republishing his lecture on Joyce,
Joyce intimo spogliato in piazza.

[6] (Translation)

'Dear Mr Mercanton: Here are the reasons for my long silence. My daughter-in-law,
in her turn gone completely mad, has been interned. The poor thing, after having
ruined her family and home and run up debts of $\frac{1}{2}$ a million francs, is out of her mind
most of the time. My son, entirely disoriented, is now in Paris with friends. He is trying
to keep busy. I have had to take over the responsibility of the child. He is at a school here
and I divide myself among here, Paris, and La Baule where my daughter still is.

You talk of a certain "novel" I wrote. Here no one has breathed a word of its
existence. I have received some more reviews among which is one very odd "contribution" from Helsinki where, happily and as the prophet foresaw, the Finn again wakes.
There was one also in the Roman review *Panorama* of 12 November. Seeing that the
whole book is founded on the work of an Italian thinker . . . ? In short, a complete
fiasco up to the present as far as European criticism is concerned. And I cannot even
get hold of my royalties because of the laws about the exportation of capital.

I will write to Francini when I find his letter again. Is he going to publish his
pamphlet in a de luxe edition, on Japan paper?

If you write me use a typewriter. If you go to Lausanne drink three litres of
Villeneuve to my three intentions. Cordially yours   James Joyce'

To DARIO DE TUONI[1]   MS. de Tuoni

20 February 1940   *Hotel de la Paix, S. Gérand-le-Puy, Allier, France*

Egregio signor de Tuoni: Dopo un buon—o piuttosto—un cattivo quarto di secolo Le sarà certo una sorpresa ricevere questa mia lettera. Fatto sta che lessi qualche tempo addietro un Suo articolo su Morand e Valery Larbaud e venerdi scorso, essendo a Vichy (20 chilometri di quà) andai a rivedere il mio amico Larbaud al quale avevo a suo tempo inviato l'articolo. Egli m'incarica di ringraziar La della Sua critica amichevole. Gli ho spiegato che noi ci conoscevamo 'in illo tempore'[2] a Trieste. La signora Larbaud[3] è genovese. Egli è stato molto ammalato da parecchi anni ma secondo me ora va per la buona strada.

Spero che Lei stia bene malgrado questo tempo che corre quando non zoppica. Mio fratello è sempre in Trieste, professore all'università. Io sono nonno di un nipotino che ha festeggiato il suo ottavo compleanno il 15 di questo mese. Ebbi recentemente una lettera di Francini il quale è tornato al suo vecchio mestiere, l'insegnamento. È maestro alla scuola dei padri 'Scalopi' a Firenze. E Tullio Silvestri? Dov'è e che cosa è diventato? Ho sempre quattro o cinque dei suoi quadri nel mio appartamento a Parigi. Era un buon pittore e anche una 'bela macia'[4] come si soleva dire.

Mando questa lettera per tramite del giornale[5] nel quale lessi il Suo articolo e così spero che, se Dio vuole, La giungerà finalmente. Me lo faccia sapere, se vuole, con un Suo cenno in riscontro all'indirizzo qui sopra.

SalutandoLa distintamente mi segno di Lei devo   JAMES JOYCE[6]

---

[1] Dario de Tuoni (b. 1892 in Innsbruck), a Triestine poet whom Joyce had met before the first World War. They were introduced by Alessandro Francini Bruni. The text of this letter is taken from Dario de Tuoni, 'James Joyce nella Vecchia Trieste', *Fiera Letteraria* (Rome) XVI. 9 (26 February 1961), 5, where most of it is reproduced photographically.

[2] This Latin phrase, meaning 'At that time', is inserted before the reading of any gospel in Catholic churches.

[3] Signora Maria Nebbia.

[4] A Triestine expression, meaning approximately, 'Some character'.

[5] De Tuoni's article appeared in the *Meridiano di Roma*.

[6] (Translation)

'Dear Mr de Tuoni: After a good—or rather—a bad quarter of a century this letter from me will certainly be a surprise for you. The fact is that I read some time ago an article of yours on Morand and Valery Larbaud and last Friday, being at Vichy (20 kilometres from here) I went to see my old friend Larbaud to whom I had previously sent your article. He charged me to thank you for your friendly criticism. I explained to him that we had known each other in that far-off time in Trieste. Signora Larbaud is Genoese. He has been very ill for several years but I believe he is now getting better.

I hope you are well in spite of time, which runs when it doesn't limp. My brother is

To Edmund Brauchbar[1]   MS. Brauchbar

30 July 1940   *Hotel du Commerce, S. Gérand-le-Puy, Allier, France*

Cher Monsieur Brauchbar: Merci de votre lettre du 21 mars et j'espère que vous allez toujours bien. Je vous avais déjà écrit à Toronto en vous envoyant une lettre que j'avais reçu de votre neveu à Dublin—la seule personne, soit dit en passant, parmi les douze ou treize que j'avais réussi à placer quelque part qui s'est dérangé jusqu'à maintenant pour savoir si j'étais même vivant.

Puisque vous me demandez de mes nouvelles nous en voilà. Ma malheureuse bru après avoir répandu autour d'elle et en pleine guerre une ruine materielle et morale indescriptible a été internée d'office par les autorités françaises comme dangereuse pour elle-même et pour les autres. Puis finalement elle a été transportée à New York par deux médecins et deux infirmières et se trouve actuellement dans une maison de santé à Connecticut. Cela s'est passé quelques jours à peine avant la debâcle ici. Ma fille se trouve avec sa maison de santé près de S. Nazaire, donc en plein zone occupée sur la côte dangereuse—et cela malgré tout ce que j'avais essayé de faire d'avance pour assurer sa tranquillité. Nous sommes ici, ma femme et moi avec notre fils et notre petit-fils et à la suite des 'evenements' je me trouve complètement isolé, coupé de mes ressources à Londres par les autorités britanniques et de mes ressources en banque ici par les autorités francaises, double blocus.

Si vous avez lu ma biographie vous avez certainement ri en lisant ce qu'écrit M. Gorman (qui, du reste, ne m'avait pas même signalé la publication ni son éditeur non plus) que l'astronome de l'Uraniaturm s'appelait . . . Siegmund Feilbogen![2]

---

still in Trieste, a professor at the university. I am the grandfather of a little grandson who celebrated his eighth birthday the 15th of this month. I had a letter recently from Francini, who has gone back to his old profession of teaching. He is an instructor at the school of the Scalopi fathers in Florence. And Tullio Silvestri? Where is he and what has become of him? I still have four or five of his paintings in my Paris flat. He was a good painter and also quite a character, as people used to say.

I am sending this letter in care of the newspaper in which I read your article, so I hope that, God willing, it will reach you sometime. Let me know, please, by acknowledging it to the above address.

With kind greetings I sign myself your devoted   James Joyce'
[1] Edmund Brauchbar (1872–1952), a Zurich businessman who studied English with Joyce during the first World War, and subsequently moved to New York. Joyce had assisted him in his efforts to aid Jewish refugees, including some of his relations, to establish themselves in other countries.
[2] Siegmund Feilbogen, a bearded messianic professor from Vienna who came to Zurich during the first World War to edit his *International Review* in both English and German. It was intended to help reconcile the two sides by persuading them that the atrocity stories of both were groundless. Joyce did some translating for the review.

Je ne sais pas ce qui est devenu mon appartement à Paris, mes livres et mes tableaux.

J'espère que notre 'tale of woes' n'est pas trop embêtant et que votre famille immédiate (puisque vos parents semblent être comme les feuilles de la forêt) se trouve, saine et sauve, autour de l'arbre maître et . . . utilisable.

Je vous serre la main cordialement   J A M E S J O Y C E[1]

To M A R I A J O L A S   MS. Jolas

7 September 1940   *Saint-Gérand-le-Puy*

Dear Mrs Jolas: Thanks for your letter of 4th just received though by your wire of 6th you are still in France. I hope you got my wire to Banyuls. It seemed useless to write to you as we never knew where you might be. I hope this finds you all safe and sound in Lisbon and about to sail. Léon and his son have gone to Paris. I hear we have all to clear out by the 20th as the landlord wants to overhaul the place. No reply from Dublin. None from Cerf or Huebsch. We got our dole on the passports, partly that is, and I paid Mme Astafiev for August. A remittance Kastor wrote he had cabled you for Giorgio has also not come. You ought to feel glad when the good ship moves off. The family is not keen on Helvetia on account of the air alarms etc. Nevertheless I wrote

[1] (Translation)

'Dear Mr Brauchbar: Thanks for your letter of 21 March and I hope you are keeping well. I had already written to Toronto sending you a letter that I had received from your nephew in Dublin—the only person, be it said in passing, among the twelve or thirteen whom I have managed to place somewhere who up to now has troubled to find out if I were still alive.

Since you ask me for my news, here we are. My unfortunate daughter-in-law after having spread around herself in the midst of war an indescribable ruin both material and moral was interned by the French authorities as dangerous to herself and others. Then finally she was taken back to New York by two doctors and two nurses and is now in a private asylum in Connecticut. That all happened hardly more than a few days before the debacle here. My daughter is with her *maison de santé* near S. Nazaire, hence deep in the occupied zone on the dangerous coast—and this in spite of everything I had tried to do in advance to assure her tranquillity. We are here, my wife and I with our son and our grandson and following the "events" I find myself entirely isolated, cut off from my resources in London by the British authorities and from my banked resources here by the French authorities, a double blockade.

If you have read my biography you have certainly laughed to read what Mr Gorman (who, indeed, did not even announce the publication to me, nor did his publisher either) writes, that the astronomer of the Uraniaturm was named . . . Siegmund Feilbogen!

I do not know what has happened to my flat in Paris, to my books and pictures.

I hope that our "tale of woe" is not too tiresome and that your immediate family (for your other relations seem to be like leaves in the forest) is clustered, safe and sound, around the paternal and . . . utilisable tree. I clasp your hand cordially   James Joyce'

to the clinique near Vallorbe. Thanks for the kind offer in your letter. At the station I literally had no breath to say what I wanted as I was doubled up by my efforts with a trunk or case. You seemed to me to be downcast. Well, if you never did anything else you made scores of children happy for many years. When they turn out to be jacobins, countesses, saints and explorers they will always remember it—'in their soberer moments'. But the Lord knows you did a lot more. I wish you all a smooth sea and a following wind! And remember me to Jolas and any others who may remember me.

Mr Huber[1] is still at work on his trunk in the lobby (it is exactly 148° in the shade today) and the day you left Mrs Huber asked me to lend her *Finnegans Wake* which I did. More anon. If you see Prince Makinsky the name of the book is *Life and Works of G. B. Vico*, on sale at 12 or 14 Troy Street, W.1. price 5/–. Osiris Jones[2] has not yet come forth by day or by night and I am waiting for a copy of that biography to be sent me by Gorman or his publisher. The Irish Legation wired again to Dublin but had no reply. If you are pressed for quarters in Lisbon probably Makinsky will be able to find you something. My friend Byrne's daughter, Phyllis, at the C.G. may also be able to help. She has been there about a year.

Dialogue. 1980. Lilac Doorway U.S.A. Time: Spring.

She: (laying aside a copy of How to Get Rid of Parasites) I have been thinking. What *was* the name of that family that was always in trouble over there in Europia?

He: (seizes jug) You're asking me.

She: The man had a wall eye, I think. Was it Wallenstein?

He: (replaces jug) Jucious!

She: Jucious! That was the name. I knew it had something to do with Scotland.

Fait rien. Bon voyage! Merci! Au revoir! Vous avez oublié le pourboire, Madame. Pour le porteur. Fait rien! . . . Cordially yours,

JAMES JOYCE

To The Mayor of Zurich   Zurich City Archives

20 December 1940   *Zürich*

Sehr verehrter Herr Stadtpräsident: Bei meiner Ankunft hier vor

---

[1] Actually Hébert; he was a Louisiana-born teacher of athletics at Mrs Jolas's school in St Gérand.

[2] Refers to a poem by Conrad Aiken, *The Coming Forth by Day of Osiris Jones* (New York, 1931).

einigen Tagen erfahre ich, dass Sie so freundlich waren, meinem Eintrittsbewilligungsgesuch bei der Behörde das Gewicht Ihrer einflussreichen Empfehlung hinzufügen, mit dem Resultat, dass ein Niederlassungsvisum in Zürich jetzt mir und meiner Familie bewilligt worden ist. Die Verbindung zwischen mir und Ihrer gastfreundlichen Stadt dehnen sich über eine Reihe von fast vierzig Jahren aus, und in diesen peinlichen Zeiten fühle ich mich sehr geehrt, dass meine Gegenwart hier zum grossen Teil ich an der persönlichen Bürgschaft Zürichs ersten Bürgers schulde.

Dankbar und hochachtungsvoll zeichne ich, sehr verehrter Herr Stadtpräsident, als   Ihr ergebener   JAMES JOYCE[1]

To STANISLAUS JOYCE[2] (Postcard)   MS. Cornell

4 January 1941   *Pension Delphin, Muhlebachstrasse 69, Zurich*

Caro fratello: Forse questi indirizzi ti saranno utili. Sono di persone che potrebbero, credo, aiutarti. Ad ogni modo prova. A. Francini, presso la Scuola dei Padri Scalopi costì, Ezra Pound, 5 via Marsala, Rapallo, Carlo Linati, 20 San Vittore, Milano, Curzio Malaparte ed Ettore Settanni, redazione di 'Prospettive' via Gregoriana 44, Roma, il primo direttore, il secondo collaboratore che fece con me (o piuttosto

[1] (Translation)
'Your Honour the Mayor: Upon my arrival here a few days ago I learnt that you were kind enough to add the weight of your influential recommendation to my request to the authorities for an entry permit, with the result that permission to reside in Zurich has now been granted to me and my family. The connection between me and your hospitable city extends over a period of nearly forty years and in these painful times I feel highly honoured that I should owe my presence here in large part to the personal guaranty of Zurich's first citizen.

With gratitude and respect I am, your Honour the Mayor, Yours faithfully
James Joyce'

[2] This postcard was Joyce's last written communication. His final illness is described in a letter of 14 January 1941 from Wilhelm Herz [William H. Hartley] to Helen Joyce's brother Robert Kastor, which says in part: 'Last Friday Grete [Mrs Herz] was in Zurich to see Stephen and just on that day the trouble started. Mr Joyce got the most terrible pains and could only be relieved by morphium. The doctors together with one of the best known surgeons held a consilium that same night and decided to take him over to the Red Cross Hospital. The condition not improving they decided to operate on him Saturday morning, January 11. They evidently found a hole in the stomach resulting from an ulcer which had as the doctors claim been there for at least seven years without being discovered, or to say the least without the correct diagnosis having been given in spite of the reiterated complaints of Mr Joyce. On Sunday, the day after the operation, the patient was very weak as was to be expected for the next 3–4 days; but during the night of Sunday to Monday the exitus was clear and Giorgio and his mother were called to the hospital. . . .' James Joyce died on 13 January 1941 and was buried two days later.

rivise) la traduzione di un brano di *Anna Livia* apparso nel fascicolo del
15 febbraio 1940 (q.v.). Saluti da tutti. Jim[1]

[1] (Translation)
'Dear brother: Possibly these addresses will be of use to you. They are of people who
might, I think, help you. Try them anyway. A. Francini, c/o Scuola dei Padri Scalopi
there, Ezra Pound, 5 via Marsala, Rapallo, Carlo Linati, 20 San Vittore, Milano,
Curzio Malaparte and Ettore Settanni, editorial office of "*Prospettive*", via Gregoriana
44, Rome. The former is the director, the latter a contributor who made with me (or
rather revised) the translation of a passage from *Anna Livia* which appeared in the
issue of 15 February 1940 (q.v.). Greetings from all of us. Jim'

INDEXES

INDEX OF CORRESPONDENTS

INDEX OF RECIPIENTS

411

GENERAL INDEX

asked for money by, 148; J hopes to conciliate, 154; is pleased with Giorgio, 156; J attends theatre with, 173; *Dubliners* rejection predicted by, 203; J encouraged by, 205; death of, 263, 360, 361; incandescent curses of, 292; J expects disapproval of *Finnegans Wake* by, 310; J owes talents to, 361; J pays for tombstone of, 364; *Ulysses* portrays friends of, 364–5; J recalls singing of, 371; his phrase 'Jesus wept', 378; Norwegian captain story of, 385 n; enjoyment of opera by, 385; in *Finnegans Wake*, 388

Joyce, Lucia Anna (J's daughter), xiii, xxix; birth of, 38; taken to Ireland, 38, 199, 291–2; J's affection for, 156, 173, 177, 203; worsening schizophrenia of, 263; interest in Napoleon of, 267; J's father writes to, 286; in summer camp, 291; in Nice with J, 292; disqualified for dance prize, 341; has eye operation, 347; writes letters for J, 356, 366–7; removed by J from Dr Codet's care, 363; designs Christmas card for Michael Healy, 368; designs lettrines for *Chaucer ABC*, 368–9, 380; J sends to Ireland, 372–3, 375–6; J's defence of, to Miss Weaver, 374–7, 380–1; J's despair over, 376–7, 380; her lettrines used in *Pomes Penyeach*, 378; J asks Curran to write to, 386; in hospital, 390; J wants to show first copy of *Finnegans Wake* to, 394; at Pornichet, 401; J tries to move to Switzerland, 401, 405–6; still at La Baule, 403

Joyce, Mabel (J's sister), 146

Joyce, Margaret ('Poppy') (J's sister), 146, 154, 162

Joyce, Mary Jane Murray (J's mother), xvi–xviii; family of, 3; final illness of, 4, 20 n; J's letters alarm, 10, 18–19; J expects parcel from, 12–13; money sent to J by, 16; J's impatience with, 16–17; J's concern for, 17, 19; J believes father's mistreatment killed, 25; J called a mocker by, 132; J pays for tombstone of, 364

Joyce, Nora Barnacle (Mrs James Joyce), xii, xiv, xvii, xviii, xix, xx, xxi, xxii–xxvi, xxvii; J's first meeting with, 5, 21 n; J's elopement with, 5, 33, 40, 49, 80; J's first letter to, 21; family and early life of, 21 n, 45–6; J's early meetings with, 21–8; J describes self to, 25–7, 28–9, 167, 169, 174, 194; J's friends critical of, 27; regards J as no different from other men, 29, 81; J expects frankness

from, 29; worried J does not love her, 30, 173; J admits his love for, 30, 53, 158 ff, 194–5, 199, 204; London employment offered to, 31; involvement in J's composition of 'The Dead', 31 n, 45, 163, 164 n, 188, 195; arrival in Zurich, 37, 40; first child born to, 37, 71; second child born to, 38, 143; J's sister to be company for, 38, 171; Ireland revisited by, 38, 199, 202–3, 204, 260, 291–4; J in Paris with, 40; news of Finn's Hotel wanted by, 44, 45, 53, 55; domestic difficulties of (Pola), 46, 66, 122, 128; J's apologetic note while dining with, 47; is indifferent to J's art, 47, 51; J quotes remarks of, 48, 51, 52, 58, 59, 60, 116; feminine reassurance needed by, 49; J praises constancy of, 49, 53, 101; writes to Mrs Murray, 50, 72, 206, 292; J describes life with, 51, 53, 54, 64–8, 69, 80, 174; relations with Cosgrave of, 52, 157–9; Stanislaus critical of, 52; possible legacy for, 60 n; J rejects marriage ceremony for, 61; landladies disapprove pregnancy of, 61, 141; believes Stanislaus mistaken about E.H., 61; J's verses written for, 63, 160–1; J thinks of leaving, 66, 74, 80–1; J's praise for, 66–7, 196, 376; is homesick for Ireland, 66, 69; J will not sacrifice his art for, 74, 80; J unselfish with, 75; Stanislaus to bring tea for, 79; J understood by, 101; unpunctuated letters of, 116, 135; anniversary celebrated by, 116; J encourages reading by, 134, 204; J compares Holy Family to, 137, 142, 188; J compares Hardy's characters to, 138; house-hunting difficulties of (Rome), 141, 145, 148, 149; J's jealousy over, 157–9, 163, 194, 195; J associates *Chamber Music* with, 160–1, 167–8, 193; Stanislaus is kind to, 163; J's gift of necklace to, 167–8, 171; J sends Donegal tweeds to, 175, 176; J's gift of gloves to, 176; J's gift of parchment MS to, 176, 180, 193; J fears being left by, 177–8, 194, 260; J's sexual images of, xxv, 180–92; J sends money to, 183; J describes Roberts interview to, 202–3; Locarno sojourn of, 215, 227; children's clothes bought by, 218; Budgen's portrait of, 239; children taken to Galway by, 260, 291; J's marriage ceremony with, 260, 357; title of *Finnegans Wake* kept secret by, 260, 395; neglects to visit Mrs Murray, 291–3; Nice sojourn of, 292; *Ulysses* not yet read by, 293, 299; is with J in

Rome, 37, 112 n, 128, 223; original of
Devan in, 40 n; Artifoni a character in,
41 n; original of Mulvey, 46 n; Mrs
Riordan in, 52 n; Heijermans' influence
on title, 58 n; Stephen's remark on
paternity in, 74 n; Abbot Joachim in,
94 n; Mr Hunter early protagonist of,
112, 131; originally a short story, 112 n;
Nora a model for Molly, 116 n; treatment of antisemitism in, 138 n; Martha
Clifford's letter in, 179 n, 215; Blackwood Price a model for Mr Deasy in,
201 n; Price's letter, 202 n; J's plan for,
209, 214; J's scholarship in, 214;
serialization, 214, 227; Paris publication, 216, 259–60; prolonged composition of, 221, 223, 224, 249, 282;
Pound's early support of, 225; Dujardin's influence on, 229 n; J's text
excised in serialization, 246; Stanislaus
reads instalments of, 246; J superstitious
about, 241, 242, 272; J defends varied
styles of, 241, 242, 284, 319; J on
pricing of, 242, 275, 285; J explicates
episodes, 242, 245, 246, 251–2, 271–2,
274, 278, 285; possible sale of MS, 245,
298; printer's errors in *Little Review*
version, 250; linkage of episodes in,
252; completion impossible in Trieste,
253; J thinks of finishing in Ireland,
254; J needs police gazette for, 255;
published on J's birthday, 260, 288; J
expects suppression of, 260; Nora
laggard in reading, 260, 293, 299;
Finnegans Wake compared with, 261,
319; Pound's advice on contract for,
265; J's schema for, 270–1; Hermes in,
272; Moly explained, 272, 273; Minerva
in, 272; limited edition of, 272, 275; J
plans entr'acte for, 273; slaughter of
suitors in, 274, 279; J promised bonus
for, 275; Larbaud's enthusiasm for, 278,
279; Bloom as immortal as Falstaff,
278; typing difficulties with, 278;
Freemasonry in, 279; J needs mathematics book for, 279; J chooses
binding, 280; J working on proofs of,
281, 287–8; Mrs Murray supplies
details for, 285–7; Larbaud's lecture on,
xix, 287–8; misprints in original
edition, 288, 299; early reviews, 288;
futurist writers influenced by, 288; early
sales, 289; Mrs Murray has not read,
291; rising market price, 291, 292, 364;
second edition sold out, 292; Major
Powell a model for Major Tweedy, 294;
English Customs confiscates, 295; J
suggests critical terms for, 297; Shaw

refuses to purchase, 302; Arnold
Bennett's review of, 303; Roth piracy of,
315, 319, 335; German translation,
315, 328; ninth printing, 324; Gilbert's
book on, 334, 343; French version, 334–
5, 342, 344; Roth piracy suit, 335–6,
349–50, 359; Polish translation, 349;
second French and German editions,
348; possible new piracy, 359; friends of
J's father in, 364–5; New York trial and
U.S. publication, 367; English copyright owned by J, 367; Pope has
blessed, 368; J sends Lucia anecdote of,
373; publication in England, 377;
possible filming of, 379; Turko pantomime in, 385. *See also*, Bloom, Leopold;
Bloom, Molly; Bloomsday; Dedalus,
Stephen

Telemachus: 'gay betrayer' phrase,
125 n; Mulligan on Stephen's mother,
143; Stephen on free thought, 152 n;
episode completed, 209

Nestor: Price a model for Mr Deasy
in, 201 n; schoolboy in, 272

Proteus: use of Aristotle in, 13 n

Hades: Morel's translation of, 310

Scylla and Charybdis: Mulligan on
Stephen and Lady Gregory, 18 n; idea
of paternity in, 74; Best in, 76 n; J to
send Pound draft of, 225; J plans
entr'acte to follow, 273

Wandering Rocks: Thomas Devin in,
40 n; Father Commee on Countess of
Belvedere in, 131 n

Sirens: phrase 'my dancing days are
over', 120; Pound is critical of, 240;
Miss Weaver's criticism of, 241; J's
difficulties in writing, 241; episode
explained, 242

Cyclops: Cusack a model for Citizen
in, 146 n; J completes episode, 238–9,
241; unnamed narrator in, 244; publication of excised version, 246; 'thrones of
alabaster' in, 268

Nausikaa: J describes style of, 242,
245; Mrs Murray to send details for, 248;
Pound sent completed episode, 249;
Miss Weaver to read, 249; New York
court action against, 275

Oxen of the Sun: Mrs Murray to
send details for, 248; most difficult
episode, 249; J wants to talk to Budgen
about, 250, 266; episode explained,
251–2; double-thudding Anglo-Saxon
in, 252; Pound sends to publisher, 254

Circe: J's difficulties with, 254, 265,
266, 269, 271–3, 274; J wants to discuss
with Budgen, 266; crowning of Bloom

in, 268 n; J considers episode his strongest writing, 269; episode explained, 271–2; whirligig movement of, 274; J's typing difficulties with, 275, 278; Larbaud's enthusiasm for, 279; J reading proofs of, 288

Eumaeus: episode written early, 266, 272; sailor in, 279; episode finished, 275, 278, 288

Ithaca: Bloom's ideal home in, 68 n; orientation of Blooms in bed in, 139 n; episode begun in Paris, 265; finished, 274; Bloom's return to, 275; episode explained, 278; J's difficulties with, 281; height of Eccles Street railing in, 286

Penelope: Lt Mulvey in, 46 n; Nora a model for Molly Bloom, 116 n; episode explained, 274, 278, 285; Molly to have last word, 274; J needs Trieste notes for, 276; J's use of Dublin originals in, 285–6; J's difficulties with proofs, 288; Miss Weaver calls prehuman, 289; Morel's criticism of, 308 n

Unicorn Press, 10, 17

United Irishman, see Sinn Féin

United States, 240, 249, 270, 352, 358, 367

Università di Trieste, 276 n

University College, Dublin, J's attendance at, 3; student magazine, 10 n; Italy refuses recognition of J's degree, 38; J wants detail about, 50; J to devote ten chapters of novel to, 58, 61; letters on coeducation in, 99; becomes part of National University, 100 n

University College, Galway, 377

Unwin, T. Fisher, 74

Vail, Laurence, 289

Valéry, Paul, 344

Vannutelli, Vincenzo (Cardinal), 24, 119

Vatican Council of 1870, 130

Vaughan, Rev. Bernard, S.J., 120–1, 129

vegetarianism, 14, 64

venereal disease, 114, 129, 146, 272, 273. *See also* syphilis

Veneziani, Gioacchino, 218

'Vengeance', J's unwritten story, 145

Venice, 63

Venture, The, 45, 53

Verbannte, see Exiles

Verdi, Giuseppe, 378

Verlaine, Paul, 103, 117 n, 274, 354 n

Vico, Giambattista, in *Finnegans Wake*, 261, 317, 321, 403; J thinks afraid of thunderstorms, 314; J wants book about, 407

Vidacovich, Nicolò, 221

Viking Press, The, 393

Vogt, Dr Alfred, eye specialist, 261, 355, 363, 390

Volpi, *see* Lauri-Volpi, Giacomo

Volta Cinematograph (Dublin), J's project for Dublin cinema, xxi, 38; J exhausted by, 187; opens, 192; Christmas crowd at, 195; J's success with, 197

Vousden, Dublin music hall singer, 386

Wagner, Richard, J requests operas of, 12; J hears *Siegfried*, 90, 252; in Moore's *The Lake*, 99; J hears *Götterdämmerung*, 149–50, 152; J's emotional response to, 150; calls *Meistersinger* pretentious, 155

Wallace, Edgar, 126, 336

Wallace, Lillian, 310

Wallace, Richard, 310

Walsh, Ernest, 308, 310, 315

Walsh, William John (Archbishop), 97, 132 n

war, J on Franco-German, 11; J's antimilitarist views, 97; J on armament expenditure, 126; internment of Stanislaus in, 39, 209, 215; J admires Tolstoy's view of, 73; Ferrero on military destructiveness, 82 n; J's Zurich residence during, 209, 213, 217; J's financial problems in, 217–18; J's Civil List grant during, 213; J's efforts for Lucia in, 263, 401, 405; J's twenty-nine words for 'Peace' in *Finnegans Wake*, 333–4; J foresees approach of new war, 377, and helps Austrian refugees, 393, 405; J's escape to Switzerland from, 402; J sees Russo-Finnish war confirming title of *Finnegans Wake*, 403; Helen Joyce's troubles during, 403, 405

Warden, Florence, 74

'Watching the Needleboats at San Sabba' (in *Pomes Penyeach*), sent to Stanislaus, 207

Weaver, Harriet Shaw, xxi, xxiii; J's financial aid from, 213, 224, 227, 254, 267, 287, 288, 298, 327, 346, 381; *A Portrait* published by, 214; J's publishing assistance from, 222–4; J's gratitude to, 224, 227, 240–1, 283; press notices forwarded by, 225, 297; identity as patron revealed, 240; J gives MS of *A Portrait* to, 241, 247; enthusiasm for *Cyclops* episode of, 244; J sent photographs of, 245, 247, 248; *Nausikaa* episode sent to, 249; *Finnegans Wake* a worry to, 261–2; Lucia nursed by, 263; *Oxen* episode sent to, 265; J describes himself to, 282–3; and report of J's